Major Problems
in American Constitutional History

MAJOR PROBLEMS IN AMERICAN HISTORY SERIES

GENERAL EDITOR
THOMAS G. PATERSON

Major Problems in American Constitutional History

Volume I: The Colonial Era Through Reconstruction

DOCUMENTS AND ESSAYS

EDITED BY

KERMIT L. HALL

UNIVERSITY OF FLORIDA

D. C. HEATH AND COMPANY
Lexington, Massachusetts   Toronto

Address editorial correspondence to:

D. C. Heath
125 Spring Street
Lexington, MA 02173

Acquisitions Editor: James Miller
Developmental Editor: Sylvia Mallory
Production Editor: Tina Beazer and Sarah Doyle
Designer: Sally Thompson Steele
Production Coordinator: Charles Dutton
Text Permissions Editor: Margaret Roll

Cover: "First State Election in Detroit, Michigan, 1837" by Thomas Mickell Burnham. The Detroit Institute of Arts. Gift of Mrs. Samuel T. Carson.

Published simultaneously in Canada.

Printed in the United States of America.

International Standard Book Number: 0-669-21209-1

Library of Congress Catalog Number: 90-86143

10 9 8 7

Preface

Almost every major problem in American history has had, in one form or another, its constitutional reflection, and those reflections have been the stuff of constitutional history. As Alexis de Tocqueville, the famous French visitor to America in the 1830s, noted, "Scarcely any political question arises in the United States that is not revolved, sooner or later, into a judicial question." The fate of slavery in the pre–Civil War era, for example, generated an almost continuous debate over constitutional principles between North and South that culminated in the Supreme Court's decision in *Scott v. Sandford* (1857). More recently, conflicts in Vietnam and the Persian Gulf have raised questions about what powers the framers in Philadelphia intended for Congress and the president in "making" and "declaring" war. In our precedent-based common law system, in order for present law to be legitimate it must have some historical connection. In other words, we achieve stability in our constitutional system by linking the past to the present. For this reason, constitutional history has figured prominently in our public life and has emerged as a source of scholarly and political controversy. Time and again public officials, whether in Congress, the White House, or the Supreme Court, have turned to the history of the federal Constitution to support their positions. Just as often, given the past's ambiguity, historians have clashed with one another about what lessons previous constitutional struggles actually teach us.

The Constitution has been both a source of authority for government and a restraint on government. A constitution is an embodiment of principles, institutions, laws, and customs that form a framework of government. What makes such a document function is the concept of constitutionalism, which holds that political authority ought to be constrained through rules and procedures. In simple terms, the law should be above persons. At important landmarks in our history—World Wars I and II, the Great Depression, the civil-rights movement of the 1960s, for example—this most basic principle of government has come under attack, with government officials invoking community needs to set aside individual rights.

The history of rights in America reminds us that we have been deeply ambivalent about them. Survey after survey has disclosed as much. For example, when asked if an individual has a right to see or show a pornographic movie or to send or receive lewd materials through the mails, a majority of Americans respond negatively. Offered a choice between liberty and community control, they often select the latter. Yet these same respondents routinely insist—and insist in overwhelming numbers—that of the Constitution's provisions, the Bill of Rights is sacred. It would seem that we love to hate those provisions of our fundamental law that we most cherish.

As the documents that follow reveal, liberty is not an absolute. Granting total freedom to any individual could theoretically result in the restriction of freedom for everyone else. Social control is essential if rights are to have meaning. The challenge for the constitutional historian, therefore, is to understand how liberty has been distributed within the social order, and in what institutions—Congress, the Supreme Court, the presidency—this task has been lodged. This tension over the distribution of rights and powers within government (who is to enjoy them, and what institution is to allocate them) lies at the core of our constitutional history.

Today public officials and constitutional historians are locked in a sustained debate about how best to balance liberty and authority amid massive social change. Conservative scholars and public officials, among them Judge Robert Bork, proffer the doctrine of original intention as the best means of striking this balance. They insist that during the Chief Justiceship of Earl Warren (1954–1969) the Supreme Court became a continuing constitutional convention, in which the justices rewrote the nation's fundamental law to suit their own prejudices and redistributed rights in ways that favored minorities. The Court, they charge, became an "imperial judiciary" awash in its own personal excesses and gripped in a rapturous fit of liberalism and welfare statism. Under these circumstances, the rights of minorities took precedence over the rights of the majority, and reverse discrimination replaced plain old discrimination. If, the conservative argument runs, the justices only heeded the wishes—the intentions—of the framers, the present mess in which we supposedly find the Supreme Court subverting community control and unfairly redistributing rights would clear up.

Liberals have taken a different tack in responding to the challenge of balancing liberty and community control. They insist that the strength of the constitutional system depends on its ability to respond to social demands for justice through law. Old law, in short, must yield to new constitutional doctrines in order for fundamental law to retain legitimacy. Former Supreme Court Justice William J. Brennan and Justice Thurgood Marshall (the only African-American ever to sit on the Court) have taken exception to the arguments of Bork and other conservatives. Justice Brennan has observed that "an awareness of history and an appreciation of the aims of the Founding Fathers seldom resolve concrete problems." Justice Marshall has argued that the miracle of the Constitution was not its birth but its life—a life nurtured through two turbulent centuries marked by a pattern in which "suffering, struggle and sacrifice . . . has triumphed over much of what was wrong with the original Constitution." Marshall reminds us that the framers in 1787 respected neither African-Americans nor women as equals to white men before the law. Liberals further insist that, considering the heavy emphasis in American government on majority will, the federal judiciary in general and Supreme Court justices in particular offer the best means of making those less equal in life more equal in law.

The documents and essays in Volume I cover the period from the United States' founding through Reconstruction. Volume II begins with the 1870s and brings the story to the present. Both volumes reveal constitutional historians of different political and scholarly persuasions challenging one another's viewpoints and, in the process, contributing to the general debate over public policy. A better and more complete understanding of America's past is sure to emerge from this lively exchange.

Each chapter opens with a brief introduction that sets the historical scene. There follow a selection of documents and two or three essays examining the chapter topic. The essays show how differing interpretations can be drawn from the same historical evidence presented in the documents. Headnotes that place the readings in historical and interpretive perspective introduce the documents and essays. Readers wishing to explore the topics in greater depth should consult the books and articles listed under the end-of-chapter Further Reading.

Numerous people contributed wise counsel and professional expertise in the development of the two volumes. Detailed and extremely helpful written reviews of draft tables of contents were provided by Herman Belz, University of Maryland, College Park; Winfred Bernhard, University of Massachusetts, Amherst; Frederick Harrod, United States Naval Academy; Mary Beth Norton, Cornell University; Michael Parrish, University of California, San Diego; David Robson, John Carroll University; Ronald Seavoy, Bowling Green State University; John Semonche, University of North Carolina, Chapel Hill; David Sterling, University of Cincinnati; and Robert P. Sutton, Western Illinois University. Additional advice was generously extended by Richard Ellis, State University of New York, Buffalo; Robert Haws, University of Mississippi; R. Kent Newmyer, University of Connecticut; John Pratt, State University of New York, Stony Brook; Rebecca Shoemaker, Indiana State University; and George Suggs, Southeast Missouri State University. Finally, Stephen Prescott and Eric Rise helped to locate and photocopy the documents and essays. I extend my thanks to them, as well as to Sylvia Mallory, James Miller, Margaret Roll, Tina Beazer, Sarah Doyle, and Karen Wise of D. C. Heath, who were encouraging, professional, and patient beyond the call of duty.

K.L.H.

Contents

C H A P T E R   4
Creating the American Republic, 1787
Page 120

C H A P T E R   5
Ratification and the Bill of Rights
Page 178

C H A P T E R   6
Freedom of Expression in the New Republic
Page 231

C H A P T E R   7
The Establishment of Federal Judicial Review
Page 276

CHAPTER 8

Andrew Jackson, the Presidency, and Separation of Powers

Page 333

CHAPTER 9

Nullification, States' Rights, and State Sovereignty

Page 364

CHAPTER 12

Race, Gender, and the Fourteenth Amendment

Page 524

APPENDIX

Page i

Major Problems
in American Constitutional History

Constitutional History
and Constitutionalism

⊹

Radical, liberal, and conservative scholars of U.S. constitutional history have yet to produce a creative synthesis. The two leading textbooks, The American Constitution, *by Herman Belz, and* A March of Liberty, *by Melvin I. Urofsky, reflect the polarization in the field. The former presents the history of constitutionalism from an essentially conservative political perspective; the latter explores it from a liberal vantage point. Never have constitutional historians disagreed so vehemently over so many issues. For example, does public law embrace certain core values of justice, equality, and fairness that elevate it above political manipulation? Are the original intentions of the framers of the Constitution and the various amendments the best guide to constitutional understanding today? Can these intentions be known to us today, in any case? Should we examine constitutional history from the perspective of judges and courts? Or should we seek the "aspirations" of the people over constitutional rights? Does the legitimacy of constitutional values endure because succeeding generations maintain fidelity to the assumptions of those who have come before them? Or does the maintenance of an effective constitutional order depend on each generation's creatively adapting federal and state constitutions to ever-changing social and economic circumstances? For the time being, constitutional historians seem to agree only that they should disagree when answering these questions.*

⊹ *E S S A Y S*

The two essays reprinted here reflect the current debate about the scope of and approaches to constitutional history. In the first selection, Hendrik Hartog, a professor of law at the University of Wisconsin, argues that constitutional historians should take seriously the development of "rights consciousness" in U.S. history by exploring how different groups interpret the Constitution. Hartog's approach, which draws from the critical legal studies perspective, underscores the ongoing conflict in the American experience about the meaning of the Constitution and the frequency with which lawmakers and ordinary citizens differ over rights. In short, Hartog emphasizes that the history of the Constitution is the history of many voices, not one, and especially not that of the Supreme Court.

Herman Belz approaches the issue of constitutionalism from a much different and politically more conservative perspective. Belz (far more than Hartog) stresses the nature of constitutionalism, but, like Hartog, he sees many connections between political life and constitutional developments. He reads the meanings differently, arguing that the interest-group pluralism that Hartog and others deplore is a vital part of the U.S. constitutional tradition. Belz dismisses charges that constitutionalism plays into the hands of those with power and influence; it merely aids those with social privilege; and it cannot deliver a meaningful solution to contemporary problems of race, gender, and economic equality. These questions of who benefits from the constitutional system, whether or not the system has been and is fair, and the extent to which it can adapt to ongoing change without losing its moorings in its historical foundations form the central issues of contemporary constitutional history.

A History of Rights Consciousness

HENDRIK HARTOG

This essay . . . suggest[s] a framework for writing a history of American constitutional rights consciousness. The first section describes characteristic practices of American constitutional rights consciousness, locating them in aspirations to freedom from bondage and from control by others. The second section poses some of the difficulties historians necessarily face in weighing the political and moral significance of those practices. The third criticizes the ordinary perspective of American constitutional history and suggests the difference that attention to constitutional rights consciousness might make.

The study of constitutional rights consciousness offers the possibility of integrating the subjects of American social history and American constitutional history. The study of constitutional rights consciousness also challenges tacit assumptions of both social and constitutional historians. Some social historians look for rights consciousness in the relative autonomy of particular social visions. They emphasize the features that, for example, differentiated black constitutional aspirations from those legitimated by a white Supreme Court, or married women's notions of their domestic rights from those of their husbands. Eventually, however, their subdiscipline ought to deal with the question of how distinctive and diverse groups learned to frame their claims in ways identified as "constitutional." They will have to deal with what binds us together as one people, as well as with what divides us. Legal scholars skeptical of the strategic value of devoting resources to claims to legal rights will have to confront groups' and individuals' convictions that constitutional struggles were meaningful. Historians certain of the transformative capacities inherent in rights discourses will have to deal with the demonstrated power of those discourses to deflect, contain, and delude those who place their hopes in rights.

Hendrik Hartog, "The Constitution of Aspiration and 'The Rights That Belong to Us All,' "
The Journal of American History, 74 (December 1987): 1013–1034. Reprinted by permission.

It is helpful to think of rights talk as a relatively stable and permanent social convention . . . . But it is important to remember the distinctiveness of *this* constitutional convention. Constitutional rights (and their denial) have constituted Americans' political identities and engaged their imaginations. Rights are almost never gained painlessly. Their apparent durability may have made them seem valuable and worth the pain. But their apparent vulnerability and fragility—their capacity to be reimagined, repossessed, redistributed—have been another part of their value to the groups struggling for constitutional rights throughout American history.

Constitutional Aspirations and Constitutional Discontent

A history of constitutional rights consciousness needs to begin by confronting the immense symbolic power of an emancipatory vision of natural rights. It is this vision that one planter identified as the freed slaves' "wild notions of rights and freedom," and that Elizabeth Cady Stanton called "the inalienable right of all to be happy." This vision has justified continued struggle by groups in the face of (presumably temporary) judicial and political defeats.

The textual expression of that vision, the constitution of aspiration and struggle—the constitution relevant to constitutional rights consciousness—emerges from only a few phrases of the federal Constitution: portions of the Bill of Rights and the Civil War Amendments, and from the Declaration of Independence, which is not officially a constitutional text at all. And even those phrases may have had to carry moral weight and meaning that would have surprised their authors. An American emancipatory tradition of constitutional meaning must be rooted in the subversive and disruptive and utopian messages that people read into constitutional texts and drew from diverse and contradictory sources, including English common law, liberalism, Enlightenment philosophy, post-Reformation theology, and the medieval peasant's vision of self-ownership and freedom.

For the past two centuries, American understandings of constitutional rights have changed as understandings of the interrelated meanings of slavery and of political freedom have changed. The identification of the Constitution with a "Great Tradition" of emancipatory aspirations apparently resulted from the happenstance that a moral critique of slavery and a celebration of the virtues of free labor developed contemporaneously with American constitutionalism. The long contest over slavery did more than any other cause to stimulate the development of an alternate, rights conscious interpretation of the federal constitution. Still, a modern American understanding of constitutional rights could only become embedded in the Constitution after the Civil War and emancipation. All the varying meanings that have been derived from the phrase "equal protection of the laws" are rooted in contending visions of what it was that was overthrown by the end of slavery.

Which groups (sharecroppers? married women? children? welfare mothers? employees?) could lay claim metaphorically to the sense of outrage that since the Civil War has attached to legalized categories of dependence and servitude? What must government do to avoid legitimating enslaving relations? Those have been crucial questions for groups claiming constitutional rights. Underneath almost any claimed constitutional right, one can find an implicit claim that not to recognize the right would be a legitimation of the "badges and incidents" of a form of slavery.

Constitutional rights consciousness—at least in its typical American forms—has started from positive notions of self-ownership and of citizenship, from the ideal of an autonomous individual capable of imagining and realizing a personal future, from the Declaration of Independence's invocation of a universal right to the pursuit of happiness. The exaltation of freedom required the antithesis of enslavement. As Stanton wrote in 1857, "When we talk of woman's rights, is not the right to her person, to her happiness, to her life, the first on the list? If you go to a southern plantation and speak to a slave of his right to property, to the elective franchise, to a thorough education, his response will be a vacant stare. . . . The great idea of his right to himself, to his personal dignity, must first take possession of his soul." Such a statement, as description and as political program, suggests an aspiration to solitude and isolation. Individual autonomy—the freedom to be left alone and to lead a "private" life—was an overarching value.

American constitutional rights consciousness began with the dream of an autonomous identity, but critiques of law and other forms of official power and violence productive of hierarchy and social division have defined its political vision. Recognition of constitutional rights required the undoing of structures of illegitimate authority. The wrongs that constitutional rights would redress have usually been tied to a structure of status and dependency (slavery, peonage, coverture, childhood) reinforced and reproduced by public power. And the constitution that claimants looked to embodied a structure of rights that rose above and countered the "real" social order of oppressive relations.

The vision of autonomy incorporated an ideal of community. Autonomous, rights-bearing individuals would live in groups and collectivities and participate in public life. Their "happiness," as Thomas Jefferson knew, required community. They would know themselves, as individuals and as citizens, through their capacity to construct intentional and voluntary forms of solidarity. And many, particularly the many in the nineteenth century raised within a powerful Christian culture, interpreted the development of individual capacities as an overarching right, because it enabled one to fulfill a variety of duties to others. One was obliged then to become an autonomous citizen, so that one could participate usefully in communities.

Who was entitled to the status of citizen and of rights bearer? At the heart of the constitutional aspiration one finds a critique of all restrictive definitions of citizenship, as reproductions of illegitimate hierarchy. Government cannot know in advance who will be capable of exercising rights. And rights holders are those who do what rights holders do. Those who act as autonomous individuals—choosing, constructing, protecting—whether through collective or solitary activities, grow entitled to rights identified with the choices they have made. More, government ought to treat as adult citizens those who take on citizenship's burdens and responsibilities, perhaps especially when they (women, minorities, children, the handicapped) fit received and legitimated categories of the naturally dependent.

The problem of dependency, what might be called the parental problem of how to prepare dependents for autonomous adulthood, strikes me as a key to a history of struggles over constitutional rights consciousness. Those who drew on visions of constitutional rights often recognized themselves as still dependent and vulnerable, even as they aspired to autonomy. They knew they needed help, and they sought to draw on (and, in the process, to construct) a continuing pragmatic tradition of care and responsibility, which many have aspired to impose on public authority. Within this tradition, government (after the Civil War, in particular the federal government) would have a particular responsibility to give dependent groups the means and the capacity for citizenship, to protect as well as to recognize.

Yet, the appropriate quantity of protection that the federal government, as well as other structures of authority, ought to provide, has also been a continuing source of division and conflict. The aspiration to undo dependency has led some to attack all governmental care as paternalistic. The desire to destroy the bonds of past legal servitudes drew Stanton and Samuel Gompers to an acceptance of a formalistic voluntarism or privatism that denied continuing dependencies. A commitment to negative liberty may justify leaving the newly enfranchised unprotected to their fates. The emancipatory project identified with constitutional rights consciousness sometimes became nothing more than the removal of formal legal constraints.

If American constitutional rights consciousness has been rooted in utopian aspirations to an autonomous life, freed of hierarchies and status, how have those aspirations been expressed in constitutional struggles? What is it that groups hoped would be the result of their recourse to rights? The papers in the symposium reveal three forms of constitutional claims made by groups seeking to realize their constitutional aspirations. By forms of constitutional claims, I do not mean the conventional lawyers' categories—free exercise, free speech, due process, equal protection—used in constitutional law, but three distinct, yet interrelated, ways of characterizing the rights required to secure constitutional aspirations. The first characterization, and the most familiar, is that of the right as a "trump," a claim that, once established, triumphs over competing values and claims. The second, and the most important for a historical understanding of American constitutional rights consciousness, is that of a right as a duty on public authority to undo—to destroy—the structures that maintain hierarchy and oppression. The third is that of a right as a duty on public authority to reconstruct itself or its relations to its citizens, or lose legitimacy. They offer three ways of describing the demand that lies behind the assertion of a claimed right. The first says, "Mine!" The second says, "Not theirs!" The third says, "Do what is necessary, or I will never again trust you!"

The first of these characterizations, the trump, is what most of us ordinarily mean when we say that we have a right. The goal of the claim is to assert the autonomy and capacity of the rights holder and the complementary disempowerment of all others, in particular of the state. That understanding of a right is implicit in the statement of the United States Supreme Court in *Pierce* v. *Society of Sisters* that Oregon had no capacity "to standardize its children by forcing them to accept instruction from public [school] teachers only." It also is what freedmen who in 1867 refused to leave a Richmond, Virginia, streetcar meant when they shouted, "Let's have our rights."

That form of asserting a right borrows from property law an almost spatial sense of the bounded self—of what in the eighteenth century were called the "fences" that constituted the liberties of free men. As with property law, the form of the constitutional claim often masks the dependence of the rights holder on a world of others. Black freedmen learned that they had a right to walk the sidewalks of southern towns as free men, but they also knew or quickly learned that that right depended, as all rights depend, on the willingness of public authority to enforce it. They knew then that their freedom rested on the temporary presence of the Union army. Likewise, the assertion of a right to a distinctive religious practice has given various devotional communities a sense of their possession of a distinctive identity. Yet, the use of secular courts to enforce rights of communities whose frames of reference place them in opposition to secular authority suggests the compromising posture of an identity founded on rights.

As with property law, the claim to a constitutional right as a trump has often been countered by assertions of a "larger" public interest, or expedience, that balanced or constrained individual freedoms and autonomy. So Mormon claims that polygamy represented the free exercise of religious beliefs and was therefore immune to challenge were countered by federal insistence that conventional Christian "monogamy was necessary for democratic and republican forms of government." Parents' insistence on a right to raise children as they see fit has regularly run up against public authority's interest in "the best interests of the child." And Stanton's belief that Radical Republicans owed her and other abolitionist women the right to vote was countered by the male apologia that securing rights for the freedman was so important that no political capital could be expended on ancillary concerns. Few rights really do trump the prudential assertions of organized public power.

Likening a constitutional claim to a property right also implies the rights holder's separation from a governing authority that can only legitimate itself by recognizing the autonomy and independence of the rights holder. Such a republican separation is assuredly what some religious minorities have hoped to realize through invocation of free exercise rights. It may also be what W. E. B. Du Bois was after when he argued that the equality guaranteed by the Fourteenth Amendment did not preclude a separate black identity. But the metaphor of property appears inconsistent with postrevolutionary notions of the sovereignty of the people. If the goal of constitutional struggle is membership in "We, the People," then it hardly seems appropriate to found one's constitutional identity on a metaphorical image of rights as possessions that isolate the holder from the larger political community.

Except for religious minorities, [no other] groups . . . devoted as much energy to gaining constitutional recognition for their rights, conceived of as private possessions, as to the destruction of the settled rights of those who oppressed them. Divesting vested rights—obtaining constitutional recognition of the "no right" of others—is thus a second way of characterizing the goals of constitutional struggles. When groups have insisted on their constitutional rights, they have usually insisted on the end to some illegitimate yet legal form of power, a form itself almost always bearing the imprimatur of a right. They have read into the Constitution an implied destabilization of those vested—and often constitutionally recognized—rights of others that constrained their capacities and their autonomy.

Establishment of a new constitutional right has often been little else than the disestablishment of an older constitutional right or structure of rights. Rights seekers, say the National Association for the Advancement of Colored People in the mid-twentieth century, have justified invoking public power by their opponents' possession of previously unquestioned rights. They knew that without a reappraisal of previously constitutional practices there could be no positive right worth having. School integration is a meaningful right only in the context of the destruction of locally imposed racial segregation. For 140 years, feminists have made male possession of their sexuality and of their wealth and of their children the hallmarks of a constitutionally corrupt society. Women's rights may have meant nothing more (or less) than the end of male patriarchal rights. When ex-slaves went out on their own, when they moved about and sought to control their work and personal lives, they were not simply asserting their possession of individual rights. Such behavior consciously challenged their ex-masters, confronting them with the destruction of previously settled rights over what was once theirs. When scholars explore labor's long struggle to establish a constitutional right to organize collectively, they may better understand that right, not as a search for a personal possession, but as a struggle to overturn a history of judicial confirmation of managerial rights over the employment relation. Even "the idea of a community right to industrial property" that Youngstown's steelworkers have recently learned to make their own is first of all about divesting steel companies of their traditional rights to do whatever they choose (including abandoning profitable factories). To reformulate such constitutional rights claims in positive and possessory terms robs them of the meanings they held for those who mobilized them.

When presented as claims to negate rights, rights readily become a focus for group organization and identity. As possessive individualists, rights holders may lack collective political identities, but to uproot common opponents they must join together. Black struggles for civil rights coalesced into a movement when leaders organized to uproot the vested rights of southern (and northern) white communities to enforce segregation by law. . . . [A]ttempts to organize a feminist antipornography movement have relied on a confrontation with the expectations of men who believe that they have a constitutional right to take erotic pleasure from whatever they choose.

. . . By focusing on the wrongs to be undone, rights claimants have transformed an inherited libertarian rhetoric, so that it could at times be made an instrument of collective organization and collective identities.

The aspiration to forms of constitutional divestment has often carried an unsettling and radical edge. When freed slaves and married women asserted their common citizenship with whites and married men, they knew (as did their opponents) that their citizenship—their potential status as members of a transformed political community—depended on taking vested and settled rights away. Likewise, both employers and employees always understood that the latters' gains derived from the formers' losses. One cannot imagine being freed from vested structures of servitude without imagining the correlative of those who have been served losing their perquisites. Masking rhetorics has sometimes allowed Americans to feel as if everyone benefited from changes in constitutional rights, but such rhetorics have been less convincing than the "instrumentalist" arguments for legal changes said to promote economic growth.

More importantly, this second form of constitutional claim suggests an apparently contradictory conception of the Constitution as a permanent structure of authority. At the same time that newly freed blacks, early feminists, and others mobilized a strategy to destabilize others' rights, they also invested the constitutional rights they sought with immanent and unchanging meaning. Many of the rights attacked by them were rights that, as in the case of the right to segregate affirmed in *Plessy* v. *Ferguson,* had been explicitly recognized by constitutional authority. If they could be changed, why not the newer rights as well?

Both the yearning for permanent statements of rights and the insistence on the contingency of present structures of authority are central features of American constitutional rights consciousness. Groups have been able to draw from constitutional language ways of demonstrating that those who exercised power over them did so illegitimately, immorally, and wrongly, and therefore had nothing worthy of recognition as vested rights. At the same time, groups have made aspirations to a life free from legally recognized hierarchies—to a life without the badges and incidents of slavery—into a super-constitution that has taken permanent precedence over any merely transitory determination of constitutional meaning. Some rights should never have been recognized. And some constitutional changes (involving the denial of previously vested rights) could only be imagined as returns to forms of permanent truth and moral meaning forgotten by earlier constitutional interpreters.

While many rights claimants have rested visions of constitutional legitimacy on the need to redistribute rights from oppressor to oppressed, few have stated their public claims so starkly. As a people, Americans may be "constitutionally" incapable of characterizing rights claims as moves in a zero-sum game. Lawyers know that a new, increased, or transformed public good must always be alleged as the necessary consequence of any recognition of previously unrecognized rights; there must be some net benefit to the public welfare. Americans have never simply righted wrongs; they have always been making things better.

Occasionally, however, particular rights claimants have gone beyond the easy and lawyerlike assertion of an increase in the public good. Instead, they have insisted on characterizing particular claims as preconditions to any future public legitimacy. This is a third way of characterizing constitutional rights. In some cases such claims have taken the form of demands for structures of effective legal remedies. For minorities and women, affirmative action today makes the formal rights secured in the constitutional order something other than empty and fraudulent assurances. Without it, they would come to see themselves as fooled by rights, as having misdirected their aspirations.

Alternatively, groups have at times declared one particular constitutional right as primary and superior to all others. Nineteenth-century feminists, for example, eventually designated the franchise as the first of all rights. Their characterization rested on the common equation of citizenship with the vote and their complementary understanding that the continuation of patriarchy was inconsistent with female citizenship. Without the ballot, women remained vulnerable and dependent, less than autonomous individuals. With it, feminists could imagine the reconstruction of a legitimate public order. Likewise, for religious minorities with deviant religious practices, the free exercise clause of the First Amendment has been seen as "the axis on which the wheel of history turns," the only foundation for life within a crushingly secular American society.

To historians, the notion that the constitutional order must legitimate itself by recognizing a particular right may suggest a strikingly tentative and contingent commitment to the American constitutional arena. Such demands imply a threat: If you (the state, the courts, the Department of Labor) don't do this one thing, then we (women, minorities, religious deviationists) will have learned the foolishness of identifying personal aspirations with constitutional rights. They imply the threat of withdrawal and of a loss of constitutional faith.

Dilemmas of a Convention

. . . [H]istorians ought not fool themselves that a return to the middle—somewhere between essential truth and no truth, somewhere between permanent moral values and aesthetics and power—will resolve their own feelings about rights. Like other Americans, they cherish deep ambivalences about the virtues of rights and rights discourses. Seeing constitutional rights consciousness as conventional in nature and structure may permit them to avoid apocalyptic excesses; it will discourage the ruminations that take some on a conceptual banister ride from rights aspirants' visions of autonomy and self-ownership to totalitarianism and despair. Yet I am sure the conflict between immanence and plasticity . . . will be recreated in the middle ground of convention. We cannot escape the conflict, because it is inherent in our inherited language of rights.

Let me briefly sketch two sources of the conflict. First, the claims of outsiders, no less than those of insiders, resonate with conceptions drawn from long-standing constitutional traditions. Those conceptions have been rooted in particular social and historical contexts and reflect the values of a variety of constitutional winners. The result is that the recourse to rights will, at times, produce distortions of outsiders' aspirations. Second, persistent struggle about conceptions of rights may call into question the value of the rights themselves, as relatively permanent measures of political stability and legitimacy.

The recourse to rights rhetoric has constrained the claims of some of those who struggled for constitutional rights, precluding some positions and cabining some aspirations. Consider the power of notions of possessive in-dividualism, for example. The Lockean tradition has lived in the constitu-tional claims Americans have made, for all of the valor and imagination of the legal and historical scholarship that has tried to recover alternative in-tellectual foundations. The inherited meanings drawn from that tradition shaped the claims of a labor movement, which from the early twentieth century on conceded many of the prerogatives of management, as the rep-resentative of company-owning shareholders. The influence of possessive individualism also helps explain the relative unavailability of constitutional language for litigants asserting the collective rights of families. Either family rights became the individualistic, libertarian rights of individuals within a family, or they were equated with the property rights of a patriarchal head of household.

To use our individualistic Bill of Rights and Fourteenth Amendment as sources of language to constitute, recognize, and legitimate group identities and to represent group aspirations is, at minimum, an odd way to articulate a collective faith. For the past century and more, lawyers have devoted much ingenuity to formulating group claims in ways that have made them appear to conform to the categories of a distinctly individualistic constitutional rights discourse. Their work has often been heroic and sometimes successful. Yet, it has also failed frequently enough that historians may wonder whether clients might not have sought better weapons in struggles for respect and legitimacy.

Using the inherited categories of rights talk as a way of articulating grievances, wants, and hopes disciplines the speaker. Not all wants can be posed as rights. Rights talk has shaped what groups demand as their rights, so that what is demanded has often ended close to what those with power wanted to give. For example, black parents in Boston (and elsewhere) who struggled for decades to compel school boards to shift resources to their impoverished and segregated schools ended up watching their children being bused to equally impoverished, but hostile, white schools. They were taught through constitutional rights litigation, as interpreted by their lawyers, that integration had to take precedence over any redistribution of resources to the education of their children. What they got was what their lawyers asked for.

Another difficulty must be faced by those who would write a "conven-tional" history of rights incorporating the struggles and achievements of constitutional outsiders. . . . Americans have often thought of the word *right* in terms of constraints and barriers against change. They have known rights as the distinctive attributes of legitimate constitutional government, because rights reveal that government's intention not to invade the private identities of its citizens. Thus, gaining a constitutional right—gaining public recognition that you have a right, and not just a want—should mean that you have gained some protection against fickle and transitory political judgments.

But such an interpretation of constitutional rights as conservative, as barriers to change, flies in the face of the histories explored in this symposium, many of which describe the articulation through rights of visions of change and transformation. Indeed, groups claiming rights have often aimed to end a preexisting regime of substantive rights. How else can we understand black freedmen's claimed right to much of the lands of their former masters? Groups wish "their" rights, once established, to be permanent and stable. They insist that only other, opposing, rights must be temporary and changeable. To make the obvious interpretive point, the attractiveness of permanence is always from a particular perspective.

To the extent then that constitutional historians integrate the perspectives of those outside the constitutional mainstream with mainstream understandings, they will, almost necessarily, weaken commitments to a traditional rights convention. At minimum, historians will have to rethink their inherited understandings of rights. At maximum, they may find themselves forced to abandon notions of a distinctively legal or constitutional history, abandoning a perspective founded on the American Constitution's separation from the indeterminacies of American social and political history.

Constitutional History from the Bottom Up

Constitutional historians have disagreed sharply over many issues: political, moral, methodological. Virtually all, however, have taken it as a given that the goal of historical inquiry should be an examination and evaluation of a body of authoritative interpretations—constitutional law—typically identified with the pronouncements of the United States Supreme Court. Largely banished from the domain of constitutional history have been the activities and beliefs of all who were not official interpreters. Thus, we have had a surfeit of studies of the racial beliefs of the drafters and official interpreters of the Fourteenth Amendment. But, until recently, we knew little of the distinctive constitutional beliefs that informed black activism in the post–Civil War period. And still, today, no constitutional historian has made Afro-American constitutional vision a prominent feature of post–Civil War constitutionalism.

The prevailing conception of constitutional history's proper subject matter has not required constitutional historians to deny the significance of social and cultural change. Today, work in constitutional history often rests on an assumption that various nonconstitutional inputs—social, cultural, ideological, economic, political—produce outputs, or constitutional texts, that are, or express, constitutional law. Insofar as conventional constitutional history has concerned itself with the constitutional faiths and values of blacks and others of the constitutionally disinherited, it has done so by considering them as inputs, helping to produce the outputs of doctrine embodied in constitutional law. The historical inquiry assesss the contribution of inputs to outputs and analyzes changes in both over time. But such historical analyses, no less than older methodologies, assume that only certain authoritative texts and certain authoritative textual interpretations can have the status of constitutional output. Recovering their meaning and their place within a continuing sequence of authoritative texts and interpretations is the proper business of constitutional history.

Scholars have often pointed to various long traditions of constitutionalism—traditions that distinguish fundamental law from (presumably democratic or, at minimum, unruly) politics—as shaping American deference to a text and to a privileged group of interpreters. The emphasis on authoritative texts tends to imply the near inevitability of the American pattern of discovering constitutional meaning and of establishing constitutional legitimacy. . . . [T]he typical forms of American constitutional history may themselves be the consequence of the machinations of two generations of jurisprudes who worked to make the federal Constitution appear an objective, external, and completed document, interpretable only by legal mandarins. One reason, then, why historians have seen the Constitution as they have is because two generations of "Framers" intended them to see it that way.

The result, in any event, is a constitutional history that provides no account of perhaps the most salient and interesting feature of American public culture: its rights consciousness. . . . Americans have been especially inclined to phrase their demands and "needs" in arguments about constitutional rights, to expect remedies for their wrongs to be provided through processes provided by formal legal institutions, and to view their activities as touching on issues of constitutional interpretation. Such consciousness has thrived among those who did not benefit from mainstream interpretations of the Constitution.

The persistent presence of constitutional rights consciousness, articulated by and embodied in a changing array of groups, ought to call into question American constitutional history's received perspective. If constitutional law were really nothing but a body of texts authoritatively interpreted by a specialized and distant elite, why would so many Americans have ceaselessly organized to validate in legal arenas distinctive constitutional claims and perceived entitlements? If American constitutionalism were really about the evolution of a univocal meaning, about getting the right historical answer to the constitutional question of the moment, could historians ever account for the contingency and the variety of wildly different right answers that have been derived from the texts over the past two centuries? If particular opinions and holdings were conclusive of struggles for legal rights, then those who lost in court should have either accepted the loss as legal and slunk into passivity or insisted on power through nonlegal means. Yet, neither alternative has attracted many groups throughout American history. . . .

Constitutional historians are so used to thinking of the business of constitutional history as explaining the origins of various statements of constitutional law doctrine that it is difficult to even imagine alternatives. To learn to see the constitutional rights consciousness as constitutional output, no less than constitutional input, would require historians to deal with the American Constitution as contested interpretive terrain, as an arena of struggle between contending and changing normative orders. They would have to recognize that constitutional history incorporates many voices, that there has rarely been a monolithic understanding of constitutional meaning, that the position of the United States Supreme Court as our preeminent constitutional interpreter is a problematic feature of our history.

Such a vision of constitutional history requires a perspective wide enough to incorporate the relations between official producers of constitutional law, and those who at particular times and in particular circumstances resisted or reinterpreted constitutional law. It would recognize the significance of a variety of groups who worked to reconstruct constitutional law for their own purposes—including the purpose of reconstructing a legitimate constitutional order. Lawyers' categories, formal legalistic language, would remain important subjects of study, but as translations and as mediations of aspirations and claims, not as the ends of inquiry.

Supreme Court cases should be only one portion of the descriptive detail of American constitutional history. As important would be the small, everyday contests, arguments, negotiations, and understandings in which legal rights and constitutional assumptions have been constructed and exercised. Labor contracts, divorce decrees, zoning variances, municipal ordinances, children's claimed right to keep their parents out of their closets, parents' exercise of their asserted right to discipline their children—all are the stuff of our constitutional history as well.

Formal constitutional rights talk translates and reconstructs conflict. It does not initiate it. Constitutional history's distinctiveness as a domain of inquiry should result from the historical experiences of groups and individuals throughout American history who have invested that arena of struggle with meaning and significance. It is not important for itself. . . . I do not believe we will ever discover a relatively stable truth about ourselves from the nature of American rights talk. We can only use American constitutional struggles as ways of learning about "the history of a people contending about power, identity, and justice."

Conclusion

. . . Our uncertainties, our discomforts, our ambivalence about the salience and significance of rights in American history should not be repressed as exploratory work proceeds. They are themselves sources of historical insight into rights' moral place. Historians cannot hope to write a social history of

American constitutional experience without confronting the peculiar eva-
nescence of rights. Constitutional rights have been valuable because they
appear as solid and permanent commitments by the society, as guarantees
of an unchanging vision of free human subjectivity. Yet we know that their
meanings have changed dramatically and frequently over time. The very
successes of particular groups in insisting on the perquisites of membership
within a common American citizenry suggest the changeability of constitutional claims.

Constitutional history has traditionally assumed responsibility for con-
serving an inherited American constitutionalism. Its practitioners have assumed the task laid out by Lincoln in his Springfield Lyceum address. What
is constitutionalism? While there are many definitions, all orient themselves
around the notion of the rule of law—around the notion that legitimate
government is, to use the famous phrase of John Adams and James Harrington, "a government of laws, not of men."

In most versions, the idea of a government of laws has been said to
lead to a vision of limited government. Government is legitimate only so
long as it recognizes that there are things that it cannot do, particularly to
the "private" identities and possessions of its citizens. At the same time,
the notion of a government of laws also has suggested a government that
must justify itself by its congruence with external standards and norms. There
is within our inherited Anglo-American notions of constitutionalism no inherent right to rule. Government, ruling, must be justified. And the right
to govern, therefore, rests on government's obligation to do particular
things—to prevent forms of bondage, to protect property rights, to guarantee
people security from the cruelty and the chaos of a life without structures
of political authority.

Can inherited notions of American constitutionalism—of the primacy
of a government of laws—coexist with a reconstructed constitutional history
founded on the study of constitutional rights consciousness? I can imagine
a constitutionalism of rights consciousness, a populist reinterpretation of the
government of laws, locating those laws in the changing aspirations of diverse
groups within the society. Yet I do not know whether such an understanding
would satisfy yearnings for stable external standards against which to hold
governmental processes.

Historians will conserve a constitutional heritage. What they conserve—
what future writings in American constitutional history will include and
exclude, what will be regarded as salient, what will be recognized as pe-
ripheral—is for them to decide. Their decisions ought to leave readers with
an understanding of the moral complexity of American constitutional experience, and the passion invested in constitutional rights, as well as the
costs of commitment to American constitutional values. The task is to interpret the constitutional history of a society that has been and remains
structured by divisions of wealth, gender, and race, yet, at the same time,
has been and remains committed to values of democracy, fairness, and
respect.

In Defense of Liberal Pluralism and Constitutionalism

HERMAN BELZ

Every state has a constitution—a body of principles, institutions, laws, and customs that forms the framework of government—but not every state is a constitutional state. The latter is distinguished by a commitment to constitutionalism, which in essence is the idea that political life ought to be carried on according to procedures and rules that paradoxically are in some degree placed beyond politics: procedures in other words that are fundamental. Nothing so positive as a written constitution, but rather the belief that the law as the embodiment of a society's most important values is powerful, characterizes government under the rule of law.

Apprehension about the future of constitutional government in the United States . . . increased in [the sixties and seventies.] Political assassination, urban riots, the resort to civil disobedience by groups as disparate as striking postal workers and university students, the idea that politics is important enough to be the object of secret intelligence operations—all of this is evidence of a crisis in which the very legitimacy of public authority is called into question. In the long run, however, perhaps even more unsettling than these turbulent events is the intellectual and ideological challenge to constitutionalism that they have produced.

This challenge appears most significantly, I believe, not in the revelations of former White House aides, alarming as these are, but rather in the crisis literature of political science [and history] which has attempted to explain the upheaval of the past several years and offer a new theory of politics. The most obvious feature of this literature is its critique of pluralism. Interest-group liberalism, the antipluralists emphatically conclude, is the dead end, not the vital center, of American democracy. Dissatisfaction with liberal pluralism is not new, however, and in the . . . literature it does not provide the special animus of the attack on the liberal state. Rather impatience with constitutionalism, which runs pretty deep amid the consciousness raising and political involvement of our time, forms the essential theme of the attack on pluralism.

The fundamental charge against pluralism is that it is not real democracy, but rather a system of special privilege by which the rich and powerful protect their interests at the expense of the people. American politics, the antipluralists insist, simply does not work the way it is supposed to in theory. It is fatuous, they say, to think that a vast number of competing and roughly equal groups interact freely in the political decision-making structure. On the contrary, a few corporate giants control the political system. An even more damning indictment of pluralism is that it excludes many groups from the political process entirely. Blacks, the poor, students, women, and sundry

Herman Belz, "New Left Reverberations in the Academy: The Antipluralist Critique of Constitutionalism," *Review of Politics*, 36 (1974): 265–283. Reprinted by permission.

minorities are all seen as relegated to a condition of noncitizenship outside the political arena.

If it is suggested that American politics is actually responsive to demands from nonelite groups, the antipluralist answer is that the system may work after a fashion, but the workings are all trivial and irrelevant. The root of the trouble is said to be the biased context in which interest-group politics operates. The political process may be open, the media relatively accessible, freedom of speech and of the press secure. All this is beside the point, however, for what is really important, say the critics, is "the other face of power," that is, the class bias of pluralist politics which prevents issues of real concern to the community from being brought into the political arena. The groups which control the system ignore problems such as urban blight, public transportation, worker alienation, and environmental destruction. What officials do not do, the argument runs—the nondecisions they make— are more important than the decisions they make about insignificant matters.

From here it is but a short distance to the doctrine of repressive tolerance. Because the political system is managed in the interests of dominant economic groups, . . . there is an objective contradiction between the political structure and the theory of pluralist toleration. In practice equality of tolerance becomes abstract and spurious, an instrument of coordination and control rather than a means of effecting change. . . . [W]hen toleration is examined in the context of liberalism, with its assumption of a utilitarian and individualistic ethic, it is revealed as negligence of the public interest. The attitude which this kind of criticism encourages will be recognized by anyone who has been on a college campus [in the late sixties and early seventies]. Student radicals take part in an election, work hard for a candidate, and then if the candidate loses decry the system for failing once again. . . . The procedures of democratic pluralism become in this view mere legitimizing rituals and the right of dissent an instrument of oppression. . . .

. . . [T]he critique of pluralism goes beyond an accounting of the specific failures of the liberal state in America. What is being challenged is the very idea of constitutionalism itself. This is most apparent in the antipluralists' preoccupation with political action.

Constitutionalism, they contend, even in its original eighteenth-century formulation, was flawed by its failure to contain a concept of political action. Beguiled by the idea of applying science to politics, the founders of constitutionalism sought to control human behavior by devising rules and procedures for the conduct of government that would eliminate the need for political leadership and citizen participation. Placing their faith in institutions rather than men, they provided no space for political action and designed a mechanistic system which depersonalized, trivialized, and fragmentized political life. Antipluralists charge further that constitutionalism comprehends and protects mere private economic interests. It thus denies the vision of politics as an educational and salvational activity, and the possibility of defining and achieving a true public purpose. In liberal society a "nondirective constitutionalism" aimed at containing competing interests is substituted for authentic political community.

Those who think of politics as the art of achieving the possible and see in the constitutional system broad scope for political action may wonder about the criteria used to reach these negative conclusions. And indeed skepticism is warranted, for the antipluralists' critique of constitutionalism depends heavily upon a conception of political action drawn more from philosophy than from ordinary language and experience.

. . . [C]ritics of pluralism hold that political action refers to acts which are novel, consequential, purposive, irreversible, and indeterminate. All else, including the routine and often predictable responses which characterize a stable constitutional regime, are defined—and dismissed—as behavior. Perhaps not every antipluralist critic would subscribe to precisely this formulation of the issue, but the demands for relevant action and meaningful change heard so often these days come pretty close to capturing the more technical definition. A corollary notion . . . is the idea of public space. As used by the antipluralists, public space refers to opportunities in which men can appear to others and disclose themselves in speech and action. This seems familiar enough, and we readily think of the range of legally protected liberties under the first and fourteenth amendments. But if speech and action and petitioning of the government avail nothing in the way of boundless, novel, unanticipated and indeterminate results—nothing that meets the criteria of political action—then there is evidently no true public space or genuine political freedom.

If constitutionalism is seen as defective in its original conception, it is criticized all the more in its present-day reality for suppressing authentic politics. This emerges most clearly in the attack on the "process theory" of democracy. Classical democratic thought, the critics argue, posited broad popular participation in politics in pursuit of the common good. In the Cold War era, however, pluralists revised the classical theory by concluding that democracy consisted in procedures and practices which assured a stable political system characterized by low popular participation. Liberal democracy became in essence a process distinguished by voter apathy and elite manipulation.

Although the antipluralists do not quite say that procedure is unimportant, they believe it has too often been honored at the expense of higher values. . . . Wilson Carey McWilliams has suggested that any solution to the contemporary political crisis must involve an abandonment of our fascination for a government of mechanical contrivances designed to avoid conflict, if not to eliminate politics altogether.

Impatient, if not scornful of procedure, antipluralists regard politics as a matter of commitment and values and substantive results. Pluralism in contrast is seen as excessively concerned with stability and efficiency and, therefore, as essentially antipolitical. Christian Bay epitomizes the antipluralist animus in condemning what he calls the liberal myth that American society is democratic and that only by working within the constitutional system can a more just society be created. The most urgent contemporary need, says Bay, is to destroy this myth.

Certainly the critics of liberal pluralism have done their demythologizing best. It remains to ask, however, what they would have in its place and how their reform ideas stand in relation to constitutionalism.

In the . . . crisis literature three tendencies can be discerned on the question, what is to be done? One looks to civil disobedience as a source of political renewal, a second contemplates the democratization of economic organizations, and a third urges a new theory of politics based upon a revival of citizenship.

Although practitioners of civil disobedience may see it as a way of bringing down the system, scholarly interpreters contend on the contrary that it can make the political system work better. Civil disobedience, they reason, can become a new form of representation with the potential to revitalize democratic citizenship. Those who engage in civil disobedience are seen as a legitimate opposition whose political actions may enlighten the government and, by informing it of its misuse of power, actually enhance the rule of law. Tyranny being the exclusion of the public from the political, reasons Wilson Carey McWilliams, we are perilously near that condition now. Yet a way out is provided by civil disobedience, which by enabling citizens to gain access to the public can be a means of constitutional reform. Hannah Arendt views civil disobedients as organized minorities expressing their disagreement with the majority. Placing recent protesters in the tradition of voluntary associations, Arendt's novel argument envisions formal recognition of a lobbyist, group representation role for civil-disobedient minorities.

The hostility that people feel toward a nameless bureaucracy may lead in the future to further spasms of civil disobedience. It is hard to take seriously, however, the suggestion that "disciplined civil disobedience is possibly a creative way to ask citizens of the state if they are satisfied with other aspects of the delegational model that has served well but which may not have produced the most equitable and efficient allocation of power and resources to deal with emergent disaffection and unmet needs in the national polity." If civil-disobedient groups do somehow become "constitutionalized" they will be part of the pluralist political structure, a curious and disappointing conclusion, it would seem, from the radical point of view. Should civil disobedience increase, however, and produce a body of concerned participating magistrates as McWilliams urges, the result will more likely be an expedient people's justice than constitutional government as we have known it historically.

A second reformist theme of the antipluralists concerns the enforcing of accountability and responsibility in the economic power structure. It has become a commonplace to observe that corporations wield political power and make policies no different in substance and effect from those of public officials. What is needed is to broaden the definition of the political to include these nominally private but actually public institutions.

One way of constitutionalizing corporations is through judicial and administrative regulation. Because this would mean more of the same sort of centralized national regulation that has seemed so ineffectual in the past, however, antipluralists take a dim view of it. They argue instead for "participatory democracy." This is surely one of the more imprecise terms of contemporary political discourse, but in the present context it means control of corporations by those who work in and are affected by them. The system of self-management that exists in Yugoslavia is taken as model. Workers would form the board of directors or governing council of a business or industry, or in larger enterprises elect delegates to a council. The point is not to redistribute property, but rather to encourage democratic participation at the place of work in order to reduce people's sense of powerlessness and contribute to their self-development. Industrial democracy would make workers citizens of the enterprise rather than corporate subjects. And by enabling them to see the relationship between public and private spheres it would in turn make them better citizens of the state.

A politically engaged citizenry, the ultimate objective of both civil disobedience strategy and participatory economic democracy, lies at the very center of the third tendency in antipluralist reformism, the quest for a new theory of politics. The immediate purpose of this quest is a regeneration of citizenship and the creation of opportunities for genuine political action. . . .

It may be, as anthropologist Stanley Diamond argues, that the rule of law is a symptom of the disorder of customary institutions and the decline of a civilization. Believing that the second coming of true democracy, community, and participation would obviate the whole rule structure of the modern liberal state, the antipluralists seem to share this view. Until our political salvation is assured, however, we are justified in asking what the implications of the new politics and the new political theory are for constitutionalism.

Although the question usually is of interest to liberals and conservatives, some radical antipluralists, despite intense criticism of the liberal state, profess concern for constitutionalism. Theorists of civil disobedience and economic democracy seek ways of legitimizing new forms of dissent and constitutionalizing the great aggregates of economic power. A few theorists of the new politics say their purpose is to revise constitutionalism to provide greater scope for political action, diminishing the height of government but not removing the restraints upon it. In fighting for their causes, moreover, radicals will rely on constitutional rules for protection. Some caution further against rejecting bourgeois liberal constitutional ideals simply because they have often been a cloak for oppression, and express concern for constitutional processes within the radical movement, lest violence and brutality obliterate peaceful procedures. This is evidence that the attack on the pluralist system does not necessarily mean repudiation of the idea of constitutionalism.

Nevertheless, the new political theory of the antipluralists contradicts the fundamental ideas of constitutionalism. Those critics who profess to revise the theory of constitutionalism are mistaken, I believe, in their understanding of its essential meaning. To them—and inferentially to the antipluralists in general—constitutionalism means, or ought to mean, the people as constituent power, the source of authority and ground of law. It means further the people creating political power by forming a social compact and exercising that power in governing themselves. The ancient notion of popular sovereignty, dating from the founding of the republic, epitomizes this conception of constitutionalism.

Its root idea is politicism, the belief, that is, that political will and the force of personality, knowledge of the good and the will to realize it in acts of wisdom, are more important for good government—and more decisive in determining the course of events—than any institutional framework or procedural arrangements. Governments are like clocks, runs the old aphorism, and go from the motion men give them, not from anything in themselves. This politicist argument has always had considerable appeal. When it is applied to the people as a whole, and they are invested with the power of political action—especially as the antipluralists would define political action—it acquires even greater force, if indeed it does not become irresistible.

But while flexibility, discretion, personal character and freedom of political action—the elements of politicism—have had a place in the constitutional tradition, they have not formed the essence of it. In essence constitutionalism has meant adherence to certain formal procedures embodying and promoting the fundamental values of liberty, equality, and justice; to ways of conducting politics and managing public affairs which preserve a space immune to or beyond politics. In order words, while the people have been the constituent power, their power to govern—popular sovereignty— has been limited by their own constitutional creation. At its inception in the eighteenth century American constitutionalism was marked by an extraordinarily democratic basis, and the people as constituent power was the most startling of the revolutionary ideas. Yet the idea that a constitution was superior to and controlling of the political power of government, even when the people themselves exercised that power either through established institutions or outside them, was also part of revolutionary constitutionalism.

In the history of Western political thought this idea of fundamental law was as remarkable an innovation as the notion of the people as constituent power. In the long run it became the truly distinctive feature of American constitutionalism. The constitution was conceived of as a means of conducting politics, but it did not consist in a mere declaration of purposes or a set of exhortations, as the French constitution of 1791 did. It was on the contrary explicitly declared to be law, the supreme law of the land along with treaties of the United States and acts of Congress made in pursuance of it. Ordinary law, as between private persons, was to be used to regulate the acts of government and the energies and passions of politics. And this political law maintaining the structure of the body politic and protecting individual liberty against encroachment by the government, a paradoxical and contradictory thing according to the best learning of the day, was to be enforced by ordinary courts of justice. It was altogether a curious amalgam which, in conjunction with the division of power between national and state governments known as federalism, effectively destroyed sovereignty as it was then known. And it meant too that popular sovereignty must be stillborn, must be placed under constitutional restraints as well.

It is the age-old politicist drive to be free of procedural restraints which informs the antipluralist appeal for a new politics. Expressing this appeal in modern terms of commitment, transcendence, and self-fulfillment, the critics resurrect the classic democratic ideal of an engaged citizenry exercising political and legal sovereignty and standing above institutions. But no better than anyone else are the antipluralists able to explain how fundamental fairness can obtain in a system of government in which all is politicized.

The essence of the political is discretion, discrimination, expediency, adjustment of conflicting claims on a pragmatic basis. The essence of the legal is general and prospective rules that result in regular and predictable procedure. A constitution must of course generate power as well as channel it. It must comprehend both the political and legal dimension. And in a strict sense we cannot say that one is more important than the other; both are essential. Yet while we can be pretty sure that political energies and passions and conflicts will continue to manifest themselves, with the insistence and power seemingly of natural forces, the experience of the twentieth century tells us that the existence of a stable and fair system for restraining these forces cannot be taken for granted. The opposite of constitutionalism— arbitrary and coercive government which denies political liberty and free public criticism—must be guarded against. And this means keeping in mind, to use the language of social science, a contrast-model.

From the 1930s to the 1950s totalitarian regimes in Europe provided a vivid contrast-model which led intellectuals in the United States to reconsider their own constitutional tradition. Instead of dismissing the rule of law as a conservative fiction and a device for maintaining the status quo, as many had done, they came to see it as a valid distinction between systems of government. A revival of interest in constitutionalism occurred which made it a principal theme in modern liberalism.

The antipluralists have reacted against liberal constitutionalism as though it were entirely ideological—a reflection of the false consciousness of its adherents—and lacking any basis in historical reality. They deny the validity of the totalitarian contrast-model on the ground that it fosters complacency and, by failing to emphasize problems, forecloses the possibility of change. Yet it is difficult to ignore recent history—right down to the latest interdiction of free speech and academic inquiry by student radicals—and hard not to be apprehensive about a political theory that exalts popular participation and political action to the extent that the new politics does. It may seem entirely clear to the heralds of the new citizenship that the mass participation of modern technological society is completely different from the true democratic participation they envision, but a skeptical view of this distinction seems warranted. How realistic is it to think that men and women will engage in politics for the sheer love of it, apart from practical purposes? Benjamin R. Barber states that "a new era of *philopoly* might help to make life for man in the post-historical epoch livable." It would be more accurate to say that only after history ends—in the world to come—will people play at politics for the love of the thing itself, as some antipluralists believe.

If the present crisis is rooted in an erosion of community which has released proliferating forces of conflict, calling into question the authority of government and politicizing all manner of social processes and relationships, the solution lies not in further encouragement of politicist tendencies but in their being brought into a more stable equilibrium with the essential ideas and procedures of constitutionalism. This will not be accomplished by stern admonitions from high officials to respect law and order, especially now in the light of the Watergate revelations. Whether the crisis can be surmounted according to prescriptions offered meanwhile by political scientists in the liberal constitutional tradition may also be doubted. These solutions range from Lowi's juridical democracy, to Friedrich's call for inspirational democratic leadership, to Tugwell's new model constitution. Appealing as these suggestions are, they seem to assume against the evidence that someone somewhere has the knowledge and power to set things right.

The crux of the matter is the tendency and habit of ordinary citizens to regard political institutions and procedures as legitimate. In the United States legitimate authority derives in large part from the direct link with the eighteenth-century framers' act of foundation and the consensual basis on which it rested. This basis has been seriously challenged, but how far the disintegration of community has gone is not clear. Probably it has not gone as far as the dramatic events [in the late sixties and early seventies] seemed to indicate. The structure of assumptions, beliefs, and practices in which constitutionalism consists may be more solidly based than it appears in the crisis literature. Nevertheless, the antipluralists' insistence on ever greater political participation and action reflects and represents a challenge to constitutionalism that is not merely academic. If the liberal constitutional order collapses, the critics of pluralism might consider, it is not at all likely that a left-wing movement dedicated to participatory democracy will take its place.

✢ *F U R T H E R   R E A D I N G*

Paul Finkelman, "The Constitution and the Intentions of the Framers: The Limits of Historical Analysis," *University of Pittsburgh Law Review* 50 (1989): 349–398

Lawrence M. Friedman, *A History of American Law,* 2nd ed. (1985)

Kermit L. Hall, *The Magic Mirror: Law in American History* (1989)

——, ed. *Main Themes in United States Constitutional and Legal History* (1987)

Michael Kammen, *A Machine That Would Go of Itself: The Constitution in American Culture* (1986)

Alfred H. Kelly, Winfred A. Harbison, and Herman J. Belz, *The American Constitution: Its Origins and Development,* 6th ed. (1983)

Melvin I. Urofsky, *A March of Liberty: A Constitutional History of the United States* (1988)

William M. Wiecek, "Clio as Hostage: The United States Supreme Court and the Uses of History," *California Western Law Review* 24 (1988): 227–276

Constitutionalism
Before the Constitution

⌗

Many Americans believe that their constitutional history began in 1787. While the delegates to the Philadelphia convention wrought powerful changes in U.S. constitutionalism, it is equally true that they built upon existing traditions of constitutional government, some of which extend to medieval history. Beginning in the thirteenth century, the English government gradually evolved policies of administration and taxation that established representative and limited government. Even more important was the colonists' practical experience with creating, and then operating, governments in the New World. Wherever one looks, therefore, constitutionalism flourished before the federal Constitution.

Historians frequently invoke the word reception *to describe the transplantation of English ideas about constitutional authority to U.S. soil. This reception metaphor emphasizes American scholars' continuing fascination with the impact of the frontier on the development of a distinctly American constitutionalism. It makes more sense, however, to emphasize the shrewdness of the colonists' legal sensibilities by stressing the ways in which they carried a constitutional tradition with them and that they molded that tradition to fit uniquely American circumstances. Such a perspective underscores the human agency involved in colonial decisions about constitutional government. The colonists, we should remember, did not come to America to create constitutions; instead, they had other objectives—some economic, others religious—that properly constituted governments could facilitate. They faced the twin problems of building structures of ordered authority on the new continent and making those structures operate within the English imperial system.*

In such a context, settlers in seventeenth-century America gradually developed ideas about the nature of representative government, the best means by which to control and regulate established authority, and the ideal way for government to promote the colonizers' goals. These matters were not easily settled, in part because each colony was organized somewhat differently, and in part because expectations about what constituted success varied from colony to colony. Yet it is clear that Americans tried to resolve these issues rapidly. What continues to fascinate historians, however, is the way in which ideas about constitu-

tionalism on the one hand, and the forces of sheer expediency on the other, combined to foster limited and representative government. We know that this combination of ideas and self-interest, when placed in the context of the New World environment, ultimately produced a distinctive form of American constitutionalism that encouraged many colonists to disavow the empire.

✠ D O C U M E N T S

Colonial Americans took from Magna Carta, excerpted here as the first document, such fundamental principles as the ideas that there could be no taxation without their consent and that there was a body of law—fundamental or natural law—not even the king could violate. Magna Carta also bequeathed to the colonists the tradition that authority and liberty must be balanced. The colonists initially stressed the former as a way of dealing with the New World's harsh conditions. Like most other colonies, Virginia's charter of 1606, excerpted here as the second document, not only established the colony as a business but also served as a governing instrument. The Virginia charter was also notable because it made little provision for local self-government.

A few years later, however, the rulers of Virginia promulgated the "Articles, Law, and Orders, Divine, Politic, and Martial" (1610–1611), reprinted here as the third selection. This document, along with the 1606 charter, gives a baseline from which to measure the progress of liberty protected by representative government in the century and a half before the American Revolution. To attract new colonists, Virginia authorities eventually instituted representative government, and in 1621 the Virginia Company issued "An Ordinance and Constitution . . . for a Council of State and General Assembly," reprinted here as the fourth reading.

The strong religious influence behind much of the settlement of New England also contributed to the early American constitutional tradition. Separatist Puritans, for example, believed in a compact theory of government, in which people agreed to join together in society and to be governed. Shortly before disembarking to settle Plymouth, they put their sentiments in writing in the Mayflower Compact of 1620, the fifth selection.

It was Connecticut's settlers, however, who first codified their fundamental law, in what is usually described as the first written constitution in America. Three years after the colony's founding in 1636, as the population of the Connecticut valley swelled, the freemen of Hartford, Windsor, and Wethersfield drew up the Fundamental Orders of Connecticut, excerpted as the sixth selection. Unlike Dale's Code and the Ordinance and Constitution of Virginia, the Fundamental Orders made no reference to the king or to the colony (Massachusetts) from which Connecticut sprang, and it carried principles of social compact and popular representation directly into the American constitutional experience.

The final two documents not only demonstrate the progress of constitutionalism over the first century of settlement but reveal the ways in which abrupt changes could and did occur in a single colony, in this instance Pennsylvania. The Frame of Government promulgated by Sir William Penn in 1682 lasted only a year and was replaced by a more flexible document the Great Charter and Frame, in 1683. Penn epitomizes the way in which settlers carried their constitutional traditions to the New World. After the passage of the Great Charter and Frame, Penn was forced by circumstances to return to England, where he lost temporary control of the colony, gaining it back only in 1694. Unable to return to Pennsyl-

in due Obedience to his Majesty, and all lawful Authority from his Majesty's Directions; and lastly, in maintaining the said People in Justice and *Christian* Conversation amongst themselves, and in Strength and Ability to withstand their Enemies. And this Council to be always, or for the most Part, residing about or near the Governor.

IV.—THE other Council, more generally to be called by the Governor once Yearly, and no oftener but for very extraordinary and important Occasions, shall consist, for the present, of the said Council of State, and of two Burgesses out of every Town, Hundred, or other particular Plantation, to be respectively chosen by the Inhabitants: Which Council shall be called THE GENERAL ASSEMBLY, wherein (as also in the said Council of State) all Matters shall be decided, determined, and ordered, by the greater Part of the Voices then present; reserving to the Governor always a Negative Voice. And this General Assembly shall have free Power to treat, consult, and conclude, as well of all emergent Occasions concerning the Publick Weal of the said Colony and every Part thereof, as also to make, ordain, and enact such general Laws and Orders for the Behoof of the said Colony, and the good Government thereof, as shall, from time to time, appear necessary or requisite;

V.—WHEREAS in all other Things, we require the said General Assembly, as also the said Council of State, to imitate and follow the Policy of the Form of Government, Laws, Customs, and Manner of Trial, and other Administration of Justice, used in the Realm of *England,* as near as may be, even as ourselves, by his Majesty's Letters Patent are required.

VI.—PROVIDED, that no Law or Ordinance, made in the said General Assembly, shall be or continue in Force of Validity, unless the same shall be solemnly ratified and confirmed in a General Quarter Court of the said Company here in *England,* and so ratified, be returned to them under our Seal; It being our Intent to afford the like Measure also unto the said Colony, that after the Government of the said Colony shall once have been well framed, and settled accordingly, which is to be done by Us, as by Authority derived from his Majesty, and the same shall have been so by us declared, no Orders of Court afterwards shall bind the said Colony, unless they be ratified in like Manner in the General Assemblies. . . .

The Mayflower Compact, 1620

In The Name of God, Amen. We, whose names are underwritten, the Loyal Subjects of our dread Sovereign Lord King *James,* by the Grace of God, of *Great Britain, France,* and *Ireland,* King, *Defender of the Faith,* &c. Having undertaken for the Glory of God, and Advancement of the Christian Faith, and the Honour of our King and Country, a Voyage to plant the first colony in the northern Parts of Virginia; Do by these Presents, solemnly and mutually in the Presence of God and one another, covenant and combine ourselves together into a civil Body Politick, for our better Ordering and Preservation, and Furtherance of the Ends aforesaid: And by Virtue hereof do enact, constitute, and frame, such just and equal Laws, Ordinances, Acts,

Constitutions, and Offices, from time to time, as shall be thought most meet and convenient for the general Good of the Colony; unto which we promise all due Submission and Obedience. In WITNESS whereof we have hereunto subscribed our names at *Cape Cod* the eleventh of *November,* in the Reign of our Sovereign Lord King *James* of *England, France,* and *Ireland,* the eighteenth and of *Scotland,* the fifty-fourth. *Anno Domini,* 1620. . . .

The Fundamental Orders of Connecticut, 1639

Forasmuch as it hath pleased the All-mighty God by the wise disposition of his divyne pruvidence so to Order and dispose of things that we the Inhabitants and Residents of Windsor, Harteford and Wethersfield are now cohabiting and dwelling in and uppon the River of Conectecotte and the Lands thereunto adioyneing; And well knowing where a people are gathered togather the word of God requires that to mayntayne the peace and union of such a people there should be an orderly and decent Government established according to God, to order and dispose of the affayres of the people at all seasons as occation shall require; doe therefore assotiate and conioyne our selves to be as one Publike State or Commonwelth; and doe, for our selves and our Successors and such as shall be adioyned to us att any tyme hereafter, enter into Combination and Confederation togather, to mayntayne and presearve the liberty and purity of the gospell of our Lord Jesus which we now professe, as also the disciplyne of the Churches, which according to the truth of the said gospell is now practised amongst us; As also in our Civell Affaires to be guided and governed according to such Lawes, Rules, Orders and decrees as shall be made, ordered & decreed, as followeth:—

1. It is Ordered . . . that there shall be yerely two generall Assemblies or Courts, the one the second thursday in Aprill, the other the second thursday in September, following; the first shall be called the Courte of Election, wherein shall be yerely Chosen . . . soe many Magestrats and other publike Officers as shall be found requisitte: Whereof one to be chosen Governour for the yeare ensueing and untill another be chosen, and noe other Magestrate to be chosen for more than one yeare; provided allwayes there be six chosen besids the Governour; which being chosen and sworne according to an Oath recorded for that purpose shall have power to administer iustice according to the Lawes here established, and for want thereof according to the rule of the word of God; which choise shall be made by all that are admitted freemen and have taken the Oath of Fidellity, and doe cohabitte within this Jurisdiction, (having beene admitted Inhabitants by the major part of the Towne wherein they live,) or the major parte of such as shall be then present.

4. It is Ordered . . . that noe person be chosen Governor above once in two yeares, and that the Governor be alwayes a member of some approved congregation, and formerly of the Magestracy within this Jurisdiction; and all the Magestrats Freemen of this Commonwelth: . . .

5. It is Ordered . . . that to the aforesaid Courte of Election the severall

Townes shall send their deputyes, and when the Elections are ended they may proceed in any publike searvice as at other Courts. Also the other Generall Courte in September shall be for makeing of lawes, and any other publike occation, which conserns the good of the Commonwelth.

7. It is Ordered . . . that after there are warrants given out for any of the said Generall Courts, the Constable . . . of ech Towne shall forthwith give notice distinctly to the inhabitants of the same, . . . that at a place and tyme by him or them lymited and sett, they meet and assemble them selves togather to elect and chuse certen deputyes to be att the Generall Courte then following to agitate the afayres of the commonwelth; which said Deputyes shall be chosen by all that are admitted Inhabitants in the severall Townes and have taken the oath of fidellity; provided that non be chosen a Deputy for any Generall Courte which is not a Freeman of this Commonwelth. . . .

8. It is Ordered . . . that Wyndsor, Hartford and Wethersfield shall have power, ech Towne, to send fower of their freemen as their deputyes to every Generall Courte; and whatsoever other Townes shall be hereafter added to this Jurisdiction, they shall send so many deputyes as the Courte shall judge meete, a resonable proportion to the number of Freemen that are in the said Townes being to be attended therein; which deputyes shall have the power of the whole Towne to give their voats and alowance to all such lawes and orders as may be for the publike good, and unto which the said Townes are to be bownd.

9. It is ordered . . . that the deputyes thus chosen shall have power and liberty to appoynt a tyme and a place of meeting togather before any Generall Courte to advise and consult of all such things as may concerne the good of the publike, as also to examine their owne Elections. . . .

10. It is Ordered . . . that every Generall Courte . . . shall consist of the Governor, or some one chosen to moderate the Court, and 4 other Magestrats at lest, with the major parte of the deputyes of the severall Townes legally chosen; and in case the Freemen or major parte of them, through neglect or refusall of the Governor and major parte of the magestrats, shall call a Courte, it shall consist of the major parte of Freemen that are present or their deputyes, with a Moderator chosen by them: In which said Generall Courts shall consist of the supreme power of the Commonwelth, and they only shall have power to make lawes or repeale them, to graunt levyes, to admitt of Freemen, dispose of lands undisposed of, to severall Townes or persons, and also shall have power to call ether Courte or Magestrate or any other person whatsoever into question for any misdemeanour, and may for just causes displace or deale otherwise according to the nature of the offence; and also may deale in any other matter that concerns the good of this commonwelth, excepte election of Magestrats, which shall be done by the whole boddy of Freemen.

In which Courte the Governour or Moderator shall have power to order the Courte to give liberty of spech, and silence unceasonable and disorderly speakeings, to put all things to voate, and in case the vote be equall to have the casting voice. But non of these Courts shall be adjorned or dissolved without the consent of the major parte of the Court.

11. It is ordered . . . that when any Generall Courte uppon the occations of the Commonwelth have agreed uppon any summe or sommes of mony to be levyed uppon the severall Townes within this Jurisdiction, that a Committee be chosen to sett out and appoynt what shall be the proportion of every Towne to pay of the said levy, provided the Committees be made up of an equall number out of each Towne.

William Penn's Preface to the Frame of Government of Pennsylvania, 1682

When the great and wise *God* had made the world, of all his creatures, it pleased him to chuse man his Deputy to rule it: and to fit him for so great a charge and trust, he did not only qualify him with skill and power, but with integrity to use them justly. This native goodness was equally his honour and his happiness; and whilst he stood here, all went well; there was no need of coercive or compulsive means; the precept of divine love and truth, in his bosom, was the guide and keeper of his innocency. But lust prevailing against duty, made a lamentable breach upon it; and the law, that before had no power over him, took place upon him, and his disobedient posterity, that such as would not live conformable to the holy law within, should fall under the reproof and correction of the just 'aw without, in a judicial administration.

This the Apostle teaches in divers of his epistles: "The law (says he) was added because of transgression": In another place, "Knowing that the law was not made for the righteous man; but for the disobedient and ungodly, for sinners, for unholy and prophane, for murderers, for whoremongers, for them that defile themselves with mankind, and for man-stealers, for lyers, for perjured persons," &c., but this is not all, he opens and carries the matter of government a little further: "Let every soul be subject to the higher powers; for there is no power but of *God.* The powers that be are ordained of *God:* whosoever therefore resisteth the power, resisteth the ordinance of *God.* For rulers are not a terror to good works, but to evil: wilt thou then not be afraid of the power? do that which is good, and thou shalt have praise of the same." "He is the minister of God to thee for good." "Wherefore ye must needs be subject, not only for wrath, but for conscience sake."

This settles the divine right of government beyond exception, and that for two ends: first, to terrify evil doers: secondly, to cherish those that do well; which gives government a life beyond corruption, and makes it as durable in the world, as good men should be. So that government seems to me a part of religion itself, a thing sacred in its institution and end. For, if it does not directly remove the cause, it crushes the effects of evil, and is as such, (though a lower, yet) an emanation of the same Divine Power, that is both author and object of pure religion; the difference lying here, that the one is more free and mental, the other more corporal and compulsive in its operations: but that is only to evil doers; government itself being otherwise as capable of kindness, goodness and charity, as a more private society. They weakly err, that think there is no other use of government, than correction, which is the coarsest part of it: daily experience tells us, that the care and regulation of many other affairs, more soft, and daily necessary, make up much of the greatest part of government; and which must have followed the peopling of the world, had Adam never fell, and will continue among men, on earth, under the highest attainments they may arrive at, by the coming of the blessed *Second Adam,* the *Lord* from heaven. Thus much of government in general, as to its rise and end.

For particular *frames* and *models,* it will become me to say little; and comparatively I will say nothing. My reasons are:

First. That the age is too nice and difficult for it; there being nothing the wits of men are more busy and divided upon. It is true, they seem to agree to the end, to wit, happiness; but, in the means, they differ, as to divine, so to this human felicity; and the cause is much the same, not always want of light and knowledge, but want of using them rightly. Men side with their passions against their reason, and their sinister interests have so strong a bias upon their minds, that they lean to them against the good of the things they know.

Secondly. I do not find a model in the world, that time, place, and some singular emergences have not necessarily altered; nor is it easy to frame a civil government, that shall serve all places alike.

Thirdly. I know what is said by the several admirers of *monarchy,* *aristocracy* and *democracy,* which are the rule of one, a few, and many, and are the three common ideas of government, when men discourse on the subject. But I chuse to solve the controversy with this small distinction, and it belongs to all three: *Any government is free to the people under it* (whatever be the frame) *where the laws rule, and the people are a party to those laws,* and more than this is tyranny, oligarchy, or confusion.

But, lastly, when all is said, there is hardly one frame of government in the world so ill designed by its first founders, that, in good hands, would not do well enough; and story tells us, the best, in ill times, can do nothing that is great or good; witness the *Jewish* and *Roman* states. Governments, like clocks, go from the motion men give them; and as governments are made and moved by men, so by them they are ruined too. Wherefore governments rather depend upon men, than men upon governments. Let men be good, and the government cannot be bad; if it be ill, they will cure it. But, if men be bad, let the government be never so good, they will endeavor to warp and spoil it to their turn.

I know some say, let us have good laws, and no matter for the men that execute them: but let them consider, that though good laws do well, good men do better: for good laws may want good men, and be abolished or evaded by ill men; but good men will never want good laws, nor suffer ill ones. It is true, good laws have some awe upon ill ministers, but that is where they have not power to escape or abolish them, and the people are generally wise and good: but a loose and depraved people (which is the question) love laws and an administration like themselves. That, therefore, which makes a good constitution, must keep it, *viz:* men of wisdom and virtue, qualities, that because they descend not with worldly inheritances, must be carefully propagated by a virtuous education of youth; for which after ages will owe more to the care and prudence of founders, and the successive magistracy, than to their parents, for their private patrimonies.

These considerations of the weight of government, and the nice and various opinions about it, made it uneasy to me to think of publishing the ensuing frame and conditional laws, forseeing both the censures, they will meet with, from men of differing humours and engagements, and the occasion they may give of discourse beyond my design.

But, next to the power of necessity, (which is a solicitor, that will take no denial) this induced me to a compliance, that we have (with reverence to God, and good conscience to men) to the best of our skill, contrived and composed the *frame* and *laws* of this government, to the great end of all government, viz: *To support power in reverence with the people, and to secure the people from the abuse of power;* that they may be free by their just obedience, and the magistrates honourable, for their just administration: for liberty without obedience is confusion, and obedience without liberty is slavery. To carry this evenness is partly owing to the constitution, and partly to the magistracy: where either of these fail, government will be subject to convulsions; but where both are wanting, it must be totally subverted; then where both meet, the government is like to endure. Which I humbly pray and hope *God* will please to make the lot of this of *Pensilvania.* Amen.

WILLIAM PENN.

Pennsylvania Charter of Liberties, 1701

. . . Know ye therefore, that for the further Well-being and good Government of the said Province, and Territories and in Pursuance of the Rights and Powers . . . , I the said *William Penn* do declare, grant and confirm, unto all the Freemen, Planters and Adventurers, and other Inhabitants of this Province and Territories, these following Liberties, Franchises and Privileges, so far as in me lieth, to be held, enjoyed and kept, by the Freemen, Planters and Adventurers, and other Inhabitants of and in the said Province and Territories thereunto annexed, for ever.

FIRST

BECAUSE no People can be truly happy, though under the greatest Enjoyment of Civil Liberties, if abridged of the Freedom of their Consciences, as to their Religious Profession and Worship: And Almighty God being the only Lord of Conscience, Father of Lights and Spirits; and the Author as well as Object of all divine Knowledge, Faith and Worship, who only doth enlighten the Minds, and persuade and convince the Understandings of People, I do hereby grant and declare, That no Person or Persons, inhabiting in this province or Territories, who shall confess and acknowledge *One* almighty God, the Creator, Upholder and Ruler of the World; and profess him or themselves obliged to live quietly under the Civil Government, shall be in any Case molested or prejudiced, in his or their Person or Estate, because of his or their conscientious Persuasion or Practice, nor be compelled to frequent or maintain any religious Worship, Place or Ministry, contrary to his or their Mind, or to do or suffer any other Act or Thing, contrary to their religious Persuasion.

AND that all Persons who also profess to believe in *Jesus Christ,* the Saviour of the World, shall be capable (notwithstanding their other Persuasions and Practices in Point of Conscience and Religion) to serve this Government in any Capacity, both legislatively and executively, he or they solemnly promising, when lawfully required, Allegiance to the King as Sovereign, and Fidelity to the Proprietary and Governor, and taking the Attests as now established by the Law made at *New-Castle,* in the Year *One Thousand and Seven Hundred,* entitled, *An Act directing the Attests of several Officers and Ministers,* as now amended and confirmed this present Assembly.

II For the well governing of this Province and Territories, there shall be an Assembly yearly chosen, by the Freemen thereof, to consist of *Four* Persons out of each County, of most Note for Virtue, Wisdom and Ability. . . . Which Assembly shall have Power to chuse a Speaker and other their Officers; and shall be Judges of the Qualifications and Elections of their own Members; sit upon their own Adjournments; appoint Committees; prepare Bills in order to pass into Laws; impeach Criminals, and redress Grievances; and shall have all other Powers and Privileges of an Assembly, according to the Rights of the free-born Subjects of *England,* and as is usual in any of the King's Plantations in *America. . . .*

III THAT the Freemen in each respective County, at the Time and Place of Meeting for Electing their Representatives to serve in Assembly, may as often as there shall be Occasion, chuse a double Number of Persons to present to the Governor for Sheriffs and Coroners to serve for *Three* Years, if so long they behave themselves well; out of which respective Elections and Presentments, the Governor shall nominate and commissionate one for each of the said Officers, the *Third* Day after such Presentment, or else the *First* named in such Presentment, for each Office as aforesaid, shall stand and serve in that Office for the Time before respectively limited; and in Case of Death or Default, such Vacancies shall be supplied by the Governor, to serve to the End of the said Term. . . .

AND that the Justices of the respective Counties shall or may nominate and present to the Governor *Three* Persons, to serve for Clerk of the Peace for the said County, when there is a Vacancy, one of which the Governor shall commissionate within *Ten* Days after such Presentment, or else the *First* nominated shall serve in the said Office during good Behavior.

IV THAT the Laws of this Government shall be in this Stile, viz. *By the Governor, with the Consent and Approbation of the Freemen in General Assembly met;* and shall be, after Confirmation by the Governor, forthwith recorded in the Rolls Office, and kept at *Philadelphia,* unless the Governor and Assembly shall agree to appoint another Place.

V THAT all Criminals shall have the same Privileges of Witnesses and Council as their Prosecutors.

VI THAT no Person or Persons shall or may, at any Time hereafter, be obliged to answer any Complaint, Matter or Thing whatsoever, relating to Property, before the Governor and Council, or in any other Place, but in ordinary Course of Justice, unless Appeals thereunto shall be hereafter by Law appointed.

VII THAT no Person within this Government, shall be licensed by the Governor to keep an Ordinary, Tavern or House of Publick Entertainment, but such who are first recommended to him, under the Hands of the Justices of the respective Counties, signed in open Court; which Justices are and shall be hereby impowered, to suppress and forbid any Person, keeping such Publick-House as aforesaid, upon their Misbehavior, on such Penalties as the Law doth or shall direct; and to recommend others from time to time, as they shall see Occasion. . . .

VIII BUT because the Happiness of Mankind depends so much upon the Enjoying of Liberty of their Consciences as aforesaid, I do hereby solemnly declare, promise and grant, for me, my Heirs and Assigns, That the *First* Article of this Charter relating to Liberty of Conscience, and every Part and Clause therein, according to the true Intent and Meaning thereof, shall be kept and remain, without any Alteration, inviolably for ever.

AND LASTLY, I the said *William Penn,* Proprietary and Governor of the Province of *Pensilvania,* and Territories thereunto belonging, for myself, my Heirs and Assigns, have solemnly declared, granted and confirmed, and do hereby solemnly declare, grant and confirm, That neither I, my Heirs or Assigns, shall procure or do any Thing or Things whereby the Liberties in this Charter contained and expressed, nor any Part thereof, shall be infringed or broken: And if any thing shall be procured or done, by any Person or Persons, contrary to these Presents, it shall be held of no Force or Effect. . . .

✠ *E S S A Y S*

In the first essay, Gary B. Nash, a professor of history at the University of California, Los Angeles, examines the pressures and influences that shaped William Penn's decisions about government in Pennsylvania. Nash stresses that Penn's ideas were often at variance with the realities he confronted, and that his inability to come to terms with those realities helps to explain why Penn had such difficulty in formulating a scheme of government that would serve liberty while attracting financial supporters and investors. In contrast, Donald S. Lutz, a professor of political science at the University of Houston, in the second essay creates a typology of colonial constitutional development that emphasizes the primacy of ideas, structures, and the common-law inheritance of England and Magna Carta, rather than direct experience and expediency, in shaping early American constitutionalism. The question still remains, which of these two competing views—experience or ideas—best explains the origin of American constitutionalism?

Expediency and Early Constitutionalism

GARY B. NASH

Little is known of the pressures and influences which bore upon William Penn as he pieced together the instruments of government for his "Holy Experiment" between March 4, 1681, when he received his charter from Charles II, and April 25, 1682, when his Frame of Government was published in London. Most historians, upon reading the widely heralded Frame of 1682, have been content to believe that Penn was given the rare opportunity of forging a government of his own and that the result was a pure distillation of his political philosophy, drawn from studies of classical Republican writers, his practical experience since 1675 in the affairs of West New Jersey, and the counsel of a few intimate advisers such as Algernon Sidney, the radical parliamentarian, and Benjamin Furly, the Rotterdam Quaker merchant.

This uncomplicated view assumes a confidence in the Quaker founder on the part of his principal supporters that probably never existed. Penn, in all likelihood, was far from a free agent in the work of constituting a government. William Markham, his cousin and a trusted adjutant in the colony for many years, indicated as much when he later wrote: "I know very well it [the Frame of Government] was forced from him by friends who unless they received all that they demanded would not have settled the country." But beyond this intriguing comment little direct evidence of such pressures survives to illuminate the government-making process in 1681 and 1682; nor is it likely that any interplay between Penn and his supporters was recorded at the time.

But what is evident from an examination of Penn's remaining correspondence and from a close analysis of the various drafts of government fashioned in 1681 and 1682 is that the ideal state which Penn had constructed theoretically in the 1670s in a series of essays and pamphlets was transmuted to a considerable degree as a consequence both of metamorphosis in his own thinking, once proprietarial authority was thrust upon him, and of the concessions he necessarily made to those whose support was indispensable in the founding of his New Jerusalem on the Delaware. The Frame of 1682, and the Frame of 1683, which was ultimately adopted in its place, represent, in effect, a failure of ideas in contact with realities.

At the root of Penn's problems in formulating a system of government was the need to capitalize his colonial enterprise. Fragmentary evidence, including the language of Penn's petition to the Crown for a patent in America, suggests that Penn himself was in financial straits in the early 1680s, perhaps because of his failing estates in Ireland and England. That he had not subscribed even a partial share in the West New Jersey enterprise, of which he was a principal mover, may be further evidence of his strained resources. And even if his finances were not in decay at the time, it would

Gary B. Nash, "The Framing of Government in Pennsylvania: Ideas in Contact with Reality," *William and Mary Quarterly,* 3d ser., 23 (1966): 183–209. Reprinted by permission of author and publisher.

have been difficult, if not impossible, for Penn to underwrite singlehandedly such an undertaking. Penn later wrote that the expenses of petitioning for his patent and launching his visionary scheme had cost him £10,000 in the first two or three years.

As a colonial promoter of no little experience, Penn must have recognized that the success of his colony hinged as much on his ability to attract wide financial support as to recruit settlers. The lessons of nearly a hundred years of English colonization were clear: success was unthinkable without the steady infusion of capital during the early years of settlement. Again and again colonial ventures had foundered on the rocks of inadequate financial backing, especially proprietary experiments such as those of Sir Ferdinando Gorges and the Carolina proprietors. Fortunately, by the 1680s English Quakerism, though identified chiefly with yeomen and shopkeeper-artisans, had attracted a considerable number of merchants and well-to-do gentry. Within a decade or so the "Richest Trading Men in London" were Quakers, according to one contemporary observer. Upon these men Penn would count for a large part of his financial support.

Penn was singularly well connected in Quaker society to make his appeal. Not only in his endeavors for West New Jersey but as one of the intellectual leaders of the Quaker movement, he had circulated for years among the most affluent Friends, establishing cordial relations with merchants of note in all the urban centers of Quakerism—Dublin, Cork, Bristol, and London—and with the Quaker gentry in the countryside. Throughout the Quaker world his name drew admiration for his courageous efforts in the law courts and at Whitehall on behalf of the faith. . . .

But even the exciting word of Penn's grant was probably not enough to attract the broad support of affluent Quakers. By 1682 a Friend intent on immigration to America or with capital to invest had a choice of three colonies dominated by Quakers: Pennsylvania, West Jersey, and East Jersey—the latter purchased by twelve Quaker proprietors, including Penn, even as plans for Pennsylvania went forward. Penn, like colonial promoters before him, had to pitch his appeal for backing on the argument that his colony was not only a haven for the oppressed but also a sound and perhaps astute investment. He had said himself in 1681 that "though I desire to extend religious freedom [in Pennsylvania], yet I want some recompense for my trouble." Similarly, Penn recognized that he could best mobilize the support of well-to-do Friends by presenting Pennsylvania not only as a religious refuge—a place for the English Quakers to build their own "city on a hill"—but also as a field ripe for economic exploitation. The same motives which induced Quaker men of means to purchase shares in East and West Jersey, and to trade them speculatively throughout the 1680s, were at play in the purchase of large blocks of land in Pennsylvania. Penn, in effect, was competing for investors with the other Quaker provinces. Thus, Robert Barclay, his promotional agent in Scotland, wrote in 1681 that the cheap price of East Jersey land "makes thine seem dear." "Thou has land enough," cautioned Barclay, "so need not be a churle if thou intend to advance thy plantation."

The success of Penn's appeal to wealthy Quakers is evident in an analysis of the men who bought property directly from Penn in the first year of settlement. . . .

This upper stratum upon which Penn depended so heavily was studded with Quaker merchants, particularly from London, and to a lesser degree from Bristol and Dublin. Regardless of which list of purchasers is used, mercantile wealth is identifiable in more than half of the names. Richard Marsh, Robert Turner, Thomas Callowhill, Samuel Carpenter, Samuel Claridge, James Claypoole, Joseph Fisher, John Fuller, James Lyell, and many more—practically a roll call of eminent Quaker merchants in England and Ireland, with a scattering from elsewhere—make up the list. The other great investors were a potpourri of professional men, well-circumstanced landowners, and Penn's relatives and personal associates. The purchases of some of these investors represented venture capital, mostly advanced for speculative purposes by men who had no intention of going to Pennsylvania. Of those who planned to take up life in the province, most, including the merchants, purchased land on the assumption that it would appreciate rapidly as new settlers sought property in Philadelphia and the surrounding countryside. A few of the gentry or prosperous yeomen, men like John Simcock, Thomas Brassey, Joseph Growden, and the landed leaders of the Welsh migration, sought a new life in the colony as country gentlemen. In short, Pennsylvania was founded primarily by yeomen and artisans who left England for both religious and economic reasons. But Penn, while seeking such sturdy settlers, relied on a far smaller number of wealthy men for the purchase of nearly half of the land and, what is more, for political leadership on the Delaware.

It is not surprising that in attempting to attract the support of the upper stratum of English Quakers Penn offered handsome rewards to those who would join him in the work of nation-building in the wilderness. It is not too much to say, in fact, that Penn, in forging plans for his colony, placed himself and his principal associates at the vital center of economic and political affairs. The distribution of land, the conferral of profitable offices, and the organization of government were all a part of this pattern.

From the earliest stages of planning, Penn conceived of a colony centering on a river capital, the seat of government and the hub of commercial activity. Property in the city was not offered for direct sale but reserved entirely for dividends meted out to the purchasers of the first 500,000 acres in proportion to country land "taken up upon rent," that is, purchased in fee simple from the proprietor and subject to an annual quit rent of one shilling per hundred acres. Buyers of these "country lots" received 2 percent of their purchase in the form of "city lots," obviously to be the most valuable real estate in the province. The larger the purchase, the greater was the dividend in the capital city.

Such an arrangement worked to the mutual benefit of Penn and the major investors. The tantalizing offer of a dominant position in city realty stimulated large purchases of land; the buyers, in turn, only one third of whom would immigrate, could anticipate a handsome return on their investment as incoming settlers bid for property in the commercial center of the province. Whether Penn at this time privately offered the largest investors first consideration in the allocation of waterfront property is not known. Such a promise is not unlikely though, for when Penn actually assigned the city lots, after his arrival in October 1682, he did just this, situating his relations and those "that he had the Greatest regard for" on the most advantageous sites.

As an additional means of welding to his interest a circle of wealthy adherents who would follow him to Pennsylvania, Penn utilized an enormous power of patronage. The proprietor, as will later be discussed, reserved for himself the right to appoint initially all proprietary, provincial, and county officers; each would serve, barring misbehavior, for life. Penn put this broad appointive power to good use. . . . [P]ositions of profit and power went almost uniformly to men whose tangible commitment to the Holy Experiment was substantial. Also noteworthy is that in striking contrast to both East and West New Jersey, the other Quaker colonies in the New World, dual officeholding was not forbidden in Pennsylvania and in fact was common practice. . . .

That Penn should establish an administrative and economic system which delivered power and advantage to those who invested most heavily in his plan is hardly surprising. Like any prudent manager of a large enterprise he sought support in the wealthiest and most experienced sector of his constituency. Conversely, these men, in return for financial backing and for their willingness to start life anew in a distant wilderness, expected compensation. Notwithstanding what has been written about Quaker equalitarianism, one searches in vain for evidence that Pennsylvania was ever conceived as an economic or political democracy in nineteenth- or twentieth-century terms. Nothing could have been more natural than the transplanting of an ordered society where position and power resided in those whose stake in the venture was the largest.

Beyond the terms of land distribution and the pattern of patronage, one must turn to the most central aspect of the governmental apparatus which was constructed in London in 1681 and 1682—the Frame of 1682, a constitutional scheme under which Pennsylvania was to be governed. The absence of conclusive evidence leaves any hypothesis open to question, but there are strong indications that Penn's circle of backers caused him to deviate markedly from his own ideas on government in favor of a system more to their liking and advantage. At the same time, in accommodating their demands, Penn seems to have taken a second hard look at the experiment he was promoting and to have sought powers as proprietor and governor that earlier he might have considered extreme.

It needs to be understood, in discussing Penn's political ideas, that consistency was never a characteristic feature of the proprietor's thinking, and that even at the time when plans for Pennsylvania were going forward Penn was capable of philosophical vacillation. On the one hand, he had long been in the vanguard of those Restoration critics who contended that English rights and liberties were being endangered by creeping licentiousness and authoritarianism. His efforts on behalf of religious toleration and civil liberties in the 1670s were unmatched by any Englishman of his time. . . . But at the same time, Penn revealed himself an essentially conservative thinker, committed to a political order based on property, in favor of a social system which upheld "all reasonable distinction and those civil degrees that are amongst people," and filled with a downright aversion to the "mob" and the "rabble." That freedom was endangered "by the ambitions of the populace which shakes the constitution," was not an atypical statement for Penn to make in the 1670s. At moments, indeed, Penn seemed to project a nostalgic longing for the feudal past with its well-ordered society and its "old time Nobility and Gentry." Even in America he likened his provincial councilors to the English "Knights of Shires." . . .

. . . By personal reference, Penn might have hewed closer to the enlightened constitutional theory of the time, which prescribed a balance of strong and independent governmental powers as the safeguard against tyranny. Just such a system was believed to be embodied, at least theoretically, in the English government—an equilibrium of monarchy, aristocracy, and democracy as represented by King, Lords, and Commons. Most of the colonies, in distributing power among governor, council, and assembly, after the English example, reflected this emphasis on equipoise. Also, Penn might logically have made other modifications of the concept of limited government simply because his charter to Pennsylvania was proprietarial in form.

Beyond such conjectures one can move to firmer ground, guided by a series of seventeen constitutional drafts in which the evolution of the Frame of 1682 can be traced. That the end product varied so significantly from Penn's expressed views of earlier years and even from his initial attempts to formulate a constitution is clear evidence that either his political philosophy underwent a complete reorientation, or, as is more likely, that he yielded to the demands of persons he was in no position to ignore.

The first draft of the Frame of 1682 projected a system far less liberal than governments in other colonies . . . . The governor was to be assisted by a parliament consisting of two houses. The upper chamber, analogous to the House of Lords, would include the first fifty purchasers of 5,000 acres or more; they would comprise a self-perpetuating aristocracy, their seats devolving to their heirs. Styled "lords," the members were to sit and adjourn at their own pleasure, nominate all officers in church and state, and delegate committees drawn from both houses to supervise financial and military affairs. Their consent was necessary to the passage of laws. The lower house contained "renters"—the smaller landowners—or their delegates. Theirs was the function of initiating laws.

Although it has been suggested that Penn was not the author of such a "government by a landed aristocracy," the two-house parliament, stripped of the hereditary feature in the upper chamber, was the essence of the next five drafts, many of them interlineated in Penn's hand. The only major innovation was the addition of a council, chosen by the proprietor from a double list of names nominated by the parliament, to assist in the executive functions of government. Untouched was the power of the lower house to initiate legislation and the right of the large landowners to sit as an upper house with power to nominate most provincial and county officers and to pass on bills presented by the lower chamber. Though somewhat unwieldy, it was a scheme of government which attempted a rough division of power among the governor, the two houses of parliament, and the executive council.

But abruptly, after the first six drafts, an entirely new direction was taken. Departing from the previous formula, the new draft greatly magnified the power of both proprietor and large landowners while reducing that of the lower house. . . .

It may have been at this point, though the absence of dates on many of the drafts makes sequential ordering indeterminable, that Penn wrote his most liberal draft of government, "The Fundamentall Constitutions of Pennsylvania." The document, which is among the most carefully wrought of Penn's constitutional drafts, is prefaced by the proprietor's reflections on theories of government—an essay which in content and phraseology closely parallels the preamble to the Frame of 1682. Central to the Fundamental Constitutions was the idea that the preponderant governmental power should rest with the freeholders. The legislative assembly would consist of two houses. The lower house, comprising 384 members, elected annually, and enjoying all the privileges known to the English House of Commons, would alone propose and pass laws. By an extraordinary clause, each member was required to bring instructions from his electors to the first session of the assembly where a copy would be made and registered. No money bill could be voted upon until referred to the freemen in each of the electoral districts. The second branch of government, the council, would include 48 members chosen by the lower house from among its own members for three-year terms. In legislative matters the council was purely a consultative body, sitting with the governor to make recommendations upon bills initiated in assembly, but possessing no negative power. Council's most important function was to exercise executive supervision in the colony through its committees of justice, trade, treasury, and "manners and education." Further articles in the Fundamental Constitutions provided for the annual election in cities and towns of justices of the peace, bailiffs, sheriffs, and constables. In the counties the governor or his deputy would choose sheriffs and justices from a double list presented by the electorate. Individual liberties were protected by guarantees of freedom of religion, due process, jury trial in the vicinage, habeas corpus, monthly sessions of county courts, and the prohibition of imprisonment for debt. That the Fundamental Constitutions contrasted so sharply with earlier drafts of government and that the document was given close consideration is indicative of Penn's fluid state of mind as blueprints for his government were on the drawing board in London.

Penn's close associate in Rotterdam, Benjamin Furly, was among those consulted in the drafting of the Fundamental Constitutions. Indeed, Furly believed that Penn had committed himself to these articles of government, which he deemed excellent. But at some point in the early months of 1682 Penn reverted to a far less liberal scheme of government. New constitutional drafts were made, providing for an upper house of the seventy-two men in the colony "most eminent for vertue Wisdom and Substance," to be elected by the freemen. The right of initiating legislation, except in bills related to "Publick moneys," was transferred from the lower to the upper house. Several drafts later the lower chamber was stripped of any role whatsoever in the initiation of legislation, leaving it with only a right of consent. The ultimate step came in the fourteenth draft. The functions of the governor's council and the upper house of the legislature were combined, fusing in one body control of legislative, executive, and judicial matters according to a pattern not unfamiliar in other colonies.

What remained was an emasculated lower house, restricted to a nine-day annual session, and allowed only to approve or negate laws proposed by council, to impeach criminals, and, after Penn died, to nominate county sheriffs, coroners, and justices of the peace. It could not initiate legislation as could Parliament at home or the lower houses in neighboring colonies. Nor could it elect its own speaker, as had been allowed in earlier drafts, or sit on its own adjournment, another right commonly enjoyed in adjacent provinces. In fact, as Penn subsequently pointed out, the lower house had no real existence of its own, but represented simply those delegates chosen annually to sit in a "General Assembly" with the councilors and to pass on laws structured by the governor and council. It did not possess the power even to debate a proposed law or to ask for the amendment of a clause within it. . . .

The council, on the other hand, was endowed with sweeping legislative, executive, and judicial powers. Included was the all-important right of initiative and also authority (with the governor) to erect courts, preserve the peace and safety of the province, situate cities, ports, and market towns, regulate all matters relating to public buildings, roads, and marketplaces, judge impeached criminals, execute the laws, and supervise the treasury. The proprietor, as governor, also possessed extensive powers. He sat as the presiding officer in council where he held a triple vote. More important he held sole power of appointment to all proprietary, provincial, and county officers—judges, treasurers, masters of the rolls, sheriffs, justices of the peace, and coroners. Only after the initial round of appointments—the appointees would serve for life barring misbehavior—would the power to nominate a double list of officers for the governor's choice devolve on council, for provincial officers, and the electorate in each county, for county officers. . . .

Penn, in short, had finally determined on a constitutional system where political power was concentrated in the governor and his council. Belatedly he had realized, or been made to understand, that neither his initial plans for a parliamentary system nor his later more liberal schemes were feasible or acceptable. Men of substance, upon whom he relied for leadership and financial backing, would not exchange carefully cultivated estates in England for the uncertainties of a proprietary wilderness unless they were conceded extensive power.

What has obscured the vision of many historians in pondering the division of power in the final frame of government is the provision that the seventy-two councilors (the council was reduced to eighteen in the first year of settlement) be elected by the freemen. Historians have sometimes read twentieth-century democracy back into seventeenth-century documents. But men of influence at the time, as Thomas Rudyard stated, knew what sort of man should and would reach office. The "Laws Agreed Upon in England," a series of forty statutes to be ratified in Pennsylvania, indicated plainly that any Christian of twenty-one years who possessed one hundred acres of land (fifty acres if he had been released from indenture within the preceding year) or who paid scot and lot, a property owners' municipal tax, was eligible to vote. This probably enfranchised about one half the adult males or one eighth of the total population. But who attained the high office of councilor was another question. Men of this era understood—and early elections in Pennsylvania would confirm their belief—that only those of considerable estate, demonstrably successful in their private affairs and proven leaders at the local level, could expect to reach the council. Early Pennsylvania was to be a deferential society, hierarchically structured and paternalistic. For Quakers had no more difficulty than did other Englishmen in reconciling spiritual equalitarianism with a traditional view of the natural ordering of social classes. An elective council little threatened the pivotal position which Penn's moneyed supporters expected to occupy. . . .

No conspiratorial overtones need be attached to this apparently conscious attempt of Penn and the principal colonizers to vest themselves with effective political control. These were men whose own sufferings as members of a persecuted sect had bred in them a keen sense of history and a watchful attitude toward their fellow men. Too, they were transferring their estates to a colony granted under semifeudal conditions. It is not surprising that those who risked their fortunes and uprooted their lives would seek every possible security for life in the Delaware wilderness. Likewise they might well have expected special concessions in the allocation of land and first consideration in the distribution of profit-bearing offices. But no advantage outweighed that of political control—of a governmental system insulated to the greatest possible degree from pressures exerted from above and below.

Penn did not find the arguments for a weak assembly and a strong council unconvincing. He was highly aristocratic himself and in political theory no dogmatist. . . .

It was [an] emphasis on the personnel rather than on the structure of government, quite the reverse of conventional Whiggish dogma, that permitted Penn to be swayed from initial plans for a government modeled on more advanced thinking. Moreover, his outlook on man at this time, while he was in the full euphoria of establishing a Quaker utopia, was Lockean rather than Hobbesian. Almost all of the great early purchasers were fellow Quakers, many of them close associates and intimate friends. Penn had every reason to believe that his Holy Experiment would be safe in their hands, especially since he planned personally to assume the role of governor in Pennsylvania. "Let men be good," he pronounced, "and the government cannot be bad."

Furthermore, Penn had compromised only one element in his plans for government. Inviolably secure was the cornerstone of religious toleration, the object of a whole decade of labors in England. Also firmly rooted were an enlightened judicial system and penal code, positive safeguards for property and individual liberty, and such Harringtonian devices as the use of the secret ballot, controls against political chicanery, and the rotation of offices. Here was a constitution which, despite its departures from his earlier concepts of government, could translate his noble vision into reality.

As complex and protracted as the organization of the machinery of government had been, a final crisis could not be averted when the Frame of 1682 was submitted for ratification in Pennsylvania. Shortly after his arrival in Pennsylvania in October 1682, Penn called for the election of seven delegates from each of the six counties erected. On December 4, 1682, the forty-two representatives gathered at Chester to confirm or revise the Frame of 1682, the "Laws Agreed upon in England" (a combined civil and criminal code, including certain fundamental laws concerned with the protection of individual rights), and a series of additional laws drafted by the proprietor after his arrival. It was no surprise that most of Penn's supporters and officeholders secured election—Holme, Taylor, More, Clarke, Simcock, Jones, Withers, Brassey, and others. But from the three Lower Counties came representatives of the older Swedish, Dutch, and English settlers, most of them apprehensive about the sudden takeover of territory and government by the proprietor and his small circle. For nearly a decade English tobacco planters had been drifting into the lower Delaware area from adjacent counties in Maryland, taking up land patents under the Duke of York's deputies and gradually replacing the Swedes. When Penn received his charter more than one thousand people populated the Lower Counties—Sussex, Kent, and Newcastle—arranged in a tier from the mouth of the Delaware Bay northward to the town of New Castle. Now their representatives seemed little ready to accede to the proprietor's requests. The speakership nearly fell to a non-Quaker, "Friends carrying it but by one voyce, and that through the absence of 2 of the other side that were not Friends," Penn wrote in dismay.

The confrontation of old and new, Quaker and non-Quaker, Penn's associates and independent adventurers, had grave consequences for the entire machinery of proprietary management. In a series of moves the convention struck at Penn's system. Proposals were made, as Benjamin Furly had predicted, to overthrow council's monopoly in initiating legislation by allowing "any Member [of the lower house to] offer any Bill, publick or private, tending to the publick Good, except in Case of levying Taxes." Nineteen of the ninety laws proposed by Penn were rejected outright. Most significant, both the Frame of 1682 and the law confirming the charter of the Free Society of Traders were voted down. Obviously a majority of representatives had arrayed themselves against central aspects of Penn's governmental system. Fissures in the community had been opened that would not quickly heal.

A new attempt to ratify the constitutional instruments was made three months later in March 1683. Recognizing that the seventy-two councilors and two hundred representatives to the General Assembly allowed by the Frame of 1682 was far too cumbersome and unrealistic a number for the sparsely populated frontier society, Penn consented to the election of three councilors and nine assemblymen from each county. When the election returns were in, it was clear that council would be dominated by Penn's associates. Half of the councilors chosen were principal officeholders and purchasers of land, while several others, Quakers who had settled on the Delaware before Penn's grant, were now equally bound to the proprietor. In the lower house of the General Assembly sat an uneasy company of Quaker and non-Quaker, new settler and old, English and non-English. One characteristic alone bound them together: almost none was tied to the proprietor by appointive office or involvement in the Free Society of Traders. Those from the upper counties were Quaker with few exceptions; from the Lower Counties came mostly non-Quaker settlers of the pre-Penn era.

The principal task of the General Assembly was to model a new frame of government in place of the rejected Frame of 1682. Debate focused on the proper distribution of power among proprietor, council, and assembly— the same thorny problem mooted so laboriously in England. But now, assent was needed from the very body which had been relegated to virtual impotency—the lower house. By rights, the matter should not have come before that body at all, for by Penn's reckoning the Frame of 1682 would be endorsed by the ratifying convention dominated by his associates. And even if the Frame should fail, Penn might logically have reasoned, the lower house would defer to the "wisdom, virtue, and ability" of the provincial councilors in the work of devising a new Frame. Now, the assembly was becoming instead the agency of antiproprietary sentiment. Half the seats were occupied by non-Quakers from the Lower Counties, and others by those eager to enlarge the assembly's role. Only an unsubstantial minority, composed of Quakers from the upper counties, remained firm in their support of Penn, demonstrating an allegiance more characteristic of the councilors. Council, though supporting Penn on the whole, sought subtle reductions of his power.

Upon one issue, the unmanageable size of both legislative houses, there was general accord. Accordingly, the council and assembly were reduced from 72 and 200, respectively, to 18 and 36 in the new Frame of Government under preparation. Agreement was reached on little else. Of foremost concern was the question of the governor's voice in legislative matters. In England, Penn, eager to promote his colony, had at first reserved for himself only a single voice in council and no negative power at all. In its final form, however, the Frame of 1682 allowed him a triple voice in council, a virtual negative in the preparing of bills, as Jasper Batt had indicated, and power to withhold approval of any constitutional alterations. Once in Pennsylvania Penn apparently took a harder look at his charter from the King. Two provisions were clear: firstly, laws were to be made by the proprietor "with the advice, assent, and approbation of the freemen." As was later pointed out, this seemed to mean that Penn was obliged by the specifications of his charter to reserve a negative power for himself. Secondly, Penn was obliged to "stand security" to the Crown for any damages resulting from colonial violations of the acts of trade, as ascertained in any English court. In effect, Penn was assuming financial liability for the behavior of his entire colony. It was a provision unknown to earlier colonial charters and reflective of attempts in England to obtain adherence to the navigation acts, frequently evaded and ignored in the colonies during the previous decade.

Meeting with council, Penn announced his intention to obtain either a negative voice in legislation or the colonists' countersecurity for observance of the navigation acts. After lengthy debate the council agreed to allow the governor a negative voice rather than cast a lien on their own estates. At the same time the councilors' appetite for power was satisfied by curbing the governor's right to act in matters of justice, trade, finance, or defense without their "advice and consent." Since virtually every public matter came under one of these heads, council obtained a large degree of control over the proprietor's executive authority.

The Assembly only reluctantly accepted the innovation of the governor's negative power in the new Frame of 1683, for a majority in that body continued to chafe at the insignificant role allowed them. Repeating a request made at the December 1682 convention, they proposed that the lower house be allowed the power of initiative. Although council and proprietor spurned this proposal, they were "condescential" to the less important request that the Assembly be allowed the privilege of conferring with the upper house. It was a concession only large enough to whet the appetite of a majority in the assembly who outspokenly cast "Reflections and Aspersions . . . upon the Governor," according to the complaint of Penn's supporters. Endorsement of the Free Society of Trader's charter could not be obtained.

On April 2, 1683, after more than three weeks of deliberations, the new constitution, called the Frame of 1683 or the Charter of Liberties, was endorsed by the General Assembly and engrossed on parchment. That evening, before the members of the General Assembly and other inhabitants of Philadelphia who attended the session, Penn signed the constitutional document under which Pennsylvania was governed until Penn's rights of government were suspended a decade later.

At best the constitution represented a bundle of compromises which failed to satisfy any of the parties involved. Nicholas More, the colony's largest landowner and one of its leaders, adamantly opposed the changes and maintained in heat that those who were party to it might be "impeacht for Treason for what you do." The allegiance of other members of the proprietary circle was no more enduring. The lower house, as the representatives to the General Assembly collectively thought of themselves, never gave up their struggle for greater power and recognition. So inflamed did subsequent relations become between the council and assembly and between factions within each body, that Penn, within two years, was imploring the colonial leaders "for the love of God, me and the poor country [to] be not so governmentish, so noisy and open in your dissatisfactions." A year later he wrote in despair at the political confusion in his colony, "It almost temps me to deliver up the colony to the K[ing]—and lett a mercenary government have the tameing of them." Already the Holy Experiment was in disarray, plagued by factionalism, disorderly pursuit of office, and acrimonious dispute over the proper form of government. From such political instability Pennsylvania would not recover for several decades.

The Idealism of Early Constitutionalism

DONALD S. LUTZ

Between 1578 and 1725 the constitutional theory evolving in British North America was a concatenation or interpenetration of charters and rules made in England, political ideas and instruments generated by the colonists themselves, English common law, and a developing theory of the colonies' place in the British political system. The manner in which these influences mixed and grew was different in the various clusters of colonies. The result was three broad "subcultures" within American constitutionalism. Their political development can, at the risk of oversimplification, be related to some basic differences in their history, geography, and demographics, just as the growth of a reasonably common political culture can be traced to some decisive similarities in the circumstances of all colonies.

Colonization began in the South and, despite an initial setback, developed rather quickly. Virginia defined the southern pattern. Initially founded by a trading company, it became in 1624 the first royal colony. By 1776, all land south of Virginia would be royal colonies based upon the Virginia model. Virginia most resembled England in its social structure. The Church of England was the established church for a number of years, and there were large landowners and thus a system that seemed at first glance similar to England's class structure. Aside from Charleston and Savannah, there were relatively few towns of any size in the South. The area looked, in short, much like the England centered on the shire or county government.

However, the South still had a number of important similarities with the rest of America. There was in fact no true aristocracy. The size and wealth of the middle strata far exceeded anything found in England. The upper class did not own or claim most of the land as the aristocracy did in England. The large landowners worked hard to maintain social distance from other Virginians, but their political interests vis-à-vis England were similar to those of middling wealth in America, a fact reflected in the operation of the colonial legislature.

The governor almost always picked the wealthier and more influential planters to serve on the Privy Council, which became a miniature upper house—a pale copy of the House of Lords. As in England, money to run the government came from taxes voted by the lower house, the House of Burgesses. But circumstances in America transformed the operation of what looked to be a typically British legislature. A pattern of uneasy cooperation and frequent conflict characterized the relationship between governor and burgesses, with the council more often than not supporting the House of Burgesses. Without the automatic support of the "better sort," the governor lacked the political base to successfully oppose the burgesses' attempts to gain political dominance. Conflict often led the governor to dismiss the legislature (which he had every right to do) and maintain his position with his own money and with funds found elsewhere.

The difference in the legislature's operation had to do with another English practice brought to America and transformed. Since the 1400s the right to vote in England had been granted to all those who owned enough land to earn at least forty shillings a year rent, usually between forty and sixty acres. In England, where a relatively small number of men were land-owners, this rule enfranchised from 2 percent to 6 percent of the adult males. In America, with plentiful land and no ancient feudal claims, the same rule enfranchised 25 percent to 35 percent of white, adult male Virginians. Although that figure was low by American standards (the percentage became higher the farther north one went), it nevertheless was a striking alteration of English political reality. Furthermore, the governor was isolated from England by the Atlantic Ocean, had few troops available to him (most of which were colonial militia anyway), and had a council disposed to support the House of Burgesses. These and other aspects of southern political life conspired to move constitutional development in a direction similar to, though distinguishable from, that found in the North.

New England developed governments that were more independent of England and more divergent from the English model. Although by 1776 a royal colony, Massachusetts was begun by a trading company; for seventy years, it functioned almost as if it were independent. When, in 1691, England ordered Plymouth colony merged with Massachusetts Bay colony, the combination maintained that strong tradition of self-government. Massachusetts, for example, used its charter of 1691 as a functioning constitution from 1776 to 1780 without readoption or alteration. In 1776 the people of Massachusetts simply acted as if they had been independent all along. New Hampshire and Maine were part of colonial Massachusetts and would later be essentially extensions of its political culture. Connecticut and Rhode Island became, through their charters from the 1660s, self-governing colonies.

Although economic opportunity was part of the motivation for settlement of New England, there were those who sought religious freedom. The population was heavily middle class in economic origins and orientation, and consisted mainly of dissenting Protestants of a radical Calvinist bent. Although many sects existed, the Calvinist base, and the common desire to involve the congregations in the running of the churches, strongly colored New England politics. That desire and the joint-stock companies led to a stronger adherence to majority rule and a broader suffrage than existed elsewhere in the colonies. The emphasis on religion meant a stronger sense of community and a greater willingness to legislate on morals, economic practices, and day-to-day behavior. Reinforcing these characteristics was the terrain, which forced the inhabitants to settle in pockets and thus live in towns.

The colonies between New England and the South developed at least half a century later. By 1776, New Jersey and New York were royal colonies, but their proprietary roots were still strong. Pennsylvania, Delaware, and Maryland were still proprietary. The most striking aspect of the middle colonies was the diversity in their respective populations. New York had a strong Dutch presence, as did northern New Jersey and Delaware. Delaware had many Swedes. Pennsylvania had many Germans—in 1776, when Pennsylvania published twenty-five thousand copies of the new state constitution, one-third were printed in German.

The middle colonies also had greater religious diversity. All the Protestant sects found in New England were there as well. The Germans, Swedes, and Dutch were members of the Protestant community, which included large numbers of Anabaptists who were not always welcome in colonies to the north and south. Another group not always welcome in New England, the Quakers, were prominent in Philadelphia politics. Finally, Maryland had originally been settled by Catholics, and though they were a minority in Maryland by 1776, they were conspicuous by their relative absence in New England and the South.

Compared to the other two sections, the middle colonies had more heterogeneous populations, relied more on export and trade, were more urbanized, and were less concerned with preserving religious or social structures. The two largest cities and economic centers in 1776 were Philadelphia and New York, and the middle states together contained approximately two-thirds of all urbanized Americans (those in cities of more than twenty-five hundred). In matters of religion, Maryland and Pennsylvania especially granted freedom of worship early on. The ethnic diversity helped create, and then fed, a greater concern for economic development than for religious, ethnic, or class hegemony. Those seeking economic opportunity as individuals were more likely to be attracted to the middle colonies. . . .

Magna Carta and the Common Law

The colonial charters invariably contained another constitutionally important provision in addition to allowing the colonists to build their own local government. The Virginia Charter of 1606 says:

> [A]ll and everie the parsons being our subjects which shall dwell and inhabit within everie or anie of the saide severall Colonies and plantacions and everie of theire children which shall happen to be borne within the limitts and precincts of the said severall Colonies and plantacions shall have and enjoy all liberties, franchises and immunities within anie of our other dominions to all intents and purposes as if they had been abiding and borne within this our realme of Englande or anie other of our saide dominions.

The phrase "all liberties, franchises and immunities" conveyed to the citizens of the New World the English common law, including the provisions of

Magna Carta. Unlike the colonists in French or Spanish settlements in America, English colonists were full citizens even though away from the mother country. It is difficult to overestimate the importance of this fact. The British government later argued that the common law did not apply in America, but the colonists insisted that the common law was theirs. The Americans, however, were selective: sometimes they argued that only the common law in effect prior to their emigration belonged to them, sometimes that all common law up to independence was theirs. They ignored the parts of Magna Carta and the common law that dealt with feudal structures, the establishment of the Anglican church, and anything else not in line with their preferences.

Virginia and Maryland had a strong common law basis to their respective legal systems from the beginning. The New England colonies initially preferred biblical sources, but their charters also implied strong ties with the common law. The middle colonies were less inclined to accept the common law of England. Nevertheless, they too managed to appropriate much of it. Starting from very different historical, social, and political circumstances, the colonies wove common law into their respective political traditions, and they all appropriated, or failed to appropriate, approximately the same parts of it.

What, precisely, was appropriated? One way to answer the question is to focus upon the parts of Magna Carta that were consistently used in colonial political systems. Until just before the Revolution, [Lord Chief Justice] Coke's commentaries [1628–1644] were the summaries of the common law. Coke, in turn, drew heavily upon Magna Carta as the centerpiece of English common law.

From Magna Carta the colonists took the fundamental principle of no taxation without consent. This was narrower than their own belief that all government should rest upon consent. It is a prime example of how they borrowed from common law on the basis of what was congruent with or supported their broader commitments. The colonists also appropriated the basic constitutional principle of the rule of law, which implied that all people, including rulers, are bound by certain legal restrictions. Part of the common law legacy to American constitutionalism, and perhaps its most important contribution, was the idea of limited government. However, the English notion encompassed only the weakest of the four senses of limited government: everyone was supposed to be subject to the same legal processes. Americans, on the other hand, believed that the majority was the source of law and that thus government was limited by majority will. There was little sense until the 1780s that the majority could also be bound by fundamental law.

The most profound effect of common law was not in principles of constitutional design or in generating the basic sense of what a constitution is. Americans used it to generate the core of their bills of rights: the right to trial by a jury of one's peers; the right to a speedy trial; prohibition of bills of attainder, *ex post facto* laws, and cruel and unusual punishment; the guarantee of habeas corpus; the rights of widows and the poor; the right to compensation for the taking of private property; and equal protection under the laws. Also taken from the common law was the notion that a judge should not have an interest in any case upon which he sits in judgment. This led to a primitive version of the separation of powers in the sense of prohibiting those in government from holding several offices at once.

These rights and legal principles existed in bills of rights throughout the colonial era, as well as in the early state constitutions. However, bills of rights were often not looked upon as part of a constitution or as having constitutional status. During the colonial era we typically find what amounts to a bill of rights embedded in a code of law written and/or approved by the legislature.

For example, the Massachusetts Body of Liberties (1641) codified and summarized the previous twenty years of legislation in the colony and added a number of new "liberties." Few people today would recognize even a resemblance to a bill of rights, yet it was perhaps the first in America. Most of its provisions dealt with defining categories of crime and the punishment each deserved. By writing down such definitions and punishments, the authors effectively created a bill of rights. First of all, the public listing of criminal behavior implicitly guaranteed that behavior not so proscribed was acceptable. It minimized the possibility of arbitrary arrest. Also, by stating the punishment for each crime, the Body of Liberties created a rough social equality. With only a few exceptions ("gentlemen" would sometimes be fined rather than receive lashes), everyone who committed a given crime would have the same punishment. In general, cruel and unusual punishments were eliminated as well. There were also recognizable rights pertaining to strangers and foreigners, indentured servants, widows and orphans, and children and women in general. Such rights might derive indirectly from the common law, since there were a number of similarities. However, the people of New England tended to rely upon the Bible for such things, and the similarity with the common law may reflect the biblical prescription in English common law as well.

These early codifications of laws functioned not only as bills of rights but also as major documents of self-definition. At first, the foundation element of self-definition was just one part of a complete foundation document, such as the Mayflower Compact. However, the matter of self-definition was so important to colonial Americans that it came to occupy longer portions of foundation documents and sometimes even a separate document.

The Pilgrim Code of Law (1636), for example, listed a number of values and rights within the body of what is otherwise a constitution, including the right to trial by jury and a commitment to equal taxation. The 1638 Act for the Liberties of the People set out for the Maryland legislature both prohibitions and goals. The most extensive was the Massachusetts Body of Liberties, though it was followed shortly by similar efforts in other colonies, to the south as well as to the north.

Through these codifications and lists of rights, we see the foundation element of self-definition being differentiated into bills of rights. However, the colonists viewed a bill of rights as a virtual celebration of the people's fundamental values. The limitation on government was, as we have seen, that certain actions were not acceptable.

Although the definition of community values was more public and insistent in New England, southerners had their equivalent documents, albeit fewer in number and less dramatic in content. The middle colonies had the example of the others as they came along later, but they also had a strong impetus for developing bills of rights.

William Penn had been the victim in England of an exceptionally unfair and politically motivated trial. Deeply traumatized by the experience, he worked hard to prevent anything similar happening in Pennsylvania. His Charter of Liberties (1682) and the Pennsylvania Frame of Government (1682) reflect a strong and independent concern for rights as we conceive of them today. Certainly Magna Carta was the source of some of his ideas, as well as his belief that he had been treated in a very un-English-like fashion. It is, however, difficult not to see direct experience as decisive in his commitment to fair and equal treatment of all citizens. Penn's ideas in this regard were influential elsewhere in the documents of the middle colonies—as, for example, the New York Charter of Liberties and Privileges (1683).

When it finally came time to write state constitutions, Americans frequently distinguished between the bill of rights and the constitution proper. The bill of rights usually came first, as part of or along with the preamble. Then the second section of the document was entitled the constitution, thus leaving open to question whether the bill of rights was part of the constitution. Of equal interest, all but two state bills of rights written before 1789 were effectively written or approved by state legislatures. That had been the practice during the colonial era—again, hardly a way to limit the legislature.

The common law embellished and deepened the American constitutional tradition, but was not its sole source. American constitutionalism is broader, more institutionally oriented, and based upon principles not generally found in Magna Carta or anywhere else in the common law. The principles underlying the colonial documents of political foundation clearly "framed" and logically preceded all but a few borrowings from Magna Carta. This is not to say that English common law had no impact. What Americans thus derived is often what they most cherished in the constitutional tradition. But the common law is only a part in the total pattern of influences on American constitutional design.

One simple way of illustrating the relative influence of common law on American constitutionalism is to consider the pattern of appropriation in the United States Bill of Rights. The ten amendments that form the Bill of Rights contain twenty-seven separate rights. Six of these rights, or about 20 percent, were first stated in Magna Carta. Twenty-one, or about 75 percent, were first found in colonial documents written before the 1689 English Bill of Rights. All but one (the Ninth Amendment) could be found in several of the state constitutions written between 1776 and 1787. When it came to matters of constitutional status, Americans drew most heavily and directly upon their own constitutional tradition, which stretched back through colonial developments. Of the many common law rights that they could have appropriated, Americans were selective. They chose in accordance with their own tradition and did not simply write the common law wholesale into their constitutions.

Saying that English common law had relatively little impact on American constitutional design does not imply a lack of effect on the legal system. English common law was used in all colonies by 1776 as the basis for court procedures, methods of appeal, legal definitions, and other key aspects. Again, however, it was selectively appropriated and blended with the colonists' principles and practices.

It is important to distinguish between the impact of common law upon the American legal system and upon American constitutional design. In England the common law was the primary means of limiting governmental power, whereas in America the means was different. The *idea* of limited government does in part derive from it. But in the American constitutional tradition, what *replaced* common law was a new political technique, the written constitution. No matter how important common law was for the operation of the American legal system, the written constitution that framed the system sprang from ideas, principles, and practices evolved primarily in America. . . .

Framing American Constitutionalism

We can usefully view the development of American constitutionalism as proceeding within a series of nested frames of influence. The outer frame was defined by the charters that provided for local self-government and the transmission of the common law to America. Within the charter framework, colonists wrote their own foundation documents, legal codes, and bills of rights. Colonial constitutionalism was thus framed by the charters, but the colonists evolved their own tradition that responded more to their own needs and desires than to English precedent. The documents the colonists wrote framed the appropriation of English common law. They did so in the manner and to the extent that common law was in accord with the evolving American constitutional tradition reflected in their own documents of foundation. Thus, portions of Magna Carta were included in many such documents.

The United States Constitution would reflect the consistent but partial appropriation of the common law that became traditional in the colonists' documents. The common law would in turn frame ideas taken from other European sources, whether Commonwealth political theory or Enlightenment thinkers. Since colonial documents of political foundation derived so heavily from covenants and compacts, and thus from the Bible, the general picture would have Montesquieu and Locke framed by Coke and Blackstone, and they in turn framed by the Bible, which was in turn framed by the civil covenants (charters) characteristic of British imperial practices between 1578 and 1725. This general model of theoretical framing will need detailed modification so we can distinguish the three clusters of colonies, but it provides a useful shorthand for sorting out the influences upon American constitutionalism.

The term *frame* or *framing* denotes a shared mental structure that is an underlying support for more complex or differentiated ideas. It not only supports but also delimits later thinking. That is, *frame* here denotes a mental disposition, a habitual inclination, that shapes or directs later thoughts in a certain way or toward a certain purpose. Furthermore, since what is framed rests upon the frame or is defined by it, the frame is like a perceptual ground for figures that otherwise could not be seen.

To say, then, that the charters frame the colonists' documents is to say that without the charters, colonists would not have written their own documents; that the charters defined what was generally possible for them to write; that the charters inclined them to view things a certain way, to consider some things problematic and others not; that the charters provide a meaningful context for what the colonists wrote. The frame does not determine what is framed, but rather delimits it. If the charters had not given as much freedom as they did to construct local government, but instead required each colony to form a military unit run according to a predetermined code of behavior, the content of the colonists' documents would have been much different.

The nature of the colonial documents did not determine how the common law was appropriated, but it did shape the colonists' thinking, direct their attention, and dispose or incline them out of habit to take some things rather than others. In effect, certain parts of the common law had special meaning because covenants, compacts, and charters led the colonists to so endow them. If those documents in turn had not framed the situation the way they did, the colonists would not have been inclined to use English common law at all, or if they had, in an entirely other way. . . .

✵ *F U R T H E R   R E A D I N G*

Stephen A. Botein, *Early American Law and Society* (1983)

Wesley Frank Craven, *The Southern Colonies in the Seventeenth Century* (1949)

George Dargo, *Roots of the Republic: A New Perspective on Early American Constitutionalism* (1974)

Jack P. Greene, *Peripheries and Center: Constitutional Development in the Extended Polities of the British Empire and the United States, 1607–1788* (1986)

George L. Haskins, *Law and Authority in Early Massachusetts: A Study in Tradition and Design* (1960)

A. E. Dick Howard, *The Road from Runnymede: Magna Carta and Constitutionalism in America* (1968)

Donald S. Lutz, ed., *Documents of Political Foundation Written by Colonial Americans* (1986)

Charles Howard McIlwain, *Constitutionalism, Ancient and Modern*, rev. ed. (1966)

CHAPTER 3

The Rise of Republican Constitutionalism

⌗

Eighteenth-century Americans refined their constitutional arguments to claim simultaneously that they had certain rights as Englishmen but should be free of tightened imperial control to pursue their burgeoning economic fortunes at will. Because colonial Americans closely identified their political fortunes with events back home, they keenly followed England's political struggles. They took particular note of the opposition Whig faction in Parliament that developed in the wake of the Glorious Revolution of 1688–1689. That bloodless event established Parliament's primacy over the crown and supposedly ushered in a new era of English politics. But a ''country'' faction soon emerged, critical of the king, his ministers, and the majority in Parliament for their corruption.

The struggle between this so-called country party (Whig opposition) and the court party in England had singular significance for the colonists, especially following the conclusion of the French and Indian War (known in Europe as the Seven Years' War) in 1763. The British government abandoned its practice of benign neglect and adopted an aggressive imperial policy designed to make the colonists pay their share of the costs of the war and future defense. This new program thrust British officials into the day-to-day affairs of the colonists, many of whom reacted strongly against new taxing measures and British authorities' efforts to rein in customs racketeering, a practice that lubricated the colonial economy. These measures, moreover, raised questions about the meaning of representation, sovereignty, and government by consent, all matters central to the colonists' understanding of their rights as Englishmen and their place within the empire under the unwritten English constitution.

Americans in this way became part of the transatlantic world, depending for their economic livelihood on England and drawing much of their political theory from the dissenting radical Whigs. The consequences of these developments for American constitutionalism have stirred substantial controversy among historians. Until the 1960s, most scholars viewed John Locke, the great English political thinker, as the patron saint of Anglo-American constitutionalism. Locke's liberal ideology stressed individuality, private rights, government by consent, and the right of revolution. The liberal view essentially held that socioeconomic griev-

ances provoked the colonists to break with England and establish a new nation. Beginning in the 1960s, however, the primacy of Locke and liberalism as the organizing ideology of early American constitutionalism came under sustained attack by the proponents of republican constitutionalism.

Scholars such as Bernard Bailyn argued that the English dissenting radical tradition was far more important to the American colonists than was Locke. The proponents of this republican school of interpretation are themselves deeply divided. They agree with the Lockean liberal interpretation that the colonists wanted to found government on the consent of the people, but they part interpretive company over the motives that spurred American constitutional development in the years immediately before the Revolution. Where the liberal intepretation stresses the individualistic and capitalistic bases of emerging constitutional thought, the republican interpretation insists that the colonists were most concerned that government had ceased to serve the public good—the commonwealth. The republican perspective, therefore, emphasizes the idealism of a people obsessed with the pursuit of virtue as the only way to sustain their English rights.

⚜ D O C U M E N T S

John Locke published his most outstanding work, *Two Treatises on Civil Government* (1690), excerpted here in the first selection, in an attempt to rationalize the Glorious Revolution. Locke contributed significantly to the development of Western constitutional thought, synthesizing existing ideas into a coherent liberal ideology that stressed the concepts of social compact, natural law, inalienable rights, government by consent, and the right of revolution. He saw civil society as arising from a double agreement, the first of which was a unanimous agreement to form society and the second of which was a majority agreement on the form of government.

American colonists, however, were quite prepared to develop their own ideas, without the direct influence of Locke. The struggle between colonial merchants and British officials over customs racketeering during and after the French and Indian War is a case in point. Massachusetts merchants hired James Otis, a well-known Boston lawyer, to defend them against the general search warrants that gave authorities open-ended access to dwellings and warehouses. At the 1761 trial of one of the indicted smugglers, Otis articulated the idea that certain fundamental principles were superior to any established legal authority (see the second document). The concept of fundamental law had a long and distinguished history in England, as we have seen with Magna Carta. Otis gave these notions a uniquely American twist, and his argument almost immediately passed into the mainstream of American constitutional thought.

The anger against British officials was also expressed at the grassroots level by what was known as "politics out-of-doors." In 1769 in Monmouth County, East Jersey, debt-ridden farmers rioted against colonial and British authorities in an effort to prevent the collection of debts by closing down the local courts. This popular resistance was also directed against lawyers and judges, who were condemned as agents of an unresponsive legal system. In the third document, the angry farmers present their grievances.

The revolutionary events of 1776, of course, were a dramatic expression of politics out-of-doors, but even at that late date Americans lacked a clearly developed rationale for breaking with the empire. Thomas Paine's *Common Sense*, an excerpt from which is reprinted in the fourth document, provided them with just that. Paine persuasively articulated the case against the king and his ministers for the suffering of American colonists and advocated a break with England as the proper remedy. Thomas Jefferson further developed these ideas in the Declaration of Independence, the fifth selection in this chapter and perhaps the most successful document of revolution in world history. In the Declaration, Jefferson succeeded in breaking the law without being illegal by arguing that the king's abuses had left Americans, as a matter of fundamental law, no choice but to rebel. The Declaration's long list of charges are particularly interesting for what they did contain. The document listed its grievances against the crown, when it had been Parliament that had caused the colonists' problems. It also did not contain an open condemnation of slavery. Jefferson had drafted one, but it was ultimately deleted.

The most immediate evidence of the new republican ideas set loose by the Revolution appeared in America's first constitutions—those of the newly independent states. Given their experiences with the unwritten English constitution, the Americans decided from the beginning to place their fundamental charters of government in writing. These state constitutions were the embodiment of the colonial experience and the prototype for the first two national constitutions, the Articles of Confederation and then the Constitution of 1787. These documents were creations of their own time and place, however, because they lodged substantial authority in the legislative branch. Such well-accepted ideas today as bicameralism and separation of powers based on an independent judiciary and executive were not fully developed. Nowhere was evidence of that clearer than in the Pennsylvania Constitution of 1776, the most democratic of the new state constitutions, which appears here as the sixth selection.

Another feature of these documents was the inclusion in most, but not all, of a separate bill of rights. The importance of such a provision was underscored in Massachusetts, where the freedmen overwhelmingly defeated the Constitution of 1778 because it lacked a bill of rights. John Adams, who had been the architect of the defeated constitution, then prepared a bill of rights that was included in a new document (the final selection here) submitted to the freedmen in 1780. Today, the Massachusetts constitution is the oldest surviving, written frame of government in the world.

John Locke on the Ends of Political Society and Government, 1690

. . . 95. Men being by nature all free, equal, and independent, no one can be put out of this state and subjected to the political power of another without his own consent. The only way one divests himself of his natural liberty and puts on the bonds of civil society is by agreeing with other men to join and unite into a community for their comfortable, safe, and peaceable living. This any number of men may do, because it injures not the freedom of the rest; they are left in the state of nature. When any number of men have so consented to make one community or government, they constitute one body politic wherein the majority have a right to act and include the rest. . . .

123. If man in the state of nature be so free, as has been said; if he be absolute lord of his own person and possessions, equal to the greatest, and subject to nobody, why will he part with his freedom and subject himself to the control of any other power? To which it is obvious to answer that though in the state of nature he had such right, yet the enjoyment of it is very uncertain and constantly exposed to the invasion of others. For all being kings as much as he, every man his equal, and the greater part of mankind no strict observers of equity and justice, the enjoyment of the property he has in this state is very unsafe, very insecure. This makes him willing to surrender this condition, which, however free, is full of fears and continual dangers. And it is not without reason that he seeks out and is willing to join in society with others who are already united, or have a mind to unite, for the mutual preservation of their lives, liberties, and estates, which I call by the general name "property."

124. The great and chief end, therefore, of men's uniting into commonwealths and putting themselves under government is the preservation of their property, to which in the state of nature there are many things lacking:

First, there is no established, settled, known law, received and agreed by common consent to be the standard of right and wrong, and the common measure to decide all controversies. For though the law of nature be plain and intelligible to all rational creatures, yet men, being biased by their interest as well as ignorant for lack of studying of it, are not apt to allow of it as a law binding to them in the application of it to their particular cases.

125. *Second,* in the state of nature there is no known and impartial judge with authority to determine all differences according to the established law. For everyone in that state being both judge and executioner of the law of nature, passion and revenge are apt to carry men too far and with too much heat in their own cases, as well as negligence and unconcernedness to make them too remiss in other men's.

126. *Thirdly,* in the state of nature, there often is no power to back and support the sentence when right, and to give it due execution. They who commit injustice will seldom lack the force to make good their injustice. Such resistance many times makes the punishment dangerous and frequently destructive to those who attempt it.

127. Thus mankind, notwithstanding all the privileges of the state of nature, being but in an ill condition while they remain in it, are quickly driven into society. Hence it comes to pass that we seldom find any number of men live any time together in this state. It is this makes them so willingly give up everyone his single power of punishing, to be exercised by such alone as shall be appointed to it among them, and by such rules as the community shall agree on. And here we have the original right of both the legislative and the executive power, as well as of governments and societies themselves.

128. In the state of nature a man has two powers: The first is to do whatsoever he thinks fit for the preservation of himself and others within

the permission of the law of nature. And, were it not for the corruption and viciousness of degenerate men, there would be no need of any other, no necessity that men should separate from this great and natural community and by positive agreements combine into smaller and divided associations.

The other power a man has in the state of nature is the power to punish the crimes committed against that law. Both these he gives up when he joins a private, if I may so call it, or particular political society and incorporates into any commonwealth separate from the rest of mankind.

129. The first power he gives up to be regulated by laws made by the society, which laws in many things confine the liberty he had by the law of nature.

130. Secondly, the power of punishing he wholly gives up, and engages his natural force to assist the executive power of the society, as the law thereof shall require.

131. But though men when they enter into society give up the equality, liberty, and executive power they had in the state of nature into the hands of the society, to be so far disposed of by the legislative as the good of the society shall require, yet it remains the intention of everyone the better to preserve himself, his liberty, and his property by entering society. Therefore, the power of that society can never be supposed to extend farther than the common good. For a government is obliged to secure everyone's property by providing against those three defects above-mentioned that made the state of nature so unsafe and uneasy. And so whoever has the legislative or supreme power of any commonwealth is bound to govern by established standing laws, promulgated and known to the people, and not by extemporary decrees; and these laws are to be administered by impartial and upright judges who are to decide controversies by these laws. The force of the community is to be employed at home only in the execution of such laws, or abroad to prevent or redress foreign injuries, and secure the community from inroads and invasion. And all this to be directed to no other end but the peace, safety, and public good of the people.

132. The majority, having the whole power of the community naturally in them, may employ all the power of the community in making laws from time to time, and executing those laws by officers of their own appointing. Then the form of government is a perfect democracy. Or else they may put the power of making laws into the hands of a few select men, and their heirs or successors, and then it is an oligarchy; or else into the hands of one man, and then it is a monarchy; if to him and his heirs, it is a hereditary monarchy; if to him only for life, but upon his death the power only of nominating a successor to return to the majority, then an elective monarchy. And so accordingly of these the community may make compounded and mixed forms of government, as they think good. For since the form of government depends on the placing of supreme power, which is the legislative—it being impossible to conceive that an inferior power should prescribe to a superior, or any but the supreme make laws—according as the power of making laws is placed, such is the form of the commonwealth. . . .

James Otis Argues Against the Writs of Assistance, 1761

1. . . . This writ is against the fundamental principles of law. The privilege of the House. A man who is quiet, is as secure in his house, as a prince in his castle—notwithstanding all his debts and civil processes of any kind. But—

For flagrant crimes and in cases of great public necessity, the privilege may be infringed on. For felonies an officer may break upon process and oath, that is, by a special warrant to search such a house, sworn to be suspected, and good grounds of suspicion appearing.

Make oath *coram* Lord Treasurer, or Exchequer in England, or a magistrate here, and get a special warrant for the public good, to infringe the privilege of house.

General warrant to search for felonies. Hawkins, Pleas of the Crown. Every petty officer, from the highest to the lowest; and if some of them are common, others are uncommon.

Government justices used to issue such perpetual edicts. (*Q*. With what particular reference.) But one precedent, and that in the reign of Charles II., when star chamber powers and all powers but lawful and useful powers, were pushed to extremity.

The authority of this modern practice of the Court of Exchequer. It has an Imprimatur. But what may not have? It may be owing to some ignorant Clerk of the Exchequer. But all precedents, and this among the rest, are under the control of the principles of law. Lord Talbot. Better to observe the known principles of law than any one precedent, though in the House of Lords.

As to Acts of Parliament. An act against the Constitution is void; an act against natural equity is void; and if an act of Parliament should be made, in the very words of this petition it would be void. The executive Courts must pass such acts into disuse.

8 Rep. 118 from Viner. Reason of the common law to control an act of Parliament. Iron manufacture. Noble Lord's proposal, that we should send our horses to England to be shod. If an officer will justify under a writ, he must return it. 12. Mod. 396, perpetual writ. Statute Charles II. We have all as good right to inform as custom-house officers, and every man may have a general irreturnable commission to break houses.

By 12 of Charles, on oath before Lord Treasurer, Barons of Exchequer, or Chief Magistrate, to break, with an officer. 14 C. to issue a warrant requiring sheriffs, &c. to assist the officers to search for goods not entered or prohibited. 7 & 8. W. & M. gives officers in plantations same powers with officers in England.

Continuance of writs and processes proves no more, nor so much, as I grant a special writ of assistance on special oath for special purpose. . . .

2. . . . In the first place, may it please your Honors, I will admit that writs of one kind may be legal; that is, special writs, directed to special officers, and to search certain houses, &c. specially set forth in the writ,

may be granted by the Court of Exchequer at home, upon oath made before the Lord Treasurer by the person who asks it, that he suspects such goods to be concealed in those very places he desires to search. The act of 14 Charles II . . . proves this. And in this light the writ appears like a warrant from a Justice of the Peace to search for stolen goods. Your Honors will find in the old books concerning the office of a Justice of the Peace, precedents of general warrants to search suspected houses. But in more modern books you will find only special warrants to search such and such houses specially named, in which the complainant has before sworn that he suspects his goods are concealed; and you will find it adjudged that special warrants only are legal. In the same manner I rely on it, that the writ prayed for in this petition, being general, is illegal. It is a power, that places the liberty of every man in the hands of every petty officer. I say I admit that special writs of assistance, to search special places, may be granted to certain persons on oath; but I deny that the writ now prayed for can be granted, for I beg leave to make some observations on the writ itself, before I proceed to other acts of Parliament. In the first place, the writ is universal, being directed "to all and singular Justices, Sheriffs, Constables, and other officers and subjects"; so, that, in short, it is directed to every subject in the King's dominions. Every one with this writ may be a tyrant; if this commission be legal, a tyrant in a legal manner also may control, imprison, or murder any one within the realm. In the next place, it is perpetual; there is no return. A man is accountable to no person for his doings. Every man may reign secure in his petty tyranny, and spread terror and desolation around him. In the third place, a person with this writ, in the daytime, may enter all houses, shops, &c. at will, and command all to assist him. Fourthly, by this writ not only deputies &c. but even their menial servants, are allowed to lord it over us. Now one of the most essential branches of English liberty is the freedom of one's house. A man's house is his castle; and whilst he is quiet, he is as well guarded as a prince in his castle. This writ, if it should be declared legal, would totally annihilate this privilege. Custom-house officers may enter our houses, when they please; we are commanded to permit their entry. Their menial servants may enter, may break locks, bars, and every thing in their way; and whether they break through malice or revenge, no man, no court, can inquire. Bare suspicion without oath is sufficient. This wanton exercise of his power is not a chimerical suggestion of a heated brain. I will mention some facts. Mr. Pew had one of these writs, and when Mr. Ware succeeded him, he endorsed this writ over to Mr. Ware; so that these writs are negotiable from one officer to another; and so your Honors have no opportunity of judging the persons to whom this vast power is delegated. Another instance is this: Mr. Justice Walley had called this same Mr. Ware before him, by a constable, to answer for a breach of Sabbath-day acts, or that of profane swearing. As soon as he had finished, Mr. Ware asked him if he had done. He replied, Yes. Well then, said Mr. Ware, I will show you a little of my power. I command you to permit me to search your house for uncustomed goods. And went on to search his house from the garret to the cellar; and then served the constable in the same manner.

But to show another absurdity in this writ; if it should be established, I insist upon it, every person by the 14 Charles II has this power as well as custom-house officers. The words are, "It shall be lawful for any person or persons authorized," &c. What a scene does this open! Every man, prompted by revenge, ill humor, or wantonness, to inspect the inside of his neighbor's house, may get a writ of assistance. Others will ask it from self-defence; one arbitrary exertion will provoke another, until society be involved in tumult and in blood.

Again, these writs are not returned. Writs in their nature are temporary things. When the purposes for which they are issued are answered, they exist no more; but these live forever; no one can be called to account. Thus reason and the constitution are both against this writ. . . .

Farmers Demand "Liberty and Property, Without Oppression": Grievances of Monmouth County, East Jersey, 1769

My dear Countrymen:

Permit me to declare to you my deep Concern for you and myself, in regard to the present deplorable and afflictive Times, which brings to my Mind the past heavy Burthens we have struggled through; it is but a few Years ago, when we were burthened with a long, tedious and expensive War, which drained our Country in a great Measure, of both Men and Money; but as it was in Defence of our Rights and Liberties, we cheerfully struggled through the same.

Secondly, we were burthened with a most Destructive, alarming, and unconstitutional Act of Parliament, (to wit the Stamp Act) and that from our Mother Country, the Thoughts of which alarmed every considerate Breast, from the highest to the lowest Rank of People, every one calling out for Liberty and Property. The Consequence of which, was, that by a steady, firm and undaunted Resolution, in Opposition to so unconstitutional an Act, we as Freemen held our Right to Freedom, and boldly withstood the Threats, and at length were heard by our Mother, our Grievance redressed, and we restored to our former Liberties.

Thirdly, We having by our Good Resolutions turned out the wounding and devouring Serpent, and then setting ourselves down easy, and not keeping out a resolute Watch, have let in Serpents seven Times more devouring than the first (to wit L—yrs), who in their daily Practice are as Private Leaches, sucking out our very Hearts Blood. Our public Houses are papered with Sheriff's Advertisements, and we daily hear our Neighbour's Lands and Goods sold for not much more than one Fourth Part of the Value, whereby the Man is ruined, and his Family turned out of Doors, and his whole Estate not amounting to more than Lawyer's and Sheriff's Fees, while the Creditor is wanting his Money; and in the next Place the Debtor is hurried to Gaol, there to starve and suffer, while his Family are in the like Condition at home. The Consideration of which makes me cry out to you my Countrymen,

Rouse, Rouse! and shake off your drowsy and stupid Delays; open your Eyes, and you will see the ruinous State of your Country, and say with David of old, that the Hand that deliver'd us out of the Paw of the Lyon and the Bear, shall he not deliver us out of the Hands of the uncircumcised L—yrs? We all of us complain of the Hardness of the Times, but not one of us offers to forward any Means to shake off the Burthen. David would never have slain the uncircumcised Philistine, had he not used Means for that Purpose; neither shall we ever overcome the ungrateful L—yrs, if we do not bestir ourselves. Consider the daily Practice of those Gentlemen of the Law, as they Stile themselves: what extravagant Bills of Cost are made, and Escapes brought against Sheriffs, when they already have got the Man's whole Estate? We are free People, & shall we be brought to Slavery, and that by a Set of People brought up among us, who are living upon the Ruins of the Poor, and will hardly look at a common Man, when they meet him, unless they can persuade him to have an Action brought against one or another of his Neighbours? We were deemed a People of good Courage and undaunted Resolution, when we withstood the Stamp-Act; and shall we now give away our all to this unconscionable Set of L—yrs? No, but let us with the same manly Spirit withstand them; and first in a friendly Manner desire them to desist their unwarrantable Practices, and if that will not take Effect, then where are all our couragious young Men? Remember the saying of Solomon of old, that Oppression maketh a wise Man mad; stand together and forbid them Practicing in our Court, and rid the County of such Barbarity, and turn them out of the County. . . .

How Matters were carried on at the Court:

The Evening before the Court, there was a Liberty Pole set up, with a Union Flag at the Head of said Pole. Tuesday the 25th of July, it being the first Day of the Court, there was no less than two or three Hundred Liberty Boys, appeared under said Flag, in Defiance of the Gentlemen called L—yrs. The Court being called, the Court with the Grand-jury were admitted peaceably to enter the Court-House, but no L—yrs were admitted to go in; upon which the Court made Proposals to the Public, with Assurances, that they would redress the Grievances of the People, as far as lay in their Power; which in some Measure appeased the People, but who could not fully consent to make Way for the Lawyers to enter the Court-House. Wednesday the 26th Day of July in the Morning, it was again warmly insisted upon, by the Court Party, that the Liberty Pole should be taken down; a Gentlemen of said County asserted to the People, that the Lawyers had given up the Point, and would not seek for an Opportunity to enter the Court. Upon which in Obedience to the Court, the Pole was taken down, and all Matters appeared quiet; but when the Liberty Boys were in a Manner all dispersed, the Court was called. The Judges coming to the House, intermixed with the Lawyers, gave some few of the Liberty Boys Reason to suspect, that the Assertion from the aforesaid Gentlemen, was not fully observed; upon which they demanded the Reason of the Lawyers coming to enter the Court, but were answered with a general Attack from Judges, Sheriff, and Lawyers; who played away so furiously, that they soon overcame the small Number that opposed them, they being four to one, and so Judges, Sheriff, and Lawyers entered the Court. . . .

Thomas Paine Calls for a Break with England, 1776

Some writers have so confounded society with government, as to leave little or no distinction between them; whereas they are not only different, but have different origins. Society is produced by our wants, and government by our wickedness; the former promotes our happiness *positively* by uniting our affections, the latter *negatively* by restraining our vices. The one encourages intercourse, the other creates distinctions. The first is a patron, the last a punisher.

Society in every state is a blessing, but Government, even in its best state, is but a necessary evil; in its worst state an intolerable one: for when we suffer, or are exposed to the same miseries *by a Government,* which we might expect in a country *without Government,* our calamity is heightened by reflecting that we furnish the means by which we suffer. Government, like dress, is the badge of lost innocence; the palaces of kings are built upon the ruins of the bowers of paradise. For were the impulses of conscience clear, uniform and irresistibly obeyed, man would need no other lawgiver; but that not being the case, he finds it necessary to surrender up a part of his property to furnish means for the protection of the rest; and this he is induced to do by the same prudence which in every other case advises him, out of two evils to choose the least. Wherefore, security being the true design and end of government, it unanswerably follows that whatever form thereof appears most likely to ensure it to us, with the least expense and greatest benefit, is preferable to all others. . . .

I draw my idea of the form of government from a principle in nature which no art can overturn, viz. that the more simple any thing is, the less liable it is to be disordered, and the easier repaired when disordered; and with this maxim in view I offer a few remarks on the so much boasted constitution of England. That it was noble for the dark and slavish times in which it was erected, is granted. When the world was overrun with tyranny the least remove therefrom was a glorious rescue. But that it is imperfect, subject to convulsions, and incapable of producing what it seems to promise, is easily demonstrated.

Absolute governments, (tho' the disgrace of human nature) have this advantage with them, they are simple; if the people suffer, they know the head from which their suffering springs; know likewise the remedy; and are not bewildered by a variety of causes and cures. But the constitution of England is so exceedingly complex, that the nation may suffer for years together without being able to discover in which part the fault lies; some will say in one and some in another, and every political physician will advise a different medicine.

I know it is difficult to get over local or long standing prejudices, yet if we will suffer ourselves to examine the component parts of the English constitution, we shall find them to be the base remains of two ancient tyrannies, compounded with some new Republican materials.

First.—The remains of Monarchical tyranny in the person of the King.

Secondly.—The remains of Aristocratical tyranny in the persons of the Peers.

Thirdly.—The new Republican materials, in the persons of the Commons, on whose virtue depends the freedom of England.

The two first, by being hereditary, are independent of the People; wherefore in a *constitutional sense* they contribute nothing towards the freedom of the State.

To say that the constitution of England is an *union* of three powers, reciprocally *checking* each other, is farcical; either the words have no meaning, or they are flat contradictions.

To say that the Commons is a check upon the King, presupposes two things.

First.—That the King is not to be trusted without being looked after; or in other words, that a thirst for absolute power is the natural disease of monarchy.

Secondly.—That the Commons, by being appointed for that purpose, are either wiser or more worthy of confidence than the Crown.

But as the same constitution which gives the Commons a power to check the King by withholding the supplies, gives afterwards the King a power to check the Commons, by empowering him to reject their other bills; it again supposes that the King is wiser than those whom it has already supposed to be wiser than him. A mere absurdity!

There is something exceedingly ridiculous in the composition of Monarchy; it first excludes a man from the means of information, yet empowers him to act in cases where the highest judgment is required. The state of a king shuts him from the World, yet the business of a king requires him to know it thoroughly; wherefore the different parts, by unnaturally opposing and destroying each other, prove the whole character to be absurd and useless.

Some writers have explained the English constitution thus: the King, say they, is one, the people another; the Peers are a house in behalf of the King, the commons in behalf of the people; but this hath all the distinctions of a house divided against itself; and though the expressions be pleasantly arranged, yet when examined they appear idle and ambiguous; and it will always happen, that the nicest construction that words are capable of, when applied to the description of something which either cannot exist, or is too incomprehensible to be within the compass of description, will be words of sound only, and though they may amuse the ear, they cannot inform the mind: for this explanation includes a previous question, viz. *how came the king by a power which the people are afraid to trust, and always obliged to check?* Such a power could not be the gift of a wise people, neither can any power, *which needs checking,* be from God; yet the provision which the constitution makes supposes such a power to exist.

But the provision is unequal to the task; the means either cannot or will not accomplish the end, and the whole affair is a *Felo de se:* for as the greater weight will always carry up the less, and as all the wheels of a machine are put in motion by one, it only remains to know which power in the constitution has the most weight, for that will govern: and tho' the others, or a part of them, may clog, or, as the phrase is, check the rapidity of its motion, yet so long as they cannot stop it, their endeavours will be ineffectual: The first moving power will at last have its way, and what it wants in speed is supplied by time.

That the crown is this overbearing part in the English constitution needs not be mentioned, and that it derives its whole consequence merely from being the giver of places and pensions is self-evident; wherefore, though we have been wise enough to shut and lock a door against absolute Monarchy, we at the same time have been foolish enough to put the Crown in possession of the key.

The prejudice of Englishmen, in favour of their own government, by King, Lords and Commons, arises as much or more from national pride than reason. Individuals are undoubtedly safer in England than in some other countries: but the will of the king is as much the law of the land in Britain as in France, with this difference, that instead of proceeding directly from his mouth, it is handed to the people under the formidable shape of an act of parliament. For the fate of Charles the First hath only made kings more subtle—not more just.

Wherefore, laying aside all national pride and prejudice in favour of modes and forms, the plain truth is that *it is wholly owing to the constitution of the people, and not to the constitution of the government* that the crown is not as oppressive in England as in Turkey.

An inquiry into the *constitutional errors* in the English form of government, is at this time highly necessary; for as we are never in a proper condition of doing justice to others, while we continue under the influence of some leading partiality, so neither are we capable of doing it to ourselves while we remain fettered by any obstinate prejudice. And as a man who is attached to a prostitute is unfitted to choose or judge of a wife, so any prepossession in favour of a rotten constitution of government will disable us from discerning a good one. . . .

As much hath been said of the advantages of reconciliation, which, like an agreeable dream, hath passed away and left us as we were, it is but right that we should examine the contrary side of the argument, and enquire into some of the many material injuries which these Colonies sustain, and always will sustain, by being connected with and dependant on Great Britain. To examine that connection and dependance, on the principles of nature and common sense, to see what we have to trust to, if separated, and what we are to expect, if dependant.

I have heard it asserted by some, that as America has flourished under her former connection with Great Britain, the same connection is necessary towards her future happiness, and will always have the same effect. Nothing can be more fallacious than this kind of argument. We may as well assert that because a child has thrived upon milk, that it is never to have meat, or that the first twenty years of our lives is to become a precedent for the next twenty. But even this is admitting more than is true; for I answer roundly that America would have flourished as much, and probably much more, had no European power taken any notice of her. The commerce by which she hath enriched herself are the necessaries of life, and will always have a market while eating is the custom of Europe.

But she has protected us, say some. That she hath engrossed us is true, and defended the Continent at our expense as well as her own, is admitted; and she would have defended Turkey from the same motive, *viz.* for the sake of trade and dominion.

Alas! we have been long led away by ancient prejudices and made large sacrifices to superstition. We have boasted the protection of Great Britain, without considering, that her motive was *interest* not *attachment;* and that she did not protect us from *our enemies* on *our account;* but from *her enemies* on *her own account,* from those who had no quarrel with us on any *other account,* and who will always be our enemies on the *same account.* Let Britain waive her pretensions to the Continent, or the Continent throw off the dependance, and we should be at peace with France and Spain, were they at war with Britain. The miseries of Hanover last war ought to warn us against connections.

It hath lately been asserted in parliament, that the Colonies have no relation to each other but through the Parent Country, *i.e.* that Pennsylvania and the Jerseys and so on for the rest, are sister Colonies by the way of England; this is certainly a very roundabout way of proving relationship, but it is the nearest and only true way of proving enmity (or enemyship, if I may so call it). France and Spain never were, nor perhaps ever will be, our enemies as *Americans,* but as our being the *subjects of Great Britain.*

But Britain is the parent country, say some. Then the more shame upon her conduct. Even brutes do not devour their young, nor savages make war upon their families. Wherefore, the assertion, if true, turns to her reproach; but it happens not to be true, or only partly so, and the phrase *parent or mother country* hath been jesuitically adopted by the King and his parasites, with a low papistical design of gaining an unfair bias on the credulous weakness of our minds. Europe, and not England, is the parent country of America. This new World hath been the asylum for the persecuted lovers of civil and religious liberty from *every part* of Europe. Hither have they fled, not from the tender embraces of the mother, but from the cruelty of the monster; and it is so far true of England, that the same tyranny which drove the first emigrants from home, pursues their descendants still. . . .

To conclude, however strange it may appear to some, or however unwilling they may be to think so, matters not, but many strong and striking reasons may be given to show that nothing can settle our affairs so expeditiously as an open and determined declaration for independence. Some of which are,

First—It is the custom of Nations, when any two are at war, for some other powers, not engaged in the quarrel, to step in as mediators, and bring about the preliminaries of a peace; But while America calls herself the subject of Great Britain, no power, however well disposed she may be, can offer her mediation. Wherefore, in our present state we may quarrel on for ever.

Secondly—It is unreasonable to suppose that France or Spain will give us any kind of assistance, if we mean only to make use of that assistance for the purpose of repairing the breach, and strengthening the connection between Britain and America; because, those powers would be sufferers by the consequences.

Thirdly—While we profess ourselves the subjects of Britain, we must, in the eyes of foreign nations, be considered as Rebels. The precedent is somewhat dangerous to their peace, for men to be in arms under the name of subjects; we, on the spot, can solve the paradox; but to unite resistance and subjection requires an idea much too refined for common understanding.

Fourthly—Were a manifesto to be published, and despatched to foreign Courts, setting forth the miseries we have endured, and the peaceful methods which we have ineffectually used for redress; declaring at the same time that not being able longer to live happily or safely under the cruel disposition of the British Court, we had been driven to the necessity of breaking off all connections with her; at the same time, assuring all such Courts of our peaceable disposition towards them, and of our desire of entering into trade with them; such a memorial would produce more good effects to this Continent than if a ship were freighted with petitions to Britain.

Under our present denomination of British subjects, we can neither be received nor heard abroad; the custom of all Courts is against us, and will be so, until by an independence we take rank with other nations.

These proceedings may at first seem strange and difficult, but like all other steps which we have already passed over, will in a little time become familiar and agreeable; and until an independence is declared, the Continent will feel itself like a man who continues putting off some unpleasant business from day to day, yet knows it must be done, hates to set about it, wishes it over, and is continually haunted with the thoughts of its necessity.

The Declaration of Independence, 1776

In Congress, July 4, 1776,

The Unanimous Declaration of the Thirteen United States of America,

When in the Course of human events, it becomes necessary for one people to dissolve the political bands which have connected them with another, and to assume among the Powers of the earth, the separate and equal station to which the Laws of Nature and of Nature's God entitle them, a decent respect to the opinions of mankind requires that they should declare the causes which impel them to the separation.

We hold these truths to be self-evident, that all men are created equal, that they are endowed by their Creator with certain unalienable Rights, that among these are Life, Liberty and the pursuit of Happiness. That to secure these rights, Governments are instituted among Men, deriving their just powers from the consent of the governed, That whenever any Form of Government becomes destructive of these ends, it is the Right of the People to alter or to abolish it, and to institute new Government, laying its foundation on such principles and organizing its powers in such form, as to them shall seem most likely to effect their Safety and Happiness. Prudence, indeed, will dictate that Governments long established should not be changed for light and transient causes; and accordingly all experience hath shown, that mankind are more disposed to suffer, while evils are sufferable, than to right themselves by abolishing the forms to which they are accustomed. But when a long train of abuses and usurpations, pursuing invariably the same Object evinces a design to reduce them under absolute Despotism, it is their right, it is their duty, to throw off such Government, and to provide new Guards for their future security.—Such has been the patient sufferance of these Colonies; and such is now the necessity which constrains them to alter their former Systems of Government. The history of the present King of Great Britain is a history of repeated injuries and usurpations, all having in direct object the establishment of an absolute Tyranny over these States. To prove this, let Facts be submitted to a candid world.

He has refused his Assent to Laws, the most wholesome and necessary for the public good.

He has forbidden his Governors to pass Laws of immediate and pressing importance, unless suspended in their operation till his Assent should be obtained; and when so suspended, he has utterly neglected to attend to them.

He has refused to pass other Laws for the accommodation of large districts of people, unless those people would relinquish the right of Representation in the Legislature, a right inestimable to them and formidable to tyrants only.

He has called together legislative bodies at places unusual, uncomfortable, and distant from the depository of their Public Records, for the sole purpose of fatiguing them into compliance with his measures.

He has dissolved Representative Houses repeatedly, for opposing with manly firmness his invasions on the rights of the people.

He has refused for a long time, after such dissolutions, to cause others to be elected; whereby the Legislative Powers, incapable of Annihilation, have returned to the People at large for their exercise; the State remaining in the mean time exposed to all the dangers of invasion from without, and convulsions within.

He has endeavoured to prevent the population of these States; for that purpose obstructing the Laws of Naturalization of Foreigners; refusing to pass others to encourage their migration hither, and raising the conditions of new Appropriations of Lands.

He has obstructed the Administration of Justice, by refusing his Assent to Laws for establishing Judiciary Powers.

He has made Judges dependent on his Will alone, for the tenure of their offices, and the amount and payment of their salaries.

He has erected a multitude of New Offices, and sent hither swarms of Officers to harass our People, and eat out their substance.

He has kept among us, in times of peace, Standing Armies without the Consent of our legislature.

He has affected to render the Military independent of and superior to the Civil Power.

He has combined with others to subject us to a jurisdiction foreign to our constitution, and unacknowledged by our laws; giving his Assent to their acts of pretended legislation:

For quartering large bodies of armed troops among us:

For protecting them, by a mock Trial, from Punishment for any Murders which they should commit on the Inhabitants of these States:

For cutting off our Trade with all parts of the world:

For imposing taxes on us without our Consent:

For depriving us in many cases, of the benefits of Trial by Jury:

For transporting us beyond Seas to be tried for pretended offences:

For abolishing the free System of English Laws in a neighbouring Province, establishing therein an Arbitrary government, and enlarging its Boundaries so as to render it at once an example and fit instrument for introducing the same absolute rule into these Colonies:

For taking away our Charters, abolishing our most valuable Laws, and altering fundamentally the Forms of our Governments:

For suspending our own Legislature, and declaring themselves invested with Power to legislate for us in all cases whatsoever.

He has abdicated Government here, by declaring us out of his Protection and waging War against us.

He has plundered our seas, ravaged our Coasts, burnt our towns, and destroyed the lives of our people.

He is at this time transporting large armies of foreign mercenaries to compleat the works of death, desolation and tyranny, already begun with circumstances of Cruelty & perfidy scarcely paralleled in the most barbarous ages, and totally unworthy the Head of a civilized nation.

He has constrained our fellow Citizens taken Captive on the high Seas to bear Arms against their Country, to become the executioners of their friends and Brethren, or to fall themselves by their Hands.

He has excited domestic insurrections amongst us, and has endeavoured to bring on the inhabitants of our frontiers, the merciless Indian Savages, whose known rule of warfare, is an undistinguished destruction of all ages, sexes and conditions.

In every stage of these Oppressions We have Petitioned for Redress in the most humble terms: Our repeated Petitions have been answered only by repeated injury. A Prince, whose character is thus marked by every act which may define a Tyrant, is unfit to be the ruler of a free People.

Nor have We been wanting in attention to our British brethren. We have warned them from time to time of attempts by their legislature to extend an unwarrantable jurisdiction over us. We have reminded them of the circumstances of our emigration and settlement here. We have appealed to their native justice and magnanimity, and we have conjured them by the ties of our common kindred to disavow these usurpations, which, would inevitably interrupt our connections and correspondence. They too have been deaf to the voice of justice and of consanguinity. We must, therefore, acquiesce in the necessity, which denounces our Separation, and hold them, as we hold the rest of mankind, Enemies in War, in Peace Friends.

We, therefore, the Representatives of the united States of America, in General Congress, Assembled, appealing to the Supreme Judge of the world for the rectitude of our intentions, do, in the Name, and by Authority of the good People of these Colonies, solemnly publish and declare, That these United Colonies are, and of Right ought to be Free and Independent States; that they are Absolved from all Allegiance to the British Crown, and that all political connection between them and the State of Great Britain, is and ought to be totally dissolved; and that as Free and Independent States, they have full Power to levy War, conclude Peace, contract Alliances, establish Commerce, and to do all other Acts and Things which Independent States may of right do. And for the support of this Declaration, with a firm reliance on the Protection of Divine Providence, we mutually pledge to each other our Lives, our Fortunes and our sacred Honor.

The Pennsylvania Constitution, 1776

Whereas all government ought to be instituted and supported for the security and protection of the community as such, and to enable the individuals who compose it to enjoy their natural rights, and the other blessings which the Author of existence has bestowed upon man; and whenever these great ends of government are not obtained, the people have a right, by common consent to change it, and take such measures as to them may appear necessary to promote their safety and happiness. AND WHEREAS the inhabitants of this commonwealth have in consideration of protection only, heretofore acknowledged allegiance to the king of Great Britain; and the said king has not only withdrawn that protection, but commenced, and still continues to carry on, with unabated vengeance, a most cruel and unjust war against them, employing therein, not only the troops of Great Britain, but foreign mercenaries, savages and slaves, for the avowed purpose of reducing them to a total and abject submission to the despotic domination of the British parliament, with many other acts of tyranny, (more fully set forth in the declaration of Congress) whereby all allegiance and fealty to the said king and his successors, are dissolved and at an end, and all power and authority derived from him ceased in these colonies. AND WHEREAS it is absolutely necessary for the welfare and safety of the inhabitants of said colonies, that they be henceforth free and independent States, and that just, permanent, and proper forms of government exist in every part of them, derived from and founded on the authority of the people only, agreeable to the directions of the honourable American Congress. We, the representatives of the freemen of Pennsylvania, in general convention met, for the express purpose of framing such a government, confessing the goodness of the great Governor of the universe (who alone knows to what degree of earthly happiness mankind may attain, by perfecting the arts of government) in permitting the people of this State, by common consent, and without violence, deliberately to form for themselves such just rules as they shall think best, for governing their future society; and being fully convinced, that it is our indispensable duty to establish such original principles of government, as will best promote the general happiness of the people of this State, and their posterity, and provide for future improvements, without partiality for, or prejudice against any particular class, sect, or denomination of men whatever, do, by virtue of the authority vested in use by our constituents, ordain, declare, and establish, the following *Declaration of Rights* and *Frame of Government,* to be the CONSTITUTION of this commonwealth, and to remain in force therein for ever, unaltered, except in such articles as shall hereafter on experience be found to require improvement, and which shall by the same authority of the people, fairly delegated as this frame of government directs, be amended or improved for the more effectual obtaining and securing the great end and design of all government, herein before mentioned.

A Declaration of the Rights of the Inhabitants of the Commonwealth, or State of Pennsylvania

I. That all men are born equally free and independent, and have certain natural, inherent and inalienable rights, amongst which are, the enjoying and defending life and liberty, acquiring, possessing and protecting property, and pursuing and obtaining happiness and safety.

II. That all men have a natural and unalienable right to worship Almighty God according to the dictates of their own consciences and understanding: And that no man ought or of right can be compelled to attend any religious worship, or erect or support any place of worship, or maintain any ministry, contrary to, or against, his own free will and consent: Nor can any man, who acknowledges the being of a God, be justly deprived or abridged of any civil right as a citizen, on account of his religious sentiments or peculiar mode of religious worship: And that no authority can or ought to be vested in, or assumed by any power whatever, that shall in any case interfere with, or in any manner controul, the right of conscience in the free exercise of religious worship.

III. That the people of this State have the sole, exclusive and inherent right of governing and regulating the internal police of the same.

IV. That all power being originally inherent in, and consequently derived from, the people; therefore all officers of government, whether legislative or executive, are their trustees and servants, and at all times accountable to them.

V. That government is, or ought to be, instituted for the common benefit, protection and security of the people, nation or community; and not for the particular emolument or advantage of any single man, family, or sett of men, who are a part only of that community; And that the community hath an indubitable, unalienable and indefeasible right to reform, alter, or abolish government in such manner as shall be by that community judged most conducive to the public weal.

VI. That those who are employed in the legislative and executive business of the State, may be restrained from oppression, the people have a right, at such periods as they may think proper, to reduce their public officers to a private station, and supply the vacancies by certain and regular elections.

VII. That all elections ought to be free; and that all free men having a sufficient evident common interest with, and attachment to the community, have a right to elect officers, or to be elected into office.

VIII. That every member of society hath a right to be protected in the enjoyment of life, liberty and property, and therefore is bound to contribute his proportion towards the expence of that protection, and yield his personal service when necessary, or an equivalent thereto: But no part of a man's property can be justly taken from him, or applied to public uses, without his own consent, or that of his legal representatives: Nor can any man who is conscientiously scrupulous of bearing arms, be justly compelled thereto, if he will pay such equivalent, nor are the people bound by any laws, but such as they have in like manner assented to, for their common good.

IX. That in all prosecutions for criminal offences, a man hath a right to be heard by himself and his council, to demand the cause and nature of his accusation, to be confronted with the witnesses, to call for evidence in his favour, and a speedy public trial, by an impartial jury of the country, without the unanimous consent of which jury he cannot be found guilty; nor can he be compelled to give evidence against himself; nor can any man be justly deprived of his liberty except by the laws of the land, or the judgment of his peers.

X. That the people have a right to hold themselves, their houses, papers, and possessions free from search and seizure, and therefore warrants without oaths or affirmations first made, affording a sufficient foundation for them, and whereby any officer or messenger may be commanded or required to search suspected places, or to seize any person or persons, his or their property, not particularly described, are contrary to that right, and ought not to be granted.

XI. That in controversies respecting property, and in suits between man and man, the parties have a right to trial by jury, which ought to be held sacred.

XII. That the people have a right to freedom of speech, and of writing, and publishing their sentiments; therefore the freedom of the press ought not to be restrained.

XIII. That the people have a right to bear arms for the defence of themselves and the state; and as standing armies in the time of peace are dangerous to liberty, they ought not to be kept up; And that the military should be kept under strict subordination to, and governed by, the civil power.

XIV. That a frequent recurrence to fundamental principles, and a firm adherence to justice, moderation, temperance, industry, and frugality are absolutely necessary to preserve the blessings of liberty, and keep a government free: The people ought therefore to pay particular attention to these points in the choice of officers and representatives, and have a right to exact a due and constant regard to them, from their legislatures and magistrates, in the making and executing such laws as are necessary for the good government of the state.

XV. That all men have a natural inherent right to emigrate from one state to another that will receive them, or to form a new state in vacant countries, or in such countries as they can purchase, whenever they think that thereby they may promote their own happiness.

XVI. That the people have a right to assemble together, to consult for their common good, to instruct their representatives, and to apply to the legislature for redress of grievances, by address, petition, or remonstrance.

Plan or Frame of Government for the Commonwealth or State of Pennsylvania

Section 1. The commonwealth or state of Pennsylvania shall be governed hereafter by an assembly of the representatives of the freemen of the same, and a president and council, in manner and form following—

Section 2. The supreme legislative power shall be vested in a house of representatives of the freemen of the commonwealth or state of Pennsylvania.

Section 3. The supreme executive power shall be vested in a president and council.

Section 4. Courts of justice shall be established in the city of Philadelphia, and in every county of this state.

Section 5. The freemen of this commonwealth and their sons shall be trained and armed for its defence under such regulations, restrictions, and exceptions as the general assembly shall by law direct, preserving always to the people the right of choosing their colonels and all commissioned officers under that rank, in such manner and as often as by the said laws shall be directed.

Section 6. Every freemen of the full age of twenty-one years, having resided in this state for the space of one whole year next before the day of election for representatives, and paid public taxes during that time, shall enjoy the right of an elector: Provided always, that sons of freeholders of the age of twenty-one years shall be intitled to vote although they have not paid taxes.

Section 7. The house of representatives of the freemen of this commonwealth shall consist of persons most noted for wisdom and virtue, to be chosen by the freemen of every city and county of this commonwealth respectively. And no person shall be elected unless he has resided in the city or county for which he shall be chosen two years immediately before the said election; nor shall any member, while he continues such, hold any other office, except in the militia.

Section 8. No person shall be capable of being elected a member to serve in the house of representatives of the freemen of this commonwealth more than four years in seven.

Section 9. The members of the house of representatives shall be chosen annually by ballot, by the freemen of the commonwealth, on the second Tuesday in October forever, (except this present year,) and shall meet on the fourth Monday of the same month, and shall be stiled, *The general assembly of the representatives of the freemen of Pennsylvania,* and shall have power to choose their speaker, the treasurer of the state, and their other officers; sit on their own adjournments; prepare bills and enact them into laws; judge of the elections and qualifications of their own members; they may expel a member, but not a second time for the same cause; they may administer oaths or affirmations on examination of witnesses; redress grievances; impeach state criminals; grant charters of incorporation; constitute towns, boroughs, cities, and counties; and shall have all other powers necessary for the legislature of a free state or commonwealth: But they shall have no power to add to, alter, abolish, or infringe any part of this constitution. . . .

And each member, before he takes his seat, shall make and subscribe the following declaration, viz:

I do believe in one God, the creator and governor of the universe, the rewarder of the good and the punisher of the wicked. And I do acknowledge the Scriptures of the Old and New Testament to be given by Divine inspiration.

And no further or other religious test shall ever hereafter be required of any civil officer or magistrate in this State.

Section 11. Delegates to represent this state in congress shall be chosen by ballot by the future general assembly at their first meeting, and annually forever afterwards, as long as such representation shall be necessary. Any delegate may be superseded at any time, by the general assembly appointing another in his stead. No man shall sit in congress longer than two years successively, nor be capable of reëlection for three years afterwards: and no person who holds any office in the gift of the congress shall hereafter be elected to represent this commonwealth in congress.

Section 12. If any city or cities, county or counties shall neglect or refuse to elect and send representatives to the general assembly, two-thirds of the members from the cities or counties that do elect and send representatives, provided they be a majority of the cities and counties of the whole state, when met, shall have all the powers of the general assembly, as fully and amply as if the whole were present.

Section 13. The doors of the house in which the representatives of the freemen of this state shall sit in general assembly, shall be and remain open for the admission of all persons who behave decently, except only when the welfare of this state may require the doors to be shut.

Section 14. The votes and proceedings of the general assembly shall be printed weekly during their sitting, with the yeas and nays, on any question, vote or resolution, where any two members require it, except when the vote is taken by ballot; and when the yeas and nays are so taken every member shall have a right to insert the reasons of his vote upon the minutes, if he desires it.

Section 15. To the end that laws before they are enacted may be more maturely considered, and the inconvenience of hasty determinations as much as possible prevented, all bills of public nature shall be printed for the consideration of the people, before they are read in general assembly the last time for debate and amendment; and, except on occasions of sudden necessity, shall not be passed into laws until the next session of assembly; and for the more perfect satisfaction of the public, the reasons and motives for making such laws shall be fully and clearly expressed in the preambles. . . .

Section 22. Every officer of state, whether judicial or executive, shall be liable to be impeached by the general assembly, either when in office, or after his resignation or removal for mal-administration: All impeachments shall be before the president or vice-president and council, who shall hear and determine the same.

Section 23. The judges of the supreme court of judicature shall have fixed salaries, be commissioned for seven years only, though capable of re-appointment at the end of that term, but removable for misbehaviour at any time by the general assembly; they shall not be allowed to sit as members in the continental congress, executive council, or general assembly, nor to hold any other office civil or military, nor to take or receive fees or perquisites of any kind.

Section 24. The supreme court, and the several courts of common pleas of this commonwealth, shall, besides the powers usually exercised by such courts, have the powers of a court of chancery, so far as relates to the perpetuating testimony, obtaining evidence from places not within this state, and the care of the persons and estates of those who are *non compotes mentis,* and such other powers as may be found necessary by future general assemblies, not inconsistent with this constitution.

Section 25. Trials shall be by jury as heretofore: And it is recommended to the legislature of this state, to provide by law against every corruption or partiality in the choice, return, or appointment of juries.

Section 26. Courts of sessions, common pleas, and orphans courts shall be held quarterly in each city and county; and the legislature shall have power to establish all such other courts as they may judge for the good of the inhabitants of the state. All courts shall be open, and justice shall be impartially administered without corruption or unnecessary delay: All their officers shall be paid an adequate but moderate compensation for their services: And if any officer shall take greater or other fees than the law allows him, either directly or indirectly, it shall ever after disqualify him from holding any office in this state.

Section 27. All prosecutions shall commence in the name and by the authority of the freemen of the commonwealth of Pennsylvania; and all indictments shall conclude with these words, *"Against the peace and dignity of the same."* The style of all process hereafter in this state shall be, *The commonwealth of Pennsylvania.*

Section 28. The person of a debtor, where there is not a strong presumption of fraud, shall not be continued in prison, after delivering up, *bona fide,* all his estate real and personal, for the use of his creditors, in such manner as shall be hereafter regulated by law. All prisoners shall be bailable by sufficient sureties, unless for capital offences, when the proof is evident, or presumption great.

Section 29. Excessive bail shall not be exacted for bailable offences: And all fines shall be moderate. . . .

Section 31. Sheriffs and coroners shall be elected annually in each city and county, by the freemen; that is to say, two persons for each office, one of whom for each, is to be commissioned by the president in council. No person shall continue in the office of sheriff more than three successive years, or be capable of being again elected during four years afterwards. The election shall be held at the same time and place appointed for the election of representatives: And the commissioners and assessors, and other officers chosen by the people, shall also be then and there elected, as has been usual heretofore, until altered or otherwise regulated by the future legislature of this state.

Section 32. All elections, whether by the people or in general assembly, shall be by ballot, free and voluntary: And any elector, who shall receive any gift or reward for his vote, in meat, drink, monies, or otherwise, shall forfeit his right to elect for that time, and suffer such other penalties as future laws shall direct. And any person who shall directly or indirectly give, promise, or bestow any such rewards to be elected, shall be thereby rendered incapable to serve for the ensuing year.

Section 33. All fees, licence money, fines and forfeitures heretofore granted, or paid to the governor, or his deputies for the support of government, shall hereafter be paid into the public treasury, unless altered or abolished by the future legislature.

Section 34. A register's office for the probate of wills and granting letters of administration, and an office for the recording of deeds, shall be kept in each city and county: The officers to be appointed by the general assembly, removable at their pleasure, and to be commissioned by the president in council.

Section 35. The printing presses shall be free to every person who undertakes to examine the proceedings of the legislature, or any part of government.

Section 36. As every freeman to preserve his independence, (if without a sufficient estate) ought to have some profession, calling, trade or farm, whereby he may honestly subsist, there can be no necessity for, nor use in establishing offices of profit, the usual effects of which are dependence and servility unbecoming freemen, in the possessors and expectants; faction, contention, corruption, and disorder among the people. But if any man is called into public service, to the prejudice of his private affairs, he has a right to a reasonable compensation: And whenever an office, through increase of fees or otherwise, becomes so profitable as to occasion many to apply for it, the profits ought to be lessened by the legislature.

Section 37. The future legislature of this state, shall regulate intails in such a manner as to prevent perpetuities.

Section 38. The penal laws as heretofore used shall be reformed by the legislature of this state, as soon as may be, and punishments made in some cases less sanguinary, and in general more proportionate to the crimes.

Section 39. To deter more effectually from the commission of crimes, by continued visible punishments of long duration, and to make sanguinary punishments less necessary; houses ought to be provided for punishing by hard labour, those who shall be convicted of crimes not capital; wherein the criminals shall be imployed for the benefit of the public, or for reparation of injuries done to private persons: And all persons at proper times shall be admitted to see the prisoners at their labour.

Section 40. Every officer, whether judicial, executive or military, in authority under this commonwealth, shall take [an] oath or affirmation of allegiance, and general oath of office before he enters on the execution of his office. . . .

Section 41. No public tax, custom or contribution shall be imposed upon, or paid by the people of this state, except by a law for that purpose: And before any law be made for raising it, the purpose for which any tax is to be raised ought to appear clearly to the legislature to be of more service to the community than the money would be, if not collected; which being well observed, taxes can never be burthens.

Section 42. Every foreigner of good character who comes to settle in this state, having first taken an oath or affirmation of allegiance to the same, may purchase, or by other just means acquire, hold, and transfer land or other real estate; and after one year's residence, shall be deemed a free denizen thereof, and entitled to all the rights of a natural born subject of this state, except that he shall not be capable of being elected a representative until after two years residence.

Section 43. The inhabitants of this state shall have liberty to fowl and hunt in seasonable times on the lands they hold, and on all other lands therein not inclosed; and in like manner to fish in all boatable waters, and others not private property.

Section 44. A school or schools shall be established in each county by the legislature, for the convenient instruction of youth, with such salaries to the masters paid by the public, as may enable them to instruct youth at low prices: And all useful learning shall be duly encouraged and promoted in one or more universities.

Section 45. Laws for the encouragement of virtue, and prevention of vice and immorality, shall be made and constantly kept in force, and provision shall be made for their due execution: And all religious societies or bodies of men heretofore united or incorporated for the advancement of religion or learning, or for other pious and charitable purposes, shall be encouraged and protected in the enjoyment of the privileges, immunities and estates which they were accustomed to enjoy, or could of right have enjoyed, under the laws and former constitution of this state.

Section 46. The declaration of rights is hereby declared to be a part of the constitution of this commonwealth, and ought never to be violated on any pretence whatever.

Section 47. In order that the freedom of the commonwealth may be preserved inviolate forever, there shall be chosen by ballot by the freemen in each city and county respectively, on the second Tuesday in October, in the year one thousand seven hundred and eighty-three, and on the second Tuesday in October, in every seventh year thereafter, two persons in each city and county of this state, to be called the COUNCIL OF CENSORS; who shall meet together on the second Monday of November next ensuing their election; the majority of whom shall be a quorum in every case, except as to calling a convention, in which two-thirds of the whole number elected shall agree: And whose duty it shall be to enquire whether the constitution has been preserved inviolate in every part; and whether the legislative and executive branches of government have performed their duty as guardians of the people, or assumed to themselves, or exercised other or greater powers than they are intitled to by the constitution: They are also to enquire whether the public taxes have been justly laid and collected in all parts of this commonwealth, in what manner the public monies have been disposed of, and whether the laws have been duly executed. For these purposes they shall have power to send for persons, papers, and records; they shall have authority to pass public censures, to order impeachments, and to recommend to the legislature the repealing such laws as appear to them to have been enacted contrary to the principles of the constitution. These powers they shall continue to have, for and during the space of one year from the day of their election and no longer: The said council of censors shall also have power to call a convention, to meet within two years after their sitting, if there appear to them an absolute necessity of amending any article of the constitution which may be defective, explaining such as may be thought not clearly expressed, and of adding such as are necessary for the preservation of the rights and happiness of the people: But the articles to be amended, and the amendments proposed, and such articles as are proposed to be added or abolished, shall be promulgated at least six months before the day appointed for the election of such convention, for the previous consideration of the people, that they may have an opportunity of instructing their delegates on the subject.

Passed in Convention the 28th day of September, 1776, and signed by their order.

The Massachusetts Bill of Rights, 1780

The end of the institution, maintenance, and administration of government, is to secure the existence of the body-politic, to protect it, and to furnish the individuals who compose it with the power of enjoying in safety and tranquillity their natural rights, and the blessings of life: and whenever these great objects are not obtained, the people have a right to alter the government, and to take measures necessary for their safety, prosperity, and happiness.

The body-politic is formed by a voluntary association of individuals; it is a social compact by which the whole people covenants with each citizen and each citizen with the whole people that all shall be governed by certain laws for the common good. It is the duty of the people, therefore, in framing a constitution of government, to provide for an equitable mode of making laws, as well as for an impartial interpretation and a faithful execution of them; that every man may, at all times, find his security in them.

We, therefore, the people of Massachusetts, acknowledging, with grateful hearts, the goodness of the great Legislator of the universe, in affording us, in the course of His Providence, an opportunity, deliberately and peaceably, without fraud, violence, or surprise, of entering into an original, explicit, and solemn compact with each other; and of forming a new constitution of civil government, for ourselves and posterity; and devoutly imploring His direction in so interesting a design, do agree upon, ordain, and establish, the following Declaration of Rights, and Frame of Government, as the Constitution of the Commonwealth of Massachusetts.

Part the First

A Declaration of the Rights of the Inhabitants of the Commonwealth of Massachusetts

Article I. All men are born free and equal, and have certain natural, essential, and unalienable rights; among which may be reckoned the right of enjoying and defending their lives and liberties; that of acquiring, possessing, and protecting property; in fine, that of seeking and obtaining their safety and happiness.

II. It is the right as well as the duty of all men in society, publicly, and at stated seasons, to worship the Supreme Being, the great Creator and Preserver of the universe. And no subject shall be hurt, molested, or restrained, in his person, liberty, or estate, for worshipping God in the manner and season most agreeable to the dictates of his own conscience; or for his religious profession of sentiments; provided he doth not disturb the public peace, or obstruct others in their religious worship. . . .

As the happiness of a people and the good order and preservation of civil government essentially depend upon piety, religion, and morality, and as these cannot be generally diffused through a community but by the institution of the public worship of God and of public instructions, in piety, religion, and morality. Therefore to promote their happiness and secure the good order and preservation of their government, the people of this commonwealth have a right to invest their legislature with power to authorize and require, and the legislature shall from time to time authorize and require, the several towns . . . and other bodies—politic or religious societies, to make suitable provision, at their own expense, for the institution of the public worship of God and the support and maintenance of public Protestant teachers of piety, religion, and morality. . . .

And the people of this commonwealth . . . do invest their legislature with authority to enjoin upon all the subjects an attendance upon the instructions of the public teachers aforesaid. . . .

And every denomination of Christians, demeaning themselves peaceably and as good subjects of the commonwealth, shall be equally under the protection of the law; and no subordination of any one sect or denomination to another shall ever be established by law.

IV. The people of this commonwealth have the sole and exclusive right of governing themselves, as a free, sovereign, and independent State, and do, and forever hereafter shall, exercise and enjoy every power, jurisdiction, and right, which is not, or may not hereafter be, by them expressly delegated to the United States of America, in Congress assembled.

V. All power residing originally in the people, and being derived from them, the several magistrates and officers of government, vested with authority, whether legislative, executive, or judicial, are their substitutes and agents, and are at all times accountable to them.

VI. No man, nor corporation, or association of men, have any other title to obtain advantages, or particular and exclusive privileges, distinct from those of the community, than what arises from the consideration of services rendered to the public; and this title being in nature neither hereditary, nor transmissible to children, or descendants, or relations by blood; the idea of a man born a magistrate, lawgiver, or judge, is absurd and unnatural.

VII. Government is instituted for the common good, for the protection, safety, prosperity, and happiness of the people and not for the profit, honor or private interest of any one man, family, or class of men; therefore the people alone have an incontestible, unalienable, and indefeasible right to institute government; and to reform, alter, or totally change the same, when their protection, safety, prosperity, and happiness require it.

VIII. In order to prevent those who are vested with authority from becoming oppressors, the people have a right, at such periods and in such manner as they shall establish by their frame of government, to cause their public officers to return to private life; and to fill up vacant places by certain and regular elections and appointments.

IX. All elections ought to be free; and all the inhabitants of this commonwealth, having such qualifications as they shall establish by their frame of government, have an equal right to elect officers, and to be elected, for public employments.

X. Each individual of the society has a right to be protected by it in the enjoyment of his life, liberty, and property. . . . No part of the property of any individual can, with justice, be taken from him, or applied to public uses, without his own consent, or that of the representative body of the people. . . . And whenever the public exigencies require that the property of any individual should be appropriated to public uses, he shall receive a reasonable compensation therefor.

XI. Every subject of the commonwealth ought to find a certain remedy, by having recourse to the laws, for all injuries or wrongs which he may receive in his person, property, or character. He ought to obtain right and justice freely, and without being obliged to purchase it; completely, and without any denial; promptly, and without delay, conformably to the laws.

XII. No subject shall be held to answer for any crimes or offence, until the same is fully and plainly . . . described to him; or be compelled to accuse, or furnish evidence against himself. And every subject shall have a right to produce all proofs that may be favorable to him; to meet the witnesses against him face to face, and to be fully heard in his defence by himself, or his counsel, at his election. And no subject shall be arrested, . . . or deprived of his life, liberty, or estate, but by the judgment of his peers, or the law of the land.

And the legislature shall not make any law that shall subject any person to a capital or infamous punishment, excepting for the government of the army and navy, without trial by jury. . . .

XIV. Every subject has a right to be secure from all unreasonable searches, and seizures, of his person, his houses, his papers, and all his possessions. . . . And no warrant ought to be issued but in cases, and with the formalities prescribed by the laws.

XV. In all controversies concerning property, and in all suits between two or more persons, . . . the parties have a right to a trial by jury; and this method of procedure shall be held sacred. . . .

XVI. The liberty of the press is essential to the security of freedom in a state it ought not, therefore, to be restricted in this commonwealth.

XVII. The people have a right to keep and to bear arms for the common defence. And as, in time of peace, armies are dangerous to liberty, they ought not to be maintained without the consent of the legislature; and the military power shall always be held in an exact subordination to the civil authority, and be governed by it.

XVIII. A frequent recurrence to the fundamental principles of the constitution, and a constant adherence to those of piety, justice, moderation, temperance, industry and frugality, are absolutely necessary to preserve the advantages of liberty, and to maintain a free government. The people ought, consequently, to have a particular attention to all those principles, in the choice of their officers and representatives: and they have a right to require of their lawgivers and magistrates an exact and constant observance of them, in the formation and execution of the laws necessary for the good administration of the commonwealth.

XIX. The people have a right, in an orderly and peaceable manner to assemble to consult upon the common good; give instructions to their representatives, and to request of the legislative body, by the way of addresses, petitions, or remonstrances, redress of the wrongs done them, and of the grievances they suffer.

XX. The power of suspending the laws, or the execution of the laws, ought never to be exercised but by the legislature, or by authority derived from it, to be exercised in such particular cases only as the legislature shall expressly provide for.

XXI. The freedom of deliberation, speech, and debate, in either house of the legislature, is so essential to the rights of the people, that it cannot be the foundation of any accusation or prosecution, action or complaint, in any other court or place whatsoever.

XXII. The legislature ought frequently to assemble for the redress of grievances, for correcting, strengthening, and confirming the laws, and for making new laws, as the common good may require.

XXIII. No subsidy, charge, tax, impost, or duties ought to be established, fixed, laid, or levied, under any pretext whatsoever, without the consent of the people or their representatives in the legislature.

XXIV. Laws made to punish for actions done before the existence of such laws, and which have not been declared crimes by preceding laws, are unjust, oppressive, and inconsistent with the fundamental principles of a free government.

XXV. No subject ought, in any case, or in any time, to be declared guilty of treason or felony by the legislature.

XXVI. No magistrate or court of law shall demand excessive bail or sureties, impose excessive fines, or inflict cruel or unusual punishments.

XXVII. In time of peace, no soldier ought to be quartered in any house without the consent of the owner; and in time of war, such quarters ought not to be made but by the civil magistrate, in a manner ordained by the legislature.

XXVIII. No person can in any case be subject to law-martial, or to any penalties or pains, by virtue of that law, except those employed in the army or navy, and except the militia in actual service, but by authority of the legislature.

XXIX. It is essential to the preservation of the rights of every individual, his life, liberty, property, and character, that there be an impartial interpretation of the laws, and administration of justice. It is the right of every citizen to be tried by judges as free, impartial, and independent as the lot of humanity will admit. It is, therefore, not only the best policy, but for the security of the rights of the people, and of every citizen, that the judges of the supreme judicial court should hold their offices as long as they behave themselves well; and that they should have honorable salaries ascertained and established by standing laws.

XXX. In the government of this commonwealth, the legislative department shall never exercise the executive and judicial powers, or either of them: the executive shall never exercise the legislative and judicial powers, or either of them: the judicial shall never exercise the legislative and executive powers, or either of them: to the end it may be a government of laws and not of men.

✣ E S S A Y S

Historians sharply disagree over the forces that spurred the development of republican constitutionalism. Fundamentally, they differ over the influence of political ideas. Among those who believe that ideas were important, debate centers on whose views counted the most and whether the ideas that did count stressed liberalism or republicanism. Scholars also disagree about whether to attribute the reconsideration of American constitutional thought to a group of virtue-obsessed republicans, or whether to assign responsibility to pent-up demands against the economic injustices of a highly stratified society.

These issues are clearly joined in the first two essays, by Bernard Bailyn and Isaac Kramnick respectively. They offer contrasting views of the pressures that brought about change in transatlantic constitutional thought in the quarter-century before the American Revolution. Pauline Maier, in the third selection, properly reminds us of the importance of politics out-of-doors in the American colonies for understanding the development of ideas about the proper relationship of the state to the individual.

The Birth of Republican Constitutionalism

BERNARD BAILYN

The word "constitution" and the concept behind it was of central importance to the colonists' political thought; their entire understanding of the crisis in Anglo-American relations rested upon it. So strategically located was this idea in the minds of both English and Americans, and so great was the pressure placed upon it in the course of a decade of pounding debate that in the end it was forced apart, along the seam of a basic ambiguity, to form the two contrasting concepts of constitutionalism that have remained characteristic of England and America ever since.

At the start of the controversy, however, the most distinguishing feature of the colonists' view of the constitution was its apparent traditionalism. Like their contemporaries in England and like their predecessors for centuries before, the colonists at the beginning of the Revolutionary controversy understood by the word "constitution" not, as we would have it, a written document or even an unwritten but deliberately contrived design of government and a specification of rights beyond the power of ordinary legislation to alter; they thought of it, rather, as the constituted—that is, existing—arrangement of governmental institutions, laws, and customs together with the principles and goals that animated them. So John Adams wrote that a political constitution is like "the constitution of the human body"; "certain contextures of the nerves, fibres, and muscles, or certain qualities of the blood and juices" some of which "may properly be called *stamina vitae,* or essentials and fundamentals of the constitution; parts without which life itself cannot be preserved a moment." A constitution of government, analogously,

Adams wrote, is "a frame, a scheme, a combination of powers for a certain end, namely,—the good of the whole community."

The elements of this definition were traditional, but it was nevertheless distinctive in its emphasis on the animating principles, the *stamina vitae,* those "fundamental laws and rules of the constitution, which ought never to be infringed." Belief that a proper system of laws and institutions should be suffused with, should express, essences and fundamentals—moral rights, reason, justice—had never been absent from English notions of the constitution. But not since the Levellers had protested against Parliament's supremacy in the mid-seventeenth century had these considerations seemed so important as they did to the Americans of the mid-eighteenth century. Nor could they ever have appeared more distinct in their content. For if the ostensible purpose of all government was the good of the people, the particular goal of the English constitution—"its end, its use, its designation, drift, and scope"—was known to all, and declared by all, to be the attainment of liberty. This was its peculiar "grandeur" and excellence; it was for this that it should be prized "next to our Bibles, above the privileges of this world." It was for this that it should be blessed, supported and maintained, and transmitted "in full, to posterity." . . .

This critical probing of traditional concepts—part of the colonists' effort to express reality as they knew it and to shape it to ideal ends—became the basis for all further discussions of enlightened reform, in Europe as well as in America. The radicalism the Americans conveyed to the world in 1776 was a transformed as well as a transforming force. . . .

The first suggestions of change came early in the period, the full conclusions only at the very end. At the start [1764] what would emerge as the central feature of American constitutionalism was only an emphasis and a peculiarity of tone within an otherwise familiar discourse. While some writers, like Richard Bland, continued to refer to "a legal constitution, that is, a legislature," and others spoke of "the English constitution . . . a nice piece of machinery which has undergone many changes and alterations," most of the writers saw the necessity of emphasizing principles above institutions, and began to grasp the consequences of doing so. The confusions and difficulties inherent in this process are dramatically illustrated in the troubled career of James Otis.

The heart of the problem Otis faced in the early 1760s was the extent to which, indeed the sense in which, the "constitution" could be conceived of as a limitation on the power of lawmaking bodies. In the writs of assistance case in 1761 he had struck a bold and confident note—so bold, indeed, that John Adams later wrote, rather romantically, that "then and there the child Independence was born." On that famous occasion Otis had said not only that an act of Parliament "against the constitution is void" but that it was the duty of the courts to "pass such acts into disuse," for the "reason of the common law [could] control an act of Parliament." But what was the "constitution" which an act of Parliament could not infringe? Was it a set of fixed principles and rules distinguishable from, antecedent to, more fundamental than, and controlling the operating institutions of government?

And was there consequently a "constitutional" limitation on Parliament's actions? Otis' answers were ambiguous, and proved to be politically disastrous. . . .

Otis, drawing the language of seventeenth-century law into the constitutional struggle of the eighteenth century, found himself veering toward positions he was neither intellectually nor politically prepared to accept. "If the reasons that can be given against an act are such," he wrote in his *Rights of the British Colonies* in 1764, "as plainly demonstrate that it is against *natural* equity, the executive courts will adjudge such act void." . . . Was this not to limit the power of Parliament by the provisions of a fixed constitution distinct from and superior to the legislature, a constitution interpreted and applied by the courts? Others, in time, would say it was. . . .

But . . . Otis . . . did not draw its implications. He ignored them, in fact, in working out his own view of the constitution and of the limits of Parliament's powers. If an act of Parliament violated natural laws, "which are *immutably* true," he wrote, it would thereby violate "eternal truth, equity, and justice," and would be "consequently void." . . .

> . . . and so it would be adjudged by the Parliament itself when convinced of their mistake. Upon this great principle Parliaments repeal such acts as soon as they find they have been mistaken . . . When such mistake is evident and palpable . . . the judges of the executive courts have declared the act "of a whole Parliament void." See here the grandeur of the British constitution! See the wisdom of our ancestors! . . . If the supreme legislative errs, it is informed by the supreme executive in the King's court of law . . . This is government! This is a constitution! to preserve which . . . has cost oceans of blood and treasure in every age; and the blood and the treasure have upon the whole been well spent.

. . . Parliament was thus itself part of the constitution, not a creature of it, and its power was "uncontrollable but by themselves, and we must obey. They only can repeal their own acts . . . let the Parliament lay what burdens they please on us, we must, it is our duty to submit and patiently bear them, till they will be pleased to relieve us." Yet Parliament's enactments against the constitution—against, that is, the whole system of laws, principles, and institutions based on reason and justice of which it was a part—were void, Otis argued; the courts will adjudge them so, and Parliament itself, by the necessity of the system, will repeal them.

It was a strange argument, comprehensible only as an effort to apply seventeenth-century assumptions to eighteenth-century problems. For Otis continued to assume, with Coke [the most distinguished English jurist of the seventeenth century], that Parliament was effectively a supreme judicial as well as a supreme legislative body and hence by definition involved in judicial processes. He continued to believe, too, that moral rights and obligations were not "differentiated as they would be today from legal rights and obligations," and that they naturally radiated from, rather than restricted, enacted law. And he expected fundamental, or higher, law to "control" positive acts of government not in the sense of furnishing judges with grounds for declaring them nonexistent because they conflicted with the "constitution" but only in the sense of providing judges with principles of interpretation by which to modify gross inequities and to interpret "unreasonableness" and self-contradiction in ways that would allow traditional qualities of justice to prevail.

But these assumptions were no longer applicable, in the same way, in the eighteenth century. Parliament was in reality no longer a court but an all powerful sovereign body, and the problem at hand concerned the structure and authority of government, not private law. Otis' theory of the constitution that included a self-correcting Parliament sensitive to the principles of justice and responsive to the admonitions of the courts was, insofar as it was realistic at all, an anachronism, and it came under attack by both the administration, which charged him with attempting to restrict the power of Parliament, and by the colonial radicals, who accused him of preaching passive obedience and nonresistance.

Otis had been faithful, in this way, to the seventeenth-century sources of constitutional thought which he, like so many Americans, revered. Others—poorer scholars, perhaps, but better judges of the circumstances that surrounded them—were less faithful, and in the end more creative. The dominant view of the constitution in 1764 was still the traditional one, unencumbered by Otis' complexities. While Otis was quoting Coke . . . without grasping the implications of their conjunction, others were referring to constitutions as "a sort of fundamental laws"; as the common law; as Parliament; and as the whole complex of existing laws and public institutions. The transition to more advanced ground was forced forward by the continuing need, after 1764, to distinguish fundamentals from institutions and from the actions of government so that they might serve as limits and controls. Once its utility was perceived and demonstrated, this process of disengaging principles from institutions and from the positive actions of government and then of conceiving of them as fixed sets of rules and boundaries, went on swiftly. . . .

Accompanying this shift in the understanding of constitutionalism, and part of it, was another change, which also began as a relocation of emphasis and ended as a contribution to the transforming radicalism of the Revolution. The *rights* that constitutions existed to protect were understood in the early years of the period, as we have seen, to be at once the inalienable, indefeasible rights inherent in all people by virtue of their humanity, and the concrete provisions of English law as expressed in statutes, charters, and court decisions; it was assumed that the "constitution" in its normal workings would specify and protect the inalienable rights of man. But what if it did not? What if this sense proved false, and it came to be believed that the force of government threatened rather than protected these rights? And what if, in addition, the protective machinery of rights—the constitution—came to be abstracted from the organs of government and to be seen not as an arrangement of institutions and enactments but as a blueprint for institutions, the ideal against which the actual was to be measured?

These questions were first posed early in the controversy, in the course of one of the most vituperative exchanges of constitutional views of the entire period. It is true, Judge Martin Howard, Jr., of Rhode Island wrote in response to Stephen Hopkins' *Rights of Colonies Examined* (1765), that the common law carries within it and guarantees with special force the "indefeasible" personal rights of men; for Britons it is the common law that makes these natural rights operative. But Parliament's power is no less a part of that same common law. "Can we claim the common law as an inheritance, and at the same time be at liberty to adopt one part of it and reject the other?" If Parliament is rejected, so too must political and even personal rights. If rights are accepted as inextricable parts of laws and institutions, the laws and institutions must be accepted in all their normal workings.

James Otis accepted the challenge. But in his stinging reply—a bitter, sarcastic, half-wild polemic—he again displayed a commitment to tradition that kept him from following through the logic of his own argument; again, he succeeded in dramatizing but not in resolving the issue. The judge's "truly *Filmerian*" performance, he wrote, has "inaccuracies in abundance, declamation and false logic without end . . . and the most indelicate fustian." His central error is that he "everywhere confounds the terms rights, liberties, and privileges, which, in legal as well as vulgar acceptation, denote very different ideas." The source of this confusion, Otis said, was a misreading of Blackstone; from his *Commentaries,* Howard had mistakenly derived the idea that the rights of natural persons are the same as those of artificial persons: that is, "bodies politic and corporate." Corporate rights are indeed "matters of the mere favor and grace of the donor or founder"; but that is not to say that the rights of natural people are too. Britons are entitled to their "natural absolute personal rights" by virtue of "the laws of God and nature, as well as by the common law and the constitution of their country so admirably built on the principles of the former." Only such a one as Judge Howard, with his "Filmerian sneer," who "cannot see any difference between power and right, between a blind, slavish submission and a loyal, generous, and rational obedience"—only such a person could fail to understand that the origin of "the inherent, indefeasible rights of the subject" lay in "the law of nature and its author. This law is the grand basis of the common law and of all other municipal laws that are worth a rush. True it is that every act of Parliament which names the colonies . . . binds them. But this is not so, strictly and properly speaking, by the common law as by the law of nature and by the constitution of a parliament or sovereign and supreme legislative in a state."

Otis had shifted the emphasis of discussion to the priority of abstract rights, but he had not attempted to follow through the implications of his own thought: he continued to assume that the actual law would express, and naturally protect, the universal rights of man. But if he did not draw the conclusions implicit in his own logic, others did: there is in the proliferating discussion of constitutionalism a steadily increasing emphasis on the universal, inherent, indefeasible qualities of rights. John Dickinson, also a lawyer—indeed, a more professionally trained lawyer than Otis—attacked in a more knowing and thorough way the idea that rights are matters of "favor and grace." True, in 1764 he had vehemently defended the charter of Pennsylvania against the attacks of Joseph Galloway and others, but not because he believed that "the liberties of the subject were mere favors granted by charters from the crown." The liberties of Pennsylvanians, he had proclaimed in a ringing oration in the Pennsylvania Assembly, are "founded on the acknowledged rights of human nature." The value of a charter like that of Pennsylvania was that it stated the true character of such liberties beyond any misunderstanding, and freed them from the entanglements of those ancient, archaic customs "that our ancestors either had not moderation or leisure enough to untwist." Two years later (1766) he elaborated the point significantly. Charters, he wrote in his *Address to the Committee of Correspondence in Barbados,* like all aspects of the law, are "*declarations* but not *gifts* of liberties." Kings and Parliaments cannot give "the *rights essential to happiness.*" . . .

> We claim them from a higher source—from the King of kings, and Lord of all the earth. They are not annexed to us by parchments and seals. They are created in us by the decrees of Providence, which establish the laws of our nature. They are born with us; exist with us; and cannot be taken from us by any human power without taking our lives. In short, they are founded on the immutable maxims of reason and justice.

Written laws—even the great declarations like Magna Carta—do not create liberties; they "must be considered as only declaratory of our rights, and in affirmance of them."

Ultimately, the conclusion to be drawn became obvious: the entire legitimacy of positive law and legal rights must be understood to rest on the degree to which they conformed to the abstract universals of natural rights. Not all were willing, even in 1775, to go as far as Alexander Hamilton, who wrote in bold, arresting words that "the sacred rights of mankind are not to be rummaged for among old parchments of musty records. They are written, as with a sunbeam, in the whole *volume* of human nature, by the hand of divinity itself, and can never be erased or obscured by mortal power." But if some found this statement too enthusiastic, few by 1774—few even of the Tories—disagreed with the calmer formulation of the same idea, by Philip Livingston. Had he understood his antagonist, the Rev. Thomas Bradbury Chandler, correctly? Had Chandler really meant to say "that any right . . . if it be not confirmed by some statute law is not a legal right"? If so, Livingston declared, "in the name of America, I deny it." Legal rights are "those rights which we are entitled to by the eternal laws of right reason"; they exist independent of positive law, and stand as the measure of its legitimacy.

Neither Hamilton nor Livingston, nor any of the other writers who touched on the subject, meant to repudiate the heritage of English common and statutory law. Their claim was only that the source of rights be recognized, in Jefferson's words, as "the laws of nature, and not as the gift of their chief magistrate," and that as a consequence the ideal must be understood to exist before the real and to remain superior to it, controlling it and limiting it. . . . In 1765 James Otis had fulminated at the mere suggestion that a document might profitably be drawn up stating the "rights of the colonies with precision and certainty." Insolence, he had called it, pedantry and nonsense; Britons had no need for "codes, pandects, novels, decretals of popes." "The common law is our birthright, and the rights and privileges confirmed and secured to us by the British constitution and by act of Parliament are our best inheritance." But thought had shifted rapidly in the decade that followed, Arthur Lee exhorting his countrymen in 1768 to draw up a petition of rights *"and never desist from the solicitation till it be confirmed into a bill of rights,"* and Andrew Eliot a year later despairing of all solutions save that of "an American bill of rights." No voice was raised in objection when in 1776 the idea was proclaimed, and acted upon, that "all the great rights . . . should be *guaranteed"* by the terms of a written constitution.

These closely related changes—in the view of what a constitution was and of the proper emphasis in the understanding of rights—were momentous; they would shape the entire future development of American constitutional thought and practice. Yet they did not seem to be momentous at the time. They were not generally experienced as intrusive or threatening alterations. They were hardly seen as changes at all: they drifted into consciousness so gradually and easily and were accepted with so little controversy that writers would soon feel called upon to remind Americans that the fundamental principles of their political and constitutional thought were "of recent date, and for [them] the world is indebted to America; for if [the distinction between constitutional law and that of the ordinary legislature] did not originate in this country, it was here that it was first reduced to practice, exemplified, and its utility and practicability first established." For in this area too, as in so many other developments in political and social thought, the way had been paved by the peculiar circumstances of colonial life. Whatever Otis may have thought of the issue when he came to consider it in theoretical terms, the fact was that written constitutions—documents not different essentially from the "codes, pandects, novels" he denounced—had existed, had been acted upon, had been assumed to be proper and necessary, for a century or more. . . .

John Locke and Liberal Constitutionalism

ISAAC KRAMNICK

For over a hundred years the world of scholarship agreed that Locke was the patron saint of Anglo-American ideology in the eighteenth century and that liberalism with its stress on individuality and private rights was the

"Republican Revisionism Revisited," by Isaac Kramnick, *American Historical Review* 87 (1982) pp. 629–645, 653, 655–664. Reprinted by permission of the American Historical Association and the author.

dominant ideal in that enlightened and revolutionary era. For the Victorian Leslie Stephen, it was self-evident that "Locke expounded the Principles of the Revolution of 1688 and his writings became the political bible of the following century." For the more recent Harold Laski, it was equally clear that Lockean liberalism dominated English political thought in the eighteenth century. Colonial Americans, it was assumed, were also schooled on Locke and became, in fact, his most self-conscious disciples. Thus, for Carl Becker, "the lineage is direct, Jefferson copied Locke," and, for Merle Curti, the "Great Mr. Locke" was "America's philosopher." Louis Hartz has summarized this scholarly consensus. "Locke," he wrote in 1955, "dominates American political thought as no thinker anywhere dominates the political thought of a nation."

As it comes to all orthodoxies, revisionism has set in, and this received wisdom has been assaulted with a vengeance. Over the last twenty years a fundamental reinterpretation of Anglo-American eighteenth-century social and political thought has occurred. The liberal individualist heritage preoccupied with private rights has, to a great extent, been replaced by a republican tradition emphasizing citizenship and public participation, a tradition with roots deep in the classical and Renaissance worlds. Fundamental to this republican revisionism has been rethinking the hegemony of Locke. As Stanley N. Katz has noted,

> *Locke et praetera nihil*, it now appears, will no longer do as a motto for the study of eighteenth century Anglo-American political thought. The state of nature, doctrine of consent, and theory of natural rights were not as important before 1776 as the ideas of mixed government, separation of powers and a balanced constitution. We are only in the opening phases of a major reassessment of our constitutional heritage.

Replacing Locke as the vital center of political discourse in the century is the country, opposition ideology of the Walpole years. In turn, these ideas are themselves read as part of a larger tradition—the civic humanist, or republican, tradition.

The revisionist school makes two distinct claims. The first de-emphasizes the role of Lockean ideas in the early eighteenth century. The second questions Locke's influence on the entire century, including the radicalism of post-Wilkes England and the ideology of the American founding. In its first claim, revisionism is on solid ground. Locke deserves the de-emphasis he has received for the early part of the century. In its second claim, however, the revisionist position is much more dubious; here it has gone too far.

The republican, revisionist reading has replaced Lockean liberalism with civic humanism. Part Aristotle, part Cicero, part Machiavelli, civic humanism conceives of man as a political being whose realization of self occurs only through participation in public life, through active citizenship in a republic. The virtuous man is concerned primarily with the public good, *res publica*, or commonweal, not with private or selfish ends. Seventeenth-century writers like James Harrington and Algernon Sidney adapted this tradition, especially under the influence of Machiavelli (according to J. G. A. Pocock), to a specifically English context. This significantly English variant of civic humanism, "neo-Machiavellianism" or "neo-Harringtonianism," became, through the writings of early eighteenth-century English Augustans like Davenant, Trenchard, Gordon, and especially Henry St. John, Viscount Bolingbroke, the ideological core of the "country" ideology that confronted Walpole and his "court" faction. Bolingbroke provided a crucial link in this intellectual chain by associating corruption with social and political themes, a critical concept in the language of eighteenth-century politics. Much richer than simple venality or fraud, the concept is enveloped by the Machiavellian image of historical change: corruption is the absence of civic virtue. Corrupt man is preoccupied with self and oblivious to the public good. Such failures of moral personality, such degeneration from the fundamental commitment to public life, fuel the decline of states and can be remedied only through periodic revitalization by returning to the original and pristine commitment to civic virtue. Calls for such renewals, for *ridurre ai principii* (Machiavelli's phrase), form the response to corruption.

Bolingbroke's achievement was to appropriate this republican and Machiavellian language for the social and economic tensions developing in Augustan England over the rise of government credit, public debt, and central banking as well as for political issues, such as Walpole's control of Parliament through patronage or concern over standing armies. Themes of independence and dependence, so critical to the republican tradition (the former essential to any commitment to the public good), were deployed by Bolingbroke into a social map of independent country proprietors opposing placemen and stock jobbers and a political map of a free Parliament opposing a despotic court. In addition, Bolingbroke stamped this eighteenth-century republican-country tradition with its socially conservative and nostalgic quality, in terms of not only its anticommercialism but also its antiegalitarianism. But this court-country reading eschews class analysis, at least in terms of the conventional dichotomy of progressive bourgeoisie and reactionary aristocracy. Its categories and frames of reference are older and more complicated.

To a great extent, the innovative scholarship of J. G. A. Pocock has shaped this new way of looking at English political thought. His writings on Harrington and his magisterial *Machiavellian Moment* (1975) have made the concept of civic humanism a strikingly useful tool with which to understand the political mind of late seventeenth- and early eighteenth-century England. The more ambitious extension of civic humanism's reign, however, is questionable. In the hands of Pocock and others, like John Murrin and Lance Banning, this insightful reading of early eighteenth-century politics through Bolingbroke's dichotomy of virtuous country and corrupt court does not stop with Augustan England. It becomes the organizing paradigm for the language of political thought in England as well as America throughout the entire century. As a result, revisionism in this second claim also insists on the irrelevance of class in political discourse, which in conventional progressive or liberal scholarship has been linked to the later decades of the century via the emergence of the Industrial Revolution. Analyses of the late eighteenth century that refer to class consciousness or conflicting class ideologies or that use concepts such as aristocracy, capitalist, feudal, or bourgeois are thus dismissed by republican scholarship as simplistic and proleptic. Challenges to the "primacy" or "omnipresence" of "civic ideology," of "Aristotelian and civic humanist values," derived throughout the century not from "simple bourgeois ideology" or from visions of "economic" or "capitalist man" but from a court ideology, part commercial and part elite, that was not representative of a class in any conventional sense. There is no dialectical tension between middle and upper classes. To claim it existed is to engage in "much distortion of history." There is for Pocock only one proper dialectical reading, which sees everywhere "the dialectic of virtue and commerce." All of Anglo-American political thought in the eighteenth century involves, then, "a continuation, larger and more irreconcilable of that Augustan debate."

Locke and possessive individualism in this scheme have obviously had to go. And a chorus of distinguished scholars have joined John Dunn in deemphasizing the importance of Locke throughout eighteenth-century Anglo-American thought. "Eighteenth century English political thought," according to Gordon Wood, "perhaps owed more to Machiavelli and Montesquieu than it did to Locke." Indeed, Bernard Bailyn has persuasively argued that "the effective triggering convictions that lay behind the [American] Revolution were derived not from common Lockean generalities but from the specific fears and formulations of the radical publicists and opposition politicians of early eighteenth century England."

J. G. A. Pocock has been the most insistent in repudiating Locke's influence on the entire century. He has seen the history of political thought "dominated by a fiction of Locke," whose importance "has been wildly distorted." He and others are engaged in what he has called "a shattering demolition of [Locke's] myth." Their concern is to prove that the predominant language of politics for the eighteenth century, even for its radicals, "is one of virtue, corruption and reform, which is Machiavellian, classical and Aristotelian, and in which Locke himself did not figure." What we have come to, Pocock has insisted, is the end of "the image of a monolithically Lockean eighteenth century," the end of "a convention of writing as if Locke dominated the thought of the eighteenth century, and imposed on it a pattern of liberal individualism." Indeed, he concluded, to understand the debates of eighteenth-century politics does "not necessitate reference to Locke at all."

Pocock has applied this revisionist verdict about Locke to an alternative reading of America and its founding. American political culture has been haunted by myths, the most mistaken of which is the role of Locke as "the patron saint of American values." The proper interpretation "stresses Machiavelli at the expense of Locke." The Revolution was, Pocock wrote, "the last great act of the Renaissance . . . emerging from a line of thought which staked everything on a positive and civic concept of the individual's virtue." The Revolution was a Machiavellian *rinnovazionne* in a new world, "a republican commitment to the renovation of virtue." America was born in a "dread of modernity," according to Pocock. In its early years "the country ideology ran riot." The debate over Hamilton's economic policies in the 1790s "was a replay of court-country debates seventy and a hundred years earlier." In Jefferson's polemics, however, "the spirit of Bolingbroke stalked on every page." John Murrin concurred. The Jeffersonians, he wrote, "like an English country opposition . . . idealized the past more than the future and feared significant change, especially major economic change, as corruption and degeneration." Welcome from this perspective, then, is Gary Wills's recent book on Jefferson's Declaration of Independence. Wills, too, got rid of Locke, but, behind Jefferson, he saw not Locke but Hutcheson and the Scottish Enlightenment. . . .

It has, indeed, been a "remarkable historiographic upheaval." Republican revisionism has sharpened our perceptions of the ideological currents operating in the eighteenth century, but its two claims must remain distinct. Revisionism has informed us of the continuity and hold of older political and cultural ideals, competing with a Lockean emphasis on natural rights and individualism, on the early eighteenth-century mind. But, in seeking to free the entire eighteenth century of Locke, of socioeconomic radicalism, and of bourgeois liberalism, this new broom has also swept away much that is truth.

There are serious difficulties in applying to Anglo-American politics after 1760 the model of court and country or the dialectic of virtue and commerce. These difficulties derive from the basic revisionist assumption of a continuous meaning throughout the century of concepts like corruption and virtue. The nostalgia, hierarchialism, and anticommercialism of the earlier part of the century cannot be that easily read into the later years of the century. A study of the writings and politics of British reformers from 1760 to 1800 illustrates the problematic nature of such a reading. Is Locke irrelevant to the reformers' radicalism? Are their ideological paradigms republicanism and civic humanism? Is theirs the politics of nostalgia untained by bourgeois liberal or individualist ideals?

The verdict of recent republican scholarship is that Locke and progressive liberal ideals were, in fact, unimportant in the agitation for parliamentary reform in Britain from the 1760s through the French Revolution. Relying heavily on the work of British historians like Herbert Butterfield and Ian Christie, the revisionists emphasize the nostalgic and even reactionary quality of the reform movement. What were being sought were lost historical rights, Anglo-Saxon rights. Alternatively, the reformers were country ideologues concerned only with mixed government and an independent House of Commons. Republican scholarship denies that any social or economic motives or grievances were at work among the reformers, either democratic or bourgeois. Continuity and nostalgia are the key, not radical appeals to abstractions like the rights of man or nature. In such a configuration of ideas, Locke is seldom to be found.

For Pocock, the reform movement was simply civic humanism and country rage. "Georgian radicals in the era of the Revolutionary War and its aftermath used a language indistinguishable from that of their American peers." That same language of corruption and virtue was being used "against the ministries of George III," by the foes of Bute "and the friends of Wilkes." This was no casual flirtation with the language of civic humanism by the radicals. Pocock has noted that the country ideology of republican virtue that the Americans adopted "had originated in England and was still very much in use there. In the minds of James Burgh, John Cartwright, or Richard Price, it was as obsessive and terrifying as in any American mind." It was "the conceptual framework" behind "radical demands for parliamentary and franchise reform." In *The Machiavellian Moment*, Wyvill, Price, and Cartwright are described as using "a vocabulary of corruption and renovation little different from that of their American contemporaries." In an earlier article, Pocock placed Burgh, Wilkes, the Yorkshire movement, the Society for Constitutional Information, and, *miracula mirabilis*, John Thelwell in the tradition of country and civic humanism. They are "key points in the long continuous history of a political language and its concepts." The terminology and ideas of country ideology, Pocock has concluded, "were extensively borrowed by the radical left when one began to appear in George III's reign."

This backward-looking reading of British reform is shared by Gordon Wood, who has also described Price, Burgh, and even Paine as members of this camp of virtue-obsessed republicans. Bernard Bailyn has agreed:

> The leaders of [American] Revolutionary movement were radicals—but they were eighteenth century radicals concerned, like the eighteenth century English radicals, not with the need to recast the social order nor with the problems of economic inequality and the injustice of stratified societies but with the need to purify a corrupt constitution and fight off the apparent growth of prerogative power.

But this essay offers a very different reading of these radicals and of British reform in general between 1760 and the French Revolution. Locke was very much alive and well in their arguments.

The radicals of the later eighteenth century, both English and American, were much more likely to base their arguments on natural rights than on historical rights; they were preoccupied less with nostalgic country concerns than with very modern socioeconomic grievances. They shared a deeply felt sense that the unreformed British constitution failed to serve the interests of the talented and hard-working middle class. Locke was, indeed, unimportant to the earlier Augustan country ideology. Its basic hierarchical commitment, in fact, led Bolingbroke to repudiate all notions of the state of nature with its egalitarian overtones. But two great historical developments operated to change the context of ideological discourse and most especially among the radicals. The 1760s represent the crucial turning point. The concerns of the earlier part of the century—the mixed constitution, annual Parliaments, the independent Commons, anti-place legislation, and the standing army controversy—were shunted aside. America and the crisis over taxation introduced new noncountry issues into politics. The taxation controversy raised to the center of debate the issue of representation, which in its trail brought to the fore basic concerns about the origins of government and authority in general. Taxation was the curse of all, yet few were enfranchised. Emphasizing taxation flew in the face of ideas of virtual representation and expanded the notion of property beyond landed wealth or freehold. What this emphasis on movable property did, as John Brewer has noted, was to enable radicals like Burgh and Cartwright to extend "the debate about parliamentary reform far beyond its previous confines." It transcended the paradigms of country ideology to more class-based categories.

The American crisis coincided with a second crucial development, the early years of the Industrial Revolution and the emergence of a new middle-class radicalism. The first decades of industrialization in England saw, as D. E. C. Eversley has calculated, a greatly expanding middling level of English society, families with an income between £50 and £400. This "free, mobile, prudent section of the population" was turning to politics. These owners of small and movable property, as well as the new entrepreneurs like Wedgwood and Wilkinson, felt excluded from a political process that affected them daily in their credit transactions, in their tax burden, and in the proliferation of intrusive statute law.

This is not to dismiss out of hand the existence of lingering country content in the radical ideology of Wilkes, Burgh, Cartwright, or Sawbridge. It had been, after all, the ideological reflex of the excluded for a century. Calls for frequent elections and a reformed suffrage along with attacks on placemen were often still uttered in the Machiavellian language of corruption, restoration of first principles, and historical analogies from Roman history. But beneath the familiar surface of the new radicalism that began to emerge during the 1760s were different themes. The new radicalism goes beyond the praise of wise and virtuous landed MPs [members of parliament] independent of both the crown and constituent pressure. It goes beyond the Rockingham Whigs' sense that all was well with the political system and that only a change of leadership in which men of virtue replaced wicked men was needed to end "the present discontents." In the new radicalism, there is a new dimension, the conviction that those now excluded—the urban and commercial interests—wanted "in," wanted to be represented in Parliament and wanted their MPs to be their spokesmen, serving their interests, not serving as wise men independent of both court and those who elected them. Thus, in their anger, the new radicals turn on *both* the landed classes and the court-government.

Precisely in this context of a critical shift in the nature and aims of the opposition, Lockean ideas made a dramatic and decisive comeback in the 1760s and 1770s. In Locke far more than in Bolingbroke and his ilk, the unenfranchised middle class and especially the Protestant dissenters found intellectual authority and legitimacy for their radical demands. Locke's ideas reflecting the revolutionary upheavals of the previous century spoke more directly to a Burgh, a Paine, or a Priestley than did the nostalgia of a St. John, a Pope, or a Swift. . . .

Locke, whose principles "so favour the natural rights of mankind," is central to this opening salvo in the campaign to reform Parliament, and his use here set the pattern for the next thirty years. His notion of contract, of governors as trustees, subject to dismissal if they forfeited this trust, was the intellectual weaponry used in the assault on the unreformed Commons. This is abundantly clear in Wilkes's agitation and its offshoot, the Society of the Supporters of the Bill of Rights. By 1771 the society, led by Horne Tooke, had moved from merely defending Wilkes's right to a seat in Commons to offering a comprehensive program for parliamentary reform. Central to that program was an oath to be required of all parliamentary candidates that they "endeavour to obtain a more fair and equal representation of the people." Echoes of the 1766 pamphlet are clear. Equitable and equal became "fair and equal." John Wilkes moved in the House of Commons on March 21, 1776, "that leave be given to bring in a bill, for a just and equal representation of the people of England in Parliament." In his speech he cited "the present unfair and inadequate state of the representation of the people in Parliament. It has now become so partial and unequal from the lapse of time." The language used in Wilkes's bill is important. For the next thirty years the reform movement used the phrases "fair and equal representation" and "just and equal representation." This abstract language of reason and nature does not derive from specific calculations from the Saxon past, and the principal author of these abstract phrases is none other than John Locke.

In a most striking case of historical oversight, few who have written on this period have noted that this formulation, so central to reform politics and writing for the remainder of the eighteenth century, is lifted directly from Locke, who in paragraphs 157 and 158 of *The Second Treatise of Government* wrote,

> It often comes to pass that in government where part of the legislative consists of representatives chosen by the people that by tract of time this representation becomes very unequal and disproportionate to the reasons it was at first established. . . . For it being the interest as well as intention of the people to have a fair and equal representative, whoever brings it nearest to that is an undoubted friend to and establisher of the government and cannot miss the consent and approbation of the community.

The key phrase of the reform movement was Locke's of nearly one hundred years earlier. Scholars' failure to note the textual derivation from Locke is all the more striking since most eighteenth-century users of the "fair and equal" demand cited Locke as their authority. So it was that Wilkes in his speech of March 21, 1776, noted that "this evil has been complained of by some of the wisest patriots our country has produced. I shall beg leave to give that close reasoner, Mr. Locke's ideas in his own words. . . . [He then read paragraphs 157 and 158.] After so great an authority as that of Mr. Locke, I shall not be treated on this occasion as a mere visionary."

Even more important than this textual linkage between Locke and the reformers, however, is the far deeper theoretical bond the reformers constructed between themselves and such Lockean themes as contract, state of nature, and natural rights and government as a trust in all of their writing on taxation and representation. This becomes evident by shifting the focus from Wilkes to more respectable and learned reformers. But Wilkes and his supporters both in London and in the provinces—by and large merchants, manufacturers, and entrepreneurs—forged the link for the enduring character of reform agitation: its antiaristocratic, middle-class bias. Wilkes the fool, Wilkes the court jester, was a living repudiation of hierarchical piety and the due subordination of rank and degree. . . .

Although now overshadowed by Godwin, Priestley, Price, and Paine, James Burgh through his *Political Disquisitions* was literally the schoolmaster for a whole generation of middle-class radicals in England and America, and it bears repeating that his critique was in large part a self-conscious apology for the assertive middle class. He railed against a British government that parceled out its profitable and prestigious jobs to the nobility and gentry who dominated Parliament. Why has the nobleman, he asked, any more claim to this respect than the artisan or manufacturer? "If the nobility and gentry declined to serve their country in the great offices of the state, without sordid hire, let the honest bourgeoisie be employed. They will themselves be sufficiently regarded by the honour done them." Rather than "half our nobility . . . and over drenched court sponges . . . being upon the parish" (that is, having public jobs), these jobs, he suggested, should go to men of merit. Burgh proposed, in fact, that public jobs, like public contracts, be filled by "sealed proposals." The talented individual most capable of serving his country would then be selected. If men of the meritorious middle class took over public service and Parliament, then public expenditures, he predicted, would decline dramatically, for these new men would not demand great salaries, they would not dance "at Mrs. Conneley's masquerades." They would "rise up early and sit up late and fill up the whole day with severe labour."

This bourgeois demand for careers open to the talented was a most critical element in British reform during this period. It is Figaro's lament to the great Count Almaviva, translated for Englishmen in 1784 by Godwin's close friend, Thomas Holcroft: "What did you do to deserve what you have— nothing but to be born." It is Tom Paine's suggestion that what "nobility" really means is "no-ability." The dissenting schoolmaster James Burgh was neither country apologist nor classical republican. His was an individualist ideology of an insurgent middle class. In America and in Britain, he wrote, the dissenters have rejected the ways of the aristocracy and the poor. They have "bounded" their "riotous appetites" and their "lusts." They have turned their backs on gaming, drunkenness, lewdness, operas, cockfighting, and the theater. Dissenter "sobriety and temperate ways of living," "their thrift and regular manner of living," their awareness "that every moment of time ought to be put to its proper use," their "industriousness," and their "order and regularity" have produced prosperity and wealth. But to what avail is such talent and merit? What are the rewards in an aristocratic society for such achievement, when "the people may be brought, by inveterate tyranny, to bear patiently to see the most worthless part of mankind (for surely the great by mere birth, in all ages and countries are commonly among the most worthless of mankind) set up above them and themselves obliged to crouch"? Sometimes, of course, such "tyranny" becomes too much to bear: "And if the people rouse to vengeance, woe to those who stand in the way. Let merit only be honoured with privilege and prerogative, and mankind will be contented."

Richard Price's *Observations on the Nature of Civil Liberty,* another critical text in the reform tradition, appeared in 1776. Price did not leave room for doubt about his source, for in his preface he noted that "the principles on which I have argued form the foundation of every state as far as it is free; and are the same with those taught by Mr. Locke." Government for Price is a trust, in which the people set up governors to serve particular ends. When the trust is betrayed, government is dissolved. Price insisted that the rights of the Americans are the natural rights of all free men, not the product of history, tradition, statute, charter, or precedent. The enemies of the colonists, like Josiah Tucker, condemned the American colonists, Price noted, by calling them "Mr. Locke's disciples." "What a glorious title," Price replied.

Price's praise of America provides an interesting insight into the Lockean world view, which so prompted British reformers to excitement when they looked to America. America was, as Locke himself had noted, as it was "in the beginning." Price and others saw America as a land of individual freedom and equality, where hierarchy and subordination were unknown. The colonies had no rich or poor, he wrote, no beggars and no "haughty grandees." The Americans were strangers to luxury, and they worked hard. There was no large government, and there were few taxes. Most important of all, Price claimed, in America merit was the only path to distinction. To his dying day, Price repeated these themes: in his speech in 1789 and in his *Discourse on the Love of Country,* which so infuriated Burke that he answered with his *Reflections on the Revolution in France.* In the sermon at Old Jewry in 1789, Price alleged that the greatest defect of the British constitution was representational inequality and that its remedy lay in a representational structure that was "fair and equal"—Locke again. . . .

[I]mportant . . . in accounting for middle-class and modernist sentiment against the debt was its symbolic role as the endless fountain of corruption, the source of jobs and patronage that not only corrupted Parliament but gave society's rewards to the untalented, those without merit. Critical here was the popular identification (well founded in fact) between the growth of the national debt and war. A vast military establishment generated the debt and left the impression in the virtuous, hard-working middle class of an immoral and unholy alliance. All of these came together in the debt. . . .

. . . [A]s is the case with Jefferson, . . . agrarian bias must again not be automatically translated into nostalgia, antimodernism, and anticommercialism, for it is by no means clear that the city was perceived in the late eighteenth century as standing for modernity and capitalism and the countryside for reaction and agrarianism. Yeoman farmers operated very much in the capitalist marketplace and had highly developed commercial networks. The yeoman ideal of both Price and Jefferson was not, as Richard Hofstadter depicted it, "non-commercial, non-pecuniary, self-sufficient." In defending American agriculture against the Hamiltonian system, Thomas Cooper recognized that encomia for farming did not necessitate a nostalgic repudiation of a commercial society. Although agriculture was a morally superior pursuit, its superiority did not lie in any more virtuous, precapitalist ideal. Commerce had less value only insofar as it drained away resources: "To foster every, or any other employment of capital at the expense of agriculture—by diminishing the savings of the farmer and forcing him to maintain the manufacturer—or by tempting the capitalist from agriculture into manufacture, is plainly contrary to our most undoubted policy."

No less committed to a commercial society than others in this period, what distinguishes the economic vision of a Price, a Cooper, a Paine, or a Jefferson is its individualistic, decentralized, and nonhierarchical flavor. Thus, Jefferson preached the virtues of unrestrained free trade in terms of an idealized, individualistic marketplace. "Our interest will be to throw open the doors of commerce, and to knock off all its shackles," he wrote, "giving perfect freedom to all persons for the vent of whatever they may choose to bring into our ports, and asking the same in theirs." So, too, Price praised America because, unlike "older countries" where rural life was graduated into ranks of "gentry, yeomanry and peasant," America had just yeomen, "all independent and nearly upon a level." The market was not the villain, hierarchy and dependence were. As Joyce Appleby has noted of Jefferson, "what was distinctive about the Republican's economic policy was not an anti-commercial bias, but a commitment to growth through the unimpeded exertions of individuals" with "access to economic opportunity."

The rural-urban dichotomy and the preference for the rural is compatible with the emerging middle-class vision. The countryside (where, after all, in England the early manufacturing occurred) represented hard work, simplicity, frugality, industry, and productivity. The city represented courts, office holders, pensioners, luxury, waste, money, and funds. In the city congregated the idle, either the very rich or the very poor. In the city were gaming, opera, theater, and other useless, time-wasting activities. To label the city corrupt and the countryside virtuous need not, then, immediately connote a dread of modernity. The ideological thrust of such activities is never simply read. Who is virtuous and who is corrupt is not reducible to who is engaged in agriculture and who in commerce, who lives on the land or who on city streets. Hard work, talent, and productivity are what are really critical in the distribution of moral worth, and the secondary distinctions based on geography have to be read in light of these much more crucial, more primary issues. . . .

Late-eighteenth-century observers thus made a clear link from Locke to British reform and socioeconomic change, a link that has been denied by the "Republican School." The real threat of Locke and his "eminent disciples" was their leveling tendencies, their assault on traditional aristocratic society. In *The True Basis of Civil Government in Opposition to the System of Mr. Locke and His Followers,* Tucker criticized the reformers for denying what he saw as basic in human nature: "a certain ascendancy in some, a kind of submissive acquiescence in others." There are, Tucker insisted, certain natural "ranks in society" and "stations in life," which contract theory undermines in its subversive preoccupation with natural freedom and equality. These critics perceptively understood the intentions of the "eminent disciples" of Locke. The praise of achievement and talent, the ideology of equal opportunity, and the cult of industry and productivity, all wrapped in doctrines of natural equality and independence, were in fact self-consciously directed at "the age of chivalry." The true nostalgics were the likes of Burke, Tucker, and Tatham. Theirs was the defense of a world with "Kings, princes, nobles and gentlemen. . . . For in the whole scale of beings, and in the nature of things, there must be regular gradations and regular distinctions." . . .

To paraphrase Mark Twain, the scholarly consensus on Locke's death in the late eighteenth century is greatly exaggerated. Late eighteenth-century English reformers dramatically worked Lockean themes into the heart of their critique of traditional England, turning to Locke because *The Second Treatise of Government* was uniquely appropriate to their peculiar problem. Parliament, the representative body, was itself the barrier to reform. Locke's belief in the residual power of the people against their governors legitimized the reformers' campaign against the unreformed House of Commons. Locke's political theory legitimated their demands, both substantive and procedural, for a reform of the suffrage and of parliamentary representation. His concept of a limited secular magistrate legitimated their demand for the separation of church and state.

The reformers also turned to Locke because their ideological concerns were similar. These spokesmen for an insurgent middle-class radicalism were drawn to this liberal theorist of possessive individualism. No one had better expressed their economic and social convictions than Locke had. His socioeconomic vision was perfectly compatible with—indeed, had helped shape—their image of a world peopled by hard-working, industrious property owners. Locke had often written on the themes of industry and talent and was perceived as a crucial part of the Protestant tradition that so informed much of this reform movement. In the libraries of the dissenting academies, Locke's works were standard references, not only for psychology and education but also for politics and commerce. Had not, in fact, *The Second Treatise* contended that God had set some men to be more industrious than others and thus to acquire more property? Locke's conviction that God "gave the world to the use of the industrious and Rational . . . , not to the Fancy or the Covetousness of the Quarrelsome and Contentious," was critical to his thought; it symbolized a central tension in his work: the struggle between the industrious and the idle—a struggle at the core of the world view of those late eighteenth-century dissenting reformers who read Locke in the libraries of their academies.

The praise of industry, of what the seventeenth and eighteenth centuries considered "skill, assiduity, perseverance and diligence," and the denunciation of idleness were, of course, by no means unique to Locke. Protestant writers, especially Puritans like Baxter, had long made them a crucial part of their notions of work, of the obligation to labor, and of the importance of one's calling. What Locke did was wed these earlier views to a political theory of private rights and individualism with his argument that property was an extension of self, the injection of personality into nature through work. Less apparent, however, is the extent to which other Lockean texts read in these dissenting academy libraries spoke to the themes of industry, idleness, and the glory of work. Indeed, so concerned with these themes was Locke that it is little exaggeration to suggest that he saw industriousness as the central characteristic of the human personality, of personal behavior, and of social and personal activity.

In his *Essay Concerning Human Understanding,* Locke linked activity to anxiety, a connection not unfamiliar to later readers of Weber and Tawney. "The chief, if not the only spur to human industry and action is," he wrote, "uneasiness." This feeling of uneasiness, a desire for "some absent good," drove men to enterprise and unrelenting activity. Once motivated, they were permanently active, for they had a never-ending "itch after honour, power and riches," which in turn unleashed more "fantastical uneasiness."

Activity and industry, according to Locke, also characterized childhood. His widely read *Thoughts Concerning Education* is a veritable diatribe against idleness. Children were the model for the species. They "generally hate to be idle. All they care then is, that their busy humour should be constantly employ'd in something of use to them." All life is industrious activity, Locke wrote; even in recreation human beings are never idle. "For *Recreation* is not being idle (as every one may observe) but easing the wearied Part by Change of Business: and he that thinks *Diversion* may not lie in hard and painful Labour, forgets the early Rising, hard Riding, Heat, Cold and Hunger of Huntsmen, which is yet known to be the constant Recreation of Men of the greatest Condition." Recreation should not just delight and provide ease, it should refresh one for "regular business" and "produce what will afterwards be profitable." Uneasiness again preoccupied Locke, as he prescribed that parents keep their children busy and fight "the dead weight of unemployed Time lying upon their hands," since "the uneasiness it is to do nothing at all."

Children should be taught to keep account books, according to Locke, which not only would keep them busy but would also teach them frugality. Such practices would contribute to the habitual and orderly management of their lives. Industriousness required that children also learn to postpone immediate gratification: "He that has not a mastery over his Inclinations, he that knows not how to *resist* the Importunity of *present Pleasure* or *Pain,* for the sake of what Reason tells him is fit to be done, wants the true Principle of Virtue and Industry."

Two groups in the community—some aristocrats and all of the poor—were not, however, active and industrious. According to Locke, they provided the "fancy or the covetousness of the Quarrelsome and contentious."

As Burgh, Price, Priestley, and all dissenting middle-class reformers eventually did, Locke divided society into an industrious, enterprising middle
beset by two idle extremes. In his essay of 1691 on lowering the interest
rate, Locke criticized the profligate aristocrat, whose plight was produced
by "debauchery and luxury beyond means." He was not criticizing the "industrious and rational" among the aristocracy, only the "covetous" and
"contentious," who "will have and by his example make it fashionable to
have more claret, spice and silk." Such men would soon lose their power
and authority to "men of lower condition who surpass them in knowledge."

While only some of the aristocracy were lazy and "debauched," Locke
presumed that most of the poor were idle and inactive, and his harshness
toward them knew no bounds. He urged that the provisions of the poor law
be made stricter so that the poor could be taught industry, hard work, and
frugality. One way to break them of their wasteful idleness was through the
establishment of what Locke called "working schools." A full century before
Bentham and his charity schools, Locke proposed that all children of the
poor "shall be obliged to come" at the age of three to live in "schools"
where the only subjects taught would be spinning and knitting. This would
cure them of idleness, for they would then "from infancy be inured to work,
which is of no small consequence to the making of them sober and industrious
all their lives after." Rounding up the children of the poor and incarcerating
them in order to teach them industry and hard work would, Locke conceded,
cost the parishes dearly; but it would ultimately prove profitable in the
account books of the spinning and knitting managers, for "the earnings of
the children [would] abat[e] the charge of their maintenance, and as much
work [would] be required of each of them as they are reasonably able to
perform," so that "it will quickly pay its own charges with an overplus."

From such Lockean schemes and the values they embody there is a
direct link not only to Bentham but to the middle-class Protestant reformers
of the late eighteenth century. . . . Middle-class reformers in the late eighteenth century were more likely to read the world and assess its institutions—
economic, social, and political—in terms of the dialectic of industry and
idleness than "virtue and commerce." Here, too, they bore the indelible
imprint of "that close reasoner, Mr. Locke." . . .

Middle-class reformers in the late eighteenth century used the older
language of civic humanism and corruption, to be sure. They and their
American friends, like Jefferson and Franklin, complained often of the corruption that hung heavy over Britain. But corruption was a very different
notion for these reformers from what it had been for the earlier Bolingbroke
and his country ideology. A corrupt man . . . was idle, profligate, unproductive, and lacking in talent and merit. A corrupt system was one in which
such drones held important public offices, one in which privilege, not merit,
distributed the prizes in the race of life, and one in which patronage insured
the rule of unproductive—that is, corrupt—men of no ability instead of
that of deserving men of talent. When Francis Place complained that "the
whole system of our Government is essentially corrupt," he was not invoking
a court-country equation with commerce and modernity, he was using a new

public language that saw government as a reserve for privileged parasites. . . . These useless idlers presided over a system that denied careers to the talented. The real nation was, as earlier in the century, seen as outside that corrupt government, but that nation was not a warmed-over Augustan country. Now it was the virtuous, hard-working, and frugal middle class and artisanry, who were as uninterested in a republican order of civic virtue as they were in an aristocratic order of deference and privilege. What they wanted was a meritocracy of talent. Had not Locke written, after all, that God "gave the world to the use of the Industrious and the Rational"?

These radical dissenters were the first fully developed theorists of the liberal ideal of equal opportunity. . . . The issue was "power, place, and influence."

Pocock and other revisionists have been quite right to see the court-commerce connection earlier in the century. But, by the late eighteenth century, the country reform tradition came to terms with the market and, indeed, in the hands of middle-class industrial dissent turned that reform tradition into a wholehearted ideology of the market. The court, while bound to the market and commerce from Walpole on, was enmeshed in the principle of patronage, which ultimately flew in the face of market notions of careers neutrally open to talent and hard work. It is here that the conflict emerges. Patronage and privilege are principles that pitted the court against the bourgeois reformers. Middle-class radicals inveighed against corrupt patronage, but it was a new sense of corruption, the corruption of jobs and places going to undeserving, untalented men of birth. It was the privileged court that in this period responded with a nostalgic defense of the ancient constitution, hierarchy, and paternalism. Its defenders ridiculed the leveling ideas of monied men and provincial bumpkins.

A court-country reading of the later eighteenth century becomes too confusing to be useful, because, with the emergence and eventual supremacy within the country "outs" of a class-conscious bourgeoisie, the court-commerce linkage becomes obsolete. In the eyes of the middle-class radical "outs," the earlier equation was reversed. The "ins," the court and all it stood for, were identified not with the market and commerce but with idle, unproductive privilege. The commercial and financial revolution stood behind the court-country split of the Augustan era. Its relevance receded, however, with the early years of the Industrial Revolution, when new dichotomous distinctions captured the fancy of reformers, not the least of which was virtuous commerce versus corrupt privilege. The marriage of industrial England with dissenter reform doomed court-country politics and introduced class politics.

What emerged in the course of the late eighteenth century—and most vividly in the writings of the middle-class radicals—was a new notion of virtue, one that dramatically rejects the assumptions of civic humanism. Citizenship and the public quest for the common good were replaced by economic productivity and hard work as the criteria of virtue. It is a mistake, however, to see this simply as a withdrawal from public activity to a private, self-centered realm. The transformation also involved a changed emphasis on the nature of public behavior. The moral and virtuous man was no longer defined by his civic activity but by his economic activity. One's duty was still to contribute to the public good, but this was best done through economic activity, which actually aimed at private gain. Self-centered economic productivity, not public citizenship, became the badge of the virtuous man.

A new cultural ideal was taking shape in the work and writings of these radicals. *Homo civicus* was being replaced by *homo oeconomicus*. In his letters, Josiah Wedgwood, Priestley's patron, described how he had "fallen in love" with and "made a mistress" of his pottery business. His productivity was merely to abide by the will of God. Wedgwood obeyed what he called the "eleventh commandment—Thou shalt not be idle." His friend, the dissenting cotton manufacturer Jedediah Strutt, was convinced, "whatever some Divines would teach to the contrary," that the "main business of the life of man was the getting of money." The early classics of children's literature produced in England from 1760 to 1800 by these very same middle-class radicals in Priestley's circle contain few lectures or parables extolling civic responsibility (unlike *Émile*), but they continually praise productive hard work. In Anna Barbauld's children's tale "True Heroism," she wrote that great men were no longer those who devote themselves to public life— "Kings, lords, generals, and prime ministers." There were new heroes, men who instead "invent useful arts, or discover important truths which may promote the comfort and happiness of unborn generations in the distant parts of the world. They act still an important part, and their claim to merit is generally more undoubted, than that of the former, because what they do is more certainly their own." A pamphleteer of 1780 spelled out even more clearly who these new heroes were: "Consider the gradual steps of civilization from barbarism to refinement and you will not fail to discover that the progress of society from its lowest and worst to its highest and most perfect state, has been uniformly accompanied and chiefly promoted by the happy exertions of man in the character of a mechanic or engineer!"

The middle-class radical praise of economic man no longer shares what Pocock described as the republican dread of Aristotle's banausic men, who are "less than citizens because they specialised in the development of one's capacity." Specialization for the radicals, far from a sign of corruption, was a characteristic of virtuous man. It did not render economic man dependent on government or make him the servant of others, like priests, lawyers, rentiers, or soldiers. The specialist, like the entrepreneur, the scientist, the engineer, the inventor, or any man of talent, was the true social hero, who through his ingenious productivity and private pursuits shaped the public good. The older praise of the public citizen as a nonspecialized amateur smacked too much of the aristocratic rule of idle and untalented privilege. A self-conscious glorification of specialization against Aristotle's "ethos of *zöon politikon*" is implicit in an ideology that extols talent, merit, and skill. Hence, not just Adam Smith but a chorus of writers in the last decades of the eighteenth century sang the praises of specialization and the division of labor. The very heart of civic humanism was repudiated and its values reversed by the radical middle-class crusade to professionalize and specialize, to replace what it saw as corrupt political man with virtuous and productive economic man.

Josiah Wedgwood approached civic life as a specialist in industry and commerce. "Sunk again I find into politicks" was how he described himself, reluctantly having to leave his business for citizenship. Not "fame" but "money getting" was his concern. When his friend, the great engineer Brindley, died, Wedgwood noted that it was talents like his that truly benefited mankind. The public good done by such men of genius, the contribution to the commonweal by such men of "ingenuity and industry," far surpassed the contribution of political men, of "many noble lords." The economic benefactors "will be remembered with gratitude and respect" when the others "are totally forgotten." For Thomas Cooper, the industrialist and scientist who like Priestley eventually settled in America, virtue and privilege were incompatible. Only those with "insatiable ambition" could be able, wise, or virtuous.

The middle class wrapped itself in this new notion of virtue. They were "not adorn'd, it's true with coats of arms and a long Parchment Pedigree of useless members of society, but deck'd with virtue and frugality." When Jedediah Strutt in composing his own epitaph wrote that "he had led a life of honesty and virtue," thoughts of country purity and citizenship could not have been further from his mind. His life was virtuous compared to the corruption of the idle nobility and the wretched poor, for he had worked harder and contributed more with his talent, ingenuity, and industry to the increased productivity and wealth of his nation than they had. He was typical of a new species of self-centered virtuous men—men like those seen in Birmingham by an eighteenth-century chronicler of the middle class:

> I was surprised at the place, but more so at the people: they were a species I had never seen: they possessed a vivacity I had never beheld: I had been among dreamers, but now I saw men awake: their very step along the street showed alacrity: Everyman seemed to know and prosecute his own affairs: the town was large, and full of inhabitants and those inhabitants full of industry.

When such self-centered, virtuous men addressed themselves to public issues, they did so less and less in terms of the paradigms and language of civic humanism or classical republicanism and more and more with the conceptual framework they knew best, the market. Joel Barlow—financial speculator, international entrepreneur, radical friend of Jefferson, Paine, Price, Wollstonecraft, Godwin, and Priestley—wrote of the French Revolution in his *Advice to the Privileged Orders in the Several States of Europe* in the language and the paradigms he knew best. He began, "It must be of vast importance to all classes of society . . . to calculate before hand what they are to gain or to lose by the approaching change; that like prudent stock jobbers, they may buy in or sell out, according as this great event shall effect them."

Barlow and his friends, British and American, knew their Aristotle, their Machiavelli, and their Montesquieu. But they also knew their Locke. The world view of liberal individualism was fast pushing aside older paradigms during the last three decades of the century in the wake of the American crisis and the inventions of Watt and Arkwright. Two hundred years later, republican revisionism depicts these late eighteenth-century figures as preoccupied with public virtue and civic humanism and as uninterested in Lockean liberal ideals. When allowed to speak for themselves, however, these radicals seem to tell a different story.

Insurrection As a Step to Constitutionalism

PAULINE MAIER

Eighteenth-century Americans accepted the existence of popular uprisings with remarkable ease. Riots and tumults, it was said, happened "in all governments at all times." To seek a world completely free of them was vain; it was to pursue "a blessing denied to this life, and reserved to complete the felicity of the next." Not that extra-legal uprisings were encouraged. They were not. But in certain circumstances, it was understood, the people would rise up almost as a natural force, much as night follows day, and this phenomenon often contributed to the public welfare. The colonists' attitude depended in large part upon a tradition of popular uprisings that also shaped the forms of popular force during the revolutionary era. The existence of such a tradition meant, moreover, that the people, or, as their opponents said, the mob, entered the struggle with Britain as an established social force, not as an agency newly invented to serve the ends of radical leadership.

Not all American eighteenth-century popular uprisings were the same, of course. Some involved no more than disorderly vandalism; some were in effect traditional brawls, like the celebrations of Pope's Day in New England every November 5; and some involved resistance to lawful authority on the part of a minority interest group. But there was yet another strain of uprisings so persistent that it became characteristic of prominent colonial incidents. Repeatedly, insurgents defended the urgent interests of their communities when lawful authorities failed to act. This had been true of the famous late-seventeenth-century Virginia tobacco uprisings: only after their provincial assembly was prevented from meeting, and thus from curtailing production so as to avert economic crisis, did insurgents begin tearing up tobacco plants. In Maryland's Prince George County, tobacco "rioting" was similarly carried on by men in "despair of any relief from the legislature." Massive rural uprisings in New Jersey and the Carolinas during the mid-eighteenth century also intervened to punish outlaws, secure land titles, or prevent the abuses of public officials only after efforts to work through established procedures failed, and the colonists became convinced that justice and security had to be imposed by the people directly. In proprietary North Carolina, the "resort to force and violence was . . . a common occurrence, almost the habit of the country"; and even after 1731, when the colony came under Crown rule,

From *From Resistance to Revolution* by Pauline Maier, pp. 3–8, 21–26. Copyright © 1972 by Pauline Maier. Reprinted by permission of Alfred A. Knopf Inc.

"scarce a decade passed that did not see the people in arms to redress official grievances." The Boston mob intervened repeatedly to keep foodstuffs in the colony during times of dearth (1710, 1713, 1729) and to destroy bawdy houses (1734, 1737, 1771); in the mid-1770s, uprisings in Marblehead, Massachusetts, and Norfolk, Virginia, acted to protect their communities from a threat of smallpox after official actions proved inadequate. And in New London, Connecticut, insurgents prevented a radical religious sect, the Rogerenes, from disturbing normal Sunday services, "a practice they . . . [had] followed more or less for many years past; and which all the laws made in that government, and executed in the most judicious manner could not put a stop to."

These incidents indicate a readiness among many Americans to act outside the bounds of law, but they cannot simply be described as antiauthoritarian. Often—as in the Boston whorehouse riot of 1734 or the Norfork smallpox incident—local magistrates openly countenanced or participated in the crowd's activities. Contemporary political structure can to a large extent explain this confluence of popular force and magijsterial inclination. Certainly within New England communities, where the town meeting ruled, and to some extent in New York, where aldermen and councilmen were annually elected, local magistrates were closely linked to the communities they served; and even in Philadelphia, with its lethargic closed corporation, or Charleston, which lacked regular town government, authority was normally exerted by provincials who had an immediate sense of local sentiment. Provincial assemblies also acted to keep public policy in accord with local demands. Of course, this identity of local magistrates with the popular will was imperfect, and occasional uprisings did turn against domestic colonial institutions—in Pennsylvania in 1764, for example, when the "Paxton Boys" complained that their assembly had failed to protect them adequately against the Indians. But uprisings over local issues proved *extra-institutional* in character more often than they were anti-institutional: they served the community where no law existed, or intervened beyond what magistrates thought they could do officially to cope with a local problem.

The case was different when imperial rule was involved. There legal authority emanated from a capital an ocean away, where the colonists had no integral voice in the formation of policy, and governmental decisions were based largely upon the reports of "King's men" who sought above all to promote the King's interests. When London's legal authority and local interest conflicted, efforts to implement the edicts of royal officials were often answered by uprisings, and it was not unusual in these cases for local magistrates to participate or openly sympathize with the insurgents. Attempts to enforce the White Pine Acts of 1722 and 1729, for example, met widespread forceful resistance, sometimes to the extent that royal officials were forced to abandon the task. Two other imperial efforts similarly provoked local uprisings in the colonies long before 1765 and continued to do so in long-established ways during the revolutionary period: impressment and customs enforcement.

As early as 1743, the colonists' violent opposition to impressment was said to indicate a "Contempt of Government." Captains had been "mobbed," the admiralty complained, "others imprisoned, and afterwards held to exorbitant Bail, and are now under Prosecutions." Colonial governors, despite their offers, furnished captains with little real aid either to procure seamen or "even protect them from the Rage and Insults of the People." Two days of severe rioting answered Commodore Charles Knowles's efforts to sweep Boston Harbor for able-bodied men in November 1747. Again in 1764, when Rear Admiral Lord Colville sent out orders to procure men in principal harbors between Casco Bay and Cape Henlopen, uprisings met the ships at every turn. When the *St. John* sent out a boat to seize a recently impressed deserter from a Newport wharf, a crowd protected him, captured the boat's officer, and hurled stones at the crew; later, fifty Newporters joined the colony's gunner at Fort George in opening fire on the King's ship itself. Under threat to her master, the *Chaleur* was forced to release four fishermen seized off Long Island; and when that ship's captain went ashore at New York, his boat was seized and burned in the Fields. In the spring of 1765, after the *Maidstone* capped a six-month siege of Newport Harbor by seizing "all the Men" out of a brigantine from Africa, a band of about five hundred men similarly seized a ship's officer and burned one of her boats on the Common. Impressment also met mass resistance at Norfolk in 1767 and was a major cause of the famous *Liberty* riot at Boston in 1768.

Like the impressment uprisings, which in most instances sought to protect or rescue men from the "press," the customs incidents tried to impede the customs service in enforcing British laws. Tactics varied; and although incidents occurred long before 1764—in 1719, for example, Caleb Heathcote reported a "riotous and tumultuous" rescue of seized claret by Newporters—their frequency increased after the Sugar Act was passed and customs enforcement efforts were tightened. The 1764 rescue of the *Rhoda* in Rhode Island preceded a theft in Dighton, Massachusetts, of the cargo from a newly seized vessel, the *Polly,* by a mob of some forty men with blackened faces. In 1766 again a customs official's home in Falmouth (Portland), Maine, was stoned while "Persons unknown and disguised" stole sugar and rum that had been impounded that morning. Attacks upon customs officials enjoyed a long history, but the punishment of informers was particularly favored: in 1770, Massachusetts's Lieutenant Governor Thomas Hutchinson noted that many persons would join in such an affair "who would scruple joining in acts of violence against any other persons." Even the South Carolina attorney general publicly attacked an informer in 1701 while crying out "this is the Informer, this is he that will ruin the country." Similar assaults on customs functionaries occurred decades later, in New Haven in 1766 and 1769, and New London in 1769, for example, and were then often distinguished by their brutality. In 1771, Providence tidesman Jesse Saville was seized, stripped, bound hand and foot, tarred and feathered, had dirt thrown in his face, then was beaten and "almost strangled." Even more thorough assaults upon two other Rhode Island tidesmen occurred in July 1770 and upon Collector Charles Dudley in April 1771. Customs vessels, too, came under direct attack: the *St. John* was shelled at Newport in 1764 where the customs ship *Liberty* was sunk in 1769—both episodes that served as prelude to the destruction of the *Gaspée* outside Providence in 1772. . . .

. . . For the most part, members of a mob clearly acted without the sanction of law. That ambiguous cases did arise, however, indicates that legitimacy and illegitimacy, *posses* and rioters, represented poles on a single spectrum. Even where their relationship to the law was doubtful, moreover, popular uprisings benefited from a certain presumptive acceptability that was founded in part on colonial experience with mass action. In words that could be drawn almost verbatim from John Locke or other English authors of similar convictions, colonial writers assumed a certain moderation and purposefulness among insurgents. "Tho' innocent Persons may sometimes suffer in popular Tumults," observed a 1768 writer in the *New York Journal,* "yet the general Resentment of the People is principally directed according to Justice, and the greatest Delinquent feels it most." More important, upheavals constituted only occasional interruptions in well-governed societies. "Good Laws and good Rulers will always be obey'd and respected"; "the Experience of all Ages proves, that Mankind are much more likely to submit to bad Laws and wicked Rulers, than to resist good ones." "Mobs and Tumults," it was often said, "never happen but thro' Oppression and a scandalous Abuse of Power."

In the hands of Locke, such remarks constituted relatively inert statements of fact. Colonial writers, however, often turned these pronouncements on their heads such that instances of popular disorder became *prima facie* indictments not of the people, but of authority. In 1747, for example, New Jersey land rioters argued that "from their Numbers, Violences, and unlawful Actions" it was "to be inferred that . . . they are wronged & oppressed, or else they would never *rebell agt. the Laws.*" When the people of any government become turbulent and uneasy, a New York writer said in 1770, it is always "a certain Sign of Maladministration." Even when disorders were not directly focused against government, they provided "strong proofs that something is much amiss in the state," as William Samuel Johnson put it; that—Samuel Adams's words—the "wheels of government" were "somewhere clogged." Americans who used this argument against Britain in the 1760s continued to depend upon it two decades later, when they reacted to Shays's Rebellion by seeking out the public "Disease" in their own independent governments that was indicated by the "Spriit of Licentiousness" in Massachusetts.

Popular turbulence seemed to follow so naturally from inadequacies of government that riots and rebellions were often described with similes from the physical world. In 1770, John Adams said that there were "Church-quakes and state-quakes in the moral and political world, as well as earthquakes, storms and tempests in the physical." Two years earlier, a writer in the *New York Journal* had likened popular tumults to "Thunder Gusts," which "do more Good than Harm." Thomas Jefferson continued the imagery in the 1780s, particularly with his famous statement that he "liked a little rebellion now and then," for it was like "a storm in the atmosphere." It was, moreover, because of the "imperfection of all things in this world" that John Adams found it vain to try to found a government totally free of tumultuousness. In effect, disorder was an integral, even predictable part of life on earth.

If popular uprisings occurred "in all governments at all times," they were nonetheless most prevalent in free governments. Tyrants imposed order and submission upon their subjects by force. Only under free governments were the people "nervous," spirited, ready and able to react against unjust provocations. As such, popular insurrections could be interpreted as "Symptoms of a strong and healthy Constitution" even while they indicated some lesser shortcoming in administration. It would be futile, Josiah Quincy, Jr., said in 1770, to expect "that pacific, timid, obsequious, and servile temper, so predominant in more despotic governments," from those who lived under free British institutions. From "our happy constitution," he claimed, there resulted as "very natural Effects" an "impatience of injuries, and a strong resentment of insults."

Occasional manifestations of this popular spirit were in fact "an evil . . . productive of good"; they clearly brought popular feelings—particularly those of the mob—to bear on public authority; and, as Thomas Jefferson argued most cogently in 1787, they tended to hold rulers "to the true principles of their institutions" and so provided "a medicine necessary for the sound health of government." Thus, members of the British House of Lords could seriously argue that "rioting is an essential part of our constitution." Even the conservative Thomas Hutchinson remarked in 1768 that "Mobs, a sort of them at least, are constitutional."

There were, however, distinct limits to colonial toleration of upheavals. It was always understood that insofar as uprisings abandoned their moderation and purposefulness, insofar as they ceased to be curative forces in society and threatened "running to such excesses, as will overturn the whole system of government," "strong discouragements" had to be provided against them. This desire to maintain the orderly rule of law led legislatures in England and the colonies to pass anti-riot statutes and to make strong efforts—in the words of a 1753 Massachusetts law—to discountenance "a mobbish temper and spirit in . . . the inhabitants," that would oppose "all government and order." . . .

Even in discouraging popular disorder, then, colonial legislators seemed as intent upon preventing any perversion of the forces of law and order by established authorities as with chastising insurgents. As such, the measures enacted by them to deal with insurrections were shaped by their experience with and understanding of popular uprisings. Since turbulence indicated above all some shortcoming in government, it was never to be met by increasing the authorities' power of suppression. It was "far less dangerous to the Freedom of a State" to allow "the laws to be trampled upon, by the licence among the rabble . . . than to dispence with their force by an act of power." Uprisings were to be answered by reform, by attacking the "disease"—to use John Jay's term of 1786—that lay behind them rather than by suppressing its "Symptoms." And ultimately, as William Samuel

Johnson observed in 1768, "the only effectual way to prevent them is to govern with wisdom, justice, and moderation."

✠ *F U R T H E R   R E A D I N G*

Willi Paul Adams, *The First American Constitutions: Republican Ideology and the Making of the State Constitutions in the Revolutionary Era* (1980)

Bernard Bailyn, *The Ideological Origins of the American Revolution* (1967)

John Murrin, "The Great Inversion, or Court Versus Country: A Comparison of the Revolution Settlements in England (1688–1721) and America (1776–1816)," in J. G. A. Pocock, ed., *Three British Evolutions: 1641, 1688, 1776* (1980): 368–455

Robert R. Palmer, "The People as Constituent Power," in Jack P. Greene, ed., *The Reinterpretation of the American Revolution, 1763–1789* (1968): 338–361.

J. G. A. Pocock, *The Machiavellian Moment: Florentine Political Thought and the Atlantic Republican Tradition* (1975)

John Phillip Reid, *The Concept of Representation in the Age of the American Revolution* (1989)

———, *The Constitutional History of the American Revolution: The Authority of Rights* (1986)

———, *The Constitutional History of the American Revolution: The Authority to Tax* (1987)

M. H. Smith, *The Writs of Assistance Case* (1978)

Corrine Comstock Weston, *English Constitutional Thought and the House of Lords, 1556–1832* (1965)

Garry Wills, *Inventing America: Jefferson's Declaration of Independence* (1979)

C H A P T E R
4

Creating the American Republic, 1787

⌗

Generations of scholars have puzzled over the intent and motivation of the framers of the Constitution. The reason for the continuing interest in the Philadelphia convention and the ratification of its work is easy to explain: because we rely on historical precedent to legitimate our constitutional order, each generation of Americans has turned with renewed interest to the perennial question of what the framers hoped to accomplish. Historians have also studied the convention as a way of gauging the meaning of the Revolution.

Earlier scholars, among them Charles A. Beard, argued that the framers undermined the localistic and democratic impulses that they believed characterized the Revolution. According to this progressive interpretation, the framers placed property interests above human liberty and weakened the local democracy and state sovereignty fostered by the Articles of Confederation. They established a central government with sufficient power to promote commerce and manufacturing at the expense of agriculture.

More recent scholarship, however, has offered a more complex view of the relationship between the Revolution and the Constitution. Scholars from the republican school of interpretation, such as Bernard Bailyn and his student Gordon Wood, agree with the progressive argument that the delegates enhanced the power of the central government to provide greater protection for property rights. The Constitution, they believe, was socially and economically conservative in thrust. Yet Wood and others argue that the document was also revolutionary in the constitutional theory that it embraced.

As such, the Constitution was a fitting climax to events begun in 1776, for the revolutionaries had intended to frame a new theory of constitutionalism that would allow them to reorder their politics. The delegates in Philadelphia succeeded in giving an entirely new meaning to ideas such as separation of powers, judicial review, federalism, representation, higher law, and popular sovereignty. As a result, the Constitution was something radically new; it was distinctive worldwide.

✠ *D O C U M E N T S*
_____

Any understanding of the convention must begin with a consideration of the document that the delegates set about revising, the Articles of Confederation—the United States' first national constitution. The Articles (which appear in the appendix of this volume) are unfortunately viewed as the scheme of government that did not work, and therefore as not worthy of consideration. But the Articles are better understood when they are juxtaposed with the Constitution and seen as an alternative approach to the problems of establishing a national political order, providing for the protection of individual rights, and dealing with a hostile world. These same considerations, of course, also figured in the constitutional convention, as the lengthy debates over the structure of the new government make clear.

Edmund Randolph submitted the large-state, or Virginia, plan, and William Paterson urged the small-state, or New Jersey, plan on the convention. Alexander Hamilton, perhaps the most aggressive proponent of a powerful national government in the convention, advocated his own scheme. Hamilton's proposal stirred little enthusiasm, but it is nonetheless an instructive counterpoint to the other plans, as well as to the document that the delegates ultimately embraced. These three blueprints for the new government are reprinted in the first selection.

Throughout the sessions, the issue of representation fueled the debates over the structure of the new government. Existing constitutional theory held that a republic could exist only in a small geographic area with a homogeneous and well-educated population. The framers—with James Madison of Virginia leading the way—exploded this theory by adopting the idea that only through a republic extended over a large geographic area could individual liberty be sustained. The debate over the direct election of members of the House of Representatives and the selection of senators by the state legislatures, presented in the second selection, reveals the way in which the delegates reshaped existing constitutional theory.

The question of representation also figured in the debates over whether or not the Constitution should support slavery (it is nowhere specifically mentioned). The debates reprinted here concern the three-fifths clause, which counted each slave as three-fifths of a person for purposes of representation. The arguments over the three-fifths clause reveal not only the founders' dilemma over slavery but also incipient sectional tensions, which would grow and become an important factor in American constitutional development throughout the Civil War era.

Finally, beyond the question of how to organize the existing states into a new Union, the delegates had to resolve how to govern new states created from unorganized territory and on what terms to admit them to the Union. The Northwest Ordinance, adopted by the Continental Congress while the convention was meeting, addressed those concerns as well as the future of slavery outside the South. Many historians believe that the ordinance, the final document in this chapter, was a crucial reason why northern delegates agreed to concessions, such as the three-fifths clause, that made the Constitution acceptable to the South.

Proposed Plans for the National Government

a. The Virginia, or Randolph, Plan, May 29, 1787

1. Resolved that the Articles of Confederation ought to be so corrected and enlarged as to accomplish the objects proposed by their institution; namely "common defence, security of liberty and general welfare."

2. Resolved therefore that the rights of suffrage in the National Legislature ought to be proportioned to the Quotas of contribution, or to the number of free inhabitants, as the one or the other rule may seem best in different cases.

3. Resolved that the National Legislature ought to consist of two branches.

4. Resolved that the members of the first branch of the National Legislature ought to be elected by the people of the several States every   for the terms of   ; to be of the age of   years at least, to receive liberal stipends by which they may be compensated for the devotion of their time to public service, to be ineligible to any office established by a particular State, or under the authority of the United States, except those peculiarly belonging to the functions of the first branch, during the term of service, and for the space of   after its expiration; to be incapable of reelection for the space of   after the expiration of their term of service, and to be subject to recall.

5. Resolved that the members of the second branch of the National Legislature ought to be elected by those of the first, out of a proper number of persons nominated by the individual Legislatures, to be of the age of   years at least; to hold their offices for a term sufficient to ensure their independency; to receive liberal stipends, by which they may be compensated for the devotion of their time to public service; and to be ineligible to any office established by a particular State, or under the authority of the United States, except those peculiarly belonging to the functions of the second branch, during the term of service, and for the space of   after the expiration thereof.

6. Resolved that each branch ought to possess the right of originating Acts; that the National Legislature ought to be impowered to enjoy the Legislative Rights vested in Congress by the Confederation and moreover to legislate in all cases to which the separate States are incompetent, or in which the harmony of the United States may be interrupted by the exercise of individual Legislation; to negative all laws passed by the several States, contravening in the opinion of the National Legislature the articles of Union; and to call forth the force of the Union against any member of the Union failing in its duty under the articles thereof.

7. Resolved that a National Executive be instituted; to be chosen by the National Legislature for the term of   years; to receive punctually, at stated times, a fixed compensation for the services rendered, in which no increase or diminution shall be made so as to affect the Magistracy, existing at the time of the increase or diminution, and to be ineligible a second time;

and that besides a general authority to execute the National laws, it ought to enjoy the Executive rights vested in Congress by the Confederation.

8. Resolved that the Executive and a convenient number of the National Judiciary, ought to compose a Council or revision with authority to examine every act of the National Legislature before it shall operate, and every act of a particular Legislature before a Negative thereon shall be final; and that the dissent of the said Council shall amount to a rejection, unless the Act of the National Legislature be passed again, or that of a particular Legislature be again negatived by   of the members of each branch.

9. Resolved that a National Judiciary be established to consist of one or more supreme tribunals, and of inferior tribunals to be chosen by the National Legislature, to hold their offices during good behaviour; and to receive punctually at stated times fixed compensation for their services, in which no increase or diminution shall be made so as to affect the persons actually in office at the time of such increase or diminution. That the jurisdiction of the inferior tribunals shall be to hear and determine in the first instance, and of the supreme tribunal to hear and determine in the dernier resort, all piracies and felonies on the high seas, captures from an enemy; cases in which foreigners or citizens of other States applying to such jurisdictions may be interested, or which respect the collection of the National revenue; impeachments of any National officers, and questions which may involve the national peace and harmony.

10. Resolved that provision ought to be made for the admission of States lawfully arising within the limits of the United States, whether from a voluntary junction of Government and Territory or otherwise, with the consent of a number of voices in the National legislature less than the whole.

11. Resolved that a Republican Government and the territory of each State, except in the instance of a voluntary junction of Government and territory, ought to be guaranteed by the United States to each State.

12. Resolved that provision ought to be made for the continuance of Congress and their authorities and privileges, until a given day after the reform of the articles of Union shall be adopted, and for the completion of all their engagements.

13. Resolved that provision ought to be made for the amendment of the Articles of Union whensoever it shall seem necessary, and that the assent of the National Legislature ought not to be required thereto.

14. Resolved that the Legislative, Executive, and Judiciary powers within the several States ought to be bound by oath to support the articles of Union.

15. Resolved that the amendments which shall be offered to the Confederation, by the Convention ought at a proper time, or times, after the approbation of Congress to be submitted to an assembly or assemblies of Representatives, recommended by the several Legislatures to be expressly chosen by the people, to consider and decide thereon.

b. The New Jersey, or Paterson, Plan, June 15, 1787

1. Resolved that the Articles of Confederation ought to be so revised, corrected, and enlarged as to render the federal Constitution adequate to the exigencies of Government, and the preservation of the Union.

2. Resolved that in addition to the powers vested in the United States in Congress, by the present existing articles of Confederation, they be authorized to pass acts for raising a revenue, by levying a duty or duties on all goods or merchandizes of foreign growth or manufacture, imported into any part of the United States, by Stamps on paper, vellum or parchment, and by a postage on all letters or packages passing through the general post-office, to be applied to such federal purposes as they shall deem proper and expedient; to make rules and regulations for the collection thereof; and the same from time to time, to alter and amend in such manner as they shall think proper: to pass Acts for the regulation of trade and commerce as well with foreign nations as with each other; provided that all punishments, fines, forfeitures and penalties to be incurred for contravening such acts rules and regulations shall be adjudged by the Common law Judiciaries of the State in which any offence contrary to the true intent and meaning of such Acts rules and regulations shall have been committed or perpetrated, with liberty of commencing in the first instance all suits and prosecutions for that purpose, in the superior common law Judiciary in such state, subject nevertheless, for the correction of errors, both in law and fact in rendering Judgement, to an appeal to the Judiciary of the United States.

3. Resolved that whenever requisitions shall be necessary, instead of the rule for making requisitions mentioned in the articles of Confederation, the United States in Congress be authorized to make such requisitions in proportion to the whole number of white and other free citizens and inhabitants of every age sex and condition including those bound to servitude for a term of years and three fifths of all other persons not comprehended in the foregoing description, except Indians not paying taxes; that if such requisitions be not complied with, in the time specified therein, to direct the collection thereof in the non-complying States and for that purpose to devise and pass acts directing and authorizing the same; provided that none of the powers hereby vested in the United States in Congress shall be exercised without the consent of at least   States, and in that proportion if the number of Confederated States should hereafter be increased or diminished.

4. Resolved that the United States in Congress be authorized to elect a federal Executive to consist of   persons, to continue in office for the term of   years, to receive punctually at stated times a fixed compensation for their services, in which no increase or diminution shall be made so as to affect the persons composing the Executive at the time of such increase or diminution, to be paid out of the federal treasury; to be incapable of holding any other office or appointment during their time of service and for   years thereafter; to be ineligible a second time, and removeable by Congress on application by a majority of the Executives of the several States; that the Executives besides their general authority to execute the

federal acts ought to appoint all federal officers not otherwise provided for, and to direct all military operations; provided that none of the persons composing the federal Executive shall on any occasion take command of any troops so as personally to conduct any enterprise as General or in other capacity.

5. Resolved that a federal Judiciary be established to consist of a supreme tribunal the Judges of which to be appointed by the Executive, and to hold their offices during good behaviour, to receive punctually at stated times a fixed compensation for their services in which no increase or diminution shall be made so as to affect persons actually in office at the time of such increase or diminution; that the Judiciary so established shall have authority to hear and determine in the first instance on all impeachments of federal officers, and by way of appeal in the dernier resort in all cases touching the rights of Ambassadors, in all cases of captures from an enemy, in all cases of piracies and felonies on the high Seas, in all cases in which foreigners may be interested, in the construction of any treaty or treaties, or which may arise on any of the Acts for regulation of trade, or the collection of the federal Revenue: that none of the Judiciary shall during the time they remain in office be capable of receiving or holding any other office or appointment during the time of service, or for thereafter.

6. Resolved that all Acts of the United States in Congress made by virtue and in pursuance of the powers hereby and by the articles of Confederation vested in them, and all Treaties made and ratified under the authority of the United States, shall be the supreme law of the respective States so far forth as those Acts or Treaties shall relate to the said States or their Citizens, and that the Judiciary of the several States shall be bound thereby in their decisions, any thing in the respective laws of the Individual States to the contrary notwithstanding; and that if any State, or any body of men in any State shall oppose or prevent carrying into execution such acts or treaties, the federal Executive shall be authorized to call forth the power of the Confederated States, or so much thereof as may be necessary to enforce and compel an obedience to such Acts or an observance of such Treaties.

7. Resolved that provision be made for the admission of new States into the Union.

8. Resolved the rule for naturalization ought to be the same in every State.

9. Resolved that a Citizen of one State committing an offence in another State of the Union, shall be deemed guilty of the same offence as if it had been committed by a Citizen of the State in which the offence was committed.

c. The Hamilton Plan, June 18, 1787

1. The Supreme Legislative power of the United States of America to be vested in two distinct bodies of men; the one to be called the Assembly, the other the Senate who together shall form the Legislature of the United

States with power to pass all laws whatsoever subject to the Negative hereafter mentioned.

2. The Assembly to consist of persons elected by the people to serve for three years.

3. The Senate to consist of persons elected to serve during good behaviour; their election to be made by electors chosen for that purpose by the people. In order to this, the States to be divided into election districts. On the death, removal or resignation of any Senator his place to be filled out of the district from which he came.

4. The supreme Executive authority of the United States to be vested in a Governor, to be elected to serve during good behaviour—His election to be made by Electors chosen by electors chosen by the people in the Election Districts aforesaid; or by electors chosen for that purpose by the respective Legislatures—provided that if an election be not made within a limited time, the President of the Senate shall be the Governor. The Governor to have a negative upon all laws about to be passed—and the execution of all laws passed—to be the Commander-in-Chief of the land and naval forces and of the militia of the United States—to have the entire direction of war when authorized or begun—to have, with the advice and approbation of the Senate, the power of making all treaties—to have the appointment of the heads or chief officers of the departments of finance, war, and foreign affairs—to have the nomination of all other officers (ambassadors to foreign nations included) subject to the approbation or rejection of the Senate—to have the power of pardoning all offences but treason, which he shall not pardon without the approbation of the Senate.

5. On the death, resignation, or removal of the Governor, his authorities to be exercised by the President of the Senate (until a successor be appointed).

6. The Senate to have the sole power of declaring war—the power of advising and approving all treaties—the power of approving or rejecting all appointments of officers except the heads or chiefs of the departments of finance, war, and foreign affairs.

7. The supreme judicial authority of the United States to be vested in twelve judges, to hold their offices during good behavior, with adequate and permanent salaries. This court to have original jurisdiction in all causes of capture, and an appellate jurisdiction (from the courts of the several States) in all causes in which the revenues of the General Government or the citizens of foreign nations are concerned.

8. The Legislature of the United States to have power to institute courts in each State for the determination of all causes of capture and of all matters relating to their revenues, or in which the citizens of foreign nations are concerned.

9. The Governor, Senators, and all officers of the United States to be liable to impeachment for mal and corrupt conduct, and upon conviction to be removed from office, and disqualified for holding any place of trust or profit. All impeachments to be tried by a court, to consist of the judges of the Supreme Court, chief or senior judge of the Superior Court of law of

each State—provided that such judge hold his place during good behavior and have a permanent salary.

10. All laws of the particular States contrary to the Constitution or laws of the United States to be utterly void. And the better to prevent such laws being passed the Governor or President of each State shall be appointed by the General Government, and shall have a negative upon the laws about to be passed in the State of which he is Governor or President.

11. No State to have any forces, land or naval—and the militia of all the States to be under the sole and exclusive direction of the United States, the officers of which to be appointed and commissioned by them.

The Debate over Establishing the Federal Legislature, May–June 1787

Thursday, May 31

Resol: 4. first clause "that the members of the first branch of the National Legislature ought to be elected by the people of the several States" being taken up,

Mr. Sherman opposed the election by the people, insisting that it ought to be by the State Legislatures. The people he said, immediately should have as little to do as may be about the Government. They want information and are constantly liable to be misled.

Mr. Gerry. The evils we experience flow from the excess of democracy. The people do not want virtue, but are the dupes of pretended patriots. In Massts. it had been fully confirmed by experience that they are daily misled into the most baneful measures and opinions by the false reports circulated by designing men, and which no one on the spot can refute. One principal evil arises from the want of due provision for those employed in the administration of Governmt. It would seem to be a maxim of democracy to starve the public servants. He [Mr. Gerry] mentioned the popular clamour in Massts. for the reduction of salaries and the attack made on that of the Govt. though secured by the spirit of the Constitution itself. He had he said been too republican heretofore: he was still however republican, but had been taught by experience the danger of the levelling spirit.

Mr. Mason, argued strongly for an election of the larger branch by the people. It was to be the grand depository of the democratic principle of the Govts. It was, so to speak, to be our House of Commons—It ought to know & sympathise with every part of the community; and ought therefore to be taken not only from different parts of the whole republic, but also from different districts of the larger members of it, which had in several instances particularly in Virga., different interests and views arising from difference of produce, of habits &c &c. He admitted that we had been too democratic but was afraid we sd. incautiously run into the opposite extreme. We ought to attend to the rights of every class of people. He had often wondered at the indifference of the superior classes of society to this dictate of humanity & policy; considering that however affluent their circumstances, or elevated their situations, might be, the course of a few years, not only might but certainly would, distribute their posterity throughout the lowest classes of Society. Every selfish motive therefore, every family attachment, ought to recommend such a system of policy as would provide no less carefully for the rights and happiness of the lowest than of the highest orders of Citizens.

Mr. Wilson contended strenuously for drawing the most numerous branch of the Legislature immediately from the people. He was for raising the federal pyramid to a considerable altitude, and for that reason wished to give it as broad a basis as possible. No government could long subsist without the confidence of the people. In a republican Government, this confidence was peculiarly essential. He also thought it wrong to increase the weight of the State Legislatures by making them the electors of the national Legislature. All interference between the general and local Governmts. should be obviated as much as possible. On examination it would be found that the opposition of States to federal measures had proceeded much more from the officers of the States, than from the people at large.

Mr. Madison considered the popular election of one branch of the National Legislature as essential to every plan of free Government. He observed that in some of the States one branch of the Legislature was composed of men already removed from the people by an intervening body of electors. That if the first branch of the general legislature should be elected by the State Legislatures, the second branch elected by the first—the Executive by the second together with the first; and other appointments again made for subordinate purposes by the Executive, the people would be lost sight of altogether; and the necessary sympathy between them and their rulers and officers, too little felt. He was an advocate for the policy of refining the popular appointments by successive filtrations, but thought it might be pushed too far. He wished the expedient to be resorted to only in the appointment of the second branch of the Legislature, and in the Executive & judiciary branches of the Government. He thought too that the great fabric to be raised woult be more stable and durable, if it should rest on the solid foundation of the people themselves, than if it should stand merely on the pillars of the Legislatures.

Mr. Gerry did not like the election by the people. The maxims taken from the British constitution were often fallacious when applied to our situation which was extremely different. Experience he said had shewn that the State legislatures drawn immediately from the people did not always possess their confidence. He had no objection however to an election by the people if it were so qualified that men of honor & character might not be unwilling to be joined in the appointments. He seemed to think the people might nominate a certain number out of which the State legislatures should be bound to choose.

Mr. Butler thought an election by the people an impracticable mode.

On the question for an election of the first branch of the national Legislature by the people.

Massts. ay. Connect. divd. N. York ay. N. Jersey no. Pena. ay. Delawe. divd. Va. ay. N. C. ay. S. C. no. Georga. ay.

The Committee proceeded to Resolution 5. "that the second, [or senatorial] branch of the National Legislature ought to be chosen by the first branch out of persons nominated by the State Legislatures."

Mr. **Spaight** contended that the 2d. branch ought to be chosen by the State Legislatures and moved an amendment to that effect.

Mr. **Wilson** opposed both a nomination by the State Legislatures, and an election by the first branch of the national Legislature, because the second branch of the latter, ought to be independent of both. He thought both branches of the National Legislature ought to be chosen by the people, but was not prepared with a specific proposition. He suggested the mode of chusing the Senate of N. York to wit of uniting several election districts, for one branch, in chusing members for the other branch, as a good model.

Mr. **Madison** observed that such a mode would destroy the influence of the smaller States associated with larger ones in the same district; as the latter would chuse from within themselves, altho' better men might be found in the former. The election of Senators in Virga. where large & small counties were often formed into one district for the purpose, had illustrated this consequence Local partiality, would often prefer a resident within the County or State, to a candidate of superior merit residing out of it. Less merit also in a resident would be more known throughout his own State.

Mr. **Sherman** favored an election of one member by each of the State Legislature.

Mr. **Pinkney** moved to strike out the "nomination by the State Legislatures." On this question.

Massts. no. Cont. no. N. Y. no. N. J. no. Pena. no. Del. divd. Va. no. N. C. no. S. C. no. Georg. no.

On the whole question for electing by the first branch out of nominations by the State Legislatures, Mass. ay. Cont. no. N. Y. no. N. Jersey. no. Pena. no. Del. no. Virga. ay. N. C. no. S. C. ay. Ga. no.

So the clause was disagreed to & a chasm left in this part of the plan.

Wednesday, June 6

Mr. **Pinkney** according to previous notice & rule obtained, moved "that the first branch of the national Legislature be elected by the State Legislatures, and not by the people." contending that the people were less fit Judges in such a case, and that the Legislature would be less likely to promote the adoption of the new Government, if they were to be excluded from all share in it.

Mr. **Rutlidge** 2ded. the motion.

Mr. **Gerry.** Much depends on the mode of election. In England, the people will probably lose their liberty from the smallness of the proportion having a right of suffrage. Our danger arises from the opposite extreme: hence in Massts. the worst men get into the Legislature. Several members of that Body had lately been convicted of infamous crimes. Men of indigence, ignorance & baseness, spare no pains, however dirty to carry their point agst. men who are superior to the artifices practised. He was not disposed to run into extremes. He was as much principled as ever agst. aristocracy and monarchy. It was necessary on the one hand that the people should appoint one branch of the Govt. in order to inspire them with the necessary confidence. But he wished the election on the other to be so modified as to secure more effectually a just preference of merit. His idea was that the people should nominate certain persons in certain districts, out of whom the State Legislature shd. make the appointment.

Mr. Wilson. He wished for vigor in the Govt., but he wished that vigorous authority to flow immediately from the legitimate source of all authority. The Govt. ought to possess not only 1st. the *force,* but 2dly. the *mind or sense* of the people at large. The Legislature ought to be the most exact transcript of the whole Society. Representation is made necessary only because it is impossible for the people to act collectively. The opposition was to be expected he said from the *Governments,* not from the Citizens of the States. The latter had parted as was observed [by Mr. King] with all the necessary powers; and it was immaterial to them, by whom they were exercised, if well exercised. The State officers were to be the losers of power. The people he supposed would be rather more attached to the national Govt. than to the State Govts. as being more important in itself, and more flattering to their pride. There is no danger of improper elections if made by *large* districts. Bad elections proceed from the smallness of the districts which give an opportunity to bad men to intrigue themselves into office.

Mr. Sherman. If it were in view to abolish the State Govt. the elections ought to be by the people. If the State Govts. are to be continued, it is necessary in order to preserve harmony between the National & State Govts. that the elections to the former shd. be made by the latter. The right of participating in the National Govt. would be sufficiently secured to the people by their election of the State Legislatures. The objects of the Union, he thought were few. 1. defence agst. foreign danger. 2 agst. internal disputes & a resort to force. 3. Treaties with foreign nations. 4 regulating foreign commerce, & drawing revenue from it. These & perhaps a few lesser objects alone rendered a Confederation of the States necessary. All other matters civil & criminal would be much better in the hands of the States. The people are more happy in small than large States. States may indeed be too small as Rhode Island, & thereby be too subject to faction. Some others were perhaps too large, the powers of Govt. not being able to pervade them. He was for giving the General Govt. power to legislate and execute within a defined province.

Col. Mason. Under the existing Confederacy, Congs. represent the *States* not the *people* of the States: their acts operate on the *States,* not the individuals. The case will be changed in the new plan of Govt. The people will be represented; they ought therefore to choose the Representatives. The requisites in actual representation are that the Reps. should sympathize with their constituents; shd. think as they think, & feel as they feel; and that for these purposes shd. even be residents among them. Much he sd. had been alledged agst. democratic elections. He admitted that much might be said;

but it was to be considered that no Govt. was free from imperfections & evils; and that improper elections in many instances, were inseparable from Republican Govts. But compare these with the advantage of this Form in favor of the rights of the people, in favor of human nature. He was persuaded there was a better chance for proper elections by the people, if divided into large districts, than by the State Legislatures. Paper money had been issued by the latter when the former were against it. Was it to be supposed that the State Legislatures then wd. not send to the Natl. legislature patrons of such projects, if the choice depended on them.

Mr. Madison considered an election of one branch at least of the Legislature by the people immediately, as a clear principle of free Govt. and that this mode under proper regulations had the additional advantage of securing better representatives, as well as of avoiding too great an agency of the State Governments in the General one.—He differed from the member from Connecticut [Mr. Sherman] in thinking the objects mentioned to be all the principal ones that required a National Govt. Those were certainly important and necessary objects; but he combined with them the necessity of providing more effectually for the security of private rights, and the steady dispensation of Justice. Interferences with these were evils which had more perhaps than any thing else, produced this convention. Was it to be supposed that republican liberty could long exist under the abuses of it practised in some of the States. The gentleman [Mr. Sherman] had admitted that in a very small State, faction & oppression wd. prevail. It was to be inferred then that wherever these prevailed the State was too small. Had they not prevailed in the largest as well as the smallest tho' less than in the smallest; and were we not thence admonished to enlarge the sphere as far as the nature of the Govt. would admit. This was the only defence agst. the inconveniencies of democracy consistent with the democratic form of Govt. All civilized Societies would be divided into different Sects, Factions, & interests, as they happened to consist of rich & poor, debtors & creditors, the landed, the manufacturing, the commercial interests, the inhabitants of this district or that district, the followers of this political leader or that political leader, the disciples of this religious Sect or that religious Sect. In all cases where a majority are united by a common interest or passion, the rights of the minority are in danger. What motives are to restrain them? A prudent regard to the maxim that honesty is the best policy is found by experience to be as little regarded by bodies of men as by individuals. Respect for character is always diminished in proportion to the number among whom the blame or praise is to be divided. Conscience, the only remaining tie, is known to be inadequate in individuals: In large numbers, little is to be expected from it. Besides, Religion itself may become a motive to persecution & oppression.—These observations are verified by the Histories of every Country antient & modern.

Mr. Read. Too much attachment is betrayed to the State Governts. We must look beyond their continuance. A national Govt. must soon of necessity swallow all of them up. They will soon be reduced to the mere office of electing the National Senate. He was agst. patching up the old federal System: he hoped the idea wd. be dismissed. It would be like putting new cloth on an old garment. The confederation was founded on temporary principles. It cannot last: it cannot be amended. If we do not establish a good Govt. on new principles, we must either go to ruin, or have the work to do over again. The people at large are wrongly suspected of being averse to a Genl. Govt. The aversion lies among interested men who possess their confidence.

Mr. Pierce was for an election by the people as to the 1st. branch & by the States as to the 2d. branch; by which means the Citizens of the States wd. be represented both *individually* & *collectively*.

General Pinkney wished to have a good National Govt. & at the same time to leave a considerable share of power in the States. An election of either branch by the people scattered as they are in many States, particularly in S. Carolina was totally impracticable. He differed from gentlemen who thought that a choice by the people wd. be a better guard agst. bad measures, than by the Legislatures. A majority of the people in S. Carolina were notoriously for paper money as a legal tender; the Legislature had refused to make it a legal tender. The reason was that the latter had some sense of character and were restrained by that consideration. The State Legislatures also he said would be more jealous, & more ready to thwart the National Govt., if excluded from a participation in it. The Idea of abolishing these Legislatures wd. never go down.

Mr. Wilson, would not have spoken again, but for what had fallen from Mr. Read; namely, that the idea of preserving the State Govts. ought to be abandoned. He saw no incompatibility between the National & State Govts. provided the latter were restrained to certain local purposes; nor any probability of their being devoured by the former. In all confederated Systems antient & modern the reverse had happened; the Generality being destroyed gradually by the usurpations of the parts composing it.

On the question for electing the 1st. branch by the State Legislatures as moved by Mr. Pinkney: it was negatived:

Mass. no. Ct. ay. N. Y. no. N. J. ay. Pa. no. Del. no. Md. no. Va. no. N. C. no. S. C. ay. Geo. no.

Thursday, June 7

The Clause providing for ye. appointment of the 2d. branch of the national Legislature, having lain blank since the last vote on the mode of electing it, to wit, by the 1st. branch, Mr. Dickenson now moved "that the members of the 2d. branch ought to be chosen by the individual Legislatures."

Mr. Sherman seconded the motion; observing that the particular States would thus become interested in supporting the national Govert. and that a due harmony between the two Governments would be maintained. He admitted that the two ought to have separate and distinct jurisdictions, but that they ought to have a mutual interest in supporting each other.

Mr. Pinkney. If the small States should be allowed one Senator only, the number will be too great, there will be 80 at least.

Mr. Dickenson had two reasons for his motion. 1. because the sense of the States would be better collected through their Governments; than immediately from the people at large; 2. because he wished the Senate to consist of the most distinguished characters, distinguished for their rank in life and their weight of property, and bearing as strong a likeness to the British House of Lords as possible; and he thought such characters more likely to be selected by the State Legislatures, than in any other mode. The greatness of the number has no objection with him. He hoped there would be 80 and twice 80. of them. If their number should be small, the popular branch could not be balanced by them. The legislature of a numerous people ought to be a numerous body.

Mr. Wilson. If we are to establish a national Government, that Government ought to flow from the people at large. If one branch of it should be chosen by the Legislatures, and the other by the people, the two branches will rest on different foundations, and dissensions will naturally arise between them. He wished the Senate to be elected by the people as well as the other branch, and the people might be divided into proper districts for the purpose & moved to postpone the motion of Mr. Dickenson, in order to take up one of that import.

Mr. Morris 2ded. him.

Mr. Madison, if the motion [of Mr. Dickenson] should be agreed to, we must either depart from the doctrine of proportional representation; or admit into the Senate a very large number of members. The first is inadmissible, being evidently unjust. The second is inexpedient.

On Mr. Dickinson's motion for an appointment of the Senate by the State Legislatures.

Mass. ay. Ct. ay. N. Y. ay. Pa. ay. Del. ay. Md. ay. Va. ay. N. C. ay. S. C. ay. Geo. ay.

The Debate over Slavery and Representation in the Constitution, June–July 1787

Saturday, June 30

Mr. Madison: But he contended that the States were divided into different interests not by their difference of size, but by other circumstances; the most material of which resulted partly from climate, but principally from the effects of their having or not having slaves. These two causes concurred in forming the great division of interests in the U. States. It did not lie between the large & small States: It lay between the Northern & Southern, and if any defensive power were necessary, it ought to be mutually given to these two interests. He was so strongly impressed with this important truth that he had been casting about in his mind for some expedient that would answer the purpose. The one which had occurred was that instead of proportioning the votes of the States in both branches, to their respective numbers of inhabitants computing the slaves in the ratio of 5 to 3, they should be represented in one branch according to the number of free inhabitants only; and in the other according to the whole no. counting the slaves as if free. By this arrangement the Southern Scale would have the advantage in one House, and the Northern in the other. He had been restrained from proposing this expedient by two considerations: one was his unwillingness to urge any diversity of interests on an occasion where it is but too apt to arise of itself—the other was, the inequality of powers that must be vested in the two branches, and which wd. destroy the equilibrium of interests.

Wednesday, July 11

Mr. Randolph's motion requiring the Legislre. to take a periodical census for the purpose of redressing inequalities in the Representation, was resumed.

Mr. Sherman was agst. shackling the Legislature too much. We ought to choose wise & good men, and then confide in them.

Mr. Mason. The greater the difficulty we find in fixing a proper rule of Representation, the more unwilling ought we to be, to throw the task from ourselves, on the Genl. Legislre. He did not object to the conjectural ratio which was to prevail in the outset; but considered a Revision from time to time according to some permanent & precise standard as essential to ye. fair representation required in the 1st. branch. According to the present population of America, the Northn. part of it had a right to preponderate, and he could not deny it. But he wished it not to preponderate hereafter when the reason no longer continued. From the nature of man we may be sure, that those who have power in their hands will not give it up while they can retain it. On the contrary we know they will always when they can rather increase it. If the S. States therefore should have $\frac{3}{4}$ of the people of America within their limits, the Northern will hold fast the majority of Representatives. $\frac{1}{4}$ will govern the $\frac{3}{4}$. The S. States will complain: but they may complain from generation to generation without redress. Unless some principle therefore which will do justice to them hereafter shall be inserted in the Constitution, disagreeable as the declaration was to him, he must declare he could neither vote for the system here, nor support it, in his State. Strong objections had been drawn from the danger to the Atlantic interests from new Western States. Ought we to sacrifice what we know to be right in itself, lest it should prove favorable to States which are not yet in existence. If the Western States are to be admitted into the Union, as they arise, they must, he wd. repeat, be treated as equals, and subjected to no degrading discriminations. They will have the same pride & other passions which we have, and will either not unite with or will speedily revolt from the Union, if they are not in all respects placed on an equal footing with their brethren. It has been said they will be poor, and unable to make equal contributions to the general Treasury. He did not know but that in time they would be both more numerous & more wealthy than their Atlantic brethren. The extent & fertility of their soil, made this probable; and though Spain might for a time deprive them of the natural outlet for their productions, yet she will, because she must, finally yield to their demands. He urged that numbers of inhabitants; though not always a precise standard of wealth was sufficiently so for every substantial purpose.

Mr. Williamson was for making it the duty of the Legislature to do what was right & not leaving it at liberty to do or not do it. He moved that Mr. Randolph's proposition be postpond. in order to consider the following "that in order to ascertain the alterations that may happen in the population & wealth of the several States, a census shall be taken of the free white inhabitants and ⅗ths. of those of other descriptions on the 1st. year after this Government shall have been adopted and every   year thereafter; and that the Representation be regulated accordingly."

Mr. Randolph agreed that Mr. Williamson's proposition should stand in the place of his. He observed that the ratio fixt for the 1st. meeting was a mere conjecture, that it placed the power in the hands of that part of America, which could not always be entitled to it, that this power would not be voluntarily renounced; and that it was consequently the duty of the Convention to secure its renunciation when justice might so require; by some constitutional provisions. If equality between great & small States be inadmissible, because in that case unequal numbers of Constituents wd. be represented by equal number of votes; was it not equally inadmissible that a larger & more populous district of America should hereafter have less representation, than a smaller & less populous district. If a fair representation of the people be not secured, the injustice of the Govt. will shake it to its foundations. What relates to suffrage is justly stated by the celebrated Montesquieu, as a fundamental article in Republican Govts. If the danger suggested by Mr. Govr. Morris be real, of advantage being taken of the Legislature in pressing moments, it was an additional reason, for tying their hands in such a manner that they could not sacrifice their trust to momentary considerations. Congs. have pledged the public faith to New States, that they shall be admitted on equal terms. They never would nor ought to accede on any other. The census must be taken under the direction of the General Legislature. The States will be too much interested to take an impartial one for themselves.

Mr. Butler & Genl. Pinkney insisted that blacks be included in the rule of Representation, *equally* with the Whites: and for that purpose moved that the words "three fifths" be struck out.

Mr. Gerry thought that ⅗ of them was to say the least the full proportion that could be admitted.

Mr. Ghorum. This ratio was fixed by Congs. as a rule of taxation. Then it was urged by the Delegates representing the States having slaves that the blacks were still more inferior to freemen. At present when the ratio of representation is to be established, we are assured that they are equal to freemen. The arguments on ye. former occasion had convinced him that $\frac{3}{5}$ was pretty near the just proportion and he should vote according to the same opinion now.

Mr. Butler insisted that the labour of a slave in S. Carola. was as productive & valuable as that of a freeman in Massts., that as wealth was the great means of defence and utility to the Nation they were equally valuable to it with freemen; and that consequently an equal representation ought to be allowed for them in a Government which was instituted principally for the protection of property, and was itself to be supported by property.

Mr. Mason, could not agree to the motion, notwithstand it was favorable to Virga. because he thought it unjust. It was certain that the slaves were valuable, as they raised the value of land, increased the exports & imports, and of course the revenue, would supply the means of feeding & supporting an army, and might in case of emergency become themselves soldiers. As in these important respects they were useful to the community at large, they ought not to be excluded from the estimate of Representation. He could not however regard them as equal to freemen and could not vote for them as such. He added as worthy of remark, that the Southern States have this peculiar species of property, over & above the other species of property common to all the States.

Mr. Williamson reminded Mr. Ghorum that if the Southn. States contended for the inferiority of blacks to whites when taxation was in view, the Eastern States on the same occasion contended for their equality. He did not however, either then or now, concur in either extreme, but approved of the ratio of $\frac{3}{5}$.

On Mr. Butler's motion for considering blacks as equal to Whites in the apportionmt. of Representation.

Massts. no. Cont. no. [N. Y. not on floor.] N. J. no. Pa. no. Del. ay. Md. no. Va. no. N. C. no. S. C. ay. Geo. ay.

Mr. Govr. Morris said he had several objections to the proposition of Mr. Williamson. 1. It fettered the Legislature too much. 2. it would exclude some States altogether who would not have a sufficient number to entitle them to a single Representative. 3. it will not consist with the Resolution passed on Saturday last authorising the Legislature to adjust the Representation from time to time on the principles of population & wealth or with the principles of equity. If slaves were to be considered as inhabitants, not as wealth, then the sd. Resolution would not be pursued: If as wealth, then why is no other wealth but slaves included? These objections may perhaps be removed by amendments. His great objection was that the number of inhabitants was not a proper standard of wealth. The amazing difference between the comparative numbers & wealth of different Countries, rendered all reasoning superfluous on the subject. Numbers might with greater propriety be deemed a measure of strength, than of wealth, yet the late defence made by G. Britain, agst. her numerous enemies proved in the clearest manner, that it is entirely fallacious even in this respect.

Mr. King thought there was great force in the objections of Mr. Govr.

Morris: he would however accede to the proposition for the sake of doing something.

Mr. Rutlidge contended for the admission of wealth in the estimate by which Representation should be regulated. The Western States will not be able to contribute in proportion to their numbers; they shd. not therefore be represented in that proportion. The Atlantic States will not concur in such a plan. He moved that "at the end of   years after the 1st. meeting of the Legislature, and of every   years thereafter, the Legislature shall proportion the Representation according to the principles of wealth & population."

Mr. Sherman thought the number of people alone the best rule for measuring wealth as well as representation; and that if the Legislature were to be governed by wealth, they would be obliged to estimate it by numbers. He was at first for leaving the matter wholly to the discretion of the Legislature; but he had been convinced by the observations of [Mr. Randolph & Mr. Mason,] that the *periods* & the *rule,* of revising the Representation ought to be fixt by the Constitution.

Mr. Reid thought the Legislature ought not to be too much shackled. It would make the Constitution like Religious Creeds, embarrassing to those bound to conform to them & more likely to produce dissatisfaction and scism, than harmony and union.

Mr. Mason objected to Mr. Rutlidge's motion, as requiring of the Legislature something too indefinite & impracticable, and leaving them a pretext for doing nothing.

Mr. Wilson had himself no objection to leaving the Legislature entirely at liberty. But considered wealth as an impracticable rule.

Mr. Ghorum. If the Convention who are comparatively so little biassed by local views are so much perplexed, How can it be expected that the Legislature hereafter under the full biass of those views, will be able to settle a standard. He was convinced by the arguments of others & his own reflections, that the Convention ought to fix some standard or other.

Mr. Govr. Morris. The argts. of others & his own reflections had led him to a very different conclusion. If we can't agree on a rule that will be just at this time, how can we expect to find one that will be just in all times to come. Surely those who come after us will judge better of things present, than we can of things future. He could not persuade himself that numbers would be a just rule at any time. The remarks of [Mr. Mason] relative to the Western Country had not changed his opinion on that head. Among other objections it must be apparent they would not be able to furnish men equally enlightened, to share in the administration of our common interests. The Busy haunts of men not the remote wilderness, was the proper school of political Talents. If the Western people get the power into their hands they will ruin the Atlantic interests. The Back members are always most averse to the best measures. He mentioned the case of Pena. formerly. The lower part of the State had ye. power in the first instance. They kept it in ye. own hands & the Country was ye. better for it. Another objection with him agst. admitting the blacks into the census, was that the people of Pena.

would revolt at the idea of being put on a footing with slaves. They would reject any plan that was to have such an effect. Two objections had been raised agst. leaving the adjustment of the Representation from time, to time, to the discretion of the Legislature. The 1. was they would be unwilling to revise it at all. The 2. that by referring to *wealth* they would be bound by a rule which if willing, they would be unable to execute. The 1st. objn. distrusts their fidelity. But if their duty, their honor & their oaths will not bind them, let us not put into their hands our liberty, and all our other great interests: let us have no Govt. at all. 2. If these ties will bind them, we need not distrust the practicability of the rule. It was followed in part by the Come. in the apportionment of Representatives yesterday reported to the House. The best course that could be taken would be to leave the interests of the people to the Representatives of the people.

On the question on the first clause of Mr. Williamson's motion as to taking a census of the *free* inhabitants; it passed in the affirmative Masts. ay. Cont. ay. N. J. ay. Pa. ay. Del. no. Md. no. Va. ay. N. C. ay. S. C. no. Geo. no.

The next clause as to ⅗ of the negroes considered.

Mr. King. being much opposed to fixing numbers as the rule of representation, was particularly so on account of the blacks. He thought the admission of them along with Whites at all, would excite great discontents among the States having no slaves. He had never said as to any particular point that he would in no event acquiesce in & support it; but he wd. say that if in any case such a declaration was to be made by him, it would be in this. He remarked that in the temporary allotment of Representatives made by the Committee, the Southern States had received more than the number of their white & three fifths of their black inhabitants entitled them to.

Mr. Sherman. S. Carola. had not more beyond her proportion than N. York & N. Hampshire, nor either of them more than was necessary in order to avoid fractions or reducing them below their proportion. Georgia had more; but the rapid growth of that State seemed to justify it. In general the allotment might not be just, but considering all circumstances, he was satisfied with it.

Mr. Ghorum supported the propriety of establishing numbers as the rule. He said that in Massts. estimates had been taken in the different towns, and that persons had been curious enough to compare these estimates with the respective numbers of people; and it had been found even including Boston, that the most exact proportion prevailed between numbers & property. He was aware that there might be some weight in what had fallen from his colleague, as to the umbrage which might be taken by the people of the Eastern States. But he recollected that when the proposition of Congs. for changing the 8th. art: of Confedn. was before the Legislature of Massts. the only difficulty then was to satisfy them that the negroes ought not to have been counted equally with whites instead of being counted in the ratio of three fifths only.*

Mr. Wilson did not well see on what principle the admission of blacks in the proportion of three fifths could be explained. Are they admitted as Citizens? then why are they not admitted on an equality with White Citizens? are they admitted as property? then why is not other property admitted into the computation? These were difficulties however which he thought must be overruled by the necessity of compromise. He had some apprehensions also from the tendency of the blending of the blacks with the whites, to give disgust to the people of Pena. as had been intimated by his Colleague [Mr. Govr. Morris]. But he differed from him in thinking numbers of inhabts. so incorrect a measure of wealth. He had seen the Western settlemts. of Pa. and on a comparison of them with the City of Philada. could discover little other difference, than that property was more unequally divided among individuals here than there. Taking the same number in the aggregate in the two situations he believed there would be little difference in their wealth and ability to contribute to the public wants.

Mr. Govr. Morris was compelled to declare himself reduced to the dilemma of doing injustice to the Southern States or to human nature, and he must therefore do it to the former. For he could never agree to give such encouragement to the slave trade as would be given by allowing them a representation for their negroes, and he did not believe those States would ever confederate on terms that would deprive them of that trade.

On Question for agreeing to include ⅗ of the blacks

Masts. no. Cont. ay. N. J. no. Pa. no. Del. no. Mard. no. Va. ay. N. C. ay. S. C. no. Geo. ay.

On the question as to taking census "the first year after meeting of the Legislature"

Masts. ay. Cont. no. N. J. ay. Pa. ay. Del. ay. Md. no. Va. ay. N. C. ay. S. ay. Geo. no.

On filling the blank for the periodical census, with "15 years," Agreed to nem. con.

Mr. Madison moved to add after "15 years," the words "at least" that the Legislature might anticipate when circumstances were likely to render a particular year inconvenient.

On this motion for adding "at least," it passed in the negative the States being equally divided.

Mas. ay. Cont. no. N. J. no. Pa. no. Del. no. Md. no. Va. ay. N. C. ay. S. C. ay. Geo. ay.

A Change of the phraseology of the other clause so as to read; "and the Legislature shall alter or augment the representation accordingly" was agreed to nem. con.

On the question on the whole resolution of Mr. Williamson as amended.

---

* They were then to have been a rule of taxation only. [Footnote by Madison.]

Mas. no. Cont. no. N. J. no. Del. no. Md. no. Va. no. N. C. no. S. C. no. Geo. no.

Thursday, July 12

Mr. Govr. Morris moved to add to the clause empowering the Legislature to vary the Representation according to the principles of wealth & number of inhabts. a "proviso that taxation shall be in proportion to Representation."

Mr. Butler contended again that Representation sd. be according to the full number of inhabts. including all the blacks; admitting the justice of Mr. Govr. Morris's motion.

Mr. Mason also admitted the justice of the principle, but was afraid embarrassments might be occasioned to the Legislature by it. It might drive the Legislature to the plan of Requisitions.

Mr. Govr. Morris, admitted that some objections lay agst. his motion, but supposed they would be removed by restraining the rule to *direct* taxation. With regard to indirect taxes on *exports* & imports & on consumption, the rule would be inapplicable. Notwithstanding what had been said to the contrary he was persuaded that the imports & consumption were pretty nearly equal throughout the Union.

General Pinkney liked the idea. He thought it so just that it could not be objected to. But foresaw that if the revision of the census was left to the discretion of the legislature, it would never be carried into execution. The rule must be fixed, and the execution of it enforced by the Constitution. He was alarmed at what was said yesterday, concerning the negroes. He was now again alarmed at what had been thrown out concerning the taxing of exports. S. Carola. has in one year exported to the amount of £600,000 Sterling all which was the fruit of the labor of her blacks. Will she be represented in proportion to this amount? She will not. Neither ought she then to be subject to a tax on it. He hoped a clause would be inserted in the system, restraining the Legislature from a taxing Exports.

Mr. Wilson approved the principle, but could not see how it could be carried into execution; unless restrained to direct taxation.

Mr. Govr. Morris having so varied his Motion by inserting the word "direct." It passd. nem. con. as follows—"provided the always that direct taxation ought to be proportioned to representation."

Mr. Davie, said it was high time now to speak out. He saw that it was meant by some gentlemen to deprive the Southern States of any share of Representation for their blacks. He was sure that N. Carola. would never confederate on any terms that did not rate them at least as $\frac{3}{5}$. If the Eastern States meant therefore to exclude them altogether the business was at an end.

Dr. Johnson, thought that wealth and population were the true, equitable rule of representation; but he conceived that these two principles resolved themselves into one; population being the best measure of wealth. He concluded therefore that ye. number of people ought to be established as the rule, and that all descriptions including blacks *equally* with the whites; ought to fall within the computation. As various opinions had been expressed on the subject, he would move that a Committee might be appointed to take them into consideration and report thereon.

Mr. Govr. Morris. It has been said that it is high time to speak out, as one member, he would candidly do so. He came here to form a compact for the good of America. He was ready to do so with all the States. He hoped & believed that all would enter into such a Compact. If they would not he was ready to join with any States that would. But as the Compact was to be voluntary, it is in vain for the Eastern States to insist on what the Southn. States will never agree to. It is equally vain for the latter to require what the other States can never admit; and he verily believed the people of Pena. will never agree to a representation of Negroes. What can be desired by these States more than has been already proposed; that the Legislature shall from time to time regulate Representation according to population & wealth.

Genl. Pinkney desired that the rule of wealth should be ascertained and not left to the pleasure of the Legislature; and that property in slaves should not be exposed to danger under a Govt. instituted for the protection of property.

The first clause in the Report of the first Grand Committee was postponed.

Mr. Elseworth. In order to carry into effect the principle established, moved to add to the last clause adopted by the House the words following "and that the rule of contribution by direct taxation for the support of the Government of the U. States shall be the number of white inhabitants, and three fifths of every other description in the several States, until some other rule that shall more accurately ascertain the wealth of the several States can be devised and adopted by the Legislature."

Mr. Butler seconded the motion in order that it might be committed.

Mr. Randolph was not satisfied with the motion. The danger will be revived that the ingenuity of the Legislature may evade or pervert the rule so as to perpetuate the power where it shall be lodged in the first instance. He proposed in lieu of Mr. Elseworth's motion, "that in order to ascertain the alterations in Representation that may be required from time to time by changes in the relative circumstances of the States, a census shall be taken within two years from the 1st. meeting of the Genl Legislature of the U.S., and once within the term of every   year afterwards, of all the inhabitants in the manner & according to the ratio recommended by Congress in their resolution of the 18th day of Apl. 1783; [rating the blacks at $\frac{2}{3}$ of their number] and, that the Legislature of the U. S. shall arrange the Representation accordingly."—He urged strenuously that express security ought to be provided for including slaves in the ratio of Representation. He lamented that such a species of property existed. But as it did exist the holders of it would require this security. It was perceived that the design was entertained by some of excluding slaves altogether; the Legislature therefore ought not to be left at liberty.

Mr. Elseworth withdraws his motion & seconds that of Mr. Randolph.

Mr. Wilson observed that less umbrage would perhaps be taken agst. an admission of the slaves into the Rule of representation, if it should be so expressed as to make them indirectly only an ingredient in the rule, by saying that they should enter into the rule of taxation: and as representation was to be according to taxation, the end would be equally attained. He accordingly moved & was 2ded. so to alter the last clause adopted by the House, that together with the amendment proposed the whole should read as follows—provided always that the representation ought to be proportioned according to direct taxation, and in order to ascertain the alterations in the direct taxation which may be required from time to time by the changes in the relative circumstances of the States. Resolved that a census be taken within two years from the first meeting of the Legislature of the U. States, and once within the term of every   years afterwards of all the inhabitants of the U. S. in the manner and according to the ratio recommended by Congress in their Resolution of April 18, 1783; and that the Legislature of the U. S. shall proportion the direct taxation accordingly."

Mr. King. Altho' this amendment varies the aspect somewhat, he had still two powerful objections agst. tying down the Legislature to the rule of numbers. 1. they were at this time an uncertain index of the relative wealth of the States. 2. if they were a just index at this time it can not be supposed always to continue so. He was far from wishing to retain any unjust advantage whatever in one part of the Republic. If justice was not the basis of the connection it could not be of long duration. He must be shortsighted indeed who does not foresee that whenever the Southern States shall be more numerous than the Northern, they can & will hold a language that will awe them into justice. If they threaten to separate now in case injury shall be done them, will their threats be less urgent or effectual, when force shall back their demands. Even in the intervening period, there will be no point of time at which they will not be able to say, do us justice or we will separate. He urged the necessity of placing confidence to a certain degree in every Govt. and did not conceive that the proposed confidence as to a periodical readjustment, of the representation exceeded that degree.

Mr. Pinkney moved to amend Mr. Randolph's motion so as to make "blacks equal to the whites in the ratio of representation." This he urged was nothing more than justice. The blacks are the labourers, the peasants of the Southern States: they are as productive of pecuniary resources as those of the Northern States. They add equally to the wealth, and considering money as the sinew of war, to the strength of the nation. It will also be politic with regard to the Northern States, as taxation is to keep pace with Representation.

Genl. Pinkney moves to insert 6 years instead of two, as the period computing from 1st. meeting of ye. Legis—within which the first census should be taken. On this question for inserting six instead of "two" in the proposition of Mr. Wilson, it passed in the affirmative

Masts. no. Ct. ay. N. J. ay. Pa. ay. Del. divd. Mayd. ay. Va. no. N. C. no. S. C. ay. Geo. no.

On a question for filling the blank for ye. periodical census with 20 years, it passed in the negative.

Masts. no. Ct. ay. N. J. ay. P. ay. Del. no. Md. no. Va. no. N. C. no. S. C. no. Geo. no.

On a question for 10 years, it passed in the affirmative.

Mas. ay. Cont. no. N. J. no. P. ay. Del. ay. Md. ay. Va. ay. N. C. ay. S. C. ay. Geo. ay.

On Mr. Pinkney's motion for rating blacks as equal to Whites instead of as $\frac{3}{5}$—

Mas. no. Cont. no. [Dr. Johnson ay] N. J. no. Pa. no. [3 agst. 2.] Del. no. Md. no. Va. no. N. C. no. S. C. ay. Geo.—ay.

Mr. Randolph's proposition as varied by Mr. Wilson being read for question on the whole.

Mr. Gerry, urged that the principle of it could not be carried into execution as the States were not to be taxed as States. With regard to taxes in imports, he conceived they would be more productive. Where there were no slaves than where there were; the consumption being greater—

Mr. Elseworth. In case of a poll tax there wd. be no difficulty. But there wd. probably be none. The sum allotted to a State may be levied without difficulty according to the plan used by the State in raising its own supplies. On the question on ye. whole proposition; as proportioning representation to direct taxation & both to the white & $\frac{3}{5}$ of black inhabitants, & requiring a Census within six years—& within every ten years afterwards.

Mas. divd. Cont. ay. N. J. no. Pa. ay. Del. no. Md. ay. Va. ay. N. C. ay. S. C. divd. Geo. ay.

The Northwest Ordinance, 1787

Be it ordained by the United States in Congress Assembled that the said territory for the purposes of temporary government be one district, subject however to be divided into two districts as future circumstances may in the opinion of Congress make it expedient. . . .

Be it ordained by the authority aforesaid, that there shall be appointed, from time to time, by Congress, a governor, whose commission shall continue in force for the term of three years, unless sooner revoked by Congress; he shall reside in the district, and have a freehold estate therein in 1000 acres of land, while in the exercise of his office.

There shall be appointed, from time to time, by Congress, a secretary, whose commission shall continue in force for four years unless sooner revoked; he shall reside in the district, and have a freehold estate therein in 500 acres of land, while in the exercise of his office; it shall be his duty to keep and preserve the acts and laws passed by the legislature, and the public records of the district, and the proceedings of the governor in his Executive department; and transmit authentic copies of such acts and proceedings, every six months, to the Secretary of Congress: There shall also be appointed a court to consist of three judges, any two of whom to form a court, who shall have a common law jurisdiction, and reside in the district, and have each therein a freehold estate in 500 acres of land while in the exercise of their offices; and their commissions shall continue in force during good behavior.

The governor and judges, or a majority of them, shall adopt and publish in the district such laws of the original States, criminal and civil, as may be necessary and best suited to the circumstances of the district, and report them to Congress from time to time: which laws shall be in force in the district until the organization of the General Assembly therein, unless disapproved of by Congress; but, afterwards, the legislature shall have authority to alter them as they shall think fit.

The governor, for the time being, shall be commander-in-chief of the militia, appoint and commission all officers in the same below the rank of general officers; all general officers shall be appointed and commissioned by Congress.

Previous to the organization of the General Assembly, the governor shall appoint such magistrates and other civil officers, in each county or township, as he shall find necessary for the preservation of the peace and good order in the same. After the General Assembly shall be organized, the powers and duties of the magistrates and other civil officers shall be regulated and defined by the said Assembly; but all . . . civil officers not herein otherwise directed shall during the continuance of this temporary government be appointed by the governor.

For the prevention of crimes and injuries the laws to be adopted or made shall have force in all parts of the district; and for the execution of process, criminal and civil, the governor shall make proper divisions thereof, and he shall proceed from time to time as circumstances may require to lay out the parts of the District in which the Indian titles shall have been extinguished into counties and townships subject however to such alterations as may thereafter be made by the legislature.

So soon as there shall be five thousand free male inhabitants of full age in the district, upon giving proof thereof to the governor, they shall receive authority with time and place to elect representatives from their counties or townships to represent them in the general Assembly, provided that for every five hundred free male inhabitants there shall be one representative; and so on progressively with the number of free male inhabitants shall the right of representation encrease until the number of representatives shall amount to twenty five, after which the number and proportion of representatives shall be regulated by the legislature; provided that no person be eligible or qualified to act as a representative unless he shall have been a citizen of one of the United States three years and be a resident in the district or unless he shall have resided in the district three years, and in either case shall likewise hold in his own right in fee simple two hundred acres of land within the same; provided also that a freehold in fifty acres of land in the district having been a citizen of one of the states and being resident in the district, or the like freehold and two years residence in the district shall be necessary to qualify a man as an elector of a representative.

The representatives thus elected shall serve for the term of two years, and in case of the death of a representative or removal from office, the governor shall issue a writ to the county or township for which he was a member, to elect another in his stead to serve for the residue of the term.

The general Assembly or legislature shall consist of the governor, legislative council and a house of representatives. The legislative council shall consist of five members to continue in Office five years unless sooner removed by Congress, any three of whom to be a quorum and the members of the council shall be nominated and appointed in the following manner, to wit: As soon as representatives shall be elected, the governor shall appoint a time and place for them to meet together; and, when met, they shall nominate ten persons, residents in the district, and each possessed of a freehold in 500 acres of land, and return their names to Congress; five of whom Congress shall appoint and commission to serve as aforesaid; and, whenever a vacancy shall happen in the council, by death or removal from office, the house of representatives shall nominate two persons, qualified as aforesaid, for each vacancy, and return their names to Congress; one of whom Congress shall appoint and commission for the residue of the term. And every five years, four months at least before the expiration of the time of service of the members of council, the said house shall nominate ten persons, qualified as aforesaid, and return their names to Congress; five of whom Congress shall appoint and commission to serve as members of the council five years, unless sooner removed. And the governor, legislative council, and house of representatives, shall have authority to make laws in all cases, for the good government of the district, not repugnant to the principles and articles in this ordinance established and declared. And all bills, having passed by a majority in the house, and by a majority in the council, shall be referred to the governor for his assent; but no bill, or legislative act whatever, shall be of any force without his assent. The governor shall have power to convene, prorogue, and dissolve the General Assembly, when, in his opinion, it shall be expedient.

The governor, judges, legislative council, secretary, and such other officers as Congress shall appoint in the district, shall take an oath or affirmation of fidelity and of office; the governor before the President of Congress, and all other officers before the governor. As soon as a legislature shall be formed in the district, the council and house assembled in one room, shall have authority, by joint ballot, to elect a delegate to Congress, who shall have a seat in Congress, with a right of debating but not of voting during this temporary government.

And, for extending the fundamental principles of civil and religious liberty, which form the basis whereon these republics, their laws and constitutions are erected; to fix and establish those principles as the basis of all laws, constitutions, and governments, which forever hereafter shall be formed in the said territory: to provide also for the establishment of States, and permanent Government therein, and for their admission to a Share in the federal Councils on an equal footing with the original States, at as early periods as may be consistent with the general interest—

It is hereby Ordained and declared by the authority aforesaid, That the following Articles shall be considered as Articles of compact between the Original States and the People and States in the said territory, and forever remain unalterable, unless by common consent, *to wit,* . . . .

Article the Fourth. The said Territory, and the States which may be formed therein, shall forever remain a part of this Confederacy . . . subject to the Articles of Confederation, and to such alterations therein as shall be constitutionally made; and to all the acts and ordinances of the United States in Congress assembled, conformable thereto. . . .

Article the Fifth. There shall be formed in the said territory, not less than three nor more than five States. . . . And, whenever any of the said States shall have 60,000 free inhabitants therein, such State shall be admitted, by its delegates, into the Congress of the United States, on an equal footing with the original States in all respects whatever, and shall be at liberty to form a permanent constitution and State government: *Provided,* the constitution and government, so to be formed, shall be republican, and in conformity to the principles contained in these articles; and, so far as it can be consistent with the general interest of the confederacy, such admission shall be allowed at an earlier period, and when there may be a less number of free inhabitants in the State than 60,000.

Article the Sixth. There shall be neither slavery nor involuntary servitude in the said territory, otherwise than in the punishment of crimes, whereof the party shall have been duly convicted: provided, always, That any person escaping into the same, from whom labor or service is lawfully claimed in any one of the original States, such fugitive may be lawfully reclaimed and conveyed to the person claiming his or her labor or service as aforesaid.

✠ E S S A Y S

Historians are a contentious lot when assessing the framers' motives, as this chapter's essays show. Charles Beard had argued that the delegates acted out of economic self-interest rather than high ideals. Subsequent scholars, however, have exploded most of Beard's arguments by showing that whether delegates were from large or small states and whether or not they owned slaves had the most to do with shaping their vision of the Constitution.

In the first essay, John P. Roche, a political scientist at Brandeis University, dismisses the entire exercise of creating typologies because of the delegates' bold unity in wishing to fashion a democratic government. Roche compares them to a political-reform caucus in a legislature, whose members worried more about current political realities than maintaining coherent ideas.

In the second selection, historian Forrest McDonald of the University of Alabama, whose research has dealt the most devastating blows to Beard's thesis, takes another view. McDonald believes that the factions into which the delegates grouped themselves were important because the delegates' behavior was closely tied to interests, and these interests were always filtered through each delegate's ideological beliefs. Unlike Roche, McDonald argues that ideas counted for a lot.

Gordon Wood, whose *Creation of the American Republic* is one of the most influential books ever written about the Constitution, concludes in the third essay that both interests and ideas were important in the convention, but he aligns these issues differently than Roche and McDonald. Wood suggests that the convention was not forward looking but rather an episode of looking backward to a classical vision of civic humanism. Creating a virtuous republic, therefore, was more important than establishing democracy.

The Practical Democracy of the Framers

JOHN P. ROCHE

Over the last century and a half, the work of the Constitutional Convention and the motives of the Founding Fathers have been analyzed under a number of different ideological auspices. To one generation of historians, the hand of God was moving in the assembly; under a later dispensation, the dialectic (at various levels of philosophical sophistication) replaced the Deity: "relationships of production" moved into the niche previously reserved for Love of Country. Thus in counterpoint to the Zeitgeist, the Framers have undergone miraculous metamorphoses: at one time acclaimed as liberals and bold social engineers, today they appear in the guise of sound Burkean conservatives, men who in our time would subscribe to *Fortune*, look to Walter Lippmann for political theory, and chuckle patronizingly at the antics of Barry Goldwater. The implicit assumption is that if James Madison were among us, he would be President of the Ford Foundation, while Alexander Hamilton would chair the Committee for Economic Development.

The "Fathers" have thus been admitted to our best circles; the revolutionary ferocity which confiscated all Tory property in reach and populated New Brunswick with outlaws has been converted by the "Miltown School" of American historians into a benign dedication to "consensus" and "prescriptive rights." The Daughters of the American Revolution have, through the ministrations of Professors Boorstin, Hartz, and Rossiter, at last found ancestors worthy of their descendants. It is not my purpose here to argue that the "Fathers" were, in fact, radical revolutionaries; that proposition has been brilliantly demonstrated by Robert R. Palmer in his *Age of the Democratic Revolution*. My concern is with the further position that not only were they revolutionaries, but also they were democrats. Indeed, in my view, there is one fundamental truth about the Founding Fathers that *every* generation of Zeitgeisters has done its best to obscure: they were first and foremost superb democratic politicians. I suspect that in a contemporary setting, James Madison would be speaker of the House of Representatives and Hamilton would be the *eminence grise* dominating (*pace* Theodore Sorenson or Sherman Adams) the Executive Office of the President. They were, with their colleagues, *political men*—not metaphysicians, disembodied conservatives or Agents of History—and as recent research into the nature of American politics in the 1780s confirms, they were committed (perhaps willy-

"The Founding Fathers: A Reform Caucus in Action," by John P. Roche, *American Political Science Review*, 55 (March 1961), pp. 799–816. Reprinted by permission.

nilly) to working within the democratic framework, within a universe of public approval. Charles Beard *and* the filiopietists to the contrary notwithstanding, the Philadelphia Convention was not a College of Cardinals or a council of Platonic guardians working within a manipulative, pre-democratic framework; it was a *nationalist* reform caucus which had to operate with great delicacy and skill in a political cosmos full of enemies to achieve the one definitive goal—popular approbation.

Perhaps the time has come, to borrow Walton Hamilton's fine phrase, to raise the Framers from immortality to mortality, to give them credit for their magnificent demonstration of the art of democratic politics. The point must be reemphasized; they *made* history and did it within the limits of consensus. There was nothing inevitable about the future in 1787; the *Zeitgeist*, that fine Hegelian technique of begging causal questions, could only be discerned in retrospect. What they did was to hammer out a pragmatic compromise which would both bolster the "National interest" and be acceptable to the people. What inspiration they got came from their collective experience as professional politicians in a democratic society. As John Dickinson put it to his fellow delegates on August 13, "Experience must be our guide. Reason may mislead us."

In this context, let us examine the problems they confronted and the solutions they evolved. The Convention has been described picturesquely as a counterrevolutionary junta and the constitution as a *coup d'état*, but this has been accomplished by withdrawing the whole history of the movement for constitutional reform from its true context. No doubt the goals of the constitutional elite were "subversive" to the existing political order, but it is overlooked that their subversion could only have succeeded if the people of the United States endorsed it by regularized procedures. Indubitably they were "plotting" to establish a much stronger central government than existed under the Articles, but only in the sense in which one could argue equally well that John F. Kennedy was, from 1956 to 1960, "plotting" to become President. In short, on the fundamental *procedural* level, the Constitutionalists had to work according to the prevailing rules of the game. Whether they liked it or not is a topic for spiritualists—and is irrelevant: one may be quite certain that had Washington agreed to play the de Gaulle (as the Cincinnati [a military society] once urged), Hamilton would willingly have held his horse, but such fertile speculation in no way alters the actual context in which events took place. . . .

II

With delegations safely named, the focus shifted to Philadelphia. While waiting for a quorum to assemble, James Madison got busy and drafted the so-called Randolph or Virginia Plan with the aid of the Virginia delegation. This was a political master-stroke. Its consequence was that once business got under way, the framework of discussion was established on Madison's terms. There was no interminable argument over agenda; instead the delegates took the Virginia Resolutions—"just for purposes of discussion"—

as their point of departure. And along with Madison's proposals, many of which were buried in the course of the summer, went his major premise: a new start on a Constitution rather than piecemeal amendment. This was not necessarily revolutionary—a little exegesis could demonstrate that a new Constitution might be formulated as "amendments" to the Articles of Confederation—but Madison's proposal that this "lump sum" amendment go into effect after approval by nine states (the Articles required unanimous state approval for any amendment) was thoroughly subversive.

Standard treatments of the Convention divide the delegates into "nationalists" and "states'-righters" with various improvised shadings ("moderate nationalists," etc.), but these are *a posteriori* categories which obfuscate more than they clarify. What is striking to one who analyzes the Convention as a case-study in democratic politics is the lack of clear-cut ideological divisions in the Convention. Indeed, I submit that the evidence—Madison's *Notes,* the correspondence of the delegates, and debates on ratification—indicates that this was a *remarkably homogeneous body on the ideological level.* Yates and Lansing, Clinton's two chaperones for Hamilton, left in disgust on July 10. (Is there anything more tedious than sitting through endless disputes on matters one deems fundamentally misconceived? It takes an iron will to spend a hot summer as an ideological *agent provocateur.*) Luther Martin, Maryland's bibulous narcissist, left on September 4 in a huff when he discovered that others did not share his self-esteem; others went home for personal reasons. But the hard core of delegates accepted a grinding regimen throughout the attrition of a Philadelphia summer precisely because they shared the Constitutionalist goal.

Basic differences of opinion emerged, of course, but these were not ideological; they were *structural.* If the so-called "states'-rights" group had not accepted the fundamental purposes of the Convention, they could simply have pulled out and by doing so have aborted the whole enterprise. Instead of bolting, they returned day after day to argue and to compromise. An interesting symbol of this basic homogeneity was the initial agreement on secrecy: these professional politicians did not want to become prisoners of publicity; they wanted to retain that freedom of maneuver which is only possible when men are not forced to take public stands in the preliminary stages of negotiation. There was no legal means of binding the tongues of the delegates: at any stage in the game a delegate with basic principled objections to the emerging project could have taken the stump (as Luther Martin did after his exit) and denounced the convention to the skies. Yet Madison did not even inform Thomas Jefferson in Paris of the course of the deliberations and available correspondence indicates that the delegates generally observed the injunction. Secrecy is certainly uncharacteristic of any assembly marked by strong ideological polarization. This was noted at the time: the *New York Daily Advertiser,* August 14, 1787, commented that the " . . . profound secrecy hitherto observed by the convention [we consider] a happy omen, as it demonstrates that the spirit of party on any great and essential point cannot have arisen to any height."

Commentators on the Constitution who have read *The Federalist* in lieu of reading the actual debates have credited the Fathers with the invention of a sublime concept called "Federalism." Unfortunately *The Federalist* is probative evidence for only one proposition: that Hamilton and Madison were inspired propagandists with a genius for retrospective symmetry. Federalism, as the theory is generally defined, was an improvisation which was later promoted into a political theory. Experts on "federalism" should take to heart the advice of David Hume, who warned in his *Of the Rise and Progress of the Arts and Sciences* that " . . . there is no subject in which we must proceed with more caution than in [history], lest we assign causes which never existed and reduce what is merely contingent to stable and universal principles." In any event, the final balance in the Constitution between the states and the nation must have come as a great disappointment to Madison, while Hamilton's unitary views are too well known to need elucidation.

It is indeed astonishing how those who have glibly designated James Madison the "father" of Federalism have overlooked the solid body of fact which indicates that he shared Hamilton's quest for a unitary central government. To be specific, they have avoided examining the clear import of the Madison-Virginia Plan, and have disregarded Madison's dogged inch-by-inch retreat from the bastions of centralization. The Virginia Plan envisioned a unitary national government effectively freed from and dominant over the states. The lower house of the national legislature was to be elected directly by the people of the states with membership proportional to population. The upper house was to be selected by the lower and the two chambers would elect the executive and choose the judges. The national government would be thus cut completely loose from the states.

The structure of the general government was freed from state control in a truly radical fashion, but the scope of the authority of the national sovereign as Madison initially formulated it was breathtaking—it was the formulation worthy of the Sage of Malmesbury himself. The national legislature was to be empowered to disallow the acts of state legislatures, and the central government was vested, in addition to the powers of the nation under the Articles of Confederation, with plenary authority wherever " . . . the separate States are incompetent or in which the harmony of the United States may be interrupted by the exercise of individual legislation." Finally, just to lock the door against state intrusion, the national Congress was to be given the power to use military force on recalcitrant states. This was Madison's "model" of an ideal national government, though it later received little publicity in *The Federalist*.

The interesting thing was the reaction of the Convention to this militant program for a strong autonomous central government. Some delegates were startled, some obviously leery of so comprehensive a project of reform, but nobody set off any fireworks and nobody walked out. Moreover, in the two weeks that followed, the Virginia Plan received substantial endorsement *en principe;* the initial temper of the gathering can be deduced from the approval "without debate or dissent," on May 31, of the Sixth Resolution which granted Congress the authority to disallow state legislation " . . . contravening *in its opinion* the Articles of Union." Indeed, an amendment was included to bar states from contravening national treaties.

The Virginia Plan may therefore be considered, in ideological terms, as the delegates' Utopia, but as the discussions continued and became more specific, many of those present began to have second thoughts. After all, they were not residents of Utopia or guardians in Plato's Republic who could simply impose a philosophical ideal on subordinate strata of the population. They were practical politicians in a democratic society, and no matter what their private dreams might be, they had to take home an acceptable package and defend it—and their own political futures—against predictable attack. On June 14, the breaking point between dream and reality took place. Apparently realizing that under the Virginia Plan, Massachusetts, Virginia and Pennsylvania could virtually dominate the national government—and probably appreciating that to sell this program to "the folks back home" would be impossible—the delegates from the small states dug in their heels and demanded time for a consideration of alternatives. One gets a graphic sense of the inner politics from John Dickinson's reproach to Madison: "You see the consequences of pushing things too far. Some of the members from the small States wish for two branches in the General Legislature and are friends to a good National Government; but we would sooner submit to a foreign power than . . . be deprived of an equality of suffrage in both branches of the Legislature, and thereby be thrown under the domination of the large States."

The bare outline of the Journal entry for Tuesday, June 14, is suggestive to anyone with extensive experience in deliberative bodies. "It was moved by Mr. Patterson [*sic*, Paterson's name was one of those consistently misspelled by Madison and everybody else] seconded by Mr. Randolph that the further consideration of the report from the Committee of the whole House [endorsing the Virginia Plan] be postponed til tomorrow, and before the question for postponement was taken, it was moved by Mr. Randolph seconded by Mr. Patterson that the House adjourn." The House adjourned by obvious prearrangement of the two principals: since the preceding Saturday when Brearley and Paterson of New Jersey had announced their fundamental discontent with the representational features of the Virginia Plan, the informal pressure had certainly been building up to slow down the streamroller. Doubtless there were extended arguments at the Indian Queen between Madison and Paterson, the latter insisting that events were moving rapidly towards a probably disastrous conclusion, towards a political suicide pact. Now the process of accommodation was put into action smoothly— and wisely, given the character and strength of the doubters. Madison had the votes, but this was one of those situations where the enforcement of mechanical majoritarianism could easily have destroyed the objectives of the majority: the Constitutionalists were in quest of a qualitative as well as a quantitative consensus. This was hardly from deference to local Quaker custom; it was a political imperative if they were to attain ratification.

III

According to the standard script, at this point the "states'-rights" group intervened in force behind the New Jersey Plan, which has been characteristically portrayed as a revision to the *status quo* under the Articles of Confederation with but minor modifications. A careful examination of the evidence indicates that only in a marginal sense is this an accurate description. It is true that the New Jersey Plan put the states back into the institutional picture, but one could argue that to do so was a recognition of political reality rather than an affirmation of states'-rights. A serious case can be made that the advocates of the New Jersey Plan, far from being ideological addicts of states'-rights, intended to substitute for the Virginia Plan a system which would both retain strong national power and have a chance of adoption in the states. The leading spokesman for the project asserted quite clearly that his views were based more on counsels of expediency than on principle; said Paterson on June 16: "I came here not to speak my own sentiments, but the sentiments of those who sent me. Our object is not such a Governmt. as may be best in itself, but such a one as our Constituents have authorized us to prepare, and as they will approve." This is Madison's version; in Yates' transcription, there is a crucial sentence following the remarks above: "I believe that a little practical virtue is to be preferred to the finest theoretical principles, which cannot be carried into effect." In his preliminary speech on June 9, Paterson had stated " . . . to the public mind we must accommodate ourselves," and in his notes for this and his later effort as well, the emphasis is the same. The *structure* of government under the Articles should be retained:

> 2. Because it accords with the Sentiments of the People
> [Proof:] 1. Coms [Commissions from state legislatures defining the jurisdiction of the delegates]
> 2. News-papers—Political Barometer. Jersey never would have sent Delegates under the first [Virginia] Plan—
> Not here to sport Opinions of my own. Wt. [What] can be done. A little practicable Virtue preferrable to Theory.

This was a defense of political acumen, not of states'-rights. In fact, Paterson's notes of his speech can easily be construed as an argument for attaining the substantive objectives of the Virginia Plan by a sound political route, i.e., pouring the new wine in the old bottles. With a shrewd eye, Paterson queries:

> Will the Operation and Force of the [central] Govt. depend upon the mode of Representn.—No—it will depend upon the Quantum of Power lodged in the leg. ex. and judy. Departments—Give [the existing] Congress the same powers that you intend to give the two Branches, [under the Virginia Plan] and I apprehend they will act with as much Propriety and more Energy . . . .

In other words, the advocates of the New Jersey Plan concentrated their fire on what they held to be the *political liabilities* of the Virginia Plan—

which were matters of institutional structure—rather than on the proposed scope of national authority. Indeed, the Supremacy Clause of the Constitution first saw the light of day in Paterson's Sixth Resolution; the New Jersey Plan contemplated the use of military force to secure compliance with national law; and finally Paterson made clear his view that under either the Virginia or the New Jersey systems, the general government would " . . . act on individuals and not on states." From the states'-rights viewpoint, this was heresy: the fundament of that doctrine was the proposition that any central government had as its constituents the states, not the people, and could only reach the people through the agency of the state government.

Paterson then reopened the agenda of the Convention, but he did so within a distinctly nationalist framework. Paterson's position was one of favoring a strong central government in principle, but opposing one which in fact *put the big states in the saddle.* (The Virginia Plan, for all its abstract merits, did very well by Virginia.) As evidence for this speculation, there is a curious and intriguing proposal among Paterson's preliminary drafts of the New Jersey Plan:

> Whereas it is necessary in Order to form the People of the U.S. of America in to a Nation, that the States should be consolidated, by which means all the Citizens thereof will become equally intitled to and will equally participate in the same Privileges and Rights . . . it is therefore resolved, that all the Lands contained within the Limits of each state individually, and of the U.S. generally be considered as constituting one Body or Mass, and be divided into thirteen or more integral parts.
>
> Resolved, That such Divisions or integral Parts shall be styled Districts.

This makes it sound as though Paterson was prepared to accept a strong unified central government along the lines of the Virginia Plan if the existing states were eliminated. He may have gotten the idea from his New Jersey colleague Judge David Brearley, who on June 9 had commented that the only remedy to the dilemma over representation was " . . . that a map of the U.S. be spread out, that all the existing boundaries be erased, and that a new partition of the whole be made into 13 equal parts. According to Yates, Brearley added at this point, " . . . then a government on the present [Virginia Plan] system will be just."

This proposition was never pushed—it was patently unrealistic—but one can appreciate its purpose: it would have separated the men from the boys in the large-state delegations. How attached would the Virginians have been to their reform principles if Virginia were to disappear as a component geographical unit (the largest) for representational purposes? Up to this point, the Virginians had been in the happy position of supporting high ideals with that inner confidence born of knowledge that the "public interest" they endorsed would nourish their private interest. Worse, they had shown little willingness to compromise. Now the delegates from the small states announced that they were unprepared to be offered up as sacrificial victims to a "national interest" which reflected Virginia's parochial ambition. Caustic Charles Pinckney was not far off when he remarked sardonically that

" . . . the whole [conflict] comes to this": "Give N. Jersey an equal vote, and she will dismiss her scruples, and concur in the Natil. system." What he rather unfairly did not add was that the Jersey delegates were not free agents who could adhere to their private convictions; they had to take back, sponsor and risk their reputations on the reforms approved by the Convention—and in New Jersey, not in Virginia.

Paterson spoke on Saturday, and one can surmise that over the weekend there was a good deal of consultation, argument, and caucusing among the delegates. One member at least prepared a full length address: on Monday Alexander Hamilton, previously mute, rose and delivered a six-hour oration. It was a remarkably apolitical speech; the gist of his position was that *both* the Virginia and New Jersey Plans were inadequately centralist, and he detailed a reform program which was reminiscent of the Protectorate under the Cromwellian *Instrument of Government* of 1653. It has been suggested that Hamilton did this in the best political tradition to emphasize the moderate character of the Virginia Plan, to give the cautious delegates something *really* to worry about; but this interpretation seems somehow too clever. Particularly since the sentiments Hamilton expressed happened to be completely consistent with those he privately—and sometimes publicly—expressed throughout his life. He wanted to take a striking phrase from a letter to George Washington, a "strong well mounted government"; in essence, the Hamilton Plan contemplated an elected life monarch, virtually free of public control, on the Hobbesian ground that only in this fashion could strength and stability be achieved. The other alternatives, he argued, would put policy-making at the mercy of the passions of the mob; only if the sovereign was beyond the reach of selfish influence would it be possible to have government in the interests of the whole community.

From all accounts, this was a masterful and compelling speech, but (aside from furnishing John Lansing and Luther Martin with ammunition for later use against the Constitution) it made little impact. Hamilton was simply transmitting on a different wavelength from the rest of the delegates; the latter adjourned after his great effort, admired his rhetoric, and then returned to business. It was rather as if they had taken a day off to attend the opera. Hamilton, never a particularly patient man or much of a negotiator, stayed for another ten days and then left, in considerable disgust, for New York. Although he came back to Philadelphia sporadically and attended the last two weeks of the Convention, Hamilton played no part in the laborious task of hammering out the Constitution. His day came later when he led the New York Constitutionalists into the savage imbroglio over ratification—an arena in which his unmatched talent for dirty political infighting may well have won the day. For instance, in the New York Ratifying Convention, Lansing threw back into Hamilton's teeth the sentiments the latter had expressed in his June 18 oration in the Convention. However, having since retreated to the fine defensive positions immortalized in *The Federalist,* the Colonel flatly denied that he had ever been an enemy of the states, or had believed that conflict between states and nation was inexorable! As Madison's authoritative *Notes* did not appear until 1840, and there had been no press coverage, there was no way to verify his assertions, so in the words of the reporter, " . . . a warm personal altercation between [Lansing and Hamilton] engrossed the remainder of the day [June 28, 1788]."

IV

On Tuesday morning, June 19, the vacation was over. James Madison led off with a long, carefully reasoned speech analyzing the New Jersey Plan which, while intellectually vigorous in its criticisms, was quite concilliatory [*sic*] in mood. "The great difficulty," he observed, "lies in the affair of Representation; and if this could be adjusted, all others would be surmountable." (As events were to demonstrate, this diagnosis was correct.) When he finished, a vote was taken on whether to continue with the Virginia Plan as the nucleus for a new constitution: seven states voted "Yes"; New York, New Jersey, and Delaware voted "No"; and Maryland, whose position often depended on which delegates happened to be on the floor, divided. Paterson, it seems, lost decisively; yet in a fundamental sense he and his allies had achieved their purpose: from that day onward, it could never be forgotten that the state governments loomed ominously in the background and that no verbal incantations could exorcise their power. Moreover, nobody bolted the convention: Paterson and his colleagues took their defeat in stride and set to work to modify the Virginia Plan, particularly with respect to its provisions on representation in the national legislature. Indeed, they won an immediate rhetorical bonus; when Oliver Ellsworth of Connecticut rose to move that the word "national" be expunged from the Third Virginia Resolution ("Resolved that a *national* Government ought to be established consisting of a *supreme* Legislative, Executive and Judiciary,") Randolph agreed and the motion passed unanimously. The process of compromise had begun.

For the next two weeks, the delegates circled around the problem of legislative representation. The Connecticut delegation appears to have evolved a possible compromise quite early in the debates, but the Virginians and particularly Madison (unaware that he would later be acclaimed as the prophet of "federalism") fought obdurately against providing for equal representation of states in the second chamber. There was a good deal of acrimony and at one point Benjamin Franklin—of all people—proposed the institution of a daily prayer; practical politicians in the gathering, however, were mediating more on the merits of a good committee than on the utility of Divine intervention. On July 2, the ice began to break when through a number of fortuitous events—and one that seems deliberate—the majority against equality of representation was converted into a dead tie. The Convention had reached the stage where it was "ripe" for a solution (presumably all the therapeutic speeches had been made), and the South Carolinians proposed a committee. Madison and James Wilson wanted none of it, but with only Pennsylvania dissenting, the body voted to establish a working party on the problem of representation.

The members of this committee, one from each state, were elected by the delegates—and a very interesting committee it was. Despite the fact that the Virginia Plan had held majority support up to that date, neither Madison nor Randolph was selected (Mason was the Virginian) and Baldwin of Georgia, whose shift in position had resulted in the tie, was chosen. From the composition, it was clear that this was not to be a "fighting" committee: the emphasis in membership was on what might be described as "second-level political entrepreneurs." On the basis of the discussions up to that time, only Luther Martin of Maryland could be described as a "bitter-ender." Admittedly, some divination enters into this sort of analysis, but one does get a sense of the mood of the delegates from these choices—including the interesting selection of Benjamin Franklin, despite his age and intellectual wobbliness, over the brilliant and incisive Wilson or the sharp, polemical Gouverneur Morris, to represent Pennsylvania. His passion for conciliation was more valuable at this juncture than Wilson's logical genius, or Morris' acerbic wit.

There is a common rumor that the Framers divided their time between philosophical discussions of government and reading the classics in political theory. Perhaps this is as good a time as any to note that their concerns were highly practical, that they spent little time canvassing abstractions. A number of them had some acquaintance with the history of political theory (probably gained from reading John Adams' monumental compilation *A Defense of the Constitutions of Government,* the first volume of which appeared in 1786), and it was a poor rhetorician indeed who could not cite Locke, Montesquieu, or Harrington *in support* of a desired goal. Yet up to this point in the deliberations, no one had expounded a defense of states'-rights or the "separation of powers" or anything resembling a theoretical basis. It should be reiterated that the Madison model had no room either for the states or for the "separation of powers": effectively *all* governmental power was vested in the national legislature. The merits of Montesquieu did not turn up until *The Federalist;* and although a perverse argument could be made that Madison's ideal was truly in the tradition of John Locke's *Second Treatise of Government,* the Locke whom the American rebels treated as an honorary president was a pluralistic defender of vested rights, not of parliamentary supremacy.

It would be tedious to continue a blow-by-blow analysis of the work of the delegates; the critical fight was over representation of the states and once the Connecticut Compromise was adopted on July 17, the Convention was over the hump. Madison, James Wilson and Gouverneur Morris of New York (who was there representing Pennsylvania!) fought the compromise all the way in a last-ditch effort to get a unitary state with parliamentary supremacy. But their allies deserted them and they demonstrated after their defeat the essentially opportunist character of their objections—using "opportunist" here in a non-pejorative sense, to indicate a willingness to swallow their objections and get on with the business. Moreover, once the compromise had carried (by five states to four, with one state divided), its advocates threw themselves vigorously into the job of strengthening the general government's substantive powers—as might have been predicted, indeed, from

Paterson's early statements. It nourishes an increased respect for Madison's devotion to the art of politics, to realize that this dogged fighter could sit down six months later and prepare essays for *The Federalist* in contradiction to his basic convictions about the true course the Convention should have taken.

V

Two tricky issues will serve to illustrate the later process of accommodation. The first was the institutional position of the Executive. Madison argued for an executive chosen by the National Legislature and on May 29 this had been adopted with a provision that after his seven-year term was concluded, the chief magistrate should not be eligible for reelection. In late July this was reopened and for a week the matter was argued from several different points of view. A good deal of desultory speechmaking ensued, but the gist of the problem was the opposition from two sources to election by the legislature. One group felt that the states should have a hand in the process; another small but influential circle urged direct election by the people. There were a number of proposals: election by the people, election by state governors, by electors chosen by state legislatures, by the National Legislature (James Wilson, perhaps ironically, proposed at one point that an Electoral College be chosen by lot from the National Legislature!), and there was some resemblance to three-dimensional chess in the dispute because of the presence of two other variables, length of tenure and reeligibility. Finally, after opening, reopening, and re-reopening the debate, the thorny probem was consigned to a committee for resolution.

The Brearley Committee on Postponed Matters was a superb aggregation of talent and its compromise on the Executive was a masterpiece of political improvisation. (The Electoral College, its creation, however, had little in its favor as an *institution*—as the delegates well appreciated.) The point of departure for all discussion about the presidency in the Convention was that in immediate terms, the problem was nonexistent; in other words, everybody present knew that under any system devised, George Washington would be President. Thus they were dealing in the future tense and to a body of working politicians the merits of the Brearley proposal were obvious: everybody got a piece of cake. (Or to put it more academically, each viewpoint could leave the Convention and argue to its constituents that it had *really* won the day.) First, the state legislatures had the right to determine the mode of selection of the electors; second, the small states received a bonus in the Electoral College in the form of a guaranteed minimum of three votes while the big states got acceptance of the principle of proportional power; third, if the state legislatures agreed (as six did in the first presidential election), the people could be involved directly in the choice of electors; and finally, if no candidate received a majority in the College, the right of decision passed to the National Legislature with each state exercising equal strength. (In the Brearley recommendation, the election went to the Senate, but a motion from the floor substituted the House; this was accepted on the ground that the Senate already had enough authority over the executive in its treaty and appointment powers.)

This compromise was almost too good to be true, and the Framers snapped it up with little debate or controversy. No one seemed to think well of the College as an *institution;* indeed, what evidence there is suggests that there was an assumption that once Washington had finished his tenure as President, the electors would cease to produce majorities and the chief executive would usually be chosen in the House. George Mason observed casually that the selection would be made in the House nineteen times in twenty and no one seriously disputed this point. The vital aspect of the Electoral College was that it got the Convention over the hurdle and protected everybody's interests. The future was left to cope with the problem of what to do with this Rube Goldberg mechanism. . . .

The second issue on which some substantial practical bargaining took place was slavery. The morality of slavery was, by design, not an issue, but in its other concrete aspects, slavery colored the arguments over taxation, commerce, and representation. The "Three-Fifths Compromise," that three-fifths of the slaves would be counted both for representation and for purposes of direct taxation (which was drawn from the past—it was a formula of Madison's utilized by Congress in 1783 to establish the basis of state contributions to the Confederation treasury) had allayed some Northern fears about Southern over-representation (no one then foresaw the trivial role that direct taxation would play in later federal financial policy), but doubts still remained. The Southerners, on the other hand, were afraid that Congressional control over commerce would lead to the exclusion of slaves or to their excessive taxation as imports. Moreover, the Southerners were disturbed over "navigation acts," i.e., tariffs or special legislation providing, for example, that exports be carried only in American ships; as a section depending upon exports, they wanted protection from the potential voracity of their commercial brethren of the Eastern states. To achieve this end, Mason and others urged that the Constitution include a proviso that navigation and commercial laws should require a two-thirds vote in Congress.

These problems came to a head in late August and, as usual were handed to a committee in the hope that, in Gouverneur Morris' words, " . . . these things may form a bargain among the Northern and Southern states." The Committee reported its measures of reconciliation on August 25, and on August 29 the package was wrapped up and delivered. What occurred can best be described in George Mason's dour version (he anticipated Calhoun in his conviction that permitting navigation acts to pass by majority vote would put the South in economic bondage to the North—it was mainly on this ground that he refused to sign the Constitution):

> The Constitution as agreed to till a fortnight before the Convention rose
> was such a one as he would have set his hand and heart to . . . [Until that
> time] The 3 New England States were constantly with us in all questions
> . . . so that it was these three States with the 5 Southern ones against
> Pennsylvania, Jersey and Delaware. With respect to the importation of
> slaves, [decision-making] was left to Congress. This disturbed the two South-

ernmost States who knew that Congress would immediately suppress the importation of slaves. Those two States therefore struck up a bargain with the three New England States. If they would join to admit slaves for some years, the two Southern-most States would join in changing the clause which required the ⅔ of the Legislature in any vote [on navigation acts]. It was done.

On the floor of the Convention there was a virtual love-feast on this happy occasion. Charles Pinckney of South Carolina attempted to overturn the committee's decision, when the compromise was reported to the Convention, by insisting that the South needed protection from the imperialism of the Northern states. But his Southern colleagues were not prepared to rock the boat and General C. C. Pinckney arose to spread oil on the suddenly ruffled waters; he admitted that:

> It was in the true interest of the S[outhern] States to have no regulation of commerce; but considering the loss brought on the commerce of the Eastern States by the Revolution, their liberal conduct towards the views of South Carolina [on the regulation of the slave trade] and the interests the weak South. States had in being united with the strong Eastern states, he thought it proper that no fetters should be imposed on the power of making commercial regulations; *and that his constituents, though prejudiced against the Eastern States, would be reconciled to this liberality.* He had himself prejudices agst the Eastern States before he came here, but would acknowledge that he had found them as liberal and candid as any men whatever. (Italics added.)

Pierce Butler took the same tack, essentially arguing that he was not too happy about the possible consequences, but that a deal was a deal. Many Southern leaders were later—in the wake of the "Tariff of Abominations"— to rue this day of reconciliation; Calhoun's *Disquisition on Government* was little more than an extension of the argument in the Convention against permitting a congressional majority to enact navigation acts.

VI

Drawing on their vast collective political experience, utilizing every weapon in the politicians' arsenal, looking constantly over their shoulders at their constituents, the delegates put together a Constitution. It was a makeshift affair; some sticky issues (for example, the qualification of voters) they ducked entirely; others they mastered with that ancient instrument of political sagacity, studied ambiguity (for example, citizenship), and some they just overlooked. . . .

The Constitution, then, was not an apotheosis of "constitutionalism," a triumph or architectonic genius; it was a patch-work sewn together under the pressure of both time and events by a group of extremely talented democratic politicians. They refused to attempt the establishment of a strong, centralized sovereignty on the principle of legislative supremacy for the excellent reason that the people would not accept it. They risked their political fortunes by opposing the established doctrines of state sovereignty because they were convinced that the existing system was leading to national impotence and probably foreign domination. For two years, they worked to get a convention established. For over three months, in what must have seemed to the faithful participants an endless process of give-and-take, they reasoned, cajoled, threatened, and bargained amongst themselves. The result was a Constitution which the people, in fact, by democratic processes, did accept, and a new and far better national government was established.

Beginning with the inspired propaganda of Hamilton, Madison and Jay, the ideological build-up got under way. *The Federalist* had little impact on the ratification of the Constitution, except perhaps in New York, but this volume had enormous influence on the image of the Constitution in the minds of future generations, particularly on historians and political scientists who have an innate fondness for theoretical symmetry. Yet, while the shades of Locke and Montesquieu *may* have been hovering in the background, and the delegates may have been unconscious instruments of a transcendent *telos,* the careful observer of the day-to-day work of the Convention finds no over-arching principles. The "separation of powers" to him seems to be a by-product of suspicion, and "federalism" he views as a *pis aller,* as the farthest point the delegates felt they could go in the destruction of state power without themselves inviting repudiation.

To conclude, the Constitution was neither a victory for abstract theory nor a great practical success. Well over half a million men had to die on the battlefields of the Civil War before certain constitutional principles could be defined—a baleful consideration which is somehow overlooked in our customary tributes to the farsighted genius of the Framers and to the supposed American talent for "constitutionalism." The Constitution was, however, a vivid demonstration of effective democratic political action, and of the forging of a national elite which literally persuaded its countrymen to hoist themselves by their own boot straps. American pro-consuls would be wise not to translate the Constitution into Japanese, or Swahili, or treat it as a work of semi-Divine origin; but when students of comparative politics examine the process of nation-building in countries newly freed from colonial rule they may find the American experience instructive as a classic example of the potentialities of a democratic elite.

The Power of Ideas in the Convention

FORREST MCDONALD

Almost all the delegates who attended the Constitutional Convention were nationalists in the narrow sense that they believed it necessary to reorganize and strengthen the central authority. A vote on that question was taken at the outset of the deliberations, and only three individuals are known to have voted in the negative. Few delegates, however, thought of themselves as

From *Novus Ordo Seclorum: The Intellectual Origins of the Constitution,* by Forrest McDonald, pp. 185–191, 199–209, University of Kansas Press, 1985. Reprinted by permission of the publisher.

representing America or the American people. The others thought of themselves as representing the people of the several states severally—or to put it differently, they were there as representatives of separate political societies—and the rules of the debates, including the rule that each state's delegation had but one vote, no matter what the number of its delegates, reflected that distinction.

Most of the delegates also attached reservations or conditions to their willingness to strengthen the central authority. Some of the reservations were ideological, though doctrinaire ideologues by no means constituted a majority of those in attendance. (Fortunately for the nation, John Adams was in London and Jefferson was in Paris, and Sam Adams, Richard Henry Lee, Patrick Henry, and most of the other archrepublican Patriot leaders of Seventy-six were either not chosen as delegates by their legislatures or declined to attend.) Other reservations arose from personal or group prejudices or interests, such as those of public-security holders, land speculators, merchants, and slave owners. The strongest reservations arose from the perceived interests, political or economic, of the individual political societies that the delegates represented. Thus, one absolutely central issue—perhaps the absolutely central issue—before the convention was the role, if any, that the states would play in the reorganized and strengthened common authority.

To understand the motives and the actions of the Framers, it is necessary to ascertain, in regard to as many of them as possible, where they stood on this issue and also where they stood in respect to the various and conflicting interests and ideological and philosophical positions that we have been considering.

Possibly the most important group of delegates consisted of those whose nationalism was undiluted or nearly so. Heading the list was Washington, who was crucial to the successful outcome of the convention even though he contributed little to the debates. Two in this group were from Massachusetts, Nathaniel Gorham and Rufus King; King had overcome the fear of an "aristocratical conspiracy" that he had so shrilly expressed in 1785, his perspective having been shifted by Shays's Rebellion, by his marriage to the daughter of a wealthy New York merchant, and by more than a year of intimate association with Alexander Hamilton. Seven were from the Middle States: Hamilton, Gouverneur Morris, Robert Morris, James Wilson, George Clymer, Thomas Fitzsimons, and George Read. Franklin should probably be added to the list, along with William R. Davie of North Carolina and perhaps William Pierce of Georgia. In several respects, Madison and Charles Pinckney can also be counted as being in this group, for they were in agreement with the nationalists on many points; but the two differed from them in certain fundamental ways, and therefore must properly be considered as being in categories by themselves.

All of these men, who might loosely be described as "court-party" nationalists, shared a complex of experiences and attitudes. In the backgrounds of all except the convert King were one or more of the following elements: they had been born or educated abroad or had traveled extensively abroad; they had served for a considerable time as officers in the Continental Line; or they had held important civilian positions in the Confederation during the climactic years 1781 to 1783. All or nearly all of them admired the British system, were somewhat elitist in their leanings (or at least wanted to create a national government that would be high-toned as well as powerful), and were concerned with national honor and glory in addition to the protection of liberty and property. They were hard-nosed and tough-minded, but they were also idealistic, some to the point of romanticism. They were practical men of experience and talent who were scornful of ideology and abstract speculation, but some of them were extremely learned in history and political thought. The intellectual influences upon them were varied. For example, Gouverneur Morris, Wilson, and Hamilton were thoroughly versed in ancient history and in English legal and constitutional history, and all three expressed ideas derived from Hume and Smith; but in other respects, Morris seems to have been most influenced by Blackstone, Wilson by Burlamaqui and Francis Hutcheson, and Hamilton by Steuart, Vattel, and Necker.

The court-party nationalists were in agreement that in framing a constitution, it was prudent to act on the assumption that most men in government would put their own interests ahead of the public interest much of the time. This way of thinking, together with the key to the problem that it posed to republican constitution makers, was familiar to them from, among other sources, Hume's essay "On the Independency of Parliament." It was a maxim, Hume wrote, "that, in contriving any system of government, and fixing the several checks and controuls of the constitution, every man ought to be supposed a *knave,* and to have no other end, in all his actions, than private interest. By this interest we must govern him, and, by means of it, make him, notwithstanding his insatiable avarice and ambition, co-operate to public good." Hume was proposing a modified Mandevillean scheme: modified in the sense that the "vice-ridden" hive was to be deliberately constructed by men who were themselves dedicated to the public good.

Several of the court-party men spoke in the convention as if they had committed Hume's essay to memory. Franklin declared that men were governed by ambition and avarice, as if he had coined the thought. Hamilton paraphrased Hume at length: "Take mankind as they are, and what are they governed by? Their passions. There may be in every government a few choice spirits, who may act from more worthy motives. One great error [however] is that we suppose mankind more honest than they are. Our prevailing passions are ambition and interest; and it will ever be the duty of a wise government to avail itself of those passions, in order to make them subservient to the public good."

It is a grave mistake, however, to assume from this that the Framers (or even the court-party nationalists or even Hamilton) cynically abandoned the whole notion of virtue in the republic and opted to substitute crass self-interest in its stead. Several historians have made that assumption, and at least one has gone so far as to pronounce the judgment that the very tradition of civic humanism, of men finding their highest fulfillment in service to the public, thereby was brought to an end. To commit that mistake is to fail to understand two subtle but crucial aspects of the concept that men are driven by their passions.

The first is the simpler of the two. Men are driven by their passions, and in devising governments, it is wise to assume that ambition and avarice are the ruling passions of all. Hume himself, however, in the very passage just cited, indicated that the assumption was "false in *fact*." To prepare for the worst was to err on the side of prudence, but the court-party nationalists actually expected something better, for men are driven by a variety of passions, and many of these—love of fame, of glory, of country, for example—are noble. When any such passion becomes a man's ruling passion, he must necessarily live his life in virtuous service to the public; and it was such men whom the nationalists counted on to govern others through their baser passions. Sir James Steuart put the matter succinctly. Self-interest, he wrote, is the "only motive which a statesman should make use of, to engage a free people to concur in the plans which he lays down for their government." But he adds, immediately: "I beg I may not here be understood to mean, that self-interest should conduct the statesman: by no means. Self-interest, when considered with regard to him, is public spirit."

It was generally agreed that the love of fame—the desire for secular immortality in the grateful remembrance of posterity—is the noblest of the passions. Fame is bestowed upon men for a variety of achievements which writers from Plutarch to Machiavelli to Sir Francis Bacon to Hume had ranked on hierarchical scales. On Bacon's scale (from the bottom upwards), those who won fame were fathers of their country, who "reign justly, and make the times good wherein they live"; champions of empire, who in honorable wars "enlarge their territories or make noble defence against invaders"; saviors of empire, who deliver their country from civil war or from tyrants; lawgivers, who provide constitutions by which they govern wisely and well after they are gone; and at the pinnacle, "FOUNDERS OF STATES AND COMMONWEALTHS." Clearly, quite a number of delegates to the convention were driven, to lesser and greater degrees, by a passion for fame, and so were many others of the founding generation. Moreover, they were convinced that—during their generation, at least—enough men were driven by the love of fame and other noble passions to permit the establishment of government on solid foundations.

As for the future, they did not propose to leave it to chance, for they had a plan, dear to Washington's heart, for training a class of *Optimates*. Concern with reforming the American public to ensure that it would contain an ample supply of virtuous men in the future had, of course, occupied the Patriot constitution makers, who had provided for educational and religious institutions that were designed to inculcate virtue. But these, by and large, aimed at the grandiose goal of remaking the whole people; in the words of Benjamin Rush, the desideratum was "to conform the principles, morals and manners of our citizens to our republican forms of government." What several of the Framers—including Madison, Washington, Wilson, and Pinckney—had in mind was more modest and seemingly more practical. They proposed to make the government conform to the existing morals and manners of the citizens, but to provide leaders for it by establishing a national university, which would select the cream of American youth, overcome the provincialism of the young men, and instill in them a love of the nation and a desire to serve it. . . .

Court-party nationalists in the convention were considerably more influential, but only slightly more numerous, than republican ideologues. In attempting to determine which delegates were of the latter description, one key issue is especially useful. Whereas the first group sought to establish a government on Humean-Mandevillean lines, moderated by Addisonian-Smithian "honor," the ideologues, taught by Bolingbroke, Montesquieu, or classical republicanism, shrank with horror at the prospect of admitting the baser passions as operating principles of government. On four occasions during the convention the delegates confronted a question that turned upon beliefs as to whether virtue or the baser passions should be depended upon as the operating principle of government. The issue was the extent to which congressmen should be excluded from holding other offices. Permeating the debates was the question of "corruption," in the British sense of the term. Bolingbroke had raged repeatedly in denunciation of "placemen," and Montesquieu had more moderately warned against entrusting people with power if it was to their personal advantage to abuse it. Both views had been accepted by the Patriots of 1776. Hume, by contrast, had contended that corruption in the form of the power to manage Parliament by passing out lucrative offices was necessary to the balance of the British constitution. Those delegates to the convention who insisted upon the absolute exclusion of congressmen from other offices during and for a time after their service in Congress can be regarded as being in the Bolingbroke-Montesquieu camp; they still hoped to found the republic upon classical principles, which is to say upon public virtue. Those who were willing to forbid dual officeholding, but who would allow congressmen to resign their seats to accept appointive offices, can be regarded as being in the Hume-Mandeville camp; they rejected as chimerical the idea that virtue alone could activate the republic, choosing instead to erect it on new principles, which is to say upon the channeling of self-interested motives. The first group might be roughly described as corresponding to the country party in England. Judging by their positions on the issue of congressional exclusion, the "country party" in the convention included Abraham Baldwin of Georgia; Pierce Butler, John Rutledge, and Charles Cotesworth Pinckney of South Carolina; Hugh Williamson of North Carolina; George Mason and Edmund Randolph of Virginia; Luther Martin and Daniel Jenifer of Maryland; John Lansing and Robert Yates of New York; Roger Sherman of Connecticut; and Elbridge Gerry of Massachusetts. The court party, by that criterion, included John Langdon and Nicholas Gilman of New Hampshire; Nathaniel Gorham, Rufus King, and Caleb Strong of Massachusetts; Oliver Ellsworth of Connecticut; Hamilton of New York; Wilson, Thomas Mifflin, and Gouverneur Morris of Pennsylvania;

ing armies in time of peace, and wanted the salaries of all officers to be fixed in the constitution but indexed to the price of wheat or some other commodity. He did not disapprove of the contract clause, but he thought it redundant, erroneously supposing that the ex post facto clause covered civil cases. He also strongly opposed the electoral-college system as adopted. Overall, of seventy-one specific proposals that Madison moved, seconded, or spoke unequivocally in regard to, he was on the losing side forty times.

As for Charles Pinckney, his attitudes and ideas about government were apparently close to those of Madison, but the subject is clouded by considerable mystery. Pinckney was a brilliant and somewhat unstable young South Carolinian who had a penchant for political theory and a pathetic craving to be admired, a craving that he was willing to satisfy by outright deceit. He lied about his age, for instance, in order to confirm his later (unfounded) claim that he had been the youngest man in the convention. More to the point, he claimed, in a paper published shortly after the convention, and claimed again many years later, that he had presented, on May 28, 1787, a plan of government that contained most of the features that were ultimately incorporated into the Constitution. The claims on both occasions were demonstrably bogus, though Pinckney did submit a plan, no authentic copy of which has survived. A close approximation of it has been reconstructed, but it is of limited value in trying to understand what Pinckney advocated, for he was a maverick in the convention, aligning himself at one time or another with members of virtually every faction. . . .

Virtue and Politics in the Convention

GORDON WOOD

. . . The founders did not intend the new Constitution to change the character of the American people. They were not naive utopians; they were, as we have often noted, realistic about human nature. They had little or no faith in the power of religion or of sumptuary or other such laws to get people to behave differently. To be sure, they believed in education, and some of them put great stock in what it might do in reforming and enlightening American people. But still they generally approached their task in the 1780s with a practical, unsentimental appreciation of the givenness of human beings. They knew they lived in an age of commerce and interests. Although some of the landed gentry like Jefferson might yearn wistfully at times for America to emulate China and "abandon the ocean altogether," most of the founders welcomed America's involvement in commerce, by which, however, they commonly meant overseas trade. They believed in the importance of such commerce, saw it as a major agent in the refining and civilizing of people, and were generally eager to use the power of government to promote

From "Interests and Disinterestedness in the Making of the Constitution," by Gordon S. Wood, pp. 81–93 in *Beyond Confederation: Origins of the Constitution and American National Identity*, edited by Richard Beeman, Stephen Botein, and Edward C. Carter II. © 1987 The University of North Carolina Press. Reprinted by permission of the publisher.

its growth. They knew too all about "interest," which Madison defined "in the popular sense" as the "immediate augmentation of property and wealth." They accepted the inevitability and the prevalence of "interest" and respected its power. "Interest," many of them said, "is the greatest tie one man can have on another." It was, they said, "the only binding cement" for states and peoples. Hamilton put it more bluntly: "He who pays is the master."

Since 1776 they had learned that it was foolish to expect most people to sacrifice their private interests for the sake of the public welfare. For the Federalists there was little left of the revolutionary utopianism of Samuel Adams. Already by the 1780s, Adams's brand of republicanism seemed archaic and Adams himself a figure from another time and place. Soon people would be shaking their heads in wonderment that such a person as Adams should have ever existed in America. "Modern times," it was said, "have produced no character like his." He was "one of Plutarch's men," a character out of the classical past. He was a Harvard-educated gentleman who devoted himself to the public. He had neither personal ambition nor the desire for wealth. He refused to help his children and gloried in his poverty. He was without interests or even private passions. Among the Revolutionary leaders he was unique. No other leader took classical republican values quite as seriously as Adams did.

In fact, the other Revolutionary leaders were very quick to expose the unreality and impracticality of Adams's kind of republican idealism. As early as 1778 Washington realized that the Revolution would never succeed if it depended on patriotism alone. "It must be aided by a prospect of interest or some reward." All men could not be like Samuel Adams. It was too bad, but that was the way it was. Human beings were like that, and by the 1780s many of the younger Revolutionary leaders like Madison were willing to look at the reality of interests with a very cold eye. Madison's *Federalist* No. 10 was only the most famous and frank acknowledgment of the degree to which interests of various sorts had come to dominate American politics.

The founders thus were not dreamers who expected more from the people than they were capable of. We in fact honor the founding fathers for their realism, their down-to-earth acceptance of human nature. Perhaps this is part of our despairing effort to make them one with us, to close that terrifying gap that always seems to exist between them and us. Nevertheless, in our hearts we know that they are not one with us, that they are separated from us, as they were separated from every subsequent generation of Americans, by an immense cultural chasm. They stood for a classical world that was rapidly dying, a world so different from what followed—and from our own—that an act of imagination is required to recover it in all its fullness. They believed in democracy, to be sure, but not our modern democracy; rather, they believed in a patrician-led classical democracy in which "virtue exemplified in government will diffuse its salutary influence through the society." For them government was not an arena for furthering the interests of groups and individuals, but a means of moral betterment. What modern American politician would say, as James Wilson said in the Philadelphia

Convention, that "the cultivation and improvement of the human mind was the most noble object" of government? Even Jefferson, who of all the founders most forcefully led the way, though inadvertently, to a popular liberal future, could in 1787 urge a Virginia colleague: "Cherish . . . the spirit of our people, and keep alive their attention. Do not be too severe upon their errors, but reclaim them by enlightening them." All the founding fathers saw themselves as moral teachers. However latently utilitarian, however potentially liberal, and however enthusiastically democratic the founders may have been, they were not modern men.

Despite their acceptance of the reality of interests and commerce, the Federalists had not yet abandoned what has been called the tradition of civic humanism—that host of values transmitted from antiquity that dominated the thinking of nearly all members of the elite in the eighteenth-century Anglo-American world. By the late eighteenth century this classical tradition was much attenuated and domesticated, tamed and eaten away by modern financial and commercial developments. But something remained, and the Federalists clung to it. Despite their disillusionment with political leadership in the states, the Federalists in 1787 had not yet lost hope that at least some individuals in the society might be worthy and virtuous enough to transcend their immediate material interests and devote themselves to the public good. They remained committed to the classical idea that political leadership was essentially one of character: "The whole art of government," said Jefferson, "consists of being honest." Central to this ideal of leadership was the quality of *disinterestedness*—the term the Federalists most used as a synonym for the classic conception of civic virtue: it better conveyed the increasing threats from interests that virtue now faced.

Dr. Johnson defined *disinterested* as being "superior to regard of private advantage; not influenced by private profit"; and that was what the founding fathers meant by the term. We today have lost most of this older meaning. Even educated people now use *disinterested* as a synonym for *uninterested,* meaning indifferent or unconcerned. It is almost as if we cannot quite conceive of the characteristic that disinterestedness describes: we cannot quite imagine someone who is capable of rising above a pecuniary interest and being unselfish and unbiased where an interest might be present. This is simply another measure of how far we have traveled from the eighteenth century.

This eighteenth-century concept of disinterestedness was not confined either to Commonwealthmen or to the country tradition (which makes our current preoccupation with these strains of thought misleading). Nor did one have to be an American or a republican to believe in disinterestedness and the other classical values that accompanied it. Virtue or disinterestedness, like the concept of honor, lay at the heart of all prescriptions for political leadership in the eighteenth-century Anglo-American world. Throughout the century Englishmen of all political persuasions—Whigs and Tories both—struggled to find the ideal disinterested political leader amid the rising and swirling currents of financial and commercial interests that threatened to engulf their societies. Nothing more enhanced William Pitt's reputation as the great patriot than his pointed refusal in 1746 to profit from the perquisites of the traditionally lucrative office of paymaster of the forces. Pitt was living proof for the English-speaking world of the possibility of disinterestedness— that a man could be a governmental leader and yet remain free of corruption.

This classical ideal of disinterestedness was based on independence and liberty. Only autonomous individuals, free of interested ties and paid by no masters, were capable of such virtue. Jefferson and other republican idealists might continue to hope that ordinary yeoman farmers in America might be independent and free enough of pecuniary temptations and interests to be virtuous. But others knew better, and if they did not, then the experience of the Revolutionary war soon opened their eyes. Washington realized almost at the outset that no common soldier could be expected to be "influenced by any other principles than those of Interest." And even among the officer corps there were only a "few . . . who act upon Principles of disinterestedness," and they were "comparatively speaking, no more than a drop in the Ocean."

Perhaps it was as Adam Smith warned: as society became more commercialized and civilized and labor more divided, ordinary people gradually lost their ability to make any just judgments about the varied interests and occupations of their country; and only "those few, who, being attached to no particular occupation themselves, have leisure and inclination to examine the occupations of other people." Perhaps then in America, as well as in Britain, only a few were free and independent enough to stand above the scramblings of the marketplace. As "Cato" had written, only "a very small Part of Mankind have Capacities large enough to judge of the Whole of Things." Only a few were liberally educated and cosmopolitan enough to have the breadth of perspective to comprehend all the different interests, and only a few were dispassionate and unbiased enough to adjudicate among these different interests and promote the public rather than a private good. Virtue, it was said as early as 1778, "can only dwell in superior minds, elevated above private interest and selfish views." Even Jefferson at one point admitted that only those few "whom nature has endowed with genius and virtue" could "be rendered by liberal education worthy to receive, and able to guard the sacred rights and liberties of their fellow citizens." In other words, the Federalists were saying that perhaps only from among the tiny proportion of the society the eighteenth century designated as "gentlemen" could be found men capable of disinterested political leadership.

This age-old distinction between gentlemen and others in the society had a vital meaning for the Revolutionary generation that we have totally lost. It was a horizontal cleavage that divided the social hierarchy into two unequal parts almost as sharply as the distinction between officers and soldiers divided the army; indeed, the military division was related to the larger social one. Ideally the liberality for which gentlemen were known connoted freedom—freedom from material want, freedom from the caprice of others, freedom from ignorance, and freedom from manual labor. The gentleman's distinctiveness came from being independent in a world of dependencies, learned in a world only partially literate, and leisured in a world of workers.

Just as gentlemen were expected to staff the officer corps of the Continental army (and expected also to provide for their own rations, clothing, and equipment on salaries that were less than half those of their British counterparts), so were independent gentlemen of leisure and education expected to supply the necessary disinterested leadership for government. Since such well-to-do gentry were "exempted from the lower and less honourable employments," wrote the philosopher Francis Hutcheson, they were "rather more than others obliged to an active life in some service to mankind. The publick has this claim upon them." Governmental service, in other words, was thought to be a personal sacrifice, required of certain gentlemen because of their talents, independence, and social preeminence.

In eighteenth-century America it had never been easy for gentlemen to make this personal sacrifice for the public, and it became especially difficult during the Revolution. Which is why many of the Revolutionary leaders, especially those of "small fortunes" who served in the Congress, continually complained of the burdens of office and repeatedly begged to be relieved from these burdens in order to pursue their private interests. Periodic temporary retirement from the cares and commotions of office to one's country estate for refuge and rest was acceptable classical behavior. But too often America's political leaders, especially in the North, had to retire not to relaxation in the solitude and leisure of a rural retreat, but to the making of money in the busyness and bustle of a city law practice.

In short, America's would-be gentlemen had a great deal of trouble in maintaining the desired classical independence and freedom from the marketplace. There were not many American gentry who were capable of living idly off the rents of tenants as the English landed aristocracy did. Of course, there were large numbers of the southern planter gentry whose leisure was based on the labor of their slaves, and these planters obviously came closest in America to fitting the classical ideal of the free and independent gentleman. But some southern planters kept taverns on the side, and many others were not as removed from the day-to-day management of their estates as their counterparts among the English landed gentry. Their overseers were not comparable to the stewards of the English gentry; thus the planters, despite their aristocratic poses, were often very busy, commercially involved men. Their livelihoods were tied directly to the vicissitudes of international trade, and they had always had an uneasy sense of being dependent on the market to an extent that the English landed aristocracy, despite its commitment to enterprising projects and improvements, never really felt. Still, the great southern planters at least approached the classical image of disinterested gentlemanly leadership, and they knew it and made the most of it throughout their history.

In northern American society such independent gentlemen standing above the interests of the marketplace were harder to find, but the ideal remained strong. In ancient Rome, wrote James Wilson, magistrates and army officers were always gentleman farmers, always willing to step down "from the elevation of office" and reassume "with contentment and with pleasure, the peaceful labours of a rural and independent life." John Dickinson's pose in 1767 as a "Pennsylvania Farmer" is incomprehensible except within this classical tradition. Dickinson, the wealthy Philadelphia lawyer, wanted to assure his readers of his gentlemanly disinterestedness by inform- ing them at the outset that he was a farmer "contented" and "undisturbed by worldly hopes or fears." Prominent merchants dealing in international trade brought wealth into the society and were thus valuable members of the community, but their status as independent gentlemen was always tainted by their concern for personal profit. Perhaps only a classical education that made "ancient manners familiar," as Richard Jackson once told Benjamin Franklin, could "produce a reconciliation between disinterestedness and commerce; a thing we often see, but almost always in men of a liberal education." Yet no matter how educated merchants were or how much leisure they managed for themselves, while they remained merchants they could never quite acquire the character of genteel disinterestedness essential for full acceptance as political leaders, and that is why most colonial mer- chants were not active in public life.

John Hancock and Henry Laurens knew this, and during the imperial crisis each shed his mercantile business and sought to ennoble himself. Han- cock spent lavishly, bought every imaginable luxury, and patronized every- one. He went through a fortune, but he did become the single most popular and powerful figure in Massachusetts politics during the last quarter or so of the eighteenth century. Laurens especially was aware of the bad image buying and selling had among southern planters. In 1764 he advised two impoverished but aspiring gentry immigrants heading for the back-country to establish themselves as planters before attempting to open a store. For them to enter immediately into "any retail Trade in those parts," he said, "would be mean, would Lessen them in the esteem of people whose respect they must endeavour to attract." Only after they were "set down in a Creditable manner as Planters" might they "carry on the Sale of many specie of European and West Indian goods to some advantage and with a good grace." In this same year, 1764, Laurens himself began to curtail his merchant operations. By the time of the Revolution he had become enough of an aristocrat that he was able to sneer at all those merchants who were still busy making money. "How hard it is," he had the gall to say in 1779, "for a rich, or covetous man to enter heartily into the kingdom of patriotism."

For mechanics and others who worked with their hands, being a dis- interested gentleman was impossible. Only when wealthy Benjamin Franklin retired from his printing business, at the age of forty-two, did "the Publick," as he wrote in his *Autobiography,* "now considering me as a Man of Leisure," lay hold of him and bring him into an increasing number of important public offices. Other artisans and petty traders who had wealth and political am- bitions, such as Roger Sherman of Connecticut, also found that retirement from business was a prerequisite for high public office.

Members of the learned professions were usually considered gentlemen, particularly if they were liberally educated. But were they disinterested? Were they free of the marketplace? Were they capable of virtuous public service? Hamilton for one argued strongly that, unlike merchants, mechanics, or farmers, "the learned professions . . . truly form no distinct interest in society"; thus they "will feel a neutrality to the rivalships between the different branches of industry" and will be most likely to be "an impartial arbiter" between the diverse interests of the society. But others had doubts. William Barton thought "a few individuals in a nation may be actuated by such exalted sentiments of public virtue, . . . but these instances must be rare." Certainly many thought lawyers did not stand above the fray. In fact, said Barton, "professional men of every description are necessarily, as such, obliged to pursue their immediate advantage."

Everywhere, men struggled to find a way of reconciling this classical tradition of disinterested public leadership with the private demands of making a living. "A Man expends his Fortune in political Pursuits," wrote Gouverneur Morris in an introspective unfinished essay. Did he do this out of "personal Consideration" or out of a desire to promote the public good? If he did it to promote the public good, "was he justifiable in sacrificing to it the Subsistence of his Family? These are important Questions; but," said Morris, "there remains one more," and that one question of Morris's threatened to undermine the whole classical tradition: "Would not as much Good have followed from an industrious Attention to his own Affairs?" Hamilton, for one, could not agree. Although he knew that most people were selfish scavengers, incapable of noble and disinterested acts, he did not want to be one of them. Thus he refused to make speculative killings in land or banking "because," as he put it in one of his sardonic moods, "there must be some *public fools* who sacrifice private to public interest at the certainty of ingratitude and obloquy—because my *vanity* whispers I ought to be one of those fools and ought to keep myself in a situation the best calculated to render service." Hamilton clung as long and as hard to this classical conception of leadership as anyone in post-Revolutionary America.

Washington too felt the force of the classical ideal and throughout his life was compulsive about his disinterestedness. Because he had not gone to college and acquired a liberal education, he always felt he had to live literally by the book. He was continually anxious that he not be thought too ambitious or self-seeking; above all, he did not want to be thought greedy or "interested." He refused to accept a salary for any of his public services, and he was scrupulous in avoiding any private financial benefits from his governmental positions.

Perhaps nothing more clearly reveals Washington's obsession with these classical republican values than his agonized response in the winter of 1784–1785 to the Virginia Assembly's gift of 150 shares in the James River and Potomac canal companies. Acceptance of the shares seemed clearly impossible. The shares might be "considered in the same light as a pension," he said. He would be thought "a dependant," and his reputation for virtue would be compromised. At the same time, however, Washington believed passionately in what the canal companies were doing; indeed, he had long dreamed of making a fortune from such canals. He thought the shares might constitute "the foundation of the *greatest* and most *certain* income" that anyone could expect from a speculative venture. Besides, he did not want to show "disrespect" to his countrymen or to appear "ostentatiously disinterested" by refusing the gift of the shares.

What should he do? Few decisions in Washington's career called for such handwringing as this one did. He sought the advice of nearly everyone he knew. Letters went out to Jefferson, to Governor Patrick Henry, to William Grayson, to Benjamin Harrison, to George William Fairfax, to Nathanael Greene, to Henry Knox, even to Lafayette—all seeking "the best information and advice" on the disposition of the shares. "How would this matter be viewed then by the eyes of the world[?]" he asked. Would not his reputation for virtue be tarnished? Would not accepting the shares "deprive me of the principal thing which is laudable in my conduct?"—that is, his disinterestedness.

The story would be comic if Washington had not been so deadly earnest. He understated the situation when he told his correspondents that his mind was "not a little agitated" by the problem. In letter after letter he expressed real anguish. This was no ordinary display of scruples such as government officials today show over a conflict of interest: in 1784–1785 Washington was not even holding public office.

These values, this need for disinterestedness in public officials, were very much on the minds of the founding fathers at the Philadelphia Convention, especially James Madison's. Madison was a tough-minded thinker, not given to illusions. He knew that there were "clashing interests" everywhere and that they were doing great harm to state legislative politics. But he had not yet given up hope that it might be possible to put into government, at the national if not at the state level, some "proper guardians of the public weal," men of "the most attractive merit, and most diffusive and established characters." We have too often mistaken Madison for some sort of prophet of a modern interest-group theory of politics. But Madison was not a forerunner of twentieth-century political scientists such as Arthur Bentley, David Truman, or Robert Dahl. Despite his hardheaded appreciation of the multiplicity of interests in American society, he did not offer America a pluralist conception of politics. He did not see public policy or the common good emerging naturally from the give-and-take of hosts of competing interests. Instead he hoped that these clashing interests and parties in an enlarged national republic would neutralize themselves and thereby allow liberally educated, rational men, "whose enlightened views and virtuous sentiments render them superior to local prejudices, and to schemes of injustice," to promote the public good in a disinterested manner. Madison, in other words, was not at all as modern as we make him out to be. He did not expect the new national government to be an integrator and harmonizer of the different interests in the society; instead he expected it to be a "disinterested and dispassionate umpire in disputes between different passions and interests in the State." Madison even suggested that the national government might play the same superpolitical, neutral role that the British king had been supposed to play in the empire.

The Federalists' plans for the Constitution, in other words, rested on their belief that there were some disinterested gentemen left in America to act as neutral umpires. In this sense the Constitution became a grand—and perhaps in retrospect a final desperate—effort to realize the great hope of the Revolution: the possibility of virtuous politics. The Constitution thus looked backward as much as it looked forward. Despite the Federalists' youthful energy, originality, and vision, they still clung to the classical tradition of civic humanism and its patrician code of disinterested public leadership. They stood for a moral and social order that was radically different from the popular, individualistic, and acquisitive world they saw emerging in the 1780s.

✛ F U R T H E R   R E A D I N G

Charles A. Beard, *An Economic Interpretation of the Constitution* (1913)
Christopher Collier and Lincoln Collier, *Decision in Philadelphia: The Constitutional Convention of 1787* (1986)
Edward S. Corwin, "The Progress of Constitutional Theory Between the Declaration of Independence and the Meeting of the Philadelphia Convention," *American Historical Review* 30 (1925): 511–536
Paul Finkelman, "Slavery and the Constitutional Convention: Making a Covenant with Death," in Richard Beeman, Stephen Botein, and Edward C. Carter, II, eds., *Beyond Confederation: Origins of the Constitution and American National Identity* (1987): 188–225
Leonard Levy, *Original Intent and the Framers' Constitution* (1988)
Forrest McDonald, *E Pluribus Unum* (1979)
Peter Onuf, *Statehood and Union: A History of the Northwest Ordinance* (1987)
J. R. Pole, *Political Representation in England and the Origins of the American Republic* (1969)
Clinton Rossiter, *1787: The Grand Convention* (1966)
Gordon Wood, *The Creation of the American Republic, 1776–1787* (1969)

CHAPTER 5

Ratification and the
Bill of Rights

⹕

Four months of intense work in Philadelphia was required to create the Consti-
tution, and ten more months passed before the necessary nine states ratified the
document. The old Articles of Confederation had provided that the Articles' pro-
visions could be changed only by the unanimous consent of the states, but the
delegates in Philadelphia realized that they could never achieve such agreement.
They also worried that if the new document was presented to the state legisla-
tures for approval, many of them would balk. Ratification, therefore, was at-
tained by separate ratifying conventions in each of the states, in a process that
gave the new Constitution an independent base of authority. The tenuous sup-
port for the Constitution was underscored by the fact that several delegates to the
Philadelphia convention opposed it. Luther Martin of Maryland, for example,
undertook an abortive effort to block ratification in his state.

Initially, the Federalists, who supported the document, achieved quick suc-
cesses in Delaware, New Jersey, and Georgia. The real struggle began in Penn-
sylvania in December 1787, when the Federalists gained approval only by
strong-arming their opponents into calling a convention and ratifying the docu-
ment. Thereafter, the ratification struggle shifted to three key states—Massachu-
setts, Virginia, and New York. In the last of these, Robert Yates and John Lan-
sing, who had left the federal convention in disgust, actively tried to block
ratification. In Massachusetts, Elbridge Gerry, who had refused to sign the Con-
stitution, also sought to prevent ratification, as did George Mason in Virginia.
Edmund Randolph, also of Virginia, initially had opposed the Constitution, but
he ultimately threw his support behind it.

The Anti-Federalist opponents of the Constitution attacked the document on
two grounds. First, they claimed that the Constitution consolidated too much
power in the hands of the national government, not only by granting excessive
authority to Congress but also by creating a strong executive and, most signifi-
cant of all, a national judiciary. The Anti-Federalists also complained that the
new Constitution, unlike most state constitutions, did not contain a bill of rights
to safeguard individual liberty from the usurpations of the national government.

The Federalists had the upper hand in the political struggle over ratifica-

tion. *They tended to come from urban, commercial, and seacoast areas where communications were effective, whereas Anti-Federalists usually hailed from outlying rural and western areas off the beaten path. Despite their organizational and communication problems, the Anti-Federalists brought sufficient pressure on the first Congress to prod it into adopting a bill of rights. Indeed, five states conditioned their ratification on just such amendments to the document. Anti-Federalists also threatened to call a second convention, with Virginia submitting its application to Congress on May 5, 1789. Two other states, North Carolina and Rhode Island, refused to ratify the Constitution because it did not contain a bill of rights. Led by James Madison, who had insisted during the constitutional convention that a bill of rights was unnecessary, the members of the First Congress ultimately agreed on twelve amendments. The ten that the states subsequently ratified became the Bill of Rights.*

✠ *D O C U M E N T S*

The ratification struggle began immediately following the Philadelphia convention in September 1787 and continued through the first meeting of Congress in 1789. Robert Yates and John Lansing, delegates to the convention from New York, not only refused to sign the document, but in a letter to the governor of New York, reprinted here as the first selection, urged that it not be ratified. Perhaps the best overview of the weaknesses of the Constitution was provided in the address of the Albany Antifederal Committee on April 26, 1788, the second document in this chapter. Virginian George Mason, who had also refused to sign the Constitution, pressed the fight against ratification in his home state, and his "Objections to the Proposed Constitution," the third selection here, was a starting point for both critics and supporters of the document. One of the most influential of the Anti-Federalist writings came from the pen of "Brutus," whose exact identity remains unknown, although scholars speculate that he was Robert Yates. In the fourth reading, "Brutus" stresses the aristocratic and undemocratic nature of the new national government.

The Anti-Federalists were concerned with Article III generally and the power of the proposed federal judiciary specifically. The fifth selection, featuring the debate in the Virginia convention between Patrick Henry, an ardent Anti-Federalist, and John Marshall, the future chief justice of the United States, illuminates these contending views of judicial authority.

The *Federalist Papers*, which were written by John Jay, Alexander Hamilton, and James Madison, offered the most persuasive case for the Constitution. The single most important of these essays was Madison's *Federalist No. 10,* the sixth selection, which deals with ideas of representation and sovereignty upon which the entire Constitution rested. Madison also orchestrated the movement in Congress for a bill of rights, and his speech of June 8, 1789, the final selection, was the most important moment in the House debates over it.

Robert Yates and John Lansing of New York Urge Against Ratification of the Constitution, 1787

. . . We beg leave, briefly, to state some cogent reasons, which, among others, influenced us to decide against a consolidation of the states. These are reducible into two heads:—

1st. The limited and well-defined powers under which we acted, and which could not, on any possible construction, embrace an idea of such magnitude as to assent to a general constitution, in subversion of that of the state.

2nd. A conviction of the impracticability of establishing a general government, pervading every part of the United States, and extending essential benefits to all.

Our powers were explicit, and confined to the sole and express purpose of revising the Articles of Confederation, and reporting such alterations and provisions therein, as should render the Federal Constitution adequate to the exigencies of government, and the preservation of the Union.

From these expressions, we were led to believe that a system of consolidated government could not, in the remotest degree, have been in contemplation of the legislature of this state; for that so important a trust, as the adopting measures which tended to deprive the state government of its most essential rights of sovereignty, and to place it in a dependent situation, could not have been confided by implication; and the circumstance, that the acts of the Convention were to receive a state approbation in the last resort, forcibly corroborated the opinion that our powers could not involve the subversion of a Constitution which, being immediately derived from the people, could only be abolished by their express consent, and not by a legislature, possessing authority vested in them for its preservation. Nor could we suppose that, if it had been the intention of the legislature to abrogate the existing confederation, they would, in such pointed terms, have directed the attention of their delegates to the revision and amendment of it, in total exclusion of every other idea.

Reasoning in this manner, we were of opinion that the leading feature of every amendment ought to be the preservation of the individual states in their uncontrolled constitutional rights, and that, in reserving these, a mode might have been devised of granting to the Confederacy, the moneys arising from a general system of revenue, the power of regulating commerce and enforcing the observance of foreign treaties, and other necessary matters of less moment.

Exclusive of our objections originating from the want of power, we entertained an opinion that a general government, however guarded by declarations of rights, or cautionary provisions, must unavoidably, in a short time, be productive of the destruction of the civil liberty of such citizens who could be effectually coerced by it, by reason of the extensive territory of the United States, the dispersed situation of its inhabitants, and the insuperable difficulty of controlling or counteracting the views of a set of men (however unconstitutional and oppressive their acts might be) possessed of all the powers of government, and who, from their remoteness from their constituents, and necessary permanency of office, could not be supposed to be uniformly actuated by an attention to their welfare and happiness; that, however wise and energetic the principles of the general government might be, the extremities of the United States could not be kept in due submission and obedience to its laws, at the distance of many hundred miles from the seat of government; that, if the general legislature was composed of so numerous a body of men as to represent the interests of all the inhabitants of the United States, in the usual and true ideas of representation, the expense of supporting it would become intolerably burdensome; and that, if a few only were vested with a power of legislation, the interests of a great majority of the inhabitants of the United States must necessarily be unknown; or, if known, even in the first stages of the operations of the new government, unattended to.

These reasons were, in our opinion, conclusive against any system of consolidated government: to that recommended by the Convention, we suppose most of them very forcibly apply. . . .

The Albany Anti-Federal Committee Outlines the Weaknesses of the Constitution, 1788

Address of the Albany Antifederal Committee
April 26, 1788

As we have been informed, that the advocates for the new constitution, have lately travelled through the several districts in the county, and propogated an opinion, that it is a good system of government: we beg leave to state, in as few words as possible, some of the many objections against it.—

The convention, who were appointed for the sole and express purpose of revising and amending the confederation, have taken upon themselves the power of making a new one.

They have not formed a *federal* but a *consolidated* government, repugnant to the principles of a republican government: not founded on the preservation but the destruction of the state governments.

The great and extensive powers granted to the new government over the lives, liberties, and property of every citizen.

These powers in many instances not defined or sufficiently explained, and capable of being interpreted to answer the most ambitious and arbitrary purposes.

The small number of members who are to compose the general legislature, which is to pass laws to govern so large and extensive a continent, inhabited by people of different laws, customs, and opinions, and many of them residing upwards of 400 miles from the seat of government.

The members of the senate are not to be chosen by the people, but appointed by the legislature of each state for the term of six years. This will destroy their responsibility, and induce them to act like the masters and not the servants of the people.

The power to alter and regulate the time, place, and manner of holding elections, so as to keep them subjected to their influence.

The power to lay poll taxes, duties, imposts, excises, and other taxes.

The power to appoint continental officers to levy and collect those taxes.

Their laws are to be *the supreme law of the land,* and the judges in every state are to be bound thereby, notwithstanding *the constitution or laws* of any state to the contrary.—A sweeping clause, which subjects every thing to the controul of the new government.

Slaves are taken into the computation in apportioning the number of representatives, whereby 50,000 slaves, give an equal representation with 30,000 freemen.

The power to raise, support, and maintain a standing army *in time of peace.* The bane of a republican government; by a standing army most of the once free nations of the globe have been reduced to bondage; and by this Britain attempted to inforce her arbitrary measures.

Men conscienciously scrupulous of bearing arms, made liable to perform military duty.

The not securing the rights of conscience in matters of religion, of granting the liberty of worshipping God agreeable to the mode thereby dictated; whereas the experience of all ages proves that the benevolence and humility inculcated in the gospel, are no restraint on the love of domination.

George Mason's Objections to the Proposed Constitution, 1787

There is no Declaration of Rights; and the Laws of the general Government being paramount to the Laws and Constitutions of the several States, the Declaration of Rights in the separate States are no Security. Nor are the people secured even in the Enjoyment of the Benefits of the common-Law: which stands here upon no other Foundation than its having been adopted by the respective Acts forming the Constitutions of the several States.

In the House of Representatives there is not the Substance, but the Shadow only of Representation; which can never produce proper Information in the Legislature, or inspire Confidence in the People: the Laws will therefore be generally made by Men little concern'd in, and unacquainted with their Effects and Consequences.

The Senate have the Power of altering all Money-Bills, and of originating Appropriations of Money and the Sallerys of the Officers of their own Appointment in Conjunction with the President of the United States; altho' they are not the Representatives of the People, or amenable to them.

These with their other great Powers (vizt. their Power in the Appointment of Ambassadors and all public Officers, in making Treaties, and in trying all Impeachments) their Influence upon and Connection with the supreme Executive from these Causes, their Duration of Office, and their being a constant existing Body almost continually sitting, joined with their being one compleat Branch of the Legislature, will destroy any Balance in the Government, and enable them to accomplish what Usurpations they please upon the Rights and Libertys of the People.

The Judiciary of the United States is so constructed and extended, as to absorb and destroy the Judiciarys of the several States; thereby rendering Law as tedious[,] intricate and expensive, and Justice as unattainable, by a great part of the Community, as in England, and enabling the Rich to oppress and ruin the Poor.

The President of the United States has no constitutional Council (a thing unknown in any safe and regular Government) he will therefore be unsupported by proper Information and Advice; and will generally be directed by Minions and Favourites—or He will become a Tool to the Senate—or a Council of State will grow out of the principal Officers of the great Departments; the worst and most dangerous of all Ingredients for such a Council, in a free Country; for they may be induced to join in any dangerous or oppressive Measures, to shelter themselves, and prevent an Inquiry into their own Misconduct in Office; whereas had a constitutional Council been formed (as was proposed) of six Members; vizt. two from the Eastern, two from the Middle, and two from the Southern States, to be appointed by Vote of the States in the House of Representatives, with the same Duration and Rotation of Office as the Senate, the Executive wou'd always have had safe and proper Information and Advice, the President of such a Council might have acted as Vice President of the United States, pro tempore, upon any Vacancy or Disability of the chief Magistrate; and long continued Sessions of the Senate wou'd in a great Measure have been prevented.

From this fatal Defect of a constitutional Council has arisen the improper Power of the Senate, in the Appointment of public Officers, and the alarming Dependence and Connection between that Branch of the Legislature, and the supreme Executive.

Hence also sprung that unnecessary and dangerous Officer, the Vice President; who for want of other Employment, is made President of the Senate; thereby dangerously blending the executive and legislative Powers; besides always giving to some one of the States an unnecessary and unjust Preeminence over the others.

The President of the United States has the unrestrained Power of granting Pardon for Treason; which may be sometimes exercised to screen from Punishment those whom he had secretly instigated to commit the Crime, and thereby prevent a Discovery of his own Guilt.

By declaring all Treaties supreme Laws of the Land, the Executive and the Senate have in many Cases, an exclusive Power of Legislation; which might have been avoided by proper Distinctions with Respect to Treaties, and requiring the Assent of the House of Representatives, where it cou'd be done with Safety.

By requiring only a Majority to make all commercial and navigation Laws, the five Southern States (whose Produce and Circumstances are totally different from that of the eight Northern and Eastern States) will be ruined; for such rigid and premature Regulations may be made, as will enable the Merchants of the Northern and Eastern States not only to demand an exorbitant Freight, but to monopolize the Purchase of the Commodities at their own Price, for many years: to the great Injury of the landed Interest, and Impoverishment of the People: and the Danger is the greater, as the

Gain on one Side will be in Proportion to the Loss on the other. Whereas requiring two thirds of the members present in both Houses wou'd have produced mutual moderation, promoted the general Interest, and removed an insuperable Objection to the Adoption of the Government.

Under their own Construction of the general Clause at the End of the enumerated powers the Congress may grant Monopolies in Trade and Commerce, constitute new Crimes, inflict unusual and severe Punishments, and extend their Power as far as they shall think proper; so that the State Legislatures have no Security for the Powers now presumed to remain to them; or the People for their Rights.

There is no Declaration of any kind for preserving the Liberty of the Press, the Tryal by Jury in civil Causes; nor against the Danger of standing Armys in time of Peace.

The State Legislatures are restrained from laying Export Duties on their own Produce.

The general Legislature is restrained from prohibiting the futher Importation of Slaves for twenty odd Years; tho' such Importations render the United States weaker, more vulnerable, and less capable of Defence.

Both the general Legislature and the State Legislatures are expressly prohibited [from] making ex post facto Laws; tho' there never was, or can be a Legislature but must and will make such Laws, when necessity and the public Safety require them; which will hereafter be a Breach of all the Constitutions in the Union, and afford precedents for other Innovations.

This Government will commence in a moderate Aristocracy; it is at present impossible to foresee whether it will, in its Operation, produce a Monarchy, or a corrupt oppressive Aristocracy; it will most probably vibrate some Years between the two, and then terminate in the one or the other.

"Brutus" Blasts the New National Government, 1787

No. 1, October 18, 1787

To the Citizens of the State of New-York.
If respect is to be paid to the opinion of the greatest and wisest men who have ever thought or wrote on the science of government, we shall be constrained to conclude, that a free republic cannot succeed over a country of such immense extent, containing such a number of inhabitants, and these encreasing in such rapid progression as that of the whole United States.

Not only the opinion of the greatest men, and the experience of mankind, are against the idea of an extensive republic, but a variety of reasons may be drawn from the reason and nature of things, against it. In every government, the will of the sovereign is the law. In despotic governments, the supreme authority being lodged in one, his will is law, and can be as easily expressed to a large extensive territory as to a small one. In a pure democracy the people are the sovereign, and their will is declared by themselves; for this purpose they must all come together to deliberate, and decide. This kind of government cannot be exercised, therefore, over a country of any considerable extent; it must be confined to a single city, or at least limited to such bounds as that the people can conveniently assemble, be able to debate, understand the subject submitted to them, and declare their opinion concerning it.

In a free republic, although all laws are derived from the consent of the people, yet the people do not declare their consent by themselves in person, but by representatives, chosen by them, who are supposed to know the minds of their constituents, and to be possessed of integrity to declare this mind.

In every free government, the people must give their assent to the laws by which they are governed. This is the true criterion between a free government and an arbitrary one. The former are ruled by the will of the whole, expressed in any manner they may agree upon; the latter by the will of one, or a few. If the people are to give their assent to the laws, by persons chosen and appointed by them, the manner of the choice and the number of chosen, must be such, as to possess, be disposed, and consequently qualified to declare the sentiments of the people; for if they do not know, or are not disposed to speak the sentiments of the people, the people do not govern, but the sovereignty is in a few. Now, in a large extended country, it is impossible to have a representation, possessing the sentiments, and of integrity, to declare the minds of the people, without having it so numerous and unwieldly, as to be subject in great measure to the inconveniency of a democratic government.

The territory of the United States is of vast extent; it now contains near three millions of souls, and is capable of containing much more than ten times that number. Is it practicable for a country, so large and so numerous as they will soon become, to elect a representation, that will speak their sentiments, without their becoming so numerous as to be incapable of transacting public business? It certainly is not.

In a republic, the manners, sentiments, and interests of the people should be similar. If this be not the case, there will be a constant clashing of opinions; and the representatives of one part will be continually striving against those of the other. This will retard the operations of government, and prevent such conclusions as will promote the public good. If we apply this remark to the condition of the United States, we shall be convinced that it forbids that we should be one government. The United States includes a variety of climates. The productions of the different parts of the union are very variant, and their interests, of consequence, diverse. Their manners and habits differ as much as their climates and productions; and their sentiments are by no means coincident. The laws and customs of the several states are, in many respects, very diverse, and in some opposite; each would be in favor of its own interests and customs, and, of consequence, a legislature, formed of representatives from the respective parts, would not only be too numerous to act with any care or decision, but would be composed of such heterogenous and discordant principles, as would constantly be contending with each other.

No. 2, November 1, 1787

If we may collect the sentiments of the people of America, from their own most solemn declarations, they hold this truth as self evident, that all men are by nature free. No one man, therefore, or any class of men, have a right, by the law of nature, or of God, to assume or exercise authority over their fellows. The origin of society then is to be sought, not in any natural right which one man has to exercise authority over another, but in the united consent of those who associate. The mutual wants of men, at first dictated the propriety of forming societies; and when they were established, protection and defence pointed out the necessity of instituting government. In a state of nature every individual pursues his own interest; in this pursuit it frequently happened, that the possessions or enjoyments of one were sacrificed to the views and designs of another; thus the weak were a prey to the strong, the simple and unwary were subject to impositions from those who were more crafty and designing. In this state of things, every individual was insecure; common interest therefore directed, that government should be established, in which the force of the whole community should be collected, and under such directions, as to protect and defend every one who composed it. The common good, therefore, is the end of civil government, and common consent, the foundation on which it is established. To effect this end, it was necessary that a certain portion of natural liberty should be surrendered, in order, that what remained should be preserved: how great a proportion of natural freedom is necessary to be yielded by individuals, when they submit to government, I shall now enquire. So much, however, must be given up, as will be sufficient to enable those, to whom the administration of the government is committed, to establish laws for the promoting the happiness of the community, and to carry those laws into effect. But it is not necessary, for this purpose, that individuals should relinquish all their natural rights. Some are of such a nature that they cannot be surrendered. Of this kind are the rights of conscience, the right of enjoying and defending life, etc. Others are not necessary to be resigned, in order to attain the end for which government is instituted, these therefore ought not to be given up. To surrender them, would counteract the very end of government, to wit, the common good. From these observations it appears, that in forming a government on its true principles, the foundation should be laid in the manner I before stated, by expressly reserving to the people such of their essential natural rights, as are not necessary to be parted with. The same reasons which at first induced mankind to associate and institute government, will operate to influence them to observe this precaution. If they had been disposed to conform themselves to the rule of immutable righteousness, government would not have been requisite. It was because one part exercised fraud, oppression, and violence on the other, that men came together, and agreed that certain rules should be formed, to regulate the conduct of all, and the power of the whole community lodged in the hands of rulers to enforce an obedience to them. But rulers have the same propensities as other men; they are as likely to use the power with which they are vested for private purposes, and to the injury and oppression of those over whom they are placed, as individuals in a state of nature are to injure and oppress one another. It is therefore as proper that bounds should be set to their authority, as that government should have at first been instituted to restrain private injuries.

This principle, which seems so evidently founded in the reason and nature of things, is confirmed by universal experience. Those who have governed, have been found in all ages ever active to enlarge their powers and abridge the public liberty. This has induced the people in all countries, where any sense of freedom remained, to fix barriers against the encroachments of their rulers. The country from which we have derived our origin, is an eminent example of this. Their magna charta and bill of rights have long been the boast, as well as the security, of that nation. I need say no more, I presume, to an American, then, that this principle is a fundamental one, in all the constitutions of our own states; there is not one of them but what is either founded on a declaration or bill of rights, or has certain express reservation of rights interwoven in the body of them. From this it appears, that at a time when the pulse of liberty beat high and when an appeal was made to the people to form constitutions for the government of themselves, it was their universal sense, that such declarations should make a part of their frames of government. It is therefore the more astonishing, that this grand security, to the rights of the people, is not to be found in this constitution.

Patrick Henry and John Marshall Debate Judicial Authority, 1788

Mr. Mason: After having read the first section, Mr. Mason asked, What is there left to the state courts? Will any gentleman be pleased, candidly, fairly, and without sophistry, to show us what remains? There is no limitation. It goes to every thing. The inferior courts are to be as numerous as Congress may think proper. They are to be of whatever nature they please. Read the 2d section, and contemplate attentively the extent of the jurisdiction of these courts, and consider if there be any limits to it.

I am greatly mistaken if there be any limitation whatsoever, with respect to the nature or jurisdiction of these courts. If there be any limits, they must be contained in one of the clauses of this section; and I believe, on a dispassionate discussion, it will be found that there is none of any check. All the laws of the United States are paramount to the laws and constitution of any single state. "The judicial power shall extend to all cases in law and equity arising under this Constitution." What objects will not this expression extend to? Such laws may be formed as will go to every object of private property.

Their *jurisdiction* further extends to controversies between citizens of different states. Can we not trust our state courts with the decision of these? If I have a controversy with a man in Maryland,—if a man in Maryland has my bond for a hundred pounds.—are not the state courts competent to try it? Is it suspected that they would enforce the payment if unjust, or refuse to enforce it if just? The very idea is ridiculous. What! carry me a thousand miles from home—from my family and business—to where, perhaps, it will be impossible for me to prove that I paid it? Perhaps I have a respectable witness who saw me pay the money; but I must carry him one thousand miles to prove it, or be compelled to pay it again. Is there any necessity for this power? It ought to have no unnecessary or dangerous power. Why should the federal courts have this cognizance? Is it because one lives on one side of the Potomac, and the other on the other? Suppose I have your bond for a thousand pounds: if I have any wish to harass you, or if I be of a litigious disposition, I have only to assign it to a gentleman in Maryland. This assignment will involve you in trouble and expense.

Mr. Henry: I consider the Virginia judiciary as one of the best barriers against strides of power—against that power which has threatened the destruction of liberty. Pardon me for expressing my extreme regret that it is in their power to take away that barrier. Gentlemen will not say that any danger can be expected from the state legislatures. So small are the barriers against the encroachments and usurpations of Congress, that, when I see this last barrier—the independency of the judges—impaired, I am persuaded I see the prostration of all our rights. In what a situation will your judges be, when they are sworn to preserve the Constitution of the state and of the general government! If there be a concurrent dispute between them, which will prevail? They cannot serve two masters struggling for the same object. The laws of Congress being paramount to those of the states, and to their constitutions also, whenever they come in competition, the judges must decide in favor of the former. This, instead of relieving or aiding me, deprives me of my only comfort—the independency of the judges. The judiciary are the sole protection against a tyrannical execution of the laws. But if by this system we lose our judiciary, and they cannot help us, we must sit down quietly, and be oppressed.

As to controversies between a state and the citizens of another state, his [Mr. Madison's] construction of it is to me perfectly incomprehensible. He says it will seldom happen that a state has such demands on individuals. There is nothing to warrant such an assertion. But he says that the state may be plaintiff only. If gentlemen pervert the most clear expressions, and the usual meaning of the language of the people, there is an end of all argument. What says the paper? That it shall have cognizance of controversies between a state and citizens of another state, without discriminating between plaintiff and defendant. What says the honorable gentleman? The contrary—that the state can only be plaintiff. When the state is debtor, there is no reciprocity. It seems to me that gentlemen may put what construction they please on it. What! is justice to be done to one party, and not to the other? If gentlemen take this liberty now, what will they not do when our rights and liberties are in their power? He said it was necessary to provide a tribunal when the case happened, though it would happen but seldom. The power is necessary, because New York could not, before the war, collect money from Connecticut! The state judiciaries are so degraded that they cannot be trusted. This is a dangerous power which is thus instituted. For what? For things which will seldom happen; and yet, because there is a possibility that the strong, energetic government may want it, it shall be produced and thrown in the general scale of power. I confess I think it dangerous.

Mr. John Marshall. Mr. Chairman, this part of the plan before us is a great improvement on that system from which we are now departing. Here are tribunals appointed for *the decision of controversies* which were before either not at all, or improperly, provided for. That many benefits will result from this to the members of the collective society, every one confesses. Unless its organization be defective, and so constructed as to injure, instead of accommodating, the convenience of the people, it merits our approbation. After such a candid and fair discussion by those gentlemen who support it,—after the very able manner in which they have investigated and examined it,—I conceived it would be no longer considered as so very defective, and that those who opposed it would be convinced of the impropriety of some of their objections. But I perceive they still continue the same opposition. Gentlemen have gone on an idea that the federal courts will not determine the causes which may come before them with the same fairness and impartiality with which other courts decide. What are the reasons of this supposition? Do they draw them from the manner in which the judges are chosen, or the tenure of their office? What is it that makes us trust our judges? Their independence in office, and manner of appointment. Are not the judges of the federal court chosen with as much wisdom as the judges of the state government? Are they not equally, if not more independent? If so, shall we not conclude that they will decide with equal impartiality and candor? If there be as much wisdom and knowledge in the United States as in a particular state, shall we conclude that the wisdom and knowledge will not be equally exercised in the selection of judges?

These, sir, are the points of *federal jurisdiction* to which he objects, with a few exceptions. Let us examine each of them with a supposition that the same impartiality will be observed there as in other courts, and then see if any mischief will result from them. With respect to its cognizance in all cases arising under the Constitution and the laws of the United States, he [Patrick Henry] says that, the laws of the United States being paramount to the laws of the particular states, there is no case but what this will extend to. Has the government of the United States power to make laws on every subject? Does he understand it so? Can they make laws affecting the mode of transferring property, or contracts, or claims, between citizens of the same state? Can they go beyond the delegated powers? If they were to make a law not warranted by any of the powers enumerated, it would be considered by the judges as an infringement of the Constitution which they are to guard. They would not consider such a law as coming under this jurisdiction. They would declare it void. It will annihilate the state courts, says the honorable gentleman. Does not every gentleman here know that the causes in our courts are more numerous than they can decide, according to their present construction? Look at the dockets. You will find them crowded with suits, which the life of man will not see determined. If some of these suits be carried to other courts, will it be wrong? They will still have business enough.

Then there is no danger that particular subjects, small in proportion, being taken out of the jurisdiction of the state judiciaries, will render them useless and of no effect. Does the gentleman think that the state courts will have no cognizance of cases not mentioned here? Are there any words in this Constitution which exclude the courts of the states from those cases which they now possess? Does the gentleman imagine this to be the case? Will any gentleman believe it? Are not controversies respecting lands claimed under the grants of different states the only controversies between citizens of the same state which the federal judiciary can take cognizance of? The case is so clear, that to prove it would be a useless waste of time. The state courts will not lose the jurisdiction of the causes they now decide. They have a concurrence of jurisdiction with the federal courts in those cases in which the latter have cognizance.

With respect to disputes between a *state and the citizens of another state,* I hope that no gentleman will think that a state will be called at the bar of the federal court. Is there no such case at present? Are there not many cases in which the legislature of Virginia is a party, and yet the state is not sued? It is not rational to suppose that the sovereign power should be dragged before a court. The intent is, to enable states to recover claims of individuals residing in other states. I contend this construction is warranted by the words. But, say they, there will be partiality in it if a state cannot be defendant— if an individual cannot proceed to obtain judgement against a state, though he may be sued by a state. It is necessary to be so, and cannot be avoided. I see a difficulty in making a state defendant, which does not prevent its being plaintiff. If this be only what cannot be avoided, why object to the system on that account? If an individual has a just claim against any particular state, is it to be presumed that, on application to its legislature, he will not obtain satisfaction? But how could a state recover any claim from a citizen of another state, without the establishment of these tribunals?

James Madison on Representation and Sovereignty, 1788

Among the numerous advantages promised by a well-constructed Union, none deserves to be more accurately developed than its tendency to break and control the violence of faction. The friend of popular governments never finds himself so much alarmed for their character and fate as when he contemplates their propensity to this dangerous vice. He will not fail, therefore, to set a due value on any plan which, without violating the principles to which he is attached, provides a proper cure for it. The instability, injustice, and confusion introduced into the public councils have, in truth, been the mortal diseases under which popular governments have everywhere perished, as they continue to be the favorite and fruitful topics from which the adversaries to liberty derive their most specious declamations. . . . However anxiously we may wish that these complaints had no foundation, the evidence of known facts will not permit us to deny that they are in some degree true. It will be found, indeed, on a candid review of our situation, that some of the distresses under which we labor have been erroneously charged on the operation of our governments; but it will be found, at the same time, that other causes will not alone account for many of our heaviest misfortunes; and, particularly, for that prevailing and increasing distrust of public engagements and alarm for private rights which are echoed from one end of the continent to the other. These must be chiefly, if not wholly, effects of the unsteadiness and injustice with which a factious spirit has tainted our public administration.

By a faction I understand a number of citizens, whether amounting to a majority or minority of the whole, who are united and actuated by some common impulse of passion, or of interest, adverse to the rights of other citizens, or to the permanent and aggregate interests of the community.

There are two methods of curing the mischiefs of faction: the one, by removing its causes; the other, by controlling its effects.

There are again two methods of removing the causes of faction: the one, by destroying the liberty which is essential to its existence; the other, by giving to every citizen the same opinions, the same passions, and the same interests.

It could never be more truly said than of the first remedy that it was worse than the disease. Liberty is to faction what air is to fire, an aliment without which it instantly expires. But it could not be a less folly to abolish liberty, which is essential to political life, because it nourishes faction than it would be to wish the annihilation of air, which is essential to animal life, because it imparts to fire its destructive agency.

The second expedient is as impracticable as the first would be unwise. As long as the reason of man continues fallible, and he is at liberty to exercise it, different opinions will be formed. As long as the connection subsists between his reason and his self-love, his opinions and his passions will have a reciprocal influence on each other; and the former will be objects to which the latter will attach themselves. The diversity in the faculties of men, from which the rights of property originate, is not less an insuperable obstacle to a uniformity of interests. The protection of these faculties is the first object of government. From the protection of different and unequal faculties of acquiring property, the possession of different degrees and kinds of property immediately results; and from the influence of these on the sentiments and views of the respective proprietors ensues a division of the society into different interests and parties.

The latent causes of faction are thus sown in the nature of man; and we see them everywhere brought into different degrees of activity, according to the different circumstances of civil society. A zeal for different opinions concerning religion, concerning government, and many other points, as well of speculation as of practice; an attachment to different leaders ambitiously contending for pre-eminence and power; or to persons of other descriptions whose fortunes have been interesting to the human passions, have, in turn, divided mankind into parties, inflamed them with mutual animosity, and rendered them much more disposed to vex and oppress each other than to co-operate for their common good. So strong is this propensity of mankind to fall into mutual animosities that where no substantial occasion presents itself the most frivolous and fanciful distinctions have been sufficient to kindle their unfriendly passions and excite their most violent conflicts. But the most common and durable source of factions has been the verious and unequal distribution of property. Those who hold and those who are without property have ever formed distinct interests in society. Those who are creditors, and those who are debtors, fall under a like discrimination. A landed interest, a manufacturing interest, a mercantile interest, a moneyed interest, with many lesser interests, grow up of necessity in civilized nations, and divide them into different classes, actuated by different sentiments and views. The regulation of these various and interfering interests forms the principal task of modern legislation and involves the spirit of party and faction in the necessary and ordinary operations of government.

No man is allowed to be a judge in his own cause, because his interest would certainly bias his judgment, and, not improbably, corrupt his integrity. With equal, nay with greater reason, a body of men are unfit to be both judges and parties at the same time; yet what are many of the most important acts of legislation but so many judicial determinations, not indeed concerning the rights of single persons, but concerning the rights of large bodies of citizens? And what are the different classes of legislators but advocates and parties to the causes which they determine? Is a law proposed concerning private debts? It is a question to which the creditors are parties on one side and the debtors on the other. Justice ought to hold the balance between them. Yet the parties are, and must be, themselves the judges; and the most numerous party, or in other words, the most powerful faction must be expected to prevail. Shall domestic manufacturers be encouraged, and in what degree, by restrictions on foreign manufacturers? are questions which would be differently decided by the landed and the manufacturing classes, and probably by neither with a sole regard to justice and the public good. The apportionment of taxes on the various descriptions of property is an act which seems to require the most exact impartiality; yet there is, perhaps, no legislative act in which greater opportunity and temptation are given to a predominant party to trample on the rules of justice. Every shilling with which they overburden the inferior number is a shilling saved to their own pockets.

It is in vain to say that enlightened statesmen will be able to adjust these clashing interests and render them all subservient to the public good. Enlightened statesmen will not always be at the helm. Nor, in many cases, can such an adjustment be made at all without taking into view indirect and remote considerations, which will rarely prevail over the immediate interest which one party may find in disregarding the rights of another or the good of the whole.

The inference to which we are brought is that the *causes* of faction cannot be removed and that relief is only to be sought in the means of controlling its *effects*.

If a faction consists of less than a majority, relief is supplied by the republican principle, which enables the majority to defeat its sinister views by regular vote. It may clog the administration, it may convulse the society; but it will be unable to execute and mask its violence under the forms of the Constitution. When a majority is included in a faction, the form of popular government, on the other hand, enables it to sacrifice to its ruling passion or interest both the public good and the rights of other citizens. To secure the public good and private rights against the danger of such a faction, and at the same time to preserve the spirit and the form of popular government, is then the great object to which our inquiries are directed. Let me add that it is the great desideratum by which alone this form of government can be rescued from the opprobrium under which it has so long labored and be recommended to the esteem and adoption of mankind.

By what means is this object attainable? Evidently by one of two only. Either the existence of the same passion or interest in a majority at the same time must be prevented, or the majority, having such coexistent passion or interest, must be rendered, by their number and local situation, unable to concert and carry into effect schemes of oppression. If the impulse and the opportunity be suffered to coincide, we well know that neither moral nor religious motives can be relied on as an adequate control. They are not found to be such on the injustice and violence of individuals, and lose their efficacy in proportion to the number combined together, that is, in proportion as their efficacy becomes needful.

From this view of the subject it may be concluded that a pure democracy, by which I mean a society consisting of a small number of citizens, who assemble and administer the government in person, can admit of no cure for the mischiefs of faction. A common passion or interest will, in almost every case, be felt by a majority of the whole; a communication and concert results from the form of government itself; and there is nothing to check the inducements to sacrifice the weaker party or an obnoxious individual. Hence it is that such democracies have ever been spectacles of turbulence and contention; have ever been found incompatible with personal security or the rights of property; and have in general been as short in their lives as they have been violent in their deaths. Theoretic politicians, who have patronized this species of government, have erroneously supposed that by reducing mankind to a perfect equality in their political rights, they would at the same time be perfectly equalized and assimilated in their possessions, their opinions, and their passions.

A republic, by which I mean a government in which the scheme of representation takes place, opens a different prospect and promises the cure for which we are seeking. Let us examine the points in which it varies from pure democracy, and we shall comprehend both the nature of the cure and the efficacy which it must derive from the Union.

The two great points of difference between a democracy and a republic are: first, the delegation of the government, in the latter, to a small number of citizens elected by the rest; secondly, the greater number of citizens and greater sphere of country over which the latter may be extended.

The effect of the first difference is, on the one hand, to refine and enlarge the public views by passing them through the medium of a chosen body of citizens, whose wisdom may best discern the true interest of their country and whose patriotism and love of justice will be least likely to sacrifice it to temporary or partial considerations. . . . On the other hand, the effect may be inverted. Men of factious tempers, of local prejudices, or of sinister designs, may, by intrigue, by corruption, or by other means, first obtain the suffrages, and then betray the interests of the people. The question resulting is, whether small or extensive republics are most favorable to the election of proper guardians of the public weal; and it is clearly decided in favor of the latter by two obvious considerations.

In the first place it is to be remarked that however small the republic may be the representatives must be raised to a certain number in order to guard against the cabals of a few; and that however large it may be they must be limited to a certain number in order to guard against the confusion of a multitude. Hence, the number of representatives in the two cases not being in proportion to that of the constituents, and being proportionally greatest in the small republic, it follows that if the proportion of fit characters be not less in the large than in the small republic, the former will present a greater option, and consequently a greater probability of a fit choice.

In the next place, as each representative will be chosen by a greater number of citizens in the large than in the small republic, it will be more difficult for unworthy candidates to practise with success the vicious arts by which elections are too often carried; and the suffrages of the people being more free, will be more likely to center on men who possess the most attractive merit and the most diffusive and established characters.

It must be confessed that in this, as in most other cases, there is a mean, on both sides of which inconveniencies will be found to lie. By enlarging too much the number of electors, you render the representative too little acquainted with all their local circumstances and lesser interests; as by reducing it too much, you render him unduly attached to these, and too little fit to comprehend and pursue great and national objects. The federal Constitution forms a happy combination in this respect; the great and aggregate interests being referred to the national, the local and particular to the State legislatures.

The other point of difference is the greater number of citizens and extent of territory which may be brought within the compass of republican than of democratic government; and it is this circumstance principally which renders factious combinations less to be dreaded in the former than in the latter. The smaller the society, the fewer probably will be the distinct parties and interests composing it; the fewer the distinct parties and interests, the more frequently will a majority be found of the same party; and the smaller the number of individuals composing a majority, and the smaller the compass within which they are placed, the more easily will they concert and execute their plans of oppression. Extend the sphere and you take in a greater variety of parties and interests; you make it less probable that a majority of the whole will have a common motive to invade the rights of other citizens; or if such a common motive exists, it will be more difficult for all who feel it to discover their own strength and to act in unison with each other. Besides other impediments, it may be remarked that, where there is a consciousness of unjust or dishonorable purposes, communication is always checked by distrust in proportion to the number whose concurrence is necessary.

Hence, it clearly appears that the same advantage which a republic has over a democracy in controlling the effects of faction is enjoyed by a large over a small republic—is enjoyed by the Union over the States composing it. Does this advantage consist in the substitution of representatives whose enlightened views and virtuous sentiments render them superior to local prejudices and to schemes of injustice? It will not be denied that the representation of the Union will be most likely to possess these requisite endowments. Does it consist in the greater security afforded by a greater variety of parties, against the event of any one party being able to outnumber and oppress the rest? In an equal degree does the increased variety of parties comprised within the Union increase this security. Does it, in fine, consist in the greater obstacles opposed to the concert and accomplishment of the secret wishes of an unjust and interested majority? Here again the extent of the Union gives it the most palpable advantage.

The influence of factious leaders may kindle a flame within their particular States but will be unable to spread a general conflagration through the other States. A religious sect may degenerate into a political faction in a part of the Confederacy; but the variety of sects dispersed over the entire face of it must secure the national councils against any danger from that source. A rage for paper money, for an abolition of debts, for an equal division of property, or for any other improper or wicked project, will be less apt to pervade the whole body of the Union than a particular member of it, in the same proportion as such a malady is more likely to taint a particular county or district than an entire State.

In the extent and proper structure of the Union, therefore, we behold a republican remedy for the diseases most incident to republican government. And according to the degree of pleasure and pride we feel in being republicans ought to be our zeal in cherishing the spirit and supporting the character of federalists.

Publius

James Madison on the Bill of Rights, 1789

. . . It will be a desirable thing to extinguish from the bosom of every member of the community, any apprehensions that there are those among his countrymen who wish to deprive them of the liberty for which they valiantly fought and honorably bled. And if there are amendments desired of such a nature as will not injure the Constitution, and they can be ingrafted so as to give satisfaction to the doubting part of our fellow-citizens, the friends of the Federal Government will envince that spirit of deference and concession for which they have hitherto been distinguished.

It cannot be a secret to the gentlemen in this House, that, notwithstanding the ratification of this system of Government by eleven of the thirteen United States, in some cases unanimously, in others by large majorities; yet still there is a great number of our constituents who are dissatisfied with it; among whom are many respectable for their talents and patriotism, and respectable for the jealousy they have for their liberty, which, though mistaken in its object, is laudable in its motive. There is a great body of the people falling under this description, who at present feel much inclined to join their support to the cause of Federalism, if they were satisfied on this one point. We ought not to disregard their inclination, but, on principles of amity and moderation, conform to their wishes, and expressly declare the great rights of mankind secured under this Constitution.

But I will candidly acknowledge, that, over and above all these considerations, I do conceive that the Constitution may be amended; that is to say, if all power is subject to abuse, that then it is possible the abuse of the powers of the General Government may be guarded against in a more secure manner than is now done, while no one advantage arising from the exercise of that power shall be damaged or endangered by it. We have in this way something to gain, and, if we proceed with caution, nothing to lose.

I believe that the great mass of the people who opposed it, disliked it because it did not contain effectual provisions against the encroachments on particular rights, and those safeguards which they have been long accustomed to have interposed between them and the magistrate who exercises the sovereign power; nor ought we to consider them safe, while a great number of our fellow-citizens think these securities necessary.

It is a fortunate thing that the objection to the Government has been made on the ground I stated; because it will be practicable, on that ground, to obviate the objection, so far as to satisfy the public mind that their liberties will be perpetual, and this without endangering any part of the Constitution, which is considered as essential to the existence of the Government by those who promoted its adoption.

The amendments which have occurred to me, proper to be recommended by Congress to the State Legislatures, are these:

First. That there be prefixed to the Constitution a declaration, that all power is originally vested in, and consequently derived from, the people.

That Government is instituted and ought to be exercised for the benefit of the people; which consists in the enjoyment of life and liberty, with the right of acquiring and using property, and generally of pursuing and obtaining happiness and safety.

That the people have an indubitable, unalienable, and indefeasible right to reform or change their Government, whenever it be found adverse or inadequate to the purposes of its institution.

Secondly. That in article 1st, section 2, clause 3, these words be struck out, to wit: "The number of Representatives shall not exceed one for every thirty thousand, but each State shall have at least one Representative, and until such enumeration shall be made," and that in place thereof be inserted these words, to wit: "After the first actual enumeration, there shall be one Representative for every thirty thousand, until the number amounts to _____, after which the proportion shall be so regulated by Congress, that the number shall never be less than, nor more than _____, but each State shall, after the first enumeration, have at least two Representatives; and prior thereto."

Thirdly. That in article 1st, section 6, clause 1, there be added to the end of the first sentence, these words, to wit: "But no law varying the compensation last ascertained shall operate before the next ensuing election of Representatives."

Fourthly. That in article 1st, section 9, between clauses 3 and 4, be inserted these clauses, to wit: The civil rights of none shall be abridged on account of religious belief or worship, nor shall any national religion be established, nor shall the full and equal rights of conscience be in any manner, or on any pretext, infringed.

The people shall not be deprived or abridged of their right to speak, to write, or to publish their sentiments; and the freedom of the press, as one of the great bulwarks of liberty, shall be inviolable.

The people shall not be restrained from peaceably assembling and consulting for their common good; nor from applying to the Legislature by petitions, or remonstrances, for redress of their grievances.

The right of the people to keep and bear arms shall not be infringed; a well armed and well regulated militia being the best security of a free country: but no person religiously scrupulous of bearing arms shall be compelled to render military service in person.

No soldier shall in time of peace be quartered in any house without the consent of the owner; nor at any time, but in a manner warranted by law.

No person shall be subject, except in cases of impeachment, to more than one punishment or one trial for the same offence; nor shall be compelled to be a witness against himself; nor be deprived of life, liberty, or property without due process of law; nor be obliged to relinquish his property, where it may be necessary for public use, without a just compensation.

Excessive bail shall not be required, nor excessive fines imposed, nor cruel and unusual punishments inflicted.

The rights of the people to be secured in their persons, their houses, their papers, and their other property, from all unreasonable searches and seizures, shall not be violated by warrants issued without probable cause, supported by oath or affirmation, or not particularly describing the places to be searched, or the persons or things to be seized.

In all criminal prosecutions, the accused shall enjoy the right to a speedy and public trial, to be informed of the cause and nature of the accusation, to be confronted with his accusers, and the witnesses against him; to have a compulsory process for obtaining witnesses in his favor; and to have the assistance of counsel for his defence.

The exceptions here or elsewhere in the Constitution, made in favor of particular rights, shall not be so construed as to diminish the just importance of other rights retained by the people, or as to enlarge the powers delegated by the Constitution; but either as actual limitations of such powers, or as inserted merely for greater caution.

Fifthly. That in article 1st, section 10, between clauses 1 and 2, be inserted this clause, to wit:

No State shall violate the equal rights of conscience, or the freedom of the press, or the trial by jury in criminal cases.

Sixthly. That, in article 3d, section 2, be annexed to the end of clause 2d, these words, to wit:

But no appeal to such court shall be allowed where the value in controversy shall not amount to _____ dollars: nor shall any fact triable by jury, according to the course of common law, be otherwise re-examinable than may consist with the principles of common law.

Seventhly. That in article 3d, section 2, the third clause be struck out, and in its place be inserted the clauses following, to wit:

The trial of all crimes (except in cases of impeachments, and cases arising in the land or naval forces, or the militia when on actual service, in time of war or public danger) shall be by an impartial jury of freeholders of the vicinage, with the requisite of unanimity for conviction, of the right of challenge, and other accustomed requisites; and in all crimes punishable with loss of life or member, presentment or indictment by a grand jury shall be an essential preliminary, provided that in cases of crimes committed within any county which may be in possession of an enemy, or in which a general insurrection may prevail, the trial may by law be authorized in some other county of the same State, as near as may be to the seat of the offence.

In cases of crimes committed not within any county, the trial may by law be in such county as the laws shall have prescribed. In suits at common law, between man and man, the trial by jury, as one of the best securities to the rights of the people, ought to remain inviolate.

Eighthly. That immediately after article 6th, be inserted, as article 7th, the clauses following, to wit:

The powers delegated by this Constitution are appropriated to the departments to which they are respectively distributed: so that the Legislative Department shall never exercise powers vested in the Executive or Judicial, nor the Executive exercise the powers vested in the Legislative or Judicial, nor the Judicial exercise the powers vested in the Legislative or Executive Departments.

The powers not delegated by this Constitution, nor prohibited by it to the States, are reserved to the States respectively.

Ninthly. That article 7th be numbered as article 8th. . . .

But I confess that I do conceive, that in a Government modified like this of the United States, the great danger lies rather in the abuse of the community than in the Legislative body. The prescriptions in favor of liberty ought to be levelled against that quarter where the greatest danger lies, namely, that which possesses the highest prerogative of power. But this is not found in either the Executive or Legislative departments of Government, but in the body of the people, operating by the majority against the minority.

It is true, the powers of the General Government are circumscribed, they are directed to particular objects; but even if Government keeps within those limits, it has certain discretionary powers with respect to the means, which may admit of abuse to a certain extent, in the same manner as the powers of the State Governments under their constitutions may to an indefinite extent; because in the Constitution of the United States, there is a clause granting to Congress the power to make all laws which shall be necessary and proper for carrying into execution all the powers vested in the Government of the United States, or in any department or officer thereof; this enables them to fulfil every purpose for which the Government was established. Now, may not laws be considered necessary and proper by Congress, (for it is for them to judge of the necessity and propriety to accomplish those special purposes which they may have in contemplation,) which laws in themselves are neither necessary nor proper; as well as improper laws could be enacted by the State Legislatures, for fulfilling the more extended objects of those Governments? I will state an instance, which I think in point, and proves that this might be the case. The General Government has a right to pass all laws which shall be necessary to collect its revenue; the means for enforcing the collection are within the direction of the Legislature: may not general warrants be considered necessary for this purpose, as well as for some purposes which it was supposed at the framing of their constitutions the State Governments had in view? If there was reason for restraining the State Governments from exercising this power, there is like reason for restraining the Federal Government.

It may be said, indeed it has been said, that a bill of rights is not necessary, because the establishment of this Government has not repealed those declarations of rights which are added to the several State constitutions; that those rights of the people which had been established by the most solemn act, could not be annihilated by a subsequent act of that people, who meant and declared at the head of the instrument, that they ordained and established a new system, for the express purpose of securing to themselves and posterity the liberties they had gained by an arduous conflict.

I admit the force of this observation, but I do not look upon it to be conclusive. In the first place, it is too uncertain ground to leave this provision upon, if a provision is at all necessary to secure rights so important as many of those I have mentioned are conceived to be, by the public in general, as well as those in particular who opposed the adoption of this Constitution. Besides, some States have no bills of rights, there are others provided with very defective ones, and there are others whose bills of rights are not only defective, but absolutely improper; instead of securing some in the full extent which republican principles would require, they limit them too much to agree with the common ideas of liberty.

It has been objected also against a bill of rights, that, by enumerating particular exceptions to the grant of power, it would disparage those rights which were not placed in that enumeration; and it might follow by implication, that those rights which were not singled out, were intended to be assigned into the hands of the General Government, and were consequently insecure. This is one of the most plausible arguments I have ever heard urged against the admission of a bill of rights into this system; but, I conceive, that it may be guarded against. I have attempted it, as gentlemen may see by turning to the last clause of the fourth resolution.

It has been said that it is unnecessary to load the Constitution with this provision, because it was not found effectual in the constitution of the particular States. It is true, there are a few particular States in which some of the most valuable articles have not, at one time or other, been violated; but it does not follow but they may have to a certain degree, a salutary effect against the abuse of power. If they are incorporated into the Constitution, independent tribunals of justice will consider themselves in a peculiar manner the guardians of those rights; they will be an impenetrable bulwark against every assumption of power in the Legislative or Executive; they will be naturally led to resist every encroachment upon rights expressly stipulated for in the Constitution by the declaration of rights. Besides this security, there is a great probability that such a declaration in the federal system would be enforced; because the State Legislatures will jealously and closely watch the operations of this Government, and be able to resist with more effect every assumption of power, than any other power on earth can do; and the greatest opponents to a Federal Government admit the State Legislatures to be sure guardians of the people's liberty. I conclude, from this view of the subject, that it will be proper in itself, and highly politic, for the tranquility of the public mind, and the stability of the Government, that we should offer something, in the form I have proposed, to be incorporated in the system of Government, as a declaration of the rights of the people.

I wish, also, in revising the Constitution, we may throw into that section, which interdicts the abuse of certain powers in the State Legislatures, some other provisions of equal, if not greater importance than those already made. The words, "No State shall pass any bill of attainder, *ex post facto* law," &c., were wise and proper restrictions in the Constitution. I think there is more danger of those powers being abused by the State Governments than by the Government of the United States. The same may be said of other powers which they possess, if not controlled by the general principle, that laws are unconstitutional which infringe the rights of the community. I should, therefore, wish to extend this interdiction, and add, as I have stated in the 5th resolution, that no State shall violate the equal right of conscience, freedom of the press, or trial by jury in criminal cases; because it is proper that every Government should be disarmed of powers which trench upon those particular rights.

[T]he State Governments are as liable to attack these invaluable privileges as the General Government is, and therefore ought to be as cautiously guarded against.

I think it will be proper, with respect to the judiciary powers, to satisfy the public mind on those points which I have mentioned. Great inconvenience has been apprehended to suitors from the distance they would be dragged to obtain justice in the Supreme Court of the United States, upon an appeal on an action for a small debt. To remedy this, declare that no appeal shall be made unless the matter in controversy amounts to a particular sum; this, with the regulations respecting jury trials in criminal cases, and suits at common law, it is to be hoped, will quiet and reconcile the minds of the people to that part of the Constitution.

I find, from looking into the amendments proposed by the State conventions, that several are particularly anxious that it should be declared in the Constitution, that the powers not therein delegated should be reserved to the several States. Perhaps other words may define this more precisely than the whole of the instrument now does. I admit they may be deemed unnecessary; but there can be no harm in making such a declaration, if gentlemen will allow that the fact is as stated. I am sure I understand it so, and do therefore propose it.

✠ E S S A Y S

Until the last twenty years, constitutional historians treated the Anti-Federalists as also-rans who were neither smart enough to appreciate the genius of the Constitution nor well organized enough to block its ratification. The Federalists, after all, were the victors. But recent scholarship has turned an increasingly sympathetic ear to the Anti-Federalists, whose concern with local control and democracy as antidotes to the growth of a consolidated central government seems particularly appealing. For these reasons, Anti-Federalist thought and behavior now appear to be integral parts of the American constitutional tradition. Might Americans have been better off if the Anti-Federalists had prevailed? Would some of the structural proposals made by the Anti-Federalists have produced a better Constitution? Should other Anti-Federalist proposals have been included in the Bill of Rights added to the Constitution?

The literature on both ratification and the Bill of Rights underscores how historians with different visions of what motivates human behavior—ideas versus economic and social interests—can shape quite different interpretations of constitutional developments. Murray Dry, a professor of political science at Middlebury College and an authority on the Anti-Federalists, stresses their political thought and their contributions, as "junior partners," to the new constitutional order. David F. Epstein, who is also a political scientist, views matters in a different way, finding much to praise in the Federalists' constitutional theory and practical politics.

The Anti-Federalists and the American Constitutional Tradition

MURRAY DRY

Until recently, little attention has been paid to the political thought of the Anti-Federalists. They were the losers in the debate over the ratification of the United States Constitution; their name, which the victorious Federalists successfully imposed upon them, gives no indication of what they stood for; and many of their major writers, who wrote under pseudonyms, have not been identified for certain.

With the publication of Herbert J. Storing's *The Complete Anti-Federalist*, it is now possible to consider the contribution of the opponents of the Constitution to American political life. We have full and accurate texts of all Anti-Federal pamphlets and all substantial newspaper essays, complete with introductory sketches and extensive cross references and annotation to the major Federalist writings, and we have Storing's own masterful account of their thought, in an essay entitled, *What the Anti-Federalists Were For*. Storing was the first to argue that the Anti-Federalists, because they played "an indispensable if subordinate part in the founding process, . . . are entitled . . . to be counted among the Founding Fathers."

The argument of this essay, while in agreement with Storing, focuses on the constitutionalism of the Anti-Federalists. It is my contention that the Anti-Federalists deserve to be considered "junior partners" in the Founding not only because their view of republican government made them thoughtful critics of the Constitution, but also because their constitutionalism survived ratification. In this essay I will elaborate on that contention by focusing on the major Anti-Federalist arguments against the Constitution and their major alternative proposals.

I. Points of Departure

By points of departure, I refer, first, to the posture taken by the Anti-Federalists toward the ratification of the proposed Constitution and, second, to their views on the fundamental principles of government. On the first point, some were candid about the need for change, while others were cautious, even defensive, about the existing constitution. On the second point, there was general agreement with the Federalists on fundamental principles but disagreement on the relative emphasis of liberty and government authority.

Murray Dry, "The Anti-Federalists and the Constitution," in *Principles of the Constitutional Order: The Ratification Debates,* ed. Robert L. Utley, Jr., 1989, pp. 68–84. Reprinted by permission of the Tocqueville Forum of Wake Forest University.

The authors of the most extensive and most thoughtful essays written in opposition to the Constitution, Brutus and The Federal Farmer, both acknowledged the inadequacy of the existing Articles of Confederation and agreed that 1787 was a critical moment in American history. "I know our situation is critical, and it behooves us to make the best of it," The Federal Farmer writes in his first letter, although he also urges deliberation and thinks that there is time for a considered judgment. Later, in the first of his *Additional Letters,* he writes that "the opposers, as well as the advocates of [the Constitution] confirm me in my opinion, that the system affords, all circumstances considered, a better basis to build upon than the confederation." Brutus opens his first letter with a reference to the people's never having seen "so critical a period in their political concerns," which he attributes to "the feebleness of the ties by which these United States are held together, and the want of sufficient energy in our present confederation, to manage, in some instances, our general concerns."

Other Anti-Federalists expressed decided reservations or opposition. Agrippa, emphasizing the tranquility of the times, urged a recommitment to a second Convention or to the Congress for necessary amendments. Impartial Examiner warned the people that "a wise nation will . . . attempt innovations of this kind with great circumspection." Centinel decried the influence of "the authority of names" in favor of the Constitution and the advocates' openness to innovation. And Patrick Henry, in his first speech in the Virginia ratification convention, argued that the danger did not come from the times but from the work of the Federal Convention: "If our situation be thus uneasy, whence has arisen this fearful jeopardy? It arises from this fatal system—it arises from this proposal to change our government:—a proposal that goes to the utter annihilation of the most solemn engagements of the States."

On the principles of government, Brutus' account of natural right and consent follows the Declaration of Independence and reveals a fundamental agreement between the Federalists and the Anti-Federalists. But Brutus also warns his readers that "when the people once part with power, they can seldom or never resume it again but by force." For a sharper version of the distinctive Anti-Federal approach to the principles of government, consider Patrick Henry's indictment of America for its willingness to consider a strong government. "When the American spirit was in its youth, the language of America was different; Liberty, Sir, was then the primary object." And, later, in the same speech: "The first thing I have at heart is American *liberty;* the second is American Union."

Henry did not oppose union, but his emphasis on liberty implied that union was dispensable. Impartial Examiner's concluding statement presented the more common Anti-Federal position. "No contention . . . subsists about supporting a *union,* but only concerning the mode; and as well those, who disapprove of the proposed plan, as those, who approve of it, consider the existence of a union as essential to their happiness."

II. Federalism and the Constitution

The last two statements reveal the Anti-Federal dilemma: they were for union and they recognized the need to strengthen the Articles of Confederation, but, in the name of liberty, they opposed the establishment of a full government for the union. As they understood it, republican liberty required a federal republic, which meant an association of small republics for certain limited purposes, mainly defense. Montesquieu's *Spirit of the Laws* was their authority on the subject. Brutus quotes one passage: "It is natural to a republic to have only a small territory, otherwise it cannot long subsist." Melancton Smith paraphrases another: "a confederated republic has all the internal advantages of a Republic, with the external force of a Monarchical Government." Such a position was widely held by the Anti-Federalists. For that reason, The Federal Farmer describes the Constitution as "appear[ing] to be a plan retaining some federal features; but to be the first important step, and to aim strongly to one consolidated government of the United States."

Consequently, Melancton Smith argued that the opponents of the Constitution "were the true Federalists, and those who advocated it Anti-Federalists." Impartial Examiner explained how they got stuck "with the epithet of anti-foederal."

> The strong desire, which has been manifested, for a union between the American states, since the revolution, affords an opportunity of making the distinction, as they imagine, to their advantage.—As *foederalists,* in their opinion, they must be deemed friendly to the *union:*—as *anti-foederal,* the opposers must, in their opinion too, be considered unfriendly. Thus on the sound of names they build their fame.

He goes on to say that the advocates are not acting on "true *foederal* principles," because the "new code" places "all sovereignty . . . in the hands of Congress," while the true federalists "desire a continuance of each distinct sovereignty" along with "such a degree of energy in the general government, as will cement the union in the strongest manner."

At the outset, then; we are faced with a terminological question—which side had the better claim to the title "federalist"? It is a question which, for once, is more than merely terminological.

The Terminological Issue.   During the confederation period, the terms *federal* and *anti-federal* referred to a willingness or unwillingness to support the instrumentality of the federation, the general government under the Articles of Confederation. The essential elements of that federal form were: (1) state equality in voting in Congress and state control, via financial support, annual elections, rotation and recall, of its congressional delegation; (2) strict construction of the powers granted to the Congress, with a nine-state requirement for approval of major matters; and (3) reliance on state requisitions for the raising of armies and money. The states were clearly the primary political units, and this was considered a strong federal system.

The origin of the terminological confusion lay in the speeches and deeds of the Framers of the new Constitution. The Federal Convention met in Philadelphia from May to September 1787; the states had petitioned Congress for such a meeting, and the Congressional Resolution of February 21, 1787, authorized a convention

> for the sole and express purpose of revising the Articles of Confederation and reporting to Congress and the several legislatures such alternatives and provisions therein, as shall, when agreed to in Congress and confirmed by the states render the federal government adequate to the exigencies of government & the preservation of the Union.

To begin with the deeds, the Federal Convention drafted an entirely new Constitution and then transmitted it to Congress to be sent on to the states for their consideration in separate ratification conventions. The Convention did not ask Congress to approve the Constitution, but merely to send it on to the states for their approbation, with the ratification of nine states, through specially elected conventions, sufficient to bring the Constitution into being. This bypassed the thirteenth article of the existing constitution, according to which amendments required the unanimous consent of the thirteen states, through their legislatures. The Anti-Federalists objected to the legality of the ratification process for this reason.

To understand the effect of the newly proposed Constitution on the federalism issue, we need to consider certain proposals and speeches at the outset of the Federal Convention and others that took place in the debate over congressional apportionment. The Virginia Plan, written by James Madison and supported by the avowed nationalists, proposed separate and independent executive and judicial branches of government, a nationally proportioned bicameral legislature, with the lower house elected by the people. The legislature was to be given a general grant of legislative power and a national negative on state laws conflicting with the articles of union. Arguing in support of the proposition that a union "merely federal" would not accomplish the objects proposed and that a national government was necessary, Gouverneur Morris "explained the difference between a *federal* and *national, supreme* Govt.; the former being a mere compact resting on the good faith of the parties; the latter having a compleat and *compulsive* operation." George Mason said virtually the same thing, and then Madison observed "that whatever reason might have existed for the equality of suffrage when the Union was a federal one among sovereign States, it must cease when a national Governt. should be put into the place." From what Madison goes on to say about the extra-legal influence of the large states under the Articles, since they are responsible for raising their own quotas of men and money, it is clear that a federal system was characterized by requisitions, or voluntary compliance by the states, and a national government was characterized by the coercion of law, acting directly on individuals.

This distinction was clear and uncontested until the Convention voted to have the State legislatures elect the senate and then turned to the rule of apportionment for that body. Oliver Ellsworth and other members of the Connecticut delegation defended equality of representation in the Senate by arguing that "we were partly national; partly federal." State equality in the Senate permitted the supporters of the Constitution to retain the term, "federal," for a new form of government. This can be seen by comparing Madison's response to the "partly national; partly federal" argument in the Convention with his own use of that argument in *The Federalist* and in the Virginia ratification convention. In the former place, he contested the partly federal description—he was arguing against equality of representation in the Senate—by claiming that the mode of operation, on individuals not states, was the sole criterion and it was entirely national. But in *Federalist* No. 39, where he could now use what he was forced to accept in defense of the Constitution, Madison introduced four other criteria for determining the character of the Constitution—mode of ratification, source of authority (which he identified with the electing agent), extent of powers, and mode of amendment—and he interpreted each of these as reflecting the federal principle to the extent that the states were recognized in the constitutional structure.

Thus, the meaning of "federal" underwent a transformation, partly, as Tocqueville put it later, because a new thing was created for which there was no new word, and partly because the supporters of the constitution could not afford to concede the "federalist" title to their opponents. Storing has pointed out that a "larceny" charge against the Federalists is overstated, since during the Confederation period "federal" referred to men and measures supportive of the government of the union. On the other hand, Storing indicates that the federal *authority* could be strengthened in such a way that the federal *principle,* requisitions, was discarded. This is what the Framers of the Constitution, and then the supporters who called themselves the Federalists, did, and with their success, a new form of federalism arose.

The Anti-Federalist position was complicated by their conceding the necessity of strengthening the Articles of Confederation. At the same time, it must be noted that those favoring modest changes were not in the forefront of the reform movement. The Federal Convention had already discussed the Virginia Plan for two weeks when William Paterson proposed the New Jersey Plan, which included a limited tax power for Congress and a plural executive, but generally stayed with the Articles of Confederation. However, the limited tax power for Congress revealed a need to go beyond the federal principle, strictly speaking.

This concession meant that the Anti-Federalists' understanding of federalism, as well as that of the Federalists, underwent a transformation. The best example comes from the "Letters of The Federal Farmer." In his first letter, The Farmer describes three plans, which he calls federal, consolidation, and partial consolidation: (1) "distinct republics connected under a federal head," or a system similar to the Articles; (2) "do away with the several state governments, and form or consolidate all the states into one entire government"; and (3) "consolidate the states as to certain national objects, and leave them severally distinct independent republics, as to internal police generally." "Touching the first, or federal plan," The Farmer says, "I do not think much can be said in its favor." He supports the third plan and charges that the Constitution will eventually produce a complete consolidation. But in the first of his *Additional Letters,* The Farmer, when he describes the parties to the contest over the Constitution, calls the third or middle ground position, federalism.

> Some of the advocates are only pretended federalists; in fact they wish for an abolition of the state governments. Some of them I believe to be honest federalists, who wish to preserve *substantially* the state governments united under an efficient federal head; and many of them are blind tools without any object. Some of the opposers also are only pretended federalists, who want no federal government, or one merely advisory. Some of them are the true federalists, their object, perhaps, more clearly seen, is the same with that of the honest federalists; and some of them, probably, have no distinct object.

Then, in his last discussion of federalism, in his seventeenth letter, The Federal Farmer returns to the distinction between consolidated government and a federal, or confederal, republic, without any reference to those who only want an advisory federal government. In a federal government, "the state governments are the basis, the pillar on which the federal head is based," and this means that men and money are raised by requisitions and the states organize and train the militia.

So, while the Federalists were taking great liberties with federalism, by calling the Constitution partly federal and partly national, even the Anti-Federalists were moving away from pure federalism. To learn more about the "new federalism," both as presented by the Constitution and as presented by the Anti-Federalists, we need to turn to the specific arguments making up the opponents' consolidation charge.

The Constitution as a Consolidated Government. The federalism issue involves the relationship between the states and the union. The Anti-Federalists argued for the primacy, or at least the equality, of the states as against the general government. We shall consider the Anti-Federal arguments about the Preamble, the enumeration of legislative powers, and the construction of the Senate.

The Preamble to the Constitution begins with "We the People of the United States," and it refers to six reasons for ordaining and establishing the Constitution: "in Order to form a more perfect Union, establish Justice, insure domestic Tranquility, provide for the common defence, promote the general Welfare, and secure the Blessings of Liberty to ourselves and our Posterity." The preamble to the Articles of Confederation referred to the delegates of the United States of America in Congress assembled, named each of the states, and was followed by an article asserting that each state retains every power "not expressly delegated." This is why Patrick Henry pounced on the Preamble to the Constitution:

> My political curiosity, exclusive of my anxious solicitude for the public welfare, leads me to ask, Who authorized them to speak the language of, *We the people,* instead of *We the states?* States are the characteristics and

the soul of a confederation. If the states be not the agents of this compact, it must be one great consolidated national government.

Brutus made the same point in more sober, constitutional terms. "If the end of government is to be learned from these words, which are clearly designed to declare it, it is obvious it has in view every object which is embraced by any government." The reference to a more perfect union suggested that "it is not an union of states or bodies corporate. . . . But it is a union of the people of the United States considered as one body, who are to ratify this constitution, if it is adopted."

Madison's remarks, in the Federal Convention, about the importance of popular ratification for establishing the supremacy of the Constitution, especially over subsequently passed state laws, lend support to the Anti-Federal argument about the preamble; it suggests a government for the people of the United States as a whole, without reference to the several states, that is, a consolidated government rather than a federal system. To consider the consolidation charge fully, however, it is necessary to turn to the enumeration of powers.

The major powers include taxing and spending for the general welfare, borrowing money, regulating commerce, declaring war, and raising and supporting armies and providing for a navy. In addition, the last clause of Article I, section 8 authorizes Congress "to make all Laws which shall be necessary and proper for carrying into Execution the foregoing Powers, and all other Powers vested by this Constitution in the Government of the United States, or in any Department or Officer thereof."

To Brutus, the necessary and proper clause, the enumerated powers, and the supremacy clause of Article VI add up to a national government of substantial powers.

> It appears from these articles that there is no need of any intervention of the state governments, between the Congress and the people, to execute any one power vested in the general government, and that the constitution and the laws of every state are nullified and declared void, so far as they are or shall be inconsistent with this constitution, or the laws made in pursuance of it, or with treaties made under the authority of the United States.—The government then, so far as it extends, is a complete one, and not a confederation. . . . It is true this government is limited to certain objects, or to speak more properly, some degree of power is left to the states, but a little attention to the powers vested in the general government, will convince every candid man, that if it is capable of being executed, all that is reserved for the individual states must very soon be annihilated, except so far as they are barely necessary to the organization of the general government.

The Anti-Federalist approach to the powers of government was to draw a line between federal and state powers, whereby only those powers which were necessary for security and defense would be assigned to the government of the union. Roger Sherman took this position in the Federal Convention, the day after the compromise on apportionment was approved. Sherman, who signed the Constitution and supported it, proposed that the legislature have the power to make laws in all cases concerning the common interests, "but not to interfere with [the Government of the individual States in any matters of internal police which respect the Govt. of such States only, and wherein the General] welfare of the U. States is not concerned."

Sherman never tried to spell out what this might look like, and, as James Monroe wrote in 1788, the task was not easy. "To mark the precise point at which the Powers of the general government shall cease, and that from whence those of the states shall commence, to poise them in such manner as to prevent either destroying the other, will require the utmost force of human wisdom and ingenuity." The Federal Farmer attempted such a delineation:

> Those respecting external, as all foreign concerns, commerce, imposts, all causes arising on the seas, peace and war, and Indian affairs, can be lodged in no where else, with any propriety, but in this government. Many powers that respect internal objects ought clearly to be lodged in it; as those to regulate trade between the states, weights and measures, the coin or current monies, post offices, naturalization, etc. These powers may be exercised without essentially effecting [sic] the internal policy of the respective states: But powers to lay and collect internal taxes, to form the militia, to make bankrupt laws, and to decide on appeals, questions arising on the internal laws of the respective states, are of a very serious nature, and carry with them almost all other powers.

The most important applications of the line-drawing approach involved the powers to tax, to raise and support armies, and to borrow money. The most common tax proposal was to limit the federal government to an impost, a tax on foreign imports, leaving internal taxes, both those on individuals and those on commodities, to the states. This would guarantee the states a source of revenue, which was important since the Anti-Federalists feared that any concurrent tax power might lead to federal preemption of the sources of taxation; it would also eliminate the need for numerous federal assessors and collectors and federal ordinances that would interfere with state laws. One specific proposal, which came out of the Massachusetts ratification convention, was that Congress could not lay direct taxes, but, if the impost did not provide sufficient funds, it could seek additional money from the states via requisitions.

As for the power to raise armies, there was substantial support for the proposition that there should be no standing armies in time of peace. Brutus proposed a limited power to raise armies to defend frontier posts and guard arsenals; to raise troops in peacetime, in anticipation of an attack or invasion, should require a two-thirds vote of both houses. Likewise, The Federal Farmer first proposed that a two-thirds or three-fourths majority be required in Congress, until the representation increased; then, in his last letter, he proposed the principle of requisitions for raising armies, with the states retaining a right to refuse, and, in addition, that land forces could not be maintained for more than a year without congressional approval.

Brutus also objected to the unlimited power to borrow money. Anticipating the debate over the assumption of state debts, he argued that "by this means [Congress] may create a national debt, so large, as to exceed the ability of the country ever to sink." He proposed that the power should be restricted to "the most urgent occasions, and then we should not borrow of foreigners if we could possibly help it."

The Anti-Federalists also objected to the provisions relating to the militia and the regulations of elections under the time, place and manner clause. Luther Martin was concerned about a state's being deprived of all of its militia; he wanted a percentage limit on the number that could be sent out of the state; The Federal Farmer was concerned about the development of a "select militia," which he regarded as inconsistent with republican government. Brutus thought that under the time, place and manner clause, the "right of election would be transferred from the people to their rulers." He argued that Congress might not permit districting for the election of the representatives. It was, interestingly, the same kind of concern, as applied to state action or inaction, which led the Federal Convention to grant Congress supervisory authority over elections.

The other major objections to the powers of government were sectional, and hence did not constitute a common Anti-Federalist position. In the North, objection was raised to counting slaves in the apportionment; in the South, objection was raised to the limit on slave importation and to the absence of special protection against tariffs (the Federal Convention rejected a proposal to require a two-thirds majority in both houses to pass navigation laws). In addition, Anti-Federalists in the Virginia convention expressed concern that the new government might negotiate away navigation rights on the Mississippi.

Turning now to the construction of the Senate, the Anti-Federalists were handicapped by the decision of the Convention, over the strenuous objection of the nationalists, to have state equality as well as election by the state legislatures. Brutus approved of equal representation, noting that it would have been inappropriate for a consolidation but was appropriate for a confederation. The Federal Farmer noted that the senators voted individually, rather than by state delegation, in a true federal manner, but he did not object. But Impartial Examiner, after contrasting the truly federal scheme of the Articles with the proposed Senate, concluded that the Senate was part of the general government, which would "participate in the sovereignty of America. Thus circumstanced, they will know not any authority superior to that, whereof they themselves possess a part." Therefore, he thought senators should be chosen by the people. He made no comment about the apportionment. Brutus, The Federal Farmer, and Smith, ignoring the point made by Impartial Examiner, went on to recommend rotation and recall and a shorter term for the Senate.

The Senate became the agency of the state governments in the federal government, and that body was also given important foreign affairs powers. This unlikely combination of traits gave rise to the following exchange in the New York convention. After Gilbert Livingston moved an amendment requiring rotation and recall, Robert Lansing, a member of the Federal Convention, who opposed the Constitution, argued in support of the motion, saying "if it was the design of the plan to make the Senate a kind of bulwark to the independence of the states; and a check to the encroachments of the general government, certainly the members of this body ought to be particularly under the control, and in strict subordination to the state who delegated them." Robert Livingston, in reply, said: "The Senate are indeed designed to represent the state governments; but they are also the representatives of the United States, and are not to consult the interest of any one state alone, but that of the Union."

III. The Anti-Federalists and Republican Government

The Anti-Federalist arguments about federalism were based, ultimately, on their understanding of republican government. In this part, we shall begin with the Anti-Federalists' general conception of republican government. Then we shall consider the two most significant constitutional contexts within which this topic was discussed: representation in the legislature and the nature of the senate and the executive branch of government.

The General Characteristics of Republican Government. For the Anti-Federalists, republican government is small in size, simple in structure, and operates with minimal coercion. On the size question, Brutus quotes from Montesquieu to the effect that "it is natural to a republic to have only a small territory," because otherwise there is an insufficient moderation of fortunes and, consequently, "the public good is sacrificed to a thousand views." Centinel advocates a unicameral legislature and legislative supremacy as examples of a simple structure. The Federal Farmer emphasizes representation and trial by jury as two essential means of assuring this mildness. For Brutus, the character of republican government precludes reliance on standing armies; one relies, instead, on "the confidence, respect, and affection of the people," and this arises from "their knowing their [rulers], from [the rulers'] being responsible to them for their conduct, and from the power they have of displacing them when they misbehave." In contrast to the Federalists, and especially to the argument of *Federalist* No. 10 and No. 51, the Anti-Federalists emphasize the attachment of the people to their country, which Montesquieu defined as virtue, i.e., political virtue. They are more concerned with this quality than they are with mechanisms aimed at restraining majority tyranny. A further illustration comes from Mercy Warren, a historian of the period who identified with the Anti-Federalists; she wrote the following in 1805:

> Nothing seemed to be wanting to the United States but a continuance of their union and virtue. It was their interest to cherish true, genuine republican virtue, in politics; and in religion, a strict adherence to a sublime code of morals, which has never been equalled by the sages of ancient time, nor can ever be abolished by the sophistical reasonings of modern philosophers.

The Anti-Federalists did not follow this public-spirited, even austere, conception of republican government without qualification, however. First, they too held to the principles of natural rights, according to which individual claims took precedence over duties. Second, several of the states were already too large for the republican form, strictly understood. Hence, they were forced to present their arguments about republican government in terms of representation, even though it may be incompatible with republican government in the strict sense. Montesquieu, who is most frequently quoted on republics, did not bring up representation in connection with the old, frugal, "small" republics; only when he discussed England, which he called a "republic disguised under the form of monarchy," did representation become prominent. Of the Anti-Federalists, only A Maryland Farmer, discussed below, takes this radical position on representation and republican government.

Representation, Aristocracy and Democracy. The first Congress was expected to have sixty-five representatives and twenty-six senators, with an increase following a census in 1790. The Anti-Federalist position was that even after the increase, and any subsequent increases, representation in the federal government was inadequate, that it was substantial in the state governments, and that therefore the powers of government should remain more evenly divided between the states and the nation. Here are two prominent examples of the Anti-Federal position on representation, from Brutus and The Federal Farmer, respectively.

> The very term, representative, implies, that the person or body chosen for this purpose, should resemble those who appoint them—a representation of the people of America, if it be a true one, must be like the people. It ought to be so constituted, that a person, who is a stranger to the country, might be able to form a just idea of their character, by knowing that of their representatives. They are the sign—the people the thing signified. . . . It must have been intended, that those who are placed instead of the people, should possess their sentiments and feelings, and be governed by their interests, or, in other words, should bear the strongest resemblance of those in whose room they are substituted.
>
> A full and equal representation, is that which possesses the same interests, feelings, opinions, and views the people themselves would were they all assembled—a fair representation therefore, should be so regulated, that every order of men, merchants, traders, farmers, mechanics, etc. to bring a just proportion of their best informed men respectively into the legislature, the representation must be considerably numerous.

In one sense, the first statement reflects no disagreement with the Federalists. In the Federal Convention, when the nationalists were arguing the importance of a direct popular election for the lower house, James Wilson said that "the legislature ought to be the most exact transcript of the whole Society. Representation is made necessary only because it is impossible for the people to act collectively." But, according to The Federal Farmer, election did not by itself guarantee an adequate representation. He praised the proposed government for being "founded on elective principles," but added that everything valuable "in this system is vastly lessened for the want of that one important feature in a free government, a representation of the people."

The Federalists had the advantage of defending a system which was thoroughly based on the elective principle; their argument equated representation with election. The Anti-Federalists were forced into a discussion of classes or orders in society in order to prove that election was not a sufficient condition for true representation. We shall examine the accounts of The Federal Farmer, Melancton Smith, and A Maryland Farmer on this subject.

After distinguishing a constitutional from a natural aristocracy, and remarking that a constitutional aristocracy does not exist "in our common acceptation of the term," The Federal Farmer presents this account of natural aristocracy and natural democracy.

> In my idea of our natural aristocracy in the United States, I include about four or five thousand men; and among those I reckon those who have been placed in the offices of governors, of members of Congress, and state senators generally, in the principal officers of Congress, of the army and militia, the superior judges, the most eminent professional men &. and men of large property.—the other persons and orders in the community form the natural democracy; this includes in general the yeomanry, the subordinate officers, civil and military, the fishermen, mechanics, and traders, many of the merchants and professional men.

The men in the first class "associate more extensively, have a high sense of honor, possess abilities, ambition, and general knowledge"; the men in the second class

> are not so much used to combining great objects . . . possess less ambition, and a larger share of honesty: their dependence is principally on middling and small estates, industrious pursuits, and hard labour, while that of the former is principally on the emoluments of large estates, and of the chief offices of government.

The Federal Farmer wanted "the two great parties" to be "balanced" and the only way to do that, he thought, was to balance the powers of the state and federal governments. This is because, and here I direct his argument to Madison's in *Federalist* No. 10, the very operation of the extended sphere, which is heralded as moderating the effect of the majority principle and refining the representation, produces an aristocratic representation, that is, a concentration of the most able, ambitious, and wealthy, as opposed to the frugal, industrious and modest democracy.

Melancton Smith described the natural aristocracy in the country similarly in the New York ratification convention. On his formulation, however, there were three classes—the aristocracy, the middling class, and the poor. He favored the representation of the middling class, or the "respectable yeomanry," on the grounds that when the interest of this part of the community is pursued, the public good is pursued. . . . No burden can be laid on the poor, but what will sensibly affect the middling class. Any law rendering property insecure, would be injurious to them. When therefore this class in society pursue their own interest, they promote that of the public, for it is involved in it.

In light of the differences between the aristocracy and the democracy, as The Federal Farmer describes them, Smith may be going too far here, since his middling class resembles The Farmer's natural democracy, but he can claim that his argument does not require a perfect reflection of the entire society, and therefore is not inconsistent with the elective principle. The middling class is likely to be more substantially represented in the several state legislatures than in Congress. Once again, this is the obverse of Madison's *Federalist* No. 10 argument.

While A Maryland Farmer's account of the classes is more elaborate than the other two, his division between aristocracy and democracy is similar. But he predicts that the aristocratic class "is nearly at the height of their power," and that "they must decline or moderate, or another revolution will ensue." And representation is rejected out of hand: "Where representation has been admitted to a component part of government, it has always proved defective, if not destructive."

The Anti-Federalist argument about representation and republican government, therefore, stands between the Federalist position, which requires no more than the elective principle, and the traditional definition of republics, which emphasizes the love of country and the obligations of citizenship more than the pursuit of interest.

The Separation of Powers and Republican Government. The Anti-Federalist critique of the constitutional separation of powers drew on a sharp distinction between republics and monarchies. As Storing put it, the Anti-Federalists believed that "the framers of the Constitution had fallen awkwardly and dangerously between the two stools of simple responsible government and genuine balanced government." Extensive checks and balances, which have the effect of shifting the powers of government from the more popular part of the government, the lower house of the legislature, to the less popular parts, the Senate and the executive, are, in this view, inappropriate for republics.

Centinel presents the clearest and fullest case for simple, responsible government. In his first letter, he attacks John Adams' notion of balanced government, which he identifies with the Constitution. "This hypothesis supposes human wisdom competent to the task of instituting three co-equal orders in government, and a corresponding weight in the community to enable them respectively to exercise their several parts. . . ." Such a plan requires "a powerful hereditary nobility" to be effective. In America, "we must recur to other principles."

A republican, or free government, can only exist where the body of the people are virtuous, and where property is pretty equally divded[;] in such a government the people are the sovereign and their sense or opinion is the criterion of every public measure. . . . The highest responsibility is to be attained, in a simple structure of government, for the great body of the people never steadily attend to the operations of government, and for want of due information are liable to be imposed on. . . .

Centinel appears to attack the whole notion of bicameralism, with Pennsylvania's unicameral legislature as his model. He also seems more concerned about the small size of the Senate than its distinctive powers. Brutus takes note of the powers, such as advice and consent for appointment and treaties, and judging impeachments, but he stops short of proposing alternatives. The Federal Farmer also expresses reservations about the Senate's powers, but he proposes rotation and recall rather than a shifting of the powers to another part of the government.

The Federal Farmer, A Maryland Farmer, and Patrick Henry all attack the Constitution for attempting checks and balances without the proper materials. Henry calls the checks "imaginary balances," says the president would have "the powers of a king," and claims that he would prefer to "have a king, lords, and commons, than a government so replete with insupportable evils." The Federal Farmer, who earlier referred to the predominance of the natural aristocracy, argues that America does not have the proper materials for a balance of classes: "the senate would be feeble, and the house powerful," if the aristocracy and democracy were assigned to each respectively. A Maryland Farmer presents the alternatives in their starkest forms: "government founded on representation" requires an executive and a senate for life, while in republican government, such as Switzerland, "the people personally exercise the powers of government." He goes on to propose a government by the freeholders, who must approve the laws, by a referendum "in their counties and cities" before they go into effect.

In addition to these general arguments, there were specific objections to the governmental structure, such as the absence of an executive council for the president and, in one case at least, the existence of the executive's qualified veto.

IV. The Bill of Rights and the Judiciary

The most common Anti-Federal argument against the Constitution concerned the absence of a Bill of Rights. The Federalists' explanation, prominently presented by James Wilson and Thomas McKean, in the Pennsylvania ratification convention, and also by Hamilton in *The Federalist*, was the weakest of any of their replies to the opponents' objections. In their ratification convention, the Massachusetts Federalists hit upon the idea of proposing unconditional ratification and submitting a list of recommended amendments; this took the place of conditional ratification, which would have necessitated a second Convention. Congressional passage of the first ten amendments, in 1789, known as the Bill of Rights, supports the contention that while the Federalists gave us the Constitution, the Anti-Federalists gave us the Bill of Rights. But the story is more complicated, since the passage of the Bill of Rights signaled the end of any sustained opposition to the Constitution, and it was Madison who led the campaign in the House for speedy passage of the Bill of Rights. In a letter to Jefferson, dated October 17, 1788, Madison said that while his "own opinion had always been in favor of a bill of rights; provided it be so named as not to imply powers not meant to be included," he also "never thought the omission a material defect."

The main Federalist arguments in defense of the Constitution without a Bill of Rights were: (1) the entire Constitution, as it provides for a well-framed government with power checking power and offices filled by election, is a bill of rights; (2) there is an internal bill of rights, especially in Article I, sections 3 and 10; and (3) unlike the state governments, the federal government is one of enumerated powers, and hence what is not enumerated is not given, and the state bills of rights remain in force. The Anti-Federal responses, in reverse order, were: (1) the clear supremacy of the federal Constitution and the extensiveness of the powers granted call into question any reliance on the state bills of rights on the one hand, or the implied restrictions on powers on the other; (2) to the extent that one might rely on the principle of implied restrictions on powers, the very fact that certain restrictions are noted, suggests, if anything, that what is not expressly reserved is granted; and (3) the general argument about a well-constructed government points back to the discussions of federalism and republican government.

An examination of some amendments proposed but not adopted illustrates the difference between the amendments preferred by the Anti-Federalists and the actual Bill of Rights. The first proposed amendment in the Massachusetts convention was "that it be explicitly declared, that all powers not expressly delegated by the aforesaid Constitution are reserved to the several states, to be by them exercised." The fourth proposed amendment limited the tax power to the impost, to be supplemented, if necessary, by a requisition on the several states, with Congress permitted to collect it only if the states failed to do so. In the New York convention, Gilbert Livingston proposed rotation and recall for the Senate.

Even as passed, however, the Bill of Rights could serve the Anti-Federalist purpose of fostering the political and moral education of the people. Having the rights provisions written into the Constitution reminds the people of the leading principles of government. But it also served to strengthen the judiciary, since it became part of the fundamental law. This was noted with favor by Thomas Jefferson, in his letter to Madison dated March 15, 1789.

> In the arguments in favor of a bill of rights, you omit one which has great weight with me, the legal check which it puts into the hands of the judiciary. This is a body, which if rendered independent, and kept strictly to their own department merits great confidence for their learning and integrity.

This argument must have impressed Madison, who led the House in its passage of the Bill of Rights in June 1789. But the position was not consistent with the Anti-Federal concern about the extensiveness of the judicial power provided for in the Constitution, to which we now turn.

Brutus provides the fullest discussion of the judiciary. He anticipates the full development of judicial review as well as the importance of the judicial branch as a vehicle for the development of the federal government's powers. Article III permits the courts "to give the constitution a legal construction," and the equity jurisdiction gives the courts power to "explain the constitution according to the reasoning spirit of it, without being confined to the words or letter." This is why Brutus claims that "the real effect of this system of government will therefore be brought home to the feelings of the people through the medium of the judicial power." The judicial power will be able to attribute certain powers to the legislature "which they have not exercised," and they will also use the preamble to expand on the legislative powers. The judicial review argument arises out of the specific language regarding equity plus the written Constitution. "It is to be observed, that the supreme court has the power, in the last resort, to determine all questions that may arise in the courts of legal discussion, on the meaning and construction of the constitution. This power they will hold under the constitution and independent of the legislature."

Brutus discusses two possible solutions to the problem of complete judicial independence: either limit the judicial tenure to a fixed term, or limit the judicial power to exclude construction of the Constitution. While Brutus indicates how the influence of the Crown introduced special problems for judicial independence in England, not applicable to the United States, he still favors appointment for good behavior. Hence, his preferred change is to leave constitutional construction to the legislature, and ultimately to the people.

Hamilton argued that the courts would do nothing more than declare laws "contrary to the manifest tenor" of the Constitution void. Brutus' account shows how much could be read into judicial power from Article III, but he did not connect his warning about the judiciary with his advocacy of the Bill of Rights.

V. Conclusion

At the outset of this essay, it was said that the Anti-Federalists deserved to be considered among the Founding Fathers because of their important part in the constitutional debate and their contribution to the finished document and its development. By way of conclusion, I should like to review the Anti-Federal arguments on the three major topics—federalism, republican government, and a bill of rights—and consider the manner in which their positions were retained, often in a different form, after the Constitution's ratification.

With respect to federalism, the Anti-Federalists were right about the novelty of the scheme, but the Federalists were able to make good use of the compromise in the construction of the Senate in order to argue that the Constitution is "partly federal; partly national." The Constitution was more an incomplete national government than a true mixture, as Tocqueville could see in 1831 and as Storing explains fully. The Anti-Federalists hammered home the point about the extensiveness of the powers, and they were right. Yet, the preservation of the Union required a stronger government, and this is why the Constitution was ratified. Ratification ended Anti-Federalist opposition to the Constitution, but it did not end the controversy over the extent of the powers of the general government. Jefferson's disagreement with Hamilton, and then Marshall, on the necessary and proper clause, in connection with the debate on the constitutionality of the national bank, is the classical source for this controversy. (Did "necessary" mean "conveni-ent," or did it mean "without which an enumerated power becomes nuga-tory"?) But the alternative to "loose construction" was not confined to Jef-ferson. Madison himself adopted the "strict construction" position in the First Congress, when the bank bill came up. Regardless of what caused Madison's shift, his taking a strict view of the powers of the national gov-ernment shows very clearly how the Anti-Federalist position was retained by being transformed; the argument shifted from a critique of the Consti-tution to an interpretation of the powers different from the original Anti-Federalist position, but to the same effect. Controversy over the extent of the federal government's powers, once thought to have been settled in 1937 in favor of congressional discretion, i.e., congressional federalism, has been renewed in recent years.

The Anti-Federalist conception of republican government emphasized smallness, simplicity, and mildness, so the people would know one another and their governing officials. The Anti-Federalists rejected as inadequate the equation of election with representation. Their discussion of aristocracy and democracy reveals a concern about character and the effects of in-equality. They wanted the agricultural middling class to set the tone in government, and hence in society as a whole. The legacy here is doubtful, since the United States has developed into a robust commercial society, which reflects the Federalist formulation. At the same time, as Storing points out, the Anti-Federalist reservations about a community based primarily on interest, as opposed to dedication to the common good, remain valid. The more heterogeneous the population, the weaker the tie of citizenship. On this key topic, the Anti-Federalists seem to have pointed to a problem for modern free government more than they have come up with a solution. While aristocracy and democracy do not describe divisions in American society accurately, the distinction between the few with substantial wealth, influence and talents and the many without them remains clear. And if we occasionally worry about the effects of unrestrained acquisitiveness, then we have returned to the Anti-Federalist reservations about the success of the large commercial republic.

Finally, the Bill of Rights appears to be the Anti-Federalists' greatest success, and yet its importance has gone hand-in-hand with the expansion of both federal power, vis-à-vis the states, and judicial power, vis-à-vis the political branches of government. To the extent that people suppose that their liberties are secure as a result of the Bill of Rights, more than as a

makers, but the result of a failure of the states spontaneously to cooperate for their common good. A government that could make the states cooperate would thwart the impulses that resisted cooperation in the first place. So strong were those impulses that Federalists bluntly predicted war among disunited American states. Commercial rivalries, disputed borders, and other particular issues of contention—as well as the general fact that neighboring countries are "natural enemies"—meant that disunited American states would be, "the victim of mutual rage, rancour, and revenge."

For example, under the Articles of Confederation importing states could raise revenue for themselves by excise taxes on imported goods that citizens of neighboring states would pay as well. Federalists appealed both to justice and to the domestic tranquility that injustice would sooner or later interrupt:

> [T]he principles of reason and justice require, that states and individuals should so exercise their rights as not to injure and depress their neighbours. If this [argument] should not induce them to adopt a proper mode of conduct, we have no doubt but argument derived from our natural strength, operating on their natural weakness will produce the desired conviction— the opinion of any statesman is not much to be regarded who supposes that a powerful and enlightened people, uncontrouled by any tie of government, will consent to become perpetual tributaries to a weaker neighbour.

Similarly, some states were endangering the others by provoking the hostility of the Indians or foreign countries. In general, the Federalists could not claim that the new government would simply preserve all the advantages enjoyed by all the states; they had to argue that the "local interests of a state ought, in every case, to give way to the interests of the Union" because the "small good ought never to oppose the great one." To this end, the new Constitution would deny the states the power to tax imports and make war, and would assign disputes between states to a national court.

But while Federalists hoped Americans would see the "necessity of sacrificing private opinions and partial interests," they did not want to see a sacrifice of anyone's *rights.* "Justice is the end of government. It is the end of civil society." The problem was not only to protect the people of some states from injustice by other states but to protect the minority of the people within each state from injustice by the majority. The same facts of human diversity and partiality that explain one state's unjust policies toward another operate in any society. The principle of popular government permits a majority of the people, moved by passionate opinion or economic interest, to violate the rights of the minority. A widely deplored example of this problem was state legislation that defrauded creditors by making paper money legal tender for debts. The "factious spirit" which had "tainted our public administration" caused a general "alarm for private rights."

Thus Federalist constitutional thought was not satisfied with the promise of a government that would promote the good of the public in general. The Federalists' more exacting standard was that government must "establish Justice," that is, protect the private rights of each individual citizen. Madison and James Wilson both explained the rights of human beings in terms of their "faculties." Government must protect "the faculties of men" by protecting their right to possess the property that they acquire by exercising their faculties. Government's task is not to satisfy human desires or needs, but only to protect men's right to exercise their human capacities so as to satisfy their own desires or needs. Thus, for example, for government to arrange" an equal division of property," whether for the moral improvement of the rich or the material satisfaction of the poor, is an "improper or wicked project." The view that government's fundamental purpose is to secure the private rights of individuals is founded on the argument made by John Locke and accepted by American founders that government is voluntarily instituted by naturally free individuals so as to secure the enjoyment of their freedom. The community as a whole ultimately exists for no other purpose, although its existence is an indispensable condition for the security of private rights and thus its common defense and even general welfare are of great importance.

Injustice not only contradicts the fundamental purpose of government, it tends to injure the general welfare and disrupt domestic tranquility— making possible a prudential argument for justice to those whose self-love attaches them to their own rights but makes them heedless of the rights of others. For example, paper money schemes that defrauded existing creditors had the additional consequence of drying up further credit. America's economic problems could be attributed in part to these policies; "if there be no confidence, property will sink in value, and there will be no inducement or emulation to industry." Moreover, the majority's oppression of the minority may cause the kind of "turbulence and contention" that made the ancient democracies "in general . . . as short in their lives as they have been violent in their deaths."

The Constitution would prohibit state governments from issuing paper money or adopting ex post facto laws or bills of attainder, and thus promised relief from those forms of injustice. James Madison offered a general argument that the new national government would be more just than the state governments. Because the new government operated over an extensive sphere of territory and population, groups of men with a particular factious motive would be less likely to constitute a majority of the entire population and less likely to find it easy to unite their efforts and carry out their plans.

Federalists did not differ from Anti-Federalists in seeing protection of ivate rights as the fundamental purpose of government; but they doubted that Anti-Federalists understood what most threatened those rights and what was necessary to protect them. Rejecting the view that strong government is the overriding danger to men's rights, Federalists insisted that rights were threatened by anarchy, by conquest, and even by the lawful majority of a heterogeneous society. Accordingly, the problem of limiting government so as to protect rights was more complicated than the Federalists' opponents assumed.

Reassurance: Limited and Popular Government

> Yet, however weak our country may be, I hope we shall never sacrifice our liberties.

To Anti-Federalists, the extensive powers conferred on the new government suggested the danger that those powers would be abused and the state governments extinguished; and the qualities of energy, stability, and wisdom emphasized by Federalists justified the suspicion that the government would be somewhat removed from the people in spirit as well as location. Much Federalist argument was devoted to refuting specific charges that seemed far-fetched—such as that the national provision for impeachment would apply to state officials, or that Congress's power over the time of elections would allow it to extend its term of office to twenty years. But these lame objections reflected the more fundamental fear that the Constitution would sooner or later replace America's local, limited, popular governments with a distant, oppressive, and aristocratic government.

The Federalists' first line of defense was that the new Constitution left the existing state governments intact and would merely secure the people's enjoyment of the benefits of those trusted, popular, local governments. The state legislatures "exclusively retain such powers as will give the states the advantages of small republics, without the danger commonly attendant on the weakness of such governments." The national government was necessary to defend the states and to serve certain national purposes, but "the Constitution does not suffer the federal powers to controul in the least, or so much as to interfere in the internal policy, jurisdiction, or municipal rights of any particular State: except where great and manifest national purposes and interests make that controul necessary." Within each state the existing form of government would rule on almost all matters; state governments could

> . . . cut canals; regulate descents and marriages; license taverns; alter the criminal law; . . . establish poor houses, hospitals, and houses of employment; regulate the police; and many other things of the utmost importance to the happiness of their respective citizens. In short, besides the particulars enumerated, every thing of a domestic nature must or can be done by them.

The fact that some constitutional provisions relied on state governments (for example, state legislative election of senators) was a further proof that the states would be preserved.

But it could not be denied that, in the name of "great and manifest national purposes and interests," the authority previously enjoyed by popular, local governments would be in some measure curtailed; and policies those governments had chosen would be changed by a newly authoritative national government. Accordingly, much Federalist argument offered reassurances about the national government's own character. In answer to a variety of charges concerning the national government's threat to liberty, the Federalists insisted that its powers were properly limited and its character "wholly popular."

In answer to the objection that the new Constitution contained no bill of rights, James Wilson offered an argument widely praised on one side and widely ridiculed on the other. The new government needed no bill of rights because all of its powers were "enumerated." In contrast to the state governments, which could exercise *any* powers except those specifically denied by a bill of rights, the national government could exercise *only* those powers specifically granted. A bill of rights that specified exceptions to national power would imply that those were the only exceptions, and thus expand rather than limit the national government's power. The problem with this argument was that the Constitution's enumeration appeared to assign broad objects or purposes to the national government, and without a bill of rights the government might choose to serve those purposes by means that would violate rights.

Eventually, Federalists temporized on this question and insisted only that universally popular amendments such as a bill of rights could easily be adopted subsequent to ratification and so ought not be made a condition for (and endanger the prospect of) ratification. But the fact that Federalists thought a bill of rights unimportant is worth noting, given the prominent place of the Bill of Rights in more recent constitutional thought. A bill of rights is "but a paper check," meaningless unless someone can be relied on to enforce it. States with bills of rights had been guilty of grossly violating them. A bill of rights is also not likely to be unequivocal in meaning; one proposed restriction on punishments would use the "expressions 'unusual and severe' or 'cruel and unusual,'" which "surely would have been too vague to have been of any consequence, since they admit of no clear and precise signification."

Moreover, some very dangerous powers of government could not prudently be limited at all. Some Anti-Federalists wanted to forbid a standing army in time of peace, and permit the national government to impose excise taxes but not direct taxes. Federalists defended granting the important powers of purse and sword "without limitation," on the grounds that *"it is impossible to foresee or to define the extent and variety of national exigencies, and the correspondent extent and variety of the means which may be necessary to satisfy them."* For example, although the national government could usually rely on excise taxes for its revenue, the additional power to impose direct taxes would be essential in time of war. And not the immediately foreseeable circumstances but the "probable exigencies of ages" should guide the assignment of the government's powers. A primary response to fears that such unlimited powers made the government dangerous was expressed by the following question: "Would any man choose a lame horse [lest] a sound one should run away with him; or will any man prefer a small tent to live in, before a large house, which may fall down and crush him in its ruins."

Federalists insisted that the form of the government—that is, its arrangement of offices, not the words that would define or limit its powers—was the people's fundamental guarantee against oppression. Thus the important question was not the extent and wording of the legislative powers, but "how are Congress formed? how far have you a control over them? Decide this, and then all the questions about their power may be dismissed for the amusement of those politicians whose business it is to catch flies. . . . " Anti-Federalists should not offer "unmeaning cavils about the extent of the powers"; they should consider whether the proposed government is "modeled in such a manner as to admit of its being safely vested with the requisite powers." The most important aspect of how that government was modeled was its representative character:

> Independent of all other reasonings on the subject, it is a full answer to those who require a more peremptory provision against military establishments in time of peace to say that the whole power of the proposed government is to be in the hands of the representatives of the people. This is the essential, and, after all, the only efficacious security for the rights and privileges of the people which is attainable in civil society.

Anti-Federalists who also saw representation as the essential security for the people's rights charged that the new government would have only a "shadow" of representation because so few officials would be elected to represent such a large and diverse population. In this view, the state governments could better be trusted with dangerous powers because they were more likely to satisfy the Anti-Federalist Brutus's standard "that those who are placed instead of the people, . . . should bear the strongest resemblance of those in whose room they are substituted." But Federalists did not accept that standard. The people's security is that representatives must answer to them, not that representatives resemble them. Federalists described representation not as an imperfect simulation of an assembled people but as a positive improvement over it. The proposed Constitution compared favorably to ancient democracies by its "*total exclusion of the people in their collective capacity,* from any share" in the government. The people participate only in their individual capacities as voters, so as to elect fit characters to serve the public good and judge their demonstrated fitness and fidelity in subsequent elections. Representatives should fully *understand* the interests and opinions of the people they represent, but should not simply convey a sample of those interests and opinions. And sufficient knowledge to support the limited tasks of the national government could be conveyed by a less minute representation than was needed by the state governments. "I apprehend it is of more consequence to be able to know the true interest of the people, than their faces, and of more consequence still, to have virtue enough to pursue the means of carrying that knowledge usefully into effect."

To the Federalists, then, representation is not a matter of reproducing or resembling the people but of being responsible to them. Rulers have room to exercise judgment, although the people's ultimate power of judgment means that "the general sense of the people will regulate the conduct of their representatives." The people are spared the task of devising policies themselves, but must judge the policies of the rulers they elect; and they can judge with the advantage of hindsight, according to their experience of the effect of those policies. Whereas Anti-Federalists doubted that the people would or should trust representatives so few, durable, and remote, Federalists thought elected officials could earn the people's trust by their deeds. The people's confidence depends not on a numerous representation but on "a good administration" and "a train of prosperous events." Moreover, it would be just as well if the people were not excessively confident of their representatives' trustworthiness. Paradoxically, it was safer to confer more dangerous powers on the less trusted federal government; such powers "had better be in those hands of which the people are most likely to be jealous than in those of which they are least likely to be jealous."

The "interior structure" of the proposed government provided additional safeguards. "A dependence on the people is, no doubt, the primary control on the government; but experience has taught mankind the necessity of auxiliary precautions." Without such auxiliary precautions, rulers might misuse their powers between elections, deceive an inattentive electorate, or even cancel future elections altogether.

One such precaution was the separation of legislative, executive, and judicial powers. The effect of this separation is that the legislators cannot dictate to whom the laws will be applied, which gives them an incentive to pass such laws as they would not mind having the executive enforce against themselves and their friends. Moreover, the people will be directly coerced or punished only by an "executive" who carries out rules made by others rather than rules according to his own whim. The executive's veto both permits him to defend his independence of the legislature and thereby preserve the advantages just mentioned, and, like the division of the legislature into two branches, serves as an additional security against oppressive laws. The judiciary's term of good behavior secures its independence of the executive and the legislature; it can judge both whether the executive's attempted executions are consistent with the law and whether the legislature's legislation is consistent with the Constitution. And the state governments will jealously watch the national government and sound an alarm among the people against any encroachments.

Without describing these checks in detail, I will summarize their nature and purpose. While elections are designed to obtain wise and virtuous rulers, they cannot be expected to yield rulers of perfect wisdom and perfect virtue. While Federalists accused Anti-Federalists of excessive distrust of elected officials, they denied expecting "nothing but the most exalted integrity and sublime virtue." Rather than simply try to calm popular suspicions concerning the private motives of potential rulers, the Federalists argued that these motives could be put to useful effect—both (as noted earlier) in provoking public service and in urging resistance to the overbearing ambitions of their fellow rulers. "Ambition must be made to counteract ambition"; "opposite and rival interests" are used to supply "the defect of better motives."

> In a compound government, such as that now recommended by the Convention, the talents, ambition, and even avarice of great men, are so balanced, restrained and opposed, that they can only be employed in promoting

the good of the community. Like a mill-race, it will convey off waters which would otherwise produce freshes and destruction, in such a manner as only to produce fruitfulness, beauty and plenty in the adjacent county.

In some cases, an official's motive in checking other rulers is a desire to preserve his own office's powers against encroachment. In other cases, he may expect to win immediate popularity by resisting another branch's assault on the people's political liberty. In this respect, "checks" serve to secure "the rights of representation" (and representation, in turn, secures "the rights of the people"). Checks may also more directly defend the people as a whole from unwise or oppressive measures instigated by hasty or ambitious representatives. Finally, and with least certainty, checks may be employed to defend a minority's rights against an overbearing majority. A majority's unjust plans can be delayed by a senate or president acting in expectation of eventual reward by a repentant people or simply from a love of justice.

But Federalists strongly insisted that none of these checks departed from the "strictly republican," "wholly popular" character of the proposed government. In contrast to the English constitution's King and Lords, in America "the whole is elective; all are dependent upon the people. The President, the Senate, the Representatives, are all creatures of the people." No "hereditary or self-appointed authority" with a "will independent of the majority—that is, of the society itself" is relied on to defend the rights of minorities—or, for that matter, to contribute the energy, wisdom, or stability traditionally attributed to monarchical or aristocratic institutions. Despite the apparent advantages of the British "mixed" constitution in these respects, the American Constitution's "strictly republican" character was given great weight:

It is evident that no other form would be reconcilable with the genius of the people of America; with the fundamental principles of the Revolution; or with that honorable determination which animates every votary of freedom to rest all our political experiments on the capacity of mankind for self-government.

I have earlier noted difficulties concerning foreign policy and minority rights which suggested that popular government is a mixed blessing when considered as a means; but in this argument popular government appears as an end in itself, both to the American people and to the votaries of freedom who address them. The Constitution is defended not simply as conducive to the people's interest, but as consistent with the people's honor.

An "honorable determination" about human "capacity" requires that government protect not only the acquisitive faculties by which men gain property but also the political faculties manifested (in different degrees) by opinionated partisans and ambitious politicians. No restrictions on suffrage are introduced by the Constitution (although existing state restrictions are deferred to); and no political offices are reserved for any hereditary or self-appointed authorities. "This new offered government is equal, every individual is a fair candidate for the highest seat in the empire, which is a matter unknown to every other nation in the world. . . . " The political opportunities a republican government preserves for its citizens as a matter of principle are desirable in themselves.

On the question of popular government Federalist reassurances should perhaps be described also as a promise. The republican governments of the states, which Anti-Federalists feared the new Constitution would destroy, were in the Federalist view unlikely to survive without the new Constitution. The danger of war between them would drive each state to "resort for repose and security to institutions which have a tendency to destroy their civil and political rights"; or factious rule within the states would bring about the same "instability, injustice, and confusion" that have "been the mortal diseases under which popular governments have everywhere perished." Only "a more perfect structure" would permit "the excellencies of republican government" to be "retained and its imperfections lessened or avoided." This would both serve the interests of America and promote the cause of popular government in general: "Republics, we trust in Heaven, can be energetic, wise and upright. Yet we must candidly acknowledge, that *it yet remains* for America to establish, by her example, the truth of this position."

The Federalists' intention to provide "energetic, wise and upright government" for America is the most conspicuous theme in their case for the Constitution. But that intention is accompanied by an "honorable determination" to vindicate republican government in general. Only if a "wholly popular" form can be designed to protect men's rights not only from overbearing government but also from foreign conquest, domestic violence, or majority faction, can "this form of government . . . be rescued from the opprobrium under which it has so long labored and be recommended to the esteem and adoption of mankind."

⊞ F U R T H E R   R E A D I N G

Douglas Adair, *Fame and the Founding Fathers,* ed., Trevor Colbourn (1974)
Irving Brant, *The Bill of Rights: Its Origins and Meaning* (1965)
John Diggins, *The Lost Soul of American Politics: Virtue, Self-Interest and the Foundations of Liberalism* (1984)
Edward Dumbald, *The Bill of Rights and What It Means Today* (1957)
David F. Epstein, *The Political Theory of the Federalist* (1984)
James H. Hutson, "Country, Court and Constitution: Antifederalism and the Historians," *William and Mary Quarterly* 38 (1981): 337–368
Jackson Turner Main, *The Antifederalists: Critics of the Constitution 1781–1788* (1961)
Robert A. Rutland, *The Birth of the Bill of Rights, 1776–1791* (1983)
———, *The Ordeal of the Constitution: The Antifederalists and the Ratification Struggle of 1787–1788* (1966)
Bernard Schwartz, ed., *The Roots of the Bill of Rights,* vol. 1 (1980)
Herbert J. Storing, ed., *The Complete Anti-Federalist,* 7 vols. (1981)
Garry Wills, *Explaining America: The Federalist* (1981)

Freedom of Expression in the New Republic

⌗

*Liberty! It was a rallying cry of the Revolution and a major concern of the fram-
ers at the Philadelphia convention. Yet these same delegates also wanted an
energetic central government capable of overcoming local interests by encouraging interstate and foreign commerce. Power and authority were in opposition to
individual liberty and freedom of expression. This tension became acute during
the 1790s as the new American nation struggled to survive in a world beset by
conflict between revolutionary France and Great Britain. The administrations of
George Washington and John Adams attempted to steer a middle course between
these two belligerents, but the Adams administration in particular sought closer
commercial ties with the English.*

*During the 1790s, therefore, political parties—which the framers had
dreaded—emerged. The Federalist party of Adams and Alexander Hamilton
wanted to cement America's trading relationship with the English and to keep
the dangerous fires of social revolution from spreading to America. The Republican party of Thomas Jefferson and James Madison, on the other hand, saluted
the ideas of liberty embodied in the French revolution.*

*These early domestic political struggles illustrated the important question of
how the leaders of the national government would deal with their political opponents. The Federalists faced an increasingly raucous Republican opposition that
even denounced the sober Washington and mocked the taciturn John Adams.
But could the Federalists abide the invective and accept the opposition as
legitimate?*

*The new Jeffersonian party questioned the constitutionality of the Alien and
Sedition Acts, which prohibited political criticism of government. English law
placed no prior restraint on seditious libel—speech or writing critical of the government or its officers. Once having spoken or printed such statements, however,
a person could be found guilty of merely having made them. In 1735 a New
York jury had taken the highly unusual step of acquitting John Peter Zenger, a
printer, for having run material that the colonial governor deemed seditious.
The jury acquitted Zenger based on the truth of the statements that he printed.
But the doctrine that truth was a defense to a seditious libel was not widely*

accepted in eighteenth-century America, and Zenger's case was little more than an interesting anomaly.

Against this background, Federalists and Jeffersonian Republicans tested the Alien and Sedition Acts against the First Amendment. The wording seemed clear: Congress was to make no law abridging freedom of speech or press. But was that prohibition meant to be absolute in light of English and American history? This question of individual expression was closely linked, moreover, to the structure of the new government. The Anti-Federalists and then the Jeffersonian Republicans claimed that since the national government's powers were strictly limited, it could not enact legislation like the Alien and Sedition Acts. They also claimed that, quite apart from the First Amendment, the protection of individual liberty rested with the states, and the Sedition Act provided further evidence of the baneful centralizing tendencies of the national government. The nation had not only its first major constitutional crisis but its first important test of the meaning of liberty and state sovereignty.

⊕ D O C U M E N T S

In the spring of 1798, the United States stood on the brink of turning an undeclared war with France into a formal conflict. To meet this crisis, as well as to put down the growing opposition from the Republican party, the Federalist-dominated Congress passed four measures directed at newspaper editors and pamphleteers critical of John Adams's administration. These measures—the Naturalization Act, the Alien Act, the Alien Enemies Act, and the Sedition Act—were repressive and controversial. The most problematic constitutionally was the Sedition Act, reprinted here as the first document, which seemed to violate both the First Amendment and the principle that the states were the primary line of defense for individual rights. Thomas Jefferson and James Madison in 1798 orchestrated the Republican response to these measures through the Kentucky and Virginia Resolutions, the second and third selections. These proclamations of constitutional principles (Jefferson wrote the former and Madison the latter.) were endorsed by the legislatures of the respective states. Both resolutions presented the classic arguments on behalf of individual liberties and states' rights.

The refusal of the vast majority of states to embrace the resolutions prompted a second and more strident round of resolutions from the Kentucky and Virginia legislatures in 1799. The Kentucky Resolution, presented as the fourth document, asserted the principle of nullification; that is, a state could declare void acts of the federal government that it considered unconstitutional. The next two documents, the responses to the resolutions by the states of Rhode Island and New Hampshire, point to the courts and not the state (or federal) legislatures as the proper place to interpret the Constitution. At the same time, the behavior of the federal courts, whose ranks were filled with Federalist judges, gave small comfort to critics of the national government. The seventh document, *Lyon's Case* (1798), is a perfect example. Matthew Lyon, a member of Congress from Vermont, was convicted of seditious libel in a federal circuit court. This sent shock waves through the Republican opposition and brought charges that the courts were mere tools of the Federalist party. Some fourteen persons were arrested under the Sedition Act, and ten of them were convicted.

The crisis of the Alien and Sedition Acts also set in motion the first sustained debate in the new nation about the scope of freedom of the press. In 1799

George Hay offered one of the most thoughtful responses to the crisis in freedom sparked by these acts. Hay was a Richmond, Virginia lawyer and the son-in-law of James Monroe, whom President Thomas Jefferson appointed as district attorney for Virginia. Hay was also one of the most gifted political writers on the Republican side, and his *Essay on the Liberty of the Press* (1799), excerpted in the eighth selection, combined themes of states' rights and individual liberty in a ringing denunciation of the Sedition Act.

The Republicans in power turned out to be almost as thin-skinned as their Federalist opponents. Republican authorities in New York brought a sedition suit against Harry Croswell, a Federalist editor from Hudson, New York, for his attacks in 1802 against President Jefferson (which may be read in the final selection) in *The Wasp*, a four-page weekly.

The Sedition Act, 1798

An Act in Addition to the Act, Entitled "An Act for the Punishment of Certain Crimes Against the United States."

Sec. 1. *Be it enacted* . . . , That if any persons shall unlawfully combine or conspire together, with intent to oppose any measure or measures of the government of the United States, which are or shall be directed by proper authority, or to impede the operation of any law of the United States, or to intimidate or prevent any person holding a place or office in or under the government of the United States, from undertaking, performing or executing his trust or duty; and if any person or persons, with intent as aforesaid, shall counsel, advise or attempt to procure any insurrection, riot, unlawful assembly, or combination, whether such conspiracy, threatening, counsel, advice, or attempt shall have the proposed effect or not, he or they shall be deemed guilty of a high misdemeanor, and on conviction, before any court of the United States having jurisdiction thereof, shall be punished by a fine not exceeding five thousand dollars, and by imprisonment during a term not less than six months nor exceeding five years; and further, at the discretion of the court may be holden to find sureties for his good behaviour in such sum, and for such time, as the said court may direct.

Sec. 2. That if any person shall write, print, utter, or publish, or shall cause or procure to be written, printed, uttered or published, or shall knowingly and willingly assist or aid in writing, printing, uttering or publishing any false, scandalous and malicious writing or writings against the government of the United States, or either house of the Congress of the United States, or the President of the United States, with intent to defame the said government, or either house of the said Congress, or the said President, or to bring them, or either of them, into contempt or disrepute; or to excite against them, or either or any of them, the hatred of the good people of the United States, or to stir up sedition within the United States, or to excite any unlawful combinations therein, for opposing or resisting any law of the United States, or any act of the President of the United States, done in pursuance of any such law, or of the powers in him vested by the constitution of the United States, or to resist, oppose, or defeat any such law or act, or to aid, encourage or abet any hostile designs of any foreign nation against the United States, their people or government, then such person, being thereof convicted before any court of the United States having jurisdiction thereof, shall be punished by a fine not exceeding two thousand dollars, and by imprisonment not exceeding two years.

Sec. 3. That if any person shall be prosecuted under this act, for the writing or publishing any libel aforesaid, it shall be lawful for the defendant, upon the trial of the cause, to give in evidence in his defence, the truth of the matter contained in the publication charged as a libel. And the jury who shall try the cause, shall have a right to determine the law and the fact, under the direction of the court, as in other cases.

Sec. 4. That this act shall continue to be in force until March 3, 1801, and no longer. . . .

The Kentucky Resolutions, November 16, 1798

I. *Resolved,* that the several States composing the United States of America, are not united on the principle of unlimited submission to their general government; but that by compact under the style and title of a Constitution for the United States and of amendments thereto, they constituted a general government for special purposes, delegated to that government certain definite powers, reserving each State to itself, the residuary mass of right to their own self-government; and that whensoever the general government assumes undelegated powers, its acts are unauthoritative, void, and of no force: That to this compact each State acceded as a State, and is an integral party, its co-States forming, as to itself, the other party: That the government created by this compact was not made the exclusive or final judge of the extent of the powers delegated to itself; since that would have made its discretion, and not the Constitution, the measure of its powers; but that as in all other cases of compact among parties having no common Judge, *each party has an equal right to judge for itself, as well of infractions as of the mode and measure of redress.*

II. *Resolved,* that the Constitution of the United States having delegated to Congress a power to punish treason, counterfeiting the securities and current coin of the United States, piracies and felonies committed on the high seas, and offenses against the laws of nations, and no other crimes whatever, and it being true as a general principle, and one of the amendments to the Constitution having also declared "that the powers not delegated to the United States by the Constitution, nor prohibited by it to the States, are reserved to the States respectively, or to the people," therefore also [the Sedition Act of July 14, 1798]; as also the act passed by them on the 27th day of June, 1798, entitled "An act to punish frauds committed on the Bank of the United States" (and all other their acts which assume to create, define, or punish crimes other than those enumerated in the Constitution), are altogether void and of no force, and that the power to create, define, and punish such other crimes is reserved, and of right appertains solely and exclusively to the respective States, each within its own Territory.

III. *Resolved,* that it is true as a general principle, and is also expressly declared by one of the amendments to the Constitution that "the powers not delegated to the United States by the Constitution, nor prohibited by it to the States, are reserved to the States respectively or to the people"; and that no power over the freedom of religion, freedom of speech, or freedom of the press being delegated to the United States by the Constitution, nor prohibited by it to the States, all lawful powers respecting the same did of right remain, and were reserved to the States, or to the people: That thus was manifested their determination to retain to themselves the right of judging how far the licentiousness of speech and of the press may be abridged without lessening their useful freedom, and how far those abuses which cannot be separated from their use should be tolerated rather than the use be destroyed; and thus also they guarded against all abridgment by the United States of the freedom of religious opinions and exercises, and retained to themselves the right of protecting the same, as this State, by a law passed on the general demand of its citizens, had already protected them from all human restraint or interference: And that in addition to this general principle and express declaration, another and more special provision has been made by one of the amendments to the Constitution which expressly declares, that "Congress shall make no law respecting an establishment of religion, or prohibiting the free exercise thereof, or abridging the freedom of speech, or of the press," thereby guarding in the same sentence, and under the same words, the freedom of religion, of speech, and of the press, insomuch, that whatever violates either, throws down the sanctuary which covers the others, and that libels, falsehoods, defamation equally with heresy and false religion, are withheld from the cognizance of Federal tribunals. That therefore [the Sedition Act], which does abridge the freedom of the press, is not law, but is altogether void and of no effect.

IV. *Resolved,* that alien friends are under the jurisdiction and protection of the laws of the State wherein they are; that no power over them has been delegated to the United States, nor prohibited to the individual States distinct from their power over citizens; and it being true as a general principle, and one of the amendments to the Constitution having also declared that "the powers not delegated to the United States by the Constitution, nor prohibited by it to the States, are reserved to the States respectively, or to the people," the [Alien Act of June 22, 1798], which assumes power over alien friends not delegated by the Constitution, is not law, but is altogether void and of no force.

V. *Resolved,* that in addition to the general principle as well as the express declaration, that powers not delegated are reserved, another and more special provision inserted in the Constitution from abundant caution has declared, "that the migration or importation of such persons as any of the States now existing shall think proper to admit, shall not be prohibited by the Congress prior to the year 1808." That this Commonwealth does admit the migration of alien friends described as the subject of the said act concerning aliens; that a provision against prohibiting their migration is a provision against all acts equivalent thereto, or it would be nugatory; that to remove them when migrated is equivalent to a prohibition of their migration, and is therefore contrary to the said provision of the Constitution, and void. . . .

VII. *Resolved,* that the construction applied by the general government (as is evinced by sundry of their proceedings) to those parts of the Constitution of the United States which delegate to Congress a power to lay and collect taxes, duties, imposts, and excises; to pay the debts, and provide for the common defense, and general welfare of the United States, and to make all laws which shall be necessary and proper for carrying into execution the powers vested by the Constitution in the government of the United States, or any department thereof, goes to the destruction of all the limits prescribed to their power by the Constitution: That words meant by that instrument to be subsidiary only to the execution of the limited powers ought not to be so construed as themselves to give unlimited powers, nor a part so to be taken as to destroy the whole residue of the instrument: That the proceedings of the general government under color of these articles will be a fit and necessary subject for revisal and correction at a time of greater tranquility, while those specified in the preceding resolutions call for immediate redress.

VIII. *Resolved,* that the preceding Resolutions be transmitted to the Senators and Representatives in Congress from this Commonwealth, who are hereby enjoined to present the same to their respective Houses, and to use their best endeavors to procure, at the next session of Congress, a repeal of the aforesaid unconstitutional and obnoxious acts.

IX. *Resolved,* lastly, that the Governor of this Commonwealth be, and is hereby authorized and requested to communicate the preceding Resolutions to the Legislatures of the several States, to assure them that this Commonwealth considers Union for specified National purposes, and particularly for those specified in their late Federal Compact, to be friendly to the peace, happiness, and prosperity of all the States: that faithful to that compact according to the plain intent and meaning in which it was understood and acceded to by the several parties, it is sincerely anxious for its preservation: that it does also believe, that to take from the States all the powers of self-government, and transfer them to a general and consolidated government, without regard to the special delegations and reservations solemnly agreed to in that compact, is not for the peace, happiness, or prosperity of these States: And that, therefore, this Commonwealth is determined, as it doubts not its co-States are, tamely to submit to undelegated and consequently unlimited powers in no man or body of men on earth: that if the acts before specified should stand, these conclusions would flow from them; that the general government may place any act they think proper on the list of crimes and punish it themselves, whether enumerated or not enumerated by the Constitution as cognizable by them: that they may transfer its cognizance to the President or any other person, who may himself be the accuser, counsel, judge, and jury, whose suspicions may be the evidence, his order the sentence, his officer the executioner, and his breast the sole record of the transaction: that a very numerous and valuable description of the inhabitants of these States being by this precedent reduced as outlaws to the absolute dominion of one man, and the barrier of the Constitution thus swept away from us all, no rampart now remains against the passions and the powers of a majority of Congress, to protect from a like exportation or other more grievous punishment the minority of the same body, the legislatures, judges, governors, and counselors of the States, nor their other peaceable inhabitants who may venture to reclaim the constitutional rights and liberties of the State and people, or who for other causes, good or bad, may be obnoxious to the views or marked by the suspicions of the President, or be thought dangerous to his or their elections or other interests, public or personal: that the friendless alien has indeed been selected as the safest subject of a first experiment, but the citizen will soon follow, or rather has already followed: for, already has a sedition act marked him as its prey: that these and successive acts of the same character, unless arrested on the threshold, may tend to drive these States into revolution and blood, and will furnish new calumnies against Republican governments, and new pretexts for those who wish it to be believed, that man cannot be governed but by a rod of iron: that it would be a dangerous delusion were a confidence in the men of our choice to silence our fears for the safety of our rights: that confidence is everywhere the parent of despotism: free government is founded in jealousy and not in confidence; it is jealousy and not confidence which prescribes limited Constitutions to bind down those whom we are obliged to trust with power: that our Constitution has accordingly fixed the limits to which and no further our confidence may go; and let the honest advocate of confidence read the alien and sedition acts, and say if the Constitution has not been wise in fixing limits to the government it created, and whether we should be wise in destroying those limits; let him say what the government is if it be not a tyranny, which the men of our choice have conferred on the President, and the President of our choice has assented to and accepted over the friendly strangers, to whom the mild spirit of our country and its laws had pledged hospitality and protection: that the men of our choice have more respected the bare suspicions of the President than the solid rights of innocence, the claims of justification, the sacred force of truth, and the forms and substance of law and justice. In questions of power then let no more be heard of confidence in man, but bind him down from mischief by the claims of the Constitution. That this Commonwealth does therefore call on its co-States for an expression of their sentiments on the acts concerning aliens, and for the punishment of certain crimes herein before specified, plainly declaring whether these acts are or are not authorized by the Federal Compact. And it doubts not that their sense will be so announced as to prove their attachment unaltered to limited government, whether general or particular, and that the rights and liberties of their co-States will be exposed to no dangers by remaining embarked on a common bottom with their own: That they will concur with this Commonwealth in considering the said acts so palpably against the Constitution as to amount to an undisguised declaration, that the compact is not meant to be the measure of the powers of the general government, but that it will proceed in the exercise over these States of all powers whatsoever: That they will view this as seizing the rights of the States and consolidating them in the hands of the general government with a power assumed to bind the States (not merely in cases made Federal) but in all cases whatsoever, by laws made, not with their consent, but by others against their consent: That this would be to surrender the form of government we have chosen, and to live under one deriving its powers from its own will, and not from our authority; and that the co-States, recurring to their natural right in cases not made Federal, will concur in declaring these acts void and of no force, and will each unite with this Commonwealth in requesting their repeal at the next session of Congress.

The Virginia Resolutions, December 24, 1798

Resolved, That the General Assembly of Virginia doth unequivocally express a firm resolution to maintain and defend the Constitution of the United States, and the Constitution of this state, against every aggression either foreign or domestic; and that they will support the Government of the United States in all measures warranted by the former.

That this Assembly most solemnly declares a warm attachment to the union of the states, to maintain which it pledges all its powers; and that, for this end, it is their duty to watch over and oppose every infraction of those principles which constitute the only basis of that Union, because a faithful observance of them can alone secure its existence and the public happiness.

That this Assembly doth explicitly and peremptorily declare that it views the powers of the Federal Government as resulting from the compact to which the states are parties, as limited by the plain sense and intention of the instrument constituting that compact; as no further valid than they are authorized by the grants enumerated in that compact; and that, in case of a deliberate, palpable, and dangerous exercise of other powers not granted by the said compact, the states, who are parties thereto, have the right and are in duty bound to interpose for arresting the progress of the evil, and for maintaining within their respective limits the authorities, rights, and liberties appertaining to them.

That the General Assembly doth also express its deep regret, that a spirit has in sundry instances been manifested by the Federal Government to enlarge its powers by forced constructions of the constitutional charter which defines them; and that indications have appeared of a design to expound certain general phrases (which, having been copied from the very limited grant of powers in the former Articles of Confederation, were the less liable to be misconstrued) so as to destroy the meaning and effect of the particular enumeration which necessarily explains and limits the general phrases; and so as to consolidate the states, by degrees, into one sovereignty, the obvious tendency and inevitable consequence of which would be to transform the present republican system of the United States into an absolute, or, at best, a mixed monarchy.

That the General Assembly doth particularly PROTEST against the palpable and alarming infractions of the Constitution in the two late cases of the "Alien and Sedition Acts," passed at the last session of Congress; the first of which exercises a power nowhere delegated to the Federal Government, and which, by uniting legislative and judicial powers to those of [the] executive, subverts the general principles of free government, as well as the particular organization and positive provisions of the Federal Constitution: and the other of which acts exercises, in like manner, a power not delegated by the Constitution, but, on the contrary, expressly and positively forbidden by one of the amendments thereto,—a power which, more than any other, ought to produce universal alarm, because it is levelled against the right of freely examining public characters and measures, and of free communication among the people thereon, which has ever been justly deemed the only effectual guardian of every other right.

That this state having, by its Convention which ratified the Federal Constitution, expressly declared that, among other essential rights, "the liberty of conscience and of the press cannot be cancelled, abridged, restrained or modified by any authority of the United States," and from its extreme anxiety to guard these rights from every possible attack of sophistry or ambition, having, with other states, recommended an amendment for that purpose, which amendment was in due time annexed to the Constitution,—it would mark a reproachful inconsistency and criminal degeneracy, if an indifference were now shown to the palpable violation of one of the rights thus declared and secured, and to the establishment of a precedent which may be fatal to the other.

That the good people of this commonwealth, having ever felt and continuing to feel the most sincere affection for their brethren of the other states, the truest anxiety for establishing and perpetuating the union of all and the most scrupulous fidelity to that Constitution, which is the pledge of mutual friendship, and the instrument of mutual happiness, the General Assembly doth solemnly appeal to the like dispositions of the other states, in confidence that they will concur with this Commonwealth in declaring, as it does hereby declare, that the acts aforesaid are unconstitutional; and that the necessary and proper measures will be taken by each for co-operating with this state, in maintaining unimpaired the authorities, rights, and liberties reserved to the states respectively, or to the people. . . .

The Kentucky Resolutions, February 22, 1799

The representatives of the good people of this commonwealth, in General Assembly convened, having maturely considered the answers of sundry states in the Union, to their resolutions passed the last session, respecting certain unconstitutional laws of Congress, commonly called the Alien and Sedition Laws, would be faithless, indeed, to themselves and to those they represent, were they silently to acquiesce in the principles and doctrines attempted to be maintained in all those answers, that of Virginia only excepted. To again enter the field of argument, and attempt more fully or forcibly to expose the unconstitutionality of those obnoxious laws, would, it is apprehended, be as unnecessary as unavailing. We cannot, however, but lament, that, in the discussion of those interesting subjects, by sundry of the legislatures of our sister states, unfounded suggestions, and uncandid insinuations, derogatory to the true character and principles of this commonwealth have been substituted in place of fair reasoning and sound argument. Our opinions of these alarming measures of the general government, together with our reasons for those opinions, were detailed with decency, and with temper, and submitted to the discussion and judgment of our fellow-citizens throughout the Union. Whether the like decency and temper have been observed in the answers of most of those States, who have denied or attempted to obviate the great truths contained in those resolutions, we have now only to submit to a candid world. Faithful to the true principles of the federal Union, unconscious of any designs to disturb the harmony of that Union, and anxious only to escape the fangs of despotism, the good people of this commonwealth are regardless of censure or calumniation. Lest, however, the silence of this commonwealth should be construed into an acquiescence in the doctrines and principles advanced and attempted to be maintained by the said answers, or at least those of our fellow-citizens throughout the Union who so widely differ from us on those important subjects, should be deluded by the expectation, that we shall be deterred from what we conceive our duty, or shrink from the principles contained in those resolutions—therefore,

Resolved, That this commonwealth considers the federal Union, upon the terms and for the purposes specified in the late compact, conducive to the liberty and happiness of the several states: That it does now unequivocally declare its attachment to the Union, and to that compact, agreeably to its obvious and real intention, and will be among the last to seek its dissolution: That if those who administer the general government be permitted to transgress the limits fixed by that compact, by a total disregard to the special delegations of power therein contained, an annihilation of the state governments, and the creation upon their ruins of a general consolidated government, will be the inevitable consequence: That the principle and construction contended for by sundry of the state legislatures, that the general government is the exclusive judge of the extent of the powers delegated to it, stop not short of *despotism*—since the discretion of those who administer the government, and not the *Constitution,* would be the measure of their powers: That the several states who formed that instrument being sovereign and independent, have the unquestionable right to judge of the infraction; and, *That a nullification of those sovereignties, of all unauthorized acts done under color of that instrument is the rightful remedy:* That this commonwealth does, under the most deliberate reconsideration, declare, that the said Alien and Sedition Laws are, in their opinion, palpable violations of the said Constitution; and, however cheerfully it may be disposed to surrender its opinion to a majority of its sister states, in matters of ordinary or doubtful policy, yet, in momentous regulations like the present, which so vitally wound the best rights of the citizen, it would consider a silent acquiescence as highly criminal: That although this commonwealth, as a party to the federal compact, will bow to the laws of the Union, yet, it does, at the same time declare, that it will not now, or ever hereafter, cease to oppose in a constitutional manner, every attempt at what quarter soever offered, to violate that compact. And, finally, in order that no pretext or arguments may be drawn from a supposed acquiescence, on the part of this commonwealth in the constitutionality of those laws, and be thereby used as precedents for similar future violations of the federal compact—this commonwealth does now enter against them its solemn PROTEST.

Rhode Island Reply to the Virginia Resolution, 1799

Certain resolutions of the Legislature of Virginia, passed on the 21st of December last, being communicated to the Assembly,—

1. *Resolved,* That, in the opinion of this legislature, the second section of the third article of the Constitution of the United States, in these words, to wit,—"The judicial power shall extend to all cases arising under the laws of the United States,"—vests in the Federal Courts, exclusively, and in the Supreme Court of the United States, ultimately, the authority of deciding on the constitutionality of any act or law of the Congress of the United States.

2. *Resolved,* That for any state legislature to assume that authority would be—

1st. Blending together legislative and judicial powers;

2d. Hazarding an interruption of the peace of the states by civil discord, in case of a diversity of opinions among the state legislatures; each state having, in that case, no resort, for vindicating its own opinions, but the strength of its own arm;

3d. Submitting most important questions of law to less competent tribunals; and,

4th. An infraction of the Constitution of the United States, expressed in plain terms.

3. *Resolved,* That, although, for the above reasons, this legislature, in their public capacity, do not feel themselves authorized to consider and decide on the constitutionality of the Sedition and Alien laws, (so called,) yet they are called upon, by the exigency of this occasion, to declare that, in their private opinions, these laws are within the powers delegated to Congress, and promotive of the welfare of the United States.

4. *Resolved,* That the governor communicate these resolutions to the supreme executive of the state of Virginia, and at the same time express to him that this legislature cannot contemplate, without extreme concern and regret, the many evil and fatal consequencies which may flow from the very unwarrantable resolutions aforesaid, of the legislature of Virginia, passed on the twenty-first day of December last.

New Hampshire Reply to the Virginia and Kentucky Resolutions, 1799

The legislature of New Hampshire, having taken into consideration certain resolutions of the General Assembly of Virginia, dated December 21, 1798; also certain resolutions of the legislature of Kentucky, of the 10th of November 1798:—

Resolved, That the legislature of New Hampshire unequivocally express a firm resolution to maintain and defend the Constitution of the United States, and the Constitution of this State, against every aggression, either foreign or domestic, and that they will support the government of the United States in all measures warranted by the former.

That the state legislatures are not the proper tribunals to determine the constitutionality of the laws of the general government; that the duty of such decision is properly and exclusively confided to the judicial department.

That, if the legislature of New Hampshire, for mere speculative purposes, were to express an opinion on the acts of the general government, commonly called "the Alien and Sedition Bills," that opinion would unreservedly be, that those acts are constitutional, and, in the present critical situation of our country, highly expedient.

That the constitutionality and expediency of the acts aforesaid have been very ably advocated and clearly demonstrated by many citizens of the United States, more especially by the minority of the General Assembly of Virginia. The legislature of New Hampshire, therefore, deem it unnecessary, by any train of arguments, to attempt further illustration of the propositions, the truth of which, it is confidently believed, at this day, is very generally seen and acknowledged.

Which report, . . . was unanimously received and adopted, one hundred and thirty-seven members being present.

Lyon's Case

U.S. Circuit Court, District of Vermont (1798)

[This was an indictment, under the act of July 14, 1798, against Matthew Lyon, for the publication of a seditious libel.]

The indictment which was found on October 5, 1798, contained three counts, the first of which, after averring the intent to be "to stir up sedition, and to bring the president and government of the United States into contempt," laid the following libellous matter: "As to the executive, when I shall see the efforts of that power bent on the promotion of the comfort, the happiness, and accommodation of the people, that executive shall have my zealous and uniform support: but whenever I shall, on the part of the executive, see every consideration of the public welfare swallowed up in a continual grasp for power, in an unbounded thirst for ridiculous pomp, foolish adulation, and selfish avarice; when I shall behold men of real merit daily turned out of office, for no other cause but independency of sentiment;

Government was deemed essential, to the peace and happiness of the people of America; not because the State institutions were defective and required amendment, not because liberty was in danger, or because character was not sufficiently guarded from defamation, but because there were many important subjects on which the State Legislatures could not act with effect. They could not make effectual provision for paying the public debt, nor regulate Commerce, nor borrow money on the credit of the United States, nor establish a system of general defence. These were the great objects which could not be attained, but by means of a Federal Government, and for the attainment of these objects a Federal Government was instituted. The powers therefore delegated to this government were special and limited, and from the state of things could not have been otherwise.

Nothing can be more obvious, and nothing has been more generally admitted, than the distinction, between the principle which is the basis of the State governments, and that which forms the basis of the Federal Constitution. To the State governments, general powers of legislation are granted, and they may legislate on all subjects, except those on which they are expressly forbidden to act. To the Federal Government, specific powers only are given, and Congress can legislate on those subjects only on which they are expressly authorised to act. The State governments possess all powers, belonging to the people, except those expressly withheld: the general government possesses those powers only which are expressly granted, or are necessary to carry a power expressly granted into effect. When therefore a doubt arises concerning the constitutionality of a Congressional law, the first question ought regularly to be, is the power to pass this law expressly granted to Congress? If it be not expressly granted in plain words for that purpose, the next question must be—Is this law necessary to carry any power expressly granted into effect? If it be not necessary, there is an end of all doubt or difficulty on the subject, and the law is absolutely void.

Let the Sedition bill be brought to the test of an examination on these principles, and the result will be, that those clauses in it, which punish insurrection or *actual* opposition to the authorised measures of government, will be found warranted by the terms and meaning of the federal compact; because the best laws would be of no avail, unless Congress possessed a power to punish those who opposed their execution. The power of punishing acts of opposition to the laws, therefore, being necessary, to carry the laws themselves into due operation, is readily conceded to belong to Congress. But the inquiry pursued farther, on the same principles, will terminate in a conviction, that so much of the Sedition Bill as relates to libels on the government, or the individuals belonging to it, is not within the words or meaning of the Constitution. It will not be said that the power of punishing libels is expressly given. Several offences are enumerated which may be defined and punished by the general government; but libels are not included. If then the power of punishing libels is not expressly given, it cannot be exercised, unless it can be shewn to be *necessary* to carry some given powers into effect. What is the power expressly given, which is carried into effect, or is in any shape aided in its operation, by the power of punishing libels?

Plain as this question is, it never has been answered. In fact it cannot be answered. Gallatin propounded it at the last session to the advocates of the Sedition Bill, with his usual perspicuity; but neither the eloquence of Otis, nor the ingenuity of Harper could be brought to encounter it! . . .

The position, that Congress can exercise no power that is not given expressly, or by *necessary* implication, tho' manifestly resulting from the nature of a federal compact, and supported by every fair and rational construction of the constitution, has, from excess of caution, been expressly recognized by the 12th article of the Amendments, which declares, "that powers not delegated to the United States by the Constitution, nor prohibited by it to the States, are reserved to the States respectively or to the people."

Solid as the foregoing principle is, and solemn as its recognition has been by the people of America, it has been boldly denied by some, and artfully evaded by others. It has been strenuously contended, that Congress had power to adopt all measures which they might think conducive to the general welfare. Mr. S. from South-Carolina was the first who openly proclaimed it as his opinion, that constitutionality and expediency were convertible terms.

Those who advocate this doctrine, endeavour to vindicate their conduct by resorting to the preamble, and to the 8th Section of the first Article of the Constitution of the United States.

But before the arguments drawn from these sources are noticed, it is proper to observe, that all reasoning on any proposition, may be reduced into the form of a syllogism; and if the first and second terms be true, and the conclusion correctly stated, the demonstration sought for is obtained; and according to all the rules of logic, and the plain dictates of common sense, principles from which a different conclusion is deduced, cannot be true.

The proposition here maintained is, that so much of the Sedition Bill as prescribes a punishment for libels is not warranted by the Federal Constitution.

To demonstrate this proposition to be true, I have recourse to the following syllogism.

1. Congress possesses no power unless it be expressly given, or necessary to carry a given power into effect. See the 1st, 2d, and 3d postulates.

2. The power of prescribing a punishment for libels is not expressly given, nor necessary to carry a given power into effect.

3. Conclusion. Therefore so much of the Sedition Bill as prescribes a punishment for libels, is not warranted by the Federal Constitution,

Upon principles of fair and logical reasoning, those who advocate the constitutionality of the Sedition Bill, must admit the conclusion here stated, unless they controvert the truth of the first or second terms of the foregoing syllogism. . . .

I contend therefore, and it appears clear, that if the words freedom of the press, have any meaning at all, they mean a total exemption from any law making any publication whatever criminal. Whether the unequivocal avowal of this doctrine in the United States would produce mischief or not, is a question which perhaps I may have leisure to discuss. I must be content here to observe, that the mischief if any, which might arise from this doctrine, could not be remedied or prevented, but by means of a power fatal to the liberty of the people.

That the real meaning of the words "freedom of the press," has been ascertained by the foregoing remarks, will appear still more clearly, if possible, from the absurdity of those constructions which have been given by the advocates of the sedition bill.

The construction clearly held out in the bill itself, is, that it does not extend to the privilege of printing facts, that are false. This construction cannot be correct. It plainly supposes that "freedom," extends only as far as the power of doing what is morally right. If, then, the freedom of the press can be restrained to the publication of facts, it follows, inevitably, that it may also be restrained to the publication of true opinions. There is truth in opinion, as well as in fact. Error in opinion may do as much harm, as falsity in fact: it may be as morally wrong, and it may be propagated from motives as malicious. It may do more harm, because the refutation of an opinion which is erroneous, is more difficult than the contradiction of a fact which is false. But the power of controlling opinions has never yet been claimed; yet it is manifest that the same construction, which warrants a control in matters of fact, does the same as to matters of opinion. In addition to this, it ought to be remarked, that the difficulty of distinguishing in many cases between fact and opinion, is extremely great, and that no kind of criterion is furnished by the law under consideration. Of this more, perhaps, will be said hereafter.

Again, if the congressional construction be right, if the freedom of the press consists in the full enjoyment of the privilege of printing facts that are true, it will be fair to read the amendment, without the words really used, after substituting those said by Congress to have the same import. The clause will then stand thus: "Congress shall make no law abridging the right of the press, to publish facts that are true!" If this was the real meaning of Congress, and the several states, when they spoke in the state constitutions, and in the amendment of the "freedom of the press," the very great solicitude on this subject displayed throughout the continent, was most irrational and absurd. If this was their meaning, the "palladium" of liberty is indeed a "wooden statue," and the bulwark of freedom is indeed a despicable fortification of paper. The officers of the government would have a right to invade this fortification, and to make prisoners of the garrison, whenever they thought that there was a failure in the duty of publishing only the truth, of which failure persons chosen by the government are to judge. This is too absurd even for ridicule.

That such was not the meaning of the convention of Virginia is manifest. They solemnly protest against any kind of legislative control, and declare, that the freedom of the press is not to be restrained or modified by any law whatever.

This venerable and enlightened assembly had too much wisdom to avow a meaning, so totally incompatible with the real object of their wishes. They knew that there never was a government in the world, however despotic, that dared to avow a design to suppress the truth: they know that the most corrupt and profligate administrations, that ever brought wretchedness and oppression upon a happy and free people, speak in their public acts the language of patriotism and virtue only, and that, although their real object is to stop inquiry, and to terrify truth into silence, the vengeance of the law *appears* to be directed against falsehood and malice only: in fact, they know, that there are many truths, important to society, which are not susceptible of that full, direct, and positive evidence, which can alone be exhibited before a court and jury:

That men might be, and often would be deterred from speaking truths, which they could prove, unless they were absolutely protected from the trouble, disgrace, losses, and expence of a prosecution:

That in the violence of party spirit which government knows too well how to produce, and to inflame evidence; the most conclusive, might be rejected, and that juries might be packed, "who would find Abel guilty of the murder of Cain:"

That nothing tends more to irritate the minds of men, and disturb the peace of society, than prosecutions of a political nature, which like prosecutions in religion, increase the evils, they were, perhaps, intended to remove:

They knew that the licentiousness of the press, though an evil, was a less evil than that resulting from any law to restrain it, upon the same principle that the most enlightened part of the world is at length convinced, that the evils arising from the toleration of heresy and atheism, are less, infinitely less, than the evils of persecution:

That the spirit of inquiry and discussion, was of the utmost importance in every free country, and could be preserved only by giving it absolute protection, even in its excesses:

That truth was always equal to the task of combating falsehood without the aid of government; because in most instances it has defeated falsehood, backed by all the power of government:

That truth cannot be impressed upon the human mind by power, with which, therefore, it disdains an alliance, but by reason and evidence only.

They knew the sublime precept inculcated by the act establishing religious freedom, that "where discussion is free, error ceases to be dangerous": and, therefore, they wisely aimed at the total exclusion of all Congressional jurisdiction.

But, it has been said, that the freedom of the press, consists not in the privilege of printing truth; but in an exemption from previous restraint, and as the sedition bill imposes no previous restraint, it does not abridge the freedom of the press. This *profound* remark is borrowed from Blackstone and De Lolme, and is gravely repeated, by those who are weak enough to take opinions upon trust.

If these writers meant to state what the law was understood to be in

England, they are correct. Even if they meant to state what the law ought to be in England, perhaps they are still correct; because it is extremely probable, that a press absolutely free, would in the short course of one year "humble in the dust and ashes," the "stupendous fabric," of the British government. But this definition does not deserve to be transplanted into America. In Britain, a legislative control over the press, is, perhaps essential to the preservation of the "present order of things"; but it does not follow, that such control is essential here. In Britain, a vast standing army is necessary to keep the people in peace, and the monarch on his throne; but it does not follow that the tranquillity of America, or the personal safety of the President, would be promoted by a similar institution.

A single remark will be sufficient to expose the extreme fallacy of the idea, when applied to the constitution of the United States. If the freedom of the press consists in an exemption from previous restraint, Congress may, without injury to the freedom of the press, punish with death any thing *actually* published, which a political inquisition may chuse to condemn.

But on what ground is this British doctrine about the freedom of the press introduced here? In Britain, the parliament is acknowledged to be omnipotent. It has exercised this omnipotence, and converted three years into seven years. In Britain there is no constitution, no limitation of legislative power; but in America, there is a constitution, the power of the legislature is limited, and the object of one limitation is to secure the freedom of the press.

If this doctrine is avowed here, under the idea that the common law of England is in force in the United States, even this idea will be of no avail. The common law knows nothing of printing or the liberty of the press. The art of printing was not discovered, until towards the close of the 15th century. It was at first in England, a subject of star-chamber jurisdiction, and afterwards put under a licencer by statute. This statute expired just before the commencement of the present century. Before this event, the rights of the press, were at the mercy of a single individual. There can be no common law, no immemorial usage or custom concerning a thing of so modern a date.

The freedom of the press, therefore, means the total exemption of the press from any kind of legislative control, and consequently the sedition bill, which is an act of legislative control, is an abridgment of its liberty, and expressly forbidden by the constitution. Which was to be demonstrated. . . .

Federalist Editor Harry Croswell Lambastes
President Thomas Jefferson, 1802

[T]he burden of the Federal song is, that Mr. Jefferson paid Callender for writing against the late administration. This is wholly false. The charge is explicitly this:—Jefferson paid Callender for calling Washington a traitor, a robber, and a perjurer—For calling Adams, a hoary headed incendiary; and for most grossly slandering the private characters of men, who, he well knew were virtuous. These charges, not a democratic editor has yet dared, or ever will dare to meet in an open [and] manly discussion. . . .

1st. He [Jefferson] ordered money to be paid out of the treasury to repair the Berceau, contrary to the clause in the constitution which gives the sole power of appropriating money to Congress.

2d. He has displaced the honest patriots of this country and appointed to succeed them foreigners and flatterers, who have always shewn themselves hostile to it, one of whom was prime agent, in raising an insurrection to oppose the constituted authorities.

3d. He planned and directed the attack on the constitution last winter, by which the independence of the judiciary was destroyed and our constitution marred and mangled.

4th. He has remitted a fine to a criminal, after the fine was collected, against the express provision of the constitution.

5th. He released Duane from a prosecution, instituted for a libel on the Senate, without the least authority from the constitution, or any law—only, because Duane had contributed his share to *lie* him into office. It would be an endless task to enumerate the many acts, in direct hostility to common sense and the constitution, of which the *"man of the people"* has been guilty—These are facts, and I now ask his friends and foes—every American—do you not blush, for your country and your President?—Do you not in all this plainly perceive the little arts—the very little arts, of a very little mind—"Alas! what will the world think of the fold if such is the shepherd."

✤ *E S S A Y S*

In the first essay, Leonard W. Levy, a historian from Claremont Graduate School, contends that the Republican opponents of the Alien and Sedition Acts wrought a fundamental change in the way Americans viewed freedom of speech and press. According to Levy the Republicans understood that, in a government based on popular sovereignty (instead of one in which there were subjects and sovereigns), the widest possible latitude had to be given to rights.

Walter Berns, a political scientist at the American Enterprise Institute, takes an entirely different tack in the second essay, discounting the transforming character of the Republican contribution to the history of liberty. He argues instead that the Republican attack on the Sedition Act was merely a way for Republicans to press their states' rights concerns. According to Berns, it was the Federalists who championed free speech and press.

The Republicans and the Transformation of Libertarian Thought

LEONARD W. LEVY

In 1798 there was a sudden break-through in American libertarian thought on freedom of speech and press—sudden, radical, and transforming, like an underwater volcano erupting its lava upward from the ocean floor to form a new island. The Sedition Act, which was a thrust in the direction of a single-party press and a monolithic party system, triggered the Republican surge. The result was the emergence of a new promontory of libertarian thought jutting out of a stagnant Blackstonian sea.

To appreciate the Republican achievement requires an understanding of American libertarian thought on the meaning and scope of freedom of political discourse. Contrary to the accepted view, neither the Revolution nor the First Amendment superseded the common law by repudiating the Blackstonian concept that freedom of the press meant merely freedom from prior restraint. There had been no rejection of the concept that government may be criminally assaulted, that is, seditiously libeled, simply by the expression of critical opinions that tended to lower it in the public's esteem.

To be sure, the principle of a free press, like flag, home, and mother, had no enemies. Only seditious libels, licentious opinions, and malicious falsehoods were condemned. The question, therefore, is not whether freedom of the press was favored but what it meant and whether its advocates would extend it to a political opponent whose criticism cut to the bone on issues that counted. Jefferson once remarked that he did not care whether his neighbor said that there are twenty gods or no God, because "It neither picks my pocket nor breaks my leg." But in drafting a constitution for Virginia in 1776 he proposed that freedom of religion "shall not be held to justify any seditious preaching or conversation against the authority of the civil government." And in the same year he helped frame a statute on treasonable crimes, punishing anyone who "by any word" or deed defended the cause of Great Britain. Apparently political opinions could break his leg or pick his pocket, thus raising the question of what he meant by freedom of the press. We can say that he and his contemporaries supported an unrestricted public discussion of issues if we understand that "unrestricted" meant merely the absence of censorship in advance of publication: no one needed a government license to express himself, but he was accountable under the criminal law for abuse of his right to speak or publish freely.

Before 1798 the *avant-garde* among American libertarians staked everything on the principles of the Zenger case, which they thought beyond improvement. No greater liberty could be conceived than the right to publish without restriction if only the defendant might plead truth as a defense in a criminal prosecution for seditious, blasphemous, obscene, or personal libel, and if the criminality of his words might be determined by a jury of his peers rather than by a judge. The substantive law of criminal libels was unquestioned.

Zengerian principles, however, were a frail prop for a broad freedom of the press. Granted, a defendant representing a popular cause against the administration in power might be acquitted, but if his views were unpopular, God help him—for a jury would not, nor would his plea of truth as a defense. A jury, then as today, was essentially a court of public opinion, often synonymous with public prejudice. Moreover, the opinions of men notoriously differ: one man's truth is another's falsehood. Indeed political opinions may be neither true nor false and are usually not capable of being proved by the rules of evidence, even if true. An indictment for seditious libel, based on a defendant's accusation of bribery or corruption by a public official, can be judged by a jury. But the history of sedition trials indicates that indictments are founded on accusations of a different order, namely, that the government, or one of its measures or officials, is unjust, tyrannical, or contrary to the public interest. Libertarians who accepted Zengerian principles painted themselves into a corner. If a jury returned a verdict of guilty despite a defense of truth, due process had been accorded, and protests were groundless, for the substance of the law that made the trial possible had not been challenged.

American acquiescence in the British or common-law definition of a free press was so widespread that even the frail Zengerian principles seemed daring, novel, and had few adherents. It was not until 1790, after the framing, but before the ratification, of the First Amendment, that the first state, Pennsylvania, took the then radical step of adopting the Zengerian principles which left the common law of seditious libel intact. The Pennsylvania provision was drafted by James Wilson, who (in the state convention that ratified the Constitution) declared, without challenge by any of the ardent proponents of a bill of rights: "what is meant by the liberty of the press is that there should be no antecedent restraint upon it; but that every author is responsible when he attacks the security or welfare of the government. . . . " The mode of proceeding, Wilson added, should be by prosecution. The state constitutional provision of 1790 reflected this proposition, as did state trials before and after 1790.

Delaware and Kentucky followed Pennsylvania's lead in 1792, but elsewhere the *status quo* prevailed. In 1789 William Cushing and John Adams worried about whether the guarantee of a free press in Massachusetts ought to mean that truth was a good defense to a charge of criminal libel, but they agreed that false publications against the government were punishable. In 1791, when a Massachusetts editor was prosecuted for a criminal libel against a state official, the Supreme Judicial Court divided on the question of truth as a defense, but, like the Pennsylvania judges, agreed that the state constitutional guarantee of a free press was merely declaratory of the common law in simply prohibiting a licensing system.

The opinions of Jefferson, the acknowledged libertarian leader in America, and of Madison, the father of the Bill of Rights, are especially significant.

Jefferson, in 1783, when proposing a new constitution for Virginia, exempted the press from prior restraints, but carefully provided for prosecution—a state criminal trial—in cases of false publication. In 1788, when urging Madison to support a bill of rights to the new federal Constitution, Jefferson made the same recommendation. Madison construed it in its most favorable light, observing: "The Exemption of the press from liability in every case for *true facts* is . . . an innovation and as such ought to be well considered." On consideration, however, he did not add truth as a defense to the amendment that he offered on the press when proposing a bill of rights to Congress. Yet his phrasing appeared too broad for Jefferson who stated that he would be pleased if the press provision were altered to exclude freedom to publish "false facts . . . affecting the peace of the confederacy with foreign nations," a clause whose suppressive possiblities can be imagined in the context of a foreign policy controversy such as the one on Jay's Treaty.

Madison fortunately ignored Jefferson's proposal but there is no evidence warranting the belief that he dissented from the universal American acceptance of the Blackstonian definition of a free press. At the Virginia ratifying convention in 1788 Madison remained silent when George Nicholas, one of his closest supporters, declared that the liberty of the press was secure because there was no power to license the press. Again Madison was silent when John Marshall rose to say that Congress would never make a law punishing men of different political opinions "unless it be such a case as much satisfy the people at large." In October 1788, when replying to Jefferson's argument that powers of the national government should be restricted by a bill of rights, Madison declared: "absolute restrictions in cases that are doubtful, or where emergencies may overrule them, ought to be avoided." When Madison proposed an amendment in Congress guaranteeing freedom of the press, he did not employ the emphatic language of the Virginia ratifying convention's recommendation that the press cannot be abridged "by any authority of the United States." The amendment, in the form in which Madison introduced it, omitted the important clause "by any authority of the United States," which would have covered the executive and the judiciary as well as Congress. The omitted clause would have prohibited the federal courts from exercising any common-law jurisdiction over criminal libels. As ratified, the First Amendment declared only that Congress should make no law abridging the freedom of speech or press.

What did the amendment mean at the time of its adoption? More complex than it appears, it meant several things, and it did not necessarily mean what it said or say what it was intended to mean. First, as is shown by an examination of the phrase "the freedom of the press," the amendment was merely an assurance that Congress was powerless to authorize restraints in advance of publication. On this point the evidence for the period from 1787 to 1791 is uniform and nonpartisan. For example, Hugh Williamson of North Carolina, a Federalist signatory of the Constitution, used freedom of the press in Blackstonian or common-law terms, as did Melancthon Smith of New York, an Antifederalist. Demanding a free press guarantee in the new federal Constitution, despite the fact that New York's constitution lacked that guarantee, Smith argued that freedom of the press was "fully defined and secured" in New York by "the common and statute law of England" and that a state constitutional provision was therefore unnecessary. No other definition of freedom of the press by anyone anywhere in America before 1798 has been discovered. Apparently there was, before that time, no dissent from the proposition that the punishment of a seditious libeler did not abridge the proper or lawful freedom of the press.

That freedom was so narrowly understood that its constitutional protection did not, per se, preclude the enactment of a sedition law. The security of the state against libelous attack was always and everywhere regarded as outweighing any social interest in completely unfettered discussion. The thought and experience of a lifetime, indeed the taught traditions of law and politics extending back many generations, supplied an unquestioned assumption that freedom of political discourse, however broadly conceived, stopped short of seditious libel.

The injunction of the First Amendment, nevertheless, was not intended to imply that a sedition act might be enacted without abridging "the freedom of the press." A sedition act would not be an abridgment, but that was not the point of the amendment. To understand its framers' intentions, the amendment should not be read with the focus on the meaning of "the freedom of the press." It should not, in other words, be read merely to mean that Congress could impose no prior restraints. It should be read, rather, with the stress on the opening clause: "Congress shall make no law . . . ." The injunction was intended and understood to prohibit any congressional regulation of the press, whether by means of a licensing law, a tax, or a sedition act. The framers meant Congress to be totally without power to enact legislation respecting the press. They intended a federal system in which the central government could exercise only such powers as were specifically enumerated or were necessary and proper to carry out the enumerated ones. Thus James Wilson declared that, because the national government had "no power whatsoever" concerning the press, "no law . . . can possibly be enacted" against it. Thus Hamilton, referring to the demand for a free press guarantee, asked, "why declare that things shall not be done which there is no power to do?" The illustrations may be multiplied fiftyfold. In other words, no matter what was meant or understood by freedom of speech and press, the national government, *even in the absence of the First Amendment,* could not make speech or press a legitimate subject of restrictive legislation. The amendment itself was superfluous. To quiet public apprehension, it offered an added assurance that Congress would be limited to the exercise of its delegated powers. The phrasing was intended to prohibit the possibility that those powers might be used to abridge speech and press. From this viewpoint, the Sedition Act of 1798 was unconstitutional.

That act was also unnecessary as a matter of law, however necessary as a matter of Federalist party policy. It was unnecessary because the federal courts exercised jurisdiction over nonstatutory or common-law crimes against the United States. At the Pennsylvania ratifying convention James Wilson declared that, while Congress could enact no law against the press, a libel against the United States might be prosecuted in the state where the offense was committed, under Article III, Section 2, of the Constitution which refers to the judicial power of the United States. A variety of common-law crimes against the United States were, in fact, tried in the federal courts during the first decade of their existence. There were, in the federal courts, even a couple of common-law indictments for the crime of seditious libel. All the early Supreme Court judges, including several who had been influential in the Philadelphia Convention, or in the state ratifying conventions, or in the Congress that passed the Judiciary Act of 1789, assumed the existence of a federal common law of crimes. Ironically, it was a case originating as a federal prosecution of Connecticut editors for seditious libels against President Jefferson that finally resulted in a ruling by a divided Supreme Court in 1812 that there was no federal common law of crimes.

There was unquestionably a federal common law of crimes at the time of the Sedition Act. Why then was the act passed if it was not legally needed? Even in England, where the criminal courts exercised an unquestioned jurisdiction over seditious libels, it was politically advisable in the 1790s to declare public policy in unmistakable terms by the enactment of sedition statutes. Legislation helped ensure effective enforcement of the law and stirred public opinion against its intended victims. The Federalists, hoping to control public opinion and elections, emulated the British model. A federal statute was expedient also because the Republicans insisted that libels against the United States might be tried only by the state courts.

This suggests another original purpose of the First Amendment. It has been said that a constitutional guarantee of a free press did not, in itself, preclude a sedition act, but that the prohibition on Congress did, though leaving the federal courts free to try cases of seditious libel. It now appears that the prohibition on Congress was motivated far less by a desire to give immunity to political expression than by a solicitude for states' rights and the federal principle. The primary purpose of the First Amendment was to reserve to the states an exclusive legislative authority in the field of speech and press.

This is clear enough from the countless states' rights arguments advanced by the Antifederalists during the ratification controversy, and it is explicit in the Republican arguments during the controversy over the Sedition Act. In the House debates on the bill, Albert Gallatin, Edward Livingston, John Nicholas, and Nathaniel Macon all agreed—to quote Macon on the subject of liberty of the press: "The States have complete power on the subject. . . . " Jefferson's Kentucky Resolutions of 1798 expressed the same proposition, as did Madison's "Address of the General Assembly to the People of the Commonwealth of Virginia" in 1799.

It is possible that the opponents of the Sedition Act did not want or believe in state prosecutions, but argued for an exclusive state power over political libels because such an argument was tactically useful as a means of denying national jurisdiction, judicial or legislative. If so, how shall we explain the Republican prosecution in New York in 1803 against Harry Croswell, a Federalist editor, for a seditious libel against President Jefferson?

How shall we explain the Blackstonian opinions of the Republican judges in that case? How shall we explain Jefferson's letter to the governor of Pennsylvania in the same year? The President, enclosing a newspaper piece that unmercifully attacked him, urged a "few prosecutions" because they "would have a wholesome effect in restoring the integrity of the presses." How shall we explain Jefferson's letter to Abigail Adams in 1804 in which he said: "While we deny that Congress have a right to controul the freedom of the press, we have ever asserted the right of the states, and their exclusive right to do so." And if exclusive state power was advanced not as a principle but as a tactic for denying federal jurisdiction, how shall we explain what Jefferson's opponents called his "reign of terror": the common-law indictments in 1806 in the United States Circuit Court in Connecticut against six men charged with seditious libel of the President? How shall we explain his letter of 1807 in which he said of the "prosecutions in the Court of the U.S." that they could "not lessen the useful freedom of the press," if truth were admitted as a defense?

Earlier, in 1798, the Federalists had also felt that the true freedom of the press would benefit if truth—their truth—were the measure of freedom. Their infamous Sedition Act, in the phrase of Gilbert and Sullivan, was the true embodiment of everything excellent. It was, that is, the very epitome of libertarian thought since the time of Zenger's case, proving that American libertarianism went from Zengerian principles to the Sedition Act in a single degeneration. Everything that the libertarians had ever demanded was, however, incorporated in the Sedition Act: a requirement that criminal intent be shown; the power of the jury to decide whether the accused's statement was libelous as a matter of law as well as of fact; and truth as a defense—an innovation not accepted in England until 1843. By every standard the Sedition Act was a great victory for libertarian principles of freedom of the press—except that libertarian standards abruptly changed because the Republicans immediately recognized a Pyrrhic victory.

The Sedition Act provoked them to develop a new libertarian theory. It began to emerge when Congressmen Albert Gallatin, John Nicholas, Nathaniel Macon, and Edward Livingston argued against the enactment of the sedition bill. It was further developed by defense counsel, most notably George Blake, in Sedition Act prosecutions. It reached its most reflective and systematic expression in tracts and books which are now unfortunately rare and little known even by historians. The main body of original Republican thought on the scope, meaning, and rationale of the First Amendment is to be found in George Hay's tract, *An Essay on the Liberty of the Press*; in Madison's *Report* on the Virginia Resolutions for the Virginia House of Delegates; in the book *A Treatise Concerning Political Enquiry, and the Liberty of the Press*, by Tunis Wortman of New York; in John Thomson's book *An Enquiry, Concerning the Liberty, and Licentiousness of the Press*; and in St. George Tucker's appendix to his edition of Blackstone's *Commentaries*, a most significant place for the repudiation of Blackstone on the liberty of the press. Of these works, Wortman's philosophical book is preeminent; it is an American masterpiece, the only equivalent on this side of the Atlantic to Milton and Mill.

The new libertarians abandoned the strait-jacketing doctrines of Blackstone and the common law, including the recent concept of a federal common law of crimes. They scornfully denounced the no prior restraints definition. Said Madison: "this idea of the freedom of the press can never be admitted to be the American idea of it" because a law inflicting penalties would have the same effect as a law authorizing a prior restraint. "It would seem a mockery to say that no laws shall be passed preventing publications from being made, but that laws might be passed for punishing them in case they should be made." As Hay put it, the "British definition" meant that a man might be jailed or even put to death for what he published provided that no notice was taken of him before he published.

The old calculus for measuring the scope of freedom was also rejected by the new libertarians. "Liberty" of the press, for example, had always been differentiated from "licentiousness," which was the object of the criminal law's sanctions. "Truth" and "facts" had always divided the realm of lawfulness from "falsehoods," and a similar distinction had been made between "good motives" and "criminal intent." All such distinctions were now discarded on grounds that they did not distinguish and, therefore, were not meaningful standards that might guide a jury or a court in judging an alleged verbal crime. The term "licentiousness," said Thomson, "is destitute of any meaning" and is used by those who wish "nobody to enjoy the liberty of the Press but such as were of their own opinion." The term "malice," Wortman wrote, is invariably confused with mistaken zeal or prejudice. It is merely an inference drawn from the supposed evil tendency of the publication itself, just a further means of punishing the excitement of unfavorable sentiments against the government even when the people's contempt of it was richly deserved. Punishment of "malice" or intent to defame the government, concluded Madison, necessarily strikes at the right of free discussion, because critics intend to excite unfavorable sentiments. Finding criminality in the tendency of words was merely an attempt to erect public "tranquility . . . upon the ruins of Civil Liberty," said Wortman.

Wholesale abandonment of the common law's limitations on the press was accompanied by a withering onslaught against the constrictions and subjectivity of Zengerian principles. The Sedition Act, Hay charged, "appears to be directed against falsehood and malice only; in fact . . . there are many truths, important to society, which are not susceptible of that full, direct, and positive evidence, which alone can be exhibited before a court and a jury. If, argued Gallatin, the administration prosecuted a citizen for his opinion that the Sedition Act itself was unconstitutional, would not a jury, composed of the friends of that administration, find the opinion "ungrounded, or, in other words, false and scandalous, and its publication malicious? And by what kind of argument or evidence, in the present temper of parties, could the accused convince them that his opinions were true?" The truth of opinions, the new libertarians concluded, could not be proved.

Allowing "truth" as a defense and thinking it to be a protection for freedom, Thomson declared, made as much sense as letting a jury decide which was "the most palatable food, agreeable drink, or beautiful color." A jury, he asserted, cannot give an impartial verdict in political trials. The result, agreed Madison, is that the "baleful tendency" of prosecutions for seditious libel "is little diminished by the privilege of giving in evidence the truth of the matter contained in political writings."

The renunciation of traditional concepts reached its climax in the assault on the very idea that there was a crime of seditious libel. That crime, Wortman concluded, could "never be reconciled to the genius and constitution of a Representative Commonwealth." He and the others constructed a new libertarianism that was genuinely radical because it broke sharply with the past and advocated an absolute freedom of political expression. One of their major tenets was that a free government cannot be criminally attacked by the opinions of its citizens. Hay, for example, insisted that freedom of the press, like chastity, was either "absolute" or did not exist. Abhorring the idea of verbal political crimes, he declared that a citizen should have a right to "say everything which his passions suggest; he may employ all his time, and all his talents, if he is wicked enough to do so, in speaking against the government matters that are false, scandalous and malicious." He should be "safe within the sanctuary of the press" even if he "condemns the principle of republican institutions. . . . If he censures the measures of our government, and every department and officer thereof, and ascribes the measures of the former, however salutary, and the conduct of the latter, however upright, to the basest motives; even if he ascribes to them measures and acts, which never had existence; thus violating at once, every principle of decency and truth."

In brief the new libertarians advocated that only "injurious conduct," as manifested by "overt acts" or deeds, rather than words, might be criminally redressable. They did not refine this proposition except to recognize that the law of libel should continue to protect private reputations against malicious falsehoods. They did not even recognize that under certain circumstances words may immediately and directly incite criminal acts.

This absolutist interpretation of the First Amendment was based on the now familiar but then novel and democratic theory that free government depends for its existence and security on freedom of political discourse. According to this theory, the scope of the amendment is determined by the nature of the government and its relationship to the people. Since the government is their servant, exists by their consent and for their benefit, and is constitutionally limited, responsible, and elective, it cannot, said Thomson, tell the citizen, "You shall not think this, or that upon certain subjects; or if you do, it is at your peril." The concept of seditiousness, it was argued, could exist only in a relationship based on inferiority, when people are subjects rather than sovereigns and their criticism implies contempt of their master. "In the United States," Madison declared, "the case is altogether different." Coercion or abridgment of unlimited political opinion, Wortman explained, would violate the very "principles of the social state," by which he meant a government of the people. Because such a government depended upon popular elections, all the new libertarians agreed that the widest possible latitude must be maintained to keep the electorate free, informed, and capable of making intelligent choices. The citizen's freedom of political expression had the same scope as the legislator's, and for the same reasons. That freedom might be dangerously abused, but the people would decide men and measures wisely if exposed to every opinion.

This brief summary of the new libertarianism scarcely does justice to its complexity, but suggests its boldness, originality, and democratic character. It developed, to be sure, as an expediency of self-defense on the part of a besieged political minority struggling to maintain its existence and right to function unfettered. But it established virtually all at once and in nearly perfect form a theory justifying the rights of individual expression and of opposition parties. That the Jeffersonians in power did not always adhere to their new principles does not diminish the enduring nobility and rightness of those principles. It proves only that the Jeffersonians set the highest standards of freedom for themselves and posterity to be measured against. Their legacy was the idea that there is an indispensable condition for the development of free men in a free society: the state must be bitted and bridled by a bill of rights which is to be construed in the most generous terms and whose protections are not to be the playthings of momentary majorities.

The Federalists and the Transformation of Libertarian Thought

WALTER BERNS

Until a few years ago it was customary, even among scholars, to regard the beginning of America as the beginning of free government, at least in the modern world. According to Lincoln, the nation was "conceived in Liberty." Seventy-five years earlier Madison, who was in a position to understand the significance of the event, said that nothing had "excited more admiration in the world, than the manner in which free governments had been established in America." It was, he continued, "the first instance from the creation of the world to the American revolution, that free inhabitants have been seen deliberating on a form of government." The Union, Charles Pinckney said, is "the temple of our freedom."

Such sentiments, and they could be collected by the thousands, constitute a major part of the American political legacy. From the beginning Americans have proclaimed liberty, have fought wars in its name, have evaluated events and institutions and policies in its light. They have convinced themselves not only that they are and have always been a free people, but that they were intended to be a free people whose institutions could serve, and were intended to serve, as a model for the world. America, Lincoln said, is "the last best hope of earth." In short, Americans were, or believed they were, the beneficiaries of a legacy of liberty.

It was, therefore, a sobering experience to be told by Professor Leonard Levy that, at least to the extent that free speech and press are essential elements of free government, Americans had been bequeathed a legacy of suppression. The Bill of Rights, with its cherished guarantee of free speech and press, according to Levy, did not mean to the men who wrote it what Americans had become accustomed to think it meant. In fact, they may only have been "the chance product of political expediency." "A broad libertarian theory of freedom of speech and press did not emerge in the United States until the Jeffersonians, when a minority party, were forced to defend themselves against the Federalist Sedition Act of 1798." According to the traditional view, the infamous Alien and Sedition Laws, certainly the latter, would have been declared unconstitutional had they ever come before the Supreme Court, assuming that the Federalist Supreme Court would succeed in putting aside its partisan prejudices. Instead, it was left to Madison and Jefferson to protest their unconstitutionality in the Virginia and Kentucky Resolutions and then to form a new political party to effect their repeal, or more precisely, their demise:

> However interesting these famous Resolutions may be for the Constitutional doctrine they contain, they were intended *primarily* as a defense, practical and spirited, of civil liberties. Some of the most severe infringements upon those liberties ever to be sanctioned by an American Congress—the Alien and Sedition Laws—were therefore more than the *occasion* of the Resolutions; they were the cause.

Yet, contrary to Professor Levy, there is reason to believe that it was not really a "broad libertarian theory" that emerged during the fight against the Alien and Sedition Laws; and that, contrary to Professors Koch and Ammon, these laws were the occasion more than the cause of Madison and Jefferson's famous resolutions. The principle on which especially Jefferson and John Taylor and some other Republican leaders based their opposition was not "a broad libertarian" version of civil liberties but the doctrine of states' rights, or nullification, or disunion. The men principally responsible for the development of a liberal law of free speech and press—for fashioning a remedy for the deprivation of the constitutional rights of freedom of speech and press—were the Federalists Alexander Hamilton and James Kent, who were able to do this because, unlike Jefferson and his colleagues and successors, they were not inhibited by an attachment to the institution of slavery.

I. The Alien and Sedition Laws

. . . The Federalists' concern with aliens and sedition gave rise to four distinct but related pieces of legislation, all enacted in less than a month's time during the summer of 1798. The first was a naturalization law that increased the period of residence required of an alien to be eligible for citizenship from five to fourteen years. The principal provision of the second, the so-called Alien Friends Act, authorized the President to deport all aliens whom he regarded as "dangerous to the peace and safety of the United States." It was a temporary measure, to be in force for two years after its passage. The third, entitled "An Act respecting Alien Enemies," was genuinely a wartime measure operative only during a "declared war" or a real or threatened invasion, which event was to be officially proclaimed by the President. It authorized him, after issuing the proclamation, to apprehend, restrain, secure, or remove any national of a country at war with the United States. The fourth was the notorious Sedition Act, consisting of four sections. The first section provided for the punishment of anyone who unlawfully combined to oppose the laws of the United States. The fourth section provided that the act was to be in force until March 3, 1801, that is, until one day before the inauguration of the next President. It is the second and third sections that have come to be known as the Sedition Act. Under these provisions indictments were brought against fourteen persons (one of them, William Duane, was indicted twice), ten of whom were convicted and sentenced to pay fines ranging from five dollars to a thousand dollars and to be imprisoned for periods ranging from six to eighteen months. No one, apparently, neither "Wild Irishman" nor "Jacobin," was deported under either of the Alien acts.

II. The Opposition to the Alien and Sedition Laws: In Congress

. . . Edward Livingston began the debate on the Sedition bill by moving to reject it in its entirety. John Allen of Connecticut responded in such a way that the issue of free expression under the Constitution was immediately joined, or at least broached. Allen quoted a typical tirade against President Adams from the New York *Time-Piece,* and asked whether anyone seriously contended that the liberty of the press extended to such publications. "Because the Constitution guarantees . . . the freedom of the press, am I at liberty to falsely call you a thief, a murderer, an atheist? . . . The freedom of the press and opinions was never understood to give the right of publishing falsehoods and slanders, nor of exciting sedition, insurrection, and slaughter, with impunity. A man was always answerable for the malicious publication of falsehood; and what more does this bill require?" Allen was followed by Harper, who, acknowledging that he had often heard in Congress and out "harangues on the liberty of the press," defined this liberty after the manner of Blackstone, which, indeed, was the accepted understanding on the subject at the time: ". . . the true meaning of [liberty of the press] is no more than that a man shall be at liberty to print what he pleases, provided he does not offend against the laws, and not that no law shall be passed to regulate this liberty of the press." Such an understanding did not preclude prosecutions of seditious libels, either at the common law or under the proposed legislation, and, according to Leonard Levy, it was only under "the pressure of the Sedition Act [that] writers of the Jeffersonian party were driven to originate so broad a theory of freedom of expression that the concept of seditious libel was, at last, repudiated." Such a theory did not, however emerge from the debates in the House. Livingston insisted that the bill violated the First Amendment, and Livingston was supported in this view by the next speaker, Nathaniel Macon of North Carolina. But the debates reveal that neither Livingston nor Macon—nor any of their Republican colleagues—adopted a broad "libertarian" understanding of the principle of freedom of expression. The bill "directly violated the letter of the Constitution," Macon said. He regretted that "at a time like this, when some gentlemen say we are at war, and when all believe we must have war, that Congress are about to pass a law which will produce more uneasiness, more irritation, than any act which ever passed the Legislature of the Union." He challenged the Federalists to show "what part of the Constitution [authorizes] the passage of a law like this." But he then acknowledged that "persons might be prosecuted for a libel under the State Governments," and questioned the necessity of a federal law. In short, he, like his colleagues during the debate on the Alien Friends bill, objected to the Sedition bill on constitutional grounds and, more precisely, on states' rights grounds, but he did not argue that such legislation was objectionable in principle. . . .

. . . The Sedition bill violated the Constitution, Livingston argued, because the power to punish libels—the power to enact criminal libel laws and to enforce them—was reserved by the Constitution to the states. Furthermore, he went on, the fair administration of justice required this arrangement:

> Suppose a libel were written against the President, where is it most probable that such an offence would receive an impartial trial? In a court, the judges of which are appointed by the President, by a jury selected by an officer holding his office at the will of the President? or in a court independent of any influence whatever?

Whether the state courts could fairly be described as "independent of any influence whatever"—that is, whether they could have provided impartial forums for the prosecution of criminal libels against the President of the Union—is a fair question. Surely they could scarcely have proved less impartial than the federal courts were soon to prove themselves to be. One historian, Charles Warren, has written that the "proper remedy for all the flood of scurrility and calumny, which swelled each succeeding year of the Adams administration, was a more rigid enforcement of the laws of criminal libel by state officials and courts," thus agreeing altogether wth Livingston. But state prosecutions depended on state officials, and no Virginia official, for example, would likely have proved assiduous in the defense of John Adams' good name. To cite another example, whereas the officials of Republican Pennsylvania did not hesitate to prosecute libels against Pennsylvania Republicans, there is no record of their being equally zealous when it came to prosecuting libels made against the Federalist officials of the national government, the capital of which was temporarily located in the state's principal city. "A criminal libel proceeding," Warren continued, "was a weapon which could be employed by both parties." He was probably correct when he added, as an account of the Federalists' motives, that they "wished absolution for their own words, and punishment only for their opponents'." But he might have said the same thing of the Republicans. The difference was (and this attests to one of the virtues of the federal system) that the Federalists with the national law, and attributing the worst of motives to them, would have silenced their opponents throughout the length and breadth of the land, whereas the Republicans would have silenced the Federalists only in those states they, the Republicans, controlled. As Jefferson was shortly to learn through his mistaken reliance on resolutions issuing from state legislatures, to be effective on a national scale requires activity on a national scale, and ultimately control of the national government. In the summer of 1798, however, he and his party were preaching states' rights and, soon to become apparent, nullification and disunion. They were not defending civil liberties—except, one must add immediately, to the extent that civil liberty, to them, depended on their states' rights view of the Constitution and the Union.

Thus, while the Jefferson party in the Congress argued the bill's unconstitutionality, insisting that no power to enact it could be found among the powers enumerated in the Constitution and that the First Amendment expressly prohibited it, they did so in the context of defending the right of the states to enact and enforce such laws. Only in one limited respect did they "originate" a broad libertarian theory in Levy's modern sense: one Virginia Republican, John Nicholas, questioned the distinction, what Levy calls the "alleged" distinction, between liberty and license, thereby challenging the prevailing Blackstonian view of the right of free expression. For, to Blackstone and the Federalists, free expression meant, to state the matter simply, no previous restraints but punishment for abuses, a view that presupposes a distinction between liberty and license and the ability of a court to discern and define it. Later the same day Gallatin pursued this point, contending that the First Amendment could not (and must not) be understood as prohibiting merely previous restraints. Whereas laws could be enacted requiring a license to print, and this would be a previous restraint on the press, what, he asked, could possibly constitute a previous restraint on the liberty of speech? Since it was impossible to conceive of such a law, he contended, and because the First Amendment forbids the abridgment of the freedom of speech as well as of the press, it must be understood to forbid more than previous restraints. Such an argument would certainly constitute evidence of the beginnings of a broader libertarian theory, simply by virtue of the fact that it rejects the essential principle of the Blackstonian "theory," except for the equally obvious fact that, having made the point, Gallatin undermined it by the characteristic Republican insistence that, anyway, the trial of criminal libels "belonged to the State courts"—exclusively. . . .

III. The Opposition to the Alien and Sedition Acts: The Virginia and Kentucky Resolutions

. . . Jefferson has never been an easy subject for his devoted portrayers. His resounding rhetoric, e.g., "I have sworn upon the altar of God, eternal hostility against every form of tyranny over the mind of man," has long made him an object of veneration among Americans. His remarks in his First Inaugural: "If there be any among us who would wish to dissolve this Union or to change its republican form, let them stand undisturbed as monuments of the safety with which error of opinion may be tolerated where reason is left free to combat it," and his views on church and state have made him the special favorite of modern liberals. Among Democrats he has long been regarded as the patron saint of their party. Among southern Democrats he has been and still is revered as the first and greatest champion of their cause, states' rights. In each case, however, with the exception of those who see him as the champion of the cause of separating church and state—an issue on which Jefferson was, even from a modern point of view, thoroughly "liberal" and consistent—it is a somewhat uneasy affiliation. Civil libertarians have been able to attribute their cause to Jefferson only by ignoring what Leonard Levy has called his "Darker Side." They and the northern Democrats generally have had to overlook his devotion to the cause of states' rights and his hatred of national power. The southerners, who extol his constitutional principles and admire the life he was able to make for himself at Monticello—with the assistance of hundreds of slaves—have difficulty accommodating themselves to his egalitarian sentiments. In these circumstances it is not strange that Jefferson lends himself readily to folklore. Among this folklore is the opinion that he drafted the Kentucky Resolutions in order to preserve "human rights" and as a "sincere champion of the highest practicable degree of human liberty in all fields." To assert that this is not true is not to suggest that Jefferson was not a champion of liberty. That would be absurd. But unless one argues that a necessary condition of liberty in America is states' sovereignty in the full Jeffersonian sense, the evidence is overwhelming that Jefferson was not acting as a champion of liberty when he drafted the Kentucky Resolutions. He drafted them to advance his states' rights view of the Constitution and to set the stage for a dissolution of the Union if this should, according to his judgment, prove necessary. This would depend, in part, on the response of the other states to the Resolutions of Kentucky and Virginia circulated during the last days of 1798.

From his point of view that response was not encouraging, and in a letter to Madison of August 23, 1799, Jefferson proposed a resumption of their efforts. More resolutions should be adopted, he said, resolutions expressing "in affectionate & conciliatory language our warm attachment to union with our sister-states," but also stating the condition of this attachment, that the "American people . . . rally with us round the true principles of our federal compact." If this did not occur, if he and Madison were "to be disappointed in this," the new resolutions must express the determination of Kentucky and Virginia at least, "to sever ourselves from that union we so much value, rather than give up the rights of self government which we have reserved, & in which alone we see liberty, safety & happiness."

Shortly after receiving this letter, Madison visited Jefferson at Monticello, and the result of that visit is reflected in a letter Jefferson wrote to Wilson Cary Nicholas on September 5. He repeated the proposals he had made two weeks earlier to Madison, and in identical language—except for the omission of the last sentence quoted above concerning a willingness to sever the union. Surely Koch and Ammon are correct in seeing this sentence as the "most extreme statement that Jefferson ever made concerning the meaning and intent of the Kentucky Resolutions," and the circumstances, plus a sentence in the letter to Nicholas, support their view that it was Madison's influence that led Jefferson to exclude the culpable sentence from the letter going to Kentucky. "Had Madison failed to argue as he did," they write, "the contention that the Virginia and Kentucky Resolutions contained in germinal form the later doctrines of nullification and secession would have rested upon firmer ground." What this means is that if Madison had not persuaded his more impetuous and less politic colleague to be circumspect in what he committed to a letter that was likely to be seen by a number of people, Jefferson's name would have been linked with that of Calhoun and Jefferson Davis. But why not? Even the resolutions as they were published were sufficient to provoke the response that Kentucky was intending to dissolve the Union, and it was public knowledge that in 1797 Kentucky was engaged in negotiations with Spain concerning the navigation of the Mississippi. Jefferson's authorship of the resolutions, rumored at the time and admitted by him in 1821, has long since been confirmed by the publication of his writings containing his two drafts of them. Even the second of these, the so-called fair copy, speaks of "nullification" and the "natural right" of each state "to nullify" acts of the national government that, in the judgment of the state, exceed the constitutional authority "delegated" to it. It calls upon the states to declare the Alien and Sedition Laws "void, and no force," and to "take measures . . . for providing that neither these acts, nor any others of the General Government not plainly and intentionally authorized by the Constitution, shall be exercised within their respective territories." It was Breckenridge who moderated Jefferson's language on this occasion by changing this call to civil disobedience into the call upon Congress to repeal the laws with which the resolutions end. But even the resolutions as Breckenridge moved them and as they were adopted by the legislature speak of "revolution and blood": "unless arrested on the threshold," these acts and others like them "may tend to drive these States into revolution and blood." South Carolina's Ordinance of Nullification in 1832 merely did what Kentucky threatened (or resolved) to do, and what Jefferson wanted Kentucky and other states to do. And the South Carolina nullifiers recognized Jefferson as the source of their principle: ". . . we must come back to Mr. Jefferson's plain, practical and downright principle, as our 'rightful remedy'—a *nullification* by the State . . . of the 'unauthorized act.' " Why, then, should he not be taxed with planting the nullification seed that germinated after his death and blossomed in civil war? Certainly he was more moderate than John Taylor to whom he wrote counseling against dissolution of the Union. But this was mainly the counsel of patience. In November of the same year, 1798, just after he had finished writing the fair copy of the resolutions, he wrote Taylor again, saying: "*For the present* I should be for resolving the alien & sedition laws to be against the constitution & merely void, and for addressing the other States to obtain similar declarations; and I would not do anything *at this moment* which should commit us further, but reserve ourselves to shape our future measures, by the events which may happen." It was eight months later that he wrote Madison calling for new resolutions threatening to dissolve the Union.

In the abstract there is no reason to be shocked by such sentiments. After all, Jefferson had already played the leading role in the dissolution of one union, a role for which he has been justly praised by his countrymen. . . . But [we should remember] that the cause for which he and his colleagues were contending was [not] liberty. . . . Their cause was states' rights, and liberty only as a function of states' rights. . . . [T]he Alien and Sedition Laws were merely the occasion of the resolutions, not the cause.

This is readily demonstrated. The Kentucky Resolutions themselves complain of the Sedition Act as a violation of the Constitution because the Constitution manifested the determination of the states and the people thereof "to retain to themselves the right of judging how far the licentiousness of speech and of the press may be abridged without lessening their useful freedom, and how far those abuses which cannot be separated from their use should be tolerated rather than the use be destroyed." And the Kentucky Resolutions themselves say, not that aliens should not be banished, but "that alien friends are under the jurisdiction and protection of the laws of the State wherein they are." The trouble with the Alien and Sedition Laws was that in enacting them the United States was assuming the powers of a sovereign nation, powers that, according to their view of the Constitution, were reserved to the states. This, Jefferson and his friends could not permit. Rather than submit to this exercise of political power or concede the constitutional theory on which it was based, they would declare the laws null and void. Failing of support in this, they would dissolve the Union. To preserve the liberty that was threatened by the Alien and Sedition Laws? Not so. Rather, to preserve the right of the states to enact and enforce their own alien and sedition laws—a right they were exercising.

The Virginia Resolutions drafted by Madison were more moderate than those of Kentucky, but the principle for which they contended was the same. In the address that accompanied them this principle is clearly stated:

> The sedition act presents a scene, which was never expected by the early friends of the constitution. It was then admitted, that the state sovereignties were only diminished, by powers specifically enumerated, or necessary to carry the specified powers into effect. Now, federal authority is deduced from implication, and from the existence of state law, it is inferred, that congress possesses a similar power of legislation; whence congress will be endowed with a power of legislation, in all cases whatsoever, and the states will be stript of every right reserved, by the concurrent claims of a paramount legislature.

In what, then, does the evil of the Sedition Act consist? In the next and summary sentence the Virginia legislature leaves no doubt of its view: "The sedition act is the offspring of these tremendous pretentions, which inflict a death wound on the sovereignty of the states." . . .

It was only after their failure to provoke a favorable response to their resolutions from the other states that the Jeffersonians—but not Jefferson—began seriously to contend against the principle of a seditious libel law. Frustrated in their attempts to impose the concept of state sovereignty on the Constitution and to persuade the other states to join them in declaring the Alien and Sedition Laws null and void, and not yet determined to force the issue by seceding from the Union (the size of the opposition in Virginia itself probably had something to do with this), some of Jefferson's followers began to direct their attention to the nature of free speech and press instead of the nature of the Union, and began to attack the Sedition Law rather than the government that enacted it. It was in the course of doing this that they began to question whether the Blackstonian view of free press as merely an uncensored press is compatible with republican government, whether state or national. It was in the course of doing this that they developed what Leonard Levy has called "the new theory of First Amendment freedoms." But even then they were a great deal less "libertarian" than Levy has asserted. . . .

The civil liberties argument that is missing in the attacks on the promulgation of the Alien and Sedition Laws is said by Levy to emerge immediately thereafter as a result of reflections on the experience of these laws. "In speeches, tracts, and books, George Blake, Albert Gallatin, Edward Livingston, Nathaniel Macon, James Madison, George Nicholas, John Thomson, St. George Tucker, and Tunis Wortman, among others, contributed brilliantly to the new theory of First Amendment freedoms."

Madison made his contribution to the "new theory" in 1800 in the Report on the Resolutions, submitted to the Virginia House of Delegates by a committee charged with dealing with the responses to the 1798 resolutions. He argued that a law of seditious libel and free republican government are incompatible, that the "security of the freedom of the press requires that it should be exempt not only from previous restraint by the Executive, as in Great Britain, but from legislative restraint also; as this exemption, to be effectual, must be an exemption not only from the previous inspection of licensers, but from the subsequent penalty of laws." Levy's failure to note the qualifications led him to attribute to Madison and some of the others a more "libertarian" position than they adopted, even after 1798. Madison went on to say that the national government is "destitute of every authority for restraining the licentiousness of the press," but he did not say this of the state governments. On the contrary, the officers of the national government, he said, can find a remedy "for their injured reputations, under the same laws, and in the same tribunals, which protect their lives, their liberties, and their properties." . . .

To cast doubt on the extent to which these Republican writers were "libertarian" in the modern sense is not to deny Levy's main point, namely, that the passage of the Sedition Law in 1798 provoked some Americans to begin thinking about the meaning of free speech and press and their place in republican government. Prior to the introduction of the question as a political issue, Americans had no practical reason for questioning the sufficiency of the Blackstonian understanding, which they accepted, to the extent to which they thought of it, as part of their legal inheritance. Yet it is not possible in the cases of Tucker and Wortman, any more than in those of the politicians Madison, Gallatin, Livingston, Macon, and Nicholas, to isolate their free speech and press arguments from the larger issues with which they were contending: the respective powers of the national and state governments. . . .

One other writer at this time presented the extreme "libertarian" argument, contending in turn against Blackstone, a legal distinction between liberty and license, criminal libel, and a privilege limited to the truth. This was George Hay, but his essays are marked by their impassioned attack on the federal government and by a support of the state-sovereignty theory of his fellow Virginians, Jefferson and Madison and the others. And even Hay, in the second edition of his essay, concedes that the state may punish libels, including libels on the President of the United States.

It is altogether proper that the passage of the Sedition Law, and especially the manner of the trials conducted under its authority, should have provoked Americans to initiate inquiry into the relation of free speech and press to free government—that is to say, into the meaning of the First Amendment. After all, even Hamilton, whom Jefferson and his party regarded as the greatest enemy of the public good as they understood it, had reservations about the wisdom of employing such legislation. He, like Marshall, may have regarded the Sedition Law as constitutional, but he did not conceal his anxieties concerning such measures from his Federalist colleagues. . . . But it is significant that these authors should have confined themselves, or in greater part confined themselves, to a denial of the national authority to punish seditious libels, while maintaining the right of the states to do so. They were far from espousing the views of modern libertarians. Nor was it they and their mentor Jefferson who provoked the salutary reforms in the law of free press, so that by the end of the nineteenth century it could be said that this law was more compatible with republican principles than it had been during the Alien and Sedition controversy. On the contrary, the Jeffersonians were responsible for the most flagrant denials of free speech and press ever perpetrated in this country, and they did this on behalf of the institution of slavery. . . .

In time the southern leaders . . . came to realize that they could not permit free discussion of the slavery issue even in the free states—and they had a number of northern allies with them on this at one time—or finally, the cruelest irony of all, in the Congress of the United States. The first of the so-called gag rules, according to which the House resolved not to entertain any petition relating to the subject of slavery or to permit any discussion of such petitions, was adopted in 1836, and it was not until December, 1845, that the last of them was rescinded, largely through the efforts of John Quincy Adams, who from the first had declared them to be "a direct violation of the constitution of the United States, the rules of this House, and the rights of my constituents." By this time, however, whether it knew it or not, the nation had in effect decided that there should be freedom for antislavery speech everywhere, which means that it had decided that either slavery would end in the South or the nation would be sundered. The divided house could no longer stand.

VI. The Liberalizing of the Law

Harry Croswell was the printer and, under a pseudonym, the editor of *The Wasp,* a Federalist newspaper published in the Republican state of New York. Shortly after Jefferson and his party had been swept into national office on their platform of save the Republic and states' rights, Croswell, in print, accused Jefferson of paying James Callender for "calling Washington a traitor, a robber, and a perjurer [and] for calling Adams a hoary-headed incendiary." He went on to say that no "democratic editor has yet dared, or ever will dare, to meet [these charges] in an open and manly discussion." He was probably right as to the editors—for Jefferson had indeed supported Callender with money—but if he expected the Republicans, who had so recently inveighed against the national Sedition Law, to remain indifferent to what was being said about them, he was quickly disabused. An indictment was brought against him in the New York courts charging him with libeling Thomas Jefferson. Croswell, the indictment ran, "being a malicious and seditious man, of a depraved mind and wicked and diabolical disposition [intended with his words] to detract from, scandalize, traduce, vilify, and to represent him, the said Thomas Jefferson, as unworthy of the confidence, respect, and attachment of the people of the said United States, and to alienate and withdraw from the said Thomas Jefferson . . . the obedience, fidelity, and allegiance of the citizens of the state of New York, and also of the said United States; and wickedly and maliciously to disturb the peace."

At the trial Croswell sought the right to call witnesses on his behalf in order to prove the truth of the accusations he had made against Jefferson, but the trial judge denied him this. The truth or falsity of the words constituting the alleged libel was irrelevant, the judge ruled, as was Croswell's intent in publishing them. This left the jury with the task of determining merely whether Croswell was indeed responsible for publishing the words and, secondly, of determining the truth of the "innuendoes"—that is to say, whether the construction put upon the published words by the prosecuting attorney was fair and acceptable. Thus, the common law of libel as understood by the state of New York was in important respects less liberal than the national Sedition Law, which permitted truth as a defense and, following Fox's Libel Act in Britain, permitted the jury "to determine the law and the fact, under the direction of the court, as in other cases." Under such conditions, and with a Republican judge presiding, it is not remarkable that Croswell was convicted. But he was not content to leave the matter there, and with the assistance of two of the leading Federalists in the country, his case was to assume a significance extending far into the future.

He petitioned for a new trial and, when this was denied as a matter of course, filed an appeal with the state supreme court. His principal defense attorney was Alexander Hamilton, and the court before which Hamilton argued included James Kent, later to become famous as Chancellor Kent and, after his retirement from the chancery bench, as the author of the extremely influential *Commentaries on American Law.* Kent's opinion in the case, built squarely and solidly on the arguments provided by Hamilton, may be said to constitute the foundation on which the American law of freedom of the press was subsequently built. This despite the fact that Kent's opinion was not controlling because the court, with only four of its five judges sitting, was evenly divided and Croswell's conviction was undisturbed. . . .

The precise question raised by the motion for a new trial was whether the trial judge had erred in denying Croswell the opportunity to prove the truth of his allegedly defamatory statements and in confining the jury to determining the fact of publication. Both Hamilton and Kent, of course, argued that he had, but their interpretation of the English precedents is not persuasive, and the reader is left with the impression that Chief Justice Lewis, who filed an opinion denying the motion, is on sounder legal grounds when, for example, he insisted that Fox's Libel Act, which in 1792 settled the question of the role of the jury in English trials, was not, as Hamilton said it was, declaratory of the English law (and therefore a common law rule in New York), but was instead a revision of the law. In fact, although in form declaratory, "it was in substance a momentous change in the law of libel." No more compelling is Hamilton's statement that the rule that truth is no defense in a libel action derives from a "polluted source," the Court of Star Chamber. Whatever its source, it had been firmly enbraced by the common law. The question could not be answered to the satisfaction of the friends of republican government by a review of the legal authorities.

The chief of these authorities, Blackstone, had recently said that freedom of the press consisted in the right to publish without a censor's imprimatur but being liable to subsequent trial and punishment for abuses of this privilege. A law embodying this understanding of freedom of the press is surely to be preferred to a licensing system, wherein nothing is publishable except that which satisfies "the hasty view of an unleisured licenser," as Milton put it. Blackstone was surely justified in looking upon the expiration in 1694 of the last of the English licensing acts and the subsequent development of a body of common law with respect to the matters formerly governed by these acts as a movement in the right direction. But it was not sufficient. He published his eleventh and last edition of his *Commentaries* in 1791, eight years after Lord Mansfield had handed down the decision in the *Dean of St. Asaph's Case,* and not many friends of republican government (although the two judges opposed to Kent in *Croswell* were exceptions) could be content with the law of that case. Especially in the trial of a seditious libel, of what benefit is the privilege to publish without the prior consent of a censor, if a judge, rather than a jury, determines whether the words are libelous? The more so if the law, as Blackstone said, is that the essence of a libel consists in its tendency to cause a "breach of the public peace" and, therefore, the question of its truth or falsity and the intent with which it was published are irrelevant in the trial. Whether Blackstone's common-law understanding of freedom of the press is, then, compatible with republican government will depend on the mode of the trial and the understanding of an abuse, or, in Blackstone's own terms, on what is understood to constitute an "improper, mischievous, or illegal publication."

By refusing to regard Croswell's case as a mere matter of defamatory libel, Hamilton and Kent reached the larger issue of freedom in a republican regime. By rejecting the authority of Blackstone, they themselves became the authorities in America. To both of them—for Kent accepted Hamilton's formulation without alteration or addition—the liberty of the press "consisted in publishing with impunity, truth with good motives, and for justifiable ends, whether it related to men or to measures." This became the basis of the law in almost every American jurisdiction.

This new law was not libertarian in the modern sense—neither Hamilton nor Kent advocated a law that would permit everyone to say anything at any, or almost any, time—but it was surely more consonant with republican government, both because it permitted truth as a defense in a trial of public or seditious libels, when it was published with good motives and for justifiable ends, and because it enlarged the role of the jury in the determination of the intent and tendency of the publication. In all criminal law, Hamilton argued, the intent constitutes the crime—homicide is not, of itself, murder. Whether intent and tendency are viewed as questions of fact, as Hamilton argued, or of law, or of a "compound of law and fact," as Kent put it, what is important in the law of criminal and especially of seditious libel is that the determination of malice and tendency not be entrusted solely to the judges who, as Hamilton said and as history confirms, "might be tempted to enter into the views of government."

A role for the jury does not by itself assure impartial trials—the experience under the Sedition Law was sufficient to prove this. But it would seem to be a prerequisite in criminal trials of what is alleged to be seditious behavior. . . . It is worth our attention to notice that while it was Jefferson who was responsible for the fact that the trials of seditious and other criminal libels would take place in state courts, it was Hamilton who was responsible for reforming the procedure in those state trials to make it conform more fully to the principles of republican government and, not accidentally, the federal Constitution.

No less essential is the other major element in the law derived from the work of Hamilton and Kent in Croswell's case: the right to offer in evidence the truth of the allegedly libelous words. The rule of the greater the truth, the greater the libel, or the more modest version in Chief Justice Lewis' opinion in *Croswell* that "truth may be as dangerous to society as falsehood," is not unreasonable in a hereditary monarchy, or in any regime that, in Burke's words, finds its "sole authority" in the fact that "it has existed time out of mind." Speaking truth there may indeed be destructive of law and government, because the regime does not rest on true principles as such, but on historical principles. The American constitutions, on the other hand, both the national and the states', were understood to rest on the laws of nature, on the self-evident truth that all men are created equal with respect to the natural rights of life, liberty, and the pursuit of happiness. Government is instituted among men to secure these rights and derives its just powers from the consent of the governed. No man is naturally exalted over another, and public officers hold their temporarily exalted stations only at the pleasure of their fellow citizens. The speaking of the truth concerning men and measures and, indeed, the very basis of the regime, cannot usually be "dangerous to society." Which means that the English law of libel, evolving in a different system, based on different principles, had to be reformed before it could be accepted in America. In Hamilton's words, "truth is [not only] a material ingredient in the evidence of intent," and must therefore be admissible on procedural grounds, but is "all-important to the liberties of the people [and] an ingredient in the eternal order of things." He hoped to see the common law "applied to the United States," and his version of the common law, whatever the case with the English version, required the rule that the defendant be permitted to prove the truth of his allegedly libelous words. The common law was "principally the application of natural law to the state and condition of society," and without adherence to its principles "the constitution would be frittered away or borne down by factions, (the evil genii, the pests of republics)." Thus, the natural law dictated the form of the Constitution and, through the vehicle of the common law, the manner in which government was to be administered under it: all men were to be free to publish opinions on public men and measures—the provisions respecting freedom of the press guaranteed this—but their publications were not to be maliciously false. The truth, or true principles, was to be the standard of political life. . . .

People vs. Croswell began as an episode in the Alien and Sedition controversy. Croswell had accused Jefferson of paying Callender, a victim of the Sedition Law, to vilify Washington and Adams. But whereas the Sedition Law had provoked nullification and even disunion sentiments in Virginia, the indictment and trial of Croswell provoked the most thoughtful consideration of the meaning of freedom of speech and press that Americans had, to that time, ever engaged in. What began as a party matter ended in the unanimous adoption of a provision embodying the principles of the arch Federalists Alexander Hamilton and James Kent. That these principles can truly be said to have embodied the considered opinion of Americans on the meaning of the freedom of speech and press is proved by the extent to which Kent's opinion in *Croswell* was cited in the future, not only in New York, but in states throughout the Union. Speech and press were to be free, republican government required it; but not everything said or published will go unpunished—the privilege might be abused. A jury of twelve peers will determine when it is abused.

⊞ *F U R T H E R   R E A D I N G*

David A. Anderson, "The Origins of the Press Clause," *UCLA Law Review* 30 (1983): 455–540

Bernard Bailyn and John B. Hench, eds., *The Press and the American Revolution* (1980)

Walter Berns, *The First Amendment and the Future of American Democracy* (1976)

Morris D. Forkosch, "Freedom of the Press: Croswell's Case," *Fordham Law Review* 33 (1965): 415–448

Alfred H. Kelly, "Constitutional Liberty and the Law of Libel," *American Historical Review* 74 (1968): 429–452

Adrienne Koch and Harry Ammon, "The Virginia and Kentucky Resolutions: An Episode in Jefferson's and Madison's Defense of Civil Liberties," *William and Mary Quarterly,* 3rd ser., 5 (1948): 145–176

Leonard W. Levy, "Did the Zenger Case Really Matter?" *William and Mary Quarterly,* 3rd ser., 17 (1960): 35–50

———, *Emergence of a Free Press* (1985)

John C. Miller, *Crisis in Freedom: The Alien and Sedition Acts* (1952)

Norman Rosenberg, *Protecting the Best Men: An Interpretive History of the Law of Libel* (1986)

Martin Shapiro, *Freedom of Speech: The Supreme Court and Judicial Review* (1966)

C H A P T E R

7

The Establishment of
Federal Judicial Review

✠

Through judicial review, the unelected justices of the Supreme Court scrutinize
state and federal legislation and the acts of state and federal executive officers to
determine whether they conflict with the Constitution. If the laws do conflict, the
Court declares them null and void. This important practice, a distinctive feature
of American constitutionalism, is nowhere provided for in the Constitution. The
framers did not even include the words judicial review *in the document. How-*
ever, they were similarly vague about other important powers, such as Con-
gress's authority to spend for the general welfare. Moreover, the framers in-
tended the Constitution to be a charter for government rather than a legalistic
code of government operations. And the framers' silence also stemmed from ne-
cessity. Nationalists at the convention understood that states' rights advocates
feared the penetration of federal judicial authority into areas previously the ex-
clusive domain of the states. An explicit *endorsement of the High Court's power*
to review state legislative and judicial pronouncements would have compounded
the already difficult task of forging agreement among the delegates.

The task of establishing judicial review was therefore left to the Court. The
two central figures in that process were Federalist Chief Justice John Marshall
(1803–1835) and, to a lesser degree, his Jacksonian Democratic successor, Roger
B. Taney (1836–1864). During their years on the bench, the High Court justices
held only forty-four laws unconstitutional—less than one-half of 1 percent of all
cases brought before them. They voided only three acts of Congress; the judicial
ax fell most often on state laws and local ordinances.

These small numbers should not obscure the justices' critical role in shaping
judicial review under the mounting pressures of social diversity, sectional conten-
tiousness, two-party activism, and robust economic development. Yet from the
beginning of the nation, federal judicial review sparked enormous controversy
because it appeared contrary to the ideals of democratic government. Why, the
argument goes, should unelected judges have the authority to overturn popularly
elected legislators? But even if we can successfully answer that question, a second
remains: should the justices of the High Court alone hold a monopoly over inter-
pretation of the Constitution?

During the past two hundred years, a judicial-monopoly theory of constitutional interpretation has replaced the departmental theory of review that prevailed during John Marshall's era. Departmental theory posited a sharp distinction between constitutional interpretation necessary for the rule of law and that associated with judicial policymaking. According to departmental theory, the political branches had responsibility for political-constitutional controversies within their spheres, and the judicial branch assumed the role of settling legal disputes, of overseeing the rule of law. According to the prevailing departmental theory at the end of the eighteenth century, judicial review was a negative, defensive practice intended to protect the courts from legislative and executive encroachments. Over time, however, the justices became important policymakers as well as arbiters of state-nation relations, and they and their court became subjects of political debate and constitutional theory.

✤ D O C U M E N T S

The distinction between law and politics captured the attention of Alexander Hamilton in No. 78 of the *Federalist Papers,* reprinted here as the first document. In a classic defense of judicial review, Hamilton argues that the power of the judiciary flowed from its apolitical character and its independence of the direct control of the political branches. Because it had neither the power of the sword nor the purse, the judiciary was the "least dangerous branch."

Critics of the judiciary, however, dismissed this notion, as the response to John Marshall's decision in *Marbury* v. *Madison* (1803), the second selection, makes clear. *Marbury* was only one of two cases in which the Supreme Court overturned an act of Congress before the Civil War, the other being *Dred Scott* v. *Sandford* (1857). Marshall's decision in *Marbury* came amidst efforts by Jeffersonian Republicans to rein in the power of the federal judiciary. The radical states' right wing of that party, for example, pushed through the Repeal Act of 1802, which wiped out the Judiciary Act of 1801. The outgoing Federalists had passed that measure to secure the federal courts against newly elected President Thomas Jefferson and his Republican majority in Congress. Moreover, the radical wing of the Republican party on March 12, 1804, engineered the impeachment of Associate Justice Samuel Chase, a Federalist who had become politically vulnerable because of his partisan oversight of several prosecutions under the Sedition Act. The third document, the eight articles of impeachment against Chase (who was subsequently acquitted by a close Senate vote) alleges no infractions of law but instead points to his oppressive conduct on the bench.

Most instances of judicial review during the Marshall and Taney years involved state laws rather than federal legislation. In *M'Culloch* v. *Maryland* (1819), this chapter's fourth selection, the Marshall Court overturned a Maryland statute that attempted to prevent the Bank of the United States from doing business. Marshall's opinion for the Court gave a ringing endorsement to the concept that the powers of Congress were broad and implied rather than limited and enumerated. His decision also asserted one of Marshall's most important values—nationalism.

Marshall's positions in *Marbury* and *M'Culloch* came under sharp attack from fellow Virginians committed to states' rights as well as from John Bannister Gibson, chief justice of the Pennsylvania Supreme Court. In the fifth document, from the *Niles' Weekly Register* of March 13, 1819, the Court is assailed for its views of national power and its intervention in the business of the state of Maryland. In the sixth selection, Judge Gibson, in *Eakin* v. *Raub* (Penna., 1825), argues that Marshall's rationale in *Marbury* could be used to reach an altogether different conclusion.

Much of the political furor surrounding early federal judicial review centered on whether the justices exercised proper standards of interpretation. Justice Joseph Story, more than any other pre–Civil War jurist, made the case that they did exercise proper standards. In the final selection, from *Commentaries on the Constitution* (1833), Story, who like Marshall was a strong nationalist, responds to Gibson and other critics by arguing that judges decided cases neither arbitrarily nor on the basis of their political beliefs. Rather, established models of interpretation guided their behavior.

Alexander Hamilton Defends Judicial Review, 1788

We proceed now to an examination of the judiciary department of the proposed government.

In unfolding the defects of the existing Confederation, the utility and necessity of a federal judicature have been clearly pointed out. It is the less necessary to recapitulate the considerations there urged as the propriety of the institution in the abstract is not disputed; the only questions which have been raised being relative to the manner of constituting it, and to its extent. To these points, therefore, our observations shall be confined.

The manner of constituting it seems to embrace these several objects: 1st. The mode of appointing the judges. 2nd. The tenure by which they are to hold their places. 3rd. The partition of the judiciary authority between different courts and their relations to each other.

First. As to the mode of appointing the judges: this is the same with that of appointing the officers of the Union in general and has been so fully discussed in the two last numbers that nothing can be said here which would not be useless repetition.

Second. As to the tenure by which the judges are to hold their places: this chiefly concerns their duration in office, the provisions for their support, the precautions for their responsibility.

According to the plan of the convention, all judges who may be appointed by the United States are to hold their offices *during good behavior;* which is conformable to the most approved of the State constitutions, and among the rest, to that of this State. Its propriety having been drawn into question by the adversaries of that plan is no light symptom of the rage for objection which disorders their imaginations and judgments. The standard of good behavior for the continuance in office of the judicial magistracy is certainly one of the most valuable of the modern improvements in the practice of government. In a monarchy it is an excellent barrier to the despotism of the prince; in a republic it is a no less excellent barrier to the encroachments and oppressions of the representative body. And it is the best expedient which can be devised in any government to secure a steady, upright, and impartial administration of the laws.

Whoever attentively considers the different departments of power must perceive that, in a government in which they are separated from each other, the judiciary, from the nature of its functions, will always be the least dangerous to the political rights of the Constitution; because it will be least in a capacity to annoy or injure them. The executive not only dispenses the honors but holds the sword of the community. The legislature not only commands the purse but prescribes the rules by which the duties and rights of every citizen are to be regulated. The judiciary, on the contrary, has no influence over either the sword or the purse; no direction either of the strength or of the wealth of the society, and can take no active resolution whatever. It may truly be said to have neither FORCE nor WILL but merely judgment; and must ultimately depend upon the aid of the executive arm even for the efficacy of its judgments.

This simple view of the matter suggests several important consequences. It proves incontestably that the judiciary is beyond comparison the weakest of the three departments of power; that it can never attack with success either of the other two; and that all possible care is requisite to enable it to defend itself against their attacks. It equally proves that though individual oppression may now and then proceed from the courts of justice, the general liberty of the people can never be endangered from that quarter; I mean so long as the judiciary remains truly distinct from both the legislature and the executive. For I agree that "there is no liberty if the power of judging be not separated from the legislative and executive powers." And it proves, in the last place, that as liberty can have nothing to fear from the judiciary alone, but would have everything to fear from its union with either of the other departments; that as all the effects of such a union must ensue from a dependence of the former on the latter, notwithstanding a nominal and apparent separation; that as, from the natural feebleness of the judiciary, it is in continual jeopardy of being overpowered, awed, or influenced by its co-ordinate branches; and that as nothing can contribute so much to its firmness and independence as permanency in office, this quality may therefore be justly regarded as an indispensable ingredient in its constitution, and, in a great measure, as the citadel of the public justice and the public security.

The complete independence of the courts of justice is peculiarly essential in a limited Constitution. By a limited Constitution, I understand one which contains certain specified exceptions to the legislative authority; such, for instance, as that it shall pass no bills of attainder, no *ex post facto* laws, and the like. Limitations of this kind can be preserved in practice no other way than through the medium of courts of justice, whose duty it must be to declare all acts contrary to the manifest tenor of the Constitution void. Without this, all the reservations of particular rights or privileges would amount to nothing.

Some perplexity respecting the rights of the courts to pronounce legislative acts void, because contrary to the Constitution, has arisen from an imagination that the doctrine would imply a superiority of the judiciary to the legislative power. It is urged that the authority which can declare the acts of another void must necessarily be superior to the one whose acts may be declared void. As this doctrine is of great importance in all the American constitutions, a brief discussion of the grounds on which it rests cannot be unacceptable.

There is no position which depends on clearer principles than that every act of a delegated authority, contrary to the tenor of the commission under which it is exercised, is void. No legislative act, therefore, contrary to the Constitution, can be valid. To deny this would be to affirm that the deputy is greater than his principal; that the servant is above his master; that the representatives of the people are superior to the people themselves; that men acting by virtue of powers may do not only what their powers do not authorize, but what they forbid.

If it be said that the legislative body are themselves the constitutional judges of their own powers and that the construction they put upon them is conclusive upon the other departments it may be answered that this cannot be the natural presumption where it is not to be collected from any particular provisions in the Constitution. It is not otherwise to be supposed that the Constitution could intend to enable the representatives of the people to substitute their *will* to that of their constituents. It is far more rational to suppose that the courts were designed to be an intermediate body between the people and the legislature in order, among other things, to keep the latter within the limits assigned to their authority. The interpretation of the laws is the proper and peculiar province of the courts. A constitution is, in fact, and must be regarded by the judges as, a fundamental law. It therefore belongs to them to ascertain its meaning as well as the meaning of any particular act proceeding from the legislative body. If there should happen to be an irreconcilable variance between the two, that which has the superior obligation and validity ought, of course, to be preferred; or, in other words, the Constitution ought to be preferred to the statute, the intention of the people to the intention of their agents.

Nor does this conclusion by any means suppose a superiority of the judicial to the legislative power. It only supposes that the power of the people is superior to both, and that where the will of the legislature, declared in its statutes, stands in opposition to that of the people, declared in the Constitution, the judges ought to be governed by the latter rather than the former. They ought to regulate their decisions by the fundamental laws rather than by those which are not fundamental.

This exercise of judicial discretion in determining between two contradictory laws is exemplified in a familiar instance. It not uncommonly happens that there are two statutes existing at one time, clashing in whole or in part with each other and neither of them containing any repealing clause or expression. In such a case, it is the province of the courts to liquidate and fix their meaning and operation. So far as they can, by any fair construction, be reconciled to each other, reason and law conspire to dictate that this should be done; where this is impracticable, it becomes a matter of necessity to give effect to one in exclusion of the other. The rule which has obtained in the courts for determining their relative validity is that the last in order of time shall be preferred to the first. But this is a mere rule of construction, not derived from any positive law but from the nature and reason of the thing. It is a rule not enjoined upon the courts by legislative provision but adopted by themselves, as consonant to truth and propriety, for the direction of their conduct as interpreters of the law. They thought it reasonable that between the interfering acts of an *equal* authority that which was the last indication of its will should have the preference.

But in regard to the interfering acts of a superior and subordinate authority of an original and derivative power, the nature and reason of the thing indicate the converse of that rule as proper to be followed. They teach us that the prior act of a superior ought to be preferred to the subsequent act of an inferior and subordinate authority; and that accordingly, whenever a particular statute contravenes the Constitution, it will be the duty of the judicial tribunals to adhere to the latter and disregard the former.

It can be of no weight to say that the courts, on the pretense of a repugnancy, may substitute their own pleasure to the constitutional intentions of the legislature. This might as well happen in the case of two contradictory statutes; or it might as well happen in every adjudication upon any single statute. The courts must declare the sense of the law; and if they should be disposed to exercise WILL instead of JUDGMENT, the consequence would equally be the substitution of their pleasure to that of the legislative body. The observation, if it proved anything, would prove that there ought to be no judges distinct from that body.

If, then, the courts of justice are to be considered as the bulwarks of a limited Constitution against legislative encroachments, this consideration will afford a strong argument for the permanent tenure of judicial offices, since nothing will contribute so much as this to that independent spirit in the judges which must be essential to the faithful performance of so arduous a duty.

This independence of the judges is equally requisite to guard the Constitution and the rights of individuals from the effects of those ill humors which the arts of designing men, or the influence of particular conjunctures, sometimes disseminate among the people themselves, and which, though they speedily give place to better information, and more deliberate reflection, have a tendency, in the meantime, to occasion dangerous innovations in the government, and serious oppressions of the minor party in the community. Though I trust the friends of the proposed Constitution will never concur with its enemies in questioning that fundamental principle of republican government which admits the right of the people to alter or abolish the established Constitution whenever they find it inconsistent with their happiness; yet it is not to be inferred from this principle that the representatives of the people, whenever a momentary inclination happens to lay hold of a majority of their constituents incompatible with the provisions in the existing Constitution would, on that account, be justifiable in a violation of those provisions; or that the courts would be under a greater obligation to connive at infractions in this shape than when they had proceeded wholly from the cabals of the representative body. Until the people have, by some solemn and authoritative act, annulled or changed the established form, it is binding upon themselves collectively, as well as individually; and no presumption, or even knowledge of their sentiments, can warrant their representatives in a departure from it prior to such an act. But it is easy to see that it would require an uncommon portion of fortitude in the judges to do their duty as faithful guardians of the Constitution, where legislative invasions of it had been instigated by the major voice of the community.

But it is not with a view to infractions of the Constitution only that the independence of the judges may be an essential safeguard against the effects of occasional ill humors in the society. These sometimes extend no farther than to the injury of the private rights of particular classes of citizens, by unjust and partial laws. Here also the firmness of the judicial magistracy is of vast importance in mitigating the severity and confining the operation of such laws. It not only serves to moderate the immediate mischiefs of those which may have been passed but it operates as a check upon the legislative body in passing them; who, perceiving that obstacles to the success of an iniquitous intention are to be expected from the scruples of the courts, are in a manner compelled, by the very motives of the injustice they meditate, to qualify their attempts. This is a circumstance calculated to have more influence upon the character of our governments than but few may be aware of. The benefits of the integrity and moderation of the judiciary have already been felt in more States than one; and though they may have displeased those whose sinister expectations they may have disappointed, they must have commanded the esteem and applause of all the virtuous and disinterested. Considerate men of every description ought to prize whatever will tend to beget or fortify that temper in the courts; as no man can be sure that he may not be tomorrow the victim of a spirit of injustice, by which he may be a gainer today. And every man must now feel that the inevitable tendency of such a spirit is to sap the foundations of public and private confidence and to introduce in its stead universal distrust and distress.

That inflexible and uniform adherence to the rights of the Constitution, and of individuals, which we perceive to be indispensable in the courts of justice, can certainly not be expected from judges who hold their offices by a temporary commission. Periodical appointments, however regulated, or by whomsoever made, would, in some way or other, be fatal to their necessary independence. If the power of making them was committed either to the executive or legislature there would be danger of an improper complaisance to the branch which possessed it; if to both, there would be an unwillingness to hazard the displeasure of either; if to the people, or to persons chosen by them for the special purpose, there would be too great a disposition to consult popularity to justify a reliance that nothing would be consulted but the Constitution and the laws.

There is yet a further and a weighty reason for the permanency of the judicial offices which is deducible from the nature of the qualifications they require. It has been frequently remarked with great propriety that a voluminous code of laws is one of the inconveniences necessarily connected with the advantages of a free government. To avoid an arbitrary discretion in the courts, it is indispensable that they should be bound down by strict rules and precedents which serve to define and point out their duty in every particular case that comes before them; and it will readily be conceived from the variety of controversies which grow out of the folly and wickedness of mankind that the records of those precedents must unavoidably swell to a very considerable bulk and must demand long and laborious study to acquire a competent knowledge of them. Hence it is that there can be but few men in the society who will have sufficient skill in the laws to qualify them for the stations of judges. And making the proper deductions for the ordinary depravity of human nature, the number must be still smaller of those who unite the requisite integrity with the requisite knowledge. These considerations apprise us that the government can have no great option between fit characters; and that a temporary duration in office which would naturally discourage such characters from quitting a lucrative line of practice to accept a seat on the bench would have a tendency to throw the administration of justice into hands less able and less well qualified to conduct it with utility and dignity. In the present circumstances of this country and in those in which it is likely to be for a long time to come, the disadvantages on this score would be greater than they may at first sight appear; but it must be confessed that they are far inferior to those which present themselves under the other aspects of the subject.

Upon the whole, there can be no room to doubt that the convention acted wisely in copying from the models of those constitutions which have established *good behavior* as the tenure of their judicial offices, in point of duration; and that so far from being blamable on this account, their plan would have been inexcusably defective if it had wanted this important feature of good government. The experience of Great Britain affords an illustrious comment on the excellence of the institution.

Marbury v. Madison, 1803

1 Cranch 137 (1803)

[Unanimous]

. . . Marshall, C. J. . . . The peculiar delicacy of this case, the novelty of some of its circumstances, and the real difficulty attending the points which occur in it, require a complete exposition of the principles on which the opinion to be given by the court is founded. . . .

In the order in which the court has viewed this subject, the following questions have been considered and decided:

1st. Has the applicant a right to the commission he demands?

2dly. If he has a right, and that right has been violated, do the laws of his country afford him a remedy?

3rdly. If they do afford him a remedy, is it a *mandamus* issuing from this court? . . .

Henry Steele Commager and Milton Cantor, eds., Documents of American History, Vol. I to 1898 (10th ed., 1988), 1: 191–195, Prentice-Hall Publishing Company.

The first object of enquiry is,

Has the applicant a right to the commission he demands? . . .

It is therefore decidedly the opinion of the court, that when a commission has been signed by the President, the appointment is made; and that the commission is complete, when the seal of the United States has been affixed to it by the secretary of state. . . .

Mr. Marbury, then, since his commission was signed by the President, and sealed by the secretary of state, was appointed; and as the law creating the office, gave the officer a right to hold for five years, independent of the executive, the appointment was not revocable; but vested in the officer legal rights, which are protected by the laws of his country.

To withhold his commission, therefore, is an act deemed by the court not warranted by law, but violative of a vested legal right.

2. This brings us to the second enquiry: which is,

If he has a right, and that right has been violated, do the laws of his country afford him a remedy? . . .

The government of the United States has been emphatically termed a government of laws, and not of men. It will certainly cease to deserve this high appellation, if the laws furnish no remedy for the violation of a vested legal right.

If this obloquy is to be cast on the jurisprudence of our country, it must arise from the peculiar character of the case. . . .

By the constitution of the United States, the President is invested with certain important political powers, in the exercise of which he is to use his own discretion, and is accountable only to his country in his political character, and to his own conscience. To aid him in the performance of these duties, he is authorized to appoint certain officers, who act by his authority and in conformity with his orders.

In such cases, their acts are his acts; and whatever opinion may be entertained of the manner in which executive discretion may be used, still there exists, and can exist, no power to control that discretion. The subjects are political. . . .

The conclusion from this reasoning is, that where the heads of departments are the political or confidential agents of the executive, merely to execute the will of the President, or rather to act in cases in which the executive possesses a constitutional or legal discretion, nothing can be more perfectly clear than that their acts are only politically examinable. But where a specific duty is assigned by law, and individual rights depend upon the performance of that duty, it seems equally clear that the individual who considers himself injured, has a right to resort to the laws of his country for a remedy. . . .

It is, then, the opinion of the Court,

1st. That by signing the commission of Mr. Marbury, the president of the United States appointed him a justice of peace for the county of Washington in the District of Columbia; and that the seal of the United States, affixed thereto by the secretary of state, is conclusive testimony of the verity of the signature, and of the completion of the appointment; and that the appointment conferred on him a legal right to the office for the space of five years.

2ndly. That, having this legal title to the office, he has a consequent right to the commission; a refusal to deliver which, is a plain violation of that right, for which the laws of his country afford him a remedy.

It remains to be enquired whether,

3rdly. He is entitled to the remedy for which he applies. This depends on

1st. The nature of the writ applied for, and

2dly. The power of this court. . . .

This, then, is a plain case for a mandamus, either to deliver the commission, or a copy of it from the record; and it only remains to be enquired,

Whether it can issue from this court.

The act to establish the judicial courts of the United States authorizes the supreme court "to issue writs of mandamus, in cases warranted by the principles and usages of law, to any courts appointed, or persons holding office, under the authority of the United States."

The secretary of state, being a person holding an office under the authority of the United States is precisely within the letter of the description; and if this court is not authorized to issue a writ of mandamus to such an officer, it must be because the law is unconstitutional, and therefore absolutely incapable of conferring the authority and assigning the duties which its words purport to confer and assign.

The constitution vests the whole judicial power of the United States in one supreme court, and such inferior courts as congress shall, from time to time, ordain and establish. This power is expressly extended to all cases arising under the laws of the United States; and consequently, in some form, may be exercised over the present case; because the right claimed is given by a law of the United States.

In the distribution of this power it is declared, that "the supreme court shall have original jurisdiction in all cases affecting ambassadors, other public ministers and consuls, and those in which a state shall be a party. In all other cases, the supreme court shall have appellate jurisdiction." . . .

If it had been intended to leave it in the discretion of the legislature to apportion the judicial power between the supreme and inferior courts according to the will of that body, it would certainly have been useless to have proceeded further than to have defined the judicial power, and the tribunals in which it should be vested. The subsequent part of the section is mere surplusage, is entirely without meaning, if such is to be the construction. If congress remains at liberty to give this court appellate jurisdiction, where the constitution has declared their jurisdiction shall be original; and original jurisdiction where the constitution has declared it shall be appellate; the distribution of jurisdiction, made in the constitution, is form without substance.

Affirmative words are often, in their operation, negative of other objects than those affirmed; and in this case, a negative or exclusive sense must be given to them or they have no operation at all.

It cannot be presumed, that any clause in the constitution is intended to be without effect; and therefore such a construction is inadmissible, unless the words require it. . . .

The authority, therefore, given to the supreme court, by the act establishing the judicial courts of the United States, to issue writs of mandamus to public officers, appears not to be warranted by the constitution; and it becomes necessary to inquire whether a jurisdiction so conferred can be exercised.

The question whether an act repugnant to the constitution can become the law of the land, is a question deeply interesting to the United States; but, happily not of an intricacy porportioned to its interest. It seems only necessary to recognize certain principles supposed to have been long and well established, to decide it.

That the people have an original right to establish for their future government such principles as, in their opinion, shall most conduce to their own happiness, is the basis on which the whole American fabric has been erected. The exercise of this original right is a very great exertion, nor can it nor ought it to be frequently repeated. The principles therefore so established are deemed fundamental. And as the authority from which they proceed is supreme and can seldom act, they are designed to be permanent.

This original and supreme will organizes the government, and assigns to different departments their respective powers. It may either stop here or establish certain limits not to be transcended by those departments.

The government of the United States is of the latter description. The powers of the legislature are defined and limited; and that those limits may not be mistaken or forgotten, the constitution is written. To what purpose are powers limited, and to what purpose is that limitation committed to writing, if these limits may, at any time, be passed by those intended to be restrained? The distinction between a government with limited and unlimited powers is abolished if those limits do not confine the persons on whom they are imposed and if acts prohibited and acts allowed are of equal obligation. It is a proposition too plain to be contested, that the constitution controls any legislative act repugnant to it; or, that the legislature may alter the constitution by an ordinary act.

Between these alternatives there is no middle ground. The constitution is either a superior paramount law, unchangeable by ordinary means, or it is on a level with ordinary legislative acts, and, like other acts, is alterable when the legislature shall please to alter it.

If the former part of the alternative be true, then a legislative act contrary to the constitution is not law; if the latter part be true, then written constitutions are absurd attempts, on the part of the people, to limit a power in its own nature illimitable.

Certainly all those who have framed written constitutions contemplate them as forming the fundamental and paramount law of the nation, and consequently the theory of every such government must be that an act of the legislature repugnant to the Constitution is void.

This theory is essentially attached to a written constitution, and is consequently to be considered, by this court as one of the fundamental principles of our society. It is not, therefore, to be lost sight of in the further consideration of this subject.

If an act of the legislature repugnant to the constitution is void, does it, notwithstanding its invalidity, bind the courts and oblige them to give it effect? Or, in other words, though it be not law, does it constitute a rule as operative as if it was a law? This would be to overthrow in fact what was established in theory, and would seem, at first view, an absurdity too gross to be insisted on. It shall, however, receive a more attentive consideration.

It is emphatically the province and duty of the judicial department to say what the law is. Those who apply the rule to particular cases must of necessity expound and interpret that rule. If two laws conflict with each other, the courts must decide on the operation of each.

So if a law be in opposition to the constitution; if both the law and the constitution apply to a particular case, so that the court must either decide that case conformably to the law, disregarding the constitution, or conformably to the constitution, disregarding the law, the court must determine which of these conflicting rules governs the case. This is of the very essence of judicial duty.

If, then, the courts are to regard the constitution, and the constitution is superior to any ordinary act of the legislature, the constitution, and not such ordinary act, must govern the case to which they both apply.

Those, then, who controvert the principle that the constitution is to be considered in court as a paramount law, are reduced to the necessity of maintaining that courts must close their eyes on the constitution and see only the law.

This doctrine would subvert the very foundation of all written constitutions. It would declare that an act which, according to the principles and theory of our government, is entirely void, is yet, in practice, completely obligatory. It would declare that if the legislature shall do what is expressly forbidden, such act, notwithstanding the express prohibition, is in reality effectual. It would be giving to the legislature a practical and real omnipotence with the same breath which professes to restrict their powers within narrow limits. It is prescribing limits and declaring that those limits may be passed at pleasure.

That it thus reduces to nothing what we have deemed the greatest improvement on political institutions, a written constitution, would of itself be sufficient, in America, where written constitutions have been viewed with so much reverence, for rejecting the construction. But the peculiar expressions of the constitution of the United States furnish additional arguments in favor of its rejection.

The judicial power of the United States is extended to all cases arising under the constitution.

Could it be the intention of those who gave this power to say that in using it the constitution should not be looked into? That a case arising under the constitution should be decided without examining the instrument under which it arises?

This is too extravagant to be maintained.

In some cases, then, the constitution must be looked into by the judges. And if they can open it at all, what part of it are they forbidden to read or to obey?

There are many other parts of the constitution which serve to illustrate this subject.

It is declared that "no tax or duty shall be laid on articles exported from any state." Suppose a duty on the export of cotton, of tobacco, or of flour, and a suit instituted to recover it, ought judgment to be rendered in such a case? Ought the judges to close their eyes on the constitution, and only see the law?

The constitution declares "that no bill of attainder or *ex post facto* law shall be passed." If, however, such a bill should be passed, and a person should be prosecuted under it, must the court condemn to death those victims whom the constitution endeavors to preserve?

"No person," says the constitution, "shall be convicted of treason unless on the testimony of two witnesses to the same overt act, or on confession in open court."

Here the language of the constitution is addressed especially to the courts. It prescribes, directly for them, a rule of evidence not to be departed from. If the legislature should change that rule, and declare one witness, or a confession out of court, sufficient for conviction, must the constitutional principle yield to the legislative act?

From these, and many other selections which might be made, it is apparent that the framers of the constitution contemplated that instrument as a rule for the government of *courts,* as well as of the legislature. Why otherwise does it direct the judges to take an oath to support it? This oath certainly applies in an especial manner to their conduct in their official character. How immoral to impose it on them if they were to be used as the instruments, and the knowing instruments, for violating what they swear to support!

The oath of office, too, imposed by the legislature, is completely demonstrative of the legislative opinion on this subject. It is in these words: "I do solemnly swear that I will administer justice without respect to persons, and do equal right to the poor and to the rich; and that I will faithfully and impartially discharge all the duties incumbent on me as ———, according to the best of my abilities and understanding, agreeably to *the constitution* and laws of the United States." Why does a judge swear to discharge his duties agreeably to the constitution of the United States, if that constitution forms no rule for his government?—if it is closed upon him, and cannot be inspected by him?

If such be the real state of things, this is worse than solemn mockery. To prescribe, or to take this oath, becomes equally a crime.

It is also not entirely unworthy of observation, that in declaring what shall be the *supreme* law of the land, the constitution itself is first mentioned, and not the laws of the United States generally, but those only which shall be made in *pursuance* of the constitution, have that rank.

Thus, the particular phraseology of the constitution of the United States confirms and strengthens the principle, supposed to be essential to all written constitutions, that a law repugnant to the constitution is void, and that courts, as well as other departments, are bound by that instrument.

[Mandamus denied.]

Articles of Impeachment Against Samuel Chase, 1803

Article I

That, unmindful of the solemn duties of his office, and contrary to the sacred obligation by which he stood bound to discharge them "faithfully and impartially, and without respect to persons," the said Samuel Chase, on the trial of John Fries, charged with treason, before the circuit court of the United States, held for the district of Pennsylvania, in the city of Philadelphia, during the months of April and May, one thousand eight hundred, whereat the said Samuel Chase presided, did, in his judicial capacity, conduct himself in a manner highly arbitrary, oppressive, and unjust, viz.

1. In delivering an opinion, in writing, on the question of law, on the construction of which the defence of the accused materially depended, tending to prejudice the minds of the jury against the case of the said John Fries, the prisoner, before counsel had been heard in his defence:

2. In restricting the counsel for the said Fries from recurring to such English authorities as they believed apposite, or from citing certain statutes of the United States, which they deemed illustrative of the positions, upon which they intended to rest the defence of their client:

3. In debarring the prisoner from his constitutional privilege of addressing the jury (through his counsel) on the law, as well as on the fact, which was to determine his guilt, or innocence, and at the same time endeavoring to wrest from the jury their indisputable right to hear argument, and determine upon the question of law, as well as the question of fact, involved in the verdict which they were required to give:

In consequence of which irregular conduct of the said Samuel Chase, as dangerous to our liberties, as it is novel to our laws and usages, the said John Fries was deprived of the right, secured to him by the eighth article amendatory of the constitution, and was condemned to death without having been heard by counsel, in his defence, to the disgrace of the character of the American bench, in manifest violation of law and justice, and in open contempt of the rights of juries, on which, ultimately, rest the liberty and safety of the American people. . . .

Article III

That, with intent to oppress and procure the conviction of the prisoner, the evidence of John Taylor, a material witness on behalf of the aforesaid Callender, was not permitted by the said Samuel Chase to be given in, on pretence that the said witness could not prove the truth of the whole of one of the charges, contained in the indictment, although the said charge embraced more than one fact.

Article IV

That the conduct of the said Samuel Chase, was marked, during the whole course of the said trial, by manifest injustice, partiality, and intemperance; viz.

1. In compelling the prisoner's counsel to reduce to writing, and submit to the inspection of the court, for their admission, or rejection, all questions which the said counsel meant to propound to the above named John Taylor, the witness.

2. In refusing to postpone the trial, although an affidavit was regularly filed, stating the absence of material witnesses on behalf of the accused; and although it was manifest, that, with the utmost diligence, the attendance of such witnesses could not have been procured at that term.

3. In the use of unusual, rude, and contemptuous expressions towards the prisoner's counsel; and in falsely insinuating that they wished to excite the public fears and indignation, and to produce that insubordination to law, to which the conduct of the judge did, at the same time, manifestly tend:

4. In repeated and vexatious interruptions of the said counsel, on the part of the said judge, which, at length, induced them to abandon their cause and their client, who was thereupon convicted and condemned to fine and imprisonment:

5. In an indecent solicitude, manifested by the said Samuel Chase, for the conviction of the accused, unbecoming even a public prosecutor, but highly disgraceful to the character of a judge as it was subversive of justice. . . .

Article VIII

And whereas mutual respect and confidence between the govenment of the United States and those of the individual states, and between the people and those governments, respectively, are highly conducive to that public harmony, without which there can be no public happiness, yet the said Samuel Chase, disregarding the duties and dignity of his judicial character, did, at a circuit court, for the district of Maryland, held at Baltimore, in the month of May, one thousand eight hundred and three, pervert his official right and duty to address the grand jury then and there assembled, on the matters coming within the province of the said jury, for the purpose of delivering to the said grand jury an intemperate and inflammatory political harangue, with intent to excite the fears and resentment of the said grand jury, and of the good people of Maryland against their state government, and constitution, a conduct highly censurable in any, but peculiarly indecent and unbecoming in a judge of the supreme court of the United States: and moreover, that the said Samuel Chase, then and there, under pretence of exercising his judicial right to address the said grand jury, as aforesaid, did, in a manner highly unwarrantable, endeavor to excite the odium of the said grand jury, and of the good people of Maryland, against the government of the United States, by delivering opinions, which, even if the judicial authority were competent to their expression, on a suitable occasion and in a proper manner, were at that time and as delivered by him, highly indecent, extra-judicial, and tending to prostitute the high judicial character with which he was invested, to the low purpose of an electioneering partizan.

And the House of Representatives, by protestation, saving to themselves the liberty of exhibiting, at any time hereafter, any farther articles, or other accusation, or impeachment, against the said Samuel Chase, and also of replying to his answers which he shall make unto the said articles, or any of them, and of offering proof to all and every the aforesaid articles, and to all and every other articles, impeachment, or accusation, which shall be exhibited by them, as the case shall require, do demand that the said Samuel Chase may be put to answer the said crimes and misdemeanors, and that such proceedings, examinations, trials, and judgments may be thereupon had and given, as are agreeable to law and justice.

This report was made the order for the 3d of December. On that and the ensuing day the House took the articles into consideration, to all of which they agreed, according to the following votes:

ARTICLE	YEAS	NAYS	ARTICLE		YEAS	NAYS
1	83	34	6	—	73	42
2	83	35	7	—	73	42
3	84	34	8	1st sect.	74	39
4	84	34	8	2d sect.	78	32
5	72	45				

M'Culloch v. *Maryland,* 1819

4 Wheaton 316 (1819)

[Unanimous]

Marshall, C. J. . . . The first question made in this cause is, has Congress power to incorporate a bank?

In discussing this question, the counsel for the State of Maryland have deemed it of some importance, in the construction of the constitution, to consider that instrument not as emanating from the people, but as the act of sovereign and independent States. The powers of the general government, it has been said, are delegated by the States, who alone are truly sovereign; and must be exercised in subordination to the States, who alone possess supreme dominion.

It would be difficult to sustain this proposition. The convention which framed the constitution was, indeed, elected by the State legislatures. But the instrument, when it came from their hands, was a mere proposal, without obligation, or pretensions to it. It was reported to the then existing Congress of the United States, with a request that it might "be submitted to a convention of Delegates, chosen in each State, by the people thereof, under the recommendation of its legislature, for their assent and ratification." This mode of proceeding was adopted; and by the Convention, by Congress, and by the State Legislatures, the instrument was submitted to the people. They acted upon it, in the only manner in which they can act safely, effectively, and wisely, on such a subject, by assembling in Convention. It is true, they assembled in their several States; and where else should they have assembled? No political dreamer was ever wild enough to think of breaking down the lines which separate the States, and of compounding the American people into one common mass. Of consequence, when they act, they act in their States. But the measures they adopt do not, on that account cease to be the measures of the people themselves, or become the measures of the state governments.

From these Conventions the constitution derives its whole authority. The government proceeds directly from the people; is "ordained and established" in the name of the people; and is declared to be ordained, "in order to form a more perfect union, establish justice, insure domestic tranquillity, and secure the blessings of liberty to themselves and to their posterity." The assent of the States, in their sovereign capacity, is implied in calling a Convention, and thus submitting that instrument to the people. But the people were at perfect liberty to accept or reject it; and their act was final. It required not the affirmance, and could not be negatived, by the State governments. The constitution, when thus adopted, was of complete obligation, and bound the State sovereignties. . . .

. . . The government of the Union, then (whatever may be the influence of this fact on the case), is emphatically and truly a government of the people. In form and in substance it emanates from them, its powers are granted by them, and are to be exercised directly on them, and for their benefit.

This government is acknowledged by all to be one of enumerated powers. The principle, that it can exercise only the powers granted to it, would seem too apparent to have required to be enforced by all those arguments which its enlightened friends, while it was depending before the people, found it necessary to urge. That principle is now universally admitted. But the question respecting the extent of the powers actually granted, is perpetually arising, and will probably continue to arise, as long as our system shall exist. In discussing these questions, the conflicting powers of the State and general governments must be brought into view, and the supremacy of their respective laws, when they are in opposition, must be settled.

If any one proposition could command the universal assent of mankind, we might expect it would be this: that the government of the Union, though limited in its powers, is supreme within its sphere of action. This would seem to result necessarily from its nature. It is the government of all; its powers are delegated by all; it represents all, and acts for all. Though any one State may be willing to control its operations, no State is willing to allow others to control them. The nation, on those subjects on which it can act, must necessarily bind its component parts. But this question is not left to mere reason: the people have, in express terms, decided it, by saying, "this constitution, and the laws of the United States, which shall be made in pursuance thereof," "shall be the supreme law of the land," and by requiring that the members of the State legislatures, and the officers of the executive and judicial departments of the States, shall take the oath of fidelity to it.

The government of the United States, then, though limited in its powers, is supreme; and its laws, when made in pursuance of the constitution, form the supreme law of the land, "anything in the constitution or laws of any State, to the contrary, notwithstanding."

Among the enumerated powers, we do not find that of establishing a bank or creating a corporation. But there is no phrase in the instrument which, like the articles of confederation, excludes incidental or implied powers; and which requires that everything granted shall be expressly and minutely described. Even the 10th amendment, which was framed for the purpose of quieting the excessive jealousies which had been excited, omits the word "expressly," and declares only that the powers "not delegated to the United States, nor prohibited to the States, are reserved to the States or to the people"; thus leaving the question, whether the particular power which may become the subject of contest, has been delegated to the one government, or prohibited to the other, to depend on a fair construction of the whole instrument. The men who drew and adopted this amendment, had experienced the embarrassments resulting from the insertion of this word in the articles of confederation, and probably omitted it to avoid those embarrassments. A constitution, to contain an accurate detail of all the subdivisions of which its great powers will admit, and of all the means by which they may be carried into execution, would partake of the prolixity of a legal code, and could scarcely be embraced by the human mind. It would probably never be understood by the public. Its nature, therefore, requires that only its great outlines should be marked, its important objects designated, and the minor ingredients which compose those objects be deduced from the nature of the objects themselves. That this idea was entertained by the framers of the American constitution, is not only to be inferred from the nature of the instrument, but from the language. Why else were some of the limitations, found in the 9th section of the first article, introduced? It is also, in some degree, warranted by their having omitted to use any restrictive term which might prevent its receiving a fair and just interpretation. In considering this question, then, we must never forget, that it is a *constitution* we are expounding.

Although, among the enumerated powers of government, we do not find the word "bank," or "incorporation," we find the great powers to lay and collect taxes; to borrow money; to regulate commerce; to declare and conduct a war; and to raise and support armies and navies. The sword and the purse, all the external relations, and no inconsiderable portion of the industry of the nation, are intrusted to its government. It can never be pretended that these vast powers draw after them others of inferior importance, merely because they are inferior. Such an idea can never be advanced. But it may, with great reason, be contended, that a government, intrusted with such ample powers, on the due execution of which the happiness and prosperity of the nation so vitally depends, must also be intrusted with ample means for their execution. The power being given, it is the interest of the nation to facilitate its execution. It can never be their interest, and cannot be presumed to have been their intention, to clog and embarrass its execution by withholding the most appropriate means. . . .

It is not denied that the powers given to the government imply the ordinary means of execution. That, for example, of raising revenue and applying it to national purposes, is admitted to imply the power of conveying money from place to place, as the exigencies of the nation may require, and of employing the usual means of conveyance. But it is denied that the government has its choice of means, or that it may employ the most convenient means, if to employ them it be necessary to erect a corporation. . . .

The government which has the right to do an act, and has imposed on it the duty of performing that act, must, according to the dictates of reason, be allowed to select the means; and those who contend that it may not select any appropriate means, that one particular mode of effecting the object is excepted, take upon themselves the burden of establishing that exception. . . .

But the constitution of the United States has not left the right of Congress to employ the necessary means, for the execution of the powers conferred on the government, to general reasoning. To its enumeration of powers is added that of making "all laws which shall be necessary and proper, for carrying into execution the foregoing powers, and all other powers vested by this constitution, in the government of the United States, or in any department thereof."

The counsel for the State of Maryland have urged various arguments, to prove that this clause, though in terms a grant of power, is not so in effect; but is really restrictive of the general right, which might otherwise be implied, of selecting means of executing the enumerated powers. . . .

But the argument on which most reliance is placed, is drawn from the peculiar language of this clause. Congress is not empowered by it to make all laws, which may have relation to the powers conferred on the government, but such only as may be *"necessary and proper"* for carrying them into execution. The word *"necessary"* is considered as controlling the whole sentence, and as limiting the right to pass laws for the execution of the granted powers, to such as are indispensable, and without which the power would be nugatory. That it excludes the choice of means, and leaves to Congress, in each case, that only which is most direct and simple.

Is it true, that this is the sense in which the word "necessary" is always used? Does it always import an absolute physical necessity, so strong, that one thing, to which another may be termed necessary cannot exist without that other? We think it does not. If reference be had to its use, in the common affairs of the world, or in approved authors, we find that it frequently imports no more than that one thing is convenient, or useful, or essential to another. To employ the means necessary to an end, is generally understood as employing any means calculated to produce the end, and not as being confined to those single means, without which the end would be entirely unattainable. Such is the character of human language, that no word conveys to the mind, in all situations one single definite idea; and nothing is more common than to use words in a figurative sense. Almost all compositions contain words, which, taken in their rigorous sense, would convey a meaning different from that which is obviously intended. It is essential to just construction, that many words which import something excessive, should be understood in a more mitigated sense—in that sense which common usage justifies. The word "necessary" is of this description. It has not a fixed character peculiar to itself. It admits of all degrees of comparison; and is often connected with other words, which increase or diminish the impression the mind receives of the urgency it imports. A thing may be necessary, very necessary, absolutely or indispensably necessary. To no mind would the same idea be conveyed, by these several phrases. . . . This word, then, like others, is used in various senses; and, in its construction, the subject, the context, the intention of the person using them, are all to be taken into view.

Let this be done in the case under consideration. The subject is the execution of those great powers on which the welfare of a nation essentially depends. It must have been the intention of those who gave these powers, to insure, as far as human prudence could insure, their beneficial execution. This could not be done by confining the choice of means to such narrow limits as not to leave it in the power of Congress to adopt any which might be appropriate, and which were conducive to the end. This provision is made in a constitution intended to endure for ages to come, and, consequently, to be adapted to the various crises of human affairs. To have prescribed the means by which government should, in all future time, execute its powers, would have been to change, entirely, the character of the instrument, and give it the properties of a legal code. It would have been an unwise attempt to provide, by immutable rules, for exigencies which, if foreseen at all, must have been seen dimly, and which can be best provided for as they occur. To have declared that the best means shall not be used, but those alone without which the power given would be nugatory, would have been to deprive the legislature of the capacity to avail itself of experience, to exercise its reason, and to accommodate its legislation to circumstances. . . .

This clause, as construed by the State of Maryland, would abridge and almost annihilate this useful and necessary right of the legislature to select its means. That this could not be intended is, we should think, had it not been already controverted, too apparent for controversy. . . .

The result of the most careful and attentive consideration bestowed upon this clause is, that if it does not enlarge, it cannot be construed to restrain the powers of Congress, or to impair the right of the legislature to exercise its best judgment in the selection of measures to carry into execution the constitutional powers of the government. If no other motive for its insertion can be suggested, a sufficient one is found in the desire to remove all doubts respecting the right to legislate on that vast mass of incidental powers which must be involved in the constitution, if that instrument be not a splendid bauble.

We admit, as all must admit, that the powers of the government are limited, and that its limits are not to be transcended. But we think the sound construction of the constitution must allow to the national legislature that discretion, with respect to the means by which the powers it confers are to be carried into execution, which will enable that body to perform the high duties assigned to it, in the manner most beneficial to the people. Let the end be legitimate, let it be within the scope of the constitution, and all means which are appropriate, which are plainly adapted to that end, which are not prohibited, but consist with the letter and spirit of the constitution, are constitutional. . . .

. . . Should Congress, in the execution of its powers, adopt measures which are prohibited by the constitution; or should Congress, under the pretext of executing its powers, pass laws for the accomplishment of objects not intrusted to the government, it would become the painful duty of this tribunal, should a case requiring such a decision come before it, to say that such an act was not the law of the land. But where the law is not prohibited, and is really calculated to effect any of the objects intrusted to the government, to undertake here to inquire into the degree of its necessity, would be to pass the line which circumscribes the judicial department, and to tread on legislative ground. This court disclaims all pretensions to such a power. . . .

After the most deliberate consideration, it is the unanimous and decided opinion of this court, that the act to incorporate the Bank of the United States is a law made in pursuance of the constitution, and is a part of the supreme law of the land. . . .

It being the opinion of the Court, that the act incorporating the bank is constitutional; and that the power of establishing a branch in the State of Maryland might be properly exercised by the bank itself, we proceed to inquire—

2. Whether the State of Maryland may, without violating the constitution, tax that branch?

That the power of taxation is one of vital importance; that it is retained by the States; that it is not abridged by the grant of a similar power to the government of the Union; that it is to be concurrently exercised by the two governments: are truths which have never been denied. But, such is the paramount character of the constitution, that its capacity to withdraw any subject from the action of even this power, is admitted. The States are expressly forbidden to lay any duties on imports or exports, except what may be absolutely necessary for executing their inspection laws. If the obligation of this prohibition must be conceded—if it may restrain a state from the exercise of its taxing power on imports and exports, the same paramount character would seem to restrain, as it certainly may restrain, a state from such other exercise of this power, as is in its nature incompatible with, and repugnant to, the constitutional laws of the Union. A law, absolutely repugnant to another, as entirely repeals that other as if express terms of repeal were used.

On this ground the counsel for the bank place its claim to be exempted from the power of a State to tax its operations. There is no express provision for the case, but the claim has been sustained on a principle which so entirely pervades the constitution, is so intermixed with the materials which compose it, so interwoven with its web, so blended with its texture, as to be incapable of being separated from it, without rending it into shreds.

This great principle is, that the constitution and the laws made in pursuance thereof are supreme; that they control the constitution and laws of the respective States, and cannot be controlled by them. From this, which may be almost termed an axiom, other propositions are deduced as corollaries, on the truth or error of which, and on their application to this case, the cause has been supposed to depend. These are, 1. That a power to create implies a power to preserve. 2. That a power to destroy, if wielded by a different hand, is hostile to, and incompatible with, these powers to create and preserve. 3. That where this repugnancy exists, that authority which is supreme must control, not yield to that over which it is supreme. . . .

The power of Congress to create, and of course to continue, the bank, was the subject of the preceding part of this opinion; and is no longer to be considered as questionable.

That the power of taxing it by the States may be exercised so as to destroy it, is too obvious to be denied. But taxation is said to be an absolute power, which acknowledges no other limits than those expressly prescribed in the constitution, and like sovereign power of every other description, is trusted to the discretion of those who use it. . . .

The argument on the part of the State of Maryland, is, not that the states may directly resist a law of Congress, but that they may exercise their acknowledged powers upon it, and that the Constitution leaves them this right in the confidence that they will not abuse it. . . .

. . . That the power to tax involves the power to destroy; that the power to destroy may defeat and render useless the power to create, that there is a plain repugnance, in conferring on one government a power to control the constitutional measures of another, which other, with respect to those very measures, is declared to be supreme over that which exerts the control, are propositions not to be denied. But all inconsistencies are to be reconciled by the magic of the word CONFIDENCE. Taxation, it is said, does not necessarily and unavoidably destroy. To carry it to the excess of destruction would be an abuse, to presume which, would banish that confidence which is essential to all government. . . .

If we apply the principle for which the State of Maryland contends, to the constitution generally, we shall find it capable of changing totally the character of that instrument. We shall find it capable of arresting all the measures of the government, and of prostrating it at the foot of the states. The American people have declared their constitution, and the laws made in pursuance thereof, to be supreme; but this principle would transfer the supremacy, in fact to the States.

If the States may tax one instrument, employed by the government in the execution of its powers, they may tax any and every other instrument. They may tax the mail; they may tax the mint; they may tax patent rights; they may tax the papers of the custom-house; they may tax judicial process; they may tax all the means employed by the government, to an excess which would defeat all the ends of government. This was not intended by the American people. They did not design to make their government dependent on the States. . . .

The question is, in truth, a question of supremacy; and if the right of the States to tax the means employed by the general government be conceded, the declaration that the constitution, and the laws made in pursuance thereof, shall be the supreme law of the land, is empty and unmeaning declamation. . . .

It has also been insisted, that, as the power of taxation in the general and State governments is acknowledged to be concurrent, every argument which would sustain the right of the general government to tax banks chartered by the States, will equally sustain the right of the States to tax banks chartered by the general government.

But the two cases are not on the same reason. The people of all the States have created the general government, and have conferred upon it the general power of taxation. The people of all the States, and the States themselves, are represented in Congress, and, by their representatives, exercise this power. When they tax the chartered institutions of the States, they tax their constituents; and these taxes must be uniform. But when a State taxes the operations of the government of the United States, it acts upon institutions created, not by their own constituents, but by people over whom they claim no control. It acts upon the measures of a government created by others as well as themselves, for the benefit of others in common with themselves. The difference is that which always exists, and always must exist, between the action of the whole on a part, and the action of a part on the whole—between the laws of a government declared to be supreme, and those of a government which, when in opposition to those laws, is not supreme. . . .

The Court has bestowed on this subject its most deliberate consideration. The result is a conviction that the States have no power, by taxation or otherwise, to retard, impede, burden, or in any manner control, the operations of the constitutional laws enacted by Congress to carry into execution the powers vested in the general government. This is, we think, the unavoidable consequence of that supremacy which the constitution has declared. We are unanimously of opinion, that the law passed by the legislature of Maryland, imposing a tax on the Bank of the United States, is unconstitutional and void. . . .

Judgment Reversed.

Niles' Weekly Register Assails the Court, 1819

An insidious dilapidation or violent dismemberment of the American union, together with a consolidation of the reserved rights and powers of the states, is the darling hope that the enemies of liberty, at home and abroad, have hugged to their heart with demoniac fervor and constancy. They have hated and still hate, the freedom of the people of the United States, on the principles with which Satan regarded the happy condition of our first parents in the garden of Eden—their own perverse dispositions not being fitted to participate in an equality of rights, or their inordinate pride rejecting every measure calculated to do away distinctions among men, save in virtue and usefulness. No part of our editorial duty has been performed with more alacrity than to combat with such, and to encourage a confidence in the perpetuity of the confederacy, in its present super-excellent form—to descant upon the inestimable advantages that must flow from a well-balanced system, with an honest administration of its principles for the common good; shewing how every part transmitted intelligence and strength to a general point, from whence the collected wisdom of the nation, with collected force, was re-transmitted to benefit every part of the common family. But, we always contended that the *living principle* was in the virtue of the people, and the sovereignty of the states—and that these were so closely united in giving order to the system, that neither could be dispensed with. The *individuals* of this country having, by the favor of Providence, and patience and per-severance, worked out their emancipation from British despotism, gave up to their state governments certain of their rights for the better preservation of those that they thought proper to retain; and the states, in like manner and for like purposes, agreed to establish a national head, to direct the *general* affairs of the confederation, in peace and in war. Here was a system that we confidently trusted was to confer happiness on many millions of freemen, to the thousandth generation. We discovered nothing which had happened to jeopardize this most splendid inheritance—and never suffered the idea to prevail that the RESERVED rights of the people, or of the states, could be *seriously* compromitted by any act of the national administration, trusting in the virtue of the *ballot* to reform abuses and punish those guilty of them. It was that thus influenced, we have labored so faithfully to build up a NATIONAL CHARACTER, to inspire a *home feeling*, a proud and jealous regard of our rights as men—rights which the people, in obedience to the will of GOD who created them free, cannot legally transfer to the keeping of others. We were aware, nevertheless, of the intrigues of the ambitious and corrupt, and had partially estimated the growing power of the rich and avaricious. We knew that few men were able to restrain, as they ought, any degree of authority which they might acquire over their fellow beings, or apply the compass to prescribe a line beyond which their unruly passions should not pass; still, we thought such might be checked, confused, and dismissed, by a redeeming spirit in the people, to whom *all* were accountable for their conduct in the public affairs.

Having so long entertained such opinions as incontrovertible truths, and as a weak, but honest apostle in the cause of mankind, endeavored to impress them upon all within our reach, the horror of an apprehension that we have deceived ourselves and others, may be better felt than described: it is like to a man discovering the infidelity of his wife whilst she reposes on his bosom, and heart seems united to heart! A deadly blow has been struck at the *sovereignty of the states,* and from a quarter so far removed from the people as to be hardly accessible to public opinion—it is needless to say that we allude to the decision of the supreme court, in the case of McCulloh *versus* the state of Maryland, by which it is established that the states cannot tax the bank of the United States.

We are yet unacquainted with the grounds of this alarming decision, but of this are resolved—that nothing but the tongue of an angel can convince us of its compatibility with the constitution of the United States, in which a power to grant acts of incorporation is not delegated, and all powers not delegated are retained.

Far be it from us to be thought as speaking disrespectfully of the supreme court, or to subject ourselves to the suspicion of a "contempt" of it. We do not impute corruption to the judges, nor intimate that they have been influenced by improper feelings—they are great and learned men: *but still, only men.* And, feeling as we do—as if the very stones would cry out if we did not speak on this subject, we will exercise our right to do it—and declare, that if the supreme court is not mistaken in its construction of the constitution of the United States, or that another definition cannot be given to it by some act of the states—their sovereignty is at the mercy of their creature— congress. . . .

Where are these things to end, and what will be the consequences of them? Every person must see in them a total prostration of the state rights, and the loss of the liberties of the nation, unless the decision turns upon some *point of common* (*not* CONSTITUTIONAL) law, in the special case that has been before the supreme court. . . .

We are awfully impressed with a conviction that the welfare of the union has received a more dangerous wound than fifty *Hartford* conventions, hateful as that assemblage was, could inflict—reaching so close to the *vitals* as seemingly to draw the heart's blood of liberty and safety, and which may be wielded to destroy the *whole revenues,* and so do away the sovereignties of the states. In the progress of this principle, we can easily anticipate the time when some daring scoundrel, having fortified himself by *soul-trading incorporations,* may seize upon these fair countries for a kingdom, and, surrounded with obedient judges and lying priests, punish his opponents, after the manner of European despots, with fines, imprisonment and tortures here, and the terrors of the *lower-world* hereafter. But we will not *despair of the republic,* nor yet *give up the ship;* no alternative, however, is left to preserve the sovereignty of the states but by amending the constitution of the United States, and more clearly defining the *original* intentions of that instrument in several respects, but especially in regard to *incorporations:*— these are evidences of sovereignty; congress has not a sovereign power, except in the cases *specially delegated.*

We repeat it—it is not on account of the bank of the United States that we are thus moved. Our sentiments are on record, that we did not wish the *destruction* of that institution; but, fearing the enormous power of the corporation, we were zealous that an authority to arrest its deleterious influence might be vested in *responsible* hands, *for it has not got any soul.* Yet this solitary institution may not subvert the liberties of our country, and command every one to bow down to it as *Baal;* it is the *principle* of it that alarms us, as operating against the unresigned rights of the states.

Eakin v. Raub, 1825

12 Sergeant & Rawle (Penna. 1825)

I am aware, that a right to declare all unconstitutional acts void, without distinction as to either constitution, is generally held as a professional dogma; but, I apprehend, rather as a matter of faith than of reason. I admit that I once embraced the same doctrine, but without examination, and I shall therefore state the arguments that impelled me to abandon it, with great respect for those by whom it is still maintained. But I may premise, that it is not a little remarkable, that although the right in question has all along been claimed by the judiciary, no judge has ventured to discuss it, except Chief Justice Marshall, ...

I begin, then, by observing that in this country, the powers of the judiciary are divisible into those that are POLITICAL and those that are purely CIVIL. Every power by which one organ of the government is enabled to control another, or to exert an influence over its acts, is a political power. . . . Our judiciary is constructed on the principles of the common law, which enters so essentially into the composition of our social institutions as to be inseparable from them, and to be, in fact, the basis of the whole scheme of our civil and political liberty. In adopting any organ or instrument of the common law, we take it with just such powers and capacities as were incident to it as the common law, except where these are expressly, or by necessary implication, abridged or enlarged in the act of adoption; and, that such act is a written instrument, cannot vary its consequences or construction. . . . Now, what are the powers of the judiciary at the common law? They are those that necessarily arise out of its immediate business; and they are therefore commensurate only with the judicial execution of the municipal law, or, in other words, with the administration of distributive justice, without extending to anything of a political cast whatever. . . . With us, although the legislature be the depository of only so much of the sovereignty as the people have thought fit to impart, it is nevertheless sovereign within the limit of its powers, and may relatively claim the same pre-eminence here that it may claim elsewhere. It will be conceded, then, that the ordinary and essential powers of the judiciary do not extend to the annulling of an act of the legislature. . . .

The constitution of *Pennsylvania* contains no express grant of political powers to the judiciary. But, to establish a grant by implication, the constitution is said to be a law of superior obligation; and, consequently, that if it were to come into collision with an act of the legislature, the latter would have to give way. This is conceded. But it is a fallacy to suppose that they can come into collision *before the judiciary*. . . .

The constitution and the right of the legislature to pass the act, may be in collision. But is that a legitimate subject for judicial determination? If it be, the judiciary must be a peculiar organ, to revise the proceedings of the legislature, and to correct its mistakes; and in what part of the constitution are we to look for this proud pre-eminence? Viewing the matter in the opposite direction, what would be thought of an act of assembly in which it should be declared that the Supreme Court had, in a particular case, put a wrong construction on the constitution of the United States, and that the judgment should therefore be reversed? It would doubtless be thought a usurpation of judicial power. But it is by no means clear, that to declare a law void which has been enacted according to the forms prescribed in the constitution, is not a usurpation of legislative power. . . .

But it has been said to be emphatically the business of the judiciary, to ascertain and pronounce what the law is; and that this necessarily involves a consideration of the constitution. It does so: but how far? If the judiciary will inquire into anything besides the form of enactment, where shall it stop? There must be some point of limitation to such an inquiry. . . .

But, in theory, all the organs of the government are of equal capacity; or, if not equal, each must be supposed to have superior capacity only for those things which peculiarly belong to it; and as legislation peculiarly involves the consideration of those limitations which are put on the law-making power, and the interpretation of the laws when made, involves only the construction of the laws themselves, it follows that the construction of the constitution in this particular belong to the legislature, which ought therefore to be taken to have superior capacity to judge of the constitutionality of its own acts. But suppose all to be of equal capacity, in every respect, why should one exercise a controlling power over the rest? That the judiciary is of superior rank, has never been pretended, although it has been said to be co-ordinate. It is not easy, however, to comprehend how the power which gives law to all the rest, can be of no more than equal rank with one which receives it, and is answerable to the former for the observance of its statutes. Legislation is essentially an act of sovereign power; but the execution of the laws by instruments that are governed by prescribed rules, and exercise no power of volition, is essentially otherwise. . . . It may be said, the power of the legislature, also, is limited by prescribed rules: it is so. But it is, nevertheless, the power of the people, and sovereign as far as it extends. It cannot be said, that the judiciary is co-ordinate merely because it is established by the constitution: if that were sufficient, sheriffs, registers of wills, and recorders of deeds, would be so too. Within the pale of their authority, the acts of these officers will have the power of the people for their support; but no one will pretend, they are of equal dignity with the acts of the legislature. Inequality of rank arises not from the manner in which the organ has been constituted, but from its essence and the nature of its functions; and the legislative organ is superior to every other, inasmuch as the power to will and to command, is essentially superior to the power to act and to obey. . . .

But what I have in view in this inquiry, is the supposed right of the judiciary to interfere, in cases where the constitution is to be carried into effect through the instrumentality of the legislature, and where that organ must necessarily first decide on the constitutionality of its own act. The oath to support the constitution is not peculiar to the judges, but is taken indiscriminately by every officer of the government, and is designed rather as a test of the political principles of the man, than to bind the officer in the discharge of his duty: otherwise it is difficult to determine what operation it is to have in the case of a recorder of deeds, for instance, who, in the execution of his office, has nothing to do with the constitution. But granting it to relate to the official conduct of the judge, as well as every other officer, and not to his political principles, still it must be understood in reference to supporting the constitution, *only as far as that may be involved in his official duty;* and, consequently, if his official duty does not comprehend an inquiry into the authority of the legislature, neither does his oath. . . .

But do not the judges do a positive act in violation of the constitution, when they give effect to an unconstitutional law? Not if the law has been passed according to the forms established in the constitution. The fallacy of the question is, in supposing that the judiciary adopts the acts of the legislature as its own; whereas the enactment of a law and the interpretation of it are not concurrent acts; and as the judiciary is not required to concur in the enactment, neither is it in the breach of the constitution which may be the consequence of the enactment. The fault is imputable to the legislature, and on it the responsibility exclusively rests. . . .

But it has been said, that this construction would deprive the citizens of the advantages which are peculiar to a written constitution, by at once declaring the power of the legislature in practice to be illimitable. . . . But there is no magic or inherent power in parchment and ink, to command respect and protect principles from violation. In the business of government a recurrence to first principles answers the end of an observation at sea with a view to correct the dead reckoning; and for this purpose, a written constitution is an instrument of inestimable value. It is of inestimable value, also, in rendering its first principles familiar to the mass of people; for, after all, there is no effectual guard against legislative usurpation but public opinion, the force of which, in this country is inconceivably great. . . . Once let public opinion be so corrupt as to sanction every misconstruction of the constitution and abuse of power which the temptation of the moment may dictate, and the party which may happen to be predominant, will laugh at the puny efforts of a dependent power to arrest it in its course.

For these reasons, I am of opinion that it rests with the people, in whom full and absolute sovereign power resides, to correct abuses in legislation, by instructing their representatives to repeal the obnoxious act. . . . On the other hand, the judiciary is not infallible; and an error by it would admit of no remedy but a more distinct expression of the public will, through the extraordinary medium of a convention; whereas, an error by the legislature admits of a remedy by an exertion of the same will, in the ordinary exercise of the right of suffrage,—a mode better calculated to attain the end, without popular excitement. . . .

But in regard to an act of [a state] assembly, which is found to be in collision with the constitution, laws, or treaties of the United States, I take the duty of the judiciary to be exactly the reverse. By becoming parties to the federal constitution, the states have agreed to several limitations of their individual sovereignty, to enforce which, it was thought to be absolutely necessary, to prevent them from giving effect to laws in violation of those limitations, through the instrumentality of their own judges. Accordingly, it is declared in the sixth article and second section of the federal constitution, that "This constitution, and the laws of the United States which shall be made in pursuance thereof, and all treaties made, or which shall be made under the authority of the United States, shall be the *supreme* law of the land; and the *judges* in every *state* shall be BOUND thereby; anything in the *laws* or *constitution* of any *state* to the contrary notwithstanding."

This is an express grant of a political power, and it is conclusive to show that no law of inferior obligation, as every state law must necessarily be, can be executed at the expense of the constitution, laws, or treaties of the United States. . . .

Justice Joseph Story Defends Judicial Standards of Interpretation, 1833

In this view of the matter, let us now proceed to consider the rules, by which it ought to be interpreted; for, if these rules are correctly laid down, it will save us from many embarrassments in examining and defining its powers. Much of the difficulty, which has arisen in all the public discussions on this subject, has had its origin in the want of some uniform rules of interpretation, expressly or tacitly agreed on by the disputants. Very different doctrines on this point have been adopted by different commentators; and not unfrequently very different language held by the same parties at different periods. In short, the rules of interpretation have often been shifted to suit the emergency; and the passions and prejudices of the day, or the favor and odium of a particular measure, have not unfrequently furnished a mode of argument, which would, on the one hand, leave the constitution crippled and inanimate, or, on the other hand, give it an extent and elasticity, subversive of all rational boundaries.

Let us, then, endeavor to ascertain, what are the true rules of interpretation applicable to the constitution; so that we may have some fixed standard, by which to measure its powers, and limit its prohibitions, and guard its obligations, and enforce its securities of our rights and liberties.

I. The first and fundamental rule in the interpretation of all instruments is, to construe them according to the sense of the terms, and the intention of the parties. Mr. Justice Blackstone has remarked, that the intention of a law is to be gathered from the words, the context, the subject-matter, the effects and consequence, or the reason and spirit of the law. . . .

Where the words are plain and clear, and the sense distinct and perfect arising on them, there is generally no necessity to have recourse to other means of interpretation. It is only, when there is some ambiguity or doubt arising from other sources, that interpretation has its proper office. There may be obscurity, as to the meaning, from the doubtful character of the words used, from other clauses in the same instrument, or from an incongruity or repugnancy between the words, and the apparent intention derived from the whole structure of the instrument, or its avowed object. In all such cases interpretation becomes indispensable. . . .

II. In construing the constitution of the United States, we are, in the first instance, to consider, what are its nature and objects, its scope and design, as apparent from the structure of the instrument, viewed as a whole, and also viewed in its component parts. Where its words are plain, clear, and determinate, they require no interpretation; and it should, therefore, be admitted, if at all, with great caution, and only from necessity, either to escape some absurd consequence, or to guard against some fatal evil. Where the words admit of two senses, each of which is conformable to common usage, that sense is to be adopted, which, without departing from the literal import of the words, best harmonizes with the nature and objects, the scope and design of the instrument. Where the words are unambiguous, but the provision may cover more or less ground according to the intention, which is yet subject to conjecture; or where it may include in its general terms more or less, than might seem dictated by the general design, as that may be gathered from other parts of the instrument, there is much more room for controversy; and the argument from inconvenience will probably have different influences upon different minds. Whenever such questions arise, they will probably be settled, each upon its own peculiar grounds; and whenever it is a question of power, it should be approached with infinite caution, and affirmed only upon the most persuasive reasons. In examining the constitution, the antecedent situation of the country, and its institutions, the existence and operations of the state governments, the powers and operations of the confederation, in short all the circumstances, which had a tendency to produce, or to obstruct its formation and ratification, deserve a careful attention. Much also, may be gathered from contemporary history and contemporary interpretation, to aid us in just conclusions. . . .

It is obvious, however, that contemporary interpretation must be resorted to with much qualification and reserve. In the first place, the private interpretation of any particular man, or body of men, must manifestly be open to much observation. The constitution was adopted by the people of the United States; and it was submitted to the whole upon a just survey of its provisions, as they stood in the text itself. In different states and in different conventions, different and very opposite objections are known to have prevailed; and might well be presumed to prevail. Opposite interpretations, and different explanations of different provisions, may well be presumed to have been presented in different bodies, to remove local objections, or to win local favor. . . . The known diversity of construction of different parts of it, as well as of the mass of its powers, in the different state conventions; the total silence upon many objections, which have since been started; and the strong reliance upon others, which have since been universally abandoned, add weight to these suggestions. Nothing but the text itself was adopted by the people. And it would certainly be a most extravagant doctrine to give to any commentary then made, and, *à fortiori,* to any commentary since made under a very different posture of feeling and opinion, an authority, which should operate as an absolute limit upon the text, or should supersede its natural and just interpretation. . . .

But to return to the rules of interpretation arising *ex directo* from the text of the constitution. And first the rules to be drawn from the nature of the instrument. It is to be construed, as a *frame,* or *fundamental law* of government, established by the PEOPLE of the United States, according to their own free pleasure and sovereign will. In this respect it is in nowise distinguishable from the constitutions of the state governments. Each of them is established by the people for their own purposes, and each is founded on their supreme authority. The powers, which are conferred, the restrictions, which are imposed, the authorities, which are exercised, the organization and distribution thereof, which are provided, are in each case for the same object, the common benefit of the governed, and not for the profit or dignity of the rulers.

And yet it has been a very common mode of interpretation to insist upon a diversity of rules in construing the state constitutions, and that of the general government. Thus, in the Commentaries of Mr. Tucker upon Blackstone, we find it laid down, as if it were an incontrovertible doctrine in regard to the constitution of the United States, that "as federal, it is to be construed *strictly,*" in all cases, where the antecedent rights of a state may be drawn in question. As a social compact, it ought likewise "to receive the same strict construction, wherever the right of personal liberty, or of personal security, or of private property may become the object of dispute; because every person, whose liberty or property was thereby rendered subject to the new government, *was antecedently a member of a civil society, to whose regulations he had submitted himself, and under whose authority and protection he still remains, in all cases not expressly submitted to the new government.*"

We here see, that the whole reasoning is founded, not on the notion, that the rights of the *people* are concerned, but the rights of the *states.* And by strict construction is obviously meant the most limited sense belonging to the words. And the learned author relies, for the support of his reasoning, upon some rules laid down by Vattel in relation to the interpretation of treaties in relation to *odious* things. It would seem, then, that the constitution of the United States is to be deemed an odious instrument. And why, it may be asked? Was it not framed for the good of the people, and by the people? . . .

. . . The state governments have no right to assume, that the power is more safe or more useful with them, than with the general government; that they have a higher capacity and a more honest desire to preserve the rights and liberties of the people, than the general government; that there is no danger in trusting them; but that all the peril and all the oppression impend on the other side. The people have not so said, or thought; and they have the exclusive right to judge for themselves on the subject. They avow, that the constitution of the United States was adopted by them, "in order to form a more perfect union, establish justice, ensure domestic tranquillity, provide for the common defence, promote the general welfare, and secure the blessings of liberty to themselves and their posterity." It would be a mockery to ask if these are odious objects. If these require every grant of power, withdrawn from the state governments, to be deemed *strictissimi juris,* and construed in the most limited sense, even if it should defeat these objects. What peculiar sanctity have the state governments in the eyes of the people beyond these objects? Are they not framed for the same general ends? Was not the very inability of the state governments suitably to provide for our national wants, and national independence, and national protection, the very groundwork of the whole system? . . .

IV. From the foregoing considerations we deduce the conclusion, that as a frame or fundamental law of government, the constitution of the United States is to receive a reasonable interpretation of its language, and its powers, keeping in view the objects and purposes, for which those powers were conferred. By a reasonable interpretation, we mean, that in case the words are susceptible of two different senses, the one strict, the other more enlarged, that should be adopted, which is most consonant with the apparent objects and intent of the constitution; that, which will give it efficacy and force, as a *government,* rather than that, which will impair its operations, and reduce it to a state of imbecility. Of course we do not mean, that the words for this purpose are to be strained beyond their common and natural sense; but keeping within that limit, the exposition is to have a fair and just latitude, so as on the one hand to avoid obvious mischief, and on the other hand to promote the public good. . . .

If, then, we are to give a reasonable construction to this instrument, as a constitution of government established for the common good, we must throw aside all notions of subjecting it to a strict interpretation, as if it were subversive of the great interests of society, or derogated from the inherent sovereignty of the people. And this will naturally lead us to some other rules properly belonging to the subject.

V. Where the power is granted in general terms, the power is to be construed, as coextensive with the terms, unless some clear restriction upon it is deducible from the context. We do not mean to assert, that it is necessary, that such restriction should be expressly found in the context. It will be sufficient, if it arise by necessary implication. But it is not sufficient to show, that there was, or might have been, a sound or probable motive to restrict it. A restriction founded on conjecture is wholly inadmissible. The reason is obvious: the text was adopted by the people in its obvious, and general sense. We have no means of knowing, that any particular gloss, short of this sense, was either contemplated, or approved by the people; and such a gloss might, though satisfactory in one state, have been the very ground of objection in another. It might have formed a motive to reject it in one, and to adopt it in another. The sense of a part of the people has no title to be deemed the sense of the whole. Motives of state policy, or state interest, may properly have influence in the question of ratifying it; but the constitution itself must be expounded, as it stands; and not as that policy, or that interest may seem now to dictate. We are to construe, and not to frame the instrument.

VI. A power, given in general terms, is not to be restricted to particular cases, merely because it may be susceptible of abuse, and, if abused, may lead to mischievous consequences. This argument is often used in public debate; and in its common aspect addressed itself so much to popular fears and prejudices, that it insensibly acquires a weight in the public mind, to which it is nowise entitled. The argument *ab inconvenienti* is sufficiently open to question, from the laxity of application, as well as of opinion, to which it leads. But the argument from a possible abuse of a power against its existence or use, is, in its nature, not only perilous, but in respect to governments, would shake their very foundation. Every form of government unavoidably includes a grant of some discretionary powers. It would be wholly imbecile without them. It is impossible to foresee all the exigencies, which may arise in the progress of events, connected with the rights, duties, and operations of a government. If they could be foreseen, it would be impossible *ab ante* to provide for them. The means must be subject to perpetual modification, and change; they must be adapted to the existing manners, habits, and institutions of society, which are never stationary; to the pressure of dangers, or necessities; to the ends in view; to general and permanent operations, as well as to fugitive and extraordinary emergencies. In short, if the whole society is not to be revolutionized at every critical period, and remodelled in every generation, there must be left to those, who administer the government, a very large mass of discretionary powers, capable of greater or less actual expansion according to circumstances, and sufficiently flexible not to involve the nation in utter destruction from the rigid limitations imposed upon it by an improvident jealousy. Every power, however limited, as well as broad, is in its own nature susceptible of abuse. No constitution can provide perfect guards against it. Confidence must be reposed some where; and in free governments, the ordinary securities against abuse are found in the responsibility of rulers to the people, and in the just exercise of their elective franchise; and ultimately in the sovereign power of change belonging to them, in cases requiring extraordinary remedies. Few cases are to be supposed, in which a power, however general, will be exerted for the permanent oppression of the people. And yet, cases may easily be put, in which a limitation upon such a power might be found in practice to work mischief; to incite foreign aggression; or encourage domestic disorder. The power of taxation, for instance, may be carried to a ruinous excess; and yet, a limitation upon that power might, in a given case, involve the destruction of the independence of the country.

VII. On the other hand, a rule of equal importance is, not to enlarge the construction of a given power beyond the fair scope of its terms, merely because the restriction is inconvenient, impolitic, or even mischievous. If it be mischievous, the power of redressing the evil lies with the people by an exercise of the power of amendment. If they do not choose to apply the remedy, it may fairly be presumed, that the mischief is less than what would arise from a further extension of the power; or that it is the least of two evils. Nor should it ever be lost sight of, that the government of the United States is one of limited and enumerated powers; and that a departure from the true import and sense of its powers is, *pro tanto,* the establishment of a new constitution. It is doing for the people, what they have not chosen to do for themselves. It is usurping the functions of a legislator, and deserting those of an expounder of the law. Arguments drawn from impolicy or inconvenience ought here to be of no weight. The only sound principle is to declare, *ita lex scripta est,* to follow, and to obey. Nor, if a principle so just and conclusive could be overlooked, could there well be found a more unsafe guide in practice, than mere policy and convenience. Men on such subjects complexionally differ from each other. The same men differ from themselves at different times. Temporary delusions, prejudices, excitements, and objects have irresistible influence in mere questions of policy. And the policy of one age may ill suit the wishes or the policy of another. The constitution is not to be subject to such fluctuations. It is to have a fixed, uniform, permanent construction. It should be, so far at least as human infirmity will allow, not dependent upon the passions or parties of particular times, but the same yesterday, to-day, and for ever. . . .

VIII. No construction of a given power is to be allowed, which plainly defeats, or impairs its avowed objects. If, therefore, the words are fairly susceptible of two interpretations, according to their common sense and use, the one of which would defeat one, or all of the objects, for which it was obviously given, and the other of which would preserve and promote all, the former interpretation ought to be rejected, and the latter be held the true interpretation. This rule results from the dictates of mere common sense; for every instrument ought to be so construed, *ut magis valeat, quam pereat.* For instance, the constitution confers on congress the power to declare war. Now the word *declare* has several senses. It may mean to proclaim, or publish. But no person would imagine, that this was the whole sense, in which the word is used in this connection. It should be interpreted in the sense, in which the phrase is used among nations, when applied to such a subject-matter. A power to declare war is a power to make, and carry on war. It is not a mere power to make known an existing thing, but to give life and effect to the thing itself. The true doctrine has been expressed by the supreme court: "If from the imperfection of human language there should be any serious doubts respecting the extent of any given power, the objects, for which it was given, especially when those objects are expressed in the instrument itself, should have great influence in the construction."

IX. Where a power is remedial in its nature, there is much reason to contend, that it ought to be construed liberally. That was the doctrine of Mr. Chief Justice Jay, in *Chisholm* v. *Georgia;* and it is generally adopted in the interpretation of laws. But this liberality of exposition is clearly inadmissible, if it extends beyond the just and ordinary sense of the terms.

X. In the interpretation of a power, all the ordinary and appropriate means to execute it are to be deemed a part of the power itself. This results from the very nature and design of a constitution. In giving the power, it does not intend to limit it to any one mode of exercising it, exclusive of all others. It must be obvious, (as has been already suggested,) that the means of carrying into effect the objects of a power may, nay, must be varied, in order to adapt themselves to the exigencies of the nation at different times. A mode efficacious and useful in one age, or under one posture of circumstances, may be wholly vain, or even mischievous at another time. Government presupposes the existence of a perpetual mutability in its own operations on those, who are its subjects; and a perpetual flexibility in adapting itself to their wants, their interests, their habits, their occupations, and their infirmities . . . .

In the practical application of government, then, the public functionaries must be left at liberty to exercise the powers, with which the people by the constitution and laws have entrusted them. They must have a wide discretion, as to the choice of means; and the only limitation upon that discretion would seem to be, that the means are appropriate to the end. And this must naturally admit of considerable latitude; for the relation between the action and the end (as has been justly remarked) is not always so direct and palpable, as to strike the eye of every observer. If the end be legitimate and within the scope of the constitution, all the means, which are appropriate, and which are plainly adapted to that end, and which are not prohibited, may be constitutionally employed to carry it into effect. When, then, it is asked, who is to judge of the necessity and propriety of the laws to be passed for executing the powers of the union, the true answer is, that the national government, like every other, must judge in the first instance of the proper exercise of its powers; and its constituents in the last. If the means are within the reach of the power, no other department can inquire into the policy or convenience of the use of them. If there be an excess by overleaping the just boundary of the power, the judiciary may generally afford the proper relief; and in the last resort the people, by adopting such measures to redress it, as the exigency may suggest, and prudence may dictate.

XI. And this leads us to remark, in the next place, that in the interpretation of the constitution there is no solid objection to implied powers. Had the faculties of man been competent to the framing of a system of government which would leave nothing to implication, it cannot be doubted, that the effort would have been made by the framers of our constitution. The fact, however, is otherwise. There is not in the whole of that admirable instrument a grant of powers, which does not draw after it others, not expressed, but vital to their exercise; not substantive and independent, indeed, but auxiliary and subordinate. There is no phrase in it, which like the articles of confederation, excludes incidental and implied powers, and which requires, that every thing granted shall be expressly and minutely described. Even the tenth admendment, which was framed for the purpose of quieting the excessive jealousies, which had been excited, omits the word "expressly," (which was contained in the articles of confederation,) and declares only, that "the powers, not delegated to the United States, nor prohibited by it to the states, are reserved to the states respectively, or to the people"; thus leaving the question, whether the particular power, which may become the subject of contest, has been delegated to the one government, or prohibited to the other, to depend upon a fair construction of the whole instrument. . . .

We may, however, lay down some few rules, deducible from what has been already said, in respect to cases of implied prohibitions upon the existence or exercise of powers by the states, as guides to aid our inquiries. (1.) Wherever the power given to the general government requires, that, to be efficacious and adequate to its end, it should be exclusive, there arises a just implication for deeming it exclusive. Whether exercised, or not, in such a case makes no difference. (2.) Wherever the power in its own nature is not incompatible with a concurrent power in the states, either in its nature or exercise, there the power belongs to the states. (3.) But in such a case, the concurrency of the power may admit of restrictions or qualifications in its nature, or exercise. In its nature, when it is capable from its general character of being applied to objects or purposes, which would control, defeat, or destroy the powers of the general government. In its exercise, when there arises a conflict in the actual laws and regulations made in pursuance of the power by the general and state governments. In the former case there is a qualification engrafted upon the generality of the power, excluding its application to such objects and purposes. In the latter, there is (at least generally) a qualification, not upon the power itself, but only upon its exercise, to the extent of the actual conflict in the operations of each. (4.) In cases of implied limitations or prohibitions of power, it is not sufficient to show a possible, or potential inconvenience. There must be a plain incompatibility, a direct repugnancy, or an extreme practical inconvenience, leading irresistibly to the same conclusion. (5.) If such incompatibility, repugnancy, or extreme inconvenience would result, it is no answer, that in the actual exercise of the power, each party may, if it chooses, avoid a positive interference with the other. The objection lies to the power itself, and not to the exercise of it. If it exist, it may be applied to the extent of controlling, defeating, or destroying the other. It can never be presumed, that the framers of the constitution, declared to be supreme, could intend to put its powers at hazard upon the good wishes, or good intentions, or discretion of the states in the exercise of their acknowledged powers. (6.) Where no such repugnancy, incompatibility, or extreme inconvenience would result, then the power in the states is restrained, not in its nature, but in its operations, and then only to the extent of the actual interference. In fact, it is obvious, that the same means may often be applied to carry into operation different powers. And a state may use the same means to effectuate an acknowledged power in itself, which congress may apply for another purpose in the acknowledged exercise of a very different power. Congress may make that a regulation of commerce, which a state may employ as a guard for its internal policy, or to preserve the public health or peace, or to promote its own peculiar interests. These rules seem clearly deducible from the nature of the instrument; and they are confirmed by the positive injunctions of the tenth amendment of the constitution. . . .

XVIII. And this leads us to remark, in the next place, that it is by no means a correct rule of interpretation to construe the same word in the same sense, wherever it occurs in the same instrument. It does not follow, either logically or grammatically, that because a word is found in one connexion in the constitution, with a definite sense, therefore the same sense is to be adopted in every other connexion, in which it occurs. This would be to suppose, that the framers weighed only the force of single words, as philologists or critics, and not whole clauses and objects, as statesmen, and practical reasoners. And yet nothing has been more common, than to subject the constitution to this narrow and mischievous criticism. Men of ingenious and subtle minds, who seek for symmetry and harmony in language, having found in the constitution a word used in some sense, which falls in with their favorite theory of interpreting it, have made that the standard, by which to measure its use in every other part of the instrument. They have thus stretched it, as it were, on the bed of Procrustes, lopping off its meaning, when it seemed too large for their purposes, and extending it, when it seemed too short. They have thus distorted it to the most unnatural shapes, and crippled, where they have sought only to adjust its proportions according to their own opinions. It was very justly observed by Mr. Chief Justice Marshall, in *The Cherokee Nation* v. *The State of Georgia,* that "it has been said, that the same words have not necessarily the same meaning attached to them, when found in different parts of the same instrument. Their meaning is controlled by the context. This is undoubtedly true. In common language, the same word has various meanings; and the peculiar sense, in which it is used in any sentence, is to be determined by the context." A very easy example of this sort will be found in the use of the word "establish," which is found in various places in the constitution. Thus, in the preamble, one object of the constitution is avowed to be "to establish justice," which seems here to mean to settle firmly, to fix unalterably, or rather, perhaps, as justice, abstractedly considered, must be considered as forever fixed and unalterable, to dispense or administer justice. Again, the constitution declares, that congress shall have power "to establish an uniform rule of naturalization, and uniform laws on the subject of bankruptcies," where it is manifestly used as equivalent to make, or form, and not to fix or settle unalterably and forever. Again, "congress shall have power to establish post-offices and post-roads," where the appropriate sense would seem to be to create, to found, and to regulate, not so much with a view to permanence of form, as to convenience of action. Again, it is declared, that "congress shall make no law respecting an establishment of religion," which seems to prohibit any laws, which shall recognize, found, confirm, or patronize any particular religion, or form of religion, whether permanent or temporary, whether already existing, or to arise in future. In this clause, establishment seems equivalent in meaning to settlement, recognition, or support. . . .

XIX. But the most important rule, in cases of this nature, is, that a constitution of government does not, and cannot, from its nature, depend in any great degree upon mere verbal criticism, or upon the import of single words. Such criticism may not be wholly without use; it may sometimes illustrate, or unfold the appropriate sense; but unless it stands well with the context and subject-matter, it must yield to the latter. While, then, we may well resort to the meaning of single words to assist our inquiries, we should never forget, that it is an instrument of government we are to construe; and, as has been already stated, that must be the truest exposition, which best harmonizes with its design, its objects, and its general structure.

The remark of Mr. Burke may, with a very slight change of phrase be addressed as an admonition to all those, who are called upon to frame, or to interpret a constitution. Government is a practical thing made for the happiness of mankind, and not to furnish out a spectacle of uniformity to gratify the schemes of visionary politicians. The business of those, who are called to administer it, is to rule, and not to wrangle. It would be a poor compensation, that one had triumphed in a dispute, whilst we had lost an empire; that we had frittered down a power, and at the same time had destroyed the republic.

⚓ *E S S A Y S*

While all constitutional historians accept that John Marshall laid the foundations for judicial review, they disagree over the nature of that foundation. Francis N. Stites, a historian at the University of California, San Diego, believes that Marshall's greatest contribution lay in adapting the ambiguous phrases of the Constitution to the circumstances he faced. According to this view, propounded in the first essay, Marshall was a skilled political figure who imposed his own will on the American people.

In the second essay, Christopher Wolfe, a political scientist at Marquette University, reads both Marshall's contribution and the early history of judicial review differently. He believes that Marshall's greatness lay in his ability to read the Constitution faithfully rather than in his judicial activism. Subsequent generations of High Court justices, Wolfe argues, have ignored Marshall's real contribution and turned judicial review into a far broader power than the great chief justice ever intended.

John Marshall and Constitutional Adaptation

FRANCIS N. STITES

John Marshall had supported the Constitution in 1788 because he believed it provided for the kind of sound representative government in which the people chose their leaders on the basis of demonstrated character, judgment, and respectability. But the mounting partisanship, the pandering to popular passions, and the growth of party organizations and newspapers jeopardized the future of the Republic, in his view. "There is a tide in the affairs of nations, of parties, and of individuals," he wrote gloomily during the savage campaign of 1800. "I fear that [tide] of real Americanism is on the ebb." As chief justice for more than a third of a century, Marshall struggled to counteract the pressures of democracy and political parties by establishing the primacy of the principles that had animated the framers of the Constitution. In so doing he established the Supreme Court as a powerful branch of the national government. . . .

Federalists—and Republicans—in 1801 were uncertain about the peaceful transfer of power. Convinced of the fragility of responsible government, Federalists believed that the Jeffersonian "artificers of ruin" planned the systematic destruction of commerce, capital, the military, and the judiciary.

Many Republicans did interpret their victory in 1800 as a mandate for radical reform. Only substantial change could reverse Federalist perversion of the principles of the Revolution. More moderate Republicans, Jefferson and Madison among them, were content to trust in the change of men in government. All Republicans had serious complaints about the Federalist judiciary, but they differed on means of redress. Moderates protested the behavior of partisan judges but did not wish to jeopardize the independence of the judiciary. Deaths and resignations would, in time, bring fair-minded judges to the federal bench. Radicals like William Branch Giles of Virginia argued that nothing short of "an absolute repeal of the whole Judiciary and terminating the present offices and creating a new system" would "redress the evil system." Giles was particularly critical of the "misapplied idea" of judicial independence.

These radical proposals suggested absolute terrorism to Marshall. If this implacable hostility to the judicial and legal systems became a part of the "new order," nothing would be left to check popular passions. Anarchy was just over the horizon.

The posture of the new president was crucial, and Marshall listened with some apprehension to the inaugural address. "Every difference of opinion is not a difference of principle," Jefferson said. "We have called by different names brethren of the same principle. We are all republicans: we are all federalists." The tone of the address, its disparagement of party, clearly placed the new executive among the moderates. Relieved, Marshall thought it "well judged and conciliatory, . . . giving the lie to the violent party declamation which has elected him, but . . . strongly characteristic of the general cast of his political theory."

These two Virginians actually had a great deal in common—beyond a mutual dislike that intensified with the years and the characteristic Virginia carelessness in attire. Both had absorbed the doctrines of liberal individualism set forth by Locke, Montesquieu, and Hume. They believed that society existed to protect the individual's natural rights. They stressed limited government, including separation of powers and an independent judiciary to protect the individual against majority excesses. Both, too, sought to preserve the federal Union, although Marshall worried more about the centrifugal tendencies in the states and Jefferson about the corruption and centralization in the national government.

Their philosophical differences arose from contrary views of human nature. "Those who know human nature, black as it is," Marshall said in his speech on the judiciary at the Virginia Convention in 1788, "must know that mankind . . . are attached to their own interests"—life, liberty of movement and opinion, and the opportunity to acquire property. An ordered and progressive society had to ignore fleeting passions and speculative theories and coldly organize itself to protect these mundane interests. Marshall had no faith in a "victory of reason over passion." He agreed wholeheartedly with Madison's statement in the tenth *Federalist* essay that the "first object of government" was "the protection of different and unequal faculties of acquiring property." Marshall wanted leadership by a natural aristocracy that earned power, wealth, and status in the competitive free market.

Jefferson was more optimistic and humanitarian, more flexible and egalitarian. He preferred the "pursuit of happiness" to the protection of property and was more willing than Marshall to limit the acquisitions of the few to ease the suffering of the many.

Jefferson was as prone as the Federalists to exaggerate his opponents' danger to the Republic. Vexed and disappointed that his old friend Adams had made so many "midnight" appointments, Jefferson determined that this "outrage on decency should not have its effect, except in life appointments [judges] which are irremovable." He immediately replaced the Federalist marshals and attorneys with Republicans. He also reduced Adams's forty-two justices of the peace to thirty but retained twenty-five of the original appointees. One of those eliminated was William Marbury, whose commission Marshall had carelessly failed to deliver. Toward the judges Jefferson remained moderate. His actions through 1801 indicated that he had not yet determined to endorse radical desires to repeal the Judiciary Act of 1801. . . .

At this critical juncture, with Jefferson and moderate congressional Republicans still hesitant, the Federalists blundered in the case of *Marbury* v. *Madison*. Marbury and three other justices of the peace whose commissions Jefferson had refused to deliver brought suit in the Supreme Court seeking a writ of mandamus (an order) requiring Secretary of State Madison to deliver their commissions. On December 17 their attorney presented a preliminary motion for a court ruling requiring Madison to show cause why the writ should not issue against him. After considering the matter for one day, the chief justice gave the Court's opinion, issued the usual order, and assigned the fourth day of the next term for argument on the question of whether Marbury was entitled to the writ.

In ordinary circumstances such a routine petition and order might have passed quietly into obscurity. But December 1801 was not an ordinary time. The timing of the suit and the mounting Federalist anxiety over a probable repeal of the 1801 act suggest that Marbury's suit was part of an effort to intimidate the president by challenging the constitutionality of his refusal to deliver the commissions.

Marshall's first *Marbury* decision excited widespread indignation and was the immediate cause for the repeal of the 1801 Judiciary Act. Even moderate Republicans thought it a "bold stroke" against the executive and a "high-handed exertion of Judiciary power." This preliminary ruling also convinced Jefferson that the pretensions of the judiciary must be curbed. The Federalists had "retired into the Judiciary as a stronghold . . . and from that battery all the works of Republicanism are to be beaten down and erased." The new Congress swiftly moved to repeal. . . .

Federalist threats of Supreme Court action alarmed Republicans. The 1801 act had changed the Supreme Court terms from February and August to December and June. Because the Repeal Act was not to take effect until July, the coming June term would provide an opportunity for a judicial strike. An Amendatory Act in April met that threat by eliminating the June term and establishing one annual term in February. The Court would not meet again until February 1803. The Amendatory Act also increased the number of circuit courts to six. Beyond those changes, the repeal of the 1801 act had simply restored the 1789 act.

Chief Justice Marshall presided over five other Federalists on the Supreme Court. William Cushing of Massachusetts was the last of the original six justices appointed by Washington and the last American to wear the full English judicial wig. William Paterson, a former governor of New Jersey, came to the Court in 1793. Samuel Chase was the most imposing and the most controversial member of the Court. Called "Bacon Face" because of his ruddy complexion, the massive, white-haired Marylander was high-handed, inflammatory, and irascible. His advocacy of the Sedition Act and his harangues to grand juries in sedition trials on circuit made him the symbol of blatant judicial partisanship to Republicans. Marshall's close friend and fellow Virginian Bushrod Washington had come to the Court in 1798. Small in stature and deferential to the chief justice during the thirty-one years he spent on the Bench, Washington was an able judge. Last and least was Alfred Moore. This distinguished North Carolinian was appointed in 1799 and resigned in 1801, leaving practically no trace. . . .

By dispossessing the circuit judges the Repeal Act had raised a serious constitutional question. But Marshall believed that the law must be tolerated and that the 1801 circuit courts should close their doors at the end of their spring sessions. This stance was a frank recognition of political realities. Any partisan move by the Court, real or apparent, would only antagonize the more powerful Republicans. His circumspection was the product of temperament and of a canvass of the other justices' views. Marshall had persuaded his colleagues to abandon seriatim opinions. He wanted the justices to confer on each case, reach a consensus, and speak authoritatively through a single majority opinion rather than express their individual opinions. This impression of impeccable unity would enhance the Court's authority.

Marshall had constitutional scruples about performing circuit court duties and was personally inclined not to resume them, but he was unwilling to refuse "without a consultation of the Judges." Exchanges with Paterson, Cushing, and Washington convinced the chief justice that the majority believed policy dictated acquiescence. Chase alone urged resistance, but in the end that old Federalist diehard deferred to the majority. . . .

But Marshall had acquitted himself well. The Court not only had acted in harmony but also had preserved its independence in the face of intense partisan pressure. . . .

When the Supreme Court began hearing argument in *Marbury* v. *Madison* on February 9, 1803, little evidence suggested that this case would become one of the most important and the most controversial in the Court's history—and the fulcrum for divergent interpretations of the judicial actions of John Marshall. The chief justice did not arrive until the day after the opening of the term on February 7. Cushing was ill and missed the entire argument. Paterson missed the first day, and Moore did not arrive until the last day of testimony on February 12. The disappointments of the preceding fourteen months had dashed Federalist hopes of using the judiciary to cancel the Repeal Act. Jefferson and Madison—more concerned with negotiations leading to the Louisiana Purchase than with arguing a "moot" case—did not even present the government side of the case. Even as a challenge to executive power, the case had lost its significance. In February 1803 Federalist senators had chosen new ground and launched an attack on Jefferson's foreign policy.

Marshall knew that the question of the Court's authority and of its relation to the other branches of government remained unanswered. He knew also that the *Marbury* case presented a unique opportunity to address that question. In addition to its other weaknesses, the Court—as distinct from the judiciary system—suffered from lack of publicity about its decisions. Reporting was unsystematic, and public information about the Court's actions depended upon reliable newspaper accounts. Because the press had riveted public attention to the judiciary since the closing days of the Adams administration, and because the *Marbury* case had long been a source of controversy, the chance existed for a full reporting of this opinion. Marshall devoted his decision of February 24 to a full exposition of the principles of good government.

The opinion answered three questions. Was Marbury entitled to his commission? Yes, said Marshall. Marbury, once appointed and confirmed, had a vested right in the office for the term fixed by statute. The president had no discretionary removal power, and the law required the secretary of state to seal and deliver the commission. Marbury, then, had sustained injury. Was he entitled to a remedy? For Marshall the "very essence of civil liberty" required that every individual have the right to "claim protection of the laws whenever he receives an injury." It was an axiom of Anglo-American law that "every right, when withheld, must have a remedy." The government of the United States, Marshall said, "has been emphatically termed a government of laws, and not of men. It will certainly cease to deserve this high appellation if the laws furnish no remedy for the violation of a vested legal right." And, he emphasized, "the question, whether a right has vested or not, is, in its nature, judicial." Was the remedy a writ of mandamus issuing from the Supreme Court? No! Marshall ruled that Section 13 of the 1789 Judiciary Act, which authorized such writs, was unconstitutional because Congress did not have the power to alter the original jurisdiction of the Supreme Court contained in Article III of the Constitution. The Constitution, he declared in a proclamation of judicial review, is "fundamental and paramount law," and it is "emphatically the province and duty of the judicial department to say what the law is."

Marshall could have first denied the Court's jurisdiction. But reversing the order of questions enabled him to scold the president for disobeying the laws. Then, by denying Marbury the writ, he gave the Republicans what they wanted—but he did so through an assertion of judicial review. Jefferson could do nothing about a decision that in its outcome was favorable.

Politics unquestionably dictated the decision and the opinion. That fact, however, does not mean that Marshall engaged in partisan sniping. The relation of the judiciary to the other branches was a serious political-constitutional problem. Marshall sought to establish "the authoritative place of a liberal Constitution kept authentic by the courts." Viewed in this light, *Marbury* v. *Madison* outlined his plan for preserving limited government against the inroads of an ever more powerful democracy.

The Constitution drafted by the enlightened statesmen at the Philadelphia Convention and ratified by the best talents in the several states at their conventions in 1788 was the product of an aristocracy natural to John Marshall. "The people" had "an original right to establish, for their future government, such principles as, in their opinion, shall most conduce to their own happiness." They had done so in 1787 and 1788. "The exercise of this original right is a very great exertion; nor can it, nor ought it to be frequently repeated. Those principles, therefore, are deemed fundamental" and "are designed to be permanent." The election of 1800 had jeopardized those principles, and Marshall knew that the Court alone could not safeguard them.

Therefore, Marshall shaped his opinion—and used the case—to enunciate fundamental principles. An initial invalidation of Section 13 would have prevented the reminder that the law obliged the president to act in certain cases. Similarly, his forced construction of Section 13 enabled Marshall to assert limits to legislative power in general and over the Court in particular. The Court would review executive and legislative actions to preserve the individual liberties guaranteed by the Constitution. On this and earlier occasions he had admitted a right of the other branches to judge certain categories of constitutional questions. "Questions, in their nature political," he said, "or which are, by the constitution and laws, submitted to the executive [and legislative], can never be made in this court." He did, though, reserve to the Court the final power to determine in individual cases which questions were "political" and which the Court could review. . . .

Jefferson and the moderate Republicans were unperturbed by Marshall's exercise of judicial review. The Court had reviewed a law pertaining only to the judiciary. That action fit perfectly with the Republican view that each branch was competent to decide constitutional questions "in their own spheres of action." . . .

[The Marshall Court's ability to shape the Constitution to meet new demands was underscored sixteen years later. Congress in 1819] was . . . now burdened by old constitutional scruples. Repeated failures to adopt a nationwide system of internal improvements revealed renewed skepticism about implied powers and the old fear of centralized government. The heart of the matter was the relation between the states and the national government. Until the Marshall Court ruled on the scope of congressional power, the capacity of the eighteenth-century Constitution to meet the demands of national growth in the nineteenth century remained unclear. The opportunity for such a ruling came in *McCulloch* v. *Maryland.*

Delirious speculation in land and paper money, overexpansion of manufacturing, the dumping of British goods on the American market, and a precipitous drop in European prices for American produce were but some of the many stages on the road to depression in 1819. Most Americans, however, blamed their economic distress on a single, tempting target—the Second Bank of the United States.

The bank was open to criticism. The nationalistic Congress of 1816 had chartered it to bring order out of monetary chaos. In its first three years this economic colossus enraged the states by establishing branches within their borders without their consent, by competing with state banks in a reckless expansion of credit, and then by bringing a number of those state banks down with a sudden, drastic credit contraction. To make matters worse the branches were guilty of fraud, embezzlement, and general mismanagement. Resentment in the South and West was so intense that state after state imposed heavy taxes on the branches within their borders. By early 1819 public outcry against the "Monster" provoked an unsuccessful congressional effort to repeal the bank's charter.

Maryland's tax brought the "Bank Case" before the Marshall Court. James McCulloch, cashier of the Baltimore branch, refused to pay. The state sued in a widely recognized test case, and, after the bank lost twice in the state courts in 1818, *McCulloch* v. *Maryland* came before the Supreme Court. Few cases attracted such public interest. When the argument began on February 22, the courtroom was suffocatingly packed. Marshall dispensed with the Court's general rule permitting only two lawyers for each side. For nine days, six of the ablest lawyers in the nation argued every facet of the controversy. William Pinkney, Daniel Webster, and Attorney General William Wirt represented the bank; Joseph Hopkinson, Walter Jones, and Luther Martin argued for the state. Pinkney closed the argument with a dazzling three-day performance in his characteristic style—without notes but with plenty of attention to the ladies in the audience.

Four days later on March 17, Marshall delivered the Court's decision upholding the incorporation of the bank and striking down the state tax. The decision was unanimous, but the opinion was unmistakably his. Its ringing defense of implied power and its elaborate discussion of the relation between the nation and the states made it the outstanding statement of his judicial nationalism.

Marshall began with a refutation of the states' rights, strict construction argument. He could not allow the narrow view to shackle the nation's growth and to reduce the Constitution to a "splendid bauble." The Constitution was not a compact between sovereign states but an instrument of government created by the people "in their highest capacity" as sovereign individuals. Reason and the supremacy clause (Article VI) established that the national government, though limited to the enumerated powers, was supreme within its sphere of action. Any lawful act by the Congress took precedence over a state law.

The question remained whether incorporation of the bank, a power not among those enumerated, was a lawful act. A government could not be supreme unless it had broad discretion to choose the means by which to carry out its powers. Implied powers were not forbidden as they had been in the Articles of Confederation. The "necessary and proper" clause, which followed the enumeration of powers in Article I, section 8, gave Congress the power to pass "all laws which shall be necessary and proper for carrying into execution the foregoing powers." Our Constitution, he reminded his audience, was intended for "ages to come" and to be adaptable to the "various *crises* of human affairs." A narrow interpretation of "necessary" would render the nation unable to meet those "exigencies." So, his famous line ran, "Let the end be legitimate, let it be within the scope of the constitution, and all means which are appropriate, which are plainly adapted to that end, which are not prohibited, but consist with the letter and spirit of the constitution, are constitutional."

The chief justice conceded that in general taxation was a concurrent power. But, because "the power to tax involves the power to destroy," the question became one of national supremacy. The "unavoidable consequence of that supremacy" was that the states had no power, "by taxation or otherwise, to retard, impede, burden, or in any manner control, the operation of the constitutional laws enacted by congress to carry into execution the powers vested in the general government." Maryland's tax on the national bank notes was unconstitutional.

There was nothing surprising in this decision upholding the constitutionality of the bank. That question was so old that Pinkney had apologized during his argument for the endless repetition of that "threadbare" topic. The incorporation of the Second Bank of the United States in 1816 showed that even Republicans had abandoned their constitutional scruples on that issue. Even the protection against state taxation was not secure until a battle with Ohio produced another decison five years later.

The chief justice's explanation and his rationale for national supremacy and implied powers made the decision a constitutional landmark. Marshall knew that the Court's influence on the vital question of congressional power depended more on the persuasiveness of its reasoning than on the result in the immediate case. *McCulloch* was certainly persuasive. Its clarity, magisterial dignity, marching logic, memorable phrases, and air of righteous certainty made it seem unanswerable. The timing was also important. Just three weeks before the decision the heated congressional debate over slavery in Missouri joined the storm over *Sturges* to revive states' rights sentiments. *Niles' Weekly Register,* edited by Hezekiah Niles and the most widely read and influential newspaper in the country, blasted the opinion for its deadly blow at state sovereignty and gave *McCulloch* more publicity than any previous judicial decision.

Marshall expected a hostile reception, especially in Virginia, the fountainhead of states' rights and so recently a challenger of the Court's authority. He was not disappointed. Shortly after returning to Richmond in mid-March, he wrote Story, "Our opinion in the bank case has roused the sleeping spirit of Virginia if indeed it ever sleeps." The Virginia politicians had "no objection to a decision in favor of the bank," Marshall wrote Bushrod Washington, but "they required an obsequious, silent opinion without reason" and now pronounced the Court's "heretical reasoning . . . damnable." Marshall's principles, not the bank, rankled Virginians.

The opening salvo in Virginia's attack came when the *Enquirer* published two letters signed "Amphictyon" on March 30 and April 2. Written by William Brockenbrough, a Richmond judge and Junto member, the "Amphictyon" essays denounced Marshall's holding that national power emanated from the people, not the states, and that the "necessary and proper" clause should be broadly interpreted. Marshall was alarmed, because whatever the *Enquirer* published was always widely reprinted. Concerned lest the states' rights poison spread through the Union, he feared that "the constitution [would] be converted into the old confederation."

In June, Spencer Roane wrote a series of articles for the *Enquirer* using the name "Hampden." Predictably he set forth the strict constructionist view that the Union was only a league of sovereign states that had delegated specific powers to the national government. Roane's prestige was too great and the issue too serious for Marshall to let the matter pass in silence. He took up the pen and wrote nine essays in reply. They appeared in the *Gazette* in Alexandria, Virginia, under the pen name "A Friend of the Constitution."

These essays confirmed the depth of his commitment to nationalism. And his careful attention to the details of formal legal learning displayed a breadth of knowledge not usually attributed to the chief justice. Most important, the exhaustive—even tedious—explanation of *McCulloch* removed all doubt about Marshall's intentions on the subject of implied powers.

Roane's principal charge was that Marshall had given the Congress carte blanche. But Marshall denied that he had construed implied powers into a plenary grant to Congress to do whatever it pleased. *Marbury* stressed the limits to executive power but allowed the president discretion in the exercise of his political powers. *McCulloch* applied the same principle to Congress. Marshall never tired of repeating that the Court had not uttered a single syllable supporting an enlargement of congressional power by construction. On the contrary, the letter and spirit of the Constitution imposed judicially enforceable limits. In *McCulloch* he said clearly that the Court would not allow Congress to "adopt measures which are prohibited by the constitution" or to "pass laws for the accomplishment of objects not intrusted to the government."

Between 1819 and 1820, broader social and economic forces such as the Missouri debates over slavery kept the agitation alive. The Virginia legislature passed resolutions in February 1820 denouncing *McCulloch* and instructing Virginia's senators to push for a constitutional amendment creating a new tribunal to adjudicate federal–state problems. John Taylor's *Construction Construed and Constitutions Vindicated,* an able but rambling defense of states' rights, devoted five of its sixteen chapters to a refutation of *McCulloch.* Jefferson applauded Taylor and chastised the Marshall Court as a "subtle corps of sappers and miners constantly working under ground to undermine the foundations of our confederated fabric." . . .

The acidity and virulence of Virginia's attack on the Court greatly distressed the chief justice. It was, he confided to Story, "a masked battery aimed at the government itself." The Court was the weakest governmental branch, "without patronage, & of course without power," and any diminution of its jurisdiction would be a "vital wound" to the Union. Story, like Marshall, feared the spread of heresy and the end of Union. "I trust in God," he wrote to the chief justice, "that the Supreme Court will continue fearlessly to do its duty; & I pray that your invaluable life may be long preserved to guide us in our defense of the Constitution."

Marshall was particularly exasperated by Jefferson's part in the business. It was not difficult, he told Story, to pinpoint the reason for Jefferson's low opinion of the Court. The "great Lama of the mountains" was among the "most ambitious" and "most unforgiving" of men. His great power was over the mass of the people, and every check on the wild impulse of the moment was a check on his own power. Hence the hostility to an independent judiciary. . . .

The Marshall Court was well-equipped to provide a blueprint for enduring growth. It had the advantage of continuous authority, which Congress lacked, and Marshall had built an institution which could speak with authority on important public issues, although only when cases came before it. Nonetheless, the unanimous decisions of 1819 to 1821 had addressed the deep social, economic, and political problems beneath the immediate cases. Marshall's searching discussions of the nature of the Union, of the scope of national power, and of the Court's role had the grand public purpose finely expressed by Story in 1815: "Let us extend the National authority over the whole extent of power given by the Constitution. . . . Let us prevent the possibility of a division, by creating great National interests which shall bind us in an indissoluble chain." Marshall wanted to demonstrate the Constitution's potential to meet the demands of a changing society. . . .

John Marshall and the Faithful Interpretation of the Constitution

CHRISTOPHER WOLFE

. . . Marshall was the greatest judicial representative of the early or traditional approach to constitutional interpretation and judicial review. He served as chief justice for thirty-five years, and his impact was felt above all in constitutional cases. The epitaph given him by his close friend and colleague Justice Joseph Story was that Marshall was "the expounder of the Constitution."

Yet Marshall is generally regarded today as the representative of views that he himself would undoubtedly disown. Commenting on Marshall's dictum that "[j]udicial power is never exercised for the purpose of giving effect . . . to the will of the judge; always for the purpose of giving effect . . . to the will of the law," the renowned modern justice Benjamin Cardozo said that

> [i]t has a lofty sound, it is well and finely said; but it can never be more than partly true. Marshall's own career is a conspicuous illustration of the fact that the ideal is beyond the reach of human faculties to attain. He gave to the constitution of the United States the impress of his own mind; and the form of our constitutional law is what it is, because he moulded it while it was still plastic and malleable in the fire of his own intense convictions.

But even the form of Cardozo's statement indicates that "objectivity" was not in fact Cardozo's ideal. The whole tenor of his remarks on Marshall's "failure" is written in the language of admiration ("the fire of his own intense conviction") rather than of criticism. More important, Cardozo subtly indicates that this "moulding" is inevitable because the Constitution is "still plastic and malleable." . . .

But this attempt to prove from Marshall's own words [in *McCulloch*] that he was intentionally a legislator who "adapted" the Constitution fails to make its case. Marshall's whole discussion of the need for adaptation appears in the context of a discussion of *Congress's* discretion to choose appropriate means to give effect to the powers granted by the Constitution. There is no word in any of Marshall's writings or opinions, nor even in first- or secondhand reports of his conversations, that suggests the duty of judges to adapt the Constitution. The recognition that "it is a *constitution* we are expounding" is no advocacy of judicial legislation, for (as we shall see) an interpreter is not a better interpreter for failing to ask whether he is interpreting a will, a deed, or a constitution—in fact, he will do a poorer job of "merely" interpreting if he does not recognize the subject matter with which he is dealing.

What is amazing is that this view of Marshall, which dismisses his own

From *The Rise of Modern Judicial Review: From Constitutional Interpretation to Judge-Made Law* by Christopher Wolfe, pp. 40–46, 90–94, 97–98, 101, 108–110, 112–113, 116–117. Copyright © 1986 by Basic Books, Inc. Reprinted by permission of Basic Books, Inc., Publishers, New York.

statements as words "well and finely said" but not to be taken seriously, is the prevalent, almost unchallenged understanding of Marshall today. Nor is it a recent view, but one that represents nearly a century of scholarship.

My contrary contention is that Marshall's words are to be taken seriously, and that his greatness lies not in shaping an ambiguous document but in reading a great document faithfully. Marshall's greatness lay in effecting not his own will but the will of the law: the Constitution. . . .

Marshall's Rules of Interpretation

A good place to start in order to understand Marshall's approach to interpreting the Constitution is with the rules of interpretation he employed in his cases. While only a reading of the cases themselves can sufficiently convey a comprehensive sense of his care in examining the document, a summary of the rules he employed can suggest the seriousness of his attempt to conform his interpretation to the meaning of the document itself. . . .

The starting point for interpretation is the examination of the words of the provision at issue. . . .

The words are to be understood in their popular usage, their "use, in the common affairs of the world, or in approved authors," for instance. Since the Constitution is the framework of a government based on the people, its words are to be understood as the people generally would understand them.

One way to obtain the popular usage is to ascertain the generally accepted usage of a word at issue in the practice of American government. . . . [I]n *Marbury* v. *Madison*, Marshall pointed to the practice of the government to illustrate the generally accepted meaning of *appointment* (specifically to determine when an appointment is completed).

Another method of ascertaining meanings of a word is to observe other examples of how it is used in the Constitution. The classic example of this occurs in *McCulloch* v. *Md.* where Marshall showed that the various gradations of *necessity* were known to the framers by pointing to the use (in art. 1, sec. 10) of the words "absolutely necessary." Why use "absolutely" unless the word "necessary" itself has a less rigorous connotation?

One aid in understanding the words employed by Marshall, though at first glance it might seem contrary to reliance on the popular usage, is to refer to the legal usage of words. Some words are connected with legal meanings even in ordinary or popular usage (for instance, there is no "popular" meaning of the term *ex post facto law* other than its ordinary legal meaning). Thus, Marshall cited legal usage of words in some opinions, as for instance in his appeal to Blackstone for the meaning of *contract* in *Fletcher* v. *Peck*.

The interpreter must employ meanings that do not render the provision absurd or meaningless or that leave it utterly without effect. Thus, Marshall noted in *Marbury* v. *Madison* that the definite constitutional division between the Supreme Court's original and appellate jurisdiction would have no operation at all unless it prevented Congress from changing the jurisdiction (that is, giving the Court original jurisdiction in cases other than those specified in the Constitution).

Finally, judges must attend to the implications of words as well as to the immediate or obvious meaning. In common language we hear such phrases as "you can't do this, because you did that." The clear implication of such a statement is that "but for doing that, you could have done this." Much of the meaning of a constitution comes not so much through direct statement as through implication. For example, Congress has power "to regulate commerce with foreign Nations, and among the several States, and with the Indian Tribes." This is an enumeration (it does not simply say the power "to regulate commerce") and therefore it may be presumed to exclude something, since otherwise the enumeration is useless. . . .

If the words of the document are clear, then the judges are bound and can do no more than apply them: "If, indeed, such be the mandate of the constitution, we have only to obey. . . ." Given, however, the "imperfection of human language," the judges may need more guidance than the words alone can provide. Where is this to be obtained? In such cases, said Marshall, "it is a well-settled rule that the objects for which it [a power] was given, especially when those objects are expressed in the instrument itself, should have great influence in the construction." Or, to use an example in which Marshall expands upon this rule, "in its construction, the subject, the context, [and] the intention of the person using them [the words], are all to be taken into view."

The easiest or most obvious of these three factors is the "context." There are several ways in which the context can be used. In *McCulloch,* for instance, Marshall relies on the narrow or immediate context of the phrase: the meaning or sense of the word *necessary* can be inferred from its connection with *proper* in the "necessary and proper clause." Since *proper* is broader or less restrictive than *necessary* ("do whatever is proper" involving more discretion than "do whatever is necessary"), the conjunction of the two suggests that *necessary* is being used in its less restrictive sense (not what is "absolutely necessary," but what is "conducive to" or useful to the end).

Another way of using context would be by observing the placement of a provision within the Constitution as a whole. By appealing to this criterion, Marshall was able to rely in *McCulloch* on the position of the necessary and proper clause in article 1, section 8 (not section 9) to defend his position that it is a grant of power rather than a restriction of power, thus making the less restrictive sense of *necessary* a more likely interpretation.

A final way of using context could be to study the position of a phrase in the kind of constitution the United States has. An example of this is Marshall's opinion in *Barron* v. *Baltimore* in which he supported his argument that the Fifth Amendment (and the rest of the Bill of Rights) does not apply to the states by noting the character of the U.S. Constitution: "The constitution was ordained and established by the people of the United States for themselves, for their own government and not for the government of the individual states." Thus, the Constitution's limitations are applicable to the "government created by the instrument."

This final and broadest sense of *context* brings us to the next factor mentioned in *McCulloch*: the subject matter. It is only common sense to relate the words being used to the subject under discussion if there is doubt about their meaning when taken alone. The word *contracts* can refer to the subject of marriage or that of commerce, and the subject under discussion will often indicate which meaning is intended.

In discussing the "subject-matter" of the Constitution, Marshall dealt particularly with two kinds of considerations (though these may be subdivided and may overlap): the nature of a constitution and the requirements of government.

Marshall's discussion of the nature of a constitution occurs especially in his two best-known cases: *Marbury* and *McCulloch*. . . . The Constitution is a particular kind of document and its nature or proper characteristics can be an aid to interpretation. In this case, Marshall argued that a constitution depends on a kind of popular action that is difficult to obtain and therefore necessarily infrequent, and that the intention of the makers of a constitution, given that difficulty and infrequency, must have been to establish *fundamental* principles that look to the distant future and not merely the moment. . . .

Marshall's most famous discussion of the nature of a constitution occurs in *McCulloch* v. *Md.*

> A constitution, to contain an accurate detail of all the subdivisions of which its great powers will admit, and of all the means by which they may be carried into execution, would partake of the prolixity of a legal code, and could scarcely be embraced by the human mind. It would probably never be understood by the public. Its nature, therefore, requires, that only its great outlines should be marked, its important objects designated, and the minor ingredients which compose those objects be deduced from the nature of the objects themselves. That this idea was entertained by the framers of the American constitution, is not only to be inferred from the nature of the instrument, but from the language. Why else were some of the limitations, found in the ninth section of the 1st article, introduced? It is also, in some degree, warranted by their having omitted to use any restrictive term which might prevent its receiving a fair and just interpretation. In considering this question, then, we must never forget that it is a *constitution* we are expounding.

Something like a "necessary and proper clause" is implicit in the nature of a constitution because governmental means could hardly all be specified in the document, and especially in the fundamental law of a democratic republic that must be "understood by the public."

Together with the consideration of the "nature of a written constitution," "the requirements of government" is an implicit part of the subject matter of constitutional provisions. This is the source of Marshall's considerations in several cases, in which he took into account the possible broad consequences of particular interpretations. . . .

[Marshall's views on constitutional interpretation are important as a limit] on judicial power in early American history if one realizes that judicial review was not then the unquestioned power that it has become. Defenders of judicial review had to make their argument strongly and to defend themselves from powerful counterattacks by exponents of other positions. . . .

The best exposition of the doctrine of legislative supremacy in early American history is generally thought to be Pennsylvania chief justice John Gibson's dissent in *Eakin* v. *Raub,* a case that dealt with judicial review in Pennsylvania state courts, but addressed itself to federal power and *Marbury* v. *Madison* as well.

Gibson distinguished between political powers (those used by one organ of government to control another) and civil powers (the ordinary and appropriate powers of a government organ according to the common law), on the principles of which our political and social institutions rest. Common law judicial powers extend only to enforcing ordinary law, and do not include any "political" powers. Does the Constitution expressly grant the power of judicial review? With one exception to be noted later, the answer is no.

The argument for judicial review has been that it is implied in the Constitution. As the Constitution is a superior law, it takes precedence in the event of a collision between it and an ordinary statute. But the question, said Gibson, is whether the collision can occur before the judiciary. On what grounds does the judiciary undertake to revise the proceedings of the legislature? If judicial review is a legitimate implication, would the same reasoning justify a legislative act overturning a judicial decision on the grounds that it misinterpreted the Constitution? Such a legislative act would be regarded by all as a usurpation of judicial power, and thus judicial review may also be regarded as usurpation of legislative power.

Each organ of government is equal, said Gibson, or at least has a superior capacity for its own functions.

> Since legislation peculiarly involves the consideration of those limitations which are put on the law-making power . . . it follows that the construction of the constitution in this particular belongs to the legislature, which ought therefore to be taken to have superior capacity to judge of the constitutionality of its own acts.

But can it even be said that the judiciary is equal? Is the power that gives the law for all the others only equal to those who receive and must obey the law? Even if all the branches equally owe their existence to the Constitution, the "essence and nature of its functions" make the legislature "superior to every other, inasmuch as the power to will and to command, is essentially superior to the power to act and obey. . . ."

Gibson argued that checks and balances have been carried too far, beyond the framer's intentions. The main check on the legislature was bicameralism. If judicial review had been intended, "the matter surely would not have been left in doubt . . . [but] have been placed on the impregnable ground of an express grant."

Nor is the argument helped by maintaining that the power is "restricted to cases that are free from doubt or difficulty. The abstract existence of the power cannot depend on the clearness or the obscurity of the case in which it is to be exercised." Such an argument "betrays a doubt of the propriety of exercising it at all."

The oath is no argument for judicial review, being intended merely to be "a test of the political principles of the man," taken by all government officials, not just judges. Even if those who take it are bound in their official conduct, the judges' official conduct should not be taken to include judicial review. The judges do not violate the Constitution by giving effect to an unconstitutional law, since enactment and interpretation are separate acts. It is the legislature alone that is responsible for the content of the law.

Does legislative supremacy take away the advantage of a written constitution by making legislative power in practice unlimited? Not at all, asserted Gibson. The chief benefit of a constitution is that it provides first principles to which the people can recur, and it renders them familiar to the citizens. In the end, after all, it is public opinion that will prevent constitutional abuses, and without the force of public opinion, the power of the judiciary would be ineffective.

Where then does the power of correcting abuses of the Constitution lie? According to Gibson, it lies "with the people, in whom full and absolute sovereign power resides . . . by instructing their representatives to repeal the obnoxious act." Gibson acknowledged that there might be some arguments for giving such a power to the judiciary: they have "habits of deliberation, and the aid derived from the arguments of counsel." But there are arguments against such judicial power too. While legislative errors can be corrected by ordinary law (and elections), judicial errors would require remedy through "the extraordinary medium of a convention." Moreover, Gibson said, the legislature is the branch closest to the people, and "it is a postulate in the theory of our government, and the very basis of the superstructure, that the people are wise, virtuous, and competent to manage their own affairs."

There is, however, one kind of "political" power that the judges have been accorded by the Constitution. Judges can strike down the acts of state assemblies that contradict the Constitution. This is specifically provided for in the Constitution itself, in article 6: judges are bound by the U.S. Constitution and laws, irrespective of state constitutions and laws.

Interestingly, Gibson eventually abandoned his position, citing as his reasons in an 1845 case, the tacit acceptance of judicial review by a subsequent Pennsylvania constitutional convention and "experience of the necessity of the case." While the latter phrase is unclear, perhaps it refers to the difficulties created for a judge when he must adjudicate a law that is clearly unjust and clearly violative of a constitutional provision.

Nonetheless his argument remains a powerful one. . . .

Judicial Review and Its Competitors: A Dialectic

An examination of the strengths and weaknesses of the arguments for judicial review, legislative supremacy, and coordinate review leads to the conclusion that judicial review is the correct constitutional doctrine. On the other hand, such an examination also suggests a particular understanding of the scope of judicial review.

Judicial review is founded on the principle of limited government, in which the limits are placed especially on the most powerful branch of the government, the legislature. The perception that the "most dangerous branch" was the legislature dominated the Convention of 1787 and such defenses of the Constitution as the *Federalist*. This was something of a shift from the primary fear of executive tyranny that had informed the state constitutional conventions of 1776 to 1787 in reaction to the antimonarchic sentiment of the Revolution. The state constitutions went so far in the direction of legislative power that even such strong democrats as Jefferson reacted against it. This prevailing fear of excessive legislative power undermines the case for legislative supremacy, and suggests that the interpretation of limits on the legislature would likely have been granted by the framers to a different branch.

The general understanding that "interpretation" of law was an essential and ordinary activity of judges would seem to suggest that the framers intended to place the power in their hands. However much the legislature and judiciary might have to do some incidental "interpreting" in their functions, common opinion associates interpretation peculiarly with judges, and rightly so.

Of the textual bases for judicial review, the strongest is undoubtedly the clause that extends the judicial power to all cases arising under the Constitution; the breadth of this clause is difficult to explain by any interpretation other than judicial review. The supremacy clause also provides strong support, (1) by indicating that the Constitution and federal laws are both part of the supreme *law* (undercutting somewhat Gibson's attempt to characterize constitution and statute as qualitatively different "laws"), (2) by referring to laws made in pursuance of the Constitution (difficult to explain in a way other than that there are laws void for unconstitutionality, since reading it as referring to the proper "form of enactment" makes its command obvious and unnecessary), and (3) by addressing itself particularly to judges (albeit state judges) and thus confirming the idea that judges have a particular responsibility in the interpretation of the Constitution and laws.

The oath is a weaker support for judicial review since it suggests a line of reasoning distinctly opposed to such review. At first glance it seems to suggest that judges should not give effect to unconstitutional laws, but, at the same time, it might suggest that no one who takes an oath should do so, thus suggesting coordinate review.

Gibson hit on another weak point in the argument when he tried to draw an unacceptable conclusion from its premises. Granting that a legislative act contrary to the Constitution may be voided by the judiciary, should not the legislature be able to void a judicial act that is unconstitutional?

One response might be that legislation precedes adjudication and that the judges act after the legislative act, whereas legislative action to reverse a final judicial decision is not appropriate because legislative action does not follow judicial action in the normal course of things. . . .

Judicial review, based on the principles of limited government and the principle that judges have a peculiar right and duty to interpret law, and supported by strong textual implications in article 3 and article 6, is ultimately the most reasonable interpretation of the Constitution. But this is so only on the condition that it not lead to an unqualified judicial supremacy in our government that could destroy the principles of republicanism and separation of powers. That is, judicial review is the proper resolution in the debate as to who should authoritatively interpret the Constitution, but that resolution must in some sense "pay its respects" to the principles underlying competing positions. . . .

Judicial review "won out" in early American history after genuine struggles, but the *form* in which it won was critical to its success. In a different form, it is likely that it would not have survived. The form it took was "moderate" judicial review, and the major qualifying components it incorporated were inherent limits of judicial power, legislative deference, and the political questions doctrine. . . .

Moderate judicial review is so called because of its very nature (ascertainment of constitutional violations through interpretation) and because of its acknowledged limitations in accord with the principles concerning legislative deference and political questions. This is the form of judicial review dominant in early American history—"mainstream" judicial review.

But if there were competitors with moderate judicial review on the "anti–judicial review" side, so there were competitors on the "ultra–judicial review" side. A more expansive notion of judicial review existed beside the mainstream, and helped eventually to pave the way for the demise of moderate judicial review. This notion was judicial review on the basis, not of violations of the Constitution itself, but of "principles of natural justice" even where these were not embodied (explicitly or implicitly) in the Constitution itself.

It is very important to make it clear from the beginning that the question here is not a dispute between those who believed in principles of natural justice and those who did not believe in them. *All* early Americans believed in such principles, and many believed that the Constitution was an embodiment of the most important ones. The question was whether or not judges could appeal to those principles of natural justice *even when they were not embodied in the Constitution* in order to declare an act unconstitutional.

My thesis in regard to this question is that such a form of judicial review did exist during early American history but that it was very rare (much rarer even than "mainstream" judicial review) and was usually combined with an argument from the Constitution itself or was sometimes simply *dicta.* These factors, I think, justify my characterization of it as outside the mainstream of early U.S. constitutional history. . . .

It is also true that the greatest constitutional jurist of the founding, Marshall, did flirt with principles of natural justice on one occasion, in *Fletcher*. Yet apparent on the face of Marshall's argument was a hesitation to put forward this argument as conclusive, in statements such as: "certain great principles . . . ought not to be *entirely* disregarded," "[i]t *may well be doubted* whether the nature of society and of government does not prescribe some limits to the legislative power; and, *if any* be prescribed, . . ." whether this act "be in the nature of the legislative power, is well *worthy of serious reflection*," "[t]he validity of this rescinding act, then, *might* well be doubted, . . ." and "*either* by general principles . . . *or* by the particular provisions" (emphasis added).

The impression of ambivalence is confirmed by the absence of appeals to natural justice (other than that included in the Constitution) in Marshall's opinions after *Fletcher*. This is true even of such cases as *Dartmouth College v. Woodward*, in which there seemed to be no less ground for relying on principles of natural justice than in *Fletcher*, but where Marshall employed only the contract clause. One can only speculate about the reasons for Marshall's ambivalence on the issue, but it seems likely that one factor would be the strength of reasoning such as Iredell's.

Last, when examining extensive discussions of judicial review by eminent jurists such as Story in his *Commentaries on the Constitution*, we find that the entire discussion seems to be discussed in terms of judicial review as described in *Marbury*. We look through such a discussion in vain, on the other hand, for a defense of judicial review based on a notion of natural rights *apart from* the Constitution.

Thus, it is possible to conclude that the normal or primary understanding of judicial review in the founding period, the predominant view, was that of *Federalist* No. 78, *Marbury* v. *Madison,* and [not judicial review based on natural justice] that was to win out, in the modern era. . . .

Conclusion

Moderate judicial review in early American history was different from "judicial supremacy." It acknowledged definite limits on itself in an effort to harmonize judicial power and independence with the legitimate autonomy of coordinate branches and the ultimate authority of the people. By this means it was hoped that the balance of our "balanced republic" could be maintained.

The subsequent history of our nation suggests that this hope was not realized, for it is a history of consistent expansion of judicial power (with only brief ebbs of judicial power for limited periods). This expansion was possible partly because "seeds" of a more expansive judicial power were sown in early American history; partly because it was a very gradual process over time, which masked the change (especially to the nonlegal public);

partly because it was carried out by a federal judiciary that was, on the whole, characterized by considerable personal and professional integrity; and partly because such a change happened to fit nicely the political agenda of influential groups during the period.

In fact, the institutional feature of American government that is referred to as "judicial review" has fundamentally changed its nature in the course of American history. . . .

✣ *F U R T H E R   R E A D I N G*

Raoul Berger, *Government by Judiciary: The Transformation of the Fourteenth Amendment* (1977)

Alexander Bickel, *The Least Dangerous Branch: The Supreme Court at the Bar of Politics* (1962)

Charles L. Black, *Structure and Relationship in Constitutional Law* (1969)

Jesse H. Choper, *Judicial Review and the National Political Process: A Functional Reconsideration of the Role of the Supreme Court* (1980)

Don E. Fehrenbacher, *The Dred Scott Case: Its Significance in American Law and Politics* (1978)

Kermit L. Hall, ed., *Judicial Review in American History: Major Historical Interpretations* (1987)

———, *The Supreme Court and Judicial Review in American History* (1985)

George L. Haskins and Herbert A. Johnson, *Foundations of Power: John Marshall, 1801–1815;* vol. II of *The Oliver Wendell Holmes Devise History of the Supreme Court of the United States* (1981)

Leonard W. Levy, "Judicial Review, History, and Democracy," in Levy, ed., *Judgments: Essays on American Constitutional History* (1972)

Gary L. McDowell, *Curbing the Courts: The Constitution and the Limits of Judicial Power* (1988)

Herbert Wechsler, "Toward Neutral Principles of Constitutional Law," *Harvard Law Review* 73 (1959): 1–41

G. Edward White, *The Marshall Court and Cultural Change, 1815–1835* (1988)

CHAPTER
8

Andrew Jackson, the Presidency, and Separation of Powers

⁜

The delegates to the Philadelphia convention in 1787 wanted to strengthen the central government without significantly diminishing either individual liberty or state sovereignty. Hence they adopted a scheme of separation of powers and checks and balances. The duties they spelled out in Article II empowered the new chief executive. The president was to be elected indirectly by the people through an electoral college composed of members from each state, with the number of delegates dependent on the state population. The president was to share certain powers, such as the appointment of judges and other high officials and the making of war, with the Congress. This hedging of presidential power reflected the ambivalence of late-eighteenth-century Americans about leadership. They recognized that the new nation would benefit from continuous, effective, and unified administration of government, but they also worried that, as the nation grew in population and territory, these same qualities might create an opportunity for one person to accumulate power sufficient to re-create the monarchical forms of Great Britain's government.

George Washington, for example, played a crucial role in developing the presidency because his actions in foreign and domestic affairs established important precedents on which subsequent presidents built. Not every president took the opportunity to expand on these precedents. Ironically, Thomas Jefferson was one who did. While a member of the emerging Republican opposition in the 1790s, Jefferson had warned against presidential power and a strong national government. Once in power, however, Jefferson contributed to the growth of the office and national authority. He negotiated the purchase of the Louisiana Territory and enforced the Embargo Act of 1807, which halted much American shipping abroad through 1809. Both measures, of course, substantially expanded congressional as well as presidential powers.

Between the end of Jefferson's administration in 1809 and the outbreak of the Civil War in 1861, Andrew Jackson contributed more than any other chief executive to the growth of the presidency. "Old Hickory" first ran for the presidency in 1824 but lost a contested election to John Quincy Adams in a highly controversial vote by the House of Representatives. Jackson charged that several

House members had engaged in a corrupt bargain that denied him victory. Four years later, Jackson turned this affair to his popular advantage and won the White House. Many scholars date the beginning of the modern presidency from Jackson's election in 1828 because, more than his predecessors, Old Hickory tested the bounds of separation of powers.

Jackson's principal weapon was the veto. The authors of the first state constitutions had sharply limited the executive veto. But the framers in Philadelphia, seeking a means of curbing legislative excesses, settled on the veto as the most appropriate tool. Whereas early presidents exercised this power only reluctantly, Jackson believed that he had the right to substitute his judgment for that of the Congress, and he took great pleasure in describing himself as the "tribune of the people." During his eight years in office, Jackson vetoed twelve measures, more than those of all his predecessors combined.

Jackson's presidential behavior also encouraged the rise of a new two-party system. Jackson's Democratic followers were committed to Jeffersonian ideals of limited government, low taxes and tariffs, and hostility to monopolies. Their Whig opponents believed in an active national government to promote economic development. By the time Jackson left office in 1837, the party battles between Democrats and Whigs demonstrated that the concept of a loyal opposition had been established in American politics, and that the constitutional doctrine of separation of powers encompassed more authority for the president than had theretofore been the case.

✠ D O C U M E N T S

In the first document, from Jackson's first message to Congress on December 8, 1829, the new president lays bare his major democratic faith that he is the "tribune of the people." An important theme of his message is his insistence, in light of his own experience with the election of 1824, on making the method of selecting the president and the vice president more responsive to popular will.

The two most famous of Jackson's vetoes dealt with the Maysville Road and the rechartering of the Second Bank of the United States. These documents, reprinted here as the second and third selections, remain classic statements of presidential power. In both instances, Jackson dresses up his expansive view of the presidency in the garb of dual federalism. This doctrine held that there existed mutually exclusive and reciprocally limiting spheres of state and federal power. Thus, neither the federal nor the state governments were superior in any categorical sense. Jackson's message vetoing the Second Bank of the United States is also important because it rejected the idea that the Supreme Court's opinions were final and binding on the other branches of government.

The documents of the nullification crisis make clear that Jackson and his followers also believed in federal sovereignty. Jackson placed his presidential authority behind the seemingly contradictory ideas that the Constitution should be construed narrowly in favor of the states while the Union itself was perpetual.

Jackson's tough stance on several issues drew increasing political and constitutional fire. In the fourth document, Senator John Tyler of Virginia—who a decade later as president adopted a veto program every bit as aggressive as that of Jackson—expresses in an 1834 letter to Dr. Henry Curtis the concern that many Whigs felt about "King Andrew." In the fifth document, dating from 1834, Whig Senator Daniel Webster calls into question the entire idea that the president was more fully empowered by the people than was the Congress. Perhaps no other figure so ably captured the constitutional changes wrought by Jackson's presidency than Alexis de Tocqueville, a French visitor to America in the mid-1830s. Tocqueville's commentary in the sixth selection offers important comparisons with the monarchical systems of Europe. Americans understood that Jackson's approach to the issue of separation of powers had altered the fundamental nature of constitutional relationships, a fact that is underscored in the final document, the brief yet prescient comments of Charles Francis Adams, a Massachusetts Whig, who criticized not only the growing openness of government but the increasing subordination of Congress and the courts to the presidency.

President Andrew Jackson
on the People's Rights, 1829

. . . I consider it one of the most urgent of my duties to bring to your attention the propriety of amending that part of our Constitution which relates to the election of President and Vice President. Our system of government was, by its framers, deemed an experiment; and they, therefore, consistently provided a mode of remedying its defects.

To the People belongs the right of electing their Chief Magistrate: it was never designed that their choice should, in any case, be defeated, either by the intervention of electoral colleges, or by the agency confided, under certain contingencies, to the House of Representatives. Experience proves, that, in proportion as agents to execute the will of the People are multiplied, there is danger of their wishes being frustrated. Some may be unfaithful: all are liable to err. So far, therefore, as the People can, with convenience, speak, it is safer for them to express their own will.

The number of aspirants to the Presidency, and the diversity of the interests which may influence their claims, leave little reason to expect a choice in the first instance: and, in that event, the election must devolve on the House of Representatives, where, it is obvious, the will of the People may not be always ascertained; or, if ascertained, may not be regarded. From the mode of voting by States, the choice is to be made by twenty-four votes; and it may often occur, that one of these will be controlled by an individual representative. Honors and offices are at the disposal of the successful candidate. Repeated ballotings may make it apparent that a single individual holds the cast in his hand. May he not be tempted to name his reward? But even without corruption—supposing the probity of the Representative to be proof against the powerful motives by which it may be assailed—the will of the People is still constantly liable to be misrepresented. One may err from ignorance of the wishes of his constituents; another, from a conviction that it is his duty to be governed by his own judgment of the fitness of the candidates: finally, although all were inflexibly honest—all accurately informed of the wishes of their constituents—yet, under the present mode of election, a minority may often elect the President; and when this happens, it may reasonably be expected that efforts will be made on the part of the majority to rectify this injurious operation of their institutions.

But although no evil of this character should result from such a perversion of the first principle of our system—*that the majority is to govern*—it must be very certain that a President elected by a minority cannot enjoy the confidence necessary to the successful discharge of his duties.

In this, as in all other matters of public concern, policy requires that as few impediments as possible should exist to the free operation of the public will. Let us, then, endeavor so to amend our system, that the office of Chief Magistrate may not be conferred upon any citizen but in pursuance of a fair expression of the will of the majority.

I would therefore recommend such an amendment of the Constitution as may remove all intermediate agency in the election of President and Vice President. The mode may be so regulated as to preserve to each State its present relative weight in the election; and a failure in the first attempt may be provided for, by confining the second to a choice between the two highest candidates. In connexion with such an amendment, it would seem advisable to limit the service of the Chief Magistrate to a single term, of either four or six years. If, however, it should not be adopted, it is worthy of consideration whether a provision disqualifying for office the Representatives in Congress on whom such an election may have devolved, would not be proper.

While members of Congress can be constitutionally appointed to offices of trust and profit, it will be the practice, even under the most conscientious adherence to duty, to select them for such stations as they are believed to be better qualified to fill than other citizens; but the purity of our Government would doubtless be promoted, by their exclusion from all appointments in the gift of the President in whose election they may have been officially concerned. The nature of the judicial office, and the necessity of securing in the Cabinet and in diplomatic stations of the highest rank, the best talents and political experience, should, perhaps, except these from the exclusion.

There are perhaps few men who can for any great length of time enjoy office and power, without being more or less under the influence of feelings unfavorable to the faithful discharge of their public duties. Their integrity may be proof against improper considerations immediately addressed to themselves; but they are apt to acquire a habit of looking with indifference upon the public interests, and of tolerating conduct from which an unpractised man would revolt. Office is considered as a species of property; and Government, rather as a means of promoting individual interests, than as an instrument created solely for the service of the People. Corruption in some, and, in others, a perversion of correct feelings and principles, divert Government from its legitimate ends, and make it an engine for the support of the few at the expense of the many. The duties of all public officers are, or, at least, admit of being made, so plain and simple, that men of intelligence may readily qualify themselves for their performance; and I cannot but believe that more is lost by the long continuance of men in office, than is generally to be gained by their experience. I submit therefore to your consideration, whether the efficiency of the Government would not be promoted, and official industry and integrity better secured, by a general extension of the law which limits appointments to four years.

In a country where offices are created solely for the benefit of the People, no one man has any more intrinsic right to official station than another. Offices were not established to give support to particular men, at the public expense. No individual wrong is therefore done by removal, since neither appointment to, nor continuance in, office, is matter of right. The incumbent became an officer with a view to public benefits; and when these require his removal, they are not to be sacrificed to private interests. It is the People, and they alone, who have a right to complain, when a bad officer is substituted for a good one. He who is removed has the same means of obtaining a living, that are enjoyed by the millions who never held office. The proposed limitation would destroy the idea of property, now so generally connected with official station; and although individual distress may be sometimes produced, it would, by promoting that rotation which constitutes a leading principle in the republican creed, give healthful action to the system. . . .

President Jackson Vetoes the Maysville Road Bill, 1830

To the House of Representatives.

Gentlemen: I have maturely considered the bill proposing to authorize "a subscription of stock in the Maysville, Washington, Paris, and Lexington Turnpike Road Company," and now return the same to the House of Representatives, in which it originated, with my objections to its passage. . . .

The constitutional power of the Federal Government to construct or promote works of internal improvement presents itself in two points of view—the first as bearing upon the sovereignty of the States within whose limits their execution is contemplated, if jurisdiction of the territory which they may occupy be claimed as necessary to their preservation and use; the second as asserting the simple right to appropriate money from the National Treasury in aid of such works when undertaken by State authority, surrendering the claim of jurisdiction. In the first view the question of power is an open one, and can be decided without the embarrassments attending the other, arising from the practice of the Government. Although frequently and strenuously attempted, the power to this extent has never been exercised by the Government in a single instance. It does not, in my opinion, possess it; and no bill, therefore, which admits it can receive my official sanction.

But in the other view of the power the question is differently situated. The ground taken at an early period of the Government was "that whenever money has been raised by the general authority and is to be applied to a particular measure, a question arises whether the particular measure be within the enumerated authorities vested in Congress. If it be, the money requisite for it may be applied to it; if not, no such application can be made." The document in which this principle was first advanced is of deservedly high authority, and should be held in grateful remembrance for its immediate agency in rescuing the country from much existing abuse and for its conservative effect upon some of the most valuable principles of the Constitution. The symmetry and purity of the Government would doubtless have been better preserved if this restriction of the power of appropriation could have been maintained without weakening its ability to fulfill the general objects of its institution, an effect so likely to attend its admission, notwithstanding its apparent fitness, that every subsequent Administration of the Government, embracing a period of thirty out of the forty-two years of its existence, has adopted a more enlarged construction of the power. It is not my purpose to detain you by a minute recital of the acts which sustain this assertion, but it is proper that I should notice some of the most prominent in order that the reflections which they suggest to my mind may be better understood. . . .

The bill before me does not call for a more definite opinion upon the particular circumstances which will warrant appropriations of money by Congress to aid works of internal improvement, for although the extension of the power to apply money beyond that of carrying into effect the object for which it is appropriated has, as we have seen, been long claimed and exercised by the Federal Government, yet such grants have always been professedly under the control of the general principle that the works which might be thus aided should be "of a general, not local, national, not State," character. A disregard of this distinction would of necessity lead to the subversion of the federal system. That even this is an unsafe one, arbitrary in its nature, and liable, consequently, to great abuses, is too obvious to require the confirmation of experience. It is, however, sufficiently definite and imperative to my mind to forbid my approbation of any bill having the character of the one under consideration. I have given to its provisions all the reflection demanded by a just regard for the interests of those of our fellow-citizens who have desired its passage, and by the respect which is due to a coördinate branch of the Government, but I am not able to view it in any other light than as a measure of purely local character; or, if it can be considered national, that no further distinction between the appropriate duties of the General and State Governments need be attempted, for there can be no local interest that may not with equal propriety be denominated national. It has no connection with any established system of improvements; is exclusively within the limits of a State, starting at a point on the Ohio River and running out 60 miles to an interior town, and even as far as the State is interested conferring partial instead of general advantages.

Considering the magnitude and importance of the power, and the embarrassments to which, from the very nature of the thing, its exercise must necessarily be subjected, the real friends of internal improvement ought not to be willing to confide it to accident and chance. . . .

In the other view of the subject, and the only remaining one which it is my intention to present at this time, is involved the expediency of embarking in a system of internal improvement without a previous amendment of the Constitution explaining and defining the precise powers of the Federal Government over it. Assuming the right to appropriate money to aid in the construction of national works to be warranted by the contemporaneous and continued exposition of the Constitution, its insufficiency for the successful prosecution of them must be admitted by all candid minds. If we look to usage to define the extent of the right, that will be found so variant and embracing so much that has been overruled as to involve the whole subject in great uncertainty and to render the execution of our respective duties in relation to it replete with difficulty and embarrassment. It is in regard to such works and the acquisition of additional territory that the practice obtained its first footing. In most, if not all, other disputed questions of appropriation the construction of the Constitution may be regarded as unsettled if the right to apply money in the enumerated cases is placed on the ground of usage. . . .

If it be the wish of the people that the construction of roads and canals should be conducted by the Federal Government, it is not only highly expedient, but indispensably necessary, that a previous amendment of the Constitution, delegating the necessary power and defining and restricting its exercise with reference to the sovereignty of the States, should be made. Without it nothing extensively useful can be effected. The right to exercise as much jurisdiction as is necessary to preserve the works and to raise funds by the collection of tolls to keep them in repair can not be dispensed with. . . .

President Jackson Vetoes the Second Bank of the United States, 1832

To the Senate:

The bill "to modify and continue" the act entitled "An act to incorporate the subscribers to the Bank of the United States" was presented to me on the 4th July instant. Having . . . come to the conclusion that it ought not to become a law, I herewith return it to the Senate, in which it originated, with my objections.

A bank of the United States is in many respects convenient for the Government and useful to the people. Entertaining this opinion, and deeply impressed with the belief that some of the powers and privileges possessed by the existing bank are unauthorized by the Constitution, subversive of the rights of the States, and dangerous to the liberties of the people, I felt it my duty at an early period of my Administration to call the attention of Congress to the practicability of organizing an institution combining all its advantages and obviating these objections. I sincerely regret that in the act before me I can perceive none of those modifications of the bank charter which are necessary, in my opinion, to make it compatible with justice, with sound policy, or with the Constitution of our country.

The present corporate body . . . enjoys an exclusive privilege of banking under the authority of the General Government, a monopoly of its favor and support, and, as a necessary consequence, almost a monopoly of the foreign and domestic exchange. The powers, privileges, and favors bestowed upon it in the original charter, by increasing the value of the stock far above its par value, operated as a gratuity of many millions to the stockholders. . . .

The act before me proposes another gratuity to the holders of the same stock, . . . On all hands it is conceded that its passage will increase at least 20 or 30 per cent more the market price of the stock, subject to the payment of the annuity of $200,000 per year secured by the act, thus adding in a moment one-fourth to its par value. It is not our own citizens only who are to receive the bounty of our Government. More than eight millions of the stock of this bank are held by foreigners. By this act the American Republic proposes virtually to make them a present of some millions of dollars. For these gratuities to foreigners and to some of our own opulent citizens the act secures no equivalent whatever. . . .

Every monopoly and all exclusive privileges are granted at the expense of the public, which ought to receive a fair equivalent. The many millions which this act proposes to bestow on the stockholders of the existing bank must come directly or indirectly out of the earnings of the American people. It is due to them, therefore, if their Government sell monopolies and exclusive privileges, that they should at least exact for them as much as they are worth in open market. The value of the monopoly in this case may be correctly ascertained. The twenty-eight millions of stock would probably be at an advance of 50 per cent, and command in market at least $42,000,000, subject to the payment of the present bonus. The present value of the monopoly, therefore, is $17,000,000, and this the act proposes to sell for three millions, payable in fifteen annual installments of $200,000 each.

It is not conceivable how the present stockholders can have any claim to the special favor of the Government. The present corporation has enjoyed its monopoly during the period stipulated in the original contract. If we must have such a corporation, why should not the Government sell out the whole stock and thus secure to the people the full market value of the privileges granted? Why should not Congress create and sell twenty-eight millions of stock, incorporating the purchasers with all the powers and privileges secured in this act and putting the premium upon the sales into the Treasury? . . .

The modifications of the existing charter proposed by this act are not such, in my view, as make it consistent with the rights of the States or the liberties of the people. The qualification of the right of the bank to hold real estate, the limitation of its power to establish branches, and the power reserved to Congress to forbid the circulation of small notes are restrictions comparatively of little value or importance. All the objectionable principles of the existing corporation, and most of its odious features, are retained without alleviation. . . .

Is there no danger to our liberty and independence in a bank that in its nature has so little to bind it to our country? The president of the bank has told us that most of the State banks exist by its forbearance. Should its influence become concentered, as it may under the operation of such an act as this, in the hands of a self-elected directory whose interests are identified with those of the foreign stockholders, will there not be cause to tremble for the purity of our elections in peace and for the independence of our country in war? Their power would be great whenever they might choose to exert it; but if this monopoly were regularly renewed every fifteen or twenty years on terms proposed by themselves, they might seldom in peace put forth their strength to influence elections or control the affairs of the nation. But if any private citizen or public functionary should interpose to curtail its powers or prevent a renewal of its privileges, it can not be doubted that he would be made to feel its influence. . . .

If we must have a bank with private stockholders, every consideration of sound policy and every impulse of American feeling admonishes that it should be *purely American*. Its stockholders should be composed exclusively of our own citizens, who at least ought to be friendly to our Government and willing to support it in times of difficulty and danger. . . . To a bank exclusively of American stockholders, possessing the powers and privileges granted by this act, subscriptions for $200,000,000 could be readily obtained. . . .

It is maintained by the advocates of the bank that its constitutionality in all its features ought to be considered as settled by precedent and by the decision of the Supreme Court. To this conclusion I can not assent. Mere precedent is a dangerous source of authority, and should not be regarded as deciding questions of constitutional power except where the acquiescence of the people and the States can be considered as well as settled. So far from this being the case on this subject, an argument against the bank might be based on precedent. One Congress, in 1791, decided in favor of a bank; another, in 1811, decided against it. One Congress, in 1815, decided against a bank; another in 1816, decided in its favor. Prior to the present Congress, therefore, the precedents drawn from that source were equal. If we resort to the States, the expressions of legislative, judicial, and executive opinions against the bank have been probably to those in its favor as 4 to 1. . . .

If the opinion on the Supreme Court covered the whole ground of this act, it ought not to control the coördinate authorities of this Government. The Congress, the Executive, and the Court must each for itself be guided by its own opinion of the Constitution. Each public officer who takes an oath to support the Constitution swears that he will support it as he understands it, and not as it is understood by others. It is as much the duty of the House of Representatives, of the Senate, and of the President to decide upon the constitutionality of any bill or resolution which may be presented to them for passage or approval as it is of the supreme judges when it may be brought before them for judicial decision. The opinion of the judges has no more authority over Congress than the opinion of Congress has over the judges, and on that point the President is independent of both. The authority of the Supreme Court must not, therefore, be permitted to control the Congress or the Executive when acting in their legislative capacities, but to have only such influence as the force of their reasoning may deserve.

But in the case relied upon the Supreme Court have not decided that all the features of this corporation are compatible with the Constitution. It is true that the court have said that the law incorporating the bank is a constitutional exercise of power by Congress; but taking into view the whole opinion of the court and the reasoning by which they have come to that conclusion, I understand them to have decided that inasmuch as a bank is an appropriate means for carrying into effect the enumerated powers of the General Government, therefore the law incorporating it is in accordance with that provision of the Constitution which declares that Congress shall have power "to make all laws which shall be necessary and proper for carrying those powers into execution." Having satisfied themselves that the word *"necessary"* in the Constitution means *"needful," "requisite," "essential," "conducive to,"* and that "a bank" is a convenient, a useful, and essential instrument in the prosecution of the Government's "fiscal operations," they conclude that to "use one must be within the discretion of Congress" and that "the act to incorporate the Bank of the United States is a law made in pursuance of the Constitution;" "but," say they, *"where the law is not prohibited and is really calculated to effect any of the objects intrusted to the Government, to undertake here to inquire into the degree of its necessity would be to pass the line which circumscribes the judicial department and to tread on legislative ground."*

The principle here affirmed is that the "degree of its necessity," involving all the details of a banking institution, is a question exclusively for legislative consideration. A bank is constitutional, but it is the province of the Legislature to determine whether this or that particular power, privilege, or exemption is "necessary and proper" to enable the bank to discharge its duties to the Government, and from their decision there is no appeal to the courts of justice. Under the decision of the Supreme Court, therefore, it is the exclusive province of Congress and the President to decide whether the particular features of this act are *necessary* and *proper* in order to enable the bank to perform conveniently and efficiently the public duties assigned to it as a fiscal agent, and therefore constitutional, or *unnecessary* and *improper,* and therefore unconstitutional.

Without commenting on the general principle affirmed by the Supreme Court, let us examine the details of this act in accordance with the rule of legislative action which they have laid down. It will be found that many of the powers and privileges conferred on it can not be supposed necessary for the purpose for which it is proposed to be created, and are not, therefore, means necessary to attain the end in view, and consequently not justified by the Constitution. . . .

The Constitution declares that "the Congress shall have power to exercise exclusive legislation in all cases whatsoever" over the District of Columbia. Its constitutional power, therefore, to establish banks in the district of Columbia and increase their capital at will is unlimited and uncontrollable by any other power than that which gave authority to the Constitution. Yet this act declares that Congress shall *not* increase the capital of existing banks, nor create other banks with capitals exceeding in the whole $6,000,000. The Constitution declares that Congress *shall* have power to exercise exclusive legislation over this District *"in all cases whatsoever,"* and this act declares they shall not. Which is the supreme law of the land? This provision can not be *"necessary"* or *"proper"* or *constitutional* unless the absurdity be admitted that whenever it be "necessary and proper" in the opinion of Congress they have a right to barter away one portion of the powers vested in them by the Constitution as a means of executing the rest. . . .

The Government is the only *"proper"* judge where its agents should reside and keep their offices, because it best knows where their presence will be *"necessary."* It can not, therefore, be *"necessary"* or *"proper"* to authorize the bank to locate branches where it pleases to perform the public service, without consulting the Government, and contrary to its will. The principle laid down by the Supreme Court concedes that Congress can not establish a bank for purposes of private speculation and gain, but only as a means of executing the delegated powers of the General Government. By the same principle a branch bank can not constitutionally be established for other than public purposes. The power which this act gives to establish two branches in any State, without the injunction or request of the Government and for other than public purposes, is not *"necessary"* to the due *execution* of the powers delegated to Congress. . . .

The principle is conceded that the States can not rightfully tax the operations of the General Government. They can not tax the money of the Government deposited in the State banks; nor the agency of those banks in remitting it; but will any man maintain that their mere selection to perform this public service for the General Government would exempt the State banks and their ordinary business from State taxation? Had the United States, instead of establishing a bank at Philadelphia, employed a private banker to keep and transmit their funds, would it have deprived Pennsylvania of the right to tax his bank and his usual banking operations? . . .

It can not be *necessary* to the character of the bank as a fiscal agent of the Government that its private business should be exempted from that taxation to which all the State banks are liable, nor can I conceive it *"proper"* that the substantive and most essential powers reserved by the States shall be thus attacked and annihilated as a means of executing the powers delegated to the General Government. It may be safely assumed that none of those sages who had an agency in forming or adopting our Constitution ever imagined that any portion of the taxing power of the States not prohibited to them nor delegated to Congress was to be swept away and annihilated as a means of executing certain powers delegated to Congress.

If our power over means is so absolute that the Supreme Court will not call in question the constitutionality of an act of Congress the subject of which "is not prohibited, and is really calculated to effect any of the objects intrusted to the Government," although, as in the case before me, it takes away powers expressly granted to Congress and rights scrupulously reserved to the States, it becomes us to proceed in our legislation with the utmost caution. Though not directly, our own powers and the rights of the States may be indirectly legislated away in the use of means to execute substantive powers. We may not enact that Congress shall not have the power of exclusive legislation over the District of Columbia, but we may pledge the faith of the United States that as a means of executing other powers it shall not be exercised for twenty years or forever. We may not pass an act prohibiting the States to tax the banking business carried on within their limits, but we may, as a means of executing our powers over other objects, place that business in the hands of our agents and then declare it exempt from State taxation in their hands. Thus may our own powers and the rights of the States, which we can not directly curtail or invade, be frittered away and extinguished in the use of means employed by us to execute other powers. That a bank of the United States, competent to all the duties which may be required by the Government, might be so organized as not to infringe on our own delegated powers or the reserved rights of the States I do not entertain a doubt. . . .

Under such circumstances the bank comes forward and asks a renewal of its charter for a term of fifteen years upon conditions which not only operate as a gratuity to the stockholders of many millions of dollars, but will sanction any abuses and legalize any encroachments. . . .

The bank is professedly established as an agent of the executive branch of the Government, and its constitutionality is maintained on that ground. Neither upon the propriety of present action nor upon the provisions of this act was the Executive consulted. It has had no opportunity to say that it neither needs nor wants an agent clothed with such powers and favored by such exemptions. There is nothing in its legitimate functions which makes it necessary or proper. Whatever interest or influence, whether public or private, has given birth to this act, it can not be found either in the wishes or necessities of the executive department, by which present action is deemed premature, and the powers conferred upon its agent not only unnecessary, but dangerous to the Government and country. . . .

There are no necessary evils in government. Its evils exist only in its abuses. If it would confine itself to equal protection, and, as Heaven does its rains, shower its favors alike on the high and the low, the rich and the poor, it would be an unqualified blessing. In the act before me there seems to be a wide and unnecessary departure from these just principles. . . .

Experience should teach us wisdom. Most of the difficulties our Government now encounters and most of the dangers which impend over our Union have sprung from an abandonment of the legitimate objects of Government by our national legislation, and the adoption of such principles as are embodied in this act. Many of our rich men have not been content with equal protection and equal benefits, but have besought us to make them richer by act of Congress. By attempting to gratify their desires we have in the results of our legislation arrayed section against section, interest against interest, and man against man, in a fearful commotion which threatens to shake the foundations of our Union. It is time to pause in our career to review our principles, and if possible revive that devoted patriotism and spirit of compromise which distinguished the sages of the Revolution and the fathers of our Union.

Senator John Tyler on "King Andrew," 1834

[To Dr. Henry Curtis.]
Washington, March 28, 1834.

My Dear Doctor:

. . . Clay finishes to-day the closing speech on the resolutions disapproving the late executive proceedings. We shall probably take the question this evening. The vote will probably be twenty-five to fifteen—a clear majority of ten. The truth is, that nobody *approves* out of the Senate chamber. *Their party* requires a different course on the part of the whole-hog men. For my own part, I can regard the questions at issue as importing nothing short of an actual change in the character of the government. Concede to the President the power to dispose of the public money as he pleases, and it is vain to talk of checker and balances. The presidential office swallows up all power, and the president becomes every inch a king. Such things as are daily transpiring want even the shadow of a precedent to repose under. The whole appointing power is exerted without the concurrence of the Senate. Four months of our session have elapsed, and no nomination of secretaries to the State or Treasury departments, or of the Attorney-General yet made. And this is justified upon the ground that these worthies, appointed during the recess, are to hold their commissions until Congress adjourns— a provision purposely introduced to enable the Senate to deliberate and to act advisedly on nominations, and resting upon the *necessity* of fixing some time for the expiration of the commission. In the meantime, every department of industry is visited by the heaviest curse, and all this brought about for no reason of law or *policy* which a bedlamite would not repudiate. I am sickened, fretted and almost angered, by the present condition of things. . . .

Yours truly,

John Tyler.

Senator Daniel Webster on Responsibility in Government, 1834

. . . The President [he stated] declares that he is "responsible for the entire action of the executive department." Responsible? What does he mean by being "responsible"? Does he mean legal responsibility? Certainly not. No such thing. Legal responsibility signifies liability to punishment for misconduct or maladministration. But the Protest does not mean that the President is liable to be impeached and punished if a secretary of state should commit treason, if a collector of the customs should be guilty of bribery, or if a treasurer should embezzle the public money. It does not mean, and cannot mean, that he should be answerable for any such crime or such delinquency. What, then, is its notion of that *responsibility* which it says the President is under for all officers, and which authorizes him to consider all officers as his own personal agents? Sir, it is merely responsibility to public opinion.

It is a liability to be blamed; it is the chance of becoming unpopular, the danger of losing a reëlection. Nothing else is meant in the world. It is the hazard of failing in any attempt or enterprise of ambition. This is all the responsibility to which the doctrines of the Protest hold the President subject. . . .

Alexis de Tocqueville Contrasts Presidency and Monarchy, 1840

The Executive Power. Dependence of the President—He Is Elective and Responsible—Free in His Own Sphere, Under the Inspection, but Not Under the Direction, of the Senate—His Salary Fixed at His Entry Into Office—Suspensive Veto

The American legislators undertook a difficult task in attempting to create an executive power dependent on the majority of the people and nevertheless sufficiently strong to act without restraint in its own sphere. It was indispensable to the maintenance of the republican form of government that the representative of the executive power should be subject to the will of the nation.

The President is an elective magistrate. His honor, his property, his liberty, and his life are the securities which the people have for the temperate use of his power. But in the exercise of his authority he is not perfectly independent; the Senate takes cognizance of his relations with foreign powers, and of his distribution of public appointments, so that he can neither corrupt nor be corrupted. The legislators of the Union acknowledge that the executive power could not fulfill its task with dignity and advantage unless it enjoyed more stability and strength than had been granted it in the separate states.

The President is chosen for four years, and he may be re-elected, so that the chances of a future administration may inspire him with hopeful undertakings for the public good and give him the means of carrying them into execution. The President was made the sole representative of the executive power of the Union; and care was taken not to render his decisions subordinate to the vote of a council, a dangerous measure which tends at the same time to clog the action of the government and to diminish its responsibility. The Senate has the right of annulling certain acts of the President; but it cannot compel him to take any steps, nor does it participate in the exercise of the executive power.

The action of the legislature on the executive power may be direct . . . but it may, on the other hand, be indirect. Legislative assemblies which have the power of depriving an officer of state of his salary encroach upon his independence; and as they are free to make the laws, it is to be feared lest they should gradually appropriate to themselves a portion of that authority

Excerpts from *Democracy in America* by Alexis de Tocqueville, edited by Jacob Peter Mayer and Max Lerner, translated by George Lawrence. Translation copyright © 1966 by Harper & Row Publishers, Inc. Reprinted by permission of HarperCollins Publishers Inc.

which the Constitution had vested in his hands. This dependence on the executive power is one of the defects inherent in republican constitutions. The Americans have not been able to counteract the tendency which legislative assemblies have to get possession of the government, but they have rendered this propensity less irresistible. The salary of the President is fixed, at the time of his entering upon office, for the whole period of his magistracy. The President, moreover, is armed with a suspensive veto, which allows him to oppose the passing of such laws as might destroy the portion of independence that the Constitution awards him. Yet the struggle between the President and the legislature must always be an unequal one, since the latter is certain of bearing down all resistance by persevering in its plans; but the suspensive veto forces it at least to reconsider the matter, and if the motion be persisted in, it must then be backed by a majority of two thirds of the whole house. The veto, moreover, is a sort of appeal to the people. The executive power, which without this security might have been secretly oppressed, adopts this means of pleading its cause and stating its motives. But if the legislature perseveres in its design, can it not always overpower all resistance? I reply that in the constitutions of all nations, of whatever kind they may be, a certain point exists at which the legislator must have recourse to the good sense and the virtue of his fellow citizens. This point is nearer and more prominent in republics, while it is more remote and more carefully concealed in monarchies; but it always exists somewhere. There is no country in which everything can be provided for by the laws, or in which political institutions can prove a substitute for common sense and public morality.

In What the Position of a President of the United States Differs from that of a Constitutional King of France. . . .

The executive power has so important an influence on the destinies of nations that I wish to dwell for an instant on this portion of my subject in order more clearly to explain the part it sustains in America. In order to form a clear and precise idea of the position of the President of the United States it may be well to compare it with that of one of the constitutional kings of France. In this comparison I shall pay but little attention to the external signs of power, which are more apt to deceive the eye of the observer than to guide his researches. When a monarchy is being gradually transformed into a republic, the executive power retains the titles, the honors, the etiquette, and even the funds of royalty long after its real authority has disappeared. The English, after having cut off the head of one king, and expelled another from his throne, were still wont to address the successors of those princes only upon their knees. On the other hand, when a republic falls under the sway of a single man, the demeanor of the sovereign remains as simple and unpretending as if his authority was not yet paramount. When the emperors exercised an unlimited control over the fortunes and the lives of their fellow citizens, it was customary to call them Cæsar in conversation; and they were in the habit of supping without formality at their friends' houses. It is therefore necessary to look below the surface.

The sovereignty of the United States is shared between the Union and the states, while in France it is undivided and compact; hence arises the first and most notable difference that exists between the President of the United States and the King of France. In the United States the executive power is as limited and exceptional as the sovereignty in whose name it acts; in France it is as universal as the authority of the state. The Americans have a Federal and the French a national government.

This cause of inferiority results from the nature of things, but it is not the only one; the second in importance is as follows. Sovereignty may be defined to be the right of making laws. In France, the King really exercises a portion of the sovereign power, since the laws have no weight if he refuses to sanction them; he is, moreover, the executor of all they ordain. The President is also the executor of the laws; but he does not really co-operate in making them, since the refusal of his assent does not prevent their passage. He is not, therefore, a part of the sovereign power, but only its agent. But not only does the King of France constitute a portion of the sovereign power; he also contributes to the nomination of the legislature, which is the other portion. He participates in it through appointing the members of one chamber and dissolving the other at his pleasure; whereas the President of the United States has no share in the formation of the legislative body and cannot dissolve it. The King has the same right of bringing forward measures as the chambers, a right which the President does not possess. The King is represented in each assembly by his ministers, who explain his intentions, support his opinions, and maintain the principles of the government. The President and his ministers are alike excluded from Congress, so that his influence and his opinions can only penetrate indirectly into that great body. The King of France is therefore on an equal footing with the legislature, which can no more act without him than he can without it. The President is placed beside the legislature like an inferior and dependent power.

Even in the exercise of the executive power, properly so called, the point upon which his position seems to be most analogous to that of the King of France, the President labors under several causes of inferiority. The authority of the King in France has, in the first place, the advantage of duration over that of the President; and durability is one of the chief elements of strength; nothing is either loved or feared but what is likely to endure. The President of the United States is a magistrate elected for four years. The King in France is a hereditary sovereign.

In the exercise of the executive power the President of the United States is constantly subject to a jealous supervision. He may prepare, but he cannot conclude, a treaty; he may nominate, but he cannot appoint, a public officer. The King of France is absolute within the sphere of executive power.

The President of the United States is responsible for his actions; but the person of the King is declared inviolable by French law.

Nevertheless, public opinion as a directing power is no less above the head of the one than of the other. This power is less definite, less evident, and less sanctioned by the laws in France than in America; but it really exists there. In America it acts by elections and decrees; in France it proceeds by revolutions. Thus, notwithstanding the different constitutions of these two countries, public opinion is the predominant authority in both of them. The fundamental principle of legislation, a principle essentially republican, is the same in both countries, although its developments may be more or less free and its consequences different. Thus I am led to conclude that France with its King is nearer akin to a republic than the Union with its President is to a monarchy.

In all that precedes I have touched only upon the main points of distinction; if I could have entered into details, the contrast would have been still more striking.

I have remarked that the authority of the President in the United States is only exercised within the limits of a partial sovereignty, while that of the King in France is undivided. I might have gone on to show that the power of the King's government in France exceeds its natural limits, however extensive these may be, and penetrates in a thousand different ways into the administration of private interests. Among the examples of this influence may be quoted that which results from the great number of public functionaries, who all derive their appointments from the executive government. This number now exceeds all previous limits; it amounts to 138,000 nominations, each of which may be considered as an element of power. The President of the United States has not the exclusive right of making any public appointments, and their whole number scarcely exceeds 12,000.

Whig Charles Francis Adams on the Ascendancy of the President, 1841

. . . To [the presidency] every other part of the system is now made in a great measure subordinate. And, instead of being regarded as the mere Executive head, charged with the duty of carrying into effect the laws, the President is looked to, by the great body of the people, as a person whose abstract sentiments upon every subject of public interest ought to be declared and made the subject of rigid examination. Should the practice of cross-questioning every candidate for the office become settled, the time will not be far distant when they will take the field in person, and solicit the people's votes. This can hardly fail to be attended with serious consequences to the Constitution, for it will have the effect of drawing the Executive and the people into a close union at the expense of the other departments of the government, as well as of consolidating the power of the national chief magistrate at the expense of that of the States. . . .

✣ *E S S A Y S*

While historians agree that Andrew Jackson transformed the presidential office and redefined the meaning of separation of powers, they disagree about his motives and the consequences of his actions. Edward Pessen, a professor of history at City University of New York, is the harshest modern critic of Jackson and the changes he wrought in the presidency. In the first essay, Pessen argues that Jackson's commitment to the people was merely rhetorical and that the expansion of presidential power accompanying his demagoguery established unfortunate precedents that have allowed modern presidents to usurp authority.

Robert V. Remini, in the second essay, takes a more charitable view of Jackson in the development of American constitutional history. Remini, who teaches history at the University of Illinois, Chicago, believes that Jackson responded to the demands of his times, bringing greater democracy to the operation of government and breaking down old lines of social deference that had impeded economic development. Jackson fashioned the presidency into an instrument of effective government by opening government to fresh, democratic breezes.

The Constitutional Expediency of Andrew Jackson

EDWARD PESSEN

. . . For all their realism, . . . the Whigs no less than their opponents did believe in certain principles. Opposition to Andrew Jackson was an expression, albeit an indistinct one, of political beliefs of sorts. The Whig charge of executive tyranny, if taken at face value, was made by men who believed in the Lockean and Jeffersonian concept of legislative dominance. Some skeptics have wondered whether Whigs would have been so opposed to a strong President had his name been Clay rather than Jackson. There is little reason to believe that any man but Jackson would have been capable of the enormities both of style and substance that he, in fact, committed as the nation's Chief Executive. Whig theories of the Executive were consistent and probably sincere expressions of constitutional convictions. It was not Andrew Jackson's person that most Whigs objected to, but his official acts. Thomas Hart Benton, who had as much reason as his brother to hate Old Hickory, did not become a Whig, after all. He belonged to that legion of men who had no fault to find with arbitrary means used to accomplish ends with which they were in sympathy.

Whig objections were not to mannerisms but to concrete policies. The precipitating issue that impelled the Administration's diverse opponents to coalesce was the removal both of the deposits as well as of the Secretaries of the Treasury who would not go along with it. No doubt some Whigs found this issue a convenient pretext essentially which might help them win office. The banking issue, for all the flaming rhetoric used to describe it, was not an ideological issue in the common meaning of the term. Rich men were on both sides of the issue and for good reason. If poor men were largely on one side of it, it was not because they should have been but rather, as Thurlow Weed had pointed out in 1832, because the demagogic phrases in Kendall's veto message had captured their imagination. Jacksonian leaders in a number of states had believed Biddle's Bank an excellent institution but not so excellent as to lead them to jeopardize their personal political careers by supporting it, after 1832. The views of the first Whig

From *Jacksonian America: Society, Personality, and Politics* by Edward Pessen, pp. 218–219, 326–333, 345–346. © 1969 The Dorsey Press. Reprinted by permission of Wadsworth, Inc.

leaders were thus not fundamentally unlike those of their Democratic opponents in the sense that Jacobin principles differed from Monarchist, or English Tory from English Whig. But if the differences between the American major parties were more over means than ends, they were real differences nonetheless.

. . . Government on the state level played a vital role in expanding and improving the nation's transportation network. Private capital, insufficient at best and made even more unlikely by the risks attendant on investment in "developmental" projects running through underdeveloped areas, could not have done the job of binding the expanding Union together. State intervention was the necessary ingredient that made possible a form of common market in which superior producers of an industrial or agricultural commodity could dispose profitably of their product in the most distant corners of the nation. The social price paid, in the form of poor construction, mismanagement, speculation, and downright corruption, cost more than the achievement warranted, according to some critics. But that kind of question is never resolved. Whether worth the cost or not, state support to the transportation revolution was indispensable.

Federal support of "internal improvements," for all the hulabaloo and controversy it engendered, was inconsistent, spasmodic, and mired in politics. Since it was a cardinal principle in Clay's American System, Jacksonians acted as though they had no alternative but to take a less than enthusiastic stand on the issue. Jackson's views changed after he moved to the White House, but too much should not be made of the Maysville veto in view of the fact that Old Hickory approved greater expenditures of internal improvements, including those purely local in character, than all previous administrations combined. Many internal improvements champions had no qualms about such vetoes. Like Cyrus King, who said, "the post roads of New England are now good . . . if they are not so elsewhere let those concerned make them so," they would not have their tax monies used to pay for projects not of direct benefit to their own states.

Attitudes toward the issue were most complex. Mississippians who eagerly sought federal assistance were dismayed but not discouraged by Maysville. Despite their disappointment at the "betrayal," many voters remained loyal to a Democracy and a Hero who pleased them in other, not always rational, respects. But Marylanders were evidently discountenanced by Jackson's veto of a bill that provided for a turnpike from Washington to Frederick. Significant defections from the Jackson party's leadership, and a decline in its voting strength, followed the veto, in a state where federal aid for internal improvements was taken seriously. In South Carolina, Virginia, and Georgia, however, strong constitutional scruples accounted for an opposition to federal roads that in some cases were badly needed. In Joseph Harrison's words, Jacksonian and particularly Van Buren's opposition to internal improvements, "however agreeable to the constitutional susceptibilities of the Southern Atlantic States, did little for their badly deficient systems of communications." Jackson's actual approval of such measures was not popular in the South, but "since its worst enemy could not accuse it [the Jackson Administration] of systematic planning . . . the South was accordingly comforted."

If national government did little for economic growth it had a much greater effect on economic stability. But its role was largely negative. Jacksonian policy and practice, in contrast to Old Hickory's rationales for them, fostered not stability but its opposite. For all the brave talk in Jacksonian utterances in praise of hard work, honest industry, frugality, modest rewards to sober enterprise, and all of the other canons of the old agrarian faith, actual Jacksonian measures either did nothing to thwart speculation or they abetted it. The Specie Circular of 1836 tried too late to call a halt to a process whereby government land offices themselves had encouraged dangerous speculation in public lands. The sudden federal refusal to accept as payment local bank notes whose overissue its own previous policy had encouraged, aggravated rather than stabilized the situation. As Harry N. Scheiber has noted, "by casting doubt on the solvency of some banks, Jackson contributed to public distrust of all banks and increased the tendency of private persons to hoard specie." Whether done grudgingly, as Jackson indicated it was, or not, the decision to distribute the federal surplus to the states only fed more fuel to the fires of inflation, promoting overextension of improvement projects as of state banks and the paper notes some of them printed in ever greater quantities. Jackson's great war on the second Bank of the United States was the federal policy that more than any other touched on the issue of stability. . . .

In his first message to Congress, Jackson charged that since the Bank had "failed in the great end of establishing a uniform and sound currency," therefore the Congress and "the people" might begin to consider whether another agency could be devised to replace it. Even a most sympathetic modern critic considers Old Hickory's currency ideas "weird." Less than three years later the Hero struck down the bill to recharter favored by the people's representatives, who obviously disagreed with him about the effect of Mr. Biddle's Bank on the nation's currency. Was Jackson's criticism valid? It is not even certain that *he* thought it was. It is altogether possible that intending to destroy the BUS [Bank of the United States] for reasons having more to do with politics or prejudice than anything else, he simply criticized it on grounds he and his political managers thought would be best accepted by the electorate. Old Hickory himself, to use an old expression, did not put his money where his mouth was. At the same time that he attacked the Bank, Jackson "continued to keep every dollar he owned in the [Bank's] Washington and Nashville branches." Apart from Democratic politicians, few knowledgeable contemporaries agreed with the President. Gallatin thought the Bank's own notes were as good as gold. William David Lewis, cashier of the Girard Bank of Philadelphia, who would subsequently be one of the beneficiaries of the removal of the deposits from the BUS when his own bank was designated an official repository of federal funds, himself had no doubts about the reliability of Biddle's notes. No modern economic historian, not even Thomas P. Govan, finds Biddle's performance as banker altogether blameless. Yet the one point banking specialists seem to agree on is that the notes of the second Bank of the United States were the soundest money not only of their own time but perhaps of the entire period prior to the Federal Reserve.

The ratio of specie or coin to the face value of the Bank's notes was generally higher than one to two, a far higher ratio than was typical for the era's money. One of the severest critics of the second Bank's performance gives it plus marks for helping to "create a sound national currency . . . by maintaining specie payments on its own notes." That its own eastern branches accepted notes from western branches at a discount of 1 percent or less in order to avoid being stripped of specie by the needier western outlets, was sensible and sound, although it "gave critics of the Bank an opportunity to accuse it of not maintaining a uniform currency." But such a charge was politically motivated rather than soundly based. The eminent John McLean, who commanded great respect from the Jacksonians, could not believe "the adversaries of the Bank in good faith," however. The Bank's effects were "obviously excellent, especially in the West where it furnishes a currency that is safe and portable." Detailed studies by modern banking specialists find that the second Bank provided a currency of high quality, its notes frequently preferred to gold. Based on ample specie reserves and domestic bills of exchange for the most part, its notes were far more sound than those of most other American banks, on the one hand, while the Bank's currency policy has been found more conducive to growth and therefore more in the national interest than the right hard money ideas of a Thomas Hart Benton, on the other.

The Bank's role in maintaining the stability of the notes of other banks was perhaps even more important in promoting a sound currency for the nation than was its policy with regard to its own notes. For as McLean observed of the BUS, "aside from its other advantages it has that of pre-venting the establishment of bad banks. It refuses to take their notes and in this way discredits them on the spot." He was describing a variation on the procedure that was later called a "self-acting" way of conducting the central banking function. As the repository of government funds, the Bank, as has been pointed out earlier, accumulated the diverse notes used in payment to customs collectors and government land offices. When the Bank of the United States required payment from the state banks which had issued the notes, in effect it compelled them to "be honest." And by punishing banks too free to print paper whether or not they had specie to back it up, the BUS certainly was forcing them in the direction of issuing a more trust-worthy currency and thus indirectly working to stabilize the economy. In-flationists and wildcat bankers, who could not care less about stability, took a dim view of the "monster" institution which thus interfered with their undisciplined schemes.

But Biddle did not inveterately insist on specie payment, thus qualifying "the automaticity of the [central banking] function." For when in his judgment it was to the interest of the nation, the economy and the BUS to loosen up credit, perhaps because specie had been drained either from the nation as a whole or from a particular section, he would exercise his discretion by simply abstaining from the demand for payment. Of course these were only technical functions capable of being performed well or badly, depending on the ability of the man at the controls. The consensus of the cognoscenti is that Nicholas Biddle was a virtuoso. He was a brilliant man and also an arrogant one, impatient, even contemptuous of the criticism directed at him by those he considered ignorant. But he was not venal. His main concerns prior to 1832 seemed always to be the interests of the economy as a whole rather than the highest possible profits for the BUS stockholders. The modest 7 percent profit that was the norm during his tenure in fact brought on his head the censure of some stockholders. He had a flair for central banking and seemed to delight in playing the game, deciding when to go easy, when to crack down. The important thing is that he played the game well. Under his guidance the BUS came close to being the "balance wheel of the banking system" that Biddle and his friends liked to think it was. In any case one can understand the contemporary viewpoint that "destroying the national bank to expel paper money was like killing the cat to keep the mice away." After the "war" was begun, Biddle hit back, launching the famous contraction of 1833 to 1834 that was designed, among other things, to demonstrate the indispensability of his Bank. That this tactic failed is another matter; modern research indicates that the so-called "Biddle depression" was slight and hardly due to his policies at all. Edward Abdy had discerned that "though President Jackson and his organs of the press . . . are declared enemies of paper money, yet his chief supporters not only maintain the system he attacks" but they perpetuate "what he professes to detest." Later critics found a terrible irony in this Jacksonian policy.

Abetted by Amos Kendall's marvelously effective Veto message, which even Jackson's warmest modern admirer concedes was essentially demagogy, the Hero succeeded not only in frustrating the Congressional majority which favored renewing the charter of the BUS, but in winning warm popular approval for his anti-Bank campaign. Certainly this was the construction he placed on his decisive electoral victory in 1832. He now decided that his next contribution to a sound currency would take the form of gradually replacing the BUS as the repository for federal funds with state banks chosen for the purpose. In his first message to Congress after his reelection, his language was reflective, questioning: in view of the Bank's abuse of its powers, might it not be wise for Congress to investigate whether the deposits of the government were safe in such an institution? Jackson's subsequent behavior shows how little these words can be credited. For when the House three months later approved a majority report by the Ways and Means Committee that an investigation had indeed established the safety of the government's deposits, Jackson was dissuaded not at all, confiding to Taney, his Attorney-General, his wish to discuss "the problem of finding safe places of deposit for the government funds." Taney proved his mastery of human nature by responding with a letter that heaped sycophantic praise on the old man, reminding him of his heroic military and political victories but evincing concern about the effect removal would have on his reputation. Since Secretary Duane was unwilling to authorize the removal, he, Taney, unqualified though he was, would stand beside his great chieftain and accept the Treasury portfolio—if the Hero thought it would be helpful. But in view of the great political risks attendant on such a policy, should Jackson jeopardize his splendid reputation? Of course, Taney hastened to assure his master, only he could slay the monster, but was the risk worth taking? One can guess Jackson's reaction!

McLane, in refusing, had argued that "no adequate reason existed for the removal." After he was moved upstairs to the State Department, William J. Duane likewise refused to be Jackson's puppet and authorize the removal of the deposits, rightly insisting that under the law he, not the President, had the responsibility for the deposits.* He refused to give a removal order, citing among other objections, his belief that "the state banks, fearing the vengeance of the Bank of the United States, would not dare to accept deposits from the government." That was all the excuse Jackson needed to send Amos Kendall on a tour of the eastern seaboard cities, to visit banks in Baltimore, Philadelphia, New York, and Boston to find out if this was so. It was not. Kendall reported back that "a considerable number of banks [were] eager to have the deposits." In view of their great joy, Kendall was here uncharacteristically guilty of understatement. Having used the pages of the *Globe* to inform the public that commencing October 1 new deposits would be placed in designated state banks, Jackson removed Duane one week prior to October 1, as was his right. He replaced him with the complaisant Taney.

Of course a storm broke out. This was not the first time deposits were to be made in a state bank, for in 1831 Lewis Cass's intervention had helped secure federal deposits for the Bank of Michigan. But that had been a most exceptional decision, not part of an anti-BUS policy. Clay compared the "daring usurpation" to the same "spirit of defiance to the Constitution and to all law" shown by Jackson "during the conduct of the Seminole War." John Derby, heretofore an ardent Jacksonian, wondered what "temporary illness and imbecility . . . persuaded [the President] to lay violent hands on the public treasure and transfer it." In New York a number of mercantile Democrats defected. A Cincinnati Whig wrote to Jackson: "Damn your . . . soul, remove them deposites back again, and recharter the bank or you will certainly be shot in less than two weeks and that by myself!!!" But such language, it goes without saying, only encouraged a man who needed no

---

* The law establishing the second Bank stated: "The deposits of the money of the United States . . . shall be made in said bank or branches thereof, unless the Secretary of the Treasury shall at any time otherwise order and direct. . . . " Later the Supreme Court in *Kendall* v. *Stokes*, 1838, took a position similar to Duane's, arguing that an appointed official was *not* a mere creature of the Executive.

encouragement to stay on the course he had decided to follow. Told of a rumor that a Baltimore "mob" intended to "lay siege to the Capitol until the deposits were restored," Jackson said, "I shall be glad to see this mob on Capitol Hill. The leaders I will hang as high as Haman to deter forever all attempts to control the Congress by intimidation." Only one man in America obviously had the right to control Congress. . . .

There is no denying that this commanding personality transformed the Presidential office. That he vetoed more bills than all previous Presidents combined and on grounds of expediency or opposition to the measures rather than to their alleged unconstitutionality was "a resounding exercise of executive authority," which infuriated Whigs and worshippers of precedent. It made the President the legislative equal not of two thirds of Congress as L. D. White wrote, but, in five cases out of six, less than one sixth of the Congress [the difference between the majority needed first to pass a bill and the two thirds to override the veto.] One writer has . . . suggested that Jackson's Presbyterianism may have accounted for his vetoes. It seems clear that it was his personality rather than a reasoned philosophy that justified, in his mind, the setting aside of Congressional measures, Supreme Court rulings, or individual officeholders he, Andrew Jackson, disagreed with or disliked. An overweening conviction of his own rightness similarly urged him on to go over the head of Congress to the people who, he was convinced, he, better than any group of elected legislators, represented.

A balanced assessment cannot condemn these Jacksonian innovations out of hand, no matter their origins or motives. The dynamic expansion of the powers of the Presidency was in fact a piece of creative statecraft that in a sense simply realized the potential latent in the Office. To Jackson as to other strong men, the "intent of the Founding Fathers" was somehow what agreed with his own interpretation. Nor is this approach inferior to an investigation of the Philadelphia Convention debate to ascertain what the Fathers really meant. Scholars, like politicians, when performing the latter exercise seem to find out that the Constitution means what they always thought it did.

The strong Presidency owes as much to Andrew Jackson as to any man. But this fateful contribution was a mixed blessing. Without a doubt it has made possible quicker responses both to domestic and international crises. But even those who approve the wars strong Presidents have led the nation into, must give pause to the upsetting of the traditional constitutional balance that has accompanied these adventures. And what happens when a "strong President" leads the nation along a dismal path—or at least one that is dismal in the judgment of most knowledgeable men—but manages through artful propaganda and news management to convince the mass of the electorate that his policy is morally good and pragmatically sound? My own reading of Jacksonian politics is that Jackson accomplished something very close to that, as he appealed to the people over the heads of his—and therefore their—enemies, oversimplifying complex issues and fighting the good fight against the forces of darkness, even though in fact the warfare was largely confined to the field of rhetoric.

Andrew Jackson as Liberator of the People and the Presidency

ROBERT V. REMINI

. . . Jackson . . . added to the power of the presidential office. His success in undermining the equal but separate doctrine of the Founding Fathers and tilting power more toward the executive was the result of the changes that had taken place in the American system of government and American society since the beginning of the century. An expanding economy had produced a rising democracy and, as a consequence, the American electorate demanded a greater say in the operation of the government. Since Jackson had become their spokesman and symbol, they were quite prepared to accept him as their representative at the seat of government. What was happening, therefore, was something that everyone sensed and accepted, even if they could not describe or define it, namely, the slow, continuing evolution of the nation from a republic into a democracy. Jackson by his conduct as President and his relations to the American people was asserting his role as the tribune of the people. And the electorate genuinely saw him as their representative. Their will was now being exercised through him, not through the legislature as was true in the past. The government had always been based on consent, right from the beginning of the American experiment, but consent was indirectly given through the legislature. Now, under Jackson, it was being expressed through the executive and in a very direct manner.

Contemporaries saw what was happening, and many expressed their horror at the possibility of the nation converting to democracy. Some resisted it, others warned of the consequences. The Washington *National Intelligencer,* an antiadministration paper, regularly sounded the alarm and predicted the rise of tyranny. "The true power of this government," preached one editorial, "*ought* to be to lie in the Congress of the United States. . . . It was never contemplated that its deliberately expressed opinions should be lightly disregarded—its well considered acts repeatedly rejected—and its legal authority overtopped by another and differently constituted power." But that is exactly what Jackson is accomplishing, said the newspaper, and he claims to be doing it in the name of the people. "Congress is the *democratic* branch of the government," the journal insisted, not the executive. "If power is safe anywhere in a Republic it is safe with the representatives."

Obviously much of the alteration of the American political system was owing to Jackson himself. He was an aggressive, forceful, and dynamic leader, accustomed to command, always prepared to expand his role to achieve the goals he envisioned for the nation. He was the right man at the most propitious moment in the ongoing development of American democracy. . . .

Jackson's novel concept about the President representing the people

Excerpts from *Andrew Jackson and the Course of American Democracy, 1833–1845,* Vol. III by Robert V. Remini, pp. 101–102, 159–161, 316–317, 338–340, 342–343. Copyright © 1984 by Robert V. Remini. Reprinted by permission of HarperCollins Publishers.

found immediate acceptance with the electorate. Perhaps the very fact that it had been stated simply and forcefully, but not argued, made it easier to gain acceptance. Clearly, its timing was perfect and eventually even the Whigs capitulated to it. Sighed Senator Leigh: "Until the President developed the faculties of the Executive power, all men thought it inferior to the legislature—he manifestly thinks it superior; and in his hands the monarchical part of Government (for the Executive is monarchical . . .) has proved far stronger than the representatives of the States." The President, not Congress, had become the instrument of popular will.

In introducing and ultimately winning acceptance of his interpretation of presidential powers, Jackson liberated the chief executive from the position of prime minister responsible only to Congress. With Jackson, the chief executive no longer served simply as the head of a coordinate branch of the government; no longer was he restricted in his actions by what the Congress would allow him. Henceforth he could assert himself as the spokesman of the people and by the skillful use of his powers force the legislature to follow his lead. This did not free him from the political necessity of working with Congress to accomplish the public will, but it did allow him to assume greater control of the government and to dominate and direct public affairs.

It was this very sense of domination and direction that so agitated the Whigs. What made it worse was the precedent Jackson was setting for future Presidents—whether they followed the precedent or not. It was there. It was waiting to be used.

All of which meant that Jackson saw himself as the head of the government, executing the popular will, and responsible only to the electorate. He truly believed himself a servant of the people—and that, in the end, is how the people saw him. They believed him "honest and patriotic; that he was the friend of the *people,* battling for them against corruption and extravagance, and opposed only by dishonest politicians. They loved him as their friend."

This mutual attitude of love and respect—amounting to a bond—between a President and the electorate was something totally novel in American history. It did not exist with Washington or Jefferson or any President previous to Jackson. And out of this special relationship forged between Old Hickory and the American people a sense of mutual dependence and commitment emerged which changed the tone and style of the government to something publicists had started to call a democracy.

. . . From the beginning of his term as President, Andrew Jackson had steadily increased his involvement in all the operations of government, whether executive, legislative, or judicial. Perhaps such intrusion might be expected from someone of his temperament and military background, from one accustomed to command. But there was more involved. Over the years Jackson had improved his political skills, and increasingly he employed them to nudge the Congress to do his bidding. With the help of an enormous propaganda machine, which he directed through the columns of the *Globe,* and with the formidable support he enjoyed from the mass electorate, he commanded unassailable advantages which few congressmen could disregard or dismiss. What aided Jackson tremendously in his vigorous assertion of presidential power was the existence of an explosive political issue which he had raised and around which he had drawn very precise and impenetrable lines. He had decreed the destruction of the BUS [Bank of the United States]. By removing the deposits he forced congressmen to come to terms with the issue and either join him in killing the monster or remove themselves from Democratic ranks. It was one or the other.

Jackson placed his entire confidence in the wisdom of a virtuous people "to arrive at right conclusions," conclusions binding on all their representatives. That was the message carried by his speeches and public pronouncements to the Democratic party and the electorate. In asserting this principle he was subverting (consciously or not) republicanism and the constitutional system as devised by the Founding Fathers. For the perceived wisdom at the time insisted that a government had been established by the Constitution which distributed power among three branches of government and provided checks and balances to keep the branches equal and prevent any one of them from dominating the others. The language of the Constitution, according to this view, *is* the will of the people. Having spoken, the people are excluded from speaking again except through the difficult, if not impossible, process of amending the Constitution. The agency or branch of government that is given the final say on the meaning of the Constitution is the Supreme Court. And the Supreme Court is the most removed body from the people.

This view Jackson totally rejected. Not only did he deny that the people may speak no more except by amending the Constitution, but he denied that the Supreme Court was the final interpreter of the meaning of the Constitution. Jackson subscribed to another view. He maintained that the people remain active in the governing process. The people are *never* excluded from the power that is theirs by right. They never surrendered that right. And they exercise that right through the ballot box which all agencies of government (including the Supreme Court) must obey. A form of government, such as the one provided by the Constitution, does not divest the people of the right to self-government. It does not give the Supreme Court, for example, the right to tell them what is or is not allowed under that form. "Forms of government," wrote George Sidney Camp in *Democracy*, a work published in 1841 and obviously written under the influence of Jacksonianism, "have been, for the most part, only so many various modes of tyranny. Where the people are everything, and political forms . . . nothing, there and there only is liberty."

That was Jackson's philosophy precisely. The people govern. Their will must be obeyed. Majority rule constitutes the only true meaning of liberty. All of which subverts the earlier notion of republicanism which did indeed provide for intermediate agencies to refine and alter the popular will when it was deemed necessary, such as occurred in 1825.

The "constant celebration" of the people, therefore, is basic to Jacksonian Democracy. And it was this celebration throughout Jackson's administration—a celebration the people enjoyed and acknowledged—that steadily advanced the march toward greater democracy in the United States.

At one point Jackson himself made a stab at defining Jacksonian Democracy and listed many of its identifying marks. If the "virtuous yeomanry of Tennessee," he wrote as he struggled with the definition, would simply ask political candidates a few basic questions, they could distinguish true Democrats from "Whiggs, nullies & blue light federalists*" by the answers they received. The people, said Jackson, "ought to enquire of them, are you opposed to a national Bank—are you in favor of a strict construction of the federal and State constitution—are you in favor of rotation in office—do you subscribe to the republican rule that the people are the sovereign power, the officers their agents, and that upon all national or general subjects, as well as local, they have a right to instruct their agents & representatives, and they are bound to obey or resign—in short are they true republicans agreeable to the true Jeffersonian creed."

Sovereign power resides with the people, declared Jackson, and that power applies to all national and local issues. Moreover, the people have a right to "instruct their agents & representatives" as to their will. It is not enough to say that once the people elect their representatives they have no further control of the governing process. For Jackson, they always retain control through the doctrine of instruction. He would take away from representatives the power or right to "correct" or alter the popular will.

Jackson would also deny the courts this power. But he made a distinction. He would allow the courts the right to review and interpret the *law* but he would not assign them ultimate authority in pronouncing "the true meaning of a doubtful clause of the Constitution" binding on all. The right to review and interpret the law may be "endured," he argued, "because it is subject to the control of the majority of the people." But pronouncing the true meaning of the Constitution was altogether objectionable because "it claims the right to bind" the states and the people with bonds that no one can loose except by amending the Constitution, a difficult process at best. To allow the Supreme Court the ultimate authority to interpret the Constitution perpetuates an aristocratic rather than a democratic system of government because four persons (five today) can dictate to a nation, with or without popular consent. And that was intolerable. As Jackson said in his Bank veto, "The Congress, the Executive, and the Court must each for itself be guided by its own opinion of the Constitution." In a truly democratic state, he argued, the people ultimately decide the question of constitutionality. And they do it through the ballot box.

In sum, then, Jackson took the position best articulated by Alexis de Tocqueville in his classic work *Democracy in America*. "The people reign in the American political world," wrote Tocqueville, "as the Deity does in

---

* Blue light Federalists supposedly signaled to the British fleet off the New England coast with blue lights during the War of 1812 to indicate a safe haven.

the universe. They are the cause and aim of all things; everything comes from them, and everything is absorbed in them." . . .

. . . [I]n addition to preaching majoritarian rule, Old Hickory cited strict construction of the Constitution as an essential article of faith. However much he himself subverted that doctrine, Jackson believed fundamentally in limited government and the necessity of keeping government spending to an absolute minimum. He also included opposition to a national bank and rotation in office as part of his creed. Rotation in office was simply his way of stating that the operation of government must be open to all. No elitism. No official class. Again, he himself may have failed to recruit from every social and economic class, but he insisted that democratizing the government be regarded as a cardinal doctrine of Jacksonianism.

Indeed, the General's views on holding office became even more democratic as he grew older. He proceeded from the premise that all offices— whether appointed or elected—must ultimately fall under the absolute control of the people. Appointed offices should be rotated, preferably every four years. Elected offices must be filled *directly* by the people. In keeping with this principle, Jackson tried to abolish the College of Electors in the selection of the chief executive by proposing a constitutional amendment. In addition, he said, the President should serve no more than a single term of either four or six years. Jackson advocated a single term in order to place the President beyond the reach of improper—"corrupting"—influences. Moreover, he believed that United States senators should be directly elected by the people. Also, their term should be limited to four years and they should be subject to removal. In Jackson's mind, the Senate was an elitist body of men committed to the principles of aristocracy and totally unrepresentative of the American people. Considering his long and bitter struggle with the upper house it is not surprising that he should feel so vehement. His thoughts on democratizing the Senate were conveyed to the electorate in the editorial columns of the *Globe*. "We say, then, to the People of the United States," wrote Blair, "is it not worthy of consideration to provide an amendment to the Constitution, limiting the senatorial term to four years and making the office elective by the People of the several States?"

Interestingly, Jackson would also require federal judges to stand for election, and presumably he would include the justices of the Supreme Court once the Constitution had been properly amended. And he would limit judicial terms to seven years but permit reelection. By this time Jackson was so totally devoted to the democratic principle of officeholding that he could conceive of no better method of preserving freedom and ensuring justice for all. His remarkably advanced views were regarded by some as very radical—if not dangerous. The historian George Bancroft interviewed Jackson on the subject and recorded some of the President's opinions. "He thinks every officer should in his turn pass before the people, for their approval or rejection," wrote Bancroft. "In England the judges should have independence to protect the people against the crown," said Jackson. But not in America. "Here the judges should not be independent of the people, but be appointed for not more than seven years. The people would always re-elect the good judges."

Jacksonian Democracy, then, stretches the concept of democracy about as far as it can go and still remain workable. Obviously, Jackson himself was far ahead of his times—and maybe further than this country can ever achieve. . . .

Because Jackson identified himself totally with the people and believed that his will represented theirs, he became increasingly intolerant of opposing political views. He labeled them conspiracies to disrupt the processes of democracy. He also presumed to interpret the Constitution for the people, and when his opinions clashed with the courts he appealed to the electorate to resolve the matter. They constituted the final court of appeal, he said. Surely, no one seriously believed that "four men who form a majority of the Supreme Court" should have "dominion . . . over the rights of the states and the rights of the majority of the people of the United States." The people rule; they decide the government they want; and all must submit. The idea of unrestrained judicial review—such as exists today—horrified him.

Jackson's constitutional views proved untenable, but they were genuinely democratic. What he did, of course, was further subvert the doctrines of republicanism. Central to the constitutional system was the notion of checks and balances, but Jackson made a shambles of that notion by insisting on his primacy as President in interpreting and executing the law because he—and he alone—represented all the people. Andrew Jackson was the great advocate of democracy. Majoritarian rule was the only thing that mattered in his thinking about the operation of government. But the democracy he practiced reduced to near ruin the kind of republic conceived by the Founding Fathers. He tilted the tripartite system in favor of the executive. In circumventing the Supreme Court, in thwarting the will of Congress and insisting on his right to direct legislation, and in riding roughshod over the claim of any state to assert its sovereignty against the collective rights of the nation, he reshaped the constitutional system into something more appropriate to a modern, democratic state, which requires strong executive leadership. He functioned under the self-imposed limitations of a laissez-faire libertarian. But self-imposed limitations hardly promote balance between three separate and equal branches of government. Within the parameters of law, if the only check upon the President is the popular will, then majoritarian democracy may have been achieved but that is not the structure of government as originally conceived. And it is certainly not republicanism as understood by Americans of the early nineteenth century.

But clearly the Americans of the Jacksonian age had advanced beyond the concerns of an earlier generation that feared popular rule. They wanted the kind of democracy their President advocated because it placed them at the very center of the governmental process. Andrew Jackson not only symbolized their age but he served as their leader and guide to a more representative society. And the final years of Old Hickory's administration witnessed the almost total victory of the forces cooperating with him in devising a more democratic government, even though many Whigs . . . denounced it as "revolution." . . .

✠ *F U R T H E R   R E A D I N G*

Matthew Crenson, *The Federal Machine: Beginnings of Bureaucracy in Jacksonian America* (1975)
James C. Curtis, *Andrew Jackson and the Search for Vindication* (1976)
Richard Hofstadter, *The American Political Tradition and the Men Who Made It* (1948)
Richard Latner, *The Presidency of Andrew Jackson: White House Politics, 1829– 1837* (1979)
Robert V. Remini, *Andrew Jackson and the Bank War: A Study in the Growth of Presidential Power* (1967)
———, *The Presidency of Andrew Jackson* (1967)
Arthur Schlesinger, Jr., *The Age of Jackson* (1945)
———, *The Imperial Presidency* (1973)
Leonard D. White, *The Jacksonians: A Study in Administrative History* (1954)

Nullification, States' Rights, and State Sovereignty

✠

The nullification crisis of 1832–1833 had its origins in the "Tariff of Abomina-tions" of 1828, which set import duties at levels far above customary standards. Many southern political leaders, such as John C. Calhoun of South Carolina, believed that the tariff benefited northern manufacturers at the expense of the southern economy. In 1832 Congress passed a new, somewhat milder tariff de-signed to mollify the South, but the measure retained the protective principle. The tariff issue also acted as a surrogate for the South's rising anxiety about slavery. The South Carolina economy weakened as slavery expanded into Missis-sippi and Alabama, and many of that state's leaders worried that a deteriorat-ing economy and an increasingly aggressive northern antislavery movement would unsettle the slave population, perhaps leading to a servile insurrection.

In simple terms, the doctrine of nullification (which owed much of its consti-tutional underpinnings to Calhoun) held that a state could invalidate an act of Congress. In essence, the states were the final interpreters of the Constitution. As a constitutional principle, nullification sharply challenged the concept of dual federalism, the perpetual nature of the Union, and judicial review by the Su-preme Court. Most of the previous debates over state-federal relations had em-phasized the rights rather than the powers of the states. By the 1830s, Whigs and Jacksonian Democrats alike held that the Constitution was a complete and executed contract, between the central government and the people, which resulted in a permanent national government. But the Democrats also believed that the states had to retain some discretion in selected areas of constitutional activity, such as slavery, internal improvements, and economic development generally.

Beginning with the nullification crisis, however, the southern wing of the Democratic party injected a new and eventually divisive theme into constitutional debate. Spokespersons such as Calhoun argued that the national government was a mere trustee for the sovereign states. State sovereignty, which was a doctrine of power rather than of right, grew in intensity in the 1840s and 1850s as the debate over the expansion of slavery into the territories accelerated. Moreover, nullification mocked the twin concepts of nationalism and federal judicial su-

premacy that Chief Justice John Marshall had been pressing. Equally significant, the behavior of the South Carolinians drew the ire of President Andrew Jackson; while a southern slaveholder sympathetic to states' rights, he was strongly nationalistic in his outlook on the Union. The fact that his vice president, John C. Calhoun, was one of the leaders of the nullification movement only aggravated Jackson's already raw political nerves.

When delegates to the South Carolina nullification convention in November 1832 declared the tariffs of 1828 and 1832 void, Jackson was also dealing with another controversial problem of state-nation relations—Indian removals. Georgia officials were refusing to obey Chief Justice Marshall's decision in Worcester v. Georgia *(1832) that the Cherokee Indians in that state constituted a distinct political nation with which only the federal government could deal. Jackson, an avid supporter of Indian removals, worried that Georgia might unite with South Carolina. The president therefore supported Georgia's defiance of the* Worcester *decision (Jackson is reputed to have said, "John Marshall has made his decision, now let him enforce it!") at the same time that he sought to crush the nullification movement in South Carolina. Old Hickory's strategy isolated South Carolina nullifiers and kept Georgia in the Union camp throughout the nullification crisis.*

Jackson dealt with the South Carolinians by persuading Congress in March 1833 to pass the Force Bill, which gave the president authority to enforce the revenue laws with the use of the military if necessary. Jackson also won agreement for the compromise Tariff of 1833. Together, these measures cooled the crisis, and the nullification convention on March 15, 1833, rescinded its original ordinance.

⚜ D O C U M E N T S

John C. Calhoun was a vigorous proponent of nullification, one of the strongest critics of federal tariff policy, and an ardent champion of slavery. In 1828 he registered his opposition and that of many South Carolinians to the "Tariff of Abominations" through the "South Carolina Protest," reprinted here as the first document. The "Protest" was placed originally as an appendix to the "South Carolina Exposition," this chapter's second document, which not only asserted the injustice of the tariff but also argued that South Carolina might nullify a federal law.

The concept of state sovereignty expounded by Calhoun and other southern senators was challenged by Whig nationalists, most notably Senator Daniel Webster of Massachusetts. In the third document, his "Reply to Robert Hayne" of 1830, Webster dramatically asserts the concept of a perpetual union and the subordination of the states to the national government in certain areas. Two years later, in October 1832, the South Carolina legislature called a nullification convention for November, which on the 24th issued an "Ordinance of Nullification," the fourth document, declaring the tariffs of 1828 and 1832 void. President Jackson in December 1832 responded with a "Proclamation to the People of South Carolina" that bluntly rejected nullification, as the fifth document reveals. Jackson's leadership worked because of strong unionist support in South Carolina and the rest of the South; Congress effectively ended the crisis by lowering the tariff. As the sixth document shows, however, South Carolina delegates to the nullification convention, after repealing their previous nullification of the tariff, reasserted their right to do so by voiding the Force Bill.

At the time of the nullification crisis, Jackson also confronted the Supreme Court's decision in *Worcester* v. *Georgia,* which appears as the final documentary selection. Jackson had outlined a plan in his first message to Congress to remove the Indians, and in 1832 he refused to acquiesce to Marshall's decision, in part because he wanted to keep Georgia outside South Carolina's constitutional orbit. A federal program to remove all the southern tribes westward, beyond the Mississippi, began shortly thereafter.

Vice President John C. Calhoun Protests the "Tariff of Abominations," 1828

The Senate and House of Representatives of South Carolina, now met, and sitting in General Assembly, through the Hon. William Smith and the Hon. Robert Y. Hayne, their representatives in the Senate of the United States, do, in the name and on behalf of the good people of the said commonwealth, solemnly PROTEST against the system of protecting duties, lately adopted by the federal government, for the following reasons:—

1st. *Because* the good people of this commonwealth believe that the powers of Congress were delegated to it in trust for the accomplishment of certain specified objects which limit and control them, and that every exercise of them for any other purposes, is a violation of the Constitution as unwarrantable as the undisguised assumption of substantive, independent powers not granted or expressly withheld.

2d. *Because* the power to lay duties on imports is, and in its very nature can be, only a means of effecting objects specified by the Constitution; since no free government, and least of all a government of enumerated powers, can of right impose any tax, any more than a penalty, which is not at once justified by public necessity, and clearly within the scope and purview of the social compact; and since the right of confining appropriations of the public money to such legitimate and constitutional objects is as essential to the liberty of the people as their unquestionable privilege to be taxed only by their consent.

3d. *Because* they believe that the tariff law passed by Congress at its last session, and all other acts of which the principal object is the protection of manufactures, or any other branch of domestic industry, if they be considered as the exercise of a power in Congress to tax the people at its own good will and pleasure, and to apply the money raised to objects not specified in the Constitution, is a violation of these fundamental principles, a breach of a well-defined trust, and a perversion of the high powers vested in the federal government for federal purposes only.

4th. *Because* such acts, considered in the light of a regulation of commerce, are equally liable to objection; since, although the power to regulate commerce may, like all other powers, be exercised so as to protect domestic manufactures, yet it is clearly distinguishable from a power to do so *eo nomine,* both in the nature of the thing and in the common acception of the terms; and because the confounding of them would lead to the most extravagant results, since the encouragement of domestic industry implies an absolute control over all the interests, resources, and pursuits of a people, and is consistent with the idea of any other than a simple, consolidated government.

5th. *Because,* from the contemporaneous exposition of the Constitution in the numbers of the *Federalist,* (which is cited only because the Supreme Court has recognized its authority), it is clear that the power to regulate commerce was considered by the Convention as only incidentally connected with the encouragement of agriculture and manufactures; and because the power of laying imposts and duties on imports was not understood to justify in any case, a prohibition of foreign commodities, except as a means of extending commerce, by coercing foreign nations to a fair reciprocity in their intercourse with us, or for some *bona fide* commercial purpose.

6th. *Because,* whilst the power to protect manufactures is nowhere expressly granted to Congress, nor can be considered as necessary and proper to carry into effect any specified power, it seems to be expressly reserved to the states, by the 10th section of the 1st article of the Constitution.

7th. *Because* even admitting Congress to have a constitutional right to protect manufactures by the imposition of duties, or by regulations of commerce, designed principally for that purpose, yet a tariff of which the operation is grossly unequal and oppressive, is such an abuse of power as is incompatible with the principles of a free government and the great ends of civil society, justice, and equality of rights and protection.

8th. *Finally,* because South Carolina, from her climate, situation, and peculiar institutions, is, and must ever continue to be, wholly dependent upon agriculture and commerce, not only for her prosperity, but for her very existence as a state; because the valuable products of her soil—the blessings by which Divine Providence seems to have designed to compensate for the great disadvantages under which she suffers in other respects—are among the very few that can be cultivated with any profit by slave labor; and if, by the loss of her foreign commerce, these products should be confined to an inadequate market, the fate of this fertile state would be poverty and utter desolation; her citizens, in despair, would emigrate to more fortunate regions, and the whole frame and constitution of her civil policy be impaired and deranged, if not dissolved entirely.

Deeply impressed with these considerations, the representatives of the good people of this commonwealth, anxiously desiring to live in peace with their fellow-citizens, and to do all that in them lies to preserve and perpetuate the union of the states, and liberties of which it is the surest pledge, but feeling it to be their bounden duty to expose and resist all encroachments upon the true spirit of the Constitution, lest an apparent acquiescence in the system of protecting duties should be drawn into precedent—do, in the name of the commonwealth of South Carolina, claim to enter upon the Journal of the Senate their *protest* against it as unconstitutional, oppressive, and unjust.

Calhoun Proposes Nullification, 1828

. . . The General Government is one of specific powers, and it can rightfully exercise only the powers expressly granted, and those that may be "necessary and proper" to carry them into effect; all others being reserved expressly to the States, or to the people. It results necessarily, that those who claim to exercise a power under the Constitution, are bound to shew, that it is expressly granted, or that it is necessary and proper, as a means to some of the granted powers. The advocates of the Tariff have offered no such proof. It is true, that the third [*sic*] section of the first article of the Constitution of the United States authorizes Congress to lay and collect an impost duty, but it is granted as a tax power, for the sole purpose of revenue; a power in its nature essentially different from that of imposing protective or prohibitory duties. The two are incompatable [*sic*]; for the prohibitory system must end in destroying the revenue from impost. It has been said that the system is a violation of the spirit and not the letter of the Constitution. The distinction is not material. The Constitution may be as grossly violated by acting against its meaning as against its letter; but it may be proper to dwell a moment on the point, in order to understand more fully the real character of the acts, under which the interest of this, and other States similarly situated, has been sacrificed. The facts are few and simple. The Constitution grants to Congress the power of imposing a duty on imports for revenue; which power is abused by being converted into an instrument for rearing up the industry of one section of the country on the ruins of another. The violation then consists in using a power, granted for one object, to advance another, and that by the sacrifice of the original object. It is, in a word, *a violation of perversion*, the most dangerous of all, because the most insidious, and difficult to resist. Others cannot be perpetrated without the aid of the judiciary; this may be, by the executive and legislative alone. The courts by their own decisions cannot look into the motives of legislators—they are obliged to take acts by their titles and professed objects, and if *they* be constitutional they cannot interpose their power, however grossly the acts may violate the Constitution. The proceedings of the last session sufficiently prove, that the House of Representatives are aware of the distinction, and determined to avail themselves of the advantage. . . .

If there be a political proposition universally true, one which springs directly from the nature of man, and is independent of circumstances, it is, that irresponsible power is inconsistent with liberty and must corrupt those who exercise it. On this great principle our political system rests. We consider all powers as delegated from the people and to be controlled by those who are interested in their just and proper exercise; and our governments, both State and General, are but a system of judicious contrivances to bring this fundamental principle into fair practical operation. . . . From diversity of interest in the several classes of the people and sections of the country, laws act differently, so that the same law, though couched in general terms and apparently fair, shall in reality transfer the power and prosperity of one class or section to another; in such case responsibility to constituents, which is but the means of enforcing the fidelity of representatives to them, must prove wholly insufficient to preserve the purity of public agents, or the liberty of the country. It would in fact be inapplicable to the evil. The disease would be in the community itself; in the constituents, not in the representatives. The opposing interest of the community would engender necessarily opposing hostile parties, organized in this very diversity of interest; the stronger of which, if the government provided no efficient check, would exercise unlimited and unrestrained power over the weaker. The relations of equality between them would thus be destroyed, and in its place there would be substituted the relation of sovereign and subject, between the stronger and the weaker interest, in its most odious and oppressive form. . . . On the great and vital point, the industry of the country, which comprehends nearly all the other interests, two great sections of the Union are opposed. We want free trade; they, restrictions. We want moderate taxes, frugality in the government, economy, accountability, and a rigid application of the public money, to the payment of the public debt, and the objects authorized by the Constitution; in all these particulars, if we may judge by experience, their views of their interest are the opposite. They act and feel on all questions connected with the American System, as sovereigns; as those always do who impose burdens on others for their own benefit; and we, on the contrary, like those on whom such burdens are imposed. In a word, to the extent stated, the country is divided and organized into two great opposing parties, one sovereign and the other subject; marked by all the characteristics which must ever accompany that relation, under whatever form it may exist. That our industry is controlled by the many, instead of one, by a majority in Congress elected by a majority in the community having an opposing interest, instead of hereditary rulers, forms not the slightest mitigation of the evil. In fact, instead of mitigating, it aggravates. In our case one opposing branch of industry cannot prevail without associating others, and thus instead of a single act of oppression we must bear many. . . . Liberty comprehends the idea of *responsible power,* that those who make and execute the laws should be controlled by those on whom they operate; that the governed should govern. Thus to prevent rulers from abusing their trust, constituents must controul [*sic*] them through elections; and so to prevent the major from oppressing the minor interests of society, the constitution must provide . . . a check founded on the same principle, and equally efficacious. In fact the abuse of delegated power, and the tyranny of the greater over the less interests of society, are the two great dangers, and the only two, to be guarded against; and if *they* be effectually guarded liberty must be *eternal.* . . . No government based on the naked principle, that the majority ought to govern, however true the maxim in its proper sense and under proper restrictions, ever preserved its liberty, even for a single generation. . . . Those governments only, which provide checks, which limit and restrain within proper bounds the power of the majority, have had a prolonged existence, and been distinguished for virtue, power and happiness. Constitutional government, and the government of a majority, are utterly incompatible, it being the sole purpose of a constitution to impose limitations and checks upon the majority. An unchecked majority, is a despotism—and government is free, and will be permanent in proportion to the number, complexity and efficiency of the checks, by which its powers are controlled. . . .

Our system, then consists of two distinct and independent sovereignties. The general powers conferred on the General Government, are subject to its sole and separate control, and the States cannot, without violating the Constitution, interpose their authority to check, or in any manner counteract its movements, so long, as they are confined to its proper sphere; so also the peculiar and local powers, reserved to the States, are subject to their exclusive control, nor can the General Government interfere with them, without on its part, also violating the Constitution. In order to have a full and clear conception of our institutions, it will be proper to remark, that there is in our system a striking distinction between the government and the sovereign power. Whatever may be the true doctrine in regard to the sovereignty of the States individually, it is unquestionably clear that while the government of the union is vested in its legislative, executive and political departments, the actual sovereign power, resides in the several States, who created it, in their separate and distinct political character. . . .

. . . The constitutional power to protect their rights as members of the confederacy, results necessarily, by the most simple and demonstrable arguments, from the very nature of the relation subsisting between the States and General Government. If it be conceded, as it must by every one who is the least conversant with our institutions, that the sovereign power is divided between the States and General Government, and that the former holds its reserved rights, in the same high sovereign capacity, which the latter does its delegated rights; it will be impossible to deny to the States the right of deciding on the infraction of their rights, and the proper remedy to be applied for the correction. The right of judging, in such cases, is an essential attribute of sovereignty of which the States cannot be divested, without losing their sovereignty itself; and being reduced to a subordinate corporate condition. In fact, to divide power, and to give to one of the parties the exclusive right of judging of the portion allotted to each, is in reality not to divide at all; and to reserve such exclusive right to the General Government, (it matters not by what department it be exercised,) is in fact to constitute it one great consolidated government, with unlimited powers, and to reduce the States to mere corporations. It is impossible to understand the force of terms, and to deny these conclusions. The opposite opinion can be embraced only on hasty and imperfect views of the relation existing between the States and the General Government. But the existence of the right of judging of their powers, clearly established from the sovereignty of the States, as clearly implies a veto, or controul on the action of the General Government on contested points of authority; and this very controul is the remedy, which the Constitution has provided to prevent the enroachment of the General Government on the reserved right of the States; and by the exercise of which, the distribution of power between the General and State Governments, may be preserved forever inviolate, as is established by the

Constitution; and thus afford effectual protection to the great minor interest of the community, against the oppression of the majority.

Senator Daniel Webster on the Nature of the Union, 1830

. . . There yet remains to be performed, Mr. President, by far the most grave and important duty, which I feel to be devolved on me by this occasion. It is to state, and to defend, what I conceive to be the true principles of the Constitution under which we are here assembled. I might well have desired that so weighty a task should have fallen into other and abler hands. I could have wished that it should have been executed by those whose character and experience give weight and influence to their opinions, such as cannot possibly belong to mine. But, Sir, I have met the occasion, not sought it; and I shall proceed to state my own sentiments, without challenging for them any particular regard, with studied plainness, and as much precision as possible.

I understand the honorable gentleman from South Carolina [Robert Hayne] to maintain, that it is a right of the State legislatures to interfere, whenever, in their judgment, this government transcends its constitutional limits, and to arrest the operation of its laws.

I understand him to maintain this right, as a right existing *under* the Constitution, not as a right to overthrow it on the ground of extreme necessity, such as would justify violent revolution.

I understand him to maintain an authority, on the part of the States, thus to interfere, for the purpose of correcting the exercise of power by the general government, of checking it, and of compelling it to conform to their opinion of the extent of its powers.

I understand him to maintain, that the ultimate power of judging of the constitutional extent of its own authority is not lodged exclusively in the general government, or any branch of it; but that, on the contrary, the States may lawfully decide for themselves, and each State for itself, whether, in a given case, the act of the general government transcends its power.

I understand him to insist, that, if the exigency of the case, in the opinion of any State government, require it, such State government may, by its own sovereign authority, annul an act of the general government which it deems plainly and palpably unconstitutional.

This is the sum of what I understand from him to be the South Carolina doctrine, and the doctrine which he maintains. I propose to consider it, and compare it with the Constitution. Allow me to say, as a preliminary remark, that I call this the South Carolina doctrine only because the gentleman himself has so denominated it. I do not feel at liberty to say that South Carolina, as a State, has ever advanced these sentiments. I hope she has not, and never may. That a great majority of her people are opposed to the tariff laws, is doubtless true. That a majority, somewhat less than that just mentioned, conscientiously believe these laws unconstitutional, may probably also be true. But that any majority holds to the right of direct

State interference at State discretion, the right of nullifying acts of Congress by acts of State legislation, is more than I know, and what I shall be slow to believe.

There may be extreme cases, in which the people, in any mode of assembling, may resist usurpation, and relieve themselves from a tyrannical government. No one will deny this. Such resistance is not only acknowledged to be just in America, but in England also. Blackstone admits as much, in the theory, and practice, too, of the English constitution. We, Sir, who oppose the Carolina doctrine, do not deny that the people may, if they choose, throw off any government when it becomes oppressive and intolerable, and erect a better in its stead. We all know that civil institutions are established for the public benefit, and that when they cease to answer the ends of their existence they may be changed. But I do not understand the doctrine now contended for to be that, which, for the sake of distinction, we may call the right of revolution. I understand the gentleman to maintain, that, without revolution, without civil commotion, without rebellion, a remedy for supposed abuse and transgression of the powers of the general government lies in a direct appeal to the interference of the State governments.

[*Mr. Hayne here rose and said: He did not contend for the mere right of revolution, but for the right of constitutional resistance. What he maintained was, that in case of a plain, palpable violation of the Constitution by the general government, a State may interpose; and that this interposition is constitutional.*

Mr. Webster resumed:]

So, Sir, I understood the gentleman, and am happy to find that I did not misunderstand him. What he contends for is, that it is constitutional to interrupt the administration of the Constitution itself, in the hands of those who are chosen and sworn to administer it, by the direct interference, in form of law, of the States, in virtue of their sovereign capacity. The inherent right in the people to reform their government I do not deny; and they have another right, and that is, to resist unconstitutional laws, without overturning the government. It is no doctrine of mine that unconstitutional laws bind the people. The great question is, Whose prerogative is it to decide on the constitutionality or unconstitutionality of the laws? On that, the main debate hinges. The proposition, that, in case of a supposed violation of the Constitution by Congress, the States have a constitutional right to interfere and annul the law of Congress, is the proposition of the gentleman. I do not admit it. If the gentleman had intended no more than to assert the right of revolution for justifiable cause, he would have said only what all agree to. But I cannot conceive that there can be a middle course, between submission to the laws, when regularly pronounced constitutional, on the one hand, and open resistance, which is revolution or rebellion, on the other.

This leads us to inquire into the origin of this government and the source of its power. Whose agent is it? Is it the creature of the State legislatures, or the creature of the people? If the government of the United States be the agent of the State governments, then they may control it, provided they can agree in the manner of controlling it; if it be the agent of the people, then the people alone can control it, restrain it, modify, or reform it. It is observable enough, that the doctrine for which the honorable gentleman contends leads him to the necessity of maintaining, not only that this general government is the creature of the States, but that it is the creature of each of the States severally, so that each may assert the power for itself of determining whether it acts within the limits of its authority. It is the servant of four-and-twenty masters, of different wills and different purposes, and yet bound to obey all.

It so happens that, at the very moment when South Carolina resolves that the tariff laws are unconstitutional, Pennsylvania and Kentucky resolve exactly the reverse. *They* hold those laws to be both highly proper and strictly constitutional. And now, Sir, how does the honorable member propose to deal with this case? How does he relieve us from this difficulty, upon any principle of his? His construction gets us into it; how does he propose to get us out?

In Carolina, the tariff is a palpable, deliberate usurpation; Carolina, therefore, may nullify it, and refuse to pay the duties. In Pennsylvania, it is both clearly constitutional and highly expedient; and there the duties are to be paid. And yet we live under a government of uniform laws, and under a Constitution too, which contains an express provision, as it happens, that all duties shall be equal in all the States. Does not this approach absurdity?

If there be no power to settle such questions, independent of either of the States, is not the whole Union a rope of sand? Are we not thrown back again, precisely, upon the old Confederation?

I must now beg to ask, Sir, Whence is this supposed right of the States derived? Where do they find the power to interfere with the laws of the Union? Sir, the opinion which the honorable gentleman maintains is a notion founded in a total misapprehension, in my judgment, of the origin of this government, and of the foundation on which it stands. I hold it to be a popular government, erected by the people; those who administer it, responsible to the people; and itself capable of being amended and modified, just as the people may choose it should be. It is as popular, just as truly emanating from the people, as the State governments. It is created for one purpose; the State governments for another. It has its own powers; they have theirs. There is no more authority with them to arrest the operation of a law of Congress, than with Congress to arrest the operation of their laws. We are here to administer a Constitution emanating immediately from the people, and trusted by them to our administration.

It is not the creature of State legislatures; nay, more, if the whole truth must be told, the people brought it into existence, established it, and have hitherto supported it, for the very purpose, amongst others, of imposing certain salutary restraints on State sovereignties. The States cannot now make war; they cannot contract alliances; they cannot make, each for itself, separate regulations of commerce; they cannot lay imposts; they cannot coin money. If this Constitution, Sir, be the creature of State legislatures, it must be admitted that it has obtained a strange control over the volitions of its creators.

This, Sir, was the first great step. By this the supremacy of the Constitution and laws of the United States is declared. The people so will it. No State law is to be valid which comes in conflict with the Constitution, or any law of the United States passed in pursuance of it. But who shall decide this question of interference? To whom lies the last appeal? This, Sir, the Constitution itself decides also, by declaring, *"that the judicial power shall extend to all cases arising under the Constitution and laws of the United States."* These two provisions cover the whole ground. They are, in truth, the keystone of the arch! With these it is a government; without them it is a confederation.

For myself, Sir, I do not admit the competency of South Carolina, or any other State, to prescribe my constitutional duty; or to settle, between me and the people, the validity of laws of Congress, for which I have voted. I decline her umpirage. I have not sworn to support the Constitution according to her construction of its clauses. I have not stipulated, by my oath of office or otherwise, to come under any responsibility, except to the people, and those whom they have appointed to pass upon the question, whether laws, supported by my votes, conform to the Constitution of the country.

And, Sir, if we look to the general nature of the case, could any thing have been more preposterous, than to make a government for the whole Union, and yet leave its powers subject, not to one interpretation, but to thirteen or twenty-four interpretations? Instead of one tribunal, established by all, responsible to all, with power to decide for all, shall constitutional questions be left to four-and-twenty popular bodies, each at liberty to decide for itself, and none bound to respect the decisions of others; and each at liberty, too, to give a new construction on every new election of its own members? Would any thing, with such a principle in it, or rather with such a destitution of all principle, be fit to be called a government? No, Sir. It should not be denominated a Constitution. It should be called, rather, a collection of topics for everlasting controversy; heads of debate for a disputatious people. It would not be a government. It would not be adequate to any practical good, or fit for any country to live under.

And now, Mr. President, let me run the honorable gentleman's doctrine a little into its practical application. Let us look at his probable *modus operandi.* If a thing can be done, an ingenious man can tell how it is to be done, and I wish to be informed how this State interference is to be put in practice, without violence, bloodshed, and rebellion. We will take the existing case of the tariff law. South Carolina is said to have made up her opinion upon it. If we do not repeal it (as we probably shall not), she will then apply to the case the remedy of her doctrine. She will, we must suppose, pass a law of her legislature, declaring the several acts of Congress, usually called the tariff laws, null and void, so far as they respect South Carolina, or the citizens thereof. So far, all is a paper transaction, and easy enough. But the collector at Charleston is collecting the duties imposed by these tariff laws. He, therefore, must be stopped. The collector will seize the goods if the tariff duties are not paid. The State authorities will undertake their rescue, the marshal, with his posse, will come to the collector's aid, and here the contest begins. The militia of the State will be called out to sustain the nullifying act. They will march, Sir, under a very gallant leader; for I believe the honorable member himself commands the militia of that part of the State.

Here would ensue a pause; for they say that a certain stillness precedes the tempest. The trumpeter would hold his breath awhile, and before all this military array should fall on the customhouse, collector, clerks, and all, it is very probable some of those composing it would request of their gallant commander-in-chief to be informed a little upon the point of law; for they have, doubtless, a just respect for his opinions as a lawyer, as well as for his bravery as a soldier. They know he has read Blackstone and the Constitution, as well as Turenne and Vauban. They would ask him, therefore, something concerning their rights in this matter. They would inquire, whether it was not somewhat dangerous to resist a law of the United States. What would be the nature of their offence, they would wish to learn, if they, by military force and array, resisted the execution in Carolina of a law of the United States, and it should turn out, after all, that the law *was constitutional?* He would answer, of course, Treason. No lawyer could give any other answer. John Fries, he would tell them, had learned that, some years ago. How, then, they would ask, do you propose to defend us? We are not afraid of bullets, but treason has a way of taking people off that we do not much relish. How do you propose to defend us? "South Carolina is a sovereign State," he would reply. That is true; but would the judge admit our plea? "These tariff laws," he would repeat, "are unconstitutional, palpably, deliberately, dangerously." That may all be so; but if the tribunal should not happen to be of that opinion, shall we swing for it? We are ready to die for our country, but it is rather an awkward business, this dying without touching the ground! After all, that is a sort of hemp tax worse than any part of the tariff.

Direct collision, therefore, between force and force, is the unavoidable result of that remedy for the revision of unconstitutional laws which the gentleman contends for. It must happen in the very first case to which it is applied. Is not this the plain result?

I profess, Sir, in my career hitherto, to have kept steadily in view the prosperity and honor of the whole country, and the preservation of our Federal Union. It is to that Union we owe our safety at home, and our consideration and dignity abroad. It is to that Union that we are chiefly indebted for whatever makes us most proud of our country. That Union we reached only by the discipline of our virtues in the severe school of adversity. It had its origin in the necessities of disordered finance, prostrate commerce, and ruined credit. Under its benign influences, these great interests immediately awoke, as from the dead, and sprang forth with newness of life. Every year of its duration has teemed with fresh proofs of its utility and its blessings; and although our territory has stretched out wider and wider, and our population spread farther and farther, they have not outrun its protection or its benefits. It has been to us all a copious fountain of national, social, and personal happiness.

I have not allowed myself, Sir, to look beyond the Union, to see what might lie hidden in the dark recess behind. I have not coolly weighed the chances of preserving liberty when the bonds that unite us together shall be broken asunder. I have not accustomed myself to hang over the precipice of disunion, to see whether, with my short sight, I can fathom the depth of the abyss below; nor could I regard him as a safe counsellor in the affairs of this government, whose thoughts should be mainly bent on considering, not how the Union may be best preserved, but how tolerable might be the condition of the people when it should be broken up and destroyed.

While the Union lasts, we have high, exciting, gratifying prospects spread out before us, for us and our children. Beyond that I seek not to penetrate the veil. God grant that in my day, at least, that curtain may not rise! God grant that on my vision never may be opened what lies behind! When my eyes shall be turned to behold for the last time the sun in heaven, may I not see him shining on the broken and dishonored fragments of a once glorious Union; on States dissevered, discordant, belligerent; on a land rent with civil feuds, or drenched, it may be, in fraternal blood! Let their last feeble and lingering glance rather behold the gorgeous ensign of the republic, now known and honored throughout the earth, still full high advanced, its arms and trophies streaming in their original lustre, not a stripe erased or polluted, nor a single star obscured, bearing for its motto, no such miserable interrogatory as "What is all this worth?" nor those other words of delusion and folly, "Liberty first and Union afterwards"; but everywhere, spread all over in characters of living light, blazing on all its ample folds, as they float over the sea and over the land, and in every wind under the whole heavens, that other sentiment, dear to every true American heart—Libery *and* Union, now and for ever, one and inseparable!

South Carolina Ordinance of Nullification, 1832

An Ordinance to Nullify Certain Acts of the Congress
of the United States, Purporting to Be Laws Laying Duties
and Imposts on the Importation of Foreign Commodities

Whereas the Congress of the United States, by various acts, purporting to be acts laying duties and imposts on foreign imports, but in reality intended for the protection of domestic manufactures, and the giving of bounties to classes and individuals engaged in particular employments, at the expense and to the injury and oppression of other classes and individuals, and by wholly exempting from taxation certain foreign commodities, such as are not produced or manufactured in the United States, to afford a pretext for imposing higher and excessive duties on articles similar to those intended to be protected, hath exceeded its just powers under the Constitution, which confers on it no authority to afford such protection, and hath violated the true meaning and intent of the Constitution, which provides for equality in imposing the burthens of taxation upon the several States and portions of the Confederacy: *And whereas* the said Congress, exceeding its just power to impose taxes and collect revenue for the purpose of effecting and accomplishing the specific objects and purposes which the Constitution of the United States authorizes it to effect and accomplish, hath raised and collected unnecessary revenue for objects unauthorized by the Constitution:—

We, therefore, the people of the State of South Carolina in Convention assembled, do declare and ordain, . . . That the several acts and parts of acts of the Congress of the United States, purporting to be laws for the imposing of duties and imposts on the importation of foreign commodities, . . . and, more especially, . . . [the tariff acts of 1828 and 1832] . . . , are unauthorized by the Constitution of the United States, and violate the true meaning and intent thereof, and are null, void, and no law, nor binding upon this State, its officers or citizens; and all promises, contracts, and cɔligations, made or entered into, or to be made or entered into, with purpose to secure the duties imposed by the said acts, and all judicial proceedings which shall be hereafter had in affirmance thereof, are and shall be held utterly null and void.

And it is further Ordained, That it shall not be lawful for any of the constituted authorities, whether of this State or of the United States, to enforce the payment of duties imposed by the said acts within the limits of this State; but it shall be the duty of the Legislature to adopt such measures and pass such acts as may be necessary to give full effect to this Ordinance, and to prevent the enforcement and arrest the operation of the said acts and parts of acts of the Congress of the United States within the limits of this State, from and after the 1st day of February next, . . .

And it is further Ordained, That in no case of law or equity, decided in the courts of this State, wherein shall be drawn in question the authority of this ordinance, or the validity of such act or acts of the Legislature as may be passed for the purpose of giving effect thereto, or the validity of the aforesaid acts of Congress, imposing duties, shall any appeal be taken or allowed to the Supreme Court of the United States, nor shall any copy of the record be printed or allowed for that purpose; and if any such appeal shall be attempted to be taken, the courts of this State shall proceed to execute and enforce their judgments, according to the laws and usages of the State, without reference to such attempted appeal, and the person or persons attempting to take such appeal may be dealt with as for a contempt of the court.

And it is further Ordained, That all persons now holding any office of honor, profit, or trust, civil or military, under this State, (members of the Legislature excepted), shall, within such time, and in such manner as the Legislature shall prescribe, take an oath well and truly to obey, execute, and enforce, this Ordinance, and such act or acts of the Legislature as may be passed in pursuance thereof, according to the true intent and meaning of the same; and on the neglect or omission of any such person or persons so to do, his or their office or offices shall be forthwith vacated, . . . and no person hereafter elected to any office of honor, profit, or trust, civil or military, (members of the Legislature excepted), shall, until the Legislature shall otherwise provide and direct, enter on the execution of his office, . . . until he shall, in like manner, have taken a similar oath; and no juror shall be empannelled in any of the courts of this State, in any cause in which shall be in question this Ordinance, or any act of the Legislature passed in pursuance thereof, unless he shall first, in addition to the usual oath, have taken an oath that he will well and truly obey, execute, and enforce this Ordinance, and such act or acts of the Legislature as may be passed to carry the same into operation and effect, according to the true intent and meaning thereof.

And we, the People of South Carolina, to the end that it may be fully understood by the Government of the United States, and the people of the co-States, that we are determined to maintain this, our Ordinance and Declaration, at every hazard, *Do further Declare* that we will not submit to the application of force, on the part of the Federal Government, to reduce this State to obedience; but that we will consider the passage, by Congress, of any act . . . to coerce the State, shut up her ports, destroy or harass her commerce, or to enforce the acts hereby declared to be null and void, otherwise than through the civil tribunals of the country, as inconsistent with the longer continuance of South Carolina in the Union: and that the people of this State will thenceforth hold themselves absolved from all further obligation to maintain or preserve their political connexion with the people of the other States, and will forthwith proceed to organize a separate Government, and do all other acts and things which sovereign and independent States may of right to do.

President Andrew Jackson's Proclamation to the People of South Carolina, 1832

Whereas a convention assembled in the State of South Carolina have passed an ordinance by which they declare "that the several acts and parts of acts of the Congress of the United States purporting to be laws for the imposing of duties and imposts on the importation of foreign commodities, . . . are unauthorized by the Constitution of the United States, and violate the true meaning and intent thereof, and are null and void and no law," nor binding on the citizens of that State or its officers; and by the said ordinance it is further declared to be unlawful for any of the constituted authorities of the State or of the United States to enforce the payment of the duties imposed by the said acts within the same State, and that it is the duty of the legislature to pass such laws as may be necessary to give full effect to the said ordinance; and

Whereas by the said ordinance it is further ordained that in no case of law or equity decided in the courts of said State wherein shall be drawn in question the validity of the said ordinance, or of the acts of the legislature that may be passed to give it effect, or of the said laws of the United States, no appeal shall be allowed to the Supreme Court of the United States, nor shall any copy of the record be permitted or allowed for that purpose, and that any person attempting to take such appeal shall be punished as for contempt of court; and . . .

Whereas the said ordinance prescribes to the people of South Carolina a course of conduct in direct violation of their duty as citizens of the United States, contrary to the laws of their country, subversive of its Constitution, and having for its object the destruction of the Union—

To preserve this bond of our political existence from destruction, to maintain inviolate this state of national honor and prosperity, and to justify the confidence my fellow-citizens have reposed in me, I, Andrew Jackson, President of the United States, have thought proper to issue this my proclamation, stating my views of the Constitution and laws applicable to the measures adopted by the convention of South Carolina and to the reasons they have put forth to sustain them, declaring the course which duty will require me to pursue, and, appealing to the understanding and patriotism of the people, warn them of the consequences that must inevitably result from an observance of the dictates of the convention. . . .

The ordinance is founded, not on the indefeasible right of resisting acts which are plainly unconstitutional and too oppressive to be endured, but on the strange position that any one State may not only declare an act of Congress void, but prohibit its execution; that they may do this consistently with the Constitution; that the true construction of that instrument permits a State to retain its place in the Union and yet be bound by no other of its laws than those it may choose to consider as constitutional. It is true, they add, that to justify this abrogation of a law it must be palpably contrary to the Constitution; but it is evident that to give the right of resisting laws of that description, coupled with the uncontrolled right to decide what laws deserve that character, is to give the power of resisting all laws; for as by the theory there is no appeal, the reasons alleged by the State, good or bad, must prevail. If it should be said that public opinion is a sufficient check against the abuse of this power, it may be asked why it is not deemed a sufficient guard against the passage of an unconstitutional act by Congress? There is, however, a restraint in this last case which makes the assumed power of a State more indefensible, and which does not exist in the other. There are two appeals from an unconstitutional act passed by Congress— one to the judiciary, the other to the people and the States. There is no appeal from the State decision in theory, and the practical illustration shows that the courts are closed against an application to review it, both judges and jurors being sworn to decide in its favor. But reasoning on this subject is superfluous when our social compact, in express terms, declares that the laws of the United States, its Constitution, and treaties made under it are the supreme law of the land, and, for greater caution, adds "that the judges in every State shall be bound thereby, anything in the constitution or laws of any State to the contrary notwithstanding." And it may be asserted without fear of refutation that no federative government could exist without a similar provision. Look for a moment to the consequence. If South Carolina considers the revenue laws unconstitutional and has a right to prevent their execution in the port of Charleston, there would be a clear constitutional objection to their collection in every other port; and no revenue could be collected anywhere, for all imposts must be equal. It is no answer to repeat that an unconstitutional law is no law so long as the question of its legality is to be decided by the State itself, for every law operating injuriously upon any local interest will be perhaps thought, and certainly represented, as unconstitutional, and, as has been shown, there is no appeal.

If this doctrine had been established at an earlier day, the Union would have been dissolved in its infancy. The excise law in Pennsylvania, the embargo and nonintercourse law in the Eastern States, the carriage tax in Virginia, were all deemed unconstitutional, and were more unequal in their operation than any of the laws now complained of; but, fortunately, none of those States discovered that they had the right now claimed by South Carolina. The war into which we were forced to support the dignity of the nation and the rights of our citizens might have ended in defeat and disgrace, instead of victory and honor, if the States who supposed it a ruinous and unconstitutional measure had thought they possessed the right of nullifying the act by which it was declared and denying supplies for its prosecution. Hardly and unequally as those measures bore upon several members of the Union, to the legislatures of none did this efficient and peaceable remedy, as it is called, suggest itself. The discovery of this important feature in our Constitution was reserved to the present day. To the statesmen of South Carolina belongs the invention, and upon the citizens of that State will unfortunately fall the evils of reducing it to practice.

If the doctrine of a State veto upon the laws of the Union carries with it internal evidence of its impracticable absurdity, our constitutional history will also afford abundant proof that it would have been repudiated with indignation had it been proposed to form a feature in our Government.

Our present Constitution was formed . . . in vain if this fatal doctrine prevails. It was formed for important objects that are announced in the preamble, made in the name and by the authority of the people of the United States, whose delegates framed and whose conventions approved it. The most important among these objects—that which is placed first in rank, on which all the others rest—is *"to form a more perfect union."* Now, is it possible that even if there were no express provision giving supremacy to the Constitution and laws of the United States over those of the States, can it be conceived that an instrument made for the purpose of *"forming a more perfect union"* than that of the Confederation could be so constructed by the assembled wisdom of our country as to substitute for that Confederation a form of government dependent for its existence on the local interest, the party spirit, of a State, or of a prevailing faction in a State? Every man of plain, unsophisticated understanding who hears the question will give such an answer as will preserve the Union. Metaphysical subtlety, in pursuit of an impracticable theory, could alone have devised one that is calculated to destroy it.

I consider, then, the power to annul a law of the United States, assumed by one State, *incompatible with the existence of the Union, contradicted expressly by the letter of the Constitution, unauthorized by its spirit, incon-*

sistent with every principle on which it was founded, and destructive of the great object for which it was formed.

After this general view of the leading principle, we must examine the particular application of it which is made in the ordinance.

The preamble rests its justification on these grounds: It assumes as a fact that the obnoxious laws, although they purport to be laws for raising revenue, were in reality intended for the protection of manufactures, which purpose it asserts to be unconstitutional; that the operation of these laws is unequal; that the amount raised by them is greater than is required by the wants of the Government; and, finally, that the proceeds are to be applied to objects unauthorized by the Constitution. These are the only causes alleged to justify an open opposition to the laws of the country and a threat of seceding from the Union if any attempt should be made to enforce them. The first virtually acknowledges that the law in question was passed under a power expressly given by the Constitution to lay and collect imposts; but its constitutionality is drawn in question from the *motives* of those who passed it. However apparent this purpose may be in the present case, nothing can be more dangerous than to admit the position that an unconstitutional purpose entertained by the members who assent to a law enacted under a constitutional power shall make that law void. For how is that purpose to be ascertained? Who is to make the scrutiny? How often may bad purposes be falsely imputed, in how many cases are they concealed by false professions, in how many is no declaration of motive made? Admit this doctrine, and you give to the States an uncontrolled right to decide, and every law may be annulled under this pretext. If, therefore, the absurd and dangerous doctrine should be admitted that a State may annul an unconstitutional law, or one that it deems such, it will not apply to the present case.

The next objection is that the laws in question operate unequally. This objection may be made with truth to every law that has been or can be passed. The wisdom of man never yet contrived a system of taxation that would operate with perfect equality. If the unequal operation of a law makes it unconstitutional, and if all laws of that description may be abrogated by any State for that cause, then, indeed, is the Federal Constitution unworthy of the slightest effort for its preservation. . . . Nor did the States, when they severally ratified it, do so under the impression that a veto on the laws of the United States was reserved to them or that they could exercise it by implication. Search the debates in all their conventions, examine the speeches of the most zealous opposers of Federal authority, look at the amendments that were proposed; they are all silent—not a syllable uttered, not a vote given, not a motion made to correct the explicit supremacy given to the laws of the Union over those of the States, or to show that implication, as is now contended, could defeat it. No; we have not erred. The Constitution is still the object of our reverence, the bond of our Union, our defense in danger, the source of our prosperity in peace. It shall descend, as we have received it, uncorrupted by sophistical construction, to our posterity; and the sacrifices of local interest, of State prejudices, of personal animosities, that were made to bring it into existence, will again be patriotically offered for its support.

The two remaining objections made by the ordinance to these laws are that the sums intended to be raised by them are greater than are required and that the proceeds will be unconstitutionally employed. . . .

The ordinance, with the same knowledge of the future that characterizes a former objection, tells you that the proceeds of the tax will be unconstitutionally applied. If this could be ascertained with certainty, the objection would with more propriety be reserved for the law so applying the proceeds, but surely can not be urged against the laws levying the duty.

These are the allegations contained in the ordinance. Examine them seriously, my fellow-citizens; judge for yourselves. I appeal to you to determine whether they are so clear, so convincing, as to leave no doubt of their correctness; and even if you should come to this conclusion, how far they justify the reckless, destructive course which you are directed to pursue. Review these objections and the conclusions drawn from them once more. What are they? Every law, then, for raising revenue, according to the South Carolina ordinance, may be rightfully annulled, unless it be so framed as no law ever will or can be framed. Congress have a right to pass laws for raising revenue and each State have a right to oppose their execution—two rights directly opposed to each other; and yet is this absurdity supposed to be contained in an instrument drawn for the express purpose of avoiding collisions between the States and the General Government by an assembly of the most enlightened statesmen and purest patriots ever embodied for a similar purpose.

In vain have these sages declared that Congress shall have power to lay and collect taxes, duties, imposts, and excises; in vain have they provided that they shall have power to pass laws which shall be necessary and proper to carry those powers into execution, that those laws and that Constitution shall be the "supreme law of the land, and that the judges in every State shall be bound thereby, anything in the constitution or laws of any State to the contrary notwithstanding"; . . . if a bare majority of the voters in any one State may, on a real or supposed knowledge of the intent with which a law has been passed, declare themselves free from its operation; . . .

The Constitution declares that the judicial powers of the United States extend to cases arising under the laws of the United States, and that such laws, the Constitution, and treaties shall be paramount to the State constitutions and laws. The judiciary act prescribes the mode by which the case may be brought before a court of the United States by appeal when a State tribunal shall decide against this provision of the Constitution. The ordinance declares there shall be no appeal—makes the State law paramount to the Constitution and laws of the United States, forces judges and jurors to swear that they will disregard their provisions, and even makes it penal in a suitor to attempt relief by appeal. It further declares that it shall not be lawful for the authorities of the United States or of that State to enforce the payment of duties imposed by the revenue laws within its limits.

Here is a law of the United States, not even pretended to be unconstitutional, repealed by the authority of a small majority of the voters of a single State. Here is a provision of the Constitution which is solemnly abrogated by the same authority.

On such expositions and reasonings the ordinance grounds not only an assertion of the right to annul the laws of which it complains, but to enforce it by a threat of seceding from the Union if any attempt is made to execute them.

This right to secede is deduced from the nature of the Constitution, which, they say, is a compact between sovereign States who have preserved their whole sovereignty and therefore are subject to no superior; that because they made the compact they can break it when in their opinion it has been departed from by the other States. Fallacious as this course of reasoning is, it enlists State pride and finds advocates in the honest prejudices of those who have not studied the nature of our Government sufficiently to see the radical error on whch it rests. . . .

The Constitution of the United States, then, forms a *government,* not a league; and whether it be formed by compact between the States or in any other manner, its character is the same. It is a Government in which all the people are represented, which operates directly on the people individually, not upon the States; they retained all the power they did not grant. But each State, having expressly parted with so many powers as to constitute, jointly with the other States, a single nation, can not, from that period, possess any right to secede, because such secession does not break a league, but destroys the unity of a nation; and any injury to that unity is not only a breach which would result from the contravention of a compact, but it is an offense against the whole Union. To say that any State may at pleasure secede from the Union is to say that the United States are not a nation, because it would be a solecism to contend that any part of a nation might dissolve its connection with the other parts, to their injury or ruin, without committing any offense. Secession, like any other revolutionary act, may be morally justified by the extremity of oppression; but to call it a constitutional right is confounding the meaning of terms, and can only be done through gross error or to deceive those who are willing to assert a right, but would pause before they made a revolution or incur the penalties consequent on a failure.

Because the Union was formed by a compact, it is said the parties to that compact may, when they feel themselves aggrieved, depart from it; but it is precisely because it is a compact that they can not. A compact is an agreement or binding obligation. It may by its terms have a sanction or penalty for its breach, or it may not. It if contains no sanction, it may be broken with no other consequence than moral guilt; if it has a sanction, then the breach incurs the designated or implied penalty. A league between independent nations generally has no sanction other than a moral one; or if it should contain a penalty, as there is no common superior it can not be enforced. A government, on the contrary, always has a sanction, express or implied; and in our case it is both necessarily implied and expressly given. An attempt, by force of arms, to destroy a government is an offense, by whatever means the constitutional compact may have been formed; and such government has the right by the law of self-defense to pass acts for punishing the offender, unless that right is modified, restrained, or resumed by the constitutional act. In our system, although it is modified in the case of treason, yet authority is expressly given to pass all laws necessary to carry its powers into effect, and under this grant provision has been made for punishing acts which obstruct the due administration of the laws.

It would seem superfluous to add anything to show the nature of that union which connects us, but as erroneous opinions on this subject are the foundation of doctrines the most destructive to our peace, I must give some further development to my views on this subject. . . .

The States severally have not retained their entire sovereignty. It has been shown that in becoming parts of a nation, not members of a league, they surrendered many of their essential parts of sovereignty. The right to make treaties, declare war, levy taxes, exercise exclusive judicial and legislative powers, were all of them functions of sovereign power. The States, then, for all these important purposes were no longer sovereign. . . . How, then, with all these proofs that under all changes of our position we had, for designated purposes and with defined powers, created national governments, how is it that the most perfect of those several modes of union should now be considered as a mere league that may be dissolved at pleasure? It is from an abuse of terms. Compact is used as synonymous with league, although the true term is not employed, because it would at once show the fallacy of the reasoning. It would not do to say that our Constitution was only a league, but it is labored to prove it a compact (which in one sense it is) and then to argue that as a league is a compact every compact between nations must of course be a league, and that from such an engagement every sovereign power has a right to recede. But it has been shown that in this sense the States are not sovereign, and that even if they were, and the national Constitution had been formed by compact, there would be no right in any one State to exonerate itself from its obligations.

This, then, is the position in which we stand: A small majority of the citizens of one State in the Union have elected delegates to a State convention; that convention has ordained that all the revenue laws of the United States must be repealed, or that they are no longer a member of the Union. The governor of that State has recommended to the legislature the raising of an army to carry the secession into effect, and that he may be empowered to give clearances to vessels in the name of the State. No act of violent opposition to the laws has yet been committed, but such a state of things is hourly apprehended. And it is the intent of this instrument to *proclaim*, not only that the duty imposed on me by the Constitution "to take care that the laws be faithfully executed" shall be performed to the extent of the powers already vested in me by law, or of such others as the wisdom of Congress shall devise and intrust to me for that purpose, but to warn the citizens of South Carolina who have been deluded into an opposition to the laws of the danger they will incur by obedience to the illegal and disorganizing ordinance of the convention; to exhort those who have refused to support it to persevere in their determination to uphold the Constitution and laws of their country; and to point out to all the perilous situation into which the good people of that State have been led, and that the course they are urged to pursue is one of ruin and disgrace to the very State whose rights they affect to support. . . .

If your leaders could succeed in establishing a separation, what would be your situation? Are you united at home? Are you free from the apprehension of civil discord, with all its fearful consequences? Do our neighboring republics, every day suffering some new revolution or contending with some new insurrection, do they excite your envy? But the dictates of a high duty oblige me solemnly to announce that you can not succeed. The laws of the United States must be executed. I have no discretionary power on the subject; my duty is emphatically pronounced in the Constitution. Those who told you that you might peaceably prevent their execution deceived you; they could not have been deceived themselves. They know that a forcible opposition could alone prevent the execution of the laws, and they know that such opposition must be repelled. Their object is disunion. But be not deceived by names. Disunion by armed force is *treason*. Are you really ready to incur its guilt? If you are, on the heads of the instigators of the act be the dreadful consequences; on their heads be the dishonor, but on yours may fall the punishment. On your unhappy State will inevitably fall all the evils of the conflict you force upon the Government of your country. It can not accede to the mad project of disunion, of which you would be the first victims. Its First Magistrate can not, if he would, avoid the performance of his duty. The consequence must be fearful for you, distressing to your fellow-citizens here and to the friends of good government throughout the world. Its enemies have beheld our prosperity with a vexation they could not conceal; it was a standing refutation of their slavish doctrines, and they will point to our discord with the triumph of malignant joy. It is yet in your power to disappoint them. . . .

Fellow-citizens of the United States, the threat of unhallowed disunion, the names of those once respected by whom it is uttered, the array of military force to support it, denote the approach of a crisis in our affairs on which the continuance of our unexampled prosperity, our political existence, and perhaps that of all free governments may depend. The conjuncture demanded a free, a full, and explicit enunciation, not only of my intentions, but of my principles of action; and as the claim was asserted of a right by a State to annul the laws of the Union, and even to secede from it at pleasure, a frank exposition of my opinions in relation to the origin and form of our Government and the construction I give to the instrument by which it was created seemed to be proper. Having the fullest confidence in the justness of the legal and constitutional opinion of my duties which has been expressed, I rely with equal confidence on your undivided support in my determination to execute the laws, to preserve the Union by all constitutional means, to arrest, if possible, by moderate and firm measures the necessity of a recourse to force; and if it be the will of Heaven that the recurrence of its primeval curse on man for the shedding of a brother's blood should fall upon our land, that it be not called down by any offensive act on the part of the United States.

Fellow-citizens, the momentous case is before you. On your undivided support of your Government depends the decision of the great question it involves—whether your sacred Union will be preserved and the blessing it secures to us as one people shall be perpetuated. No one can doubt that the unanimity with which that decision will be expressed will be such as to inspire new confidence in republican institutions, and that the prudence, the wisdom, and the courage which it will bring to their defense will transmit them unimpaired and invigorated to our children.

May the Great Ruler of Nations grant that the signal blessings with which He has favored ours may not, by the madness of party or personal ambition, be disregarded and lost; and may His wise providence bring those who have produced this crisis to see the folly before they feel the misery of civil strife, and inspire a returning veneration for that Union which, if we may dare to penetrate His designs, He has chosen as the only means of attaining the high destinies to which we may reasonably aspire.

South Carolina's Ordinance to Nullify the Force Bill, 1833

We, the People of the State of South Carolina in Convention assembled, do *Declare and Ordain,* that the Act of the Congress of the United States, entitled "An Act further to provide for the collection of duties on imports," approved the second day of March, 1833, is unauthorized by the Constitution of the United States, subversive of that Constitution, and destructive of public liberty; and that the same is, and shall be deemed, null and void, within the limits of this State; and it shall be the duty of the Legislature, at such time as they may deem expedient, to adopt such measures and pass such acts as may be necessary to prevent the enforcement thereof, and to inflict proper penalties on any person who shall do any act in execution or enforcement of the same within the limits of this State.

We do further Declare and Ordain, That the allegiance of the citizens of this State, while they continue such, is due to the said State; and that obedience only, and not allegiance, is due by them to any other power or authority, to whom a control over them has been, or may be delegated by the State; and the General Assembly of the said State is hereby empowered, from time to time, when they may deem it proper, to provide for the administration to the citizens and officers of the State, or such of the said officers as they may think fit, of suitable oaths or affirmations, binding them to the observance of such allegiance; and abjuring all other allegiance; and, also, to define what shall amount to a violation of their allegiance, and to provide the proper punishment for such violation.

Worcester v. *Georgia,* 1832

6 PETERS 515 (1832)

[5-1: Marshall, Duvall, McLean,
Thompson, Story; Baldwin]

Marshall, C. J. This cause, in every point of view in which it can be placed, is of the deepest interest.

The defendant is a State, a member of the Union, which has exercised the powers of government over a people who deny its jurisdiction, and are under the protection of the United States.

The plaintiff is a citizen of the State of Vermont, condemned to hard labor for four years in the penitentiary of Georgia under color of an act which he alleges to be repugnant to the Constitution, laws, and treaties of the United States.

The legislative power of a State, the controlling power of the Constitution and laws of the United States, the rights, if they have any, the political existence of a once numerous and powerful people, the personal liberty of a citizen, all are involved in the subject now to be considered. . . .

We must inquire and decide whether the act of the Legislature of Georgia under which the plaintiff in error has been prosecuted and condemned, be consistent with, or repugnant to the Constitution, laws and treaties of the United States.

It has been said at the bar that the acts of the Legislature of Georgia seize on the whole Cherokee country, parcel it out among the neighboring counties of the State, extend her code over the whole country, abolish its institutions and its laws, and annihilate its political existence.

If this be the general effect of the system, let us inquire into the effect of the particular statute and section on which the indictment is founded.

It enacts that "all white persons, residing within the limits of the Cherokee Nation on the 1st day of March next, or at any time thereafter, without a licence or permit from his excellency the governor . . . and who shall not have taken the oath hereinafter required, shall be guilty of a high misdemeanor, and upon conviction thereof, shall be punished by confinement to the penitentiary at hard labor for a term not less than four years." . . .

The extraterritorial power of every Legislature being limited in its action to its own citizens or subjects, the very passage of this act is an assertion of jurisdiction over the Cherokee Nation, and of the rights and powers consequent on jurisdiction.

The first step, then, in the inquiry which the Constitution and the laws impose on this court, is an examination of the rightfulness of this claim. . . .

From the commencement of our government Congress has passed acts to regulate trade and intercourse with the Indians; which treat them as nations, respect their rights, and manifest a firm purpose to afford that protection which treaties stipulate. All these acts, and especially that of 1802, which is still in force, manifestly consider the several Indian nations as distinct political communities, having territorial boundaries, within which their authority is exclusive, and having a right to all the lands within those boundaries, which is not only acknowledged, but guaranteed by the United States. . . .

The Cherokee Nation, then, is a distinct community, occupying its own territory, with boundaries accurately described, in which the laws of Georgia can have no force, and which the citizens of Georgia have no right to enter but with the assent of the Cherokees themselves or in conformity with treaties and with the acts of Congress. The whole intercourse between the United States and this nation is, by our Constitution and laws, vested in the government of the United States.

The act of the State of Georgia under which the plaintiff in error was prosecuted is consequently void, and the judgement a nullity. . . . The Acts of Georgia are repugnant to the Constitution, laws, and treaties of the United States.

They interfere forcibly with the relations established between the United States and the Cherokee Nation, the regulation of which according to the settled principles of our Constitution, are committed exclusively to the government of the Union.

They are in direct hostility with treaties, repeated in a succession of years, which mark out the boundary that separates the Cherokee country from Georgia; guarantee to them all the land within their boundary; solemnly pledge the faith of the United States to restrain their citizens from trespassing on it; and recognize the preexisting power of the nation to govern itself.

They are in equal hostility with the acts of Congress for regulating this intercourse, and giving effect to the treaties.

The forcible seizure and abduction of the plaintiff, who was residing in the nation with its permission, and by authority of the President of the United States, is also a violation of the acts which authorize the chief magistrate to exercise this authority. . . .

Judgement reversed.

⌗ E S S A Y S

On first impression, it would seem that Jackson and the Unionists prevailed in the nullification crisis. On closer examination, however, the story becomes considerably more complex. As this chapter's two contrasting essays show, historians' disagreements about the crisis are rooted in contending views about the nature of the states' right debate. In the first essay, Robert V. Remini, the leading modern biographer of Andrew Jackson, interprets events in a way that gives Jackson high marks for maintaining the Union and asserting the supremacy of the national government. Jackson had been equally successful, according to Remini, in propounding the view that the Union was perpetual.

Richard Ellis, a historian at the State University of New York at Buffalo, in the second essay takes strong exception to Remini's arguments. He believes that the crisis did little to establish the permanency of the Union, and he chastises other historians for portraying the event as a struggle between adherents of a strong national government and proponents of states' rights. Instead, Ellis believes that the conflict largely raged between states' rights groups, and that it was the exponents of secession—a doctrine even more radical than nullification—who won the day. Ellis's essay also accurately situates the nullification crisis in the pre–Civil War debate about the Supreme Court's powers of constitutional interpretation.

Nullification Defeated

ROBERT V. REMINI

. . . The central question of the nullification controversy, raised by the tariff dispute, was whether the states had the right to declare federal law invalid within their boundaries (and, if necessary, to secede from the Union) in order to protect their rights, particularly their property rights. And Congress could not provide the answer. The sense of the members as a group was unclear and inexact. There were three distinct viewpoints: one class of politician contended for the "inalienable & indefensible right of a state to secede at pleasure;—another class, that there is no such right, consistent with the constitution, or theory of the Government—and a third class seem disposed to admit the right to secede, but maintain the right of the other states, on the first principle of self preservation, to whip the seceding states into submission."

Andrew Jackson had an absolutely clear conception of his position on this question. It was simple, direct, and logical. It may not have been historically accurate, but he sincerely believed it to be so. Most important, it proceeded from his commitment to democratic principles. The federal government, he said, was "based on a confederation of perpetual union" by an act of the people. A state may never secede, and that was final. Moreover, the people, not the states, granted sovereignty to the federal government through the Constitution. They called the Union into existence, they created the federal government, and they granted federal power. These actions, he insisted, were taken by the people at conventions that ratified the Constitution. And in ratifying the Constitution the people automatically amended their state constitutions to accord with the new arrangement.

Jackson felt totally comfortable with this position. He believed it to be the only one guaranteed to safeguard the liberty and rights of all. And he was sure the American electorate supported his view.

One day he was visited by an old army comrade, General Sam Dale. The nullification controversy clearly troubled the President, and he expressed his concern over what might happen if his theory of government did not in fact command popular support. But the doubting thought was instantly dismissed. "General Dale," Jackson said, "if this thing goes on, our country will be like a bag of meal with both ends open. Pick it up in the middle or endwise, and it will run out. I must tie the bag and save the country."

Excerpts from *Andrew Jackson and the Course of American Democracy, 1833–1845,* Vol. III. by Robert V. Remini, pp. 16–23, 44. Copyright © 1984 by Robert V. Remini. Reprinted by permission of HarperCollins Publishers.

Dale tried to reassure him by expressing the hope that things eventually would go right.

"They SHALL go right, sir," Jackson cried. And he reacted so passionately that he shivered his pipe upon the table.

To make things "go right," Jackson prepared for immediate executive action. "As soon as it can be had in authentic form," he wrote in a private memorandum, referring to the Ordinance of Nullification, "meet it with a proclamation."

A presidential proclamation to the people of South Carolina was what he had in mind. A bold, forthright statement of what nullification entailed in terms of inevitable bloodshed and civil war. More than that, the proclamation was meant to generate a "moral force" in the country to counteract the forces of disunion; it was meant to reach out to all Americans—not simply South Carolinians—and rally them to the defense of the Union and the Constitution.

Jackson had no way of knowing beforehand whether such a proclamation would actually create this "moral force" and unite the people behind him. But he sensed instinctively that this was the proper action for him to take. He knew precisely what he wanted to say in his proclamation. It was just a matter of finding the right words. Unlike his fourth annual message to Congress, which had soft-pedaled the issue and which some interpreted as "a complete surrender to the nullifiers," the proclamation must carry a strong and eloquent statement to excite the entire nation.

Naturally, as he had done so often in the past, Jackson turned first for assistance to his Kitchen Cabinet, in particular Amos Kendall. The astute, energetic, and reform-minded Kendall was a vigorous writer whose previous efforts, such as the Bank veto, were much admired by the President. But on this occasion Kendall failed him. His attempt was too restrained, too muted, too similar to the annual message. Jackson wanted something more thrusting, something so eloquent as to "strike to the heart and speak to the feelings" of all Americans. So he turned to Edward Livingston, his secretary of state.

A plain-looking man, but not unattractive, with a prominent nose and expansive forehead, Livingston was a brilliant scholar of the law. Among his friends and admirers he was known as Beau Ned because of the fastidiousness of his dress and the elegance of his manner. As a member of the cabinet, as a writer whose style frequently matched the grace and refinement of his bearing, and as one of the nation's outstanding constitutional minds, he could give the proclamation authority, grandeur, learning. But it must have fire. That above all.

Not that Livingston needed to provide the ideas for this proclamation. That the President would take care of himself. In fact Jackson closeted himself in his office and scribbled page after page of what he wanted said. Writing rapidly and with great emotion, he poured out his ideas about the Union, its preservation, and the rights of the states. His entire being vibrated with the intensity of his thought and conviction. After he had written fifteen or twenty pages, he was interrupted by a visitor who noted that three of the pages were still glistening with wet ink. "The warmth, the glow, the passion, the eloquence" of the proclamation shone bright on those still-moist sheets.

Gathering these pages, along with the sheaves of notes and memoranda that he normally wrote on all major issues, Jackson presented them to Livingston and asked him to shape the proclamation into an authoritative and persuasive presidential paper. Livingston was honored, and said so. He took the sheets to his office, labored over them for three or four days, and then returned the finished product to Old Hickory.

In the quiet of his study, with no one to disturb him, Jackson scrutinized the finished product. As he read a look of disappointment flickered across his face. He was clearly dissatisfied. The work did not convey the full essence of his intent. Jackson fidgeted in his seat, he rose and paced the floor, and then he turned to Major Lewis's room to share his disappointment with his old friend.

Livingston had not correctly understood his notes, he complained. Parts of the draft did not express his views with the precision and passion that he wanted. After a moment's pause and a comment or two from Lewis, the President decided to ask for extensive revisions. He summoned Livingston and informed him that certain passages would have to be rewritten. He needed to rally public sentiment to the defense of the Union and the draft had not provided it. Livingston expressed his regrets over his failure and said he would try again.

Jackson returned to his own room and struggled to find the exact words he wanted. On such occasions he worked long into the night with only a servant nearby to keep the fire going. On the evening of Tuesday, December 4, 1832, Jackson composed a conclusion to the proclamation and sent it to Livingston with his instructions. The document carried the full thrust of his intent.

for the conclusion of the proclamation

Seduced as you have been, my fellow countryment by the delusive theories and misrepresentation of ambitious, *deluded* & designing men, I call upon you in the language of truth, and with the feelings of a Father to retrace your steps. As you value liberty and the blessings of peace blot out from the page of your history a record so fatal to their security as this ordinance will become if it be obeyed. Rally again under the banners of the union whose obligations you in common with all your countrymen have, with an appeal to heaven, sworn to support, and which must be indesoluble as long as we are capable of enjoying freedom.

Recollect that the first act of resistance to the laws which have been denounced as void by those who abuse your confidence and falsify your hopes is Treason, and subjects you to all the pains and penalties that are provided for the highest offence against your country. Can the descendants of the Rutledges, the Pinckneys, the Richardsons, the Middletons, the Sumpters, the Marions, the Pickens, the Bratons, the Taylors, the Haynes, the Gadsdens, the Bratons [*sic*] the Winns, the Hills, the Kershaws, and the Crawfords, with the descendants of thousands more of the patriots of the revolution that might be named, consent to become Traitors? Forbid it Heaven!

Dr Sir-

I submit the above as the conclusion of the proclamation for your amendment & revision. Let it receive your best flight of eloquence to strike to the heart, & speak to the feelings of my deluded countrymen of South Carolina—The Union must be preserved, without blood if this be possible—but it must be preserved at all hazards and at any price yours with high regard

> Andrew Jackson
> Decb. 4th 1832
> 11 oclock P.M.

Edward Livingston Esqr—

Jackson carefully noted the precise time of day that he signed this document. He knew the significance of his proclamation and appreciated its historic moment. In fact, on many of the documents and letters he wrote during the crisis, he carefully recorded the day, date, and time.

Livingston took Jackson's written conclusion and extensively revised it, eliminating most of the names of the distinguished South Carolinians that Jackson had laboriously included. But the fire and temper of the presidential piece was retained.

At 4 P.M., Friday, December 7, 1832, Livingston returned with a second draft. After a slow and thoughtful reading, Jackson pronounced it satisfactory, although he asked for a few further changes in the final paragraphs. The opening sections needed nothing more and Jackson turned them over to Major Andrew Jackson Donelson, his secretary and former ward, and asked that they be copied. At this point Jackson emphasized speed. He was very anxious to issue the proclamation as quickly as possible. "The Message [to Congress] having been made public on the 4th," he explained to Livingston, "it is desirable, whilst it is drawing the attention of the people in South Carolina, that their minds should be drawn to their *real situation*, before their leaders can, by false theories, delude them again. Therefore it is, to prevent blood from being shed, & positive treason committed, that I wish to draw the attention of the people of South Carolina to their danger, that no blame can attach to me, by being silent. From these reasons you can judge of my anxiety to have this to follow the Message."

These words clearly show how anxious Jackson was to avoid not only bloodshed but the accusation that he had failed to exert himself sufficiently to prevent the crisis from escalating. It was never his desire to seek a confrontation. He did everything in his power to avoid conflict because he knew how easy it was for such things to fly out of hand and lead to irreversible calamity.

As these final preparations for the publication of the proclamation took place, Major Lewis politely suggested to Jackson that he delete those portions of the message that might offend the "States-rights party." No need to antagonize them, he said.

The President glowered. "Those are my views," he rumbled, "and I will not change them nor strike them out."

It was at moments like these that his colleagues in the cabinet recognized the true quality of Jackson's statemanship. "The President has much more sagacity in civil affairs," wrote one astute observer, "and a much fuller acquaintance with the principles and practice of the government than many of his opponents are willing to concede. He is very firm in his opinions— inflexibly upright—devoted to his public duties."

The proclamation, dated December 10, 1832, was published on December 11. It is one of the most significant presidential documents in American history and has been frequently compared to Lincoln's inaugural addresses. It contains the subtlety of language to make its legal and constitutional arguments both impressive and persuasive. Yet it contains enough Jacksonian passion to give it spirit and life. Much of the wording and subtlety of expression should be credited to Livingston, but the ideas of government, the conviction of its sentiment, and the weight of its thought belong to Jackson.

The proclamation opened by declaring the actions of the nullifying convention inconsistent with the duty of citizens, subversive of the Constitution, and aimed ultimately at the destruction of the Union. To prevent this destruction and maintain the honor and prosperity of the nation and justify the confidence placed in the President by the American people, "I, Andrew Jackson, President of the United States, have thought it proper to issue this my proclamation" and state "my views of the Constitution" and its laws and declare the course this administration will pursue.

"Strict duty" required "nothing more," the President said, than the exercise of his powers to preserve peace and enforce the nation's laws. Then he slammed head on against the argument of the nullifiers—and pronounced it false. "I consider, then, the power to annul a law of the United States, assumed by one State, *incompatible with the existence of the Union, contradicted expressly by the letter of the Constitution, unauthorized by its spirit, inconsistent with every principle on which it was founded, and destructive of the great object for which it was formed.*"

In directing the publication of his proclamation the President personally ordered these words italicized. He wanted the people of South Carolina— indeed the entire nation—to appreciate the import of what he was saying.

The people of the United States, Jackson went on, formed the Constitution, acting through their respective states. "We are *one people* in the choice of President and Vice President." The people, he declared, not the states, are represented in the executive branch. This assertion culminated Jackson's efforts to redefine the presidency and the relation of the American people to their government. It was another appeal for recognition that it was the presidential office—not the legislature, no matter what Webster or Clay or Calhoun argued—that embodies all the people. The President is the representative of the American electorate and directly responsible to them. By his actions and words he articulates and executes their will.

The Constitution, he continued, "forms a *government*, not a league," a government in which all the people are represented and which operates directly on the people themselves, not upon the states. A "single nation" having been formed, it follows that the states do not "possess any right to secede."

In addressing the question of secession and whether it was included among the rights of the states, Jackson was treading on very thin ice. And he knew it. Still he felt obliged as President to state his views since South Carolina had already declared that it would secede if force were applied to collect the tariff duties. "Surely then if the Proclamation were necessary to show the country what the Executive would do in the case of Nullification, it was also necessary to indicate his course in the event of secession." And the right of secession did not belong to the states, he argued. For if South Carolina could secede for Congress's levying tariff duties, then Rhode Island could secede "for taking them off," and that was absurd.

Nor, the President went on, have the states retained their entire sovereignty. They surrendered "essential parts of sovereignty" in "becoming parts of a nation," such as the right to declare war, make treaties, and exercise exclusive judicial and legislative powers. The allegiance of their citizens was also altered. It was transferred to the government of the United States. Their citizens became American citizens and owed obedience to the Constitution and its laws.

Again and again Jackson struck at the very root of the nullification argument. Again and again he stated his fundamental creed: The people are sovereign. The Union is perpetual.

Jackson's proclamation comes close, contends one modern historian, "to being the definitive statement of the case for perpetuity" of the Union. Among the many presentations decades later of the argument of a perpetual Union, the proclamation "stands above the rest for its incisiveness, coherence, and comprehensiveness." So complete is it, that the Supreme Court in 1869 could find no additional argument of any moment or significance.

The Union is older than the states, Jackson declared. Its political character commenced long before the adoption of the Constitution. "Under the royal Government we had no separate character; our opposition to its oppressions began as *united colonies.* We were the *United States* under the Confederation, and the name was perpetuated and the Union rendered more perfect by the Federal Constitution."

Here, then, is Jackson's unique contribution to a more profound understanding and appreciation of the American experiment in democracy and constitutional government. He was the first American statesman to offer the doctrine of the Union as a perpetual entity. His arguments and conclusions provide a complete brief against the right of a state to secede. In terms of constitutional arguments, Jackson's statement is far greater than Daniel Webster's more famous second reply to Hayne. Webster relied on a sentimental appeal, arguing for the Union "as a blessing to mankind." Jackson went beyond sentiment. He offered history and a dynamic new reading of constitutional law.

Jackson's extraordinary understanding of what is meant by "the United States" did not arise from some profound intellectual exercise or a mastery of history and political science. Rather it was something that emanated directly from his background and education as lawyer, judge, legislator, military commander and politician. He simply knew as a fact, revealed by "common sense," that the people had called the Union into existence, and that only they could alter or dissolve it. To argue otherwise, he said, "reduces every thing to anarchy & strikes at the very existence of society."

Having forcefully refuted the leading arguments of the nullifiers, Jackson concluded the proclamation with a direct appeal to the people of South Carolina. The mood and tone of the message changed dramatically, and here Jackson's own hand can be seen guiding the sentiment behind the words. Like a sorrowing but resolute parent, he warns his children of the consequence of their folly. It pains him to speak so harshly, he said, but he is determined that they behave like responsible and dutiful children. "Fellow-citizens of my native State," he began, "let me not only admonish you as the First Magistrate of our common country, not to incur the penalty of its laws, but use the influence that a father would over his children whom he saw rushing to certain ruin. In that paternal language, with that paternal feeling, let me tell you, my countrymen, that you are deluded by men who are either deceived themselves or wish to deceive you. Mark under what pretenses you have been led on to the brink of insurrection and treason on which you stand."

Behold this happy country, he enthused. See the asylum where the wretched and oppressed find refuge. Look and say, *"We too are citizens of America.* Carolina is one of these proud States; her arms have defended, her best blood has cemented, this happy Union. And then add, if you can . . . this happy Union we will dissolve; this picture of peace and prosperity we will deface; this free intercourse we will interrupt; these fertile fields we will deluge with blood; the protection of that glorious flag we renounce; the very name of Americans we discard."

This powerful nationalistic thrust, this appeal to sentiment and patriotism reached far beyond the people of South Carolina. It deeply affected citizens in every state. It rallied nationalists everywhere.

Then Jackson's tone darkened. The laws of the United States must be executed, he declared. "I have no discretionary power on the subject; my duty is emphatically pronounced in the Constitution." Let there be no misunderstanding of what is involved. Let the truth be known as to what will happen if the laws are disobeyed.

> Those who told you that you might peaceably prevent their execution deceived you; they could not have been deceived themselves. They know that a forcible opposition could alone prevent the execution of the laws, and they know that such opposition must be repelled. Their object is disunion. But be not deceived by names. Disunion by armed force is *treason.* Are you really ready to incur its guilt? If you are, on the heads of the instigators of the act be the dreadful consequences; on their heads be the dishonor, but on yours may fall the punishment. On your unhappy State will inevitably fall all the evils of the conflict you force upon the Government of your country. It can not accede to the mad project of disunion, of which you

would be the first victims. Its First Magistrate can not, if he would, avoid the performance of his duty. . . . There is yet time to show that the descendants of the Pinckneys, the Sumpters, the Rutledges, and of the thousand other names which adorn the pages of your Revolutionary history will not abandon that Union to support which so many of them fought and bled and died. I adjure you, as you honor their memory, as you love the cause of freedom, to which they dedicated their lives, as you prize the peace of your country, the lives of its best citizens, and your own fair fame, to retrace your steps.

The decision is yours, he concluded, "whether your sacred Union will be preserved and perpetuated." May the "Great Ruler of Nations" bring those who have produced this crisis to their senses and see their folly "before they feel the misery of civil strife."

Jackson never so much deserved the trust and confidence and love of the American people as he did at this moment. It was a superb state paper. Little in it needed improvement. Indeed, Abraham Lincoln later extracted from it the basic argument he needed to explain and justify his intended course of action to meet secession in 1861. The proclamation is a major statement in constitutional law. It came about only because Jackson was a statesman of the first rank. And, as many Americans promptly acknowledged, they were fortunate to have him at the head of the government at this moment of crisis. "The dauntless spirit of resolution" presided over the nation in the person of General Andrew Jackson, protecting the Union and the people in his care.

. . . But Andrew Jackson had not only maintained the pride and dignity of the American name and preserved the Union from dismemberment; he had powerfully and successfully driven home the argument that the Union is perpetual.

Nullification Triumphant

RICHARD ELLIS

The nullification crisis certainly was not simply, and perhaps not even mainly, a struggle between the proponents of nationalism and states' rights. In a very fundamental way it also involved a struggle between advocates of different kinds of states' rights thought. It also was not an isolated, if dramatic, episode that took place during Andrew Jackson's presidency. Nor should it be viewed only as a precursor of what was to occur on a much broader and even more serious scale in 1860–61. Rather it was an integral event of the Jacksonian era that both reflected and had an enormous impact upon various ideological, constitutional, political, and even economic aspects of the 1820s and 1830s. The importance of the Bank War and the struggle over state

From *The Union at Risk: Jacksonian Democracy, States' Rights, and the Nullification Crisis* by Richard E. Ellis. Copyright © 1987 by Richard E. Ellis. Reprinted by permission of Oxford University Press, Inc.

banking and financial policy for understanding what was involved in Jacksonian Democracy has long been recognized by scholars. Not so the nullification crisis. This is unfortunate, for while the confrontation between Jackson and South Carolina on the issue of nullification took place over a much shorter time span than the struggle over the rechartering of the Second Bank of the United States, the removal of the deposits, and the attempt to implement a hard money policy, it was a much more intense and volatile crisis, and it had equally far reaching consequences.

I

Andrew Jackson's attitude toward nullification is the necessary starting point for understanding the significance of the crisis. For, like almost everything else during his two terms as President, it was how the Old Hero responded to a particular issue or development that determined the context in which that matter was to be handled and discussed, so powerful was his personality. Although sincerely committed to states' rights himself, Jackson was deeply hostile to Calhoun and South Carolina's version of the doctrine because it was a way of thwarting majority rule and because he believed the claim that secession was a legal right that could be peacefully exercised threatened the existence of the Union. Personal and political considerations also contributed to Jackson's dislike of Calhoun. These, however, were less a cause for his hostility to nullification than they were factors that determined the fierceness of his reaction to South Carolina's actions in the winter of 1832–33.

Jackson's official response to the Ordinances that declared the tariffs of 1828 and 1832 unconstitutional came on December 10, 1832, in a document that is known as the Nullification Proclamation, a powerful and cogently argued statement denying to any state the right to disobey a federal law and denouncing secession as treason. The Proclamation was also more than simply an attack upon the specific actions of South Carolina. Determined to assert the power of the national government and to march down to South Carolina to hang Calhoun and his co-conspirators for treasonous activities, Jackson, in the Proclamation, focused on nullification as a doctrine *"incompatible with the existence of the Union,"* rejected the compact theory of the origins of the Union, and generally downplayed the states' rights position he had taken throughout his first administration. Further, in the process of attacking the concept of secession, Jackson seemed now to be endorsing a nationalist theory of the origins of the Union: the nation came before the states and the national government was sovereign, and that sovereignty was indivisible because it was granted by the people and not the states.

So different in content was the Nullification Proclamation from anything the President had previously espoused that a number of people expressed disbelief when they first saw it. Moreover, it immediately won the warm endorsement of nationalists like John Quincy Adams, John Marshall, Joseph Story, and most important of all, Daniel Webster, while at the same time causing consternation among traditional states' rights advocates and good Jacksonians like Martin Van Buren, Thomas Hart Benton, and Thomas

Ritchie. In fact, so confusing was the alignment on the reception of the Proclamation that many people during the next few months believed they were in the midst of a major political revolution. As a result ideological confusion and division spread through the Democratic party. Across the country Jacksonians were either uneasy with or were outright critical of the Proclamation, with especially vociferous opposition to the President during the crisis coming from the southern wing of the party.

Conventional wisdom would have it that South Carolina was completely isolated during the nullification crisis. This is true only in the narrow sense that no other state formally endorsed its controversial doctrines. This, however, is only part of the story. In addition to shrill criticism of the Proclamation, there was widespread opposition, an opposition that prevailed in the end, to Jackson's repeated threats to use force against South Carolina. The unwillingness to going along with the use of force extended not only to traditional states' rights Jacksonians, who favored an immediate and sharp reduction of the tariff as the best way to compromise the crisis, but also to many nationalists and high tariff supporters. Webster, the great spokesman for a nationalist interpretation of the origins of the Constitution and opponent of any kind of tarriff reduction in the face of South Carolina's threats, never explicitly endorsed the use of force during the crisis. Young Henry Barnard, who was to become the famous educator, was traveling through Washington at the time. A New Englander and a nationalist, he was very critical of South Carolina's actions. Nonetheless, he expressed the belief "Jackson is the most abandoned tyrant at heart on earth, and I am not sure if he gets the power, but what he would seize upon any occasion to hang Hayne etc.-etc." And Massachusetts congressman Edward Everett, a hard-line opponent of nullification and a strong protectionist who believed the nullifiers should be tried for treason, nonetheless also indicated that after a fair trial and conviction they should be pardoned. He separated himself from Jackson's more bloody-minded approach to the problem by observing, "I do not wish them to die, in the first ditch nor the last; nor in fact in any ditch at all." In many ways, by the end of the crisis it was Jackson, not the nullifiers, who was isolated.

An unwillingness to authorize Jackson to use force and a fear of civil war were the underlying concerns that dominated the country during the winter of 1833. As a consequence it soon became clear to the President that he was not going to get his own way during the nullification crisis, and he reluctantly agreed to accept the compromise of 1833, upon the terms of which he was only marginally influential.

The resolution of the crisis in this manner had important political ramifications. In several ways the crisis turned out to be a victory for the nullifiers, and especially for Calhoun. South Carolina, as a consequence of the crisis, had forced the federal government to lower the tariff, succeeded in nullifying the Force Act, and was not required to recant on any aspect of its controversial theory of the nature of the Union. Furthermore, in the years following the crisis, the nullifiers effectively consolidated their political control of South Carolina. They did this by accusing their Unionist opponents of having been "disloyal" and by adopting a test oath in 1834 which required state militia men and civil officeholders to, in essence, swear primary allegiance to the state and only conditional allegiance to the federal government, something most Unionists could not do in good conscience, and which, therefore, effectively proscribed them from holding key offices. Calhoun, in particular, emerged from the crisis in a strong political position. During the 1820s, despite his national prominence, Calhoun had all kinds of political problems in his home state: traditional states' rights types opposed him because of his earlier nationalism while the more extreme nullifiers distrusted him. But he proved himself, at least where most of the nullifiers were concerned, by his successful advocacy of South Carolina's cause during the crisis. As a result, in the years after 1833 Calhoun was able to pursue his presidential ambitions, albeit unsuccessfully, and various other stratagems, like trying to unite the South on the issue of slavery from an extremely secure political base, something he had lacked in the earlier part of his career.

For Jackson, on the other hand, the nullification crisis, in a number of important ways, turned into a serious political setback, although the President made much of the fact that the Force Act had been adopted by what he called an "unparalleled majority" and claimed it vindicated his position during the crisis. But this could not obscure the fact that, in the end, it was the President who had backed down or been defeated on the most important points. Jackson at the beginning of the crisis had been extremely combatative and argued openly and belligerently that the mere raising of troops on the part of a state to resist the laws of the federal government was rebellion and in itself justified the use of force on his part. Yet when it became clear that this point of view did not have either popular or congressional support, and that it frightened many people and was wisely criticized as dangerous, the President formally requested Congress to authorize his using force should South Carolina actually oppose the authority of the federal government. Again, however, Jackson was rebuffed, and in the end the Force Act was passed, mainly as a face-saving device for the President, only after it had become clear that the crisis had already been effectively resolved through the adoption of a tariff acceptable to the nullifiers. By the end of February 1833, although Jackson continued to denounce the doctrine of nullification, he had dropped all threats of military coercion and, like everybody else, had become eager to compromise the issue as quickly as possible in order to get out of an adverse political situation.

The resolution of the nullification crisis by compromise was an embarrassing defeat for Jackson in yet another sense: he had to abandon the Unionists of South Carolina. They had been among the President's most loyal supporters before and during the crisis, and Jackson had frequently assured them that he would protect not only their lives and property but their political rights as well. Throughout the crisis the *Globe* defended Jackson's harsh attitude toward the nullifiers in part on the grounds that they did not really represent the will of the people of South Carolina and that they had intimidated the Unionists and violated their constitutional rights. But when the end of the crisis left the nullifiers in total control of the state, and they proceeded to proscribe and reduce the political influence of the Unionists, Jackson, with the exception of singling out a few individuals for federal appointment, could do nothing about it. As a military commander Jackson had always demanded the utmost loyalty from his subordinates and in return was protective and generous with those who stood by him. By going along with compromise in 1833, the President, in practical terms, deserted the Unionists and left them to the mercy of their opponents. . . .

II

The nullification crisis also had significant constitutional ramifications. It was the single most important time in American history when the two different conceptions of states' rights—one democratic and committed to the idea of a perpetual union and the other providing a mechanism for the protection of minority interests and espousing secession as a constitutional right—confronted each other.

For their part, the nullifiers claimed that their doctrines flowed naturally and inexorably from the Jeffersonian heritage as manifested in the Kentucky and Virginia Resolutions, and they did their best to avoid any discussion of how their controversial doctrine might differ from the more traditional and democratic kind of states' rights. These differences were precisely what the traditional states' rights spokesmen, critical of nullification, stressed. Between 1828, when the doctrine of nullification was first announced in the *South Carolina Exposition and Protest,* and the beginning of the crisis in December 1832, these spokesmen, led by the likes of James Madison, Edward Livingston, Levi Woodbury, Martin Van Buren, Thomas Ritchie, William Cabell Rives, and Andrew Jackson, denied that any legitimate connection existed between nullification and states' rights. Then, in his zeal to crush the nullifiers and to preserve the Union, Jackson issued his famous Proclamation which tended to endorse a nationalist interpretation of the origins and nature of the Constitution, and which embarrassed most traditional states' rights advocates. Ideological and political confusion followed, after which the crisis was resolved through a political compromise that failed to provide answers to the complex constitutional questions that had been raised in the debate over the legitimacy of nullification.

The seemingly inconclusive outcome of the nullification crisis, especially where constitutional issues are involved, should not obscure the fact that it basically worked to the advantage of the nullifiers. Calhoun and his supporters may have made some concessions on the tariff in 1833, but they had not been forced to back down in any way on their controversial assertions about the relationship of nullification and states' rights. Moreover, during the nullification crisis Jackson and his followers failed to articulate adequately the difference between their own commitment to states' rights and what South Carolina advocated. Their most serious attempt to do this came in speeches by Grundy and especially Rives on the Force bill, but its significance was lost in the political maneuverings that dominated Congress during February of 1833. For their part, in their speeches, Calhoun and his followers ignored the issues raised by the traditional advocates of states' rights; instead they focused on the nationalists' interpretation of the nature of the Union as advocated by Daniel Webster, John Quincy Adams, and others. In other words, the inability of the Jackson administration to articulate its own constitutional position effectively during the crisis allowed Calhoun to polarize the debate in terms of a struggle between a nationalist and states' rights interpretation of the Constitution, and for South Carolina to emerge as the advocate of states' rights thought in general and not just a particular variety of the doctrine. The significance of this became clear to Chief Justice Marshall early on in the crisis. "Our people," he wrote, "will be inextricably entangled in the labyrinth of their state right theories, and the feeble attachment they still retain for the union will be daily weakened. We have fallen on evil times."

Immediately following the conclusion of the crisis, traditional states' righters urged the President to make use of his second inaugural address to clarify the confusion on constitutional questions, and especially the role of the states in the federal system of government, that had concerned so many Democrats in recent months. Although the President obliged, the results were disappointing. It was a very brief speech, and while it acknowledged the rights of the states it did not contain a creed like his fourth annual message; moreover, it also stressed the importance of maintaining the Union at all costs, thereby indicating the President was unwilling to recant on the principles of the Proclamation. The fact of the matter is that Jackson emerged from the nullification crisis extremely unhappy over the manner in which it had been settled. He was angry over the failure of key Democrats to give him their unqualified support in the confrontation with South Carolina, and was unwilling to admit that there was any justice in the criticism of the Proclamation. He refused to discuss the matter with Van Buren, and as for the extensive debate on the issue of states' rights going on in the Old Dominion he is reported to have observed "what has Virginia to do with this matter? It is no business of hers. And there is Tom Ritchie talking about *state rights.* I have no patience to read *such stuff.* I fling his paper against the wall."

A major exception to the President's reluctance to discuss the nullification crisis and its ramifications took place in an exchange of letters between him and Nathaniel Macon. Macon, a former Speaker of the House of Representatives and a retired North Carolina senator, was, like John Randolph, highly regarded by Jackson and other important Democrats as a long-standing critic of the nationalist tendencies of the American System. A vigorous advocate of states' rights, Macon had been openly critical of nullification and a strong defender of most of Jackson's policies. But he did not like the Proclamation and was openly critical of it. Specifically, he took issue with the President's unwillingness to recognize South Carolina's claim that secession was a constitutional right. "Sovereign power," Macon asserted, "cannot commit treason or rebellion or be subject to the laws relating to either. . . . If South Carolina would not permit the laws of the United States to be enforced within her limits, she was out of the Union and ought to

have been treated as a foreign power." Jackson's strongly worded response
to Macon indicated that the right of secession continued to remain a central
issue in his debate with the nullifiers:

> In my opinion the admission of the right of secession is a virtual dissolution
> of the Union. . . . If the federal government and its laws are to be deprived
> of all authority in a state by its mere declaration *that* it *secedes,* the union
> and all its attributes, depend upon the breath of every faction which may
> maintain a momentary ascendancy in any one state of the confederacy. To
> insist that secession is a reserved right, is to insist, that each state reserved
> the right to put an end to the government established for the benefit of all
> and that there are no common obligations among the states. I hold that the
> states expressly gave up the right to secede when they entered into the
> compact binding them in articles of "perpetual union" and more especially
> when the present constitution was adopted to establish "a more perfect
> union" equally unlimited as to duration.

Ironically, it was on the issue of secession, on which Jackson had such
strong feelings, that South Carolina emerged triumphant from the nullification crisis. Prior to the espousal of the doctrine by the South Carolina
nullifiers, most assertions of secession had taken the form of rhetorical
flourishes, political ploys, and logical extensions of arguments not fully understood or thought out. Moreover, secession before 1828–1833 was not a
doctrine that was associated with a particular interest group or section of
the country. A number of the more vociferous New England opponents of
the War of 1812 had spoken of it, but the moderates who controlled the
Hartford Convention rejected the doctrine, and the entire movement was
soon disgraced and lost in the nationalist fervor that swept the country after
1815. By the time of the nullification crisis most New Englanders were either
nationalists or strong Union supporters. In the South, however, as a consequence of South Carolina's being able to more than hold its own in the
constitutional debate with Jackson, the doctrine of secession gained both
converts and respectability after 1833, and included many who were critical
of nullification. The long-range implications of the linking up of secession
with states' rights were clear to one particularly prescient congressman: "It
is quite remarkable to witness the composure with which a dissolution of
the Union is spoken of here—I think the present disturbances will be settled,
or got over; but it seems to me that the sound feeling which the Union ever
inspired, is irrevocably gone." The doctrine of secession was asserted with
great vigor and clarity during the nullification crisis; and since the Compromise of 1833 did not deal with it in any way, it came to play an increasingly
important role in the political and ideological culture of the country during
the second third of the nineteenth century.

On the other side of the political spectrum, those who argued that the
Supreme Court of the United States should be the final arbiter of constitutional questions were also inadvertent beneficiaries of the various compromises that brought an end to the nullification crisis. This had been the
nationalist position since the adoption of the United States Constitution in
1788; however, it was rejected by states' rights spokesmen, both tradition-

alists and nullifiers. Although the Supreme Court had declared part of a federal law unconstitutional in 1803 in *Marbury* v. *Madison,* the decision was in many ways very ambiguous. While the United States Supreme Court claimed for itself the right to oversee the Constitution, it did not claim that its power to do so was either exclusive or final. Moreover, the actual holding of the case worked to the advantage of the Republican administration, for the Court turned down the request of the disappointed Federalist appointees for a *writ of mandamus* ordering the secretary of state to hand over the commissions of several justices of the peace that had been signed by Federalist President John Adams, but which Thomas Jefferson refused to deliver. After the Civil War the decision in *Marbury* v. *Madison* took on enormous significance as triumphant nationalists pointed to it as an important first precedent in their successful drive to, in fact, make the Supreme Court the final arbiter in constitutional disputes, but at the time the decision was handed down it was considered, if anything, a defeat for the more belligerent members of the Federalist party and a conciliatory gesture on the part of the Supreme Court toward the new administration.

This conciliatory gesture worked, for Jefferson and especially Madison successfully headed off attempts by radicals and states' rights Old Republicans to dismantle the federal judiciary. During the four administrations of Madison and his successor James Monroe, the Supreme Court handed down a series of important decisions that significantly tilted the distribution of powers between the states and the federal government in a nationalist direction. There was a strong reaction to this development during the 1820s, when states' rights advocates vigorously denied any claims that the Supreme Court should be viewed as the final arbiter of constitutional disputes, especially those involving the state and federal governments. Proponents of states' rights also sponsored various pieces of legislation and even amendments to the Constitution to circumscribe the Supreme Court's power but without much success, for at no time did these measures have the support of an incumbent President. Most critics of the Supreme Court supported Andrew Jackson for the presidency in 1828, and his election was a definite victory for the concept of states' rights over a strong and active national government. Despite this, Jackson did not go out of his way to seek a confrontation with the Supreme Court, at least not in the same way that he tended to with the issues of a federal program of internal improvements or the Bank. Still, the general states' rights thrust of must of his other policies made it highly likely that some kind of confrontation with the Supreme Court would eventually have to take place. The specific issue that emerged was the High Court's decision in *Worcester* v. *Georgia* that directly contradicted the President's Indian removal policy. An actual confrontation, however, was avoided at the last minute by the intervention of the nullification crisis, when ideological confusion and political expediency required both sides in the controversy—nationalists and traditional states' rights spokesmen—to work out a compromise.

This was an important development for the Supreme Court's long-term well being. For should an actual crisis have occurred, that is, should an attempt have been made to force Jackson's hand in the Worcester case, it is highly probable that he would have refused on the grounds that the President of the United States was not bound by the Court's decisions, as he had indicated in his Bank veto message when he rejected the argument that *McCulloch* v. *Maryland* had established the Bank's constitutionality. This would have exposed, for all to see, the Supreme Court's lack of political power and its dependency upon the other branches of the government to enforce its decisions. It also would have created a very important and dangerous precedent, for until this point no incumbent President had explicitly refused to uphold the Court's authority. It might even have so angered Jackson as to cause him to initiate, as many of his closest advisers favored, legislation or an amendment to the Constitution restricting the authority of the Supreme Court in cases dealing with federal-state relations.

The various political and ideological issues raised by the nullification crisis were the main cause for the compromise that took place on the *Worcester* decision. The compromise allowed the Court to emerge from the Jacksonian era relatively unscathed. This, of course, in no sense established what we today term judicial supremacy: the idea that the Supreme Court is the final arbiter of constitutional questions. But it was an important step in the long and arduous journey that the Court made during the *antebellum* period to emerge with its various powers and claims to powers virtually intact. The significance of this became clear after the Civil War, when with the states' rights thought in general thoroughly discredited, the Supreme Court in fact as well as theory began to become the final arbiter in all constitutional matters. . . .

✠ *F U R T H E R   R E A D I N G*

C. S. Boucher, *The Nullification Controversy in South Carolina* (1919)

Richard H. Brown, "The Missouri Crisis, Slavery, and the Politics of Jacksonianism," *South Atlantic Quarterly* 65 (Winter 1966): 55–72

Edward S. Corwin, "National Power and State Interposition, 1787–1861," *Michigan Law Review* 10 (1912): 535–551

William W. Freehling, *Prelude to Civil War: The Nullification Crisis in South Carolina, 1816–1836* (1965)

Kermit L. Hall, "Andrew Jackson and the Judiciary: The Michigan Territorial Judiciary as a Test Case, 1828–1832," *Michigan History* 59 (Fall 1975): 177–186

George Kateb, "The Majority Principle: Calhoun and His Antecedents," *Political Science Quarterly* 84 (1969): 583–605

Richard B. Latner, "The Nullification Crisis and Republican Subversion," *Journal of Southern History* 43 (1977): 19–38

Edwin A. Miles, "After John Marshall's Decision: Worcester v. Georgia and the Nullification Crisis," *Journal of Southern History* 39 (1973): 519–544

Paul C. Nagel, *One Nation Indivisible: The Union in American Thought* (1964)

Michael Paul Rogin, *Fathers and Children: Andrew Jackson and the Subjugation of the American Indian* (1975)

Ronald Satz, *American Indian Policy in the Jacksonian Era* (1975)

Kenneth N. Stampp, "The Concept of a Perpetual Union," *Journal of American History* 65 (1978): 5–33

James B. Stewart, "A Great Talking and Eating Machine: Patriarchy, Mobilization and the Dynamics of Nullification in South Carolina," *Civil War History* 27 (1981): 197–220

Property, Economy, and Culture in the Marshall and Taney Eras

✢

With independence, Americans achieved one of the crucial goals of the Revolution: control over their economic destinies. Signs of economic transformation studded nineteenth-century America's bountiful landscape. The personal, informal, and local dealings of the colonial era yielded to an increasingly impersonal national and international commercial market economy. By 1850 the value of manufactured goods surpassed that of agricultural produce for the first time in the nation's brief history.

This economic transformation raised new questions about the relationship of private economic rights to the public welfare. The privatization of economic decisionmaking was one of the most important features of the antebellum marketplace. Merchants and consumers, lenders and borrowers, and farmers and planters made decisions about their own individual fortunes that had far-reaching economic consequences. With privatization, the distribution of economic rights flowed from agreements reached among individuals rather than by government fiat. The colonial experience had taught many Americans that the enhancement of private economic decisionmaking was an essential check on governmental authority. Antebellum Americans did not embrace a strict theory of laissez-faire, however; instead, they participated in a mixed economy where the government played an important but limited role in adjusting supply and demand. The scope of even this limited intervention was a hotly contested constitutional question, and it surfaced regularly as an incident of the larger constitutional turmoil over state-nation relations. Equally important was the question of how the government should maintain property rights while distributing in a just way the costs, benefits, and rewards of economic development.

First under Chief Justice John Marshall and then under Roger B. Taney, the Supreme Court had to deal with competing visions of property rights and distributive economic justice. One school of thought, associated with the Whig party, believed that the government could best encourage economic development by granting monopolies to those persons willing to bear the risks of that development. The Jacksonian Democrats, on the other hand, insisted that monopolies subverted the public interest by discouraging new entrepreneurs with better technology from entering the marketplace. According to this view, a granting of privilege to run a ferry, operate a steamboat, or collect tolls on a bridge might encourage initial development, but it stifled subsequent competition, kept prices artificially high, and discouraged inventiveness.

The long-term pattern of development in the Supreme Court was clear. Government-sanctioned monopolies gradually disappeared as Jacksonian Democrats filled the bench. This process of political and constitutional change was never smooth, as the case of Charles River Bridge v. Warren Bridge *(1837) reveals. Of course, debate over distributive justice and property rights persists even today.*

✠ D O C U M E N T S

The three Supreme Court cases in this chapter not only involve questions of private property rights but also stand among the most important decisions of the pre–Civil War era. The first of these, the *Dartmouth College* case, had its origins in an 1816 act of the New Hampshire legislature that altered a supposedly perpetual charter granted by King George III almost a half-century earlier. The college's board of trust was dominated by Federalists, whereas the legislature was heavily Republican. The New Hampshire Superior Court sustained the new law, and the old board members appealed to the Supreme Court on the grounds that the 1816 act violated the contract clause of the federal Constitution. The Supreme Court, however, decided in favor of the old trustees. The important question is, why? Whose economic interests were favored by such a decision?

The *Dartmouth College* decision appeared to protect monopoly vested rights, and corporations of all kinds insisted that their charters had to be broadly construed. Some state legislatures attempted to limit these corporate demands by passing laws and constitutional amendments providing for the states alone to interpret or alter charter provisions. The Marshall Court, backing away from *Dartmouth College,* encouraged this process in *Providence Bank* v. *Billings* (1830), reprinted here as the second document. In 1791 Rhode Island had chartered the Providence Bank, but in 1822 the legislature had passed a bank tax that the Providence Bank refused to pay on the grounds that it violated its original charter and was, as a result, an impairment of contract. John Marshall's opinion found to the contrary, and so began the process by which the Court limited claims of privilege by state-chartered corporations.

This process reached a crescendo in Chief Justice Taney's first opinion as a member of the Court in *Charles River Bridge* v. *Warren Bridge* (1837), the third document in this chapter. The Massachusetts legislature in 1786 had given the proprietors of the Charles River Bridge a charter to operate a bridge between Charlestown and Boston and promised that they could charge tolls for forty years, later extended to seventy years. In 1828 the legislature responded to popular pressure by chartering the Warren Bridge Company to build a new bridge alongside the old structure and authorizing it to charge tolls for only six years, to cover the costs of construction. Thereafter, crossing the Warren Bridge would be free. The proprietors of the Charles River Bridge claimed that their original charter, by implication, gave them the privilege of collecting tolls without any competition. Taney and a majority of the Court disagreed.

What goals was Taney trying to achieve? What brought about the seemingly dramatic change from *Dartmouth College* to *Charles River Bridge*? The key to answering these questions can be found in Justice Joseph Story's famous dissent. As you read it, ask yourself whether Story was most concerned with cultural and moral issues or with economic matters. Is it possible to reconcile Marshall's position in *Dartmouth College* with Taney's in *Charles River Bridge*?

Dartmouth College v. *Woodward*, 1819

4 WHEATON 518 (1819)

[5-1: Marshall, Duvall, Johnson, Livingston,
Story; Todd]

The opinion of the court was delivered by Marshall, Ch. J.—   This court can be insensible neither to the magnitude nor delicacy of this question. The validity of a legislative act is to be examined; and the opinion of the highest law tribunal of a state is to be revised—an opinion which carries with it intrinsic evidence of the diligence, of the ability, and the integrity, with which it was formed. On more than one occasion, this court has expressed the cautious circumspection with which it approaches the consideration of such questions; and has declared, that in no doubtful case, would it pronounce a legislative act to be contrary to the constitution. But the American people have said, in the constitution of the United States, that "no state shall pass any bill of attainder, *ex post facto* law, or law impairing the obligation of contracts." In the same instrument, they have also said, "that the judicial power shall extend to all cases in law and equity arising under the constitution." On the judges of this court, then, is imposed the high and solemn duty of protecting, from even legislative violation, those contracts which the constitution of our country has placed beyond legislative control; and, however irksome the task may be, this is a duty from which we dare not shrink.

The title of the plaintiffs originates in a charter dated the 13th day of December, in the year 1769, incorporating twelve persons therein mentioned, by the name of "The Trustees of Dartmouth College," granting to them and their successors the usual corporate privileges and powers, and authorizing the trustees, who are to govern the college, to fill up all vacancies which may be created in their own body.

The defendant claims under three acts of the legislature of New Hampshire, the most material of which was passed on the 27th of June 1816, and is entitled, "an act to amend the charter, and enlarge and improve the corporation of Dartmouth College." Among other alterations in the charter, this act increases the number of trustees to twenty-one, gives the appointment of the additional members to the executive of the state, and creates a board of overseers, with power to inspect and control the most important acts of the trustees. This board consists of twenty-five persons. The president of the senate, the speaker of the house of representatives, of New Hampshire, and the governor and lieutenant-governor of Vermont, for the time being, are to be members *ex officio*. The board is to be completed by the governor and council of New Hampshire, who are also empowered to fill all vacancies which may occur. The acts of the 18th and 26th of December are supplemental to that of the 27th of June, and are principally intended to carry that act into effect. The majority of the trustees of the college have refused to accept this amended charter, and have brought this suit for the corporate property, which is in possession of a person holding by virtue of the acts which have been stated.

It can require no argument to prove, that the circumstances of this case constitute a contract. An application is made to the crown for a charter to incorporate a religious and literary institution. In the application, it is stated, that large contributions have been made for the object, which will be conferred on the corporation, as soon as it shall be created. The charter is granted, and on its faith the property is conveyed. Surely, in this transaction every ingredient of a complete and legitimate contract is to be found. The points for consideration are, 1. Is this contract protected by the constitution of the United States? 2. Is it impaired by the acts under which the defendant holds?

1. On the first point, it has been argued, that the word "contract," in its broadest sense, would comprehend the political relations between the government and its citizens, would extend to offices held within a state, for state purposes, and to many of those laws concerning civil institutions, which must change with circumstances, and be modified by ordinary legislation; which deeply concern the public, and which, to preserve good government, the public judgment must control. That even marriage is a contract, and its obligations are affected by the laws respecting divorces. That the clause in the constitution, if construed in its greatest latitude, would prohibit these laws. Taken in its broad, unlimited sense, the clause would be an unprofitable and vexatious interference with the internal concerns of a state, would unnecessarily and unwisely embarrass its legislation, and render immutable those civil institutions, which are established for purposes of internal government, and which, to subserve those purposes, ought to vary with varying circumstances. That as the framers of the constitution could never have intended to insert in that instrument, a provision so unnecessary, so mischievous, and so repugnant to its general spirit, the term "contract" must be understood in a more limited sense. That it must be understood as intended to guard against a power, of at least doubtful utility, the abuse of which had been extensively felt; and to restrain the legislature in future from violating the right to property. That, anterior to the formation of the constitution, a course of legislation had prevailed in many, if not in all, of the states, which weakened the confidence of man in man, and embarrassed all transactions between individuals, by dispensing with a faithful performance of engagements. To correct this mischief, by restraining the power which produced it, the state legislatures were forbidden "to pass any law impairing the obligation of contracts," that is, of contracts respecting property, under which some individual could claim a right to something beneficial to himself;

and that, since the clause in the constitution must in construction receive some limitation, it may be confined, and ought to be confined, to cases of this description; to cases within the mischief it was intended to remedy.

The general correctness of these observations cannot be controverted. That the framers of the constitution did not intend to restrain the states in the regulation of their civil institutions, adopted for internal government, and that the instrument they have given us, is not to be so construed, may be admitted. The provision of the constitution never has been understood to embrace other contracts, than those which respect property, or some object of value, and confer rights which may be asserted in a court of justice. . . .

The parties in this case differ less on general principles, less on the true construction of the constitution in the abstract, than on the application of those principles to this case, and on the true construction of the charter of 1769. This is the point on which the cause essentially depends. If the act of incorporation be a grant of political power, if it create a civil institution, to be employed in the administration of the government, or if the funds of the college be public property, or if the state of New Hampshire, as a government, be alone interested in its transactions, the subject is one in which the legislature of the state may act according to its own judgment, unrestrained by any limitation of its power imposed by the constitution of the United States.

But if this be a private eleemosynary institution, endowed with a capacity to take property, for objects unconnected with government, whose funds are bestowed by individuals, on the faith of the charter; if the donors have stipulated for the future disposition and management of those funds, in the manner prescribed by themselves; there may be more difficulty in the case, . . . It becomes then the duty of the court, most seriously to examine this charter, and to ascertain its true character.

From the instrument itself, it appears, that about the year 1754, the Rev. Eleazer Wheelock established, at his own expense, and on his own estate, a charity school for the instruction of Indians in the Christian religion. The success of this institution inspired him with the design of soliciting contributions in England, for carrying on and extending his undertaking. In this pious work, he employed the Rev. Nathaniel Whitaker, who, by virtue of a power of attorney from Dr. Wheelock, appointed the Earl of Dartmouth and others, trustees of the money, which had been, and should be, contributed; which appointment Dr. Wheelock confirmed by a deed of trust, authorizing the trustees to fix on a site for the college. They determined to establish the school on Connecticut river, in the western part of New Hampshire; that situation being supposed favorable for carrying on the original design among the Indians, and also for promoting learning among the English; and the proprietors in the neighborhood having made large offers of land, on condition, that the college should there be placed. Dr. Wheelock then applied to the crown for an act of incorporation; and represented the expediency of appointing those whom he had, by his last will, named as trustees in America, to be members of the proposed corporation. "In consideration of the premises," "for the education and instruction of the youth of the Indian tribes," &c., "and also of English youth, and any others," the charter was granted, and the trustees of Dartmouth College were, by that name, created a body corporate, with power, for the use of the said college, to acquire real and personal property, and to pay the president, tutors and other officers of the college, such salaries as they shall allow.

The charter proceeds to appoint Eleazer Wheelock, "the founder of said college," president thereof, with power, by his last will, to appoint a successor, who is to continue in office, until disapproved by the trustees. In case of vacancy, the trustees may appoint a president, and in case of the ceasing of a president, the senior professor or tutor, being one of the trustees, shall exercise the office, until an appointment shall be made. The trustees have power to appoint and displace professors, tutors and other officers, and to supply any vacancies which may be created in their own body, by death, resignation, removal or disability; and also to make orders, ordinances and laws for the government of the college, the same not being repugnant to the laws of Great Britain, or of New Hampshire, and not excluding any person on account of his speculative sentiments in religion, or his being of a religious profession different from that of the trustees. This charter was accepted, and the property, both real and personal, which had been contributed for the benefit of the college, was conveyed to, and vested in, the corporate body.

From this brief review of the most essential parts of the charter, it is apparent, that the funds of the college consisted entirely of private donations. It is, perhaps, not very important, who were the donors. The probability is, that the Earl of Dartmouth, and the other trustees in England, were, in fact, the largest contributors. . . . But be this as it may, Dartmouth College is really endowed by private individuals, who have bestowed their funds for the propagation of the Christian religion among the Indians, and for the promotion of piety and learning generally. From these funds, the salaries of the tutors are drawn; and these salaries lessen the expense of education to the students. It is then an eleemosynary (1 Bl. Com. 471), and so far as respects its funds, a private corporation.

Whence, then, can be derived the idea, that Dartmouth College has become a public institution, and its trustees public officers, exercising powers conferred by the public for public objects? Not from the source whence its funds were drawn; for its foundation is purely private and eleemosynary— not from the application of those funds; for money may be given for education, and the persons receiving it do not, by being employed in the education of youth, become members of the civil government. Is it from the act of incorporation? Let this subject be considered.

A corporation is an artificial being, invisible, intangible, and existing only in contemplation of law. Being the mere creature of law, it possesses only those properties which the charter of its creation confers upon it, either expressly, or as incidental to its very existence. These are such as are supposed best calculated to effect the object for which it was created. Among the most important are immortality, and, if the expression may be allowed, individuality; properties, by which a perpetual succession of many persons are considered as the same, and may act as a single individual. They enable a corporation to manage its own affairs, and to hold property, without the perplexing intricacies, the hazardous and endless necessity, of perpetual conveyances for the purpose of transmitting it from hand to hand. It is chiefly for the purpose of clothing bodies of men, in succession, with these qualities and capacities, that corporations were invented, and are in use. By these means, a perpetual succession of individuals are capable of acting for the promotion of the particular object, like one immortal being. But this being does not share in the civil government of the country, unless that be the purpose for which it was created. Its immortality no more confers on it political power, or a political character, than immortality would confer such power or character on a natural person. It is no more a state instrument, than a natural person exercising the same powers would be. If, then, a natural person, employed by individuals in the education of youth, or for the government of a seminary in which youth is educated, would not become a public officer, or be considered as a member of the civil government, how is it, that this artificial being, created by law, for the purpose of being employed by the same individuals, for the same purposes, should become a part of the civil government of the country? Is it because its existence, its capacities, its powers, are given by law? Because the government has given it the power to take and to hold property, in a particular form, and for particular purposes, has the government a consequent right substantially to change that form, or to vary the purposes to which the property is to be applied? This principle has never been asserted or recognised, and is supported by no authority. Can it derive aid from reason?

The objects for which a corporation is created are universally such as the government wishes to promote. They are deemed beneficial to the country; and this benefit constitutes the consideration, and in most cases, the sole consideration of the grant. In most eleemosynary institutions, the object would be difficult, perhaps unattainable, without the aid of a charter of incorporation. Charitable or public-spirited individuals, desirous of making permanent appropriations for charitable or other useful purposes, find it impossible to effect their design securely and certainly, without an incorporating act. They apply to the government, state their beneficent object, and offer to advance the money necessary for its accomplishment, provided the government will confer on the instrument which is to execute their designs the capacity to execute them. The proposition is considered and approved. The benefit to the public is considered as an ample compensation for the faculty it confers, and the corporation is created. If the advantages to the public constitute a full compensation for the faculty it gives, there can be no reason for exacting a further compensation, by claiming a right to exercise over this artificial being, a power which changes its nature, and touches the fund, for the security and application of which it was created. There can be no reason for implying in a charter, given for a valuable consideration, a power which is not only not expressed, but is in direct contradiction to its express stipulations.

From the fact, then, that a charter of incorporation has been granted, nothing can be inferred, which changes the character of the institution, or transfers to the government any new power over it. The character of civil institutions does not grow out of their incorporation, but out of the manner in which they are formed, and the objects for which they are created. The right to change them is not founded on their being incorporated, but on their being the instruments of government, created for its purposes. The same institutions, created for the same objects, though not incorporated, would be public institutions, and, of course, be controllable by the legislature. The incorporating act neither gives nor prevents this control. Neither, in reason, can the incorporating act change the character of a private eleemosynary institution.

We are next led to the inquiry, for whose benefit the property given to Dartmouth College was secured? The counsel for the defendant have insisted, that the beneficial interest is in the people of New Hampshire. The charter, after reciting the preliminary measures which had been taken, and the application for an act of incorporation, proceeds thus: "Know ye, therefore, that we, considering the premises, and being willing to encourage the laudable and charitable design of spreading Christian knowledge among the savages of our American wilderness, and also that the best means of education be established in our province of New Hampshire, for the benefit of said province, do, of our special grace," &c. Do these expressions bestow on New Hampshire any exclusive right to the property of the college, any exclusive interest in the labors of the professors? Or do they merely indicate a willingness that New Hampshire should enjoy those advantages which result to all from the establishment of a seminary of learning in the neighborhood? On this point, we think it impossible to entertain a serious doubt. The words themselves, unexplained by the context, indicate, that the "benefit intended for the province" is that which is derived from "establishing the best means of education therein"; that is, from establishing in the province, Dartmouth College, as constituted by the charter. But, if these words, considered alone, could admit of doubt, that doubt is completely removed, by an inspection of the entire instrument.

The particular interests of New Hampshire never entered into the mind of the donors, never constituted a motive for their donation. The propagation of the Christian religion among the savages, and the dissemination of useful knowledge among the youth of the country, were the avowed and the sole objects of their contributions. In these, New Hampshire would participate; but nothing particular or exclusive was intended for her. Even the site of the college was selected, not for the sake of New Hampshire, but because it was "most subservient to the great ends in view," and because liberal donations of land were offered by the proprietors, on condition that the institution should be there established. . . .

From this review of the charter, it appears, that Dartmouth College is an eleemosynary institution, incorporated for the purpose of perpetuating the application of the bounty of the donors, to the specified objects of that bounty; that its trustees or governors were originally named by the founder, and invested with the power of perpetuating themselves; that they are not public officers, nor is it a civil institution, participating in the administration of government; but a charity school, or a seminary of education, incorporated for the preservation of its property, and the perpetual application of that property to the objects of its creation.

Yet a question remains to be considered, of more real difficulty, on which more doubt has been entertained, than on all that have been discussed. The founders of the college, at least, those whose contributions were in money, have parted with the property bestowed upon it, and their representatives have no interest in that property. The donors of land are equally without interest, so long as the corporation shall exist. Could they be found, they are unaffected by any alteration in its constitution, and probably regardless of its form, or even of its existence. The students are fluctuating, and no individual among our youth has a vested interest in the institution, which can be asserted in a court of justice. Neither the founders of the college, nor the youth for whose benefit it was founded, complain of the alteration made in its charter, or think themselves injured by it. The trustees alone complain, and the trustees have no beneficial interest to be protected. Can this be such a contract, as the constitution intended to withdraw from the power of state legislation? Contracts, the parties to which have a vested beneficial interest, and those only, it has been said, are the objects about which the constitution is solicitous, and to which its protection is extended.

According to the theory of the British constitution, their parliament is omnipotent. To annul corporate rights might give a shock to public opinion, which that government has chosen to avoid; but its power is not questioned. Had parliament, immediately after the emanation of this charter, and the execution of those conveyances which followed it, annulled the instrument, so that the living donors would have witnessed the disappointment of their hopes. The perfidy of the transaction would have been universally acknowledged. Yet, then, as now, the donors would have no interest in the property; then, as now, those who might be students would have had no rights to be violated; then, as now, it might be said, that the trustees, in whom the rights of all were combined, possessed no private, individual, beneficial interests in the property confided to their protection. Yet the contract would, at that time, have been deemed sacred by all. What has since occurred, to strip it of its inviolability? Circumstances have not changed it. In reason, in justice, and in law, it is now, what it was in 1769.

The opinion of the court, after mature deliberation, is, that this is a contract, the obligation of which cannot be impaired, without violating the constitution of the United States. This opinion appears to us to be equally supported by reason, and by the former decisions of this court.

2. We next proceed to the inquiry, whether its obligation has been

impaired by those acts of the legislature of New Hampshire, to which the special verdict refers?

On the effect of this law, two opinions cannot be entertained. Between acting directly, and acting through the agency of trustees and overseers, no essential difference is perceived. The whole power of governing the college is transferred from trustees, appointed according to the will of the founder, expressed in the charter, to the executive of New Hampshire. The management and application of the funds of this eleemosynary institution, which are placed by the donors in the hands of trustees named in the charter, and empowered to perpetuate themselves, are placed by this act under the control of the government of the state. The will of the state is substituted for the will of the donors, in every essential operation of the college. This is not an immaterial change. The founders of the college contracted, not merely for the perpetual application of the funds which they gave, to the objects for which those funds were given; they contracted also, to secure that application by the constitution of the corporation. They contracted for a system, which should, so far as human foresight can provide, retain for ever the government of the literary institution they had formed, in the hands of persons approved by themselves. This system is totally changed. The charter of 1769 exists no longer. It is re-organized; and re-organized in such a manner, as to convert a literary institution, moulded according to the will of its founders, and placed under the control of private literary men, into a machine entirely subservient to the will of government. This may be for the advantage of this college in particular, and may be for the advantage of literature in general; but it is not according to the will of the donors, and is subversive of that contract, on the faith of which their property was given.

It results from this opinion, that the acts of the legislature of New Hampshire, which are stated in the special verdict found in this cause, are repugnant to the constitution of the United States; and that the judgment on this special verdict ought to have been for the plaintiffs. The judgment of the state court must, therefore, be reversed.

Providence Bank v. Billings, 1830

4 PETERS 516 (1830)

[Unanimous]

Mr Chief Justice Marshall delivered the opinion of the Court.   . . . In November 1791 the legislature of Rhode Island granted a charter of incorporation to certain individuals, who had associated themselves together for the purpose of forming a banking company. They are incorporated by the name of the "President, Directors, and Company of the Providence Bank"; and have the ordinary powers which are supposed to be necessary for the usual objects of such associations.

In 1822 the legislature of Rhode Island passed "an act imposing a duty on licensed persons and others, and bodies corporate within the state"; in which, among other things, it is enacted that there shall be paid, for the use of the state, by each and every bank within the state, except the Bank of the United States, "the sum of fifty cents on each and every thousand dollars of the capital stock actually paid in." This tax was afterwards augmented to one dollar and twenty-five cents. . . .

It has been settled that a contract entered into between a state and an individual, is as fully protected by the tenth section of the first article of the constitution, as a contract between two individuals; and it is not denied that a charter incorporating a bank is a contract. Is this contract impaired by taxing the banks of the state?

This question is to be answered by the charter itself.

It contains no stipulation promising exemption from taxation. The state, then, has made no express contract which has been impaired by the act of which the plaintiffs complain. No words have been found in the charter, which, in themselves, would justify the opinion that the power of taxation was in the view of either of the parties; and that an exemption of it was intended, though not expressed. The plaintiffs find great difficulty in showing that the charter contains a promise, either express or implied, not to tax the bank. The elaborate and ingenious argument which has been urged amounts, in substance, to this. The charter authorises the bank to employ its capital in banking transactions, for the benefit of the stockholders. It binds the state to permit these transactions for this object. Any law arresting directly the operations of the bank would violate this obligation, and would come within the prohibition of the constitution. But, as that cannot be done circuitously which may not be done directly, the charter restrains the state from passing any act which may indirectly destroy the profits of the bank. A power to tax the bank may unquestionably be carried to such an excess as to take all its profits, and still more than its profits for the use of the state; and consequently destroy the institution. Now, whatever may be the rule of expediency, the constitutionality of a measure depends, not on the degree of its exercise, but on its principle. A power therefore which may in effect destroy the charter, is inconsistent with it; and is impliedly renounced by granting it. Such a power cannot be exercised without impairing the obligation of the contract. When pushed to its extreme point, or exercised in moderation, it is the same power, and is hostile to the rights granted by the charter. This is substantially the argument for the bank. The plaintiffs cite and rely on several sentiments expressed, on various occasions by this court, in support of these positions.

The claim of the Providence Bank is certainly of the first impression. The power of taxing moneyed corporations has been frequently exercised; and has never before, so far as is known, been resisted. Its novelty, however, furnishes no conclusive argument against it.

That the taxing power is of vital importance; that it is essential to the existence of government; are truths which it cannot be necessary to reaffirm. They are acknowledged and asserted by all. It would seem that the relinquishment of such a power is never to be assumed. We will not say that a state may not relinquish it; that a consideration sufficiently valuable to induce a partial release of it may not exist: but as the whole community is interested in retaining it undiminished; that community has a right to insist that its abandonment ought not to be presumed, in a case in which the deliberate purpose of the state to abandon it does not appear.

The plaintiffs would give to this charter the same construction as if it contained a clause exempting the bank from taxation on its stock in trade. But can it be supposed that such a clause would not enlarge its privileges? They contend that it must be implied; because the power to tax may be so wielded as to defeat the purpose for which the charter was granted. And may not this be said with equal truth of other legislative powers? Does it not also apply with equal force to every incorporated company? A company may be incorporated for the purpose of trading in goods as well as trading in money. If the policy of the state should lead to the imposition of a tax on unincorporated companies, could those which might be incorporated claim an exemption, in virtue of a charter which does not indicate such an intention? The time may come when a duty may be imposed on manufactures. Would an incorporated company be exempted from this duty, as the mere consequence of its charter?

The great object of an incorporation is to bestow the character and properties of individuality on a collective and changing body of men. This capacity is always given to such a body. Any privileges which may exempt it from the burthens common to individuals, do not flow necessarily from the charter, but must be expressed in it, or they do not exist.

If the power of taxation is inconsistent with the charter, because it may be so exercised as to destroy the object for which the charter is given; it is equally inconsistent with every other charter, because it is equally capable of working the destruction of the objects for which every other charter is given. If the grant of a power to trade in money to a given amount, implies an exemption of the stock in trade from taxation, because the tax may absorb all the profits; then the grant of any other thing implies the same exemption; for that thing may be taxed to an extent which will render it totally unprofitable to the grantee. Land, for example, has, in many, perhaps in all the states, been granted by government since the adoption of the constitution. This grant is a contract, the object of which is that the profits issuing from it shall enure to the benefit of the grantee. Yet the power of taxation may be carried so far as to absorb these profits. Does this impair the obligation of the contract? The idea is rejected by all; and the proposition appears so extravagant, that it is difficult to admit any resemblance in the cases. And yet if the proposition for which the plaintiffs contend be true, it carries us to this point. That proposition is, that a power which is in itself capable of being exerted to the total destruction of the grant, is inconsistent with the grant; and is therefore impliedly relinquished by the grantor, though the language of the instrument contains no allusion to the subject. If this be an abstract truth, it may be supposed universal. But it is not universal; and therefore its truth cannot be admitted, in these broad terms, in any case.

We must look for the exemption in the language of the instrument; and if we do not find it there, it would be going very far to insert it by construction.

The power of legislation, and consequently of taxation, operates on all the persons and property belonging to the body politic. This is an original principle, which has its foundation in society itself. It is granted by all, for the benefit of all. It resides in government as a part of itself, and need not be reserved when property of any description, or the right to use it in any manner, is granted to individuals or corporate bodies. However absolute the right of an individual may be, it is still in the nature of that right, that it must bear a portion of the public burthens; and that portion must be determined by the legislature. This vital power may be abused; but the constitution of the United States was not intended to furnish the corrective for every abuse of power which may be committed by the state governments. The interest, wisdom, and justice of the representative body, and its relations with its constituents, furnish the only security, where there is no express contract, against unjust and excessive taxation; as well as against unwise legislation generally. . . .

We have reflected seriously on this case, and are of opinion that the act of the legislature of Rhode Island, passed in 1822, imposing a duty on licensed persons and others, and bodies corporate within the state, does not impair the obligation of the contract created by the charter granted to the plaintiffs in error. It is therefore the opinion of this court, that there is no error in the judgment of the supreme judicial court for the state of Rhode Island, affirming the judgment of the circuit court in this case; and the same is affirmed; and the cause is remanded to the said supreme judicial court, that its judgment may be finally entered. . . .

Proprietors of the Charles River Bridge v. Proprietors of the Warren Bridge, 1837

11 PETERS 420 (1837)

[4-3: Taney, Baldwin, Barbour, Wayne;
McLean, Story, Thompson]

Chief Justice Taney delivered the opinion of the Court.   The questions involved in this case are of the gravest character, and the court have given to them the most anxious and deliberate consideration. The value of the right claimed by the plaintiffs is large in amount; and many persons may no doubt be seriously affected in their pecuniary interests by any decision which the court may pronounce; and the questions which have been raised as to the power of the several States, in relation to the corporations they have charted, are pregnant with important consequences; not only to the individuals who are concerned in the corporate franchises, but to the communities in which they exist. The court are fully sensible that it is their duty, in exercising the high powers conferred on them by the constitution of the United States, to deal with these great and extensive interests with the utmost caution; guarding, as far as they have the power to do so, the rights of property, and at the same time carefully abstaining from any encroachment on the rights reserved to the States. . . .

Borrowing, as we have done, our system of jurisprudence from the English law; and having adopted, in every other case, civil and criminal, its rules for the construction of statutes; is there any thing in our local situation, or in the nature of our political institutions, which should lead us to depart from the principle where corporations are concerned? Are we to apply to acts of incorporation, a rule of construction differing from that of the English law, and, by implication, make the terms of a charter in one of the States, more unfavorable to the public, than upon an act of parliament, framed in the same words, would be sanctioned in an English court? Can any good reasons be assigned for excepting this particular class of cases from the operation of the general principle; and for introducing a new and adverse rule of construction in favor of corporations, while we adopt and adhere to the rules of construction known to the English common law, in every other case, without exception? We think not; and it would present a singular spectacle, if, while the courts in England are restraining, within the strictest limits, the spirit of monopoly, and exclusive privileges in nature of monopolies, and confining corporations to the privileges plainly given to them in their charter; the courts of this country should be found enlarging these privileges by implication; and construing a statute more unfavorably to the public, and to the rights of the community, than would be done in a case in an English court of justice.

But we are not now left to determine, for the first time, the rules by which public grants are to be construed in this country. The subject has already been considered in this court; and the rule of construction, above stated, fully established. In the case of the *United States* v. *Arredondo,* 6 Pet. 738, the leading cases upon this subject are collected together by the learned judge who delivered the opinion of the court; and the principle recognized, that in grants by the public, nothing passes by implication. . . .

But the case most analogous to this, and in which the question came more directly before the court, is the case of the *Providence Bank* v. *Billings.* . . .

It may, perhaps, be said, that in the case of the Providence Bank, this court were speaking of the taxing power; which is of vital importance to the very existence of every government. But the object and end of all government is to promote the happiness and prosperity of the community by which it is established; and it can never be assumed, that the government intended to diminish its power of accomplishing the end for which it was created. And in a country like ours, free, active, and enterprising, continually advancing in numbers and wealth, new channels of communication are daily found necessary, both for travel and trade; and are essential to the comfort, convenience, and prosperity of the people. A State ought never to be presumed to surrender this power, because, like the taxing power, the whole community have an interest in preserving it undiminished. And when a corporation alleges, that a State has surrendered for seventy years, its power of improvement and public accommodation, in a great and important line of travel, along which a vast number of its citizens must daily pass; the community have a right to insist, in the language of this court above quoted, "that its abandonment ought not to be presumed, in a case, in which the deliberate purpose of the State to abandon it does not appear." The continued existence of a government would be of no great value, if by implications and presumptions, it was disarmed of the powers necessary to accomplish the ends of its creation; and the functions it was designed to perform, transferred to the hands of privileged corporations. The rule of construction announced by the court, was not confined to the taxing power; nor is it so limited in the opinion delivered. On the contrary, it was distinctly placed on the ground that the interests of the community were concerned in preserving, undiminished, the power then in question; and whenever any power of the State is said to be surrendered or diminished, whether it be the taxing power or any other affecting the public interest, the same principle applies, and the rule of construction must be the same. No one will question that the interests of the great body of the people of the State, would, in this instance, be affected by the surrender of this great line of travel to a single corporation, with the right to exact toll, and exclude competition for seventy years. While the rights of private property are sacredly guarded, we must not forget that the community also have rights, and that the happiness and well being of every citizen depends on their faithful preservation.

Adopting the rule of construction above stated as the settled one, we proceed to apply it to the charter of 1785, to the proprietors of the Charles River Bridge. This act of incorporation is in the usual form, and the privileges such as are commonly given to corporations of that kind. It confers on them the ordinary faculties of a corporation, for the purpose of building the bridge; and establishes certain rates of toll, which the company are authorized to take. This is the whole grant. There is no exclusive privilege given to them over the waters of Charles River, above or below their bridge. No right to erect another bridge themselves, nor to prevent other persons from erecting one. No engagement from the State that another shall not be erected; and no undertaking not to sanction competition, nor to make improvements that may diminish the amount of its income. Upon all these subjects the charter is silent; and nothing is said in it about a line of travel, so much insisted on in the argument, in which they are to have exclusive privileges. No words are used, from which an intention to grant any of these rights can be inferred. If the plaintiff is entitled to them, it must be implied, simply, from the nature of the grant; and cannot be inferred from the words by which the grant is made.

The relative position of the Warren Bridge has already been described. It does not interrupt the passage over the Charles River Bridge, nor make the way to it or from it less convenient. None of the faculties or franchises granted to that corporation have been revoked by the legislature, and its right to take the tolls granted by the charter remains unaltered. In short, all the franchises and rights of property enumerated in the charter, and there mentioned to have been granted to it, remain unimpaired. But its income is destroyed by the Warren Bridge; which, being free, draws off the passengers and property which would have gone over it, and renders their franchise of no value. This is the gist of the complaint. For it is not pretended that the erection of the Warren Bridge would have done them any injury, or in any degree affected their right of property, if it had not diminished the amount of their tolls. In order then to entitle themselves to relief, it is necessary to show that the legislature contracted not to do the act of which they complain, and that they impaired, or, in other words, violated that contract by the erection of the Warren Bridge.

The inquiry then is, Does the charter contain such a contract on the part of the State? Is there any such stipulation to be found in that instrument? It must be admitted on all hands that there is none,—no words that even relate to another bridge, or to the diminution of their tolls, or to the line of travel. If a contract on that subject can be gathered from the charter, it must be by implication, and cannot be found in the words used. Can such an agreement be implied? The rule of construction before stated is an answer to the question. In charters of this description, no rights are taken from the public, or given to the corporation, beyond those which the words of the charter, by their natural and proper construction, purport to convey. There are no words which import such a contract as the plaintiffs in error contend for, and none can be implied; and the same answer must be given to them that was given by this court to the Providence Bank. 4 Pet. 514. The whole community are interested in this inquiry, and they have a right to require that the power of promoting their comfort and convenience, and of advancing the public prosperity, by providing safe, convenient, and cheap ways for the transportation of produce and the purposes of travel, shall not be construed to have been surrendered or diminished by the State, unless it shall appear by plain words that it was intended to be done. . . .

Can the legislature be presumed to have taken upon themselves an implied obligation, contrary to its own acts and declarations contained in the same law? It would be difficult to find a case justifying such an implication, even between individuals; still less will it be found where sovereign rights are concerned, and where the interests of a whole community would be deeply affected by such an implication. It would, indeed, be a strong exertion of judicial power, acting upon its own views of what justice required, and the parties ought to have done, to raise, by a sort of judicial coercion, an implied contract, and infer from it the nature of the very instrument in which the legislature appear to have taken pains to use words which disavow and repudiate any intention, on the part of the State, to make such a contract.

Indeed, the practice and usage of almost every State in the Union, old enough to have commenced the work of internal improvements, is opposed to the doctrine contended for on the part of the plaintiffs in error. Turnpike roads have been made in succession on the same line of travel; the later one interfering materially with the profits of the first. These corporations have, in some instances, been utterly ruined by the introduction of newer and better modes of transportation and travelling. In some cases, railroads have rendered the turnpike roads on the same line of travel so entirely useless, that the franchise of the turnpike corporation is not worth preserving. Yet in none of these cases have the corporation supposed that their privileges were invaded, or any contract violated on the part of the State. Amid the multitude of cases which have occurred, and have been daily occurring for the last forty or fifty years, this is the first instance in which such an implied contract has been contended for, and this court called upon to infer it from an ordinary act of incorporation, containing nothing more than the usual stipulations and provisions to be found in every such law. The absence of any such controversy, when there must have been so many occasions to give rise to it, proves that neither States, nor individuals, nor corporations, ever imagined that such a contract could be implied from such charters. It shows that the men who voted for these laws, never imagined that they were forming such a contract; and if we maintain that they have made it, we must create it by a legal fiction, in opposition to the truth of the fact, and the obvious intention of the party. We cannot deal thus with the rights reserved to the States, and by legal intendments and mere technical reasoning, take away from them any portion of that power over their own internal police and improvement, which is so necessary to their well being and prosperity.

And what would be the fruits of this doctrine of implied contracts on the part of the States, and of property in a line of travel by a corporation, if it should now be sanctioned by this court? To what results would it lead us? If it is to be found in the charter to this bridge, the same process of reasoning must discover it in the various acts which have been passed, within the last forty years, for turnpike companies. And what is to be the extent of the privileges of exclusion on the different sides of the road? The counsel who have so ably argued this case have not attempted to define it by any certain boundaries. How far must the new improvement be distant from the old one? How near may you approach without invading its rights in the privileged line? If this court should establish the principles now contended for, what is to become of the numerous railroads established on the same line of travel with turnpike companies; and which have rendered the franchises of the turnpike corporations of no value? Let it once be understood that such charters carry with them these implied contracts, and give this unknown and undefined property in a line of travelling, and you will soon find the old turnpike corporations awakening from their sleep, and calling upon this court to put down the improvements which have taken their place. The millions of property which have been invested in railroads and canals, upon lines of travel which had been before occupied by turnpike corporations, will be put in jeopardy. We shall be thrown back to the improvements of the last century, and obliged to stand still, until the claims of the old turnpike corporations shall be satisfied, and they shall consent to permit these States to avail themselves of the lights of modern science, and to partake of the benefit of those improvements which are now adding to the wealth and prosperity, and the convenience and comfort of every other part of the civilized world. Nor is this all. This court will find itself compelled to fix, by some arbitrary rule, the width of this new kind of property in a line of travel; for if such a right of property exists, we have no lights to guide us in marking out its extent, unless, indeed, we resort to the old feudal grants, and to the exclusive rights of ferries, by prescription, between towns; and are prepared to decide that when a turnpike road from one town to another had been made, no railroad or canal, between these two points, could afterwards be established. This court are not prepared to sanction principles which must lead to such results. . . .

[Justice Story dissenting.]   . . . It is a well known rule in the construction of private grants, if the meaning of the words be doubtful, to construe them most strongly against the grantor. . . .

In the case of a legislative grant, there is no ground to impute surprise, imposition or mistake to the same extent as in a mere private grant of the crown. The words are the words of the legislature, upon solemn deliberation, and examination, and debate. Their purport is presumed to be well known, and the public interests are watched, and guarded by all the varieties of local, personal and professional jealousy; as well as by the untiring zeal of numbers, devoted to the public service.

It should also be constantly kept in mind, that in construing this charter, we are not construing a statute involving political powers and sovereignty, like those involved in the case of the Elsebe . . . . We are construing a grant of the legislature, which though in the form of a statute, is still but a solemn contract. In such a case, the true course is to ascertain the sense of the parties from the terms of the instrument; and that once ascertained, to give it full effect. Lord Coke, indeed, recommends this as the best rule, even in respect to royal grants. "The best exposition" (says he,) "of the king's charter is, upon the consideration of the whole charter, to expound the charter by the charter itself; every material part thereof [being] explained according to the true and genuine sense, which is the best method." . . .

But with a view to induce the Court to withdraw from all the common rules of reasonable and liberal interpretation in favour of grants, we have been told at the argument, that this very charter is a restriction upon the legislative power; that it is in derogation of the rights and interests of the state, and the people; that it tends to promote monopolies, and exclusive privileges; and that it will interpose an insuperable barrier to the progress of improvement. Now, upon every one of these propositions, which are assumed, and not proved, I entertain a directly opposite opinion; and, if I did not, I am not prepared to admit the conclusion for which they are adduced. If the legislature has made a grant, which involves any or all of these consequences, it is not for courts of justice to overturn the plain sense of the grant, because it has been improvidently or injuriously made.

But I deny the very ground work of the argument. This charter is not (as I have already said) any restriction upon the legislative power; unless it be true, that because the legislature cannot grant again, what it has already granted, the legislative power is restricted. If so, then every grant of the public land is a restriction upon that power; a doctrine, that has never yet been established, nor (as far as I know) ever contended for. Every grant of a franchise is, so far as that grant extends, necessarily exclusive; and cannot be resumed, or interfered with. All the learned judges in the state court admitted, that the franchise of Charles River Bridge, whatever it be, could not be resumed, or interfered with. The legislature could not recall its grant, or destroy it. It is a contract, whose obligation cannot be constitutionally impaired. In this respect, it does not differ from a grant of lands. In each case, the particular land, or the particular franchise, is withdrawn from the legislative operation. The identical land, or the identical franchise, cannot be regranted, or avoided by a new grant. But the legislative power remains unrestricted. The subject matter only (I repeat it) has passed from the hands of the government. If the legislature should order a government debt to be paid by a sale of the public stock, and it is so paid, the legislative power over the funds of the government remains unrestricted, although it has ceased over the particular stock, which has been thus sold. For the present, I pass over all further consideration of this topic, as it will necessarily come again under review, in examining an objection of a more broad and comprehensive nature.

Then, again, how is it established that this is a grant in derogation of the rights and interests of the people? No individual citizen has any right to build a bridge over navigable waters; and consequently he is deprived of no right, when a grant is made to any other persons for that purpose. Whether it promotes or injures the particular interest of an individual citizen, constitutes no ground for judicial or legislative interference, beyond what his own rights justify. When, then, it is said, that such a grant is in derogation of the rights and interests of the people, we must understand that reference is had to the rights and interests common to the whole people, as such, (such as the right of navigation,) or belonging to them as a political body; or, in other words, the rights and interests of the state. Now, I cannot understand how any grant of a franchise is a derogation from the rights of the people of the state, any more than a grant of public land. The right, in each case, is gone to the extent of the thing granted, and so far may be said to derogate from, that is to say, to lessen the rights of the people, or of the state. But that is not the sense in which the argument is pressed; for, by derogation, is here meant an injurious or mischievous detraction from the sovereign rights of the state. On the other hand, there can be no derogation from the rights of the people, as such, except it applies to rights common there before; which the building of a bridge over navigable waters certainly is not. If it had been said that the grant of this bridge was in derogation of the common right of navigating the Charles River, by reason of its obstructing, pro tanto, a free and open passage, the ground would have been intelligible. So, if it had been an exclusive grant of the navigation of that stream. But, if at the same time, equivalent public rights of a different nature, but of greater public accommodation and use, had been obtained; it could hardly have been said, in a correct sense, that there was any derogation from the rights of the people, or the rights of the state. It would be a mere exchange of one public right for another.

Then, again, as to the grant being against the interests of the people. I know not how that is established; and certainly it is not to be assumed.

It will hardly be contended that every grant of the government is injurious to the interests of the people; or that every grant of a franchise must necessarily be so. The erection of a bridge may be of the highest utility to the people. It may essentially promote the public convenience, and aid the public interests, and protect the public property. And if no persons can be found willing to undertake such a work, unless they receive in return the exclusive privilege of erecting it, and taking toll; surely it cannot be said, as of course, that such a grant, under such circumstances, is, per se, against the interests of the people. Whether the grant of a franchise is, or is not, on the whole, promotive of the public interests; is a question of fact and judgment, upon which different minds may entertain different opinions. It is not to be judicially assumed to be injurious, and then the grant to be reasoned down. It is a matter exclusively confided to the sober consideration of the legislature; which is invested with full discretion, and possesses ample means to decide it. For myself, meaning to speak wth all due deference for others, I know of no power or authority confided to the judicial department, to rejudge the decisions of the legislature upon such a subject. It has an exclusive right to make the grant, and to decide whether it be, or be not, for the public interests. It is to be presumed, if the grant is made, that it is made from a high sense of public duty, to promote the public welfare, and to establish the public prosperity. In this very case, the legislature has, upon the very face of the act, made a solemn declaration as to the motive for passing it; that—"The erecting of a bridge over Charles River, &c., will be of great public utility."

What court of justice is invested with authority to gainsay this declaration? To strike it out of the act, and reason upon the other words, as if it were not there? To pronounce that a grant is against the interests of the people, which the legislature has declared to be of great utility to the people? It seems to me to be our duty to interpret laws, and not to wander into speculations upon their policy. And where, I may ask, is the proof that Charles River Bridge has been against the interests of the people? The record contains no such proof; and it is, therefore, a just presumption that it does not exist.

Again, it is argued that the present grant is a grant of a monopoly, and of exclusive privileges; and therefore to be construed by the most narrow mode of interpretation. The sixth article of the bill of rights of Massachusetts has been supposed to support the objection; "No man, nor corporation, or association of men, have any other title to obtain advantages or particular and exclusive privileges distinct from those of the community, than what arises from the consideration of services rendered to the public; and this title being in nature neither hereditary nor transmissive to children, or descendants, or relations by blood, the idea of a man born a magistrate, lawgiver, or judge, is absurd and unnatural." Now, it is plain, that taking this whole clause together, it is not an inhibition of all legislative grants of exclusive privileges; but a promulgation of the reasons why there should be no hereditary magistrates, legislators, or judges. But it admits, by necessary implication, the right to grant exclusive privileges for public services, without ascertaining of what nature those services may be. It might be sufficient to say, that all the learned judges in the state court, admitted that the grant of an exclusive right to take toll at a ferry, or a bridge, or a turnpike, is not a monopoly which is deemed odious in law; nor one of the particular and exclusive privileges, distinct from those of the community, which are reprobated in the bill of rights. All that was asserted by the judges, opposed to a liberal interpretation of this grant, was, that it tended to promote monopolies. . . .

No sound lawyer will, I presume, assert that the grant of a right to erect a bridge over a navigable stream, is a grant of a common right. Before such grant, had all the citizens of the state a right to erect bridges over navigable streams? Certainly they had not; and, therefore, the grant was no restriction of any common right. It was neither a monopoly; nor, in a legal sense, had it any tendency to a monopoly. It took from no citizen what he possessed before; and had no tendency to take it from him. It took, indeed, from the legislature the power of granting the same identical privilege or franchise to any other persons. But this made it no more a monopoly, than the grant of the public stock or funds of a state for a valuable consideration. Even in cases of monopolies, strictly so called, if the nature of the grant be such that it is for the public good, as in cases of patents for inventions, the rule has always been to give them a favourable construction in support of the patent . . . .

But it has been argued, and the argument has been pressed in every form which ingenuity could suggest, that if grants of this nature are to be construed liberally, as conferring any exclusive rights on the grantees, it will interpose an effectual barrier against all general improvements of the country. For myself, I profess not to feel the cogency of this argument; either in its general application to the grant of franchises, or in its special application to the present grant. This is a subject upon which different minds may well arrive at different conclusions, both as to policy and principle. Men may, and will, complexionally differ upon topics of this sort, according to their natural and acquired habits of speculation and opinion. For my own part, I can conceive of no surer plan to arrest all public improvements, founded on private capital and enterprise, than to make the outlay of that capital uncertain, and questionable both as to security, and as to productiveness. No man will hazard his capital in any enterprise, in which, if there be a loss, it must be borne exclusively by himself; and if there be success, he has not the slightest security of enjoying the rewards of that success for a single moment. If the government means to invite its citizens to enlarge the public comforts and conveniences, to establish bridges, or turnpikes, or canals, or railroads, there must be some pledge, that the property will be safe; that the enjoyment will be co-extensive with the grant: and that success will not be the signal of a general combination to overthrow its rights, and to take away its profits. The very agitation of a question of this sort, is sufficient to alarm every stockholder in every public enterprise of this sort, throughout the whole country. Already, in my native state, the legislature has found it necessary expressly to concede the exclusive privilege here contended against; in order to insure the accomplishment of a rail road for the benefit of the public. And yet, we are told, that all such exclusive grants are to the detriment of the public.

But if there were any foundation for the argument itself in a general view, it would totally fail in its application to the present case. Here, the grant, however exclusive, is but for a short and limited period, more than two-thirds of which have already elapsed; and, when it is gone, the whole property and franchise are to revert to the state. The legislature exercised a wholesome foresight on the subject; and within a reasonable period it will have an unrestricted authority to do whatever it may choose, in the appropriation of the bridge and its tolls. There is not, then, under any fair aspect of the case, the slightest reason to presume that public improvements either can, or will, be injuriously retarded by a liberal construction of the present grant.

I have thus endeavoured to answer, and I think I have successfully answered all the arguments, (which indeed run into each other) adduced to justify a strict construction of the present charter. I go further, and maintain not only, that it is not a case for strict construction; but that the charter upon its very face, by its terms, and for its professed objects, demands from the Court, upon undeniable principles of law, a favourable construction for the grantees. In the first place, the legislature has declared, that the erecting of the bridge will be of great public utility; and this exposition of its own motives for the grant, requires the Court to give a liberal interpretation, in order to promote, and not to destroy an enterprise of great public utility. In the next place, the grant is a contract for a valuable consideration, and a full and adequate consideration. The proprietors are to lay out a large sum of money, (and in those times it was a very large outlay of capital,) in erecting a bridge; they are to keep it in repair during the whole period of forty years; they are to surrender it in good repair at the end of that period to the state, as its own property; they are to pay, during the whole period, an annuity of two hundred pounds to Harvard college; and they are to incur other heavy expenses and burthens, for the public accommodation. In return for all these charges, they are entitled to no more than the receipt of the tolls during the forty years, for their reimbursement of capital, interest and expenses. With all this they are to take upon themselves the chances of success; and if the enterprise fails, the loss is exclusively their own. Nor let any man imagine, that there was not, at the time when this charter was granted, much solid ground for doubting success. In order to entertain a just view of this subject, we must go back to that period of general bankruptcy, and distress and difficulty. The constitution of the United States was not only not then in existence, but it was not then even dreamed of. The union of the states was crumbling into ruins, under the old confederation. Agriculture, manufactures and commerce, were at their lowest ebb. There was infinite danger to all the states from local interests and jealousies, and from the apparent impossibility of a much longer adherence to that shadow of a government, the continental congress. And even four years afterwards, when every evil had been greatly aggravated, and civil war was added to other calamities, the constitution of the United States was all but shipwrecked in passing through the state conventions. It was adopted by very slender majorities. These are historical facts which required no colouring to give them effect, and admitted of no concealment to seduce men into schemes of future aggrandizement. I would even now put it to the common sense of every man, whether, if the constitution of the United States had not been adopted, the charter would have been worth a forty years' purchase of the tolls.

This is not all. It is well known, historically, that this was the very first bridge ever constructed in New England, over navigable tide waters so near the sea. The rigours of our climate, the dangers from sudden thaws and freezing, and the obstructions from ice in a rapid current, were deemed by many persons to be insuperable obstacles to the success of such a project. It was believed, that the bridge would scarcely stand a single severe winter. And I myself am old enough to know, that in regard to other arms of the sea, at much later periods, the same doubts have had a strong and depressing influence upon public enterprises. If Charles River Bridge had been carried away during the first or second season after its erection, it is far from being certain, that up to this moment another bridge, upon such an arm of the sea, would ever have been erected in Massachusetts. I state these things which are of public notoriety, to repel the notion that the legislature was surprised into an incautious grant, or that the reward was more than adequate to the perils. There was a full and adequate consideration, in a pecuniary sense, for the charter. But, in a more general sense, the erection of the bridge, as a matter of accommodation, has been incalculably beneficial to the public. Unless, therefore, we are wholly to disregard the declarations of the legislature, and the objects of the charter, and the historical facts of the times; and indulge in mere private speculations of profit and loss by our present lights and experience; it seems to me, that the Court is bound to come to the interpretation of this charter, with a persuasion that it was granted in furtherance, and not in derogation of the public good.

But I do not insist upon any extraordinary liberality in interpreting this charter. All I contend for is that it shall receive a fair and reasonable interpretation; so as to carry into effect the legislative intention, and secure to the grantees a just security for their privileges. I might, indeed, well have spared myself any investigation of the principles upon which royal and legislative grants are ordinarily to be construed; for this Court has itself furnished an unequivocal rule for interpreting all public contracts. The present grant is confessedly a contract. . . .

The legislature understood itself to be granting a boon; and not making a bargain, or asking a favour. It was liberal, because it meant to be just, in a case of acknowledged hazard, and of honourable enterprise, very beneficial to the public. To suppose, that the plaintiffs meant to surrender their present valuable and exclusive right of franchise for thirty-four remaining years, and to put it in the power of the legislature, the next day, or the next year, to erect a bridge, toll or free, which by its contiguity should ruin theirs, or take away all their profits; is a supposition, in my judgment, truly extravagant, and without a scintilla of evidence to support it. The burdens of maintaining the bridge were to remain; the payment of the annuity to Harvard college was to remain: and yet, upon this supposition, the extension of the term of their charter, granted in the shape of a bounty, would amount to a right to destroy the franchise the next day, or the next hour, at the pleasure of the legislature. I cannot perceive, upon what ground such an implication can be made; an implication, not arising from any words or intent expressed on the face of the act, or fairly inferrible from its purposes; and wholly repugnant to the avowed objects of the grant, which are to confer a benefit, and not to impose an oppressive burden, or create a ruinous competition.

Upon the whole, my judgment is, that the act of the legislature of Massachusetts granting the charter of Warren Bridge, is an act impairing the obligation of the prior contract and grant to the proprietors of Charles River Bridge; and, by the constitution of the United States, it is, therefore, utterly void. I am for reversing the decree of the state court, (dismissing the bill;) and for remanding the cause to the state court for further proceedings, as to law and justice shall appertain.

⊞ E S S A Y S

Since vested property rights yielded new technology, it is easy to dismiss rights proponents and to applaud what Professor Stanley I. Kutler of the University of Wisconsin, Madison, terms the "creative destruction" of property rights in *Charles River Bridge.* According to the view of Kutler and others, the Marshall and Taney courts wanted economic development, but disagreed about how best to realize it. R. Kent Newmyer, a historian at the University of Connecticut, argues that this interpretation, while useful in studying the economic basis of constitutional change, fails to capture the cultural and moral differences underlying the debate about property rights. Newmyer's essay spotlights Justice Joseph Story, the key dissenter in *Charles River Bridge,* and argues that the differences separating Marshall and Taney were about ends rather than means. Story's dissent, rather than simply an instance of trying to use old law to salvage the doctrine of vested rights, represented an entirely different view of the relationship between law and economic change.

Law as an Economic Instrument

STANLEY I. KUTLER

The Supreme Court's decision in 1837 involved a full-scale debate between Chief Justice Taney and Justice Story on the substantive issues, the nature of public policy, and the judicial function. The clash marked an institutional watershed. After John Marshall became Chief Justice in 1801, he introduced the custom of a single opinion by the justices in contrast to the earlier

Excerpt from *Privilege and Creative Destruction: The Charles River Bridge Case* by Stanley I. Kutler. Copyright © 1971 by the J. B. Lippincott Company, pp. 85–101. Reprinted by permission of HarperCollins Publishers.

practice of delivering opinions *seriatim.* To be sure, there were occasional dissents in the Marshall years, and the Chief Justice often trimmed his views in order to secure unanimity. But by 1837, the justices' political genealogy spanned three decades, which in turn reinforced the diversity of their views. The Charles River Bridge case may well mark the origins of dissent over basic values within the Supreme Court. At no time prior to 1837 had the disagreement in a major case been so sharp and fundamental. The Charles River Bridge decision thus demolished the illusion of consensus within the judiciary, just as certainly as the Bank War had exposed it within other political, social, and economic spheres of American life.

Chief Justice Taney's opinion for the Court combined specific legal principles with emerging general concepts involving the role of government and the public interest. He applied these specific principles and general concepts in order to serve particular purposes of the society and the economy. He utilized the law as a handmaiden for change, progress, and growth. As a specimen of judicial craftsmanship, Taney's opinion was of the highest caliber, dexterously joining *stare decisis* to a recognition of changes in American life that demanded legal accommodation. Actually, Taney offered little that was doctrinally new. He fashioned his views from early state court decisions, on English precedent, opinions by John Marshall and his colleagues, and the arguments of counsel. Taney's opinion marked not the emergence of a new idea, but rather the triumph of a competing idea, now propelled by a decisive political—and judicial—majority.

However much political considerations may have influenced Taney's opinion, it is worth noting that his remarks were almost devoid of Jacksonian rhetoric. Indeed, it may not be stretching the point too far to suggest that John Marshall could have written the same opinion. But Taney's views of economic progress, technological change, and the interwoven responsibilities of government were not uniquely his or those of a "Jacksonian Democrat." Marshall, the anachronistic Virginia Federalist, and Taney, the Maryland Democrat, who only recently and reluctantly had shed his Federalist label, simply were not very far apart on these problems in the 1830s.

At the outset, Taney acknowledged that the case presented questions of the "gravest character." He also noted that great pecuniary interests were at stake and, as in most legal choices, all sides would be affected, and someone harmed. Taney phrased the choices a bit more abstractly: the Court, he said, must guard "the rights of property, and at the same time carefully . . . [abstain] from any encroachment on the rights reserved to the States." It should be emphasized that Taney's conception of state rights in no way corresponds to the modern, and essentially negativist, connotation of the term. As evidenced by the whole of his opinion, Taney had clearly in mind an active and positive view of state *powers.*

The Chief Justice reduced the plaintiffs' argument to two basic propositions. First, the 1650 grant to Harvard entitled the college to a perpetual and exclusive right to operate a ferry between Charlestown and Boston. Massachusetts, in turn, transferred and vested those rights in the Charles

River Bridge proprietors, thus giving the latter exclusive rights in the line of travel. Second, and independent of the ferry rights, the proprietors claimed that the acts of 1785 and 1792 "necessarily implied" that the legislature would not authorize a competing bridge. In any event, the original charter was a contract and the grant to the Warren Bridge group thus impaired the obligation of the contract. But Taney, after summarizing the position of the proprietors, immediately indicated that nothing would pass by implication. The plaintiffs, he said, must "show that the State had entered into a contract with them . . . not to establish a free bridge. . . . Such, and such only, are the principles upon which the plaintiffs . . . can claim relief."

Taney declared quite simply that the ferry rights were nonexistent; therefore the proprietors had no claim to them whatsoever. The bridge itself, he maintained, had destroyed the ferry when it took its place and assumed its same functions. With the ferry destroyed, how could rights incidental to it have survived? Whatever exclusive privileges attached to the ferry followed the fate of the ferry. "The privilege of exclusion could not remain in the hands of [the] . . . assignees," Taney said, "if those assignees destroyed the ferry."

Taney could not resist the irony of the proprietors' claims to Harvard's privileges. The state had chartered the Charles River Bridge because of public need when the ferry proved inadequate. When the prospective proprietors petitioned the legislature in 1785, they had ignored Harvard's claims and stressed the greater demands of public interest and convenience and the superior advantages of a bridge over a ferry. The legislature had in turn accepted and then acted upon these principles. The bridge charter was not dependent upon Harvard's consent. The legislature, with the acquiescence of the proprietors, treated the subject as wholly within its power and ignored any claims of exclusive rights. In short, it considered the ferry rights extinguished by the bridge grant. The legislature compensated the college for the loss of its ferry operation, but nothing in the legislative documents in 1785, or thereafter, indicated an intent to reserve or later continue the ferry rights. The ferry, Taney concluded, "with all its privileges was intended to be forever at an end." In effect, the Chief Justice contended that the state had resumed the ferry privilege in order to construct a bridge in its place.

Taney concluded his discussion of the ferry rights by insisting upon a narrow construction of the charter. "The charter to the bridge is a written instrument which must speak for itself, and be interpreted by its own terms." Nothing in the charter associated the rights of the college with the bridge proprietors, and Taney noted that there was "no rule of legal interpretation" which authorized the Court even to infer such an association. This narrow construction was the theoretical basis for Taney's whole point of view in the case. And just as he used it to dispose of the question of the continuity of ferry rights, so he employed it to reject the proprietors' contention that the charter "necessarily implied" an exclusive control over the line of travel to the Charles River Bridge Company.

Throughout his opinion Taney confidently asserted that the "rule" of narrow construction in cases that involved the public interest was well-settled.

For particular support he relied on an English case and recent Marshall Court decisions. Interestingly enough, the English case, *Stourbridge Canal v. Wheeley,* proved as useful to Story in his dissent as it did to the Chief Justice. Taney, however, noted that the English court considered the established rule of construction as one resolving any ambiguity in a public contract in favor of the public, and that the grantees could "claim nothing that is not clearly given them in the act." The facts and issues of the English case were not at all analogous to the bridge controversy. It involved an attempt by canal proprietors to charge tolls for use of their waterways when boats did not pass through the company's locks. The court held that the charter did not authorize such charges, either specifically or by clear "inference" from some of its provisions. Taney exploited the court's doctrine of strict construction, whereas Story grasped the English judge's acknowledgment of resulting rights when they could be clearly implied.*

A common ploy of a Supreme Court justice is to use the decisions and language of a distinguished predecessor to make a different goal more palatable to the public or to his colleagues. In the 1920s Chief Justice William Howard Taft consistently qualified the traditional doctrine that production could not be regulated under the interstate commerce power of the federal government. Chief Justice Charles Evans Hughes, in 1937, approvingly quoted Taft's *dicta* in order to overthrow completely the same doctrine and open the path for massive federal regulation of the economy. To offset the vigorous protest within his own court and the outraged cries of a large part of the legal and business community, Hughes deftly utilized the language of Taft, that impeccable constitutionalist.

Similarly, in 1837, Chief Justice Taney shrewdly invoked the decisions of his predecessor, the most important of which was Marshall's Providence Bank opinion of 1830. Taney insisted that the state action in the Charles River Bridge case was analogous to Rhode Island's bank tax. The proprietors' arguments were the same as those of the bank; that is, the state's power, if it existed, could destroy the franchise it had granted. But Taney, like Marshall, treated this only as a consequential, or incidental, effect. That the

---

* The Stourbridge Canal case was an action of assumpsit brought by the canal proprietors against coal transporters who had refused to pay tolls. The parliamentary act chartering the canal provided that the proprietors could charge tolls for passage through any of the canal's locks. The defendants, however, had used a collateral cut of the Stourbridge, containing no locks, to link up to another canal. The proprietors maintained that only those who passed through the locks, and therefore paid tolls, were entitled to navigate the canal or any of its cuts. The defendants insisted that the canal was a public utility and that all persons were eligible to use it, paying rates only when properly authorized. The judge framed the conflict within the question of charter construction. For charters of public utility, he contended that the rule of strict construction was fully established: "that any ambiguity in the terms of the contract must operate against the adventurers, and in favor of the public; and the plaintiffs can claim nothing which is not *clearly* given them by the act." All this, of course, was most useful for Taney. But after the English judge found that the plaintiffs had no express right to receive compensation except for passage through the locks, he was willing for them to demonstrate "a right *clearly* given by inference" from other clauses of the charter. The implications, however, were not apparent enough and the judge held that the company could impose no burdens on the canal users, for its own benefit, except those clearly specified in the charter. *The Proprietors of the Stourbridge Canal* against *Wheely and others* (2 Barn. & Ald. 792).

power might be exercised so as to destroy the franchise could not, he concluded, "in any degree affect the principle."

In the Providence Bank case, Marshall had been concerned with the power of taxation, a power basic and crucial for the existence of government. Taney, however, raised Marshall's use of a specific power to a general proposition involving the total power and purpose of government. The power to tax is essential if government is to function in behalf of the whole community. But Taney saw taxation as only one means to a larger end, and the power to serve such ends could not be diminished: "[T]he object and end of all government," he insisted, "is to promote the happiness and prosperity of the community by which it is established; and it can never be assumed, that the government intended to diminish its power of accomplishing the end for which it was created." Taney shrewdly perceived the vital role of government in stimulating the release of energy needed to serve and satisfy the requirements of a growing, free, active, and enterprising nation. Specifically, new channels of communication—"safe, convenient, and cheap"— were needed to maintain such activity; they served both travel and trade and were "essential to the comfort, convenience, and prosperity of the people." No government, Taney reiterated, could presume to surrender its power to provide for or encourage the development of these channels of communication. As with the power of taxation, "the whole community have an interest in preserving it undiminished."

Nothing more infuriated, or perhaps embarrassed, Taney's Whig detractors than his use of Marshall to complement and secure what some of them saw as exclusively Jacksonian rhetoric and doctrine. They insisted, for example, that the cases were not analogous; the taxation in the bank case did not indicate a certain tendency and intent to destroy the institution as did the chartering of the Warren Bridge. The chief criticism came down to a conflict as old as government itself. The purpose of government is to maintain an ordered community so as to better insure the freedom and happiness of its individual constituents. But to what extent may government diminish or harm the rights and well-being of any individual, or group of individuals, in order that the community at large may benefit?

One Whig critic flatly maintained that "government becomes subversive of its own end, when its purpose is bent to destruction." Marshall, he contended, never sanctioned governmental power or action that was confiscatory in its result. Anticipating this line, Taney refused to distinguish the power to tax from "any other affecting the public interest." The principles were the same, he said, and the rule of charter construction must be the same. Turning to the Massachusetts case, Taney argued that the "interests" of a large part of the community were unquestionably affected if the state should surrender control of a line of travel, for profit, to a corporation for its exclusive operation during seventy years. Taney paid his respects to individual rights—and there is no reason to doubt his commitment—but he emphasized their qualified character: "While the rights of private property are sacredly guarded, we must not forget that the community also have rights, and that the happiness and well being of every citizen depends on their faithful preservation."

The argument was complementary: on one hand, the community benefits when it maintains individual rights; but individual rights must, of necessity, sometimes bow to the needs and well-being of the community. The resolution, then as always, was a practical one, and here Taney saw the "rights" of the community as paramount. Summing up his views of "positive" government and community rights, the Chief Justice neatly combined older Federalist notions with the leaven of Jacksonian rhetoric: "The continued existence of a government would be of no great value, if by implications and presumptions, it was disarmed of the powers necessary to accomplish the ends of its creations; and the functions it was designed to perform, transferred to the hands of privileged corporations." In effect Taney recognized the existence of both focused interests or claims, and the framework or supporting interests necessary for an effective existence and pursuit of the specific ones. His decision was practical because it acknowledged the necessity for maintaining the functions and needs of social organization or social infrastructure, on which the more particular activities and relations depend.

Firmly establishing the principles of narrow construction and the inviolability of certain governmental functions, Taney proceeded to refute the claims of the Charles River Bridge proprietors. Their charter provided no exclusive privileges over the river, no right to erect another bridge for themselves, or to prevent others from doing so. Furthermore, the charter did not expressly prohibit the state from building another bridge. The plaintiffs could only infer such conditions, and in this case, obviously nothing would pass by implication. Taney also cited the charter of the West Boston Bridge in 1792 to prove that the state had not intended to deprive itself of making further improvements over the river. When the state extended the Charles River Bridge charter at the same time, Taney noted that the legislature's language carefully avoided any implication that the extension amounted to a compromise or compensation.

Taney's opinion, however, was somewhat ambiguous as to whether the state could ever specifically surrender, even for a limited period of time, its power to make improvements or any other power basic to the "happiness and prosperity" of the community. He recognized throughout, as he did in similar opinions as attorney general, that government could grant certain privileges to individuals who embarked on enterprises of value to the community. Furthermore, while he specifically acknowledged that the state's power of "promoting the comfort and convenience" of the people could not be surrendered or diminished, he added, as a qualification, "unless it shall appear by plain words that it was intended to be done." Taney's language in the Charles River Bridge case, and his decisions in future cases, clearly illustrate that the contract clause of the federal constitution still had force. The chief limitation was that nothing could be implied when the public interest was at stake. This limitation, incidentally, is related to Taney's conception of the judicial function. To infer from a contract things that a legislature had presumably avoided implying with great care, would constitute an excess of judicial power, acting upon its own prejudices with "a sort of judicial coercion." The proprietors' alleged privilege of exclusivity for bridge transportation would have vitally affected a broad array of interests. Accordingly, such an impact required a clear decision for such a right from the broadly-represented lawmaking body. Courts had much less claim to such representativenes than legislatures and Taney properly hesitated to sustain implicatory claims.

The touchstone of Taney's opinion was its practicality, its responsiveness to contemporary reality—in short, it was a document of public policy. The material progress of society, Taney observed, is prompted by technological change and improvement. Law should be a spur, not an impediment. It should allow for some loss, some sacrifice in order to make way for the new. In the past, successive turnpikes followed the same routes; then, in some cases, railroads ruined the turnpike corporations. New techniques provide the *raison d'être* for internal improvements. If the Charles River Bridge proprietors carried their point, Taney rightly feared that the courts would face all sorts of suits. He envisioned, for example, turnpike corporations "awakening from their sleep and calling upon this court to put down the improvements which have taken their place." Property and capital invested in railroads and canals would be jeopardized; more than that, venture capital would be discouraged. The prospects were grim, Taney noted: "We shall be thrown back to the improvements of the last century, and obliged to stand still, until the claims of the old turnpike corporations shall be satisfied, and they shall consent to permit these States to avail themselves of the lights of modern science, and to partake of the benefit of those improvements which are now adding to the wealth and prosperity, and the convenience and comfort of every other part of the civilized world." The Supreme Court, he concluded, would not "sanction principles which must lead to such results." Taney cast the law with the new entrepreneurs, the present rather than the past risk-takers, as the preferred agents for material progress. Only thus could technological advances be applied rapidly. One writer has put it more bluntly: Justice Story and those who supported the Charles River Bridge stood for the "horse and buggy," while Taney cleared the path for the "onrushing railroad."

Given the materialistic drives and dreams of the Americans—a people "forever moving on"—the Taney arguments made sense. He allied our laws with broadened entrepreneurial opportunity, even at the expense of past commitments of assets. Americans in the nineteenth century faced a land of rich and boundless opportunities for material reward. Nothing so threatened the aspirations of nineteenth century Americans as the scarcity of capital; nothing, therefore, required greater legal encouragement than venture capital, subject to the normal risks and vicissitudes of the market. It was this that took a local dispute over a free bridge out of its provincial setting and thrust it into the larger debate over political economy. Retrospectively, in a century that put a premium on "progress," and the release of creative human energy to propel that progress, the decision was inevitable.

Taney's Charles River Bridge opinion helped free new forms of property from the impeding, sometimes aggressive claims of obsolescent corporations that desperately tried to preserve exclusive earning opportunities. Such corporations often had vague and amgibuous charters, and represented the kind of abstraction cited by Taney in his example of turnpike roads and railroads. The plaintiff's claims in the Maryland case of *The Washington and Baltimore Turnpike Co. v. The Baltimore and Ohio Railroad* two years afterwards vindicated Taney's fears. The title of the case neatly summed up the issues. A Maryland turnpike company, chartered in 1812, brought an action of trespass against the railroad for building its route between the two cities and connected by the turnpike's line of travel. The railroad had done so under authority of four charters granted by Maryland between 1827 and 1833. The turnpike company charged that the railroad charters impaired its contract, threatened its existence, and so amounted to a deprivation of property without compensation. The situation paralleled that of the Charles River Bridge in that the new competition was destructive of an existing (although physically different) property form. A Maryland county court ingnored the turnpike company's claim and found for the railroad. The Maryland high court subsequently affirmed the decision without opinion. Cognizant of community desires for the obvious advantages of the railroad, the courts refused to intervene in behalf of the extravagantly obstructionist claims of established competing interests.

As a problem of public policy, the Charles River Bridge decision was the practical one in terms of broad public policy needs. Still, "legal doctrine" needed some support, and Taney found such support in the tool of strict construction. This enabled him to work out the balance between competing private interests and community needs. Despite the Chief Justice's rough handling of the proprietor's claims, his dictum that the "rights of private property must be sacredly guarded" was not an empty one on his part. He neither denied Webster's argument, nor refuted Story's opinion, that investors would be discouraged if they found their property insecure every time the state or community desired a change. If titles were valid, if charter rights and privileges were explicit, Taney never would have approved their arbitrary destruction. In such cases, Taney and his judicial contemporaries, federal and state, insisted upon the implementation of eminent domain, that is, the taking of private property for public use but with compensation to the owners. Eminent domain is an equitable resolution of the constant tension between the demands of the community and the prerogatives of private property, and as the rate of technological innovation increased and new communities developed in the nineteenth century, it was increasingly employed. It applied, however, only in cases of indisputable rights and prerogatives of ownership. In cases such as the Charles River Bridge, courts have dismissed eminent domain as irrelevant, as Taney did in his one reference to it. Compensation here depended solely upon the beneficence of the state. But in no manner was the Charles River Bridge case a requiem for private property in the United States.

The Charles River Bridge decision was a crushing blow to Justice Story. "A case of grosser injustice, or more oppressive legislation, never existed," he wrote to his wife. "I feel humiliated, as I think every one here is, by the Act which has now been confirmed." Story, his judicial world collapsing about him, despaired for the Court and the nation. Soon after the decision, he talked about resigning, but McLean and others dissuaded him. Webster, of course, remained loyal and admiring. He told Story that his opinion was the "ablest, and best written" he had ever delivered. But Webster, too, was melancholy about the future: "The intelligent part of the profession will all be with you," Webster said. "There is no doubt of that; but then the decision of the Court will have completely overturned, in my judgment, one great provision of the Constitution." Story felt keenly the loss of past values. "I am the last of the old race of judges," he lamented to Harriet Martineau. "I stand their solitary representative, with a pained heart, and a subdued confidence."

Story's opinion was substantially the one he had prepared in 1831, tailored somewhat to respond to Taney. The thrust, however, was the same. In 1831, when the Court divided, Story revealed that the conflict revolved around the problem of strict construction of charters. Then and later he believed that three centuries of law and practice, English and American, favored a liberal construction in behalf of grantees. The confrontation between Taney and Story thus resulted in a debate over economic theory and the purposes of public policy. Story's massive documentation of the common law, along with English and American precedents, probably gave him the better of the doctrinal contest—or in what Story himself called the "old law." But Story bucked a powerful tide of opinion and was wholly out of line with the prevailing commercial ethos. Yet with a tenacity born of deep-rooted conviction, with an adherence to older and more experienced values, and with a sense of history, Story pursued his cause in spite of his isolation.

At the onset of his opinion, Story challenged the Chief Justice's version of charter construction. The original Charles River Bridge charter, he argued, dictated a liberal construction. He correctly observed that the charter was vague as to the obvious purpose and intent. The act nowhere really conferred an authority upon the corporation to build a bridge, except by "inference and implication" from the preamble. For Story, this was "irresistible proof" that the court must resort "to the common principles of interpretation, and imply and presume things, which the legislature has not expressly declared." In a real sense, Story tried to preserve a judicial role in the interpretation of charters. He recognized a certain sterility, a kind of built-in judicial obsolescence, in Taney's conception of strict construction. If courts and judges were not at liberty to presume and imply meanings of charters, there would be, he said, an end to the case. From this, Story launched a long explanation and support for what he considered the proper rules of interpretation.

Story's opinion was a veritable treatise. Extensively researched, it offered a parade of precedents, all marshaled in an imposing array to support the most extravagant claims for entrepreneurial privilege. Story metaphorically worshipped at the altar of the common law, indulging in constant references to, for example, the "doctrine of my Lord Coke, and of the venerable sages of the law in other times."

Story contended that the Charles River Bridge grant was one of contract, and not of bounty. In exchange for the grant, the proprietors had offered a valuable consideration to the state, that is, a satisfaction of public need and convenience that would encourage enterprise and commerce. He compared this to a royal grant in which the king received some consideration, as opposed to one of mere donation flowing from the bounty of the crown. The latter, he acknowledged, allowed a construction wholly in the king's favor. But in cases where valuable consideration was received, the grant was the same as any private one and was to be construed in favor of the grantee. "It would be to the dishonour of the government," Story said, "that it should pocket a fair consideration, and then quibble as to the obscurities and implications of its own contract." Republican justice, he added, should be no less than that of monarchy.

In classical Whig fashion, Story polarized the conflict as a simple one between lawful vested rights on the one hand, and arbitrary capricious prerogative on the other. He thought this indulgence of American legislative prerogative infinitely worse than the greatest excesses of Tudor and Stuart monarchs. For him, the battles against despotism were over and the lessons and principles clear. "I stand upon the old law; upon law established more than three centuries ago, in cases contested with as much ability and learning as any in the annals of our jurisprudence, in resisting any such encroachments upon the rights and liberties of the citizens, secured by public grants. I will not," he vowed, "consent to shake their title deeds by any speculative niceties or novelties." Story's target here, of course, was Taney's doctrine of community rights and interest. So it is not surprising that despite his massive documentation, Story ignored the Marshall Court decisions that sustained such a view, decisions to which Story had at the time acquiesced.

Story profoundly disliked the "new" doctrine and betrayed his impatience with the voguish premium on "progress." He insisted that the grant be examined within its original context. The risks had been great when the state had approved the venture. Economic conditions in the 1780s were not exactly propitious and the risk was further increased by the political instability that obtained under the Confederation. In addition, the very idea was technically hazardous; no one rightly knew for certain that the bridge could be built. Story emphasized these facts in order to refute any notion that the legislature had been deceived into an unwise grant, or that the proprietors' prospective rewards were out of proportion to their imediate perils. If the whole venture failed, the proprietors alone assumed the loss; the community's risk was nil and the public stood only to gain. The grant was only "in furtherance, and not in derogation of the public good."

Story believed that "natural" law and the "first principles of justice" forbade the legislature from doing indirectly what it could not do directly. From that, his conclusions fell neatly into line. He cited the decision in *Fletcher* v. *Peck* to deny that a legislature could revoke its own grant. Furthermore, he maintained that when a state granted privilege, it implicitly gave whatever was necessary for taking and enjoying it. In the case of the Charles River Bridge, the unimpaired taking of tolls was indispensable for the full enjoyment of the proprietors' rights to conduct their transport facility. If denied the tolls, directly or indirectly, the franchise was worthless. It was this right that was exclusive and to deny it was, in effect, to impair the obligation of the contract. The rights over the whole river, he added, need not be exclusive. He believed that the grant implied an exclusive franchise to a reasonable distance so that the owners would not be injured by competition. He thus applied the common law of ferry rights to bridges: "Wherever any other bridge or ferry is so near that it injures the franchise, or diminishes the toll in a positive and essential degree, there it is a nuisance, and is actionable. It invades the franchise, and ought to be abated."

Story had a powerful point. Suppose, he hypothesized, the legislature said to investors: build a bridge, bear the burdens of maintenance, and collect the tolls. Suppose the legislature offered no guarantee that the corporation could receive its tolls and reserved the right to erect competing bridges anywhere. "[I]s there a man living, of ordinary discretion or prudence, who would have accepted such a charter upon such terms," Story asked. And what legislature, in its right senses, he continued, would have ever inserted such a qualification and expected a response from private capital and patronage? When the legislature chartered the Warren Bridge in 1828, and provided that it ultimately be free, the effect on the Charles River Bridge tolls was the same as if the legislature had directly abrogated them.

Significantly, Taney had avoided any direct treatment of this consideration, but he probably subscribed to the underlying assumptions of the free bridge proponents in the local squabble. The proprietors had taken a great risk but had been amply rewarded beyond their expectations. The stock values had risen excessively on speculations of even greater prospects as the community developed. The proprietors and their immediate heirs had profited handsomely, and with that consideration, the community was scarcely obligated to continue paying a tribute to an unproductive, uncreative *rentier* class. Taney ignored the theoretical implications, and like the community, undoubtedly preferred to think in terms of practical and current conditions.

Story apparently realized that his common law erudition and scholarship amounted to an exercise in futility. And he was not totally obtuse toward the temper of the times. He realized the impact of technological change and the need for its implementation; he was certainly not adverse to material progress. Though Taney did stand for the "onrushing railroad," it is unfair to stigmatize Story as a "horse and buggy" judge. Taney and Story disagreed on the judicial interpretation of charters and contracts. But it was a difference over the means to the same end. Both favored a public policy that would encourage and foster improvements. Taney emphasized opportunity—immediate opportunity—as the chief inducement for investments, whereas

Story recognized security of title and full enjoyment of existing property as paramount.

Story confidently believed that investors must be assured the security and productiveness of their capital; otherwise public improvements based on private capital would come to a halt. He found it paradoxical that a successful venture should threaten the security of investments: "If the government means to invite its citizens to enlarge the public comforts and conveniences, to establish bridges, turnpikes, or canals, or railroads, there must be some pledge, that the property will be safe; that the enjoyment will be coextensive with the grant, and that success will not be the signal of a general combination to overthrow its rights, and to take away its profits." The current agitation against corporate privileges, he warned, would only alarm potential investors against participating in public enterprises. Yet Story knew better. In his own way, he perceived the irony and sham of the Charles River Bridge controversy when he observed that his native Massachusetts, in order to assure improvements, made grants of exclusive privileges to the new railroads.

Story, moreover, recognized the problems raised by obsolete privileges, such as those of turnpike and canal companies. But the just manner of treating such impediments to progress and public improvements, Story believed, lay within the state's power of eminent domain. In this manner the state served the community's purpose and protected the rights of property. He dismissed the defendants' contention that the damage caused by the new bridge was merely consequential and therefore the state was not liable. Once again, Story refused to recognize any distinction between a direct and an indirect method. The "eternal principles of justice," he averred, required compensation.

Story simply discounted the potentially staggering social and economic costs to the community inherent in a universal application of eminent domain—even if those costs restrained and inhibited further development. The difference with Taney is again significant. The Chief Justice ignored the question of eminent domain in part because it was not at issue; the state was not a party in the case. Furthermore, once he determined the proper means of charter construction, Taney could avoid the issue of eminent domain. Carrying the Court with him on the validity of strict construction, Taney disposed of the compensation question and focused on the need for recognizing broadly-shared commonwealth values. His abiding concern was with the will and needs of the larger community; some individuals' rights had to be sacrificed in behalf of ambitious other individuals. Allegedly, this would better serve the needs of the whole community. To the very end, however, Story emphasized the rights of individuals and a potential legislative despotism. The burden was on the state to prevent any misconception of public intentions. If the legislature did not mean to grant exclusive rights, it should say so. The grantees, he added, then act at their own peril, and they "must abide the results of their overweening confidence, indiscretion, and zeal."

Story's tragic sense of moral decay in the midst of commercial greed and untoward ambitions echoed the simple messages of honor and duty. The price of honor for him was no less than the value Taney placed on progress. Perhaps, though, like Taney, Story understood the political and social pressures that had so often dominated the bridge controversy. If so, he undoubtedly considered them beneath contempt. They did violence to the law he revered, a law he believed had amply and usefully fostered growth, progress, and above all, justice.

Law as a Cultural Delineator

R. KENT NEWMYER

Justice Joseph Story's dissent in the *Bridge Case* pioneered no new law. Nor did it successfully reaffirm the old—although conservatives like Webster and Kent clung to it as legal gospel. Its importance has not been in law, then, but in legal history, where it has served as a benchmark from which historians have measured the distance and direction travelled by American law in the Age of Jackson.

The well-known question in the *Bridge Case* was whether the new free bridge encroached upon the allegedly exclusive toll rights of the earlier bridge, in violation of the contract clause of the Constitution, as interpreted in *Dartmouth College* v. *Woodward*. On this question the essential difference between Taney and Story, so most scholars argue, was over means, not ends: Both, the argument goes, liked the corporation and assumed that the function of the law was to facilitate economic progress by releasing its productive energies. This could be done best, asserted Taney, by preventing existing corporations from holding back dynamic capital and technology by inferring monopoly claims from their charters; accordingly, he refused the old bridge company's claim. Story insisted that corporate expansion required a favorable environment for investment, which depended in turn on stable, predictable legislative charters, and accordingly he upheld the implied charter rights asked for by the Charles River Bridge Company.

The Chief Justice opted for "creative destruction," as one . . . scholar put it, which is to say that he laid the unavoidable social costs of economic growth upon static capital. By supporting "privilege" Story made the public pay—either by foregoing a second bridge and continuing to pay tolls or by footing the bill for compensating the old bridge company under eminent domain. Taney's law was flexible, pragmatic, and instrumental—simultaneously accommodating the dynamic capital and state-based legislative democracy ushered in by the Jacksonians. Story's black letter *tour de force* comes off as impractical, inflexible, and nostalgic; Story as the "last of the old race of judges," grinding out "old law" to save vested property rights.

Insightful and useful though it is, this interpretation, especially as it concerns Story, is incomplete and in some important respects misleading. It

Kent Newmyer, "Justice Joseph Story, the Charles River Bridge Case and the Crisis of Republicanism," *American Journal of Legal History* 17 (July 1973), pp. 232–245. Reprinted by permission.

is history written by the winners: the post-1837 corporate boom is equated with progress, and Taney, *post hoc ergo propter hoc*, is given credit for it. Because Story differed from Taney, because he wrongly prophesied Taney's law would produce economic stagnation, his own legal position has been dismissed as backward-looking and unworkable. His dissent, in fact, appears more as a symbolic foil to the majority's opinion than a serious and possibly viable alternative to it.

The problem is to avoid anachronism, to take Story seriously, to reread his opinion with an open mind and to see the *Bridge Case* as he saw it— as part of a desperate struggle for the preservation of Republican society itself. To do so, I argue here, would show (1) that the legal debate between Story and Taney was more fundamental than is generally noted and that the difference between Taney in the *Bridge Case* and Marshall in the *Dartmouth College Case* was basically irreconcilable; (2) that Story and Taney differed on cultural objectives as well as legal means; (3) that Story's dissent was less inflexible, more workable, and less preoccupied with privilege and property and more with morality than is generally believed. In short, another look at Story's dissent might throw some light on his legal thinking, his place in American legal history, and at the same time illuminate something of the interrelation of law and cultural change in the early nineteenth century United States.

I

The *Bridge Case* for Story was part of an unmistakable pattern of disaster, which included the resurgence of political parties, the election of Andrew Jackson, the rise of states' rights and nullification, the defeat of the Cherokees, the destruction of the Second Bank of the United States and national economic planning, the movement for codification of the common law, the death of Marshall and the emergence of the Jacksonian Court. Economic expansion was the issue in the *Bridge Case,* to be sure, but more fundamentally it raised the question of who should make and maintain the rules of republican society. By what system was the course of American history to be guided? As Story put it, while listening to arguments of counsel, "The only question here is of sheer power."

The power struggle which Story saw, I contend, was between law and politics—a struggle which originated in the ambiguities and tensions within Republicanism itself. The original and fundamental principle of Republican political theory was sovereignty of the people, but what the Framers gave to the people with one hand they took back with the other, for the corollary to popular sovereignty was the axiom that law, not men, governed. The American people were sovereign but they could speak in their sovereign capacity only in organic convention and had spoken only in their Constitution. Beneath this supreme law, permeating and informing it, was the common law, which the newly-constituted states made the foundation of their respective jurisdictions. Law, then, and the system of courts designed to administer and maintain it, provided the basic framework of public and private action—one designed, first, to maximize the individual energies unleashed by the Revolution (and both the Constitution and the common law took on this promotive function), and second, to prevent the abuse of public power by both the magistrates and the people.

No sooner had the Republican system been instituted than the conflict between popular sovereignty and rule of law began to manifest itself. Political party was the catalyst: by fusing factions into a national majority, party organization subverted Madison's principle that the size of the American republic would prevent majority tyranny. Party could be effectively used to harmonize the executive and Congress, thus short-circuiting the constitutional system of checks and balances. Nor could *noblesse oblige* be counted on to preserve rule of law because party undercut the system of deference by substituting service to party organization for proven social status as the test of leadership. And the same erosive effects were visible on the state as well as national level. With democracy let loose, the whole system of rule by law seemed in jeopardy. The people seemed bent on claiming and using their sovereignty. One by one the barriers fell: Congress, where parties originated, was the first to go—the Senate proved no more resistant than the House. State government, already parochial in outlook and mediocre in talent, was debilitated further by party influence. The presidency, rather than rising above party, as the Framers planned, had, by the time of Jackson, become the prize of party and the nerve center of its operations. The basic Republican principle that the sovereign people spoke only in constitutional convention was forgotten as the new breed of professional politicians claimed sovereignty for themselves by virtue of their election. Republicanism succumbed to democracy, law to politics.

But not quite. Congress, the presidency, *noblesse oblige* were gone, to be sure, but the Court remained. Under Marshall it had become the final arbiter and guardian of the American legal system. Only it could bring the people back to their Republican senses and restore the system of law which kept republican citizens moral and virtuous. Or so Justice Story and other conservatives desperately hoped—which brings us to the *Charles River Bridge Case.*

II

If indeed the *Bridge Case* reflected a crisis of Republicanism, as I argue, that fact should be apparent in the legal debate between Story and Taney. The argument could not be merely a debate over how best to facilitate corporate growth, nor could it, so far as Story is concerned, be simply a question of securing property rights. Careful scrutiny of Story's dissent, in fact, shows that the disagreement was about fundamentals—about basic legal issues, about the role of the law and the Court in the social-political order— in short, about law and history.

What appeared on the surface to be a dispute between Story and Taney over legal rules was in fact a profound disagreement over law. Although the case was constitutional, both agreed that the common law should resolve the issue whether the Charles River Bridge charter by implication conveyed the exclusive right to collect tolls. But beyond this they disagreed sharply. Taney's interpretation of the charter rested on the common law of royal grants. Story turned to the law of contract. Before he did, however, he met the Chief Justice on his own ground (a fact which worked to disguise the deep chasm separating their legal positions). The weakness of Taney's analysis of the law of royal grants, Story argued, was that he took "a single insulated position" as a "general axiom." Traversing the whole field of authorities which Taney ignored, Story concluded that Taney's rule of law— that in doubtful cases the benefit goes to the King and against the adventurers—was "exclusively confined to cases of mere *donation,* flowing from the bounty of the crown." When the grant turned upon valuable consideration, Taney's rule ceases and "the grant is expounded exactly as it would be in the case of a private grant—favorable to the grantee."

Story's scholarly dispute with Taney over authorities is significant in itself, as I hope to show later, but what must be emphasized, what Story took pains to emphasize, was that he differed with Taney's entire legal frame of reference. The crucial point was, he declared emphatically, that a bridge charter was "not the case of a royal grant" and consequently "the rules of common law in relation to royal grants have, therefore, in reality, nothing to do with the case." Rather, "we are construing a grant of a legislature, which though in the form of a statute, is still but a solemn contract." It followed that the majority's arguments about axioms of strict construction, their theories of public welfare which turned on the analogy of a charter to a royal grant were out-of-bounds.

By resting his argument on private contract, Story raised a different set of questions and established different ground rules for their resolution. The legal confrontation was not between the state and the individual, not between ruler and subject (as in the royal grant analogy), but between contracting parties of equal authority. The problem, therefore, was not to define special prerogatives belonging to the state but to determine what two contracting parties (presumed to be equal in their capacity to negotiate and honorable in their intentions) meant by their agreement: what was given and what taken. On this question Story had no trouble in showing that inferential reasoning was no extraordinary concession demanded by the counsel for the old bridge but a necessary and legitimate common law tool of interpretation. As Oliver Wendell Holmes put it in his discussion of contract in *The Common Law.* "The very office of construction is to work out, from what is expressly said and done, what would have been said with regard to events not definitely before the minds of the parties, if these events had been considered." Common reason, good sense, embodied in common law axioms of construction, guided the inquiry into intent.

Given his premise that private contract law governed the case, Story's argument is all but irresistible. Mutuality of interest existed, a meeting of minds and an exchange for consideration had taken place: The legislature wanted a bridge built across the Charles; the bridge company wanted to make a profit. For building the bridge, keeping it in repair, and giving it to

the state after forty years (later extended to seventy), the legislature granted
the company the right to collect tolls. The contingency "not definitely before
the minds of the parties" was whether the toll right was exclusive to the
extent that it prohibited the legislature from chartering an adjacent toll-free
bridge. Story put it to the common law and to "the common sense of every
man." Would any sensible business man, he asked, venture capital in a risky
enterprise (which bridging the Charles in 1785 was), in which the sole profit
was the right to collect tolls, if the legislature reserved the right to destroy
those tolls at any time by chartering an adjacent free bridge? Even without
explicitly saying so, the legislature recognized the company's exclusive right
to take tolls, Story argued, because it was equipped with the same common
sense that the businessmen had and because, in the eyes of the law, it was
presumed to have bargained in good faith. Any doubt about the legislature's
intent to grant exclusive tolls was removed by the compensation awarded
to Harvard for destroying its ferry rights by chartering the Charles River
Bridge and by the thirty-year extension of the original charter to the old
Bridge Company as compensation for chartering another bridge across the
Charles in 1792 which might have diminished the old company's tolls. And
when the exclusive right was given, "the law giveth, impliedly, whatever is
necessary for the taking and enjoying the same."

Story's argument not only follows *Dartmouth College* but lays bare the
radical implications of that decision. Not merely were grants and charters
within the meaning of Article I, Section 10 of the Constitution, but they
were to be interpreted according to private law. Taney and the majority
refused to be bound by this logic. They did not overrule *Dartmouth College*,
to be sure, but neither did they merely refuse to extend it by implication.
By talking royal grants instead of private contract, Taney's opinion simply
ignored *Dartmouth College* altogether—which is what Story perceived.

III

He also perceived with even greater distress that Taney's refusal to apply
the rigorous logic of contract undercut the moral foundations of Republicanism. For no other area of law in the nineteenth century was so laden
with cultural baggage, none so congenial to Republican society, as was
contract. As Western and American society moved from corporateness to
individualism, as the model of the new American man changed from a
passive, delimited, class bound one to a rational, self-sufficient creature of
volition, contract emerged as the necessary basis of social order. The movement of history in the eighteenth and nineteenth centuries was, in fact, as
Sir Henry Maine aptly phrased it, from status to contract.

By the contract device, American Puritans established their individual
and collective relationship to their God and bound themselves together in
churches and civil communities. From religion, the colonial experience, the
English legal heritage, and the influence of John Locke, contract entered
into the fabric of Republican political thought. To be sure, Republicanism
emphasized individual responsibility to a greater whole, and the principles

of popular sovereignty and representative government somewhat undercut the contractual relationship between the rulers and the people. But contract was made to justify the Revolution itself and it was the Lockean theory of social contract that best explained how a nation of free, rational, individual men could form itself into the collective sovereign people. What was true politically was equally true economically. As the American people moved progressively toward *laissez faire* capitalism, contract emerged as that area of law central to economic expansion. As such it was—along with provisions against retrospective legislation, which is in fact part of contract in the broadest sense—guaranteed by the Constitution itself. When Marshall applied the law of private contract to governmental economic activities, then he was merely following the syntactic imperative of culture to integrate and harmonize: private law became public law; common law infused constitutional law; private morality became synonymous with public, republican morality.

It was this permeating morality of contract which Story aimed to preserve in his *Bridge* dissent (and both he and Kent used the word "moral" to describe the contract issue). By shifting from contract to royal grant, Taney subtly but surely effected a shift in cultural values from a social order based on a buyer-seller model—where the individual was the basic unit of social organization, where contract was the means of collective action, and moral standards and legal ones, too, were internal and individualized—to the ruler-subject model which introduced a notion of public good outside and beyond individuals, one subject to state determination.

Story's repudiation of this cultural shift was explicit. He did not deny that the legislature could enter into the individualistic, *laissez faire* economic process, indeed assumed that it would do so to stimulate individual activity and thus promote public welfare (as when it chartered the Charles River Bridge Company). But once the legislature entered the economic arena through grants and charters, it was governed by the same laws as applied to individuals—that is, by private contract law. "Our legislatures neither have, nor affect to have, any royal prerogatives," declared Story, referring to Taney's mistaken analogy of a legislative charter to a royal grant. Indeed, the Massachusetts legislature has no claim to sovereignty whatsoever. Only the people are sovereign, he continued—applying the Federalist constitutional theory of 1787 to the states—and the people in their sovereign capactiy speak only in their constitutions. "What solid ground is there to say [then], that the words of a grant, in the mouth of a citizen, shall mean one thing, and in the mouth of the legislature shall mean another thing? In short, public welfare was not some external value which a sovereign legislature could call on when it pleased to control the economic process. Public economic good was the collective product of individual effort and of contractual relationships between individuals (under which category Story put both the state legislatures and the business corporations). There was no disjunction between mercantilism and free enterprise. One morality governed all—or with the help of the law might be made to do so. What Story wanted to achieve through law was not just economic expansion, as some historians have assumed, but economic expansion *and* the preservation of Republican morality. Indeed, in his dire forecast about the effect of Taney's opinion, he went the final step to argue that *only* with such morality could progress be achieved.

History disproved Story's proposition that contractual morality as he laid it out in his dissent was the *sine qua non* of corporate expansion. But what about his formula for a moral economic growth, i.e., economic expansion that would not undercut the basic principle of private contract? Two arguments against its viability need to be considered briefly: first, that Story's legal formula for morality worked only against the legislature and not the corporation, and, second, that it would not work at all.

Concerning the allegation that Story's morality was mainly a device for obscuring his pro-corporate, private property bias: Assuredly, Story worked through the law (public and private) to make the corporation an effective vehicle for capitalist expansion. Nor can it be denied that he viewed state legislatures as obstacles to corporate growth. But it did not follow that he wanted an unregulated corporation, one free from the constraints of Republican morality. After all, it was Story's concurrence in *Dartmouth College* that recognized the right of state legislatures to reserve, in their charters, the power to regulate corporations—providing only that the reservation clause was explicit, so that the corporation could accept or reject legislative terms. In Story's scheme, however, it was not the legislature but the courts, working especially in the realm of private contract law, that would mainly hold corporations to their moral duties. Using much the same reasoning he applied against the legislature in the *Bridge Case*—that is, by using the rational, fair-minded, practical individual as the rule-giving model—Story worked to enlarge corporate duties and responsibilities. In *Bank of Columbia v. Patterson's Administrator* (1813), the Judge departed from existing authorities to make corporations liable for contracts not under corporate seal made by their authorized agents. His *Bank of the United States* v. *Dandridge* opinion (1827) extended that principle to cover obligations entered into by cashiers of banking corporations. In effect both cases established contractual duties by construction and implication, by the same reasoning, in short, that would guide Story in the *Bridge Case*. He also worked to hold corporations to a strict performance of contracts made with private parties as in his pioneering opinion in *Mumma* v. *The Potomac Company* (1834), which announced the doctrine that a corporation's contract survives its dissolution and that the capital stock of dissolved corporations becomes a trust fund for the satisfaction of debts against the corporation. Story also accepted the doctrine emerging in state courts of corporate liability for torts, and he knew and counted on the traditional common law writ of mandamus and the doctrine of *ultra vires* as remedies against corporations that exceeded their charter rights or failed to perform duties imposed upon them. In short, Story made the same Republican assumptions about corporations that he made about individuals and legislatures—that law, especially law administered by the courts, could make them responsible and moral.

Now what about the argument that Story's dissent would not have worked at all—that it would have forestalled corporate expansion by fortifying existing corporations with monopoly protection? It cannot be denied that Story's ruling would have worked to slow down and restrain corporate growth; and in a real sense that was his intention. But it does not follow that his dissent precluded considerable economic advancement. Even in the area of most obvious applicability—that of bridges—Story's opinion offered no absolute monopoly protection to existing corporations. First, an implied grant of exclusive rights, even if successfully claimed, would last only for the period of time set by legislative discretion. (For example, the Charles River Bridge would have reverted to the state in 1855.) And if existing charters were subject to monopolistic interpretations, future ones could explicitly deny such interpretations if the legislature so willed. Nor did Story's ruling preclude the building of other bridges even during the period of the grant and such bridges had, in fact, been built across the Charles. Whether existing bridges could claim monopoly rights against new bridges depended on the extent to which a second bridge damaged the revenue of existing bridges, which was necessarily a question of degree—a question, in short, for future courts to decide on new facts. Story made clear, both in his manuscript notes on the arguments and in his opinion, that the Court's decision was limited strictly to the case at hand and was "not to decide the principles for all cases. . . ." His ruling put no dead hand on future courts.

If Story's concession to the old bridge company did not rule out new bridges, then how can historians be so certain that it would have unreasonably curtailed the growth of railroad corporations? The fact that existing canal and turnpike companies tried to stop railroads by arguing implied monopoly does not prove the point. It is one thing to argue that a charter to a canal corporation would by implication preclude parallel canals (for the duration of the grant), quite another that such a charter would automatically preclude parallel railroads. The important point is that future courts could distinguish between a canal and a railroad in such matters as function and termini, and Story's contention about the limited scope of the Bridge ruling would invite them to do so. Certainly the touchstones of common sense and business acumen by which the common law presumed to read the mind of contracting parties would not apply so irresistibly as in the *Bridge Case*. And perhaps most importantly, legislatures could and surely would make sure in future charters to guarantee against implied monopoly in areas of new technology.

The argument is speculative of necessity, but the idea that Story saw and provided for controlled economic growth is certainly consistent with the promotive thrust of his entire legal system. At the very least, doesn't he deserve a "Scotch verdict" on the question of workability?

IV

Story's dissent reveals much about his system of law and about the role he designed for the Court (which follows logically from his system). The law which Story fashioned to save the Republic from the onslaught of democracy in the *Bridge* dissent was neither moral and idealistic, scientific and rational, nor pragmatic and instrumental—it was all of these together. And it was,

I suggest, the same ingredients fashioned in the same organic manner that constitute Story's larger system of law as revealed in his remarkable and varied legal career as judge, scholar, and teacher.

Certainly no lawyer of the age save Kent was so committed to making law technically, scientifically pure. Witness his teaching at Harvard Law School, his series of commentaries on various branches of the law, his popular articles in encyclopedias, law journals, and general periodicals, and especially his scholarly opinions (and more especially his opinions on circuit), which were designed to educate as much as to decide the controversies. But legal science was not an end in itself. The first lesson Story learned from his tutor Sam Sewall, the same he saw practiced in the court of Chief Justice Theophilus Parsons, was that inherited legal principles, even from the superb Blackstone, were imperfect and incomplete and would have to be shaped and molded to fit the special needs of the American people. As judge and jurist, he made scholarship walk in the street, the marketplace, and the counting house. While he started his legal inquiries with black letter, he was also guided by the usages of commerce and business with which he was intimately acquainted. And for all his respect for inherited principles, he never hesitated to depart from or go beyond them if practical necessity required—as in his conception of public and private corporations, his doctrine of the contractual responsibilities of corporate agents, or the binding nature of parole contracts. It was this very same practical, creative legal scientist who argued strenuously that Christianity was a part of the common law, who, of all judges of the period, revered and retained natural law notions of the eternal, unchanging and moral principles of jurisprudence.

Story never got his system entirely together, unfortunately never analyzed it or philosophized about it, never resolved the tensions within it which came from his effort to fuse so many divergent ingredients. Story the lawyer was like a geographer and map maker. He looked idealistically to the day when the whole of God's creation would be explored and mapped out with scientific rules and precise predictable relationships so that human action might be rational, equitable and productive. But he knew in fact that the job was not done, that old maps would have to be modified and new areas charted. Law was both substance and process; fixed rules and the science of modifying and making them; map making and the final map; science and mystery.

If Republican law was so complex and so delicate, and if legal science was so demanding, it followed that lawyers and judges, not professional politicians and legislators, should be entrusted with the main duty of law-keeping and law-making. And herein lay Story's final argument with Taney in the *Bridge Case*, for the Chief Justice conceded too much authority to the legislature and professional politicians who then ruled there. By arguing that there was some principle of public welfare beyond the operation of the buyer-seller contractual process and by conceding that the legislature had some special prerogative to voice that principle, Taney came dangerously close to the ultimate democratic heresy—the very one presumably stamped out by Republican constitutional theory—that the legislature itself and not the people was sovereign.

But even more troubling to Story than Taney's concession to legislative power was his demonstrated incompetence in the *Bridge* opinion to exercise the responsibilities that Story would have given to the Court. It was a matter of scholarship. That Taney should misread the authorities on royal grants was one thing, but not to consult them was another, and to misconstrue the entire legal framework of the case was even worse. Taney was either cynical or incompetent; though Story did not say so, it is a good guess that he agreed with Webster that Taney's performance, however "plausible," was ultimately "cunning and jesuitical." But whether cynical or inept, the result was disastrous, for by abandoning the rational system of scientific inquiry and the struggle for objectivity, the Court launched itself on a turbulent sea of judicial subjectivism. Without scholarship and legal science, political opinion would take over. Rather than controlling politics and party, Taney and the majority now invited them into the temple. Tragic enough it would have been had the Court gone to defeat doing its moral duty (as in the *Cherokee Indian Case*), but to surrender without battle was ignominy. The old Republic seemed lost.

V

Story's position in the 1830s was remarkably analogous to Jonathan Edwards' in the Great Awakening in that both attempted to maintain the unity and coherence of an earlier social system which was disintegrating under the impact of rapid historical change. Edwards wanted to preserve Puritanism as a way of life: Story aimed to save Republicanism. For Edwards, society's salvation lay in the permeating spirit of true religion; for Story in true law. Story's system of law like Edwards' theology was organic and synthetic like the culture it hoped to conserve—that is to say, it reached out to integrate politics, economics, and other aspects of society into a harmonious and moral community.

Story's undertaking was conservative in the largest sense (perhaps American conservatism comes of age with him). But it does not follow that his legal system was static or retrogressive. Natural law assumptions of the eighteenth century permeated his legal thinking, to be sure, but he harmonized them, as Blackstone did earlier, with rational, systematic legal science. And to this fusion of morality and science he added a pragmatic instrumentalism quite alien to the eighteenth century common law—a pragmatism which was designed to bring law into harmony with the unique demands of American history. His own protestations to the contrary notwithstanding, Story was not "the last of the old race of judges" but was a transitional figure who was simultaneously a rationalist and a romantic idealist, a conservative and an innovator, who at a particularly fertile moment in American history tried to fashion an American jurisprudence. His system of law, the parts of which never quite coalesced, is not so much an indication to legal historians of what American law *was,* as a creative vision of what it might have been.

Antebellum law—of which Taney's *Bridge* opinion was an intimation—moved away from Story's organic model: Instrumentalism broke the moral confines Story attempted to impose and American law took its character more and more, as Willard Hurst shows, from the chaotic forces of economic expansion. A new model of the law of economic growth responsive to new technology and mature capital replaced the old commercial one designed to promote investment by securing it absolutely. Natural law thinking fell into the background where it served to legitimize the new law (and not incidentally to obscure the realities of legal development and retard the rise of a self-conscious jurisprudence). At the same time, law-making initiative began to shift from the Court (to which Story had entrusted his delicately balanced system) to the legislature, where the new forces of instrumentalism operated with less hindrance and restraint. Story's model lawyer-statesman—a moral and virtuous natural aristocrat who mastered all branches of law, knew the real world, and devoted himself to polite learning and public service—gave way to legal specialists and lawyer-politicians.

To be sure, bits and pieces of Story's system would be incorporated into the main stream of American law. His arguments would bolster future judicial conservatives in their battle against legislative dominance. But his system, the legal cosmology he fashioned to save the old Republic, would become a relic of history, a curiosity on Clio's junkpile. But still history's losers deserve their day if only to show the complex process by which the victors carried the field—and possibly to show the price paid for their victory.

➯ *F U R T H E R   R E A D I N G*

Gerald T. Dunne, *Joseph Story and the Rise of the Supreme Court* (1970)
Oscar and Mary Handlin, *Commonwealth: A Study of the Role of Government in the American Economy: Massachusetts, 1774–1861* (1947)
Morton Horwitz, *The Transformation of American Law: 1790–1860* (1976)
James Willard Hurst, *Law and the Conditions of Freedom in the Nineteenth Century United States* (1956)
Leonard Levy, *The Law of the Commonwealth and Chief Justice Shaw* (1967)
James McClelland, *Joseph Story and the American Constitution: A Study in Political and Legal Thought with Selected Writings* (1971)
R. Kent Newmyer, *Supreme Court Justice Joseph Story: Statesman of the Old Republic* (1985)
———, *The Supreme Court Under Marshall and Taney* (1968)
Harry N. Scheiber, "The Road to MUNN: Eminent Domain and the Concept of Public Purpose in the State Courts," in Donald Fleming and Bernard Bailyn, eds., *Law in American History* (1971), pp. 121–321
Ronald Seavoy, *The Origins of the American Business Corporation, 1784–1855* (1985)
Francis N. Stites, *Private Interest and Public Gain: The Dartmouth College Case, 1819* (1972)
Carl B. Swisher, *The Taney Period, 1836–1864* (1974)
Jamil Zainaldin, *Law in Antebellum Society* (1983)

CHAPTER
11

State Sovereignty, Slavery, and Secession

⌗

In the mid-nineteenth century, Alexis de Tocqueville wrote that "scarcely any political question arises in the United States that is not resolved, sooner or later, into a judicial question." That was certainly the case with slavery. By 1860 the struggle over slavery had produced a far-reaching realignment of the political universe. The Republican party, which had its sole base of support in the free states, adopted the position that liberty and Union were one and inseparable. The Democratic party, the last institution binding North and South, snapped apart. Southern Democrats insisted that liberty was more important than Union, although they simply ignored the logical problem of professing such beliefs when more than 4 million blacks were held in bondage. The traditional "federal consensus"—that slavery was local; and freedom, national—collapsed. Southern Democrats, drawing on the inheritance of John C. Calhoun and the nullification controversy, expected the national government, as trustee for the states, to return escaped slaves and open the territories to the "peculiar institution." Faced with declining strength in Congress, the South found judicial support in a Supreme Court dominated by southerners and their northern Democratic sympathizers. The result was Justice Roger B. Taney's infamous decision in Dred Scott v. Sandford *(1857).*

The election of Republican presidential candidate Abraham Lincoln in 1860 proved to be the last straw for the South. Despite feverish efforts to achieve a compromise—including an agreement by Lincoln to support an amendment to the Constitution guaranteeing slavery's future—the movement for southern independence became unstoppable. Lincoln argued that the Union was perpetual and that secession was therefore constitutionally impossible. Southerners, on the other hand, painted themselves as the true inheritors of the revolutionary republican tradition of 1776.

For practical purposes, however, the root of the sectional conflict lay in the weakness rather than the strength of the federal government. President Andrew Jackson in the nullification crisis, and the Supreme Court under John Marshall (and a lesser extent, Roger B. Taney), had scored significant victories for national authority. But in practical terms, the framers in 1787 had failed to vest

*sufficient constitutional strength in the central government. In most instances, lo-
cal rather than national government was most important in the day-to-day conduct of public affairs. Ironically, the southerners who argued for the demise of
the Union did so on the grounds that the national government had not done
enough to place southern interests over those of the free states.*

✠ D O C U M E N T S

The documents in this chapter shed light on three interrelated constitutional questions involving slavery. The first matter was the extent of the federal government's responsibility to aid masters in securing the return of escaped slaves. As
antislavery agitation mounted in the 1830s and free-state representation in Congress swelled, slaveholders wanted the federal government to protect their minority
property rights in slaves. That proposition received its first important constitutional test in *Prigg* v. *Pennsylvania,* reprinted here as the first document, in which
the Supreme Court weighed the meaning of Article IV, Section 2, of the Constitution and the scope of the federal government's responsibility to return escaped
slaves under the Fugitive Slave Act of 1793. Justice Joseph Story's decision in
Prigg, which drew the ire of Chief Justice Roger B. Taney, held that the federal
government had preempted the states on the matter of fugitive slavery. Story's
decision offered free states the option of refusing to enforce the 1793 act. In
1850, however, southerners secured a new fugitive slave law as part of a complicated political compromise—the Compromise of 1850—that, among other provisions, ended the selling of slaves in the nation's capital. You may read the text of
the Fugitive Slave Act in the second document.

The next block of documents focuses on the status of slavery in the territories. Territorial growth generated new pressure on Congress to decide whether the
lands ceded from Mexico would be slave or free. The Free Soil party and the
antislavery northern Whigs and Democrats resisted the notion of congressional decisionmaking, which promised to open vast new stretches of territory to slavery at
just the time when the free states were winning a majority in Congress. The
Compromise of 1850 represented only a temporary solution. In 1854 Democratic
Senator Stephen A. Douglas of Illinois, harboring ambitions of building a trans-
continental railroad that would have its terminus in his home state, predicated the
controversial Kansas-Nebraska Act, the third selection here, on the doctrine of
territorial, or popular, sovereignty. The act opened an area once forbidden to
slavery (Kansas), subject only to popular vote of the territory's residents at the
time of statehood.

In the fourth document, *Dred Scott* v. *Sandford* (1857), the Supreme Court
plunged into the political maelstrom created by the Kansas-Nebraska Act. The
case involved a suit for freedom brought by a Missouri slave, Dred Scott, against
his nominal owner, John F. V. A. Sanford (his name was misspelled by the court
reporter). Scott claimed that he was a citizen and that, as a result of his having
traveled in free territory, he had become a free person. Chief Justice Taney, himself a slaveholder, wrote the Court's opinion, which provided that Congress could
not restrict slavery in the territories and that blacks, because they were of African
descent, could never be citizens and hence could not sue in federal courts. Justices Benjamin R. Curtis and John McLean denounced Taney's opinion. The
Court's decision, along with its professed role as the ultimate interpreter of the
Constitution, was at the center of the 1858 Illinois senatorial debates between Re-

publican Abraham Lincoln and Democrat Stephen A. Douglas, excerpted in the fifth selection.

Secession was the third consequence of the slavery-expansion controversy. The sixth selection, the South Carolina Declaration of Causes of Secession, December 24, 1860, demonstrates the connection between state sovereignty and slavery. In the next document, Lincoln's first inaugural address of March 4, 1861, the new president rejects secession as a constitutional impossibility but offers to guarantee slavery where it stood.

The most tangible constitutional product of southern secession was the Confederate constitution, reprinted here as the final document. Although similar to the United States Constitution, it differed in several fundamental respects. What were these differences? Among others, the document provided for a "Superior Court" of appeal with powers surprisingly broader than those of the federal Supreme Court, but the Confederate congress—reflecting the South's traditional fear of a national judiciary as a threat to state sovereignty—never carried out the constitutional provisions to put that court in operation. Ironically, the Confederate constitution did not explicitly grant the right of secession.

Prigg v. *Pennsylvania,* 1842

16 PETERS 536 (1842)

[6-3: Story, McLean, Baldwin, Wayne, Catron,
McKinley; Taney, Daniel, Thompson]

. . . The facts are briefly these: the plaintiff in error was indicted in the Court of Oyer and Terminer for York County for having, . . . taken and carried away from that county to the State of Maryland, a certain negro woman, named Margaret Morgan, with a design and intention of selling and disposing of, and keeping her as a slave or servant for life, contrary to a statute of Pennsylvania, passed on the 26th of March 1826. That statute in the first section, . . . provides, that if any person or persons shall from and after the passing of the act, by force and violence take and carry away . . . and shall by fraud and false pretense seduce . . . any negro or mulatto from any part of that Commonwealth, . . . shall on conviction thereof, be deemed guilty of a felony, and shall forfeit and pay a sum not less than five hundred, nor more than one thousand dollars; . . . and shall be confined and kept to hard labor, etc. . . .

The plaintiff in error pleaded not guilty to the indictment; and at the trial the jury found a special verdict, which, in substance, states, that the negro woman, Margaret Morgan was a slave for life, and held to labor and service . . . to a certain Margaret Ashmore, a citizen of Maryland; that the slave escaped and fled from Maryland into Pennsylvania in 1832; that the plaintiff in error . . . caused the said negro woman to be taken . . . as a fugitive from labor by a State constable under a warrant from a Pennsylvania magistrate; that the said negro woman was thereupon brought before the said magistrate who refused to take further cognizance of the case; and thereupon the plaintiff . . . did . . . carry away the said negro woman and her children out of Pennsylvania into Maryland. . . . The special verdict further finds, that one of the children was born in Pennsylvania, more than a year after the said negro woman had fled and escaped from Maryland. . . .

The question arising in the case as to the constitutionality of the statute of Pennsylvania, has been most elaborately argued at the bar. The counsel for the plaintiff have contended that the statute of Pennsylvania is unconstitutional; First, because Congress has the exclusive power of legislation upon the subject matter under the constitution of the United States, and under the act of the 12th of February 1793, which was passed in pursuance thereof; second, that if this power is not exclusive in Congress, still the concurrent power of the State Legislatures is suspended by the actual exercise of the power by Congress; and third, that if not suspended, still the statute of Pennsylvania, in all its provisions applicable to this case, is in direct collision with the act of Congress, and therefore is unconstitutional and void. The counsel for Pennsylvania maintain the negative of all these points.

Few questions which have ever come before this court involve more delicate and important considerations; and few upon which the public at large may be presumed to feel a more profound and pervading interest. . . .

[U]nder and in virtue of the constitution, the owner of a slave is clothed with entire authority, in every State in the Union, to seize and recapture his slave, whenever he can do it without any breach of the peace or any illegal violence. In this sense, and to this extent this clause of the constitution may properly be said to execute itself, and to require no aid from legislation, State or national. . . .

If, indeed, the constitution guarantees the right, and if it requires the delivery upon the claim of the owner, (as cannot well be doubted), the natural inference certainly is, that the national government is clothed with the appropriate authority and functions to enforce it. The fundamental principle, applicable to all cases of this sort, would seem to be, that where the end is required, the means are given; and where the duty is enjoined, the ability to perform it is contemplated to exist on the part of the functionaries to whom it is intrusted. The clause is found in the national constitution, and not in that of any State. It does not point out any state functionaries, or any state action to carry its provisions into effect. The States cannot, therefore, be compelled to enforce them; and it might well be deemed an unconstitutional exercise of the power of interpretation, to insist that the States are bound to provide means to carry into effect the duties of the national government, nowhere delegated or intrusted to them by the constitution. On the contrary, the natural, if not the necessary conclusion is, that the national government, in the absence of all positive provisions to the contrary, is bound, through its own proper departments, legislative, judicial, or executive, as the case may require, to carry into effect all the rights and duties imposed upon it by the constitution. . . .

The remaining question is, whether the power of legislation upon this subject is exclusive in the national government, or concurrent in the States, until it is exercised by congress. In our opinion it is exclusive; and we shall now proceed briefly to state our reasons for that opinion. The doctrine stated by this court, in *Sturges* v. *Crowninshield*, 4 Wheat. 122, 193, contains the true, although not the sole rule or consideration, which is applicable to this particular subject. "Wherever," said Mr. Chief Justice Marshall, in delivering the opinion of the court, "the terms in which a power is granted to congress, or the nature of the power, require that it should be exercised exclusively by congress, the subject is as completely taken from the state legislatures as if they had been forbidden to act." The nature of the power, and the true objects to be attained by it, are then as important to be weighed, in considering the question of its exclusiveness, as the words in which it is granted.

In the first place, it is material to state, (what has been already incidentally hinted at), that the right to seize and retake fugitive slaves, and the duty to deliver them up, in whatever State of the Union they may be found, and of course the corresponding power in congress to use the appropriate means to enforce the right and duty, derive their whole validity and obligation exclusively from the constitution of the United States, and are there for the first time, recognized and established in that peculiar character. Before the adoption of the constitution, no State had any power whatsoever over the subject, except within its own territorial limits, and could not bind the sovereignty or the legislation of other States. Whenever the right was acknowledged or the duty enforced in any State, it was a matter of comity and favor, and not as a matter of strict moral, political, or international obligation or duty. . . .

In the next place, the nature of the provision and the objects to be attained by it, require that it should be controlled by one and the same will, and act uniformly by the same system of regulations throughout the Union. If, then, the States have a right, in the absence of legislation by congress, to act upon the subject, each State is at liberty to prescribe just such regulations as suit its own policy, local convenience, and local feelings. The legislation of one State may not only be different from, but utterly repugnant to and incompatible with that of another. The time, and mode, and limitation of the remedy, the proofs of the title, and all other incidents applicable thereto, may be prescribed in one State, which are rejected or disclaimed in another. One State may require the owner to sue in one mode, another in a different mode. One State may make a statute of limitations as to the remedy, in its own tribunals, short and summary; another may prolong the period, and yet restrict the proofs. Nay, some States may utterly refuse to act upon the subject at all; and others may refuse to open its courts to any remedies *in rem,* because they would interfere with their own domestic policy, institutions, or habits. The right, therefore, would never, in a practical sense, be the same in all the States. It would have no unity of purpose, or uniformity of operation. The duty might be enforced in some States; retarded or limited in others; and denied, as compulsory in many, if not in all. Consequences like these must have been foreseen as very likely to occur in the nonslaveholding States, where legislation, if not silent on the subject, and purely voluntary, could scarcely be presumed to be favorable to the exercise of the rights of the owner. . . .

To guard, however, against any possible misconstruction of our views, it is proper to state, that we are by no means to be understood in any manner whatsoever to doubt or to interfere with the police power belonging to the States, in virtue of their general sovereignty. That police power extends over all subjects within the territorial limits of the States, and has never been conceded to the United States. It is wholly distinguishable from the right and duty secured by the provision now under consideration, which is exclusively derived from and secured by the constitution of the United States, and owes its whole efficacy thereto. We entertain no doubt whatsoever, that the States, in virtue of their general police power, possess full jurisdiction to arrest and restrain runaway slaves, and remove them from their borders, and otherwise to secure themselves against their depredations and evil example, as they certainly may do in cases of idlers, vagabonds, and paupers. The rights of the owners of fugitive slaves are in no just sense interfered with, or regulated by such a course; and in many cases, the operations of this police power, although designed generally for other purposes, for the protection, safety, and peace of the State, may essentially promote and aid the interests of the owners. But such regulations can never be permitted to interfere with or to obstruct the just rights of the owner to reclaim his slave, derived from the constitution of the United States, or with the remedies prescribed by congress to aid and enforce the same. . . .

Mr. Chief Justice Taney.   I concur in the opinion pronounced by the Court, that the law of Pennsylvania, under which the plaintiff in error was indicted, is unconstitutional and void; and that the judgment against him must be reversed. But as the questions before us arise upon the construction of the Constitution of the United States, and as I do not assent to all the principles contained in the opinion just delivered, it is proper to state the points on which I differ. . . .

But, as I understand the opinion of the Court, it goes further, and decides that the power to provide a remedy for this right is vested exclusively in Congress; and that all laws upon the subject passed by a state, since the adoption of the Constitution of the United States, are null and void; even although they were intended, in good faith, to protect the owner in the exercise of his rights of property, and do not conflict in any degree with the act of Congress.

I do not consider this question as necessarily involved in the case before us; for the law of Pennsylvania, under which the plaintiff in error was prosecuted, is clearly in conflict with the Constitution of the United States, as well as with the law of 1793. But as the question is discussed in the opinion of the Court, and as I do not assent either to the doctrine or the reasoning by which it is maintained, I proceed to state very briefly my objections.

The opinion of the Court maintains that the power over this subject is so exclusively vested in Congress, that no state, since the adoption of the Constitution, can pass any law in relation to it. In other words, according to the opinion just delivered, the state authorities are prohibited from interfering for the purpose of protecting the right of the master and aiding him in the recovery of his property. I think the states are not prohibited; and that, on the contrary, it is enjoined upon them as a duty to protect and support the owner when he is endeavouring to obtain possession of his property found within their respective territories.

The language used in the Constitution does not, in my judgment, justify the construction given to it by the Court. It contains no words prohibiting the several states from passing laws to enforce this right. They are in express terms forbidden to make any regulation that shall impair it. But there the prohibition stops. And according to the settled rules of construction for all written instruments, the prohibition being confined to laws injurious to the right, the power to pass laws to support and enforce it, is necessarily implied. And the words of the article which direct that the fugitive "shall be delivered up," seem evidently designed to impose it as a duty upon the people of the several states to pass laws to carry into execution, in good faith, the compact into which they thus solemnly entered with each other. The Constitution of the United States, and every article and clause in it, is a part of the law of every state in the Union; and is the paramount law. The right of the master, therefore, to seize his fugitive slave, is the law of each state; and no state has the power to abrogate or alter it. And why may not a state protect a right of property, acknowledged by its own paramount law? Besides, the laws of the different states, in all other cases, constantly protect the citizens of other states in their rights of property, when it is found within their respective territories; and no one doubts their power to do so. And in the absence of any express prohibition, I perceive no reason for establishing, by implication, a different rule in this instance; where, by the national compact, this right of property is recognised as an existing right in every state of the Union.

I do not speak of slaves whom their masters voluntarily take into a non-slaveholding state. That case is not before us. I speak of the case provided for in the Constitution; that is to say, the case of a fugitive who has escaped from the service of his owner, and who has taken refuge and is found in another state.

Moreover, the clause of the Constitution of which we are speaking, does not purport to be a distribution of the rights of sovereignty by which certain enumerated powers of government and legislation are exclusively confided to the United States. It does not deal with that subject. It provides merely for the rights of individual citizens of different states, and places them under the protection of the general government; in order more effectually to guard them from invasion by the states. There are other clauses in the Constitution in which other individual rights are provided for and secured in like manner; and it never has been suggested that the states could not uphold and maintain them, because they were guaranteed by the Constitution of the United States. On the contrary, it has always been held to be the duty of the states to enforce them; and the action of the general government has never been deemed necessary except to resist and prevent their violation. . . .

Indeed, if the state authorities are absolved from all obligation to protect this right, and may stand by and see it violated without an effort to defend it, the act of Congress of 1793 scarcely deserves the name of a remedy. The state officers mentioned in the law are not bound to execute the duties imposed upon them by Congress, unless they choose to do so, or are required to do so by a law of the state; and the state legislature has the power, if it thinks proper, to prohibit them. The act of 1793, therefore, must depend altogether for its execution upon the officers of the United States named in it. And the master must take the fugitive, after he has seized him, before a judge of the District or Circuit Court, residing in the state, and exhibit his proofs, and procure from the judge his certificate of ownership, in order to obtain the protection in removing his property which this act of Congress professes to give.

Now, in many of the states there is but one district judge, and there are only nine states which have judges of the Supreme Court residing within them. The fugitive will frequently be found by his owner in a place very distant from the residence of either of these judges; and would certainly be removed beyond his reach, before a warrant could be procured from the judge to arrest him, even if the act of Congress authorized such a warrant. But it does not authorize the judge to issue a warrant to arrest the fugitive; but evidently relied on the state authorities to protect the owner in making the seizure. And it is only when the fugitive is arrested and brought before the judge that he is directed to take the proof, and give the certificate of ownership. It is only necessary to state the provisions of this law in order to show how ineffectual and delusive is the remedy provided by Congress, if state authority is forbidden to come to its aid.

But it is manifest from the face of the law, that an effectual remedy was intended to be given by the act of 1793. It never designed to compel the master to encounter the hazard and expense of taking the fugitive in all cases, to the distant residence of one of the judges of the Courts of the United States; for it authorized him, also, to go before any magistrate of the county, city, or town corporate wherein the seizure should be made. And Congress evidently supposed that it had provided a tribunal at the place of the arrest, capable of furnishing the master with the evidence of ownership to protect him more effectually from unlawful interruption. So far from regarding the state authorities as prohibited from interfering in cases of this description, the Congress of that day must have counted upon their cordial co-operation. They legislated with express reference to state support. And it will be remembered, that when this law was passed, the government of the United States was administered by the men who had but recently taken a leading part in the formation of the Constitution. And the reliance obviously placed upon state authority for the purpose of executing this law, proves that the construction now given to the Constitution by the Court had not entered into their minds. Certainly, it is not the construction which it received in the states most interested in its faithful execution. Maryland, for example, which is substantially one of the parties to this case, has continually passed laws, ever since the adoption of the Constitution of the United States, for the arrest of fugitive slaves from other states as well as her own. Her officers are by law required to arrest them when found within her territory;

and her magistrates are required to commit them to the public prison, in order to keep them safely until the master has an opportunity of reclaiming them. And if the owner is not known, measures are directed to be taken by advertisement to apprize him of the arrest; and if known, personal notice to be given. And as fugitives from the more southern states, when endeavouring to escape into Canada, very frequently pass through her territory, these laws have been almost daily in the course of execution in some part of the state. But if the states are forbidden to legislate on this subject, and the power is exclusively in Congress, then these state laws are unconstitutional and void; and the fugitive can only be arrested, according to the provisions of the act of Congress. By that law the power to seize is given to no one but the owner, his agent, or attorney. And if the officers of the state are not justified in acting under the state laws, and cannot arrest the fugitive, and detain him in prison without having first received an authority from the owner; the territory of the state must soon become an open pathway for the fugitives escaping from other states. For they are often in the act of passing through it by the time that the owner first discovers that they have absconded; and in almost every instance, they would be beyond its borders (if they were allowed to pass through without interruption) before the master would be able to learn the road they had taken.

I am aware that my brethren of the majority do not contemplate these consequences; and do not suppose that the opinion they have given will lead to them. And it seems to be supposed that laws nearly similar to those I have mentioned, might be passed by the state in the exercise of her powers over her internal police, and by virtue of her right to remove from her territory disorderly and evil-disposed persons, or those who, from the nature of her institutions, are dangerous to her peace and tranquillity. But it would be difficult perhaps to bring all the laws I have mentioned within the legitimate scope of the internal powers of police. The fugitive is not always arrested in order to prevent a dangerous or evil-disposed person from remaining in her territory. He is himself most commonly anxious to escape from it; and it often happens that he is seized near the borders of the state when he is endeavouring to leave it, and is brought back and detained until he can be delivered to his owner. He may sometimes be found travelling peaceably along the public highway on his road to another state, in company with and under the protection of a white man who is abetting his escape. And it could hardly be maintained that the arrest and confinement of the fugitive in the public prison, under such circumstances, until he could be delivered to his owner, was necessary for the internal peace of the state; and therefore a justifiable exercise of its powers of police.

It has not heretofore been supposed necessary, in order to justify these laws, to refer them to such questionable powers of internal and local police. They were believed to stand upon surer and firmer grounds. They were passed, not with reference merely to the safety and protection of the state itself; but in order to secure the delivery of the fugitive slave to his lawful owner. They were passed by the state in the performance of a duty believed to be enjoined upon it by the Constitution of the United States.

It is true that Maryland as well as every other slaveholding state, has a deep interest in the faithful execution of the clause in question. But the obligation of the compact is not confined to them. It is equally binding upon the faith of every state in the Union; and has heretofore, in my judgment, been justly regarded as obligatory upon all.

I dissent therefore, upon these grounds, from that part of the opinion of the Court which denies the obligation and the right of the state authorities to protect the master, when he is endeavouring to seize a fugitive from his service, in pursuance of the right given to him by the Constitution of the United States;—provided the state law is not in conflict with the remedy provided by Congress. . . .

The Fugitive Slave Act, 1850

. . . Section 5. That it shall be the duty of all marshals and deputy marshals to obey and execute all warrants and precepts issued under the provisions of this act, when to them directed; and should any marshal or deputy marshal refuse to receive such warrant, or other process, when tendered, or to use all proper means diligently to execute the same, he shall, on conviction thereof, be fined in the sum of one thousand dollars, to the use of such claimant, . . . and after arrest of such fugitive, by such marshal or his deputy, or whilst at any time in his custody under the provisions of this act, should such fugitive escape, whether with or without the assent of such marshal or his deputy, such marshal shall be liable, on his official bond, to be prosecuted for the benefit of such claimant, for the full value of the service or labor of said fugitive in the State, Territory, or District whence he escaped: and the better to enable the said commissioners, when thus appointed, to execute their duties faithfully and efficiently, in conformity with the requirements of the Constitution of the United States and of this act, they are hereby authorized and empowered, within their counties respectively, to appoint, . . . any one or more suitable persons, from time to time, to execute all such warrants and other process as may be issued by them in the lawful performance of their respective duties; with authority to such commissioners, or the persons to be appointed by them, to execute process as aforesaid, to summon and call to their aid the bystanders, or *posse comitatus* of the proper county, when necessary to ensure a faithful observance of the clause of the Constitution referred to, in conformity with the provisions of this act; and all good citizens are hereby commanded to aid and assist in the prompt and efficient execution of this law, whenever their services may be required, as aforesaid, for that purpose; and said warrants shall run, and be executed by said officers, any where in the State within which they are issued.

Section 6. That when a person held to service or labor in any State or Territory of the United States, has heretofore or shall hereafter escape into another State or Territory of the United States, the person or persons to whom such service or labor may be due, . . . may pursue and reclaim such fugitive person, either by procuring a warrant from some one of the courts, judges, or commissioners aforesaid, of the proper circuit, district, or county, for the apprehension of such fugitive from service or labor, or by seizing and arresting such fugitive, where the same can be done without process, and by taking, or causing such person to be taken, forthwith before such court, judge, or commissioner, whose duty it shall be to hear and determine the case of such claimant in a summary manner; and upon satisfactory proof being made, by deposition or affidavit, in writing, to be taken and certified by such court, judge, or commissioner, or by other satisfactory testimony, duly taken and certified by some court, . . . and with proof, also by affidavit, of the identity of the person whose service or labor is claimed to be due as aforesaid, that the person so arrested does in fact owe service or labor to the person or persons claiming him or her, in the State or Territory from which such fugitive may have escaped as aforesaid, and that said person escaped, to make out and deliver to such claimant, his or her agent or attorney, a certificate setting forth the substantial facts as to the service or labor due from such fugitive to the claimant, and of his or her escape from the State or Territory in which he or she was arrested, with authority to such claimant, . . . to use such reasonable force and restraint as may be necessary, under the circumstances of the case, to take and remove such fugitive person back to the State or Territory whence he or she may have escaped as aforesaid. In no trial or hearing under this act shall the testimony of such alleged fugitive be admitted in evidence; and the certificates in this and the first [fourth] section mentioned, shall be conclusive of the right of the person or persons in whose favor granted, to remove such fugitive to the State or Territory from which he escaped, and shall prevent all molestation of such person or persons by any process issued by any court, judge, magistrate, or other person whomsoever.

Section 7. That any persons who shall knowingly and willingly obstruct, hinder, or prevent such claimant, his agent or attorney, or any person or persons lawfully assisting him, her, or them, from arresting such a fugitive from service or labor, either with or without process as aforesaid, or shall rescue, or attempt to rescue, such fugitive from service or labor, from the custody of such claimant, . . . or other person or persons lawfully assisting as aforesaid, when so arrested, . . . or shall aid, abet, or assist such person so owing service or labor as aforesaid, directly or indirectly, to escape from such claimant, . . . or shall harbor or conceal such fugitive, so as to prevent the discovery and arrest of such person, after notice or knowledge of the fact that such person was a fugitive from service or labor . . . shall, for either of said offences, be subject to a fine not exceeding one thousand dollars, and imprisonment not exceeding six months . . . ; and shall moreover forfeit and pay, by way of civil damages to the party injured by such illegal conduct, the sum of one thousand dollars, for each fugitive so lost as aforesaid. . . .

Section 9. That, upon affidavit made by the claimant of such fugitive, . . . that he has reason to apprehend that such fugitive will be rescued by force from his or their possession before he can be taken beyond the limits of the State in which the arrest is made, it shall be the duty of the officer making the arrest to retain such fugitive in his custody, and to remove him to the State whence he fled, and there to deliver him to said claimant, his agent, or attorney. And to this end, the officer aforesaid is hereby authorized and required to employ so many persons as he may deem necessary to overcome such force, and to retain them in his service so long as circumstances may require. . . .

Section 10. That when any person held to service or labor in any State or Territory, or in the District of Columbia, shall escape therefrom, the party to whom such service or labor shall be due, . . . may apply to any court of record therein, . . . and make satisfactory proof to such court, . . . of the escape aforesaid, and that the person escaping owed service or labor to such party. Whereupon the court shall cause a record to be made of the matters so proved, and also a general description of the person so escaping, with such convenient certainty as may be; and a transcript of such record, . . . being produced in any other State, Territory, or district in which the person so escaping may be found, . . . shall be held and taken to be full and conclusive evidence of the fact of escape, and that the service or labor of the person escaping is due to the party in such record mentioned. And upon the production by the said party of other and further evidence if necessary, either oral or by affidavit, in addition to what is contained in the said record of the identity of the person escaping, he or she shall be delivered up to the claimant. And the said court, commissioner, judge, or other person authorized by this act to grant certificates to claimants of fugitives, shall, upon the production of the record and other evidences aforesaid, grant to such claimant a certificate of his right to take any such person identified and proved to be owing service or labor as aforesaid, which certificate shall authorize such claimant to seize or arrest and transport such person to the State or Territory from which he escaped. . . .

The Kansas-Nebraska Act, 1854

An Act to Organize the Territories of Nebraska and Kansas

Be it enacted . . . , That all that part of the territory of the United States included within the following limits, except such portions thereof as are hereinafter expressly exempted from the operations of this act, to wit: beginning at a point in the Missouri River where the fortieth parallel of north latitude crosses the same; thence west on said parallel to the east boundary of the Territory of Utah, on the summit of the Rocky Mountains; thence on said summit northward to the forty-ninth parallel of north latitude; thence east on said parallel to the western boundary of the territory of Minnesota; thence southward on said boundary to the Missouri River; thence down the main channel of said river to the place of beginning, be, and the same is hereby, created into a temporary government by the name of the Territory of Nebraska; and when admitted as a State or States, the said Territory, or any portion of the same, shall be received into the Union with or without slavery, as their constitution may prescribe at the time of their admission: . . .

Section 14. *And be it further enacted,* . . . That the Constitution, and all laws of the United States which are not locally inapplicable, shall have the same force and effect within the said Territory of Nebraska as elsewhere within the United States, except the eighth section of the act preparatory to the admission of Missouri into the Union, approved March 6, 1820, which, being inconsistent with the principle of nonintervention by Congress with slavery in the States and Territories, as recognized by the legislation of eighteen hundred and fifty, commonly called the Compromise Measures, is hereby declared inoperative and void; it being the true intent and meaning of this act not to legislate slavery into any Territory or State, nor to exclude it therefrom, but to leave the people thereof perfectly free to form and regulate their domestic institutions in their own way, subject only to the Constitution of the United States: *Provided,* That nothing herein contained shall be construed to revive or put in force any law or regulation which may have existed prior to the act of March 6, 1820, either protecting, establishing, prohibiting, or abolishing slavery. . . .

Section 19. *And be it further enacted,* That all that part of the Territory of the United States included within the following limits, except such portions thereof as are hereinafter expressly exempted from the operations of this act, to wit, beginning at a point on the western boundary of the State of Missouri, where the thirty-seventh parallel of north latitude crosses the same; thence west on said parallel to the eastern boundary of New Mexico; thence north on said boundary to latitude thirty-eight; thence following said boundary westward to the east boundary of the Territory of Utah, on the summit of the Rocky Mountains; thence northward on said summit to the fortieth parallel of latitude; thence east on said parallel to the western boundary of the State of Missouri; thence south with the western boundary of said State to the place of beginning, be, and the same is hereby, created into a temporary government by the name of the Territory of Kansas; and when admitted as a State or States, the said Territory, or any portion of the same, shall be received into the Union with or without slavery, as their constitution may prescribe at the time of their admission: . . .

Dred Scott v. *Sandford,* 1857

19 HOWARD 393 (1857)

[7-2: Taney, Catron, Grier, Nelson, Daniel, Campbell, Wayne; Curtis, McLean]

Mr. Chief Justice Taney Delivered the Opinion of the Court.　The question is simply this: Can a negro, whose ancestors were imported into this country, and sold as slaves, become a member of the political community formed and brought into existence by the constitution of the United States, and as such become entitled to all the rights, and privileges, and immunities, guaranteed by that instrument to the citizen? One of which rights is the privilege of suing in a court of the United States in the cases specified in the constitution.

It will be observed, that the plea applies to that class of persons only whose ancestors were negroes of the African race, and imported into this country, and sold and held as slaves. The only matter in issue before the court, therefore, is, whether the descendants of such slaves, when they shall be emancipated, or who are born of parents who had become free before their birth, are citizens of a State, in the sense in which the word citizen is used in the constitution of the United States. And this being the only matter in dispute on the pleadings, the court must be understood as speaking in this opinion of that class only, that is, of those persons who are the descendants of Africans who were imported into this country, and sold as slaves. . . .

The words "people of the United States" and "citizens" are synonymous terms, and mean the same thing. They both describe the political body who, according to our republican institutions, form the sovereignty, and who hold the power and conduct the government through their representatives. They are what we familiarly call the "sovereign people," and every citizen is one of this people, and a constituent member of this sovereignty. The question before us is, whether the class of persons described in the plea in abatement compose a portion of this people, and are constituent members of this sovereignty? We think they are not, and that they are not included, and were not intended to be included, under the word "citizens" in the constitution, and can therefore claim none of the rights and privileges which that instrument provides for and secures to citizens of the United States. On the contrary, they were at that time considered as a subordinate and inferior class of beings, who had been subjugated by the dominant race, and, whether emancipated or not, yet remained subject to their authority, and had no rights or privileges but such as those who held the power and the government might choose to grant them.

It is not the province of the court to decide upon the justice or injustice, the policy or impolicy, of these laws. The decision of that question belonged to the political or law-making power; to those who formed the sovereignty and framed the constitution. The duty of the court is, to interpret the instrument they have framed, with the best lights we can obtain on the subject, and to administer it as we find it, according to its true intent and meaning when it was adopted.

In discussing this question, we must not confound the rights of citizenship which a State may confer within its own limits, and the rights of citizenship as a member of the Union. It does not by any means follow, because he has all the rights and privileges of a citizen of a State, that he must be a citizen of the United States. He may have all of the rights and privileges of the citizen of a State, and yet not be entitled to the rights and privileges of a citizen in any other State. For, previous to the adoption of the constitution of the United States, every State had the undoubted right to confer on whomsoever it pleased the character of citizen, and to endow him with all its rights. But this character of course was confined to the boundaries of the State, and gave him no rights or privileges in other States beyond those secured to him by the laws of nations and the comity of States. Nor have the several States surrendered the power of conferring these rights and privileges by adopting the constitution of the United States. . . .

It is very clear, therefore, that no State can, by any act or law of its own, passed since the adoption of the constitution, introduce a new member into the political community created by the constitution of the United States. It cannot make him a member of this community by making him a member of its own. And for the same reason it cannot introduce any person, or description of persons, who were not intended to be embraced in this new political family, which the constitution brought into existence, but were intended to be excluded from it.

The question then arises, whether the provisions of the constitution, in relation to the personal rights and privileges to which the citizen of a State should be entitled, embraced the negro African race, at that time in this country, or who might afterwards be imported, who had then or should afterwards be made free in any State; and to put it in the power of a single State to make him a citizen of the United States, and endue him with the full rights of citizenship in every other State without their consent? Does the constitution of the United States act upon him whenever he shall be made free under the laws of a State, and raised there to the rank of a citizen, and immediately clothe him with all the privileges of a citizen in every other State, and in its own courts?

The court think the affirmative of these propositions cannot be maintained. And if it cannot, the plaintiff in error could not be a citizen of the State of Missouri, within the meaning of the constitution of the United States, and, consequently, was not entitled to sue in its courts.

It is true, every person, and every class and description of persons, who were at the time of the adoption of the constitution recognized as citizens in the several States, became also citizens of this new political body; but none other; it was formed by them, and for them and their posterity, but for no one else. And the personal rights and privileges guaranteed to citizens of this new sovereignty were intended to embrace those only who were then members of the several State communities, or who should afterwards by birthright or otherwise become members, according to the provisions of the constitution and the principles on which it was founded. It was the union of those who were at that time members of distinct and separate political communities into one political family, whose power, for certain specified purposes, was to extend over the whole territory of the United States. And it gave to each citizen rights and privileges outside of his State which he did not before possess, and placed him in every other State upon a perfect equality with its own citizens as to rights of person and rights of property; it made him a citizen of the United States. . . .

In the opinion of the court, the legislation and histories of the times, and the language used in the declaration of independence, show, that neither the class of persons who had been imported as slaves, nor their descendants, whether they had become free or not, were then acknowledged as a part of the people, nor intended to be included in the general words used in that memorable instrument. . . .

They had for more than a century before been regarded as beings of an inferior order, and altogether unfit to associate with the white race, either in social or political relations; and so far inferior, that they had no rights which the white man was bound to respect; and that the negro might justly and lawfully be reduced to slavery for his benefit. . . .

The legislation of the different colonies furnishes positive and indisputable proof of this fact. . . .

The language of the declaration of independence is equally conclusive. . . .

But it is too clear for dispute, that the enslaved African race were not intended to be included, and formed no part of the people who framed and adopted this declaration; for if the language, as understood in that day, would embrace them, the conduct of the distinguished men who framed the declaration of independence would have been utterly and flagrantly inconsistent with the principles they asserted; and instead of the sympathy of mankind, to which they so confidently appealed, they would have deserved and received universal rebuke and reprobation. . . .

This state of public opinion had undergone no change when the constitution was adopted, as is equally evident from its provisions and language. . . .

But there are two clauses in the constitution which point directly and specifically to the negro race as a separate class of persons, and show clearly that they were not regarded as a portion of the people or citizens of the government then formed.

One of these clauses reserves to each of the thirteen States the right to import slaves until the year 1808, if it thinks proper. . . . And by the other provision the States pledge themselves to each other to maintain the right of property of the master, by delivering up to him any slave who may have escaped from his service, and be found within their respective territories. . . .

The only two provisions which point to them and include them, treat them as property, and make it the duty of the government to protect it; no other power, in relation to this race, is to be found in the constitution; and as it is a government of special, delegated, powers, no authority beyond these two provisions can be constitutionally exercised. The government of the United States had no right to interfere for any other purpose but that of protecting the rights of the owner, leaving it altogether with the several States to deal with this race, whether emancipated or not, as each State may think justice, humanity, and the interests and safety of society, require. The States evidently intended to reserve this power exclusively to themselves. . . .

[U]pon a full and careful consideration of the subject, the court is of opinion, that, upon the facts stated . . . , Dred Scott was not a citizen of Missouri within the meaning of the constitution of the United States, and not entitled as such to sue in its courts; and, consequently, that the circuit court had no jurisdiction of the case, and that the judgment on the plea in abatement is erroneous. . . .

We proceed . . . to inquire whether the facts relied on by the plaintiff entitled him to his freedom. . . .

The act of Congress, upon which the plaintiff relies, declares that slavery and involuntary servitude, except as a punishment for crime, shall be forever prohibited in all that part of the territory ceded by France, under the name of Louisiana, which lies north of thirty-six degrees thirty minutes north latitude and not included within the limits of Missouri. And the difficulty which meets us at the threshold of this part of the inquiry is whether Congress was authorized to pass this law under any of the powers granted to it by the Constitution; for, if the authority is not given by that instrument, it is the duty of this Court to declare it void and inoperative and incapable of conferring freedom upon anyone who is held as a slave under the laws of any one of the states.

The counsel for the plaintiff has laid much stress upon that article in the Constitution which confers on Congress the power "to dispose of and make all needful rules and regulations respecting the territory or other property belonging to the United States"; but, in the judgment of the Court, that provision has no bearing on the present controversy, and the power there given, whatever it may be, is confined, and was intended to be confined, to the territory which at that time belonged to, or was claimed by, the United States and was within their boundaries as settled by the treaty with Great Britain and can have no influence upon a territory afterward acquired from a foreign government. It was a special provision for a known and particular territory, and to meet a present emergency, and nothing more. . . .

We do not mean, however, to question the power of Congress in this respect. The power to expand the territory of the United States by the admission of new states is plainly given; and in the construction of this power by all the departments of the government, it has been held to authorize the acquisition of territory, not fit for admission at the time, but to be admitted as soon as its population and situation would entitle it to admission. It is acquired to become a state and not to be held as a colony and governed by Congress with absolute authority; and, as the propriety of admitting a new state is committed to the sound discretion of Congress, the power to acquire territory for that purpose, to be held by the United States until it is in a suitable condition to become a state upon an equal footing with the other states, must rest upon the same discretion. It is a question for the political department of the government, and not the judicial; and whatever the political department of the government shall recognize as within the limits of the United States, the judicial department is also bound to recognize, and to administer in it the laws of the United States, so far as they apply, and to maintain in the territory the authority and rights of the government, and also the personal rights and rights of property of individual citizens, as secured by the Constitution. All we mean to say on this point is that, as there is no express regulation in the Constitution defining the power which the general government may exercise over the person or property of a citizen in a territory thus acquired, the Court must necessarily look to the provisions and principles of the Constitution, and its distribution of powers, for the rules and principles by which its decision must be governed.

Taking this rule to guide us, it may be safely assumed that citizens of the United States who migrate to a territory belonging to the people of the United States cannot be ruled as mere colonists, dependent upon the will of the general government, and to be governed by any laws it may think proper to impose. The principle upon which our governments rest, and upon which alone they continue to exist, is the union of states, sovereign and independent within their own limits in their internal and domestic concerns, and bound together as one people by a general government, possessing certain enumerated and restricted powers, delegated to it by the people of the several states, and exercising supreme authority within the scope of the powers granted to it, throughout the dominion of the United States. A power, therefore, in the general government to obtain and hold colonies and dependent territories, over which they might legislate without restriction, would be inconsistent with its own existence in its present form. Whatever it acquires, it acquires for the benefit of the people of the several states who created it. It is their trustee acting for them and charged with the duty of promoting the interests of the whole people of the Union in the exercise of the powers specifically granted. . . .

But the power of Congress over the person or property of a citizen can never be a mere discretionary power under our Constitution and form of government. The powers of the government and the rights and privileges of the citizen are regulated and plainly defined by the Constitution itself. And, when the territory becomes a part of the United States, the federal government enters into possession in the character impressed upon it by those who created it. It enters upon it with its powers over the citizen strictly defined and limited by the Constitution, from which it derives its own existence, and by virtue of which alone it continues to exist and act as a government and sovereignty. It has no power of any kind beyond it; and it cannot, when it enters a territory of the United States, put off its character and assume discretionary or despotic powers which the Constitution has denied to it. It cannot create for itself a new character separated from the citizens of the United States and the duties it owes them under the provisions of the Constitution. The territory, being a part of the United States, the government and the citizen both enter it under the authority of the Constitution, with their respective rights defined and marked out; and the federal government can exercise no power over his person or property, beyond what that instrument confers, nor lawfully deny any right which it has reserved. . . .

These powers, and others, in relation to rights of person, which it is not necessary here to enumerate, are, in express and positive terms, denied to the general government; and the rights of private property have been guarded with equal care. Thus the rights of property are united with the rights of person and placed on the same ground by the Fifth Amendment to the Constitution, which provides that no person shall be deprived of life, liberty, and property without due process of law. And an act of Congress which deprives a citizen of the United States of his liberty or property, without due process of law, merely because he came himself or brought his property into a particular territory of the United States, and who had committed no offense against the laws, could hardly be dignified with the name of due process of law. . . .

The powers over person and property of which we speak are not only not granted to Congress but are in express terms denied, and they are forbidden to exercise them. And this prohibition is not confined to the states, but the words are general and extend to the whole territory over which the Constitution gives it power to legislate, including those portions of it remaining under territorial government as well as that covered by states. . . .

It seems, however, to be supposed that there is a difference between property in a slave and other property and that different rules may be applied to it in expounding the Constitution of the United States. And the laws and usages of nations, and the writings of eminent jurists upon the relation of master and slave and their mutual rights and duties, and the powers which governments may exercise over it, have been dwelt upon in the argument.

But, in considering the question before us, it must be borne in mind that there is no law of nations standing between the people of the United States and their government and interfering with their relation to each other. The powers of the government and the rights of the citizen under it are positive and practical regulations plainly written down. The people of the United States have delegated to it certain enumerated powers and forbidden it to exercise others. It has no power over the person or property of a citizen but what the citizens of the United States have granted. And no laws or usages of other nations, or reasoning of statesmen or jurists upon the relations of master and slave, can enlarge the powers of the government or take from the citizens the rights they have reserved. And if the Constitution recognizes the right of property of the master in a slave, and makes no distinction between that description of property and other property owned by a citizen, no tribunal, acting under the authority of the United States, whether it be legislative, executive, or judicial, has a right to draw such a distinction or deny to it the benefit of the provisions and guarantees which have been provided for the protection of private property against the encroachments of the government.

Now, as we have already said in an earlier part of this opinion, upon a different point, the right of property in a slave is distinctly and expressly affirmed in the Constitution. The right to traffic in it, like an ordinary article of merchandise and property, was guaranteed to the citizens of the United States, in every state that might desire it, for twenty years. And the government in express terms is pledged to protect it in all future time if the slave escapes from his owner. That is done in plain words—too plain to be misunderstood. And no word can be found in the Constitution which gives Congress a greater power over slave property or which entitles property of that kind to less protection than property of any other description. The only power conferred is the power coupled with the duty of guarding and protecting the owner in his rights.

Upon these considerations it is the opinion of the Court that the act of Congress which prohibited a citizen from holding and owning property of this kind in the territory of the United States north of the line therein mentioned is not warranted by the Constitution and is therefore void; and that neither Dred Scott himself, nor any of his family, were made free by being carried into this territory; even if they had been carried there by the owner with the intention of becoming a permanent resident. . . .

Abraham Lincoln and Stephen A. Douglas Debate the *Dred Scott* Decision, 1858

1. The Second Joint Debate, Freeport, August 27, 1858 Lincoln's Opening Speech and Douglas's Reply

Mr. Lincoln's Speech

. . . I now proceed to propound to the Judge the interrogatories, so far as I have framed them. I will bring forward a new installment when I get them ready. I will bring them forward now only reaching to number four.

The first one is:

Question 1.—If the people of Kansas shall, by means entirely unobjectionable in all other respects, adopt a State constitution, and ask admission into the Union under it, *before* they have the requisite number of inhabitants according to the English bill,—some ninety-three thousand,—will you vote to admit them?

Q. 2. Can the people of a United States Territory, in any lawful way, against the wish of any citizen of the United States, exclude slavery from its limits prior to the formation of a State constitution?

Q. 3. If the Supreme Court of the United States shall decide that States cannot exclude slavery from their limits, are you in favor of acquiescing in, adopting, and following such decision as a rule of political action?

Q. 4. Are you in favor of acquiring additional territory, in disregard of how such acquisition may affect the nation on the slavery question? . . .

Senator Douglas's Reply

First, he desires to know if the people of Kansas shall form a constitution by means entirely proper and unobjectionable, and ask admission into the Union as a State, before they have the requisite population for a member of Congress, whether I will vote for that admission. . . . I will answer his question. In reference to Kansas, it is my opinion that as she has population enough to constitute a slave State, she has people enough for a free State. I will not make Kansas an exceptional case to the other States of the Union. I hold it to be a sound rule, of universal application, to require a Territory to contain the requisite population for a member of Congress before it is admitted as a State into the Union. I made that proposition in the Senate in 1856, and I renewed it during the last session, in a bill providing that no Territory of the United States should form a constitution and apply for admission until it had the requisite population. On another occasion I proposed that neither Kansas nor any other Territory should be admitted until it had the requisite population. Congress did not adopt any of my propositions containing this general rule, but did make an exception of Kansas. I will stand by that exception. Either Kansas must come in as a free State, with whatever population she may have, or the rule must be applied to all the other Territories alike. I therefore answer at once, that, it having been decided that Kansas has people enough for a slave State, I hold that she has enough for a free State. I hope Mr. Lincoln is satisfied with my answer; . . .

The next question propounded to me by Mr. Lincoln is, Can the people of a Territory in any lawful way, against the wishes of any citizen of the United States, exclude slavery from their limits prior to the formation of a State constitution? I answer emphatically, as Mr. Lincoln has heard me answer a hundred times from every stump in Illinois, that in my opinion the people of a Territory can, by lawful means, exclude slavery from their limits prior to the formation of a State constitution. Mr. Lincoln knew that I had answered that question over and over again. He heard me argue the Nebraska Bill on that principle all over the State in 1854, in 1855, and in 1856, and he has no excuse for pretending to be in doubt as to my position on that question. It matters not what way the Supreme Court may hereafter decide as to the abstract question whether slavery may or may not go into a Territory under the Constitution, the people have the lawful means to introduce it or exclude it as they please, for the reason that slavery cannot exist a day or an hour anywhere unless it is supported by local police regulations. Those police regulations can only be established by the local legislature; and if the people are opposed to slavery, they will elect representatives to that body who will by unfriendly legislation effectually prevent the introduction of it into their midst. If, on the contrary, they are for it, their legislation will favor its extension. Hence, no matter what the decision of the Supreme Court may be on that abstract question, still the right of the people to make a slave Territory or a free Territory is perfect and complete under the Nebraska Bill. I hope Mr. Lincoln deems my answer satisfactory on that point. . . .

. . . The third question which Mr. Lincoln presented is, if the Supreme Court of the United States shall decide that a State of this Union cannot exclude slavery from its own limits, will I submit to it? . . . He casts an imputation upon the Supreme Court of the United States, by supposing that they would violate the Constitution of the United States. I tell him that such a thing is not possible. It would be an act of moral treason that no man on the bench could ever descend to. Mr. Lincoln himself would never in his partisan feelings so far forget what was right as to be guilty of such an act.

The fourth question of Mr. Lincoln is, Are you in favor of acquiring additional territory, in disregard as to how such acquisition may affect the Union on the slavery question? This question is very ingeniously and cunningly put.

The Black Republican creed lays it down expressly that under no circumstances shall we acquire any more territory, unless slavery is first prohibited in the country. . . . I answer that whenever it becomes necessary, in our growth and progress, to acquire more territory, that I am in favor of it, without reference to the question of slavery; and when we have acquired it, I will leave the people free to do as they please, either to make it slave or free territory, as they prefer. It is idle to tell me or you that we have territory enough. . . . I tell you, increase, and multiply, and expand, is the law of this nation's existence. You cannot limit this great Republic by mere boundary lines, saying, "Thus far shalt thou go, and no farther." Any one of you gentlemen might as well say to a son twelve years old that he is big enough, and must not grow any larger; and in order to prevent his growth, put a hoop around him to keep him to his present size. What would be the result? Either the hoop must burst and be rent asunder, or the child must die. So it would be with this great nation. With our natural increase, growing with a rapidity unknown in any part of the globe, with the tide of emigration that is fleeing from despotism in the Old World to seek refuge in our own, there is a constant torrent pouring into this country that requires more land, more territory upon which to settle; and just as fast as our interests and our destiny require additional territory in the North, in the South, or on the islands of the ocean, I am for it; and when we acquire it, will leave the people, according to the Nebraska Bill, free to do as they please on the subject of slavery and every other question. . . .

2. The Third Joint Debate, Jonesboro, September 15, 1858

Lincoln's Reply to Douglas

. . . At Freeport I propounded four interrogatories to him, claiming it as a right that he should answer as many interrogatories for me as I did for him, and I would reserve myself for a future installment when I got them ready. The Judge, in answering me upon that occasion, put in what I suppose he intends as answers to all four of my interrogatories. The first one of these interrogatories I have before me, and it is in these words:

"*Question* 1. If the people of Kansas shall, by means entirely unobjectionable in all other respects, adopt a State constitution, and ask admission into the Union under it, *before* they have the requisite number of inhabitants according to the English bill,"—some ninety-three thousand,—"will you vote to admit them?"

As I read the Judge's answer in the newspaper, and as I remember it as pronounced at the time, he does not give any answer which is equivalent to yes or no,—I will or I won't. He answers at very considerable length, rather quarrelling with me for asking the question, and insisting that Judge Trumbull had done something that I ought to say something about, and finally getting out such statements as induce me to infer that he means to be understood he will, in that supposed case, vote for the admission of Kansas. I only bring this forward now for the purpose of saying that if he chooses to put a different construction upon his answer, he may do it. But if he does not, I shall from this time forward assume that he will vote for the admission of Kansas in disregard of the English bill. He has the right to remove any misunderstanding I may have. I only mention it now, that I may hereafter assume this to be the true construction of his answer, if he does not now choose to correct me.

The second interrogatory that I propounded to him was this:

"*Question* 2. Can the people of a United States Territory, in any lawful way, against the wish of any citizen of the United States, exclude slavery from its limits prior to the formation of a State Constitution?"

To this Judge Douglas answered that they can lawfully exclude slavery from the Territory prior to the formation of a constitution. He goes on to tell us how it can be done. As I understand him, he holds that it can be done by the Territorial Legislature refusing to make any enactments for the protection of slavery in the Territory, and especially by adopting unfriendly legislation to it. For the sake of clearness, I state it again: that they can exclude slavery from the Territory, 1st, by withholding what he assumes to be an indispensable assistance to it in the way of legislation; and, 2d, by unfriendly legislation. If I rightly understand him, I wish to ask your attention for a while to his position.

In the first place, the Supreme Court of the United States has decided that any Congressional prohibition of slavery in the Territories is unconstitutional; that they have reached this proposition as a conclusion from their former proposition, that the Constitution of the United States expressly recognizes property in slaves, and from that other Constitutional provision, that no person shall be deprived of property without due process of law. Hence they reach the conclusion that as the Constitution of the United States expressly recognizes property in slaves, and prohibits any person from being deprived of property without due process of law, to pass an Act of Congress by which a man who owned a slave on one side of a line would be deprived of him if he took him on the other side, is depriving him of that property without due process of law. That I understand to be the decision of the Supreme Court. I understand also that Judge Douglas adheres most firmly to that decision; and the difficulty is, how is it possible for any power to exclude slavery from the Territory, unless in violation of that decision? That is the difficulty. . . .

I hold that the proposition that slavery cannot enter a new country without police regulations is historically false. It is not true at all. I hold that the history of this country shows that the institution of slavery was originally planted upon this continent *without* these "police regulations" which the Judge now thinks necessary for the actual establishment of it. Not only so, but is there not another fact: how came this Dred Scott decision to be made? It was made upon the case of a negro being taken and actually held in slavery in Minnesota Territory, claiming his freedom because the Act of Congress prohibited his being so held there. *Will the Judge pretend that Dred Scott was not held there without police regulations?* There is at least one matter of record as to his having been held in slavery in the Territory, not only without police regulations, but in the teeth of Congressional legislation supposed to be valid at the time. This shows that there is vigor enough in slavery to plant itself in a new country even against unfriendly legislation. It takes not only law, but the *enforcement* of law to keep it out. That is the history of this country upon the subject.

I wish to ask one other question. It being understood that the Constitution of the United States guarantees property in slaves in the Territories, if there is any infringement of the right of that property, would not the United States courts, organized for the government of the Territory, apply such remedy as might be necessary in that case? It is a maxim held by the courts that there is no wrong without its remedy; and the courts have a remedy for whatever is acknowledged and treated as a wrong.

Again: I will ask you, my friends, if you were elected members of the Legislature, what would be the first thing you would have to do before entering upon your duties? *Swear to support the Constitution of the United States.* Suppose you believe, as Judge Douglas does, that the Constitution of the United States guarantees to your neighbor the right to hold slaves in that Territory; that they are his property: how can you clear your oaths unless you give him such legislation as is necessary to enable him to enjoy that property? What do you understand by supporting the Constitution of a State, or of the United States? Is it not to give such constitutional helps to the rights established by that Constitution as may be practically needed? Can you, if you swear to support the Constitution, and believe that the Constitution establishes a right, clear your oath, without giving it support? Do you support the Constitution if, knowing or believing there is a right established under it which needs specific legislation, you withhold that legislation? Do you not violate and disregard your oath? I can conceive of nothing plainer in the world. There can be nothing in the words "support the Constitution," if you may run counter to it by refusing support to any right established under the Constitution. And what I say here will hold with still more force against the Judge's doctrine of "unfriendly legislation." How could you, having sworn to support the Constitution, and believing it guaranteed the right to hold slaves in the Territories, assist in legislation *intended to defeat that right?* That would be violating your own view of the Constitution. Not only so, but if you were to do so, how long would it take the courts to hold your votes unconstitutional and void? Not a moment.

Lastly, I would ask: Is not Congress itself under obligation to give legislative support to any right that is established under the United States Constitution? I repeat the question: Is not Congress itself bound to give legislative support to any right that is established in the United States Constitution? A member of Congress swears to support the Constitution of the United States: and if he sees a right established by that Constitution which needs specific legislative protection, can he clear his oath without giving that protection? Let me ask you why many of us who are opposed to slavery upon principle give our acquiescence to a Fugitive Slave law? Why do we hold ourselves under obligations to pass such a law, and abide by it when it is passed? Because the Constitution makes provision that the owners of slaves shall have the right to reclaim them. It gives the right to reclaim slaves; and that right is, as Judge Douglas says, a barren right, unless there is legislation that will enforce it.

The mere declaration, "No person held to service or labor in one State under the laws thereof, escaping into another, shall in consequence of any law or regulation therein be discharged from such service or labor, but shall be delivered up on claim of the party to whom such service or labor may be due," is powerless without specific legislation to enforce it. Now, on what ground would a member of Congress, who is opposed to slavery in the abstract, vote for a Fugitive law, as I would deem it my duty to do? Because there is a constitutional right which needs legislation to enforce it. And although it is distasteful to me, I have sworn to support the Constitution; and having so sworn, I cannot conceive that I do support it if I withhold from that right any necessary legislation to make it practical. And if that is true in regard to a Fugitive Slave law, is the right to have fugitive slaves reclaimed any better fixed in the Constitution than the right to hold slaves in the Territories? For this decision is a just exposition of the Constitution, as Judge Douglas thinks. Is the one right any better than the other? Is there any man who, while a member of Congress, would give support to the one any more than the other? If I wished to refuse to give legislative support to slave property in the Territories, if a member of Congress, I could not do it, holding the view that the Constitution establishes that right. If I did it at all, it would be because I deny that this decision properly construes the Constitution. But if I acknowledge, with Judge Douglas, that this decision properly construes the Constitution, I cannot conceive that I would be less than a perjured man if I should refuse in Congress to give such protection to that property as in its nature it needed.

3. The Seventh Joint Debate, Alton, October 15, 1858 Douglas's Speech, Lincoln's Reply, and Douglas's Rejoinder

Senator Douglas's Speech

Ladies and Gentlemen: It is now nearly four months since the canvass between Mr. Lincoln and myself commenced. On the 16th of June the Republican Convention assembled at Springfield and nominated Mr. Lincoln as their candidate for the United States Senate, and he, on that occasion, delivered a speech in which he laid down what he understood to be the Republican creed, and the platform on which he proposed to stand during the contest. The principal points in that speech of Mr. Lincoln's were: First, that this government could not endure permanently divided into free and slave States, as our fathers made it; that they must all become free or all become slave; all become one thing, or all become the other,—otherwise this Union could not continue to exist. I give you his opinions almost in the identical language he used. His second proposition was a crusade against the Supreme Court of the United States because of the Dred Scott decision, urging as an especial reason for his opposition to that decision that it deprived the negroes of the rights and benefits of that clause in the Constitution of the United States which guarantees to the citizens of each State all the rights, privileges, and immunities of the citizens of the several States. On the 10th of July I returned home, and delivered a speech to the people of Chicago, in which I announced it to be my purpose to appeal to the people of Illinois to sustain the course I had pursued in Congress. In that speech I joined issue with Mr. Lincoln on the points which he had presented. Thus there was an issue clear and distinct made up between us on these two propositions laid down in the speech of Mr. Lincoln at Springfield, and controverted by me in my reply to him at Chicago. On the next day, the 11th of July, Mr. Lincoln replied to me at Chicago, explaining at some length and reaffirming the positions which he had taken in his Springfield speech. In that Chicago speech he even went further than he had before, and uttered sentiments in regard to the negro being on an equality with the white man. He adopted in support of this position the argument which Lovejoy and Codding and other Abolition lecturers had made familiar in the northern and central portions of the State: to wit, that the Declaration of Independence having declared all men free and equal, by divine law, also that negro equality was an inalienable right, of which they could not be deprived. He insisted, in that speech, that the Declaration of Independence included the negro in the clause asserting that all men were created equal, and went so far as to say that if one man was allowed to take the position that it did not include the negro, others might take the position that it did not include other men. He said that all these distinctions between this man and that man, this race and the other race, must be discarded, and we must all stand by the Declaration of Independence, declaring that all men were created equal.

The issue thus being made up between Mr. Lincoln and myself on three points, we went before the people of the State. During the following seven weeks, between the Chicago speeches and our first meeting at Ottawa, he and I addressed large assemblages of the people in many of the central counties. In my speeches I confined myself closely to those three positions which he had taken, controverting his proposition that this Union could not exist as our fathers made it, divided into free and slave States, controverting his proposition of a crusade against the Supreme Court because of the Dred Scott decision, and controverting his proposition that the Declaration of Independence included and meant the negroes as well as the white men, when it declared all men to be created equal. . . . I took up Mr. Lincoln's three propositions in my several speeches, analyzed them, and pointed out what I believed to be the radical errors contained in them. First, in regard to his doctrine that this government was in violation of the law of God, which says that a house divided against itself cannot stand, I repudiated it as a slander upon the immortal framers of our Constitution. I then said, I have often repeated, and now again assert, that in my opinion our government can endure forever, divided into free and slave States as our fathers made it,—each State having the right to prohibit, abolish, or sustain slavery, just as it pleases. This government was made upon the great basis of the sovereignty of the States, the right of each State to regulate its own domestic institutions to suit itself; and that right was conferred with the understanding and expectation that, inasmuch as each locality had separate interests, each locality must have different and distinct local and domestic institutions, corresponding to its wants and interests. Our fathers knew when they made the government that the laws and institutions which were well adapted to the Green Mountains of Vermont were unsuited to the rice plantations of South Carolina. They knew then, as well as we know now, that the laws and institutions which would be well adapted to the beautiful prairies of Illinois would not be suited to the mining regions of California. They knew that in a republic as broad as this, having such a variety of soil, climate, and interest, there must necessarily be a corresponding variety of local laws,—the policy and institutions of each State adapted to its condition and wants. For this reason this Union was established on the right of each State to do as it pleased on the question of slavery, and every other question; and the various States were not allowed to complain of, much less interfere with, the policy of their neighbors. . . .

. . . These measures [Compromise of 1850] passed on the joint action of the two parties. They rested on the great principle that the people of each State and each Territory should be left perfectly free to form and regulate their domestic institutions to suit themselves. You Whigs and we Democrats justified them in that principle. In 1854, when it became necessary to organize the Territories of Kansas and Nebraska, I brought forward the bill on the same principle. In the Kansas-Nebraska Bill you find it declared to be the true intent and meaning of the act not to legislate slavery into any State or Territory, nor to exclude it therefrom, but to leave the people thereof perfectly free to form and regulate their domestic institutions in their own way. I stand on that same platform in 1858 that I did in 1850, 1854, and 1856. . . . It has occurred to me that in 1854 the author of the Kansas and Nebraska Bill was considered a pretty good Democrat. It has occurred to me that in 1856, when I was exerting every nerve and every energy for James Buchanan, standing on the same platform then that I do now, that I was a pretty good Democrat. They now tell me that I am not a Democrat, because I assert that the people of a Territory, as well as those of a State, have the right to decide for themselves whether slavery can or cannot exist in such Territory. . . .

I . . . further . . . say that while, under the decision of the Supreme Court, as recorded in the opinion of Chief Justice Taney, slaves are property like all other property, and can be carried into any Territory of the United States the same as any other description of property, yet when you get them there they are subject to the local law of the Territory just like all other property. You will find in a recent speech delivered by that able and eloquent statesman Hon. Jefferson Davis, at Bangor, Maine, that he took the same view of this subject that I did in my Freeport speech. He there said:

"If the inhabitants of any Territory should refuse to enact such laws and police regulations as would give security to their property or to his, it would be rendered more or less valueless in proportion to the difficulties of holding it without such protection. In the case of property in the labor of man, or what is usually called slave property, the insecurity would be so great that the owner could not ordinarily retain it. Therefore, though the right would remain, the remedy being withheld, it would follow that the owner would be practically debarred, by the circumstances of the case, from taking slave property into a Territory where the sense of the inhabitants was opposed to its introduction. So much for the oft-repeated fallacy of forcing slavery upon any community."

You will also find that the distinguished Speaker of the present House of Representatives, Hon. Jas. L. Orr, construed the Kansas and Nebraska Bill in this same way in 1856, and also that great intellect of the South, Alex. H. Stephens, put the same construction upon it in Congress that I did in my Freeport speech. The whole South are rallying to the support of the doctrine that if the people of a Territory want slavery, they have a right to have it, and if they do not want it, that no power on earth can force it upon them. I hold that there is no principle on earth more sacred to all the friends of freedom than that which says that no institution, no law, no constitution, should be forced on an unwilling people contrary to their wishes; and I assert that the Kansas and Nebraska Bill contains that principle. It is the great principle contained in that bill. It is the principle on which James Buchanan was made President. Without that principle, he never would have been made President of the United States. I will never violate or abandon that doctrine, if I have to stand alone. I have resisted the blandishments and threats of power on the one side, and seduction on the other, and have stood immovably for that principle, fighting for it when assailed by Northern mobs, or threatened by Southern hostility. I have defended it against the North and the South, and I will defend it against whoever assails it, and I will follow it wherever its logical conclusions lead me. I say to you that there is but one hope, one safety for this country, and that is to stand immovably by that principle which declares the right of each State and each Territory to decide these questions for themselves. This government was founded on that principle, and must be administered in the same sense in which it was founded. . . .

Mr. Lincoln's Reply

. . . Now, irrespective of the moral aspect of this question as to whether there is a right or wrong in enslaving a negro, I am still in favor of our new Territories being in such a condition that white men may find a home,— may find some spot where they can better their condition; where they can settle upon new soil and better their condition in life. I am in favor of this, not merely (I must say it here as I have elsewhere) for our own people who are born amongst us, but as an outlet for *free white people everywhere*— the world over—in which Hans, and Baptiste, and Patrick, and all other men from all the world, may find new homes and better their conditions in life.

I have stated upon former occasions, and I may as well state again, what I understand to be the real issue in this controversy between Judge Douglas and myself. . . . The real issue in this controversy—the one pressing upon every mind—is the sentiment on the part of one class that looks upon the institution of slavery *as a wrong,* and of another class that *does not* look upon it as a wrong. The sentiment that contemplates the institution of slavery in this country as a wrong is the sentiment of the Republican party. It is the sentiment around which all their actions, all their arguments, circle, from which all their propositions radiate. They look upon it as being a moral, social, and political wrong; and while they contemplate it as such, they nevertheless have due regard for its actual existence among us, and the difficulties of getting rid of it in any satisfactory way, and to all the constitutional obligations thrown about it. Yet, having a due regard for these, they desire a policy in regard to it that looks to its not creating any more danger. They insist that it should, as far as may be, *be treated* as a wrong; and one of the methods of treating it as a wrong is to *make provision that it shall grow no larger.* They also desire a policy that looks to a peaceful end of slavery at some time, as being wrong. These are the views they entertain in regard to it as I understand them; and all their sentiments, all their arguments and propositions, are brought within this range. I have said, and I repeat it here, that if there be a man amongst us who does not think that the institution of slavery is wrong in any one of the aspects of which I have spoken, he is misplaced, and ought not to be with us. And if there be a man amongst us who is so impatient of it as a wrong as to disregard its actual presence among us and the difficulty of getting rid of it suddenly in a satisfactory way, and to disregard the constitutional obligations thrown about it, that man is misplaced if he is on our platform. We disclaim sympathy with him in practical action. He is not placed properly with us.

On this subject of treating it as a wrong, and limiting its spread, let me say a word. Has anything ever threatened the existence of this Union save and except this very institution of slavery? What is it that we hold most dear amongst us? Our own liberty and prosperity. What has ever threatened our liberty and prosperity, save and except this institution of slavery? If this is true, how do you propose to improve the condition of things by enlarging slavery,—by spreading it out and making it bigger? You may have a wen or cancer upon your person, and not be able to cut it out, lest you bleed to death; but surely it is no way to cure it, to engraft it and spread it over your whole body. That is no proper way of treating what you regard a wrong. You see this peaceful way of dealing with it as a wrong,—restricting the spread of it, and not allowing it to go into new countries where it has not already existed. That is the peaceful way, the old-fashioned way, the way in which the fathers themselves set us the example.

On the other hand, I have said there is a sentiment which treats it as *not* being wrong. That is the Democratic sentiment of this day. . . .

. . . The Democratic policy in regard to that institution will not tolerate the merest breath, the slightest hint, of the least degree of wrong about it. Try it by some of Judge Douglas's arguments. He says he "don't care whether it is voted up or voted down" in the Territories. I do not care myself, in dealing with that expression, whether it is intended to be expressive of his individual sentiments on the subject, or only of the national policy he desires to have established. It is alike valuable for my purpose. Any man can say that who does not see anything wrong in slavery; but no man can logically say it who does see a wrong in it, because no man can logically say he don't care whether a wrong is voted up or voted down. He may say he don't care whether an indifferent thing is voted up or down, but he must logically have a choice between a right thing and a wrong thing. He contends that whatever community wants slaves has a right to have them. So they have, if it is not a wrong. But if it is a wrong, he cannot say people have a right to do wrong. He says that upon the score of equality slaves should be allowed to go in a new Territory, like other property. This is strictly logical if there is no difference between it and other property. If it and other property are equal, this argument is entirely logical. But if you insist that one is wrong and the other right, there is no use to institute a comparison between right and wrong. You may turn over everything in the Democratic policy from beginning to end, whether in the shape it takes on the statute book, in the shape it takes in the Dred Scott decision, in the shape it takes in conversation, or the shape it takes in short maxim-like arguments,—it everywhere carefully excludes the idea that there is anything wrong in it.

That is the real issue. That is the issue that will continue in this country when these poor tongues of Judge Douglas and myself shall be silent. It is the eternal struggle between these two principles—right and wrong—throughout the world. They are the two principles that have stood face to face from the beginning of time, and will ever continue to struggle. The one is the common right of humanity, and the other the divine right of kings. . . . And whenever we can get rid of the fog which obscures the real question, when we can get Judge Douglas and his friends to avow a policy looking to its perpetuation,—we can get out from among that class of men and bring them to the side of those who treat it as a wrong. Then there will soon be an end of it, and that end will be its "ultimate extinction." Whenever the issue can be distinctly made, and all extraneous matter thrown out so that men can fairly see the real difference between the parties, this controversy will soon be settled, and it will be done peaceably too. There will be no war, no violence. It will be placed again where the wisest and best men of the world placed it. . . .

I understand I have ten minutes yet. I will employ it in saying something about this argument Judge Douglas uses, while he sustains the Dred Scott decision, that the people of the Territories can still somehow exclude slavery. The first thing I ask attention to is the fact that Judge Douglas constantly said, before the decision, that whether they could or not, *was a question for the Supreme Court.* But after the court had made the decision he virtually says it is *not* a question for the Supreme Court, but for the people. And how is it he tells us they can exclude it? He says it needs "police regulations," and that admits of "unfriendly legislation." Although it is a right established by the Constitution of the United States to take a slave into a Territory of the United States and hold him as property, yet unless the Territorial Legislature will give friendly legislation and more especially if they adopt unfriendly legislation, they can practically exclude him. Now, without meeting this proposition as a matter of fact, I pass to consider the real constitutional obligation. Let me take the gentleman who looks me in the face before me, and let us suppose that he is a member of the Territorial Legislature. The first thing he will do will be to swear that he will support the Constitution of the United States. His neighbor by his side in the Territory has slaves and needs Territorial legislation to enable him to enjoy that constitutional right. Can he withhold the legislation which his neighbor needs for the enjoyment of a right which is fixed in his favor in the Constitution of the United States which he has sworn to support? Can he withhold it without violating his oath? And, more especially, can he pass unfriendly legislation to violate his oath? Why, this is a *monstrous* sort of talk about the Constitution of the United States! *There has never been as outlandish or lawless a doctrine from the mouth of any respectable man on earth.* I do not believe it is a constitutional right to hold slaves in a Territory of the United States. I believe the decision was improperly made and I go for reversing it. Judge Douglas is furious against those who go for reversing a decision. But he is for legislating it out of all force while the law itself stands. I repeat that there has never been so monstrous a doctrine uttered from the mouth of a respectable man. . . .

I say that no man can deny his obligation to give the necessary legislation to support slavery in a Territory, who believes it is a constitutional right to have it there. No man can, who does not give the Abolitionists an argument to deny the obligation enjoined by the Constitution to enact a Fugitive State law. Try it now. It is the strongest Abolition argument ever made. I say if that Dred Scott decision is correct, then the right to hold slaves in a Territory is equally a constitutional right with the right of a slaveholder to have his runaway returned. No one can show the distinction between them. The one is express, so that we cannot deny it. The other is construed to be in the Constitution, so that he who believes the decision to be correct believes in the right. And the man who argues that by unfriendly legislation, in spite of that constitutional right, slavery may be driven from the Territories, cannot avoid furnishing an argument by which Abolitionists may deny the obligation to return fugitives, and claim the power to pass laws unfriendly to the right of the slaveholder to reclaim his fugitive. I do not know how such an argument may strike a popular assembly like this, but I defy anybody to go before a body of men whose minds are educated to estimating evidence and reasoning, and show that there is an iota of difference between the constitutional right to reclaim a fugitive and the constitutional right to hold a slave, in a Territory, provided this Dred Scott decision is correct. I defy any man to make an argument that will justify unfriendly legislation to deprive a slaveholder of his right to hold his slave in a Territory, that will not equally, in all its length, breadth, and thickness, furnish an argument for nullifying the Fugitive Slave law. Why, there is not such an Abolitionist in the nation as Douglas, after all!

Mr. Douglas's Rejoinder

Mr. Lincoln tries to avoid the main issue by attacking the truth of my proposition that our fathers made this government divided into free and slave States, recognizing the right of each to decide all its local questions for itself. Did they not thus make it? It is true that they did not establish slavery in any of the States, or abolish it in any of them; but finding thirteen States, twelve of which were slave and one free, they agreed to form a government uniting them together as they stood, divided into free and slave States, and to guarantee forever to each State the right to do as it pleased on the slavery question. Having thus made the government, and conferred this right upon each State forever, I assert that this government can exist as they made it, divided into free and slave States, if any one State chooses to retain slavery. He says that he looks forward to a time when slavery shall be abolished everywhere. I look forward to a time when each State shall be allowed to do as it pleases. If it chooses to keep slavery forever, it is not my business, but its own; if it chooses to abolish slavery, it is its own business,—not mine. I care more for the great principle of self-government, the right of the people to rule, than I do for all the negroes in Christendom. I would not endanger the perpetuity of this Union, I would not blot out the great inalienable rights of the white man, for all the negroes that ever existed. Hence, I say, let us maintain this government on the principles that our fathers made it, recognizing the right of each State to keep slavery as long as its people determine, or to abolish it when they please. But Mr. Lincoln says that when our fathers made this government they did not look forward to the state of things now existing, and therefore he thinks the doctrine was wrong; . . . Our fathers, I say, made this government on the principle of the right of each State to do as it pleases in its own domestic affairs, subject to the Constitution, and allowed the people of each to apply to every new change of circumstances such remedy as they may see fit to improve their condition. This right they have for all time to come.

Mr. Lincoln went on to tell you that he does not at all desire to interfere with slavery in the States where it exists, nor does his party. I expected him to say that down here. Let me ask him, then, how he expects to put slavery in the course of ultimate extinction everywhere, if he does not intend to interfere with it in the States where it exists? He says that he will prohibit it in all Territories, and the inference is, then, that unless they make free States out of them he will keep them out of the Union; for, mark you, he did not say whether or not he would vote to admit Kansas with slavery or not, as her people might apply (he forgot that, as usual, etc.): he did not say whether or not he was in favor of bringing the Territories now in existence into the Union on the principle of Clay's Compromise measures on the slavery question. I told you that he would not. His idea is that he will prohibit slavery in all the Territories and thus force them all to become free States, surrounding the slave States with a cordon of free States, and hemming them in, keeping the slaves confined to their present limits whilst they go on multiplying, until the soil on which they live will no longer feed them, and he will thus be able to put slavery in a course of ultimate extinction by starvation. He will extinguish slavery in the Southern States as the French general exterminated the Algerines when he smoked them out. He is going to extinguish slavery by surrounding the Slave States, hemming in the slaves, and starving them out of existence, as you smoke a fox out of his hole. He intends to do that in the name of humanity and Christianity, in order that we may get rid of the terrible crime and sin entailed upon our fathers of holding slaves. . . .

I ask you to look into these things, and then tell me whether the Democracy or the Abolitionists are right. I hold that the people of a Territory, like those of a State . . . have the right to decide for themselves whether slavery shall or shall not exist within their limits. The point upon which Chief Justice Taney expresses his opinion is simply this, that slaves, being property, stand on an equal footing with other property, and consequently that the owner has the same right to carry that property into a Territory that he has any other, subject to the same conditions. Suppose that one of your merchants was to take fifty or one hundred thousand dollars' worth of liquors to Kansas. He has a right to go there, under that decision; but when he gets there he finds the Maine liquor law in force, and what can he do with his property after he gets it there? He cannot sell it, he cannot use it; it is subject to the local law, and that law is against him, and the best thing he can do with it is to bring it back into Missouri or Illinois and sell it. If you take negroes to Kansas, as Colonel Jefferson Davis said in his Bangor speech, from which I have quoted to-day, you must take them there subject to the local law. If the people want the institution of slavery, they will protect and encourage it; but if they do not want it, they will withhold that protection, and the absence of local legislation protecting slavery excludes it as completely as a positive prohibition. You slaveholders of Missouri might as well understand, what you know practically, that you cannot carry slavery where the people do not want it. All you have a right to ask is that the people shall do as they please: if they want slavery, let them have it; if they do not want it, allow them to refuse to encourage it.

My friends, if, as I have said before, we will only live up to this great fundamental principle, there will be peace between the North and the South. Mr. Lincoln admits that, under the Constitution, on all domestic questions, except slavery, we ought not to interfere with the people of each State. What right have we to interfere with slavery any more than we have to interfere with any other question? He says that this slavery question is now the bone of contention. Why? Simply because agitators have combined in all the free States to make war upon it. Suppose the agitators in the States should combine in one half of the Union to make war upon the railroad system of the other half? They would thus be driven to the same sectional strife. Suppose one section makes war upon any other peculiar institution of the opposite section, and the same strife is produced. The only remedy and safety is that we shall stand by the Constitution as our fathers made it, obey the laws as they are passed, while they stand the proper test, and sustain the decisions of the Supreme Court and the constituted authorities.

South Carolina Declaration of Causes of Secession, 1860

The people of the State of South Carolina in Convention assembled, on the 2d day of April, A.D. 1852, declared that the frequent violations of the Constitution of the United States by the Federal Government, and its encroachments upon the reserved rights of the States, fully justified this State in their withdrawal from the Federal Union; but in deference to the opinions and wishes of the other Slaveholding States, she forbore at that time to exercise this right. Since that time these encroachments have continued to increase, and further forbearance ceases to be a virtue.

And now the State of South Carolina having resumed her separate and equal place among nations, deems it due to herself, to the remaining United States of America, and to the nations of the world, that she should declare the immediate causes which have led to this act.

In 1787, Deputies were appointed by the States to revise the articles of Confederation; and on 17th September, 1787, these Deputies recommended, for the adoption of the States, the Articles of Union, known as the Constitution of the United States.

. . . Thus was established by compact between the States, a Government with defined objects and powers, limited to the express words of the grant. . . . We hold that the Government thus established is subject to the two great principles asserted in the Declaration of Independence; and we hold further, that the mode of its formation subjects it to a third fundamental principle, namely, the law of compact. We maintain that in every compact between two or more parties, the obligation is mutual; that the failure of one of the contracting parties to perform a material part of the agreement, entirely releases the obligation of the other; and that, where no arbiter is provided, each party is remitted to his own judgment to determine the fact of failure, with all its consequences.

In the present case, that fact is established with certainty. We assert that fourteen of the States have deliberately refused for years past to fulfil their constitutional obligations, and we refer to their own statutes for the proof.

The Constitution of the United States, in its fourth Article, provides as follows:

"No person held to service or labor in one State under the laws thereof, escaping into another, shall, in consequence of any law or regulation therein, be discharged from such service or labor, but shall be delivered up, on claim of the party to whom such service or labor may be due."

This stipulation was so material to the compact that without it that compact would not have been made. The greater number of the contracting parties held slaves, and they had previously evinced their estimate of the value of such a stipulation by making it a condition in the Ordinance for the government of the territory ceded by Virginia, which obligations, and the laws of the General Government, have ceased to effect the objects of the Constitution. The States of Maine, New Hampshire, Vermont, Massachusetts, Connecticut, Rhode Island, New York, Pennsylvania, Illinois, Indiana, Michigan, Wisconsin and Iowa, have enacted laws which either nullify the acts of Congress, or render useless any attempt to execute them. In many of these States the fugitive is discharged from the service of labor claimed, and in none of them has the State Government complied with the stipulation made in the Constitution. The State of New Jersey, at an early day, passed a law in conformity with her constitutional obligation; but the current of Anti-Slavery feeling has led her more recently to enact laws which render inoperative the remedies provided by her own laws and by the laws of Congress. In the State of New York even the right of transit for a slave has been denied by her tribunals; and the States of Ohio and Iowa have refused to surrender to justice fugitives charged with murder, and with inciting servile insurrection in the State of Virginia. Thus the constitutional compact has been deliberately broken and disregarded by the non-slaveholding States; and the consequence follows that South Carolina is released from her obligation. . . .

We affirm that these ends for which this Government was instituted have been defeated, and the Government itself has been destructive of them by the action of the non-slaveholding States. Those States have assumed the right of deciding upon the propriety of our domestic institutions; and have denied the rights of property established in fifteen of the States and recognized by the Constitution; they have denounced as sinful the institution of Slavery; they have permitted the open establishment among them of societies, whose avowed object is to disturb the peace of and eloin the property of the citizens of other States. They have encouraged and assisted thousands of our slaves to leave their homes; and those who remain, have been incited by emissaries, books, and pictures, to servile insurrection.

For twenty-five years this agitation has been steadily increasing, until it has now secured to its aid the power of the common Government. Observing the *forms* of the Constitution, a sectional party has found within that article establishing the Executive Department, the means of subverting the Constitution itself. A geographical line has been drawn across the Union, and all the States north of that line have united in the election of a man to the high office of President of the United States whose opinions and purposes are hostile to Slavery. He is to be intrusted with the administration of the common Government, because he has declared that "Government cannot endure permanently half slave, half free," and that the public mind must rest in the belief that Slavery is in the course of ultimate extinction.

This sectional combination for the subversion of the Constitution has been aided, in some of the States, by elevating to citizenship persons who, by the supreme law of the land, are incapable of becoming citizens; and their votes have been used to inaugurate a new policy, hostile to the South, and destructive of its peace and safety.

On the 4th of March next this party will take possession of the Government. It has announced that the South shall be excluded from the common territory, that the Judicial tribunal shall be made sectional, and that a war must be waged against Slavery until it shall cease throughout the United States.

The guarantees of the Constitution will then no longer exist; the equal rights of the States will be lost. The Slaveholding States will no longer have the power of self-government, or self-protection, and the Federal Government will have become their enemy.

Sectional interest and animosity will deepen the irritation; and all hope of remedy is rendered vain, by the fact that the public opinion at the North has invested a great political error with the sanctions of a more erroneous religious belief.

We, therefore, the people of South Carolina, by our delegates in Convention assembled, appealing to the Supreme Judge of the world for the rectitude of our intentions, have solemnly declared that the Union heretofore existing between this State and the other States of North America is dissolved, and that the State of South Carolina has resumed her position among the nations of the world, as a separate and independent state, with full power to levy war, conclude peace, contract alliances, establish commerce, and to do all other acts and things which independent States may of right do.

President Lincoln Rejects Secession: The First Inaugural Address, 1861

Fellow-Citizens of the United States:

—In compliance with a custom as old as the Government itself, I appear before you to address you briefly, and to take in your presence the oath prescribed by the Constitution of the United States to be taken by the President "before he enters on the execution of his office." . . .

Apprehension seems to exist among the people of the Southern States that by the accession of a Republican administration their property and their peace and personal security are to be endangered. There has never been any reasonable cause for such apprehension. Indeed, the most ample evidence to the contrary has all the while existed and been open to their inspection. It is found in nearly all the published speeches of him who now addresses you. I do but quote from one of those speeches when I declare that "I have no purpose, directly or indirectly, to interfere with the institution of slavery in the States where it exists. I believe I have no lawful right to do so, and I have no inclination to do so." . . .

I now reiterate these sentiments; and, in doing so, I only press upon the public attention the most conclusive evidence of which the case is susceptible, that the property, peace and security of no section are to be in any wise endangered by the now incoming administration. I add, too, that all the protection which, consistently with the Constitution and the laws, can be given, will be cheerfully given to all the States when lawfully demanded, for whatever cause—as cheerfully to one section as to another. . . .

I take the official oath to-day with no mental reservations, and with no purpose to construe the Constitution or laws by any hypercritical rules. And, while I do not choose now to specify particular acts of Congress as proper to be enforced, I do suggest that it will be much safer for all, both in official and private stations, to conform to and abide by all those acts which stand unrepealed, than to violate any of them, trusting to find impunity in having them held to be unconstitutional. . . .

A disruption of the Federal Union, heretofore only menaced, is now formidably attempted.

I hold that, in contemplation of universal law and of the Constitution, the Union of these States is perpetual. Perpetuity is implied, if not expressed, in the fundamental law of all national governments. It is safe to assert that no government proper ever had a provision in its organic law for its own termination. Continue to execute all the express provisions of our national Constitution, and the Union will endure forever—it being impossible to destroy it except by some action not provided for in the instrument itself.

Again, if the United States be not a government proper, but an association of States in the nature of contract merely, can it as a contract be peaceably unmade by less than all the parties who made it? One party to a contract may violate it—break it, so to speak; but does it not require all to lawfully rescind it?

Descending from these general principles, we find the proposition that in legal contemplation the Union is perpetual confirmed by the history of the Union itself. The Union is much older than the Constitution. It was formed, in fact, by the Articles of Association in 1774. It was matured and continued by the Declaration of Independence in 1776. It was further matured, and the faith of all the then thirteen States expressly plighted and engaged that it should be perpetual, by the Articles of Confederation in 1778. And, finally, in 1787 one of the declared objects for ordaining and establishing the Constitution was "to form a more perfect Union."

But if the destruction of the Union by one or by a part only of the States be lawfully possible, the Union is less perfect than before the Constitution, having lost the vital element of perpetuity.

It follows from these views that no State upon its own mere motion can lawfully get out of the Union; that resolves and ordinances to that effect are legally void; and that acts of violence, within any State or States, against the authority of the United States, are insurrectionary or revolutionary, according to circumstances.

I therefore consider that, in view of the Constitution and the laws, the Union is unbroken; and to the extent of my ability I shall take care, as the Constitution itself expressly enjoins upon me, that the laws of the Union be faithfully executed in all the States. Doing this I deem to be only a simple duty on my part; and I shall perform it so far as practicable, unless my rightful masters, the American people, shall withhold the requisite means, or in some authoritative manner direct the contrary. I trust this will not be regarded as a menace, but only as the declared purpose of the Union that it will constitutionally defend and maintain itself.

In doing this there needs to be no bloodshed or violence; and there shall be none, unless it be forced upon the national authority. The power confided to me will be used to hold, occupy, and possess the property and places belonging to the Government, and to collect the duties and imposts; but beyond what may be necessary for these objects, there will be no invasion, no using of force against or among the people anywhere. Where hostility to the United States, in any interior locality, shall be so great and universal as to prevent competent resident citizens from holding the Federal offices, there will be no attempt to force obnoxious strangers among the people for that object. While the strict legal right may exist in the government to enforce the exercise of these offices, the attempt to do so would be so irritating, and so nearly impracticable withal, that I deem it better to forego for the time the uses of such offices.

The mails, unless repelled, will continue to be furnished in all parts of the Union. So far as possible, the people everywhere shall have that sense of perfect security which is most favorable to calm thought and reflection. The course here indicated will be followed unless current events and experience shall show a modification or change to be proper, and in every case and exigency my best discretion will be exercised according to circumstances actually existing, and with a view and a hope of a peaceful solution of the national troubles and the restoration of fraternal sympathies and affections.

That there are persons in one section or another who seek to destroy the Union at all events, and are glad of any pretext to do it, I will neither affirm nor deny; but if there be such, I need address no word to them. To those, however, who really love the Union may I not speak?

Before entering upon so grave a matter as the destruction of our national fabric, with all its benefits, its memories, and its hopes, would it not be wise to ascertain precisely why we do it? Will you hazard so desperate a step while there is any possibility that any portion of the ills you fly from have no real existence? Will you, while the certain ills you fly to are greater than all the real ones you fly from—will you risk the commission of so fearful a mistake?

All profess to be content in the Union if all constitutional rights can be maintained. Is it true, then, that any right, plainly written in the Constitution, has been denied? I think not. Happily the human mind is so constituted that no party can reach to the audacity of doing this. Think, if you can, of a single instance in which a plainly written provision of the Constitution has ever been denied. If by the mere force of numbers a majority should deprive a minority of any clearly written constitutional right, it might, in a moral point of view, justify revolution—certainly would if such a right were a vital one. But such is not our case. All the vital rights of minorities and of individuals are so plainly assured to them by affirmations and negations, guarantees and prohibitions, in the Constitution, that controversies never arise concerning them. But no organic law can ever be framed with a provision specifically applicable to every question which may occur in practical administration. No foresight can anticipate, nor any document of reasonable length contain, express provisions for all possible questions. Shall fugitives from labor be surrendered by national or by State authority? The Constitution does not expressly say. *May* Congress prohibit slavery in the Territories? The Constitution does not expressly say. *Must* Congress protect slavery in the Territories? The Constitution does not expressly say.

From questions of this class spring all our constitutional controversies, and we divide upon them into majorities and minorities. If the minority will not acquiesce, the majority must, or the Government must cease. There is no other alternative; for continuing the Government is acquiescence on one side or the other.

If a minority in such case will secede rather than acquiesce, they make a precedent which in turn will divide and ruin them; for a minority of their own will secede from them whenever a majority refuses to be controlled by such minority. For instance, why may not any portion of a new confederacy a year or two hence arbitrarily secede again, precisely as portions of the present Union now claim to secede from it? All who cherish disunion sentiments are now being educated to the exact temper of doing this.

Is there such perfect identity of interests among the States to compose a new Union as to produce harmony only, and prevent renewed secession?

Plainly, the central idea of secession is the essence of anarchy. A majority held in restraint by constitutional checks and limitations, and always changing easily with deliberate changes of popular opinions and sentiments, is the only true sovereign of a free people. Whoever rejects it does, of necessity, fly to anarchy or to despotism. Unanimity is impossible; the rule of a minority, as a permanent arrangement, is wholly inadmissible; so that, rejecting the majority principle, anarchy or despotism in some form is all that is left.

I do not forget the position assumed by some, that constitutional questions are to be decided by the Supreme Court; nor do I deny that such decisions must be binding, in any case, upon the parties to a suit, as to the object of that suit, while they are also entitled to a very high respect and consideration in all parallel cases by all other departments of the government. And, while it is obviously possible that such decision may be erroneous in any given case, still the evil effect following it, being limited to that particular case, with the chance that it may be overruled and never became a precedent for other cases, can better be borne than could the evils of a different practice. At the same time, the candid citizen must confess that if the policy of the government, upon vital questions affecting the whole people, is to be irrevocably fixed by the decisions of the Supreme Court, the instant they are made, in ordinary litigation between parties in personal actions, the people will have ceased to be their own rulers, having to that extent practically resigned the government into the hands of that eminent tribunal. Nor is there in this view any assault upon the court or the judges. It is a duty from which they may not shrink to decide cases properly brought before them, and it is no fault of theirs if others seek to turn their decisions to political purposes.

One section of our country believes slavery is right, and ought to be extended, while the other believes it is wrong, and ought not to be extended. This is the only substantial dispute. The fugitive slave clause of the Constitution and the law for the suppression of the foreign slave trade are each as well enforced, perhaps, as any law can ever be in a community where the moral sense of the people imperfectly supports the law itself. The great body of the people abide by the dry legal obligation in both cases, and a few break over in each. This, I think, cannot be perfectly cured; and it would be worse in both cases after the separation of the sections than before. The foreign slave trade, now imperfectly suppressed, would be ultimately revived, without restriction, in one section, while fugitive slaves, now only partially surrendered, would not be surrendered at all by the other.

Physically speaking, we cannot separate. We cannot remove our respective sections from each other, nor build an impassable wall between them. A husband and wife may be divorced and go out of the presence and beyond the reach of each other; but the different parts of our country cannot do this. They cannot but remain face to face, and intercourse, either amicable or hostile, must continue between them. Is it possible, then, to make that intercourse more advantageous or more satisfactory after separation than before? Can aliens make treaties easier than friends can make laws? Can treaties be more faithfully enforced between aliens than laws can among friends? Suppose you go to war, you cannot fight always; and when, after much loss on both sides, and no gain on either, you cease fighting, the identical old questions as to terms of intercourse are again upon you.

This country, with its institutions, belongs to the people who inhabit it. Whenever they shall grow weary of the existing government, they can exercise their constitutional right of amending it, or their revolutionary right to dismember or overthrow it. I cannot be ignorant of the fact that many worthy and patriotic citizens are desirous of having the national Constitution amended. While I make no recommendation of amendments, I fully recognize the rightful authority of the people over the whole subject, to be exercised in either of the modes prescribed in the instrument itself, and I should, under existing circumstances, favor rather than oppose a fair opportunity being afforded the people to act upon it. I will venture to add that to me the convention mode seems preferable, in that it allows amendments to originate with the people themselves, instead of only permitting them to take or reject propositions originated by others not especially chosen for the purpose, and, which might not be precisely such as they would wish to either accept or refuse. I understand a proposed amendment to the Constitution—which amendment, however, I have not seen—has passed Congress, to the effect that the Federal Government shall never interfere with the domestic institutions of the States, including that of persons held to service. To avoid misconstruction of what I have said, I depart from my purpose not to speak of particular amendments so far as to say that, holding such a provision to now be implied constitutional law, I have no objection to its being made express and irrevocable. . . .

Why should there not be a patient confidence in the ultimate justice of the people? Is there any better or equal hope in the world? In our present differences is either party without faith of being in the right? If the Almighty Ruler of nations, with his eternal truth and justice, be on your side of the North, or on yours of the South, that truth and that justice will surely prevail by the judgment of this great tribunal of the American people.

By the frame of the government under which we live, this same people have wisely given their public servants but little power for mischief; and have, with equal wisdom, provided for the return of that little to their own hands at very short intervals. While the people retain their virtue and vigilance, no administration, by any extreme of wickedness or folly, can very seriously injure the government in the short space of four years.

My countrymen, one and all, think calmly and well upon this whole subject. Nothing valuable can be lost by taking time. If there be an object to hurry any of you in hot haste to a step which you would never take deliberately, that object will be frustrated by taking time; but no good object can be frustrated by it. Such of you as are now dissatisfied still have the old Constitution unimpaired, and, on the sensitive point, the laws of your own framing under it; while the new administration will have no immediate power, if it would, to change either. If it were admitted that you who are dissatisfied hold the right side in the dispute, there still is no single good reason for precipitate action. Intelligence, patriotism, Christianity, and a firm reliance on Him who has never yet forsaken this favored land, are still competent to adjust in the best way all our present difficulty.

In your hands, my dissatisfied fellow-countrymen, and not in mine, is the momentous issue of civil war. The government will not assail you. You can have no conflict without being yourselves the aggressors. You have no oath registered in heaven to destroy the government, while I shall have the most solemn one to "preserve, protect, and defend" it.

I am loath to close. We are not enemies, but friends. We must not be enemies. Though passion may have strained, it must not break, our bonds of affection. The mystic chords of memory, stretching from every battle-field and patriot grave to every living heart and hearthstone all over this broad land, will yet swell the chorus of the Union when again touched, as surely they will be, by the better angels of our nature.

The Confederate Constitution, 1861

We, the people of the Confederate States, each State acting in its sovereign and independent character, in order to form a permanent federal government, establish justice, insure domestic tranquillity, and secure the blessings of liberty to ourselves and our posterity—invoking the favor and guidance of Almighty God—do ordain and establish this Constitution for the Confederate States of America.

Article I

Section 2. (5) The House of Representatives shall choose their Speaker and other officers; and shall have the sole power of impeachment; except that any judicial or other federal officer resident and acting solely within the limits of any State, may be impeached by a vote of two-thirds of both branches of the Legislature thereof. . . .

Section 7. (2) . . . The President may approve any appropriation and disapprove any other appropriation in the same bill. In such case he shall, in signing the bill, designate the appropriations disapproved; and shall return a copy of such appropriations, with his objections, to the House in which the bill shall have originated; and the same proceedings shall then be had as in case of other bills disapproved by the President. . . .

Section 8. The Congress shall have power—

(1) To lay and collect taxes, duties, imposts, and excises, for revenue

necessary to pay the debts, provide for the common defence, and carry on the Government of the Confederate States; but no bounties shall be granted from the treasury; nor shall any duties or taxes on importations from foreign nations be laid to promote or foster any branch of industry; and all duties, imposts, and excises shall be uniform throughout the Confederate States. . . .

(3) To regulate commerce with foreign nations, and among the several States, and with the Indian tribes; but neither this, nor any other clause contained in the Constitution shall be construed to delegate the power to Congress to appropriate money for any internal improvement intended to facilitate commerce; except for the purpose of furnishing lights, beacons, and buoys, and other aids to navigation upon the coasts, and the improvement of harbors, and the removing of obstructions in river navigation, in all which cases, such duties shall be laid on the navigation facilitated thereby, as may be necessary to pay the costs and expenses thereof.

(4) To establish uniform laws of naturalization, and uniform laws on the subject of bankruptcies throughout the Confederate States, but no law of Congress shall discharge any debt contracted before the passage of the same. . . .

(7) To establish post-offices and post-routes; but the expenses of the Post-office Department, after the first day of March, in the year of our Lord eighteen hundred and sixty-three, shall be paid out of its own revenues. . . .

Section 9. (1) The importation of negroes of the African race, from any foreign country, other than the slaveholding States or Territories of the United States of America, is hereby forbidden; and Congress is required to pass such laws as shall effectually prevent the same.

(2) Congress shall also have power to prohibit the introduction of slaves from any State not a member of, or Territory not belonging to, this Confederacy. . . .

(4) No bill of attainder, or *ex post facto* law, or law denying or impairing the right of property in negro slaves shall be passed. . . .

(6) No tax or duty shall be laid on articles exported from any State, except by a vote of two-thirds of both Houses.

(7) No preference shall be given by any regulation of commerce or revenue to the ports of one State over those of another. . . .

(9) Congress shall appropriate no money from the treasury except by a vote of two-thirds of both Houses, taken by yeas and nays, unless it be asked and estimated for by some one of the heads of departments, and submitted to Congress by the President; or for the purpose of paying its own expenses and contingencies; or for the payment of claims against the Confederate States, the justice of which shall have been judicially declared by a tribunal for the investigation of claims against the Government, which it is hereby made the duty of Congress to establish.

(10) All bills appropriating money shall specify in federal currency the exact amount of each appropriation and the purposes for which it is made; and Congress shall grant no extra compensation to any public contractor, officer, agent, or servant, after such contract shall have been made or such service rendered. . . .

[Paragraphs 12 through 19 incorporate the first 8 amendments to the U.S. Constitution.]

(20) Every law, or resolution having the force of law, shall relate to but one subject, and that shall be expressed in the title.

Section 10. (3) No State shall, without the consent of Congress, lay any duty on tonnage, except on sea-going vessels, for the improvement of its rivers and harbors navigated by the said vessels; but such duties shall not conflict with any treaties of the Confederate States with foreign nations; and any surplus of revenue, thus derived, shall, after making such improvement, be paid into the common treasury; nor shall any State keep troops or ships of war in time of peace, enter into any agreement or compact with another State, or with a foreign power, or engage in war, unless actually invaded, or in such imminent danger as will not admit of delay. But when any river divides or flows through two or more States, they may enter into compacts with each other to improve the navigation thereof.

Article II

Section 1. (1) The Executive power shall be vested in a President of the Confederate States of America. He and the Vice-President shall hold their offices for the term of six years; but the President shall not be reeligible. . . .

[Paragraph 3 incorporates the twelfth amendment.]

(7) No person except a natural born citizen of the Confederate States, or a citizen thereof, at the time of the adoption of this Constitution, or a citizen thereof born in the United States prior to the 20th December, 1860, shall be eligible to the office of President. . . .

Section 2. (3) The principal officer in each of the Executive Departments, and all persons connected with the diplomatic service, may be removed from office at the pleasure of the President. All other civil officers of the Executive Department may be removed at any time by the President, or other appointing power, when their services are unnecessary, or for dishonesty, incapacity, inefficiency, misconduct, or neglect of duty; and when so removed, the removal shall be reported to the Senate, together with the reasons therefor.

(4) The President shall have power to fill all vacancies that may happen during the recess of the Senate, by granting commissions which shall expire at the end of the next session; but no person rejected by the Senate shall be reappointed to the same office during their ensuing recess. . . .

Article III

[Section 2, paragraph 1 incorporates the eleventh amendment.]

Article IV

Section 2. (1) The citizens of each State shall be entitled to all the privileges and immunities of citizens of the several States, and shall have the right of transit and sojourn in any State of this Confederacy, with their slaves and other property; and the right of property in said slaves shall not be thereby impaired. . . .

(3) No slave or other person held to service or labor in any State or Territory of the Confederate States, under the laws thereof, escaping or unlawfully carried into another, shall, in consequence of any law or regulation therein, be discharged from such service or labor; but shall be delivered up on claim of the party to whom such slave belongs, or to whom such service or labor may be due.

Section 3. (1) Other States may be admitted into this Confederacy by a vote of two-thirds of the whole House of Representatives, and two-thirds of the Senate, the Senate voting by States. . . .

(2) The Congress shall have power to dispose of and make all needful rules and regulations concerning the property of the Confederate States, including the lands thereof.

(3) The Confederate States may acquire new territory; and Congress shall have power to legislate and provide governments for the inhabitants of all territory belonging to the Confederate States, lying without the limits of the several States, and may permit them, at such times, and in such manner as it may by law provide, to form States to be admitted into the Confederacy. In all such territory, the institution of negro slavery, as it now exists in the Confederate States, shall be recognized and protected by Congress and by the territorial government; and the inhabitants of the several Confederate States and Territories shall have the right to take to such territory any slaves lawfully held by them in any of the States or Territories of the Confederate States. . . .

Article V

Section 1. (1) Upon the demand of any three States, legally assembled in their several Conventions, the Congress shall summon a Convention of all the States, to take into consideration such amendments to the Constitution as the said States shall concur in suggesting at the time when the said demand is made; and should any of the proposed amendments to the Constitution be agreed on by the said Convention—voting by States—and the same be ratified by the Legislatures of two-thirds of the several States, or by conventions in two-thirds thereof—as the one or the other mode of ratification may be proposed by the general convention—they shall thenceforward form a part of this Constitution. But no State shall, without its consent, be deprived of its equal representation in the Senate.

Article VI

(1) The Government established by this Constitution is the successor of the Provisional Government of the Confederate States of America, and all the laws passed by the latter shall continue in force until the same shall be repealed or modified; and all the officers appointed by the same shall remain in office until their successors are appointed and qualified, or the offices abolished. . . .

[Paragraph 5 incorporates the ninth amendment.]

(6) The powers not delegated to the Confederate States by the Constitution, nor prohibited by it to the States, are reserved to the States, respectively, or to the people thereof.

Article VII

(2) When five States shall have ratified this Constitution in the manner before specified, the Congress, under the provisional Constitution, shall prescribe the time for holding the election of President and Vice-President, and for the meeting of the electoral college, and for counting the votes and inaugurating the President. They shall also prescribe the time for holding the first election of members of Congress under this Constitution, and the time for assembling the same. Until the assembling of such Congress, the Congress under the provisional Constitution shall continue to exercise the legislative powers granted them; not extending beyond the time limited by the Constitution of the Provisional Government.

✠ E S S A Y S

Secession and the Civil War marked the nation's greatest constitutional crises— ever. The period of Reconstruction after the war was just as traumatic, if less bloody. Indeed, at no other time has the nation undergone such a searching examination of its constitutional values. Historians sharply disagree, however, about how the Constitution figured in the decision of people to enter into the conflict. For some scholars, among them Arthur Bestor, Jr., professor emeritus of history at the University of Washington, the answer lies in understanding the configurative role of the Constitution. In the first essay, Bestor argues that secession is best understood as one of three national constitutional crises, each of them shaped by the structure of the Constitution.

Phillip S. Paludan, a historian at the University of Kansas, in the second essay sees the legal/constitutional meaning of secession in an entirely different way. He links the northern response to the secession crisis to a profound local concern in that section with self-government and law and order. Secession therefore was more than an abstract argument about the constitutional nature of the Union. It constituted such a threat to the existing local social order that northerners felt their traditions of government and social stability gravely menaced.

Secession and the Civil War as a Constitutional Crisis

ARTHUR BESTOR, JR.

Within the span of a single generation—during the thirty-odd years that began with the annexation of Texas in 1845 and ended with the withdrawal of the last Union troops from the South in 1877—the United States under-

Arthur Bestor, Jr., "The Civil War as a Constitutional Crisis," *American Historical Review* 69 (1964): 327–352.

went a succession of constitutional crises more severe and menacing than any before or since. From 1845 on, for some fifteen years, a constitutional dispute over the expansion of slavery into the western territories grew increasingly tense until a paralysis of normal constitutional functioning set in. Abruptly, in 1860–1861, this particular constitutional crsis was transformed into another: namely, that of secession. Though the new crisis was intimately linked with the old, its constitutional character was fundamentally different. The question of how the Constitution ought to operate as a piece of working machinery was superseded by the question of whether it might and should be dismantled. A showdown had come, and the four-year convulsion of Civil War ensued. Then, when hostilities ended in 1865, there came not the hoped for dawn of peace, but instead a third great constitutional struggle over Reconstruction, which lasted a dozen years and proved as harsh and divisive as any cold war in history. When the nation finally emerged from three decades of corrosive strife, no observer could miss the profound alterations that its institutions had undergone. Into the prodigious vortex of crisis and war every current of American life had ultimately been drawn.

So all-devouring was the conflict and so momentous its effects, that to characterize it (as I have done) as a series of constitutional crises will seem to many readers an almost irresponsible use of language, a grotesque belittling of the issues. Powerful economic forces, it will be pointed out, were pitted against one another in the struggle. Profound moral perplexities were generated by the existence of slavery, and the attacks upon it had social and psychological repercussions of incredible complexity. The various questions at issue penetrated into the arena of politics, shattering established parties and making or breaking the public careers of national and local leaders. Ought so massive a conflict to be discussed in terms of so rarified an abstraction as constitutional theory?

To ask such a question, however, is to mistake the character of constitutional crises in general. When or why or how should they arise if not in a context of social, economic, and ideological upheaval? A constitution, after all, is nothing other than the aggregate of laws, traditions, and understandings—in other words, the complex of institutions and procedures—by which a nation brings to political and legal decision the substantive conflicts engendered by changes in all the varied aspects of its societal life. In normal times, to be sure, routine and recurrent questions of public policy are not thought of as constitutional questions. Alternative policies are discussed in terms of their wisdom or desirability. Conflicts are resolved by the ordinary operation of familiar constitutional machinery. A decision is reached that is essentially a political decision, measuring, in some rough way, the political strength of the forces that are backing or opposing some particular program of action, a program that both sides concede to be constitutionally possible, though not necessarily prudent or desirable.

When controversies begin to cut deep, however, the constitutional legitimacy of a given course of action is likely to be challenged. Questions of policy give place to questions of power; questions of wisdom to questions of legality. Attention shifts to the Constitution itself, for the fate of each particular policy has come to hinge upon the interpretation given to the fundamental law. In debating these constitutional questions, men are not evading the substantive issues. They are facing them in precisely the manner that the situation now requires. A constitutional dispute has been superadded to the controversies already present.

Should the conflict become so intense as to test the adequacy of existing mechanisms to handle it at all, then it mounts to the level of a constitutional crisis. Indeed the capability of producing a constitutional crisis is an ultimate measure of the intensity of the substantive conflicts themselves. If, in the end, the situation explodes into violence, then the catastrophe is necessarily a constitutional one, for its very essence is the failure and the threatened destruction of the constitutional framework itself.

The secession crisis of 1860–1861 was obviously an event of this kind. It was a constitutional catastrophe in the most direct sense, for it resulted in a civil war that destroyed, albeit temporarily, the fabric of the Union.

There is, however, another sense—subtler, but perhaps more significant—in which the American Civil War may be characterized as a constitutional crisis. To put the matter succinctly, the very form that the conflict finally took was determined by the pre-existing form of the constitutional system. The way the opposing forces were arrayed against each other in war was a consequence of the way the Constitution had operated to array them in peace. Because the Union could be, and frequently had been, viewed as no more than a compact among sovereign states, the dissolution of the compact was a conceivable thing. It was constitutional theorizing, carried on from the very birth of the Republic, which made secession the ultimate recourse of any group that considered its vital interests threatened.

Since the American system was a federal one, secession, when it finally occurred, put the secessionists into immediate possession of fully organized governments, capable of acting as no *ad hoc* insurrectionary regime could possibly have acted. Though sometimes described as a "Rebellion" and sometimes as a "Civil War," the American conflict was, in a strict sense, neither. It was a war between pre-existing political entities. But it was not (to use a third description) a "War between the States," for in war the states did not act severally. Instead, the war was waged between two federations of these states: one the historic Union, the other a Confederacy that, though newly created, was shaped by the same constitutional tradition as its opponent. In short, only the pre-existing structure of the American Constitution can explain the actual configuration even of the war itself.

The *configurative* role that constitutional issues played is the point of crucial importance. When discussed in their own terms and for their own sakes, constitutional questions are admittedly theoretical questions. One may indeed say (borrowing a phrase that even academicians perfidiously employ) that they are academic questions. Only by becoming involved with other (and in a sense more "substantive") issues, do they become highly charged. But when they do become so involved, constitutional questions turn out to be momentous ones, for every theoretical premise draws after it a train of practical consequences. Abstract though constitutional issues may be, they exert a powerful shaping effect upon the course that events will in actuality take. They give a particular direction to forces already at work. They impose upon the conflict as a whole a unique, and an otherwise inexplicable, pattern or configuration.

To speak of a configuration of forces in history is to rule out, as essentially meaningless, many kinds of questions that are popularly supposed to be both answerable and important. In particular, it rules out as futile any effort to decide which one of the various forces at work in a given historical situation was "*the* most important cause" of the events that followed, or "*the* decisive factor" in bringing them about, or "*the* crucial issue" involved. The reason is simple. The steady operation of a single force, unopposed and uninterrupted, would result in a development so continuous as to be, in the most literal sense, eventless. To produce an event, one force must impinge upon at least one other. The event is the consequence of their interaction. Historical explanation is, of necessity, an explanation of such interactions.

If interaction is the crucial matter, then it is absurd to think of assigning to any factor in history an intrinsic or absolute weight, independent of its context. In the study of history, the context is all-important. Each individual factor derives its significance from the position it occupies in a complex structure of interrelationships. The fundamental historical problem, in short, is not to measure the relative weight of various causal elements, but instead to discover the pattern of their interaction with one another.

A cogent illustration of this particular point is afforded by the controversy over slavery, which played so significant a role in the crisis with which this paper deals. Powerful emotions, pro and con, were aroused by the very existence of slavery. Powerful economic interests were involved with the fate of the institution. Nevertheless, differences of opinion, violent though they were, cannot, by themselves, account for the peculiar configuration of events that historically occurred. The forces unleashed by the slavery controversy were essentially indeterminate; that is to say, they could lead to any number of different outcomes, ranging from simple legislative emancipation to bloody servile insurrection. In the British West Indies the former occurred; in Haiti, the latter. In the United States, by contrast with both, events took an exceedingly complicated course. The crisis can be said to have commenced with a fifteen-year dispute not over slavery itself, but over its expansion into the territories. It eventuated in a four-year war that was avowedly fought not over the issue of slavery, but over the question of the legal perpetuity of the Union. The slavery controversy, isolated from all other issues, cannot begin to explain why events followed so complex and devious a course. On the other hand, though other factors must be taken into account in explaining the configuration of events, these other factors, isolated from those connected with slavery, cannot explain why tensions mounted so high as to reach the breaking point of war.

No single factor, whatever its nature, can account for the distinctive form that the mid-nineteenth-century American crisis assumed. Several forces converged, producing a unique configuration. Men were debating a variety of issues simultaneously, and their various arguments intertwined.

Each conflict tended to intensify the others, and not only to intensify them but also to alter and deflect them in complicated ways. The crisis was born of interaction. . . .

When the historical record is as vast as the one produced by the mid-nineteenth-century American crisis—when arguments were so wearisomely repeated by such multitudes of men—it is sheer fantasy to assume that the issues discussed were not the real issues. The arguments of the period were public ones, addressed to contemporaries and designed to influence their actions. If these had not touched upon genuine issues, they would hardly have been so often reiterated. Had other lines of argument possessed a more compelling force, they would certainly have been employed.

The only tenable assumption, one that would require an overwhelming mass of contrary evidence to rebut, is that men and women knew perfectly well what they were quarreling about. And what do we find? They argued about economic measures—the tariff, the banking system, and the Homestead Act—for the obvious reason that economic interests of their own were at stake. They argued about slavery because they considered the issues it raised to be vital ones—vital to those who adhered to the ideal of a free society and vital to those who feared to disturb the *status quo*. They argued about the territories because they felt a deep concern for the kind of social order that would grow up there. They argued about the Constitution because they accepted its obligations (whatever they considered them to be) as binding.

These are the data with which the historian must reckon. Four issues were mentioned in the preceding paragraph: the issue of economic policy, the issue of slavery, the issue of the territories, and the issue of constitutional interpretation. At the very least, the historian must take all these into account. Other factors there indubitably were. To trace the interaction of these four, however, will perhaps suffice to reveal the underlying pattern of the crisis and to make clear how one of these factors, the constitutional issue, exerted a configurative effect that cannot possibly be ignored.

Conflicts over economic policy are endemic in modern societies. They formed a recurrent element in nineteenth-century American political conflict. To disregard them would be an even greater folly than to assume that they determined, by themselves, the entire course of events. Between a plantation economy dependent upon the sale of staples to a world market and an economy in which commerce, finance, and manufacturing were rapidly advancing, the points of conflict were numerous, real, and important. At issue were such matters as banks and corporations, tariffs, internal improvements, land grants to railroads, and free homesteads to settlers. In a general way, the line of division on matters of economic policy tended, at mid-century, to coincide with the line of division on the question of slavery. To the extent that it did so (and it did so far less clearly than many economic determinists assume), the economic conflict added its weight to the divisive forces at work in 1860–1861.

More significant, perhaps, was another and different sort of relationship between the persistent economic conflict and the rapidly mounting crisis before the Civil War. To put the matter briefly, the constitutional theories that came to be applied with such disruptive effects to the slavery dispute had been developed, in the first instance, largely in connection with strictly economic issues. Thus the doctrine of strict construction was pitted against the doctrine of loose construction as early as 1791, when Alexander Hamilton originated the proposal for a central bank. And the doctrine of nullification was worked out with ingenious thoroughness in 1832 as a weapon against the protective tariff. Whatever crises these doctrines precipitated proved to be relatively minor ones so long as the doctrines were applied to purely economic issues. Within this realm, compromise always turned out to be possible. The explosive force of irreconcilable constitutional theories became apparent only when the latter were brought to bear upon the dispute over slavery.

Inherent in the slavery controversy itself (the second factor with which we must reckon) were certain elements that made compromise and accommodation vastly more difficult than in the realm of economic policy. To be sure, slavery itself had its economic aspect. It was, among other things, a labor system. The economic life of many regions rested upon it. The economic interests that would be affected by any tampering with the institution were powerful interests, and they made their influence felt.

Nevertheless, it was the noneconomic aspect of slavery that made the issues it engendered so inflammatory. As Ulrich B. Phillips puts it, "Slavery was instituted not merely to provide control of labor but also as a system of racial adjustment and social order." The word "adjustment" is an obvious euphemism; elsewhere Phillips speaks frankly of "race control." The effort to maintain that control, he maintains, has been "the central theme of Southern history." The factor that has made the South "a land with a unity despite its diversity," Phillips concludes, is "a common resolve indomitably maintained—that it shall be and remain a white man's country."

It was this indomitable resolve—say rather, this imperious demand—that lay at the heart of the slavery controversy, as it lies at the heart of the struggle over civil rights today. To put the matter bluntly, the demand was that of a master race for a completely free hand to deal as it might choose with its own subject population. The word "sovereignty" was constantly on the lips of southern politicians. The concept they were invoking was one that Blackstone had defined as "supreme, irresistible, absolute, uncontrolled authority." This was the kind of authority that slaveholders exercised over their chattels. What they were insisting on, in the political realm, was that the same species of power should be recognized as belonging to the slave-holding states when dealing with their racial minorities. "State Sovereignty" was, in essence, the slaveowner's authority writ large.

If slavery had been a static system, confined geographically to the areas where the institution was an inheritance from earlier days, then the demand of the slaveholding states for unrestricted, "sovereign" power to deal with it was a demand to which the majority of Americans would probably have reconciled themselves for a long time. In 1861, at any rate, even Lincoln and the Republicans were prepared to support an ironclad guarantee that the Constitution would never be amended in such a way as to interfere with the institution within the slaveholding states. An irrepealable amendment to that effect passed both houses of Congress by the necessary two-thirds vote during the week before Lincoln's inauguration. The incoming President announced that he had "no objection" to the pending amendment and three states (two of them free) actually gave their ratifications in 1861 and 1862. If the problems created by slavery had actually been, as slaveowners so vehemently maintained, of a sort that the slaveholding states were perfectly capable of handling by themselves, then the security offered by this measure might well have been deemed absolute.

As the historical record shows, however, the proposed amendment never came close to meeting the demands of the proslavery forces. These demands, and the crisis they produced, stemmed directly from the fact that slavery was *not* a static and local institution; it was a prodigiously expanding one. By 1860 the census revealed that more than half the slaves in the nation were held in bondage *outside* the boundaries of the thirteen states that had composed the original Union. The expansion of slavery meant that hundreds of thousands of slaves were being carried beyond the territorial jurisdictions of the states under whose laws they had originally been held in servitude. Even to reach another slaveholding state, they presumably entered the stream of "Commerce . . . among the several States," which the Constitution gave Congress a power "to regulate." If they were carried to United States territories that had not yet been made states, their presence there raised questions about the source and validity of the law that kept them in bondage.

Territorial expansion, the third factor in our catalogue, was thus a crucial element in the pattern of interaction that produced the crisis. The timing of the latter, indeed, indicates clearly the role that expansion played. . . .

This prospect of continuing expansion is sometimes forgotten by historians who regard the issue of slavery in the territories as somehow bafflingly unreal. Since 1854, it is true, no contiguous territory has actually been added to the "continental" United States. No one in the later 1850s, however, could know that this was to be the historic fact. There were ample reasons to expect otherwise. A strong faction had worked for the annexation of the whole of Mexico in 1848. Filibustering expeditions in the Caribbean and Central America were sporadic from 1849 to 1860. As if to spell out the implications of these moves, the notorious Ostend Manifesto of 1854 had announced (over the signatures of three American envoys, including a future President) that the United States could not "permit Cuba to be Africanized" (in plainer language, could not allow the slaves in Cuba to become free of white domination and control), and had defiantly proclaimed that if Spain should refuse to sell the island, "then, by every law, human and divine, we shall be justified in wresting it from Spain if we possess the power." This was "higher law" doctrine with a vengeance.

Behind the intransigent refusal of the Republicans in 1860–1861 to accept any sort of compromise on the territorial question lay these all too recent developments. Lincoln's letters during the interval between his election and his inauguration contained pointed allusions to filibustering and to Cuba.

And his most explicit instructions on policy, written on February 1, 1861, to William H. Seward, soon to take office as his Secretary of State, were adamant against any further extension of slavery in any manner:

> I say now, . . . as I have all the while said, that on the territorial question—
> that is, the question of extending slavery under the national auspices—I
> am inflexible. I am for no compromise which *assists* or *permits* the extension
> of the institution on soil owned by the nation. And any trick by which the
> nation is to acquire territory, and then allow some local authority to spread
> slavery over it, is as obnoxious as any other.

The obnoxious "trick" that Lincoln feared was, of course, the acceptance of Stephen A. Douglas' doctrine of popular sovereignty. The supreme importance that Lincoln attached to the territorial issue was underlined by the final paragraph of his letter, wherein he discussed four other issues on which antislavery feeling ran high: the Fugitive Slave Act, the existence of slavery in the national capital, the domestic slave trade, and the slave code that the territorial legislature of New Mexico had enacted in 1859. Concerning these matters, Lincoln wrote Seward:

> As to fugitive slaves, District of Columbia, slave trade among the slave
> states, and whatever springs of necessity from the fact that the institution
> is amongst us, I care but little, so that what is done be comely, and not
> altogether outrageous. Nor do I care much about New-Mexico, if further
> extension were hedged against.

The issues raised by territorial expansion were, however, not merely prospective ones. Expansion was a present fact, and from 1845 onward its problems were immediate ones. Population was movin so rapidly into various parts of the newly acquired West, most spectacularly into California, that the establishment of civil governments within the region could hardly be postponed. Accordingly, within the single decade already delimited (that is, from the beginning of 1845 until the end of 1854), state or territorial forms of government were actually provided for every remaining part of the national domain, except the relatively small enclave known as the Indian Territory (now Oklahoma). The result was an actual doubling of the area of the United States within which organized civil governments existed. This process of political creation occurred not only in the new acquisition, but it also covered vast areas, previously acquired, that had been left unorganized, notably the northern part of the old Louisiana Purchase. There, in 1854, the new territories of Kansas and Nebraska suddenly appeared on the map. With equal suddenness these new names appeared in the newspapers, connected with ominous events.

The process of territorial organization brought into the very center of the crisis a fourth factor, the last in our original catalogue, namely, the constitutional one. The organization of new territories and the admission of new states were, after all, elements in a constitution-making process. Territorial expansion drastically changed the character of the dispute over slavery by entangling it with the constitutional problem of devising forms of government for the rapidly settling West. Slavery at last became, in the most direct and immediate sense, a constitutional question, and thus a question capable of disrupting the Union. It did so by assuming the form of a question about the power of Congress to legislate for the territories.

This brings us face to face with the central paradox in the pre–Civil War crisis. Slavery was being attacked in places where it did not, in present actuality, exist. The slaves, close to four million of them, were in the states, yet responsible leaders of the antislavery party pledged themselves not to interfere with them there. In the territories, where the prohibition of slavery was being so intransigently demanded and so belligerently resisted, there had never been more than a handful of slaves during the long period of crisis. Consider the bare statistics. The census of 1860, taken just before the final descent into Civil War, showed far fewer than a hundred slaves in all the territories, despite the abrogation of restrictions by the Kansas-Nebraska Act and the Dred Scott decision. Especially revealing was the situation in Kansas. Though blood had been spilled over the introduction of slavery into that territory, there were actually only 627 colored persons, slave or free, within its boundaries on the eve of its admission to statehood (January 29, 1861). The same situation obtained throughout the West. In 1846, at the time the Wilmot Proviso was introduced, the Union had comprised twenty-eight states. By the outbreak of the Civil War, more than two and a third million persons were to be found in the western areas beyond the boundaries of these older twenty-eight states, yet among them were only 7,687 Negroes, free or slave. There was much truth in the wry observation of a contemporary: "The whole controversy over the Territories . . . related to an imaginary negro in an impossible place."

The paradox was undeniable, and many historians treat it as evidence of a growing retreat from reality. . . . As [James G.] Randall sees it, the struggle "centered upon a political issue which lent itself to slogan making rather than to political analysis."

Slogan making, to be sure, is an important adjunct of political propaganda, and slogans can easily blind men to the relatively minor character of the tangible interests actually at stake. Nevertheless, a much more profound force was at work, shaping the crisis in this peculiar way. This configurative force was the constitutional system itself. The indirectness of the attack upon slavery, that is to say, the attack upon it in the territories, where it was merely a future possibility, instead of in the states, where the institution existed in force, was the unmistakable consequence of certain structural features of the American Constitution itself.

A centralized national state could have employed a number of different methods of dealing with the question of slavery. Against most of these, the American Constitution interposed a barrier that was both insuperable and respected. By blocking every form of frontal attack, it compelled the adoption of a strategy so indirect as to appear on the surface almost timid and equivocal. In effect, the strategy adopted was a strategy of "containment." Lincoln traced it to the founding fathers themselves. They had, he asserted, put into effect a twofold policy with respect to slavery: "restricting it from the new Territories where it had not gone, and legislating to cut off its source by the abrogation of the slave trade." Taken together, these amounted to "putting the seal of legislation against its spread." The second part of their policy was still in effect, but the first, said Lincoln, had been irresponsibly set aside. To restore it was his avowed object:

> I believe if we could arrest the spread [of slavery] and place it where Washington, and Jefferson, and Madison placed it, it would be in the course of ultimate extinction, and the public mind would, as for eighty years past, believe that it was in the course of ultimate extinction. The crisis would be past.

Whether or not slavery could have been brought to an end in this manner is a totally unanswerable question, but it requires no answer. The historical fact is that the defenders of slavery regarded the policy of containment as so dangerous to their interests that they interpreted it as signifying "that a war must be waged against slavery until it shall cease throughout the United States." On the other hand, the opponents of slavery took an uncompromising stand in favor of this particular policy because it was the only one that the Constitution appeared to leave open. To retreat from it would be to accept as inevitable what Lincoln called "the perpetuity and nationalization of slavery."

To understand the shaping effect of the Constitution upon the crisis, one must take seriously not only the ambiguities that contemporaries discovered in it, but also the features that all alike considered settled. The latter point is often neglected. Where constitutional understandings were clear and unambiguous, responsible leaders on both sides accepted without serious question the limitations imposed by the federal system. The most striking illustration has already been given. Antislavery leaders were willing to have written into the Constitution an absolute and perpetual ban upon congressional interference with slavery inside the slaveholding states. They were willing to do so because, as Lincoln said, they considered "such a provision to now be implied constitutional law," which might without objection be "made express, and irrevocable."

Equally firm was the constitutional understanding that Congress had full power to suppress the foreign slave trade. On the eve of secession, to be sure, a few fire-eaters proposed a resumption of the importation of slaves. The true index of southern opinion, however, is the fact that Constitution of the Confederate States outlawed the foreign trade in terms far more explicit than any found in the Constitution of the United States.

Far more surprising, to a modern student, is a third constitutional understanding that somehow held firm throughout the crisis. The Constitution grants Congress an unquestioned power "To regulate Commerce with foreign Nations, and among the several States, and with the Indian Tribes." Employing this power, Congress had outlawed the foreign slave trade in 1808, with the general acquiescence that we have just noted. To anyone familiar with twentieth-century American constitutional law, the commerce clause would seem to furnish an obvious weapon for use against the domestic slave trade as well. Since the 1890s the power of Congress to regulate interstate commerce has been directed successively against lotteries, prostitution, child labor, and innumerable other social evils that are observed to propagate themselves through the channels of interstate commerce.

The suppression of the domestic slave trade, moreover, would have struck a far more telling blow at slavery than any that could possibly have been delivered in the territories. Only the unhampered transportation and sale of slaves from the older seaboard regions can account for the creation of the black belt that stretched westward through the new Gulf States. By 1840 there were already as many slaves in Alabama and Mississippi together, as in Virginia. During the twenty years that followed, the number of slaves in the two Gulf States almost doubled, while the number of slaves in Virginia remained almost stationary.

The migration of slaveholding families with the slaves they already possessed can account for only part of this change. The domestic slave trader was a key figure in the process. His operations, moreover, had the indirect effect of pouring money back into older slaveholding states like Virginia, where slavery as an economic system had seemed, in the days of the Revolution, on the verge of bankruptcy. Furthermore, a direct attack upon the domestic slave trade might well have aroused less emotional resentment than the attack actually made upon the migration of slaveholders to the territories, for the slave trader was a universally reprobated figure, the object not only of antislavery invective but even of southern distrust and aversion.

No serious and sustained effort, however, was ever made to employ against the domestic slave trade the power of Congress to regulate interstate commerce. The idea was suggested, to be sure, but it never received significant support from responsible political leaders or from public opinion. . . .

Various other constitutional understandings weathered the crisis without particular difficulty, but to catalogue them is needless. The essential point has been made. The clearly stated provisions of the Constitution were accepted as binding. So also were at least two constitutional principles that rested upon no specific written text, but were firmly ingrained in public opinion; the plenary authority of the slaveholding states over the institution within their boundaries and the immunity of the domestic slave trade to federal interference.

In the Constitution as it stood, however, there were certain ambiguities and certain gaps. These pricked out, as on a geological map, the fault line along which earthquakes were likely to occur, should internal stresses build up to the danger point.

Several such points clustered about the fugitive slave clause of the Constitution. Clear enough was the principle that slaves might not secure their freedom by absconding into the free states. Three vital questions, however, were left without a clear answer. In the first place, did responsibility for returning the slaves to their masters rest with the states or the federal government? As early as 1842, the Supreme Court, in [*Prigg* v. *Pennsylvania*], placed responsibility upon the latter. This decision brought to the fore a second question. How far might the free states go in refusing co-operation and even impeding the process of rendition? The so-called "personal liberty laws" of various northern states probed this particular constitutional question. Even South Carolina, originator of the doctrine of nullification, saw no inconsistency in its wrathful denunciation of these enactments, "which either nullify the Acts of Congress or render useless any attempt to execute them." A third question arose in connection with the measures adopted by Congress to carry out the constitutional provision, notably the revised Fugitive Slave Act of 1850. Were the methods of enforcement prescribed by federal statute consistent with the procedural guarantees and undrlying spirit of the Bill of Rights? From the twentieth-century viewpoint, this was perhaps the most profound of all the constitutional issues raised by the slavery dispute. It amounted to a direct confrontation between the philosophy of freedom and the incompatible philosophy of slavery. Important and disturbing though the issues were, the mandate of the fugitive slave clause was sufficiently clear and direct to restrain all but the most extreme leaders from outright repudiation of it.

Of all the ambiguities in the written Constitution, therefore, the most portentous proved in fact to be the ones that lurked in the clause dealing with territory: "The Congress shall have Power to dispose of and make all needful Rules and Regulations respecting the Territory or other Property belonging to the United States." At first glance the provision seems clear enough, but questions were possible about its meaning. Eventually they were raised, and when raised they turned out to have so direct a bearing upon the problem of slavery that they would not down. What did the Constitution mean by mingling both "Territory" and "other Property," and speaking first of the power "to dispose of" such property? Was Congress in reality given a power to govern, or merely a proprietor's right to make regulations for the orderly management of the real estate he expected eventually to sell? If it were a power to govern, did it extend to all the subjects on which a full-fledged state was authorized to legislate? Did it therefore endow Congress with powers that were not federal powers at all but municipal ones, normally reserved to the states? In particular, did it bestow upon Congress, where the territories were concerned, a police power competent to deal with domestic relations and institutions like slavery?

This chain of seemingly trivial questions, it will be observed, led inexorably to the gravest question of the day: the future of slavery in an impetuously expanding nation. On many matters the decisions made by territorial governments might be regarded as unimportant, for the territorial stage was temporary and transitional. With respect to slavery, however, the initial decision was obviously a crucial one. A single article of the Ordinance of 1787 had eventuated in the admission of one free state after another in the Old Northwest. The omission of a comparable article from other territorial enactments had cleared the way for the growth of a black belt of slavery from Alabama through Arkansas. An identical conclusion was drawn by both sides. The power to decide the question of slavery for the territories was the power to determine the future of slavery itself.

In whose hands, then, had the Constitution placed the power of decision with respect to slavery in the territories? This was, in the last analysis, the constitutional question that split the Union. To it, three mutually irreconcilable answers were offered.

The first answer was certainly the most straightforward. The territories were part of the "Property belonging to the United States." The Constitution gave Congress power to "make all needful Rules and Regulations" respecting them. Only a definite provision of the Constitution, either limiting this power or specifying exceptions to it, could destroy the comprehensiveness of the grant. No such limitations or exceptions were stated. Therefore, Congress was fully authorized by the Constitution to prohibit slavery in any or all of the territories, or to permit its spread thereto, as that body, in exercise of normal legislative discretion, might decide.

This was the straightforward answer; it was also the traditional answer. The Continental Congress had given that answer in the Ordinance of 1787, and the first Congress under the Constitution had ratified it. For half a century thereafter the precedents accumulated, including the precedent of the Missouri Compromise of 1820. Only in the 1840s were these precedents challenged.

Because this was the traditional answer, it was (by definition, if you like) the conservative answer. When the breaking point was finally reached in 1860–1861 and four identifiable conflicting groups offered four constitutional doctrines, two of them accepted this general answer, but each gave it a peculiar twist.

Among the four political factions of 1860, the least well-organized was the group that can properly be described as the genuine conservatives. Their vehicle in the election of 1860 was the Constitutional Union party, and a rattletrap vehicle it certainly was. In a very real sense, however, they were the heirs of the old Whig party and particularly of the ideas of Henry Clay. Deeply ingrained was the instinct for compromise. They accepted the view just stated, that the power of decision with respect to slavery in a particular territory belonged to Congress. But they insisted that one additional understanding, hallowed by tradition, should likewise be considered constitutionally binding. In actually organizing the earlier territories, Congress had customarily balanced the prohibition of slavery in one area by the erection elsewhere of a territory wherein slaveholding would be permitted. To conservatives, this was more than a precedent; it was a constitutional principle. When, on December 18, 1860, the venerable John J. Crittenden offered to the Senate the resolutions summing up the conservative answer to the crisis, he was not in reality offering a new plan of compromise. He was, in effect, proposing to write into the Constitution itself the understandings that had governed politics in ealier, less crisis-ridden times. The heart of his plan was the re-establishment of the old Missouri Compromise line, dividing free territories from slave. An irrepealable amendment was to change this from a principle of policy into a mandate of constitutional law.

That Congress was empowered to decide the question of slavery for the territories was the view not only of the conservatives, but also of the Republicans. The arguments of the two parties were identical, up to a point; indeed, up to the point just discussed. Though territories in the past had been apportioned between freedom and slavery, the Republicans refused to consider this policy as anything more than a policy, capable of being altered at any time. The Wilmot Proviso of 1846 announced, in effect, that the time had come to abandon the policy. Radical though the proviso may have been in a political sense, it was hardly so in a constitutional sense. The existence of a congressional power is the basic constitutional question. In arguing for the existence of such a power over slavery in the territories, the Republicans took the same ground as the conservatives. In refusing to permit mere precedent to hamper the discretion of Congress in the *use* of that power, they broke with the conservatives. But the distinction they made between power and discretion, that is, between constitutional law and political policy, was neither radical nor unsound.

One innovation did find a place in antislavery, and hence in Republican, constitutional doctrine. Though precedent alone ought not to hamper the discretion of Congress, specific provisions of the Constitution could, and in Republican eyes did, limit and control that discretion. With respect to congressional action on slavery in the territories, so the antislavery forces maintained, the due process clause of the Fifth Amendment constituted such an express limitation. "Our Republican fathers," said the first national platform of the new party in 1856, "ordained that no person shall be deprived of life, liberty, or property, without due process of law." To establish slavery in the territories "by positive legislation" would violate this guarantee. Accordingly the Constitution itself operated to "deny the authority of Congress, of a Territorial Legislation [*sic*], of any individual, or association of individuals, to give legal existence to Slavery in any Territory of the United States." The Free Soil platform of 1848 had summed the argument up in an aphorism: "Congress has no more power to make a SLAVE than to make a KING; no more power to institute or establish SLAVERY, than to institute or establish a MONARCHY." As a doctrine of constitutional law, the result was this: the federal government had full authority over the territories, but so far as slavery was concerned, Congress might exercise this authority in only one way, by prohibiting the institution there.

The conservatives and the Republicans took the constitutional system as it stood, a combination of written text and historical precedent, and evolved their variant doctrines therefrom. By contrast, the two other factions of 1860—the northern Democrats under Stephen A. Douglas, and the southern Democrats whose senatorial leader was Jefferson Davis and whose presidential candidate was John C. Breckinridge—appealed primarily to constitutional theories above and beyond the written document and the precedents. If slogans are meaningfully applied, these two factions (each in its own way) were the ones who, in 1860, appealed to a "higher law."

For Douglas, this higher law was the indefeasible right of every community to decide for itself the social institutions it would accept and establish. "Territorial Sovereignty" (a more precise label than "popular sovereignty") meant that this right of decision on slavery belonged to the settlers in a new territory fully as much as to the people of a full-fledged state. At bottom the argument was one from analogy. The Constitution assigned responsibility for national affairs and interstate relations to the federal government; authority over matters of purely local and domestic concern were reserved to the states. So far as this division of power was concerned, Douglas argued, a territory stood on the same footing as a state. It might not yet have sufficient population to entitle it to a vote in Congress, but its people were entitled to self-government from the moment they were "organized into political communities." Douglas took his stand on what he regarded as a fundamental principle of American political philosophy: "that the people of every separate political community (dependent colonies, Provinces, and Territories as well as sovereign States) have an inalienable right to govern themselves in respect to their internal polity."

Having thus virtually erased the constitutional distinction between a territory and a state—a distinction that was vital (as we shall see) to the state sovereignty interpretation—Douglas proceeded to deal with the argument that since a territorial government was a creation of Congress, the powers it exercised were delegated ones, which Congress itself was free to limit, to overrule, or even to exercise through direct legislation of its own. He met the argument with an ingenious distinction. "Congress," he wrote, "may institute governments for the Territories," and, having done so, may "invest them with powers which Congress does not possess and can not exercise under the Constitution." He continued: "The powers which Congress may thus *confer* but can not *exercise,* are such as relate to the domestic affairs and internal polity of the Territory." Their sorce is not to be sought in any provision of the written Constitution, certainly not in the so-called territorial clause, but in the underlying principle of self-government.

Though Douglas insisted that the doctrine of popular sovereignty embodied "the ideas and principles of the fathers of the Revolution," his appeal to history was vitiated by special pleading. In his most elaborate review of the precedents, he passed over in silence the Northwest Ordinance of 1787, with its clear-cut congressional ban on slavery. Douglas chose instead to dwell at length upon the "Jeffersonian Plan of government for the Territories," embodied in the Ordinance of 1784. This plan, it is true, treated the territories as virtually equal with the member states of the Union, and thus supported (as against subsequent enactments) Douglas' plea for the largest measure of local self-government. When, however, Douglas went on to imply that the "Jeffersonian Plan" precluded, in principle, any congressional interference with slavery in the territories, he was guilty of outright misrepresentation. Jefferson's original draft (still extant in his own hand) included a forthright prohibition of slavery in all the territories. The Continental Congress, it is true, refused at the time to adopt this particular provision, a fact that Douglas mentioned, but there is no evidence whatever to show that they believed they lacked the power to do so. Three years later, the same body exercised this very power by unanimous vote of the eight states present.

Disingenuousness reached its peak in Douglas' assertion that the Ordinance of 1784 "stood on the statute book unrepealed and irrepealable . . . when, on the 14th day of May, 1787, the Federal Convention assembled at

Philadelphia and proceeded to form the Constitution under which we now live." Unrepealed the ordinance still was, and likewise unimplemented, but irrepealable it was not. Sixty days later, on July 13, 1787, Congress repealed it outright and substituted in its place the Northwest Ordinance, which Douglas chose not to discuss.

Despite these lapses, Douglas was, in truth, basing his doctrine upon one undeniably important element in the historic tradition of American political philosophy. In 1860 he was the only thoroughgoing advocate of local self-determination and local autonomy. He could justly maintain that he was upholding this particular aspect of the constitutional tradition not only against the conservatives and the Republicans, but also (and most emphatically) against the southern wing of his own party, which bitterly repudiated the whole notion of local self-government, when it meant that the people of a territory might exclude slavery from their midst.

This brings us to the fourth of the parties that contested the election of 1860, and to the third and last of the answers that were given to the question of where the Constitution placed the power to deal with slavery in the territories.

At first glance there would appear to be only two possible answers. Either the power of decision lay with the federal government, to which the territories had been ceded or by which they had been acquired; or else the decision rested with the people of the territories, by virtue of some inherent right of self-government. Neither answer, however, was acceptable to the proslavery forces. By the later 1850s they were committed to a third doctrine, state sovereignty.

The theory of state sovereignty takes on a deceptive appearance of simplicity in most historical accounts. This is because it is usually examined only in the context of the secession crisis. In that situation the corollaries drawn from the theory of state sovereignty were, in fact, exceedingly simple. If the Union was simply a compact among states that retained their ultimate sovereignty, then one or more of them could legally and peacefully withdraw from it, for reasons which they, as sovereigns, might judge sufficient. Often overlooked is the fact that secession itself was responsible for reducing the argument over state sovereignty to such simple terms. The right to secede was only one among many corollaries of the complex and intricate doctrine of the sovereignty of the states. In the winter and spring of 1860–1861, this particular corollary, naked and alone, became the issue on which events turned. Earlier applications of the doctrine became irrelevant. As they dropped from view, they were more or less forgotten. The theory of state sovereignty came to be regarded simply as a theory that had to do with the perpetuity of the Union.

The simplicity of the theory is, however, an illusion. The illusion is a consequence of reading history backward. The proslavery constitutional argument with respect to slavery in the territories cannot possibly be understood if the fifteen years of debate prior to 1860 are regarded simply as a dress rehearsal for secession. When applied to the question of slavery, state sovereignty was a positive doctrine, a doctrine of power, specifically, a doctrine designed to place in the hands of the slaveholding states a power sufficient to uphold slavery and promote its expansion *within* the Union. Secession might be an ultimate recourse, but secession offered no answer whatever to the problems of power that were of vital concern to the slave-holding states so long as they remained in the Union and used the Constitution as a piece of working machinery.

As a theory of how the Constitution should operate, as distinguished from a theory of how it might be dismantled, state sovereignty gave its own distinctive answer to the question of where the authority lay to deal with matters involving slavery in the territories. All such authority, the theory insisted, resided in the sovereign states. But how, one may well ask, was such authority to be exercised? The answer was ingenious. The laws that maintained slavery—which were, of course, the laws of the slaveholding states—must be given extraterritorial or extrajurisdictional effect. In other words, the laws that established a property in slaves were to be respected, and if necessary enforced, by the federal government, acting as agent for its principals, the sovereign states of the Union. . . .

. . . In effect, the laws of slavery were to become an integral part of the laws of the Union, so far as the territories were concerned.

Four irreconcilable constitutional doctrines were presented to the American people in 1860. There was no consensus, and the stage was set for civil war. The issues in which the long controversy culminated were abstruse. They concerned a seemingly minor detail of the constitutional system. The arguments that supported the various positions were intricate and theoretical. But the abstractness of constitutional issues has nothing to do, one way or the other, with the role they may happen to play at a moment of crisis. The sole question is the load that events have laid upon them. Thanks to the structure of the American constitutional system itself, the abstruse issue of slavery in the territories was required to carry the burden of well-nigh all the emotional drives, well-nigh all the political and economic tensions, and well-nigh all the moral perplexities that resulted from the existence in the United States of an archaic system of labor and an intolerable policy of racial subjection. To change the metaphor, the constitutional question of legislative authority over the territories became, so to speak, the narrow channel through which surged the torrent of ideas and interests and anxieties that flooded down from every drenched hillside upon which the storm cloud of slavery discharged its poisoned rain.

Secession as a Crisis of Local Authority

PHILLIP S. PALUDAN

Despite thousands of volumes written about the Civil War we still know almost nothing about one of the central questions that that struggle poses: why did men rush to fight for their endangered country? Indeed why did they believe that secession endangered it? We know with some precision

"The American Civil War Considered as a Crisis in Law and Order," *American Historical Review* 77 by Dr. Phillip Paludan, (1972), pp. 1013–1034. Reprinted by permission of the author.

why the South seceded. The answer is obvious at first glance and remains clear upon deeper investigation—the South seceded because it saw in the election of Lincoln a threat to the survival of slavery, the foundation for the Southern way of life. Tradition, psychology, and economics all spoke clearly the same message—without slavery we cannot survive. And so secession came.

But a description of the decision for secession is not a description of why the war came. Although the South prepared for war there would be none unless the North contested the Southern action. Lincoln's assertion that "both parties deprecated war; but one of them would make war rather than let the nation survive; and the other would accept war rather than let it perish," is imprecise and thus misleading. The decision to make war for the Union was made not in Richmond or Montgomery but in Washington, and Boston and New York, and Indianapolis, and Columbus, and Springfield. This decision was made by Lincoln and by thousands of men who throughout the secession winter and especially after Sumter rushed to the colors. To understand why the war came we must look not at secession but at the Northern response to it.

In that response, as we shall see, the concept of law and order loomed large. The concept is a complex one, contemporary political rhetoric to the contrary notwithstanding. The order of a society depends on more than the rigid enforcement of all its laws. It depends on maintaining an enduring consensus about a people's fundamental goals and beliefs, and hence on the success of the institutions created to secure this consensus. Fundamental to social stability is the family with its role of passing on ideals and attitudes about the nature of man, the relationship between man and God, and the duties, roles, and responsibilities of individuals to themselves and to others. In inculcating these ideas the family is supported by a whole environment including schools, churches, and informal and formal groups. Together these social institutions engender a collection of usually unexamined beliefs that act as society's silent, internal police. They say, "You must," "Thou shalt or shalt not," or "This is not done," and they operate wherever men carry their consciences.

Although order depends most fundamentally on these social institutions, any society that advances beyond a primitive level requires the creation of a political order and of institutions that secure it. These institutions provide the means for resolving intergroup conflicts, for utilizing the power of government to achieve the ambitions of society, and for preserving whatever freedom its citizens demand. As the political theorist Carl Friedrich points out, political order is "a term suited to designate the political situation of the community in which component parts, or units, are arranged in such a way that the actions required for the attainment of the purposes of the community will be taken."

In discussing the issue of law and order in the Civil War era it is useful to take Friedrich's definition as a focus. Specifically, order in the nineteenth-century United States refers to a condition in which the people were convinced that those institutions were secure that stabilized the protean nature of their society, restrained the potential for conflict in an environment that encouraged avarice, harmonized the diversity of opinions and influences fostered by a free society, and gave them a voice in determining their future. It is my contention that secession and the firing on Sumter provoked a crisis in which all these things seemed threatened and that, because of the widespread involvement of Northern citizens in the creation and maintenance of legal and political order, saving the Union was not merely an abstract issue but a matter of compelling personal concern.

An investigation of the reasons for this intense personal interest in the survival of the Union reveals serious shortcomings in existing descriptions of the Northern decision to fight for the Union. The traditional way that historians have looked at the reasons the North went to war has been to ask "What did 'Union' mean to Northerners who fought for it?" Thus we have studies of the idea of Union by Paul Nagel and of American nationalism by Merle Curti, Hans Kohn, and Yehoshua Arieli. All of these works describe in one fashion or another the ideas people had about the United States that made them willing to fight to keep it united. Through these works we discover the many images that came to Northerners when they said "Union" or "United States." Northerners visualized a large, prosperous, magisterial land whose continued success depended on unity. They saw the nation as "the last best hope" of democracy in the world, a country with a mission to demonstrate that a nation "dedicated to the proposition that all men are created equal" might work. They believed that here individualism and nationalism were mutually agreeable, not in conflict; that the nation did not submerge but rather expanded the individual by maximizing his opportunities to achieve his dreams. Such inquiries are thoughtful analyses of the issue. But they share what I believe are enfeebling faults. First, insofar as they deal directly with the question, they analyze why the common man went to war by reporting what intellectuals wrote about an idea of national union. Second, they focus their studies of nationalism in the United States too much on the nation as a whole and insufficiently on local experience.

The first of these faults is the least serious. There are, of course, obvious differences between the attitudes of Emerson, Lowell, Hawthorne, and Melville and those of the average American of their time—differences in values seen in the criticism that these men leveled against the excessive materialism of the years from the 1830s to the 1860s. Still, both intellectuals and common people shared a common experience, and while some intellectuals might deplore and common people revel in the potentials for acquisition, we may see the fact and dimensions of materialism in the culture of the time. Emerson's observations of that world are expressed in language more refined than the common man might use, but the crude materialism of Emerson's world is not altered by his intellectual approach. Yet the concept of the Union held by intellectuals is really only secondhand information on why those who fought, fought. Without study of a vital aspect of the daily experience of the future soldiers—their daily involvement with the process of governing—we should suspect the adequacy of such observations.

The weakness that arises from too nationalistic a focus is that the nation these historians describe was a federal union of states with a national government singularly inactive, a prevailing constitutional philosophy that discouraged national activity, and a population that feared its excesses. "States' rights and sovereignty" was a potent rallying cry whose validity and attraction was not diminished but rather demonstrated by the fact that all sections used it when it suited their purposes. In addition the excessively national orientation defies even one of the most tenacious of nineteenth-century images of nationhood. What many Americans admired about their nation was its federal nature, the tradition that kept in local hands the administration of local problems and that gave the people control over their own destiny. This is seen most clearly in discussions over why the nation could and should expand. To assertions that expansion would create tyranny, supporters of manifest destiny replied with discourses on the merits of federalism. Nationalist Edward Everett well expressed their arguments. "By the wise and happy partition of powers between the national and state governments, in virtue of which the national government is relieved of all the odium of administration, and the state governments are spared the conflicts of foreign politics, all bounds seem removed from the possible extension of our country, but the geographical limits of the continent."

In addition the trouble with emphasizing the nation when discussing pre–Civil War nationalism is that such an emphasis misconstrues the nature of loyalty and allegiance. It implies that loyalty to the nation precludes other loyalties, that the dilemma of Robert E. Lee about whether to join his state or his nation describes a necessary dichotomy. But from what social sciences suggest about loyalty it is likely that Lee and those attracted by his agonizing decision saw the problem too simply. . . . [M]ultiple loyalties are possible and indeed . . . loyalties to things familiar and nearby are the imperative foundations for attachments to larger and more general and hence more vague ideals and entities. Page Smith, discussing the American Revolution, insists that the creation of local communities that attracted the intense devotion of the colonists was indispensable for generating the "power of common action" that resulted in successful rebellion. Martin Buber adds his insight concerning the inextricable connection between local and national loyalty with the observation that "a nation is a community to the degree that it is a community of communities." Such observations were predicted in the nineteenth century by Tocqueville. With characteristic insight he observed, "Public spirit in the Union is, in a sense, only summing up of provincial patriotism. Every citizen of the United States may be said to transfer the concern inspired in him by his little republic into his love of the common motherland."

If we are to understand the reason that the North went to war for the Union we need to follow such suggestions and direct our attention toward the local experience, toward the environments in which the majority of Northerners lived. To focus locally is to ask the question about why men fought for the Union in a different and I hope more useful and precise way. The question changes from the general "Why fight for the Union?" to "What was there in the daily experience of most Northerners that made them sensitive and responsive to those images the Union evoked?"

As the North reacted to the secession crisis one theme was repeated constantly, and it suggests a crucial fact about Northern society. Again and again newspaper editors and political leaders discussed the degree to which secession was likely to produce disorder, anarchy, and a general disrespect for democratic government. . . .

These warnings and fears, intense as they were, still did not sound the depths of outrage and concern over the threat of lawlessness. It took the firing on Sumter to do that. Until early April men were still debating the question of secession with hope that its potential for disorder might be defused. Many who feared the precedent of successful lawbreaking that secession portended sought to solve the problem by transforming the crime into a lawful act. Newspapers, private citizens, and public figures asked for constitutional amendments that would legalize secession.

The cannonades from Charleston ended such equivocation. Now the issue was not the validity of one constitutional view as opposed to another but the need to uphold government and the rule of law against forceful disruption. Earlier warnings of anarchy were multiplied and intensified. From Chicago: "Without a Union that is free, without a Constitution that can be enforced, without an authority to command respect and obedience . . . our Republic ceases to be a government, our freedom will be quickly supplanted by anarchy and despotism." From Madison, Wisconsin: "This contest is not so much about territorial limits as to demonstrate whether we have government or not." From Indianapolis: "We are fighting for the existence of our own government, and not for the destruction of that at Montgomery." Roxbury, Massachusetts: "Every man instinctively feels that the moment has at last arrived for crushing treason and asserting the supremacy of law and the constitution." Cincinnati: "If [the] doctrine of secession as illustrated and enforced by [its] practice, is true, then there is no such thing as government authority or social obligation. . . . *A surrender to Secession is the suicide of government.*" Philadelphia: "Establish the authority of the Constitution and laws over violence and anarchy." The Republican parties of Indiana, Ohio, and Illinois rallied around the cry "enforce the laws." Two hundred thousand people attended a rally at Union Square in New York City on April 20, 1860, and listened for hours to speakers from throughout the North asserting that the rule of law was at stake. Orators such as the New York Democrat John A. Dix, the Whig attorney William Evarts, the city's mayor and future Copperhead Fernando Wood, the Ohio politician Robert Schenck, the Oregon senator Edward Baker, and many others supported the contention of the lifelong Democrat, Robert J. Walker, that "we must resist and subdue [secession] or our government will be but an organized anarchy." On April 17 the New York *Tribune* had summarized the prevailing sentiment: "We have a civil war on our hands. There is no use looking away from the fact. For this year the Chief Business of the American people must be proving that they have a Government, and that freedom is not another name for anarchy."

Did secession in fact threaten the order of society in the North? Not this particular secession; a section different in so many ways from the North might justify its departure by pointing to the conflicts that its presence produced. Whatever the reality, however, the factor motivating the Northern response was what men then believed secession might mean and what they foresaw as its consequences. The idea of secession, applied generally, suggested that conflicts between parties should be settled not by harmonizing differences in the service of higher ends but by ignoring those ends in the service of the quarrel of the moment. What community was safe if such a pattern were established and endorsed? But despite this fear, it is possible that peaceful secession would have been tolerated if some regular procedure for division had been adopted or if a way of giving the action some semblance of legality and regularity had been discovered and utilized. The firing on Sumter eliminated this possibility. The issue was now no longer the means of division or the justice of the cause of secession or the right of the national government to use its power to hold a state that sought to depart. The issue after Sumter was, can the country permit force to settle its disputes, cannons to resolve its differences? No people so dependent for success and stability on respecting and adhering to the processes of self-government, in the absence of any other compulsion, could afford to say yes. . . .

Northern determination to uphold government and order against the threat of anarchy was not simply rhetoric. Both speakers and listeners responded to such sentiments naturally, for in talking about the need for order and stable government they were discussing the topic about which the vast majority of Northerners were experts in practice if not in theory. In raising the issue of law and order the speakers struck Northerners quite literally where they lived. No issue, with the possible exception of acquiring wealth, had attracted so much energy and debate in the prewar years. From the Mayflower Compact and the organization of colonial governments through the writing of the Articles of Confederation, the creation of the Constitution, the ratification of thirty-two state constitutions from 1776 to 1860 in the states that did not secede (fifteen in the last fifteen years before secession), the debates and elections over constitutions that failed, the countless creations of county, town, and city governments, these Americans had been engaged in government-making. Add to this the millions of words expended debating constitutional questions in the prewar era, the numerous court cases that attracted national attention, the almost constant elections in the country with their concomitant discussions of governmental issues, and it is possible to describe the prewar years as a time of continual concern with questions of government, order, and law.

Although the South shared this history and shared also some of the characteristics of Northern society to be described, Southern fears of losing slavery ultimately overwhelmed countercurrents of loyalty and unionism and a respect for law and order. Had the North been similarly threatened it is probable that Northerners would have risked political disorder to preserve societal order. Many Southerners made this choice reluctantly and seem to have worried about the political disruption secession might provoke. Instead of following their secessionist ideas to logical conclusions, they made sure that no provision for secession would exist in the Confederate constitution.

Forsaking uncharted paths they wrote a document that copied in many ways the Constitution of the United States. And again and again they insisted that they were not violating the Philadelphia document but rather upholding its true principles against the lawbreakers of the North. As Confederate President Jefferson Davis told his constituents, "The Constitution formed by our forefathers is that of these Confederate states." Surely the South shared with the North a devotion to the established legal order that only a threat to its way of life could shake.

Yet there were differences in attitudes toward and experience with law and government that may help explain the diminished unionism of the South. Charles Sydnor points to Southern views of law that emphasized unwritten rules of conduct and elevated private over public law codes, the practice of dueling being the most obvious example. He notes the impact of slavery in making every master, and most white men, a law unto themselves when it came to dealing with blacks. Southerners also had fewer opportunities for involvement in the legal-political process than did Northerners. There were fewer towns per capita in the South, less rotation in office, and lower participation in voting—all factors worth exploring to test the degree of personal involvement in issues of order, government, and law in the South. That task, however, must be put off until another time. The focus here is on why the North fought to save the Union, not why Southerners tried to divide it.

The avalanche of oratory debating questions of law, government, and the Constitution had special meaning for Northerners. It was not merely theorizing about ideals but was a practical debate about the way they lived. Government in the pre–Civil War North was not "them"; it was "us." The national government was days if not weeks away, and its constitutional powers were strictly limited. It regulated interstate commerce, ran the post office, dealt with Indians, conducted such foreign policy as there was, and paid and administered an army and navy that totaled around 28,000 men as of 1860. In 1861 there were about 36,500 paid civilian employees of the national government, and approximately 30,000 of these were local postmasters. The national government did not tax the public at large. It had no powers in matters of health, education, welfare, morals, sanitation, safety, or local transportation. In short, practically every activity that affected the lives of Americans was the province of either state or local government—and more often than not it was local. . . .

. . . [A]gain and again Americans proved to themselves that they were lawmakers—that the law and order of their communities was their personal responsibility and depended on their actions and efforts. Their connection with the preservation of that order was intimate, vital, and compelling. This is made even more clear when we consider the way in which Americans gave passionate attention not only to the creation of an ordered community but to the legal battles that continued in the towns after they had been established.

Court terms at county seats in the prewar years were gala social events. People drove or walked into town in large numbers. Big wagons filled with women and children and loaded with provisions entered the town from every direction. People followed their favorite lawyers like modern sports stars and demanded of them not only courtroom performance but speeches in the evenings after the courts had closed. The people knew these lawyers, and it was eminently to the advantage of lawyers to be well known and popular, as practically all cases were decided by juries. The system of legal education that prevailed at the time further encouraged a familiar and popular image of the law. Lawyers were preponderantly local men who received their legal training at the hands of neighbors who were established attorneys. They thus became as familiar with and sensitive to local customs and ideas as they were with Blackstone, Coke, and Littleton, for their success was more dependent on such informal awareness than on formal knowledge. In addition opposing lawyers and judges all knew each other well, usually living together in the same boarding house during the court term. Plaintiffs and defendants were often well acquainted, and all figures in most cases were familiar to the people of the area. The jury system, intense popular interest, local training, and the social intimacy produced by a nation that was essentially a nation of small towns and farmers thus all encouraged a law that tended to mirror the judgment and mores of the town or locality. Page Smith's conclusion rings true: "In the small town law was what the community had ordained, growing directly out of the needs and aspirations of the people. It was not something remote, alien, imposed from without."

Popular involvement in questions of the legal order of course transcended concern with judicial proceedings. More than simply jurors and witnesses, these people themselves were the makers of the law they observed being contested. The creation of communities had meant more than providing a police and judicial function; it meant establishing and manning the institutions that made the community function. For every community that was created there were problems of education, health, housing, and municipal services to be solved and offices to be sought and staffed. The extent of involvement the citizens demonstrated and their interest in the survival and prospering of their governmental order was the measure of community services. . . .

In the prewar period, then, Americans made their own governments, enforced their own laws, staffed their own institutions, and gave intense attention to questions of government, politics, and law. There existed compelling personal reasons to be devoted to the preservation of law and order.

There was violence in prewar American society—a great deal of it. Indians, abolitionists, immigrants, Negroes, Mormons, Masons, as well as the WASP majority all received their share. But violence is not necessarily the opposite of law and order. Modern riots and disruptions have provoked and energized a "law-and-order" movement, but that should suggest that violence may be the instrument of stability as well as disorder. In fact, when we look carefully at the violence of the pre–Civil War years, as well as our own, we discover how much of it, though not all, resulted from efforts to preserve, not to destroy, the existing order. Abolitionists were attacked by "gentlemen of property and standing" for threatening the existing economic and racial status quo. Indians were seen as savage threats to the expansion of prosperous and comparatively well-organized society. Immigrants threatened to inject foreign ideas and practices into a political system that demanded consensus. Mormons outraged the morals of their neighbors and seemed to endanger the prevailing ideology by their exclusiveness. Masons were charged with an anarchistic atheism that would destroy the Christian sinews of society. And Negroes who forgot their assigned place knew that their punishment would not be restrained by charity.

Much of this violence was part of the persistent vigilante tradition in American society. Although hardly the sort of law and order that civil libertarians admire, vigilantism is "as American as cherry pie" and springs from the same sentiment that is the focus of this essay—the belief that individual Americans are responsible for the preservation of stability, that the law is an expression of popular sentiment, and that the people have the duty to maintain it even if procedural due process is not respected. Vigilantism is, as Richard M. Brown argues, socially conservative—an attempt to secure and maintain a society that respects property, stability, and order. To the degree that he feels personally responsible for maintaining order, therefore, every American is potentially a vigilante. Michel Chevalier saw this in 1833 and thought that it was admirable. Local saloonkeepers, he observed, were often the "police commissioner," and the tavern regulars "would in case of necessity be ready to act the part of constables." In a society that lacked a powerful state, he concluded, "This is real self-government; these are the obligations and responsibilities that every citizen takes upon himself when he disarms authority." . . .

. . . Despite the protean nature of prewar society visitors noted again and again the ease with which Americans preserved and developed the tools of self-rule. They were struck especially by the facility with which the American people created the communities and associations they needed. "These people associate as easily as they breathe," Fredrika Bremer noted. The need for American settlers to work together, encouraged by the absence of government energy, produced a capacity for self-generated unity that overcame the natural centrifugal tendencies of equality, Tocqueville observed. After over twenty years in this country, the German-American political thinker Francis Lieber was still struck by "the thousandfold evidences of an all pervading associative spirit in all moral and practical spheres."

What they were describing of course was the fact of democratic government—the constantly demonstrated ability of the people to make government and use it for their purposes. On the national level, as representatives from Maine tried to solve the issue of Southern slavery and senators from Alabama sought to establish a government for Kansas territory, in short, as national legislators wrestled with moral issues fomenting in places unfamiliar to them, democratic government was demonstrating its limitations. But in the range of life most people lived, self-government was creating abilities and commitments that would ensure that democratic government would endure in the United States whatever its national infirmities. Men were developing a sense that government was them and that they were responsible for order.

This personal experience with self-government was of course local, as it must be. How could one feel that he was a meaningful part of a government of thirty million people? How could one feel that his wishes were known and respected in a national government that elected presidents through electoral colleges, senators through state legislatures, and in which the only popularly elected national officials, members of the House of Representatives, represented, at the minimum, thirty thousand people? Men will always view larger concepts and institutions through the prism of their own experience.

And yet when the Union was attacked Northerners equated an attack on the national government with a threat to the self-government they had experienced. Why? The question of course defies absolute answer, but some speculation is in order. . . . Among other things the blossoming national economy undoubtedly provided many of them with personal experience of connections with other states, other regions. And migration certainly was a factor. Many citizens of the West had been born in other parts of the country; their experience of what the nation comprehended was thus broader than their present locality.

But what is striking is the fact that throughout the disunion crisis of 1860–61 men spoke not merely of a national economy or of the ties of sentiment that bound them to their birthplace but constantly and passionately of the destruction of self-government should secession succeed. They were thus seriously concerned with the preservation of the institutions of government that they were a part of, and they linked their experience with that government to the survival of the Union. Local personal experience was somehow bound to the preservation of national institutions. How?

First of all, they knew that the Union was a federal union, that local government performed administrative functions that Washington could not, and should not, supply. Local government was an inextricable part of the nation's governing process. Functions of local and national government were divided, and debates raged over state versus national rights and powers. Yet the division of power and responsibility existed not for its own sake but because men believed that a national government could not function, nor could it remain the government of a free people, if it took to itself the governing of a vast continent. Men wanted to preserve local government so that the nation could function and continue to be free.

Second, and perhaps of greatest importance in establishing the connection between local self-government and the survival of the Union, was this fact: not only was local government an administrative necessity; it was the fundamental characteristic of this nation. The country had been founded with the ideal of self-rule in mind, had fought a revolution to secure it, and had created a constitution that respected it. Americans endorsed and validated this national ideal every time they established institutions of self-government.

Americans were not attached to a place; constant migration demonstrated that. They were not devoted to the land; the image of the land as real estate, the continuing land speculation attested to that. What made them Americans was that they ruled themselves wherever they went. The Scotsman Alexander McKay saw this with notable insight. What distinguished this people, he observed, was "the feeling which they cherish towards their institutions." Europeans loved the land that they and their ancestors had occupied for centuries. But "the American exhibits little or none of the local attachments which distinguish the European. His feelings are more centered upon his institutions than his mere country. . . . His affections have more to do with the social and political system with which he is connected than with the soil he inhabits." Europeans tended to be miserable when separated for long periods from their birthplace, but "give the American his institutions and he cares but little where you place him." McKay admitted that in places like New England there was strong local feeling but what was "astonishing" was "how readily even there an American makes up his mind to try his fortunes elsewhere, particularly if he contemplates removal to another part of the Union, no matter how remote . . . providing the flag of his country waves over it, and republican institutions accompany him on his wanderings." Local institutions of democratic self-government were thus a nationalizing force, and devotion to them was the imperative bond of union.

Of course not every Northern soldier would go to war against the South with the words "law and order" on his lips. Many would enlist in the excitement of the moment. Many would seek the cheap glory of a short war and sign up for ninety days to march under the banner "the Union forever." A response of simple outrage at being attacked was natural enough and was probably widespread. Many believed that the time had come when war might purge the nation of many of its corrupting impurities—the willingness to value material wealth over nobility of character, the inclination to serve personal selfishness rather than the good of society. Republicans naturally were unwilling to destroy their party and repudiate the principles on which they had been elected by yielding to Southern threats and then rebel gunfire. The vast majority accepted the assertion of Richard Henry Dana that the North should not "buy the right to carry on the government, by any concession to slavery." For these reasons and others men went to war.

Yet admitting these expressions of anti-Southern sentiment does not weaken the argument so far advanced for the importance of the idea of law and order in generating a willingness to fight. The source of much of this sentiment was a widespread fear that the institutions of self-government that maintained ordered liberty were threatened by slavery and the South. To describe the incidents of the 1850s that spawned or encouraged anti-Southern feelings is practically to catalog apparent threats by slavery on such Northern institutions.

The outrage against the Fugitive Slave Law was provoked in part by the Northern belief that this law defied local custom and traditions of self-government. The Kansas crisis was often described as proof that local government might be despoiled by slavery and its supporters. When Presidents

Pierce and Buchanan supported the proslavery government in Kansas, despite the Free-Soil majority in the territory, their action was taken by many as a sign that the corrupting hand of slavery had captured the nation's executive office. When the Supreme Court produced the Dred Scott decision opponents saw evidence that courts were not immune from the same corruption. When Charles Sumner was attacked in Congress the event was described as more than the beating of one fire-eater by another: it was declared to be one more Southern attack on the principle of free speech in a free government and hence on Congress itself. The impact of these events would lead many of the North's conservative legal thinkers, men devoted to the preservation of existing legal and governmental institutions, to take anti-Southern positions even though they deplored the extremism of abolitionism. A potent source of anti-Southern sentiment was thus a widespread fear that slavery and its proponents endangered the institutions of self-government of the nation. Such a threat, of course, would shake Northerners profoundly, for it involved institutions that were an inextricable part of their experience as citizens of a democracy.

Examining the strengths of democracy on the eve of secession one perceptive author hit the mark: More than any other government, wrote Henry Flanders, democracy identified the citizen with his government and thus instilled a powerful patriotism. The citizen in such a state was "an indirect but influential agent in the administration of its affairs, watches with eager interest its course and whenever difficulty or danger impends, with something more than a sense of duty or spirit of loyalty, acts boldly and greatly in its service." Such people were deeply devoted to the law, he continued, for "in doing homage to law, they do homage to themselves, the creators and preservers of law." Three years later, with the war raging, Andrew Preston Peabody was equally struck by the way in which self-government created patriotic citizens. Men who made the laws themselves felt personally responsible for them and their survival. Peabody's language was ornate, but the meaning for the war was precise: "He in whom resides an aliquot portion of the sovereignty," he wrote, "will bear his kingly estate in mind on the numerous occasions in daily life on which he might else forget even his manhood."

Urging the energetic prosecution of the war James Russell Lowell had observed that "our Constitution claims our allegiance because it is law and order." Northerners did not forget their responsibility for that law and order. Foreign observers might have doubted that the nation with the least powerful national government in the world, a nation apparently so centrifugal, could and would find soldiers for a struggle to maintain unity, but those who knew the nation were not surprised. Exulting in the proof of strength that was indubitable by 1864 an obscure writer in the *Atlantic Monthly* remarked, "The bubble of Republicanism, which was to display such alacrity at bursting, is not the childish thing it was once deemed. . . . We have proved that we are a nation equal to the task of self-discipline and self-control." The daily experience of Americans with self-government, with fashioning and maintaining law and order, had done its work well.

✠ *F U R T H E R   R E A D I N G*

William L. Barney, *The Road to Secession: A New Perspective on the Old South* (1972)

Don E. Fehrenbacher, *The Dred Scott Case: Its Significance in American Law and Politics* (1978)

Paul Finkelman, *An Imperfect Union: Slavery, Federalism, and Comity* (1981)

———, "*Prigg* v. *Pennsylvania* and Northern State Courts: Anti-Slavery Use of a Pro-Slavery Opinion," *Civil War History* 25 (March 1979): 5–14, 19–35

Larry Gara, "The Fugitive Slave Law: A Double Paradox," *Civil War History* 10 (September 1964): 229–240

Harold M. Hyman and William M. Wiecek, *Equal Justice Under Law: Constitutional Development, 1835–1875* (1982)

Charles R. Lee, *The Confederate Constitution* (1963)

Donald Nieman, "Republicanism, the Confederate Constitution, and the American Constitutional Tradition," in Kermit L. Hall and James W. Ely, Jr., eds., *An Uncertain Tradition: Constitutionalism and the History of the South* (1989): 201–224

David M. Potter, *The South and the Sectional Conflict* (1968)

Robert B. Russell, "Constitutional Doctrines with Regard to Slavery in the Territories," *Journal of Southern History* 32 (November 1966): 466–486

David L. Smiley, "Revolutionary Origins of the South's Constitutional Defenses," *North Carolina Historical Review* 44 (1967): 256–269

Kenneth L. Stampp, *And the War Came: The North and the Secession Crisis, 1860–1861* (1950)

Carl B. Swisher, *The Taney Period, 1836–1864* (1974)

William M. Wiecek, "Slavery and Abolition Before the United States Supreme Court, 1820–1860," *Journal of American History* 65 (June 1978): 34–59

———, *The Sources of Antislavery Constitutionalism in America, 1760–1848* (1977)

Ralph A. Wooster, *The Secession Conventions of the South* (1962)

Race, Gender,
and the Fourteenth Amendment

✠

The Civil War obliterated the institution of slavery and the doctrines of state sovereignty and secession that supported it. Such sweeping changes forced a wholesale reexamination of federalism and civil rights that lasted for almost a quarter-century. The entire process was indubitably political. Moderate and radical Republicans viewed the Confederacy's collapse as an opportunity to build a new political following in the South. To secure the political support of the more than 4 million newly freed slaves, the Republicans had to transform the South's social order. That social revolution, in turn, depended on a redefinition of the federal government's responsibility for civil rights. The Dred Scott precedent, for example, denied blacks (slave or free) rights of citizenship that went as a matter of course to white male Americans.

Former Confederates and their northern Democratic allies had other ambitions. Southerners, while militarily defeated, clung proudly to their traditions, including white social and political control. Much to Republicans' consternation, ex-Confederates immediately assumed prominent positions of authority in state governments that swiftly passed black codes restricting the rights of the freedmen. The efforts of the former Confederates received the blessing of President Andrew Johnson, a closet Democrat from Tennessee who approached Reconstruction as a political opportunity to forge alliances with ex-Confederates. Johnson's resistance to Republican initiatives finally brought about his impeachment by Congress in 1868.

Greater congressional attention to blacks' civil rights necessarily prompted interest in the constitutional status of another long neglected group—women. The connection between black and female civil rights had its roots in the antebellum era, when Elizabeth Cady Stanton and Susan B. Anthony played key roles in the antislavery movement. Women of all races did not enjoy equality in either state or federal law. Instead, they occupied a private, ''separate sphere'' of home and children. Pre–Civil War culture dictated that public affairs were the exclusive province of men. The federal constitutional system almost totally ignored women, and when all-male state lawmakers did advance women's interests, as with the passage of the married women's property acts, they did so out of a spirit of paternalism rather than a commitment to gender equality.

Even with the demise of state sovereignty as a constitutional theory, extending federal rights to freedmen and women raised difficult questions about the nature of American federalism. The states continued to enjoy (and to claim) significant authority. Nonetheless, the Republican program was comprehensive. Congress passed a blizzard of legislation, as well as the Thirteenth, Fourteenth, and Fifteenth amendments.

Of these Reconstruction amendments, the Fourteenth was as important then as it is controversial now. Until its passage, the states had almost total control over civil rights; the Supreme Court in Barron v. Baltimore (1833) held that the federal Bill of Rights applied only with regard to the national government, not the states. The Fourteenth Amendment, however, contained a "state action" clause, which empowered the federal government to scrutinize states' actions based on due process of law, equal protection of the laws, and the privileges and immunities accorded to U.S. citizens. The congressional debates over the Fourteenth Amendment and what they reveal about the intentions of its framers are as closely studied today as are the records of the Philadelphia convention.

While Congress was innovative in the area of civil rights, almost all of its legislative measures were eventually tested before the Supreme Court. By the end of the century, the court declared that the Fourteenth Amendment protected corportions against state regulation, but not the rights of blacks, for whom the amendment was originally intended, and of women.

⌖ D O C U M E N T S

The connection between the civil rights of women and of blacks was made well before the Civil War. At the 1840 World Anti-Slavery Convention in London, a group of American women delegates were excluded, and they determined that the cause of emancipation affected them as much as it did slaves. The result was the 1848 Seneca Falls Declaration of Sentiments and Resolutions, the first documentary reading in this chapter.

The Emancipation Proclamation of 1863 freed the slaves only in those areas under Confederate control, as the second document reveals. It received an unenthusiastic welcome from race-conscious Americans, as the third selection, an excerpt from President Lincoln's hometown newspaper, *The Illinois State Register*, makes clear. The Civil Rights Act of 1866, the fourth document, was the first major piece of federal legislation designed to promote equality before the law without regard to race or color, but it did nothing to enhance the rights of women. While modest by today's standards, the act was greeted as a revolutionary measure of debatable constitutional authority. President Johnson's message of March 27, 1866, reprinted here as the fifth selection, invoked several constitutional arguments, but Congress easily overrode his veto.

Moderate and radical Republicans alike were sufficiently impressed by Johnson's arguments that they passed the Fourteenth Amendment. The excerpts in the sixth document from the House and Senate debates over the amendment touch upon critical questions such as whether the framers wanted to make the federal Bill of Rights apply to the states, whether they intended *persons* to mean women as well as blacks, and what limits they wanted to place on the federal enforcement of civil rights.

The seventh document, *Slaughterhouse Cases,* marked the first, most important interpretation by the Court of the new amendment. The litigation had nothing to do with blacks or women; instead, it involved a Louisiana state regulation that so improved the sanitary conditions of New Orleans's slaughterhouse business that many butchers lost their jobs. The butchers sued, claiming that they had been denied a property right in violation of the privileges-or-immunities and due-process clauses of the Fourteenth Amendment. Justice Samuel F. Miller's majority opinion held that the amendment had been passed solely for the protection of black freedmen and that the protection of most privileges and immunities fell to the states. Justices Stephen J. Field and Joseph Bradley dissented on the grounds that the amendment's framers intended the term *person* to be broadly rather than narrowly construed.

Even when blacks were involved, the justices continued to interpret state action, due process of law, and privileges and immunities narrowly. For example, in the 1883 *Civil Rights Cases,* the Court overturned the Civil Rights Act of 1875 on the grounds that Congress had far exceeded the authority granted it by the amendment. Nor did the Court take a generous view of the application of the amendment's protection to women, rejecting claims by women to vote (*Minor* v. *Happersett* [1875]) and to practice law (*Bradwell* v. *Illinois* [1873]).

The Seneca Falls Declaration of Sentiments and Resolutions, 1848

1. Declaration of Sentiments

When, in the course of human events, it becomes necessary for one portion of the family of man to assume among the people of the earth a position different from that which they have hitherto occupied, but one to which the laws of nature and of nature's God entitle them, a decent respect to the opinions of mankind requires that they should declare the causes that impel them to such a course.

We hold these truths to be self-evident: that all men and women are created equal; that they are endowed by their Creator with certain inalienable rights; that among these are life, liberty, and the pursuit of happiness; that to secure these rights governments are instituted, deriving their just powers from the consent of the governed. Whenever any form of government becomes destructive of these ends, it is the right of those who suffer from it to refuse allegiance to it, and to insist upon the institution of a new government, laying its foundation on such principles, and organizing its powers in such form, as to them shall seem most likely to effect their safety and happiness. Prudence, indeed, will dictate that governments long established should not be changed for light and transient causes; and accordingly all experience hath shown that mankind are more disposed to suffer while evils are sufferable, than to right themselves by abolishing the forms to which they are accustomed. But when a long train of abuses and usurpations, pursuing invariably the same object, evinces a design to reduce them under absolute despotism, it is their duty to throw off such government, and to provide new guards for their future security. Such has been the patient sufferance of the women under this government, and such is now the necessity which constrains them to demand the equal station to which they are entitled.

The history of mankind is a history of repeated injuries and usurpations on the part of man toward woman, having in direct object the establishment of an absolute tyranny over her. To prove this, let facts be submitted to a candid world.

He has never permitted her to exercise her inalienable right to the elective franchise.

He has compelled her to submit to laws, in the formation of which she had no voice.

He has withheld from her rights which are given to the most ignorant and degraded men—both natives and foreigners.

Having deprived her of this first right of a citizen, the elective franchise, thereby leaving her without representation in the halls of legislation, he has oppressed her on all sides.

He has made her, if married, in the eye of the law, civilly dead.

He has taken from her all right in property, even to the wages she earns.

He has made her, morally, an irresponsible being, as she can commit many crimes with impunity, provided they be done in the presence of her husband. In the covenant of marriage, she is compelled to promise obedience to her husband, he becoming, to all intents and purposes, her master—the law giving him power to deprive her of her liberty, and to administer chastisement.

He has so framed the laws of divorce, as to what shall be the proper causes, and in case of separation, to whom the guardianship of the children shall be given, as to be wholly regardless of the happiness of women—the law, in all cases, going upon a false supposition of the supremacy of man, and giving all power into his hands.

After depriving her of all rights as a married woman, if single, and the owner of property, he has taxed her to support a government which recognizes her only when her property can be made profitable to it.

He has monopolized nearly all the profitable employments, and from those she is permitted to follow, she receives but a scanty remuneration. He closes against her all the avenues to wealth and distinction which he considers most honorable to himself. As a teacher of theology, medicine, or law, she is not known.

He has denied her the facilities for obtaining a thorough education, all colleges being closed against her.

He allows her in Church, as well as State, but a subordinate position, claiming Apostolic authority for her exclusion from the ministry, and, with some exceptions, from any public participation in the affairs of the Church.

He has created a false public sentiment by giving to the world a different code of morals for men and women, but which moral delinquencies which exclude women from society, are not only tolerated, but deemed of little account in man.

He has usurped the prerogative of Jehovah himself, claiming it as his right to assign for her a sphere of action, when that belongs to her conscience and to her God.

He has endeavored, in every way that he could, to destroy her confidence in her own powers, to lessen her self-respect and to make her willing to lead a dependent and abject life.

Now, in view of this entire disfranchisement of one-half the people of this country, their social and religious degradation—in view of the unjust laws above mentioned, and because women do feel themselves aggrieved, oppressed, and fraudulently deprived of their most sacred rights, we insist that they have immediate admission to all the rights and privileges which belong to them as citizens of the United States.

In entering upon the great work before us, we anticipate no small amount of misconception, misrepresentation, and ridicule; but we shall use every instrumentality within our power to effect our object. We shall employ agents, circulate tracts, petition the State and National legislatures, and endeavor to enlist the pulpit and the press in our behalf. We hope this Convention will be followed by a series of Conventions embracing every part of the country.

2. Resolutions

Whereas, the great precept of nature is conceded to be, that "man shall pursue his own true and substantial happiness." Blackstone in his Commentaries remarks, that this law of Nature being coeval with mankind, and dictated by God himself, is of course superior in obligation to any other. It is binding over all the globe, in all countries and at all times; no human laws are of any validity if contrary to this, and such of them as are valid, derive all their force, and all their validity, and all their authority, mediately and immediately, from this original; therefore,

Resolved, That all laws which prevent woman from occupying such a station in society as her conscience shall dictate, or which place her in a position inferior to that of man, are contrary to the great precept of nature, and therefore of no force or authority.

Resolved, That woman is man's equal—was intended to be so by the Creator, and the highest good of the race demands that she should be recognized as such.

Resolved, That the women of this country ought to be enlightened in regard to the laws under which they live, that they may no longer publish their degradation by declaring themselves satisfied with their present position, nor their ignorance, by asserting that they have all the rights they want.

Resolved, That inasmuch as man, while claiming for himself intellectual superiority, does accord to woman moral superiority, it is pre-eminently his duty to encourage her to speak and teach, as she has an opportunity, in all religious assemblies.

Resolved, That the same amount of virtue, delicacy, and refinement of behavior that is required of woman in the social state, should also be required of man, and the same transgressions should be visited with equal severity on both man and woman.

Resolved, That the objection of indelicacy and impropriety, which is so often brought against woman when she addresses a public audience, comes with a very ill-grace from those who encourage, by their attendance, her appearance on the stage, in the concert, or in feats of the circus.

Resolved, That woman has too long rested satisfied in the circumscribed limits which corrupt customs and a perverted application of the Scriptures have marked out for her, and that it is time she should move in the enlarged sphere which her great Creator has assigned her.

Resolved, That it is the duty of the women of this country to secure to themselves their sacred right to the elective franchise.

Resolved, That the equality of human rights results necessarily from the fact of the identity of the race in capabilities and responsibilities.

Resolved, That the speedy success of our cause depends upon the zealous and untiring efforts of both men and women, for the overthrow of the monopoly of the pulpit, and for the securing to women an equal participation with men in the various trades, professions, and commerce.

Resolved, therefore, That, being invested by the creator with the same capabilities, and the same consciousness of responsibility for their exercise, it is demonstrably the right and duty of woman, equally with man, to promote every righteous cause by every righteous means; and especially in regard to the great subjects of morals and religion, it is self-evidently her right to participate with her brother in teaching them, both in private and in public, by writing and by speaking, by any instrumentalities proper to be used, and in any assemblies proper to be held; and this being a self-evident truth growing out of the divinely implanted principles of human nature, any custom or authority adverse to it, whether modern or wearing the hoary sanction of antiquity, is to be regarded as a self-evident falsehood, and at war with mankind.

The Emancipation Proclamation, 1863

Whereas on the twenty-second day of September, A.D. eighteen hundred and sixty two, a proclamation was issued by the President of the United States, containing, among other things, the following, to wit:

"That on the first day of January, A.D. 1863, all persons held as slaves within any State or designated part of a State the people whereof shall then be in rebellion against the United States shall be then, thenceforward, and forever free; and the executive government of the United States, including the military and naval authority thereof, will recognize and maintain the freedom of such persons and will do no act or acts to repress such persons, or any of them, in any efforts they may make for their actual freedom.

"That the executive will on the first day of January aforesaid, by proclamation, designate the States and parts of States, if any, in which the people thereof, respectively, shall then be in rebellion against the United States;" . . .

Now, therefore, I, Abraham Lincoln, President of the United States, by virtue of the power in me vested as Commander-in-Chief of the Army and Navy of the United States in time of actual armed rebellion against the authority and government of the United States, and as a fit and necessary war measure for suppressing said rebellion, do . . . order and declare that all persons held as slaves within said designated States and parts of States are, and henceforward shall be, free; and that the Executive Government of the United States, including the military and naval authorities thereof, will recognize and maintain the freedom of said persons.

And I hereby enjoin upon the people so declared to be free to abstain from all violence, unless in necessary self-defense; and I recommend to them that, in all cases when allowed, they labor faithfully for reasonable wages.

And I further declare and make known that such persons of suitable condition will be received into the armed service of the United States to garrison forts, positions, stations, and other places, and to man vessels of all sorts in said service.

And upon this act, sincerely believed to be an act of justice, warranted by the Constitution upon military necessity, I invoke the considerate judgment of mankind and the gracious favor of Almighty God.

The *Illinois State Register* Denounces the Emancipation Proclamation, 1863

Resolved: That the emancipation proclamation of the president of the United States is as unwarrantable in military as in civil law; a gigantic usurpation, at once converting the war, professedly commenced by the administration for the vindication of the authority of the constitution, into the crusade for the sudden, unconditional and violent liberation of three millions of negro slaves; a result which would not only be a total subversion of the Federal Union but a revolution in the social organization of the southern states, the immediate and remote, the present and far-reaching consequences of which to both races cannot be contemplated without the most dismal foreboding of horror and dismay. The proclamation invites servile insurrection as an element in this emancipation crusade—a means of warfare, the inhumanity and diabolism of which are without example in civilized warfare, and which we denounce, and which the civilized world will denounce, as an ineffaceable disgrace to the American name.

The Civil Rights Act of 1866

14 U.S. Statutes at Large 1868

Be it enacted by the Senate and House of Representatives of the United States of America in Congress assembled, That all persons born in the United States and not subject to any foreign power, excluding Indians not taxed, are hereby declared to be citizens of the United States; and such citizens, of every race and color, without regard to any previous condition of slavery or involuntary servitude, except as a punishment for crime whereof the party shall have been duly convicted, shall have the same right, in every State and Territory in the United States, to make and enforce contracts, to sue, be parties, and give evidence, to inherit, purchase, lease, sell, hold, and convey real and personal property, and to full and equal benefit of all laws and proceedings for the security of person and property, as is enjoyed by white citizens, and shall be subject to like punishment, pains, and penalties, and to none other, any law, statute, ordinance, regulation, or custom, to the contrary notwithstanding.

Section 2. *And be it further enacted,* That any person who, under color of any law, statute, ordinance, regulation, or custom, shall subject, or cause to be subjected, any inhabitant of any State or Territory to the deprivation of any right secured or protected by this act, or to different punishment, pains, or penalties on account of such person having at any time been held in a condition of slavery or involuntary servitude, except as a punishment for crime whereof the party shall have been duly convicted, or by reason of his color or race, than is prescribed for the punishment of white persons, shall be deemed guilty of a misdemeanor, and, on conviction, shall be punished by fine not exceeding one thousand dollars, or imprisonment not exceeding one year, or both, in the discretion of the court. . . .

President Andrew Johnson Vetoes the Civil Rights Act, 1866

To the Senate of the United States:

I regret that the bill, which has passed both Houses of Congress, entitled "An act to protect all persons in the United States in their civil rights and furnish the means of their vindication," contains provisions which I can not approve consistently with my sense of duty to the whole people and my obligations to the Constitution of the United States. I am therefore constrained to return it to the Senate, the House in which it originated, with my objections to its becoming a law.

By the first section of the bill all persons born in the United States and not subject to any foreign power, excluding Indians not taxed, are declared to be citizens of the United States. . . . It does not purport to give these classes of persons any status as citizens of States, except that which may result from their status as citizens of the United States. The power to confer the right of State citizenship is just as exclusively with the several States as the power to confer the right of Federal citizenship is with Congress.

The right of Federal citizenship thus to be conferred on the several excepted races before mentioned is now for the first time proposed to be given by law. If, as is claimed by many, all persons who are native born already are, by virtue of the Constitution, citizens of the United States, the passage of the pending bill can not be necessary to make them such. If, on the other hand, such persons are not citizens, as may be assumed from the proposed legislation to make them such, the grave question presents itself whether, when eleven of the thirty-six States are unrepresented in Congress at the present time, it is sound policy to make our entire colored population and all other excepted classes citizens of the United States. Four millions of them have just emerged from slavery into freedom. . . . It may also be asked whether it is necessary that they should be declared citizens in order that they may be secured in the enjoyment of the civil rights proposed to be conferred by the bill. Those rights are, by Federal as well as State laws, secured to all domiciled aliens and foreigners, even before the completion of the process of naturalization; and it may safely be assumed that the same enactments are sufficient to give like protection and benefits to those for whom this bill provides special legislation. Besides, the policy of the Government from its origin to the present time seems to have been that persons who are strangers to and unfamiliar with our institutions and our laws should pass through a certain probation, at the end of which, before attaining the coveted prize, they must give evidence of their fitness to receive and to exercise the rights of citizens as contemplated by the Constitution of the United States. The bill in effect proposes a discrimination against large numbers of intelligent, worthy, and patriotic foreigners, and in favor of the negro, to whom, after long years of bondage, the avenues to freedom and intelligence have just now been suddenly opened. . . .

The first section of the bill also contains an enumeration of the rights to be enjoyed by these classes so made citizens "in every State and Territory in the United States." These rights are "to make and enforce contracts; to sue, be parties, and give evidence; to inherit, purchase, lease, sell, hold, and convey real and personal property," and to have "full and equal benefit of all laws and proceedings for the security of person and property as is enjoyed by white citizens." So, too, they are made subject to the same punishment, pains, and penalties in common with white citizens, and to none other. Thus a perfect equality of the white and colored races is attempted to be fixed by Federal law in every State of the Union over the vast field of State jurisdiction covered by these enumerated rights. In no one of these can any State ever exercise any power of discrimination between the different races. . . .

Hitherto every subject embraced in the enumeration of rights contained in this bill has been considered as exclusively belonging to the States. They all relate to the internal police and economy of the respective States. They are matters which in each State concern the domestic condition of its people, varying in each according to its own peculiar circumstances and the safety and well-being of its own citizens. I do not mean to say that upon all these subjects there are not Federal restraints—as, for instance, in the State power of legislation over contracts there is a Federal limitation that no State shall pass a law impairing the obligations of contracts; and, as to crimes, that no State shall pass an *ex post facto* law; and, as to money, that no State shall make anything but gold and silver a legal tender; but where can we find a Federal prohibition against the power of any State to discriminate, as do most of them, between aliens and citizens, between artificial persons, called corporations, and natural persons, in the right to hold real estate? If it be granted that Congress can repeal all State laws discriminating between whites and blacks in the subjects covered by this bill, why, it may be asked, may not Congress repeal in the same way all State laws discriminating between the two races on the subjects of suffrage and office? If Congress can declare by law who shall hold lands, who shall testify, who shall have capacity to make a contract in a State, then Congress can by law also declare who, without regard to color or race, shall have the right to sit as a juror or as a judge, to hold any office, and, finally, to vote "in every State and Territory of the United States." As respects the Territories, they come within the power of Congress, for as to them the lawmaking power is the Federal power; but as to the States no similar provision exists vesting in Congress the power "to make rules and regulations" for them.

The object of the second section of the bill is to afford discriminating protection to colored persons in the full enjoyment of all the rights secured to them by the preceding section. . . .

This provision of the bill seems to be unnecessary, as adequate judicial remedies could be adopted to secure the desired end without invading the immunities of legislators, always important to be preserved in the interest of public liberty; without assailing the independence of the judiciary, always essential to the preservation of individual rights; and without impairing the efficiency of ministerial officers, always necessary for the maintenance of public peace and order. The remedy proposed by this section seems to be in this respect not only anomalous, but unconstitutional; for the Constitution guarantees nothing with certainty if it does not insure to the several States the right of making and executing laws in regard to all matters arising within their jurisdiction, subject only to the restriction that in cases of conflict with the Constitution and constitutional laws of the United States the latter should be held to be the supreme law of the land. . . .

It is clear that in States which deny to persons whose rights are secured by the first section of the bill any one of those rights all criminal and civil cases affecting them will, by the provisions of the third section, come under the exclusive cognizance of the Federal tribunals. It follows that if, in any State which denies to a colored person any one of all those rights, that person should commit a crime against the laws of a State—murder, arson, rape, or any other crime—all protection and punishment through the courts of the State are taken away, and he can only be tried and punished in the Federal courts. How is the criminal to be tried? If the offense is provided for and punished by Federal law, that law, and not the State law, is to govern. It is only when the offense does not happen to be within the purview of Federal law that the Federal courts are to try and punish him under any other law. Then resort is to be had to "the common law, as modified and changed" by State legislation, "so far as the same is not inconsistent with the Constitution and laws of the United States." So that over this vast domain of criminal jurisprudence provided by each State for the protection of its own citizens and for the punishment of all persons who violate its criminal laws, Federal law, whenever it can be made to apply, displaces State law. The question here naturally arises, from what source Congress derives the power to transfer to Federal tribunals certain classes of cases embraced in this section. . . . This section of the bill undoubtedly comprehends cases and authorizes the exercise of powers that are not, by the Constitution, within the jurisdiction of the courts of the United States. To transfer them to those courts would be an exercise of authority well calculated to excite distrust and alarm on the part of all the States, for the bill applies alike to all of them—as well to those that have as to those that have not been engaged in rebellion. . . .

The fourth section of the bill provides that officers and agents of the Freedmen's Bureau shall be empowered to make arrests, and also that other officers may be specially commissioned for that purpose by the President of the United States. It also authorizes circuit courts of the United States and the superior courts of the Territories to appoint, without limitation, commissioners, who are to be charged with the performance of *quasi* judicial duties. The fifth section empowers the commissioners so to be selected by the courts to appoint in writing, under their hands, one or more suitable persons from time to time to execute warrants and other processes described by the bill. These numerous official agents are made to constitute a sort of police, in addition to the military, and are authorized to summon a *posse comitatus,* and even to call to their aid such portion of the land and naval forces of the United States, or of the militia, "as may be necessary to the performance of the duty with which they are charged." This extraordinary power is to be conferred upon agents irresponsible to the Government and to the people, to whose number the discretion of the commissioners is the only limit, and in whose hands such authority might be made a terrible engine of wrong, oppression, and fraud. . . .

The ninth section authorizes the President, or such person as he may empower for that purpose, "to employ such part of the land or naval forces of the United States, or of the militia, as shall be necessary to prevent the violation and enforce the due execution of this act." This language seems to imply a permanent military force, that is to be always at hand, and whose only business is to be the enforcement of this measure over the vast region where it is intended to operate. . . .

In all our history, in all our experience as a people living under Federal and State law, no such system as that contemplated by the details of this bill has ever before been proposed or adopted. They establish for the security of the colored race safeguards which go infinitely beyond any that the General Government has ever provided for the white race. In fact, the distinction of race and color is by the bill made to operate in favor of the colored and against the white race. They interfere with the municipal legislation of the States, with the relations existing exclusively between a State and its citizens, or between inhabitants of the same State—an absorption and assumption of power by the General Government which, if acquiesced in, must sap and destroy our federative system of limited powers and break down the barriers which preserve the rights of the States. It is another step, or rather stride, toward centralization and the concentration of all legislative powers in the National Government. The tendency of the bill must be to resuscitate the spirit of rebellion and to arrest the progress of those influences which are more closely drawing around the States the bonds of union and peace. . . .

Congress Debates the Fourteenth Amendment, 1866

February 27, 1866

Mr. Hale. What is the effect of the amendment which the committee on reconstruction propose for the sanction of this House and the States of the Union? I submit that it is in effect a provision under which all State legislation, in its codes of civil and criminal jurisprudence and procedure, affecting the individual citizen, may be overridden, may be repealed or abolished, and the law of Congress established instead. I maintain that in this respect it is an utter departure from every principle ever dreamed of by the men who framed our Constitution.

Mr. Stevens. Does the gentleman mean to say that, under this provision, Congress could interfere in any case where the legislation of a State was equal, impartial to all? Or is it not simply to provide that, where any State makes a distinction in the same law between different classes of individuals, Congress shall have power to correct such discrimination and inequality? Does this proposition mean anything more than that?

Mr. Hale. I will answer the gentleman. In my judgment it does go much further than the remarks of the gentleman would imply: but even if it goes no further than that—and I will discuss this point more fully before I conclude—it is still open to the same objection, that it proposes an entire departure from the theory of the Federal Government in meddling with these matters of State jurisdiction at all.

Now, I say to the gentleman from Pennsylvania [Mr. Stevens] that reading the language in its grammatical and legal construction it is a grant of the fullest and most ample power to Congress to make all laws "necessary and proper to secure to all persons in the several States protection in the rights of life, liberty, and property," with the simple proviso that such protection shall be equal. It is not a mere provision that when the States undertake to give protection which is unequal Congress may equalize it: it is a grant of power in general terms—a grant of the right to legislate for the protection of life, liberty and property, simply qualified with the condition that it shall be equal legislation. That is my construction of the proposition as it stands here. It may differ from that of other gentlemen.

Mr. Eldridge. Mr. Speaker, let me go a little further here. If it be true that the construction of this amendment, which I understand to be claimed by the gentlemen from Ohio, [Mr. Bingham] who introduced it, and which I infer from his question is claimed by the gentleman from Pennsylvania. [Mr. Stevens:] if it be true that that is the true construction of this article, is it not even then introducing a power never before intended to be conferred upon Congress. For we all know it is true that probably every State in this

Union fails to give equal protection to all persons within its borders in the rights of life, liberty, and property. It may be a fault in the States that they do not do it. A reformation may be desirable, but by the doctrines of the school of politics in which I have been brought up, and which I have been taught to regard was the best school of political rights and duties in this Union, reforms of this character should come from the States, and not be forced upon them by the centralized power of the Federal Government.

Take a single case by way of illustration, and I take it simply to illustrate the point, without expressing any opinion whatever on the desirability or undesirability of a change in regard to it. Take the case of the rights of married women: did any one ever assume that Congress was to be invested with the power to legislate on that subject, and to say that married women, in regard to their rights of property, should stand on the same footing with men and unmarried women? There is not a State in the Union where disability of married women in relation to the rights of property does not to a greater or less extent still exist. Many of the States have taken steps for the partial abolition of that distinction in years past, some to a greater extent and others to a less. But I apprehend there is not to-day a State in the Union where there is not a distinction between the rights of married women, as to property, and the rights of *femmes sole* and men.

Mr. Stevens. If I do not interrupt the gentleman I will say a word. When a distinction is made between two married people or two *femmes sole,* then it is unequal legislation: but where all of the same class are dealt with in the same way then there is no pretense of inequality.

Mr. Hale. The gentleman will pardon me: his argument seems to me to be more specious than sound. The language of the section under consideration gives to *all persons* equal protection. Now, if that means you shall extend to one married woman the same protection you extend to another, and not the same you extend to unmarried women or men, then by parity of reasoning it will be sufficient if you extend to one negro the same rights you do to another, but not those you extend to a white man. I think, if the gentleman from Pennsylvania claims that the resolution only intends that all of a certain class shall have equal protection, such class legislation may certainly as easily satisfy the requirements of this resolution in the case of the negro as in the case of the married woman. The line of distinction is, I take it, quite as broadly marked between negroes and white men as between married and unmarried women.

Mr. Hale. It is claimed that this constitutional amendment is aimed simply and purely toward the protection of "American citizens of African descent" in the States lately in rebellion. I understand that to be the whole intended practical effect of the amendment.

Mr. Bingham. It is due to the committee that I should say that it is proposed as well to protect the thousands and tens of thousands and hundreds of thousands of loyal white citizens of the United States whose property, by State legislation, has been wrested from them under confiscation, and protect them also against banishment.

Mr. Hale. I trust that when the gentlemen comes to reply, he will give me as much of his time as he takes of mine. As he has the reply, I do not think he ought to interject his remarks into my speech. I will modify my statement and say that this amendment is intended to apply solely to the eleven States lately in rebellion, so far as any practical benefit to be derived from it is concerned. The gentleman from Ohio can correct me if I am again in error.

Mr. Bingham. It is to apply to other States also that have in their constitutions and laws to-day provisions in direct violation of every principle of our Constitution.

Mr. Rogers. I suppose this gentleman refers to the State of Indiana!

Mr. Bingham. I do not know: it may be so. It applies unquestionably to the State of Oregon.

Mr. Hale. Then I will again modify my correction and say that it is intended to apply to every State which, in the judgment of the honorable member who introduced this measure, has failed to provide equal protection to life, liberty, and property. And here we come to the very thing for which I denounce this proposition, that it takes away from these States the right to determine for themselves what their institutions shall be.

February 28, 1866

Mr. Bingham. Excuse me. Mr. Speaker, we have had some most extraordinary arguments against the adoption of the proposed amendment.

But, say the gentleman, if you adopt this amendment you give to Congress the power to enforce all the rights of married women in the several States. I beg the gentleman's pardon. He need not be alarmed at the condition of married women. Those rights which are universal and independent of all local State legislation belong, by the gift of God, to every woman, whether married or single. The rights of life and liberty are theirs whatever States may enact. But the gentleman's concern is as to the right of property in married women.

Although this word property has been in your bill of rights from the year 1789 until this hour, who ever heard it intimated that anybody could have property protected in any State until he owned or acquired property there according to its local law or according to the law of some other State which he may have carried thither? I undertake to say no one.

As to real estate, every one knows that its acquisition and transmission under every interpretation ever given to the word property, as used in the Constitution of the country, are dependent exclusively upon the local law of the States, save under a direct grant of the United States. But suppose any person has acquired property not contrary to the laws of the State, but in accordance with its law, are they not to be equally protected in the enjoyment of it, or are they to be denied all protection? That is the question, and the whole question, so far as that part of the case is concerned.

Mr. Speaker. I speak in behalf of this amendment in no party spirit, in no spirit of resentment toward any State or the people of any State, in no spirit of innovation, but for the sake of a violated Constitution and a wronged and wounded country whose heart is now smitten with a strange, great sorrow. I urge the amendment for the enforcement of these essential provisions of your Constitution, divine in their justice, sublime in their humanity, which declare that all men are equal in the rights of life and liberty before the majesty of American law.

Representatives, to you I appeal, that hereafter, by your act and the approval of the loyal people of this country, every man in every State of the Union, in accordance with the written words of your Constitution, may, by the national law, be secured in the equal protection of his personal rights. Your Constitution provides that no man, no matter what his color, no matter beneath what sky he may have been born, no matter in what disastrous conflict or by what tyrannical hand his liberty may have been cloven down, no matter how poor, no matter how friendless, no matter how ignorant, shall be deprived of life or liberty or property without due process of law— law in its highest sense, that law which is the perfection of human reason, and which is impartial, equal, exact justice; that justice which requires that every man shall have his right: that justice which is the highest duty of nations as it is the imperishable attribute of the God of nations.

Mr. Hale. Before the gentleman takes his seat will he allow me to ask a single question pertinent to this subject?

Mr. Bingham. Yes sir.

Mr. Hale. I desire after hearing the gentleman's argument, in which I have been much interested as a very calm, lucid, and logical vindication of the amendment, to ask him, as an able constitutional lawyer, which he has proved himself to be, whether in his opinion this proposed amendment to the Constitution does not confer upon Congress a general power of legislation for the purpose of securing to all persons in the several States protection of life, liberty, and property, subject only to the qualification that that protection shall be equal.

Mr. Bingham. I believe it does in regard to life and liberty and property as I have heretofore stated it: the right to real estate being dependent on the State law except when granted by the United States.

Mr. Hale. Excuse me. If I understand the gentleman, he now answers that it does confer a general power to legislate on the subject in regard to life and liberty, but not in regard to real estate. I desire to know if he means to imply that it extends to personal estate.

Mr. Bingham. Undoubtedly it is true. Let the gentleman look to the great Mississippi case, Slaughter and another, which is familiar doubtless, to all the members of the House, and he will find that under the Constitution the personal property of a citizen follows its owner, and is entitled to be protected in the State into which he goes.

Mr. Hale. The gentleman misapprehends my point, or else I misapprehend his answer. My question was whether this provision, if adopted, confers upon Congress general powers of legislation in regard to the protection of life, liberty, and personal property.

Mr. Bingham. It certainly does this: it confers upon Congress power to see to it that the protection given by the laws of the United States shall be equal in respect to life and liberty and property to all persons.

Mr. Hale. Then will the gentleman point me to that clause or part of this resolution which contains the doctrine he here announces?

Mr. Bingham. The words "equal protection" contain it, and nothing else.

May 8, 1866

Mr. Stevens. Let us now refer to the provisions of the proposed amendment.

The first section prohibits the States from abridging the privileges and immunities of citizens of the United States, or unlawfully depriving them of life, liberty, or property, or of denying to any person within their jurisdiction the "equal" protection of the laws.

I can hardly believe that any person can be found who will not admit that every one of these provisions is just. They are all asserted, in some form or other, in our DECLARATION or organic law. But the Constitution limits only the action of Congress, and is not a limitation on the States. This amendment supplies that defect, and allows Congress to correct the unjust legislation of the States, so far that the law which operates upon one man shall operate *equally* upon all. Whatever law punishes a white man for a crime shall punish the black man precisely in the same way and to the same degree. Whatever law protects the white man shall afford "equal" protection to the black man. Whatever means of redress is afforded to one shall be afforded to all. Whatever law allows the white man to testify in court shall allow the man of color to do the same. These are great advantages over their present codes. Now different degrees of punishment are inflicted, not on account of the magnitude of the crime, but according to the color of the skin. Now color disqualifies a man from testifying in courts, or being tried in the same way as white men. I need not enumerate these partial and oppressive laws. Unless the Constitution should restrain them those States will all, I fear, keep up this discrimination, and crush to death the hated freedmen. Some answer, "Your civil rights bill secures the same things." That is party true, but a law is repealable by a majority. And I need hardly say that the first time that the South with their copperhead allies obtain the command of Congress it will be repealed. The veto of the President and their votes on the bill are conclusive evidence of that.

Mr. Garfield. Sir. I believe that the right to vote, if it be not indeed one of the natural rights of all men, is so necessary to the protection of their natural rights as to be indispensable, and therefore equal to natural rights. I believe that the golden sentence of John Stuart Mill, in one of his greatest works, ought to be written on the constitution of every State, and on the Constitution of the United States as the greatest and most precious of truths. "That the ballot is put into the hands of men, not so much to enable them to govern others as that he may not be misgoverned by others." I believe that suffrage is the shield, the sword, the spear, and all the panoply that best befits a man for his own defense in the great social organism to which he belongs. And I profoundly regret that we have not been enabled to write it and engrave it upon our institutions, and imbed it in the imperishable bulwarks of the Constitution as a part of the fundamental law of the land.

But I am willing, as I said once before in this presence, when I cannot get all I wish to take what I can get. And therefore I am willing to accept the propositions that the committee have laid before us, though I desire one amendment which I will mention presently.

I am glad to see this first section here which proposes to hold over every American citizen, without regard to color, the protecting shield of law. The gentleman who has just taken his seat [Mr. Finck] undertakes to show that because we propose to vote for this section we therefore acknowledge that the civil rights bill was unconstitutional. He was anticipated in that objection by the gentleman from Pennsylvania [Mr. Stevens]. The civil rights bill is now a part of the law of the land. But every gentleman knows it will cease to be a part of the law whenever the sad moment arrives when that gentleman's party comes into power. It is precisely for that reason that we propose to lift that great and good law above the reach of political strife, beyond the reach of the plots and machinations of any party, and fix it in the serene sky, in the eternal firmament of the Constitution, where no storm of passion can shake it and no cloud can obscure it. For this reason, and not because I believe the civil rights bill unconstitutional, I am glad to see that first section here.

Mr. Thayer. With regard to the second section of the proposed amendment to the Constitution, it simply brings into the Constitution what is found in the bill of rights of every State of the Union. As I understand it, it is but incorporating in the Constitution of the United States the principle of the civil rights bill which has lately become a law, and that, not as the gentleman from Ohio [Mr. Finck] suggested, because in the estimation of this House that law cannot be sustained as constitutional, but in order, as was justly said by the gentleman from Ohio who last addressed the House [Mr. Garfield.] that that provision so necessary for the equal administration of the law, so just in its operation, so necessary for the protection of the fundamental rights of citizenship, shall be forever incorporated in the Constitution of the United States. But, sir, that subject has already been fully discussed. I have upon another occasion expressed my views upon it, and I do not propose to detain the House with any further remarks of my own upon it.

May 10, 1866

Mr. Bingham. The necessity for the first section of this amendment to the Constitution, Mr. Speaker, is one of the lessons that have been taught to your committee and taught to all the people of this country by the history of the past four years of terrific conflict—that history in which God is, and in which He teaches the profoundest lessons to men and nations. There was a want hitherto, and there remains a want now, in the Constitution of our country, which the proposed amendment will supply. What is that? It is the power in the people, the whole people of the United States, by express authority of the Constitution to do that by congressional enactment which hitherto they have not had the power to do, and have never even attempted to do; that is, to protect by national law the privileges and immunities of all the citizens of the Republic and the inborn rights of every person within its jurisdiction whenever the same shall be abridged or denied by the unconstitutional acts of any State.

Allow me, Mr. Speaker, in passing, to say that this amendment takes from no State any right that ever pertained to it. No State ever had the right, under the forms of law or otherwise, to deny to any freeman the equal protection of the laws or to abridge the privileges or immunities of any citizen of the Republic, although many of them have assumed and exercised the power, and that without remedy. The amendment does not give, as the second section shows, the power to Congress of regulating suffrage in the several States.

The second section excludes the conclusion that by the first section suffrage is subjected to congressional law: save, indeed, with this exception, that as the right in the people of each State to a republican government and to choose their Representatives in Congress is of the guarantees of the Constitution, by this amendment a remedy might be given directly for a case supposed by Madison, where treason might change a State government from a republican to a despotic government, and thereby deny suffrage to the people. Why should any American citizen object to that? But, sir, it has been suggested, not here, but elsewhere, if this section does not confer suffrage the need of it is not perceived. To all such I beg leave again to say, that many instances of State injustice and oppression have already occurred in the State legislation of this Union, of flagrant violations of the guaranteed privileges of citizens of the United States, for which the national Government furnished and could furnish by law no remedy whatever. Contrary to the express letter of your Constitution, "cruel and unusual punishments" have been inflicted under State laws within this Union upon citizens, not only for crimes committed, but for sacred duty done, for which and against which the Government of the United States had provided no remedy and could provide none.

Sir, the words of the Constitution that "the citizens of each State shall be entitled to all privileges and immunities of citizens in the several States" include, among other privileges, the right to bear true allegiance to the Constitution and laws of the United States, and to be protected in life, liberty, and property. Next, sir, to the allegiance which we all owe to God our Creator, is the allegiance which we owe to our common country.

The time was in our history, thirty-three years ago, when, in the State of South Carolina, by solemn ordinance adopted in a convention held under the authority of State law, it was ordained, as a part of the fundamental law of that State, that the citizens of South Carolina, being citizens of the United States as well, should abjure their allegiance to every other government or authority than that of the State of South Carolina.

That ordinance contained these words:

"The allegiance of the citizens of this State is due to the State: and no allegiance is due from them to any other Power or authority: and the General Assembly of said State is hereby empowered from time to time, when they may deem it proper, to provide for the administration to the citizens and officers of the State, or such of the said officers, as they may think fit, of suitable oaths or affirmations, binding them to the observance of such allegiance, and abjuring all other allegiance; and also to define what shall amount to a violation of their allegiance, and to provide the proper punishment for such violation."

There was also, as gentlemen know, an attempt made at the same time by that State to nullify the revenue laws of the United States. What was the legislation of Congress in that day to meet this usurpation of authority by that State, violative alike of the rights of the national Government and of the rights of the citizen?

In that hour of danger and trial to the country there was as able a body of men in this Capitol as was ever convened in Washington, and of these were Webster, Clay, Benton, Silas Wright, John Quincy Adams, and Edward Livingston. They provided a remedy by law for the invasion of the rights of the Federal Government and for the protection of its officials and those assisting them in executing the revenue laws. (See 4 Statutes-at-Large, 632–33.) No remedy was provided to protect the citizen. Why was the act to provide for the collection of the revenue passed, and to protect all acting under it, and no protection given to secure the citizen against punishment for fidelity to his country? But one answer can be given. There was in the Constitution of the United States an express grant of power to the Federal Congress to lay and collect duties and imposts and to pass all laws necessary to carry that grant of power into execution. But, sir, that body of great and patriotic men looked in vain for any grant of power in the Constitution by which to give protection to the citizens of the United States resident in South Carolina against the infamous provision of the ordinance which required them to abjure the allegiance which they owed their country. It was an opprobrium to the Republic that for fidelity to the United States they could not by national law be protected against the degrading punishment inflicted on slaves and felons by State law. That great want of the citizen and stranger, protection by national law from unconstitutional State enactments, is supplied by the first section of this amendment. That is the extent that it hath, no more; and let gentlemen answer to God and their country who oppose its incorporation into the organic law of the land.

May 23, 1866

Mr. Howard. The first clause of this section relates to the privileges and immunities of citizens of the United States as such, and as distinguished from all other persons not citizens of the United States.

It would be a curious question to solve what are the privileges and immunities of citizens of each of the States in the several States. I do not propose to go at any length into that question at this time. It would be a somewhat barren discussion. But it is certain the clause was inserted in the Constitution for some good purpose. It has in view some results beneficial to the citizens of the several States, or it would not be found there; yet I am not aware that the Supreme Court have ever undertaken to define either the nature or extent of the privileges and immunities thus guaranteed. Indeed, if my recollection serves me, that court, on a certain occasion not many years since, when this question seemed to present itself to them, very modestly declined to go into a definition of them, leaving questions arising under the clause to be discussed and adjudicated when they should happen practically to arise. But we may gather some intimation of what probably will be the opinion of the judiciary by referring to a case adjudged many years ago in one of the circuit courts of the United States by Judge Washington: and I will trouble the Senate but for a moment by reading what that very learned and excellent judge says about these privileges and immunities of the citizens of each State in the several States. It is the case of *Corfield* v. *Coryell.*

Such is the character of the privileges and immunities spoken of in the second section of the fourth article of the Constitution. To these privileges and immunities, whatever they may be—for they are not and cannot be fully defined in their entire extent and precise nature—to these should be added the personal rights guaranteed and secured by the first eight amendments of the Constitution; such as the freedom of speech and of the press; the right of the people peaceably to assemble and petition the Government for a redress of grievances, a right appertaining to each and all the people; the right to keep and to bear arms; the right to be exempted from the quartering of soldiers in a house without the consent of the owner; the right to be exempt from unreasonable searches and seizures, and from any search or seizure except by virtue of a warrant issued upon a formal oath or affidavit: the right of an accused person to be informed of the nature of the accusation against him, and his right to be tried by an impartial jury of the vicinage; and also the right to be secure against excessive bail and against cruel and unusual punishments.

Now, sir, here is a mass of privileges, immunities, and rights, some of them secured by the second section of the fourth article of the Constitution, which I have recited, some by the first eight amendments of the Constitution; and it is a fact well worthy of attention that the course of decision of our courts and the present settled doctrine is, that all these immunities, privileges, rights, thus guaranteed by the Constitution or recognized by it, are secured to the citizen solely as a citizen of the United States and as a party in their courts. They do not operate in the slightest degree as a restraint or prohibition upon State legislation. States are not affected by them, and it has been repeatedly held that the restriction contained in the Constitution against the taking of private property for public use without just compensation is not a restriction upon State legislation, but applies only to the legislation of Congress.

Now, sir, there is no power given in the Constitution to enforce and to carry out any of these guarantees. They are not powers granted by the Constitution to Congress, and of course do not come within the sweeping clause of the Constitution authorizing Congress to pass all laws necessary and proper for carrying out the foregoing or granted powers, but they stand simply as a bill of rights in the Constitution, without power on the part of Congress to give them full effect; while at the same time the States are not restrained from violating the principles embraced in them except by their own local constitutions, which may be altered from year to year. The great object of the first section of this amendment is, therefore, to restrain the power of the States and compel them at all times to respect these great fundamental guarantees. How will it be done under the present amendment? As I have remarked, they are not powers granted to Congress, and therefore it is necessary, if they are to be effectuated and enforced, as they assuredly ought to be, that additional power should be given to Congress to that end. This is done by the fifth section of this amendment, which declares that "the Congress shall have power to enforce by appropriate legislation the provisions of this article." Here is a direct affirmative delegation of power to Congress to carry out all the principles of all these guarantees, a power not found in the Constitution.

The last two clauses of the first section of the amendment disable a State from depriving not merely a citizen of the United States, but any person, whoever he may be, of life, liberty, or property without due process of law, or from denying to him the equal protection of the laws of the State. This abolishes all class legislation in the States and does away with the injustice of subjecting one caste of persons to a code not applicable to another. It prohibits the hanging of a black man for a crime for which the white man is not to be hanged. It protects the black man in his fundamental rights as a citizen with the same shield which it throws over the white man. Is it not time, Mr. President, that we extend to the black man, I had almost called it the poor privilege of the equal protection of the law? Ought not the time to be now passed when one measure of justice is to be meted out to a member of one caste while another and a different measure is meted out to the member of another caste, both castes being alike citizens of the United States, both bound to obey the same laws, to sustain the burdens of the same Government, and both equally responsible to justice and to God for the deeds done in the body?

But, sir, the first section of the proposed amendment does not give to either of these classes the right of voting. The right of suffrage is not, in law, one of the privileges or immunities thus secured by the Constitution.

It is merely the creature of law. It has always been regarded in this country as the result of positive local law, not regarded as one of those fundamental rights lying at the basis of all society and without which a people cannot exist except as slaves, subject to a despotism.

As I have already remarked, section one is a restriction upon the States, and does not, of itself, confer any power upon Congress. The power which Congress has, under this amendment, is derived, not from that section, but from the fifth section, which gives it authority to pass laws which are appropriate to the attainment of the great object of the amendment. I look upon the first section, taken in connection with the fifth, as very important. It will, if adopted by the States, forever disable every one of them from passing laws trenching upon those fundamental rights and privileges which pertain to citizens of the United States, and to all persons who may happen to be within their jurisdiction. It establishes equality before the law, and it gives to the humblest, the poorest, the most despised of the race the same rights and the same protection before the law as it gives to the most powerful, the most wealthy, or the most haughty. That, sir, is republican government, as I understand it, and the only one which can claim the praise of a just Government. Without this principle of equal justice to all men and equal protection under the shield of the law, there is no republican government and none that is really worth maintaining.

May 30, 1866

Mr. Doolittle. As I understand, a member from Ohio, Mr. Bingham, who in a very able speech in the House maintained that the civil rights bill was without any authority in the Constitution, brought forward a proposition in the House of Representatives to amend the Constitution so as to enable Congress to declare the civil rights of all persons, and that the constitutional amendment, Mr. Bingham being himself one of the committee of fifteen, was referred by the House to that committee, and from the committee it has been reported. I say I have a right to infer that it was because Mr. Bingham and others of the House of Representatives and other persons upon the committee had doubts, at least, as to the constitutionality of the civil rights bill that this proposition to amend the Constitution now appears to give it validity and force. It is not an imputation upon any one.

Mr. Grimes. It is an imputation upon every member who voted for the bill, the inference being legitimate and logical that they violated their oaths and knew they did so when they voted for the civil rights bill.

Mr. Doolittle. The Senator goes too far. What I say is that they had doubts.

Mr. Fessenden. I will say to the Senator one thing: whatever may have been Mr. Bingham's motives in bringing it forward, he brought it forward some time before the civil rights bill was considered at all and had it referred to the committee, and it was discussed in the committee long before the civil rights bill was passed. Then I will say to him further, that during all the discussion in the committee that I heard nothing was ever said about the civil rights bill in connection with that. It was placed on entirely different grounds.

Mr. Doolittle. I will ask the Senator from Maine this question: if Congress, under the Constitution now has the power to declare that "all persons born in the United States, and not subject to any foreign Power, excluding Indians not taxed, are hereby declared to be citizens of the United States," what is the necessity of amending the Constitution at all on this subject?

Mr. Fessenden. I do not choose that the Senator shall get off from the issue he presented. I meet him right there on the first issue. If he wants my opinion upon other questions, he can ask it afterward. He was saying that the committee of fifteen brought this proposition forward for a specific object.

Mr. Doolittle. I said the committee of fifteen brought it forward because they had doubts as to the constitutional power of Congress to pass the civil rights bill.

Mr. Fessenden. Exactly: and I say, in reply, that if they had doubts, no such doubts were stated in the committee of fifteen, and the matter was not put on that ground at all. There was no question raised about the civil rights bill.

Mr. Doolittle. Then I put the question to the Senator: if there are no doubts, why amend the Constitution on that subject?

Mr. Fessenden. That question the Senator may answer to suit himself. It has no reference to the civil rights bill.

Mr. Doolittle. That does not meet the case at all. If my friend maintains that at this moment the Constitution of the United States, without amendment, gives all the power you ask, why do you put this new amendment into it on that subject?

Mr. Howard. If the Senator from Wisconsin wishes an answer, I will give him one such as I am able to give.

Mr. Doolittle. I was asking the Senator from Maine.

Mr. Howard. I was a member of the same committee, and the Senator's observations apply to me equally with the Senator from Maine. We desired to put this question of citizenship and the right of citizens and freedmen under the civil rights bill beyond the legislative power of such gentlemen as the Senator from Wisconsin, who would pull the whole system up by the roots and destroy it, and expose the freedmen again to the oppressions of their old masters.

The Slaughterhouse Cases, 1873

16 WALLACE 36 (1873)

[5-4: Miller, Hunt, Clifford, Strong, Davis;
Bradley, Field, Swayne, Chase]

[Justice Miller for the Court]. . . . This statute is denounced not only as creating a monopoly and conferring odious and exclusive privileges upon a small number of persons at the expense of the great body of the community of New Orleans, but it is asserted that it deprives a large and meritorious class of citizens—the whole of the butchers of the city—of the right to exercise their trade, the business to which they have been trained and on which they depend for the support of themselves and their families; and that the unrestricted exercise of the business of butchering is necessary to the daily subsistence of the population of the city.

But a critical examination of the act hardly justifies these assertions. . . .

It is . . . the slaughter-house privilege, which is mainly relied on to justify the charges of gross injustice to the public, and invasion of private right.

It is not, and cannot be successfully controverted, that it is both the right and the duty of the legislative body—the supreme power of the State or municipality—to prescribe and determine the localities where the business of slaughtering for a great city may be conducted. To do this effectively it is indispensable that all persons who slaughter animals for food shall do it in those places *and nowhere else.* . . .

The wisdom of the monopoly granted by the legislature may be open to question, but it is difficult to see a justification for the assertion that the butchers are deprived of the right to labor in their occupation, or the people of their daily service in preparing food, or how this statute, with the duties and guards imposed upon the company, can be said to destroy the business of the butcher, or seriously interfere with its pursuit.

The power here exercised by the legislature of Louisiana is, in its essential nature, one which has been, up to the present period in the constitutional history of this country, always conceded to belong to the States, however it may *now* be questioned in some of its details. . . .

This power is, and must be from its very nature, incapable of any very exact definition or limitation. Upon it depends the security of social order, the life and health of the citizen, the comfort of an existence in a thickly populated community, the enjoyment of private and social life, and the beneficial use of property. . . .

The regulation of the place and manner of conducting the slaughtering of animals, and the business of butchering within a city, and the inspection of the animals to be killed for meat, and of the meat afterwards, are among the most necessary and frequent exercises of this power. . . .

It cannot be denied that the statute under consideration is aptly framed to remove from the more densely populated part of the city, the noxious slaughter-houses, and large and offensive collections of animals necessarily incident to the slaughtering business of a large city, and to locate them where the convenience, health, and comfort of the people require they shall be located. And it must be conceded that the means adopted by the act for this purpose are appropriate, are stringent, and effectual. But it is said that in creating a corporation for this purpose, and conferring upon it exclusive privileges—privileges which it is said constitute a monopoly—the legislature has exceeded its power. If this statute had imposed on the city of New Orleans precisely the same duties, accompanied by the same privileges, which it has on the corporation which it created, it is believed that no question would have been raised as to its constitutionality. In that case the effect on the butchers in pursuit of their occupation and on the public would have been the same as it is now. Why cannot the legislature confer the same powers on another corporation, created for a lawful and useful public object, that it can on the municipal corporation already existing? That wherever a legislature has the right to accomplish a certain result, and that result is best attained by means of a corporation, it has the right to create such a corporation, and to endow it with the powers necessary to effect the desired and lawful purpose, seems hardly to admit of debate. The proposition is ably discussed and affirmed in the case of *McCulloch* v. *The State of Maryland*, in relation to the power of Congress to organize the Bank of the United States to aid in the fiscal operations of the government.

It can readily be seen that the interested vigilance of the corporation created by the Louisiana legislature will be more efficient in enforcing the limitation prescribed for the stock-landing and slaughtering business for the good of the city than the ordinary efforts of the officers of the law.

Unless, therefore, it can be maintained that the exclusive privilege granted by this charter to the corporation, is beyond the power of the legislature of Louisiana, there can be no just exception to the validity of the statute. And in this respect we are not able to see that these privileges are especially odious or objectionable. The duty imposed as a consideration for the privilege is well defined, and its enforcement well guarded. The prices or charges to be made by the company are limited by the statute, and we are not advised that they are on the whole exorbitant or unjust. . . .

It may, therefore, be considered as established, that the authority of the legislature of Louisiana to pass the present statute is ample, unless some restraint in the exercise of that power be found in the constitution of that State or in the amendments to the Constitution of the United States, adopted since the date of the decisions we have already cited.

If any such restraint is supposed to exist in the constitution of the State, the Supreme Court of Louisiana having necessarily passed on that question, it would not be open to review in this court.

The plaintiffs in error accepting this issue, allege that the statute is a violation of the Constitution of the United States in these several particulars:

That it creates an involuntary servitude forbidden by the thirteenth article of amendment;

That it abridges the privileges and immunities of citizens of the United States;

That it denies to the plaintiffs the equal protection of the laws; and,

That it deprives them of their property without due process of law; contrary to the provisions of the first section of the fourteenth article of amendment.

This court is thus called upon for the first time to give construction to these articles.

We do not conceal from ourselves the great responsibility which this duty devolves upon us. No questions so far-reaching and pervading in their consequences, so profoundly interesting to the people of this country, and so important in their bearing upon the relations of the United States, and of the several States to each other and to the citizens of the States and of the United States, have been before this court during the official life of any of its present members. We have given every opportunity for a full hearing at the bar; we have discussed it freely and compared views among ourselves; we have taken ample time for careful deliberation, and we now propose to announce the judgments which we have formed in the construction of those articles, so far as we have found them necessary to the decision of the cases before us, and beyond that we have neither the inclination nor the right to go.

Twelve articles of amendment were added to the Federal Constitution soon after the original organization of the government under it in 1789. Of these all but the last were adopted so soon afterwards as to justify the statement that they were practically contemporaneous with the adoption of the original; and the twelfth, adopted in eighteen hundred and three, was so nearly so as to have become, like all the others, historical and of another age. But within the last eight years three other articles of amendment of vast importance have been added by the voice of the people to that now venerable instrument.

The first section of the fourteenth article, to which our attention is more specially invited, opens with a definition of citizenship—not only citizenship of the United States, but citizenship of the States. No such definition was previously found in the Constitution, nor had any attempt been made to define it by act of Congress. It had been the occasion of much discussion in the courts, by the executive departments, and in the public journals. It had been said by eminent judges that no man was a citizen of the United States, except as he was a citizen of one of the States composing the Union. Those, therefore, who had been born and resided always in the District of Columbia or in the Territories, though within the United States, were not citizens. Whether this proposition was sound or not had never been judicially decided. But it had been held by this court, in the celebrated Dred Scott case, only a few years before the outbreak of the civil war, that a man of African descent, whether a slave or not, was not and could not be a citizen of a State or of the United States. This decision, while it met the condemnation of some of the ablest statesmen and constitutional lawyers of the country, had never been overruled; and if it was to be accepted as a constitutional limitation of the right of citizenship, then all the negro race who had recently been made freemen, were still, not only not citizens, but were incapable of becoming so by anything short of an amendment to the Constitution.

To remove this difficulty primarily, and to establish a clear and comprehensive definition of citizenship which should declare what should constitute citzenship of the United States, and also citizenship of a State, the first clause of the first section was framed.

"All persons born or naturalized in the United States, and subject to the jurisdiction thereof, are citizens of the United States and of the State wherein they reside."

The first observation we have to make on this clause is, that it puts at rest both the questions which we stated to have been the subject of differences of opinion. It declares that persons may be citizens of the United States without regard to their citizenship of a particular State, and it overturns the Dred Scott decision by making *all persons* born within the United States and subject to its jurisdiction citizens of the United States. That its main purpose was to establish the citizenship of the negro can admit of no doubt. The phrase, "subject to its jurisdiction" was intended to exclude from its operation children of ministers, consuls, and citizens or subjects of foreign States born within the United States.

The next observation is more important in view of the arguments of counsel in the present case. It is, that the distinction between citizenship of the United States and citizenship of a State is clearly recognized and established. Not only may a man be a citizen of the United States without being a citizen of a State, but an important element is necessary to convert the former into the latter. He must reside within the State to make him a citizen of it, but it is only necessary that he should be born or naturalized in the United States to be a citizen of the Union.

It is quite clear, then, that there is a citizenship of the United States, and a citizenship of a State, which are distinct from each other, and which depend upon different characteristics or circumstances in the individual.

We think this distinction and its explicit recognition in this amendment of great weight in this argument, because the next paragraph of this same section, which is the one mainly relied on by the plaintiffs in error, speaks only of privileges and immunities of citizens of the United States, and does not speak of those of citizens of the several States. The argument, however, in favor of the plaintiffs rests wholly on the assumption that the citizenship is the same, and the privileges and immunities guaranteed by the clause are the same.

The language is, "No State shall make or enforce any law which shall abridge the privileges or immunities of citizens of *the United States.*" It is a little remarkable, if this clause was intended as a protection to the citizen of a State against the legislative power of his own State, that the word citizen of the State should be left out when it is so carefully used, and used in contradistinction to citizens of the United States, in the very sentence which precedes it. It is too clear for argument that the change in phraseology was adopted understandingly and with a purpose.

Of the privileges and immunities of the citizen of the United States, and of the privileges and immunities of the citizen of the State, and what they respectively are, we will presently consider; but we wish to state here that it is only the former which are placed by this clause under the protection of the Federal Constitution, and that the latter, whatever they may be, are not intended to have any additional protection by this paragraph of the amendment.

If, then, there is a difference between the privileges and immunities belonging to a citizen of the United States as such, and those belonging to the citizen of the State as such, the latter must rest for their security and protection where they have heretofore rested; for they are not embraced by this paragraph of the amendment.

The first occurrence of the words "privileges and immunities" in our constitutional history, is to be found in the fourth of the articles of the old Confederation.

It declares "that the better to secure and perpetuate mutual friendship and intercourse among the people of the different States in this Union, the free inhabitants of each of these States, paupers, vagabonds, and fugitives from justice excepted, shall be entitled to all the privileges and immunities of free citizens in the several States; and the people of each State shall have free ingress and regress to and from any other State, and shall enjoy therein all the privileges of trade and commerce, subject to the same duties, impositions, and restrictions as the inhabitants thereof respectively."

In the Constitution of the United States, which superseded the Articles of Confederation, the corresponding provision is found in section two of the fourth article, in the following words: "The citizens of each State shall be entitled to all the privileges and immunities of citizens of the several States."

There can be but little question that the purpose of both these provisions is the same, and that the privileges and immunities intended are the same in each. In the article of the Confederation we have some of these specifically mentioned, and enough perhaps to give some general idea of the class of civil rights meant by the phrase.

Fortunately we are not without judicial construction of this clause of the Constitution. The first and the leading case on the subject is that of *Corfield* v. *Coryell,* decided by Mr. Justice Washington in the Circuit Court for the District of Pennsylvania in 1823.

"The inquiry," he says, "is, what are the privileges and immunities of citizens of the several States? We feel no hesitation in confining these expressions to those privileges and immunities which are *fundamental;* which belong of right to the citizens of all free governments, and which have at all times been enjoyed by citizens of the several States which compose this Union, from the time of their becoming free, independent, and sovereign. What these fundamental principles are, it would be more tedious than difficult to enumerate. They may all, however, be comprehended under the following general heads: protection by the government, with the right to acquire and possess property of every kind, and to pursue and obtain happiness and safety, subject, nevertheless, to such restraints as the government may prescribe for the general good of the whole."

This definition of the privileges and immunities of citizens of the States is adopted in the main by this court in the recent case of *Ward* v. *The State of Maryland,* while it declines to undertake an authoritative definition beyond what was necessary to that decision. The description, when taken to include others not named, but which are of the same general character, embraces nearly every civil right for the establishment and protection of which organized government is instituted. They are, in the language of Judge Washington, those rights which are fundamental. Throughout his opinion, they are spoken of as rights belonging to the individual as a citizen of a State.

They are so spoken of in the constitutional provision which he was construing. And they have always been held to be the class of rights which the State governments were created to establish and secure.

In the case of *Paul* v. *Virginia,* the court, in expounding this clause of the Constitution, says that "the privileges and immunities secured to citizens of each State in the several States, by the provision in question, are those privileges and immunities which are common to the citizens in the latter States under their constitution and laws by virtue of their being citizens."

The constitutional provision there alluded to did not create those rights, which it called privileges and immunities of citizens of the States. It threw around them in that clause no security for the citizen of the State in which they were claimed or exercised. Nor did it profess to control the power of the State governments over the rights of its own citizens.

Its sole purpose was to declare to the several States, that whatever those rights, as you grant or establish them to your own citizens, or as you limit or qualify, or impose restrictions on their exercise, the same, neither more nor less, shall be the measure of the rights of citizens of other States within your jurisdiction.

It would be the vainest show of learning to attempt to prove by citations of authority, that up to the adoption of the recent amendments, no claim or pretence was set up that those rights depended on the Federal government for their existence or protection, beyond the very few express limitations which the Federal Constitution imposed upon the States—such, for instance, as the prohibition against ex post facto laws, bills of attainder, and laws impairing the obligation of contracts. But with the exception of these and a few other restrictions, the entire domain of the privileges and immunities of citizens of the States, as above defined, lay within the constitutional and legislative power of the States, and without that of the Federal government. Was it the purpose of the fourteenth amendment, by the simple declaration that no State should make or enforce any law which shall abridge the privileges and immunities of *citizens of the United States,* to transfer the security and protection of all the civil rights which we have mentioned, from the States to the Federal government? And where it is declared that Congress shall have the power to enforce that article, was it intended to bring within the power of Congress the entire domain of civil rights heretofore belonging exclusively to the States?

All this and more must follow, if the proposition of the plaintiffs in error be sound. For not only are these rights subject to the control of Congress whenever in its discretion any of them are supposed to be abridged by State legislation, but that body may also pass laws in advance, limiting and restricting the exercise of legislative power by the States, in their most ordinary and usual functions, as in its judgment it may think proper on all such subjects. And still further, such a construction followed by the reversal of the judgments of the Supreme Court of Louisiana in these cases, would constitute this court a perpetual censor upon all legislation of the States, on the civil rights of their own citizens, with authority to nullify such as it did not approve as consistent with those rights, as they existed at the time of the adoption of this amendment. The argument we admit is not always the most conclusive which is drawn from the consequences urged against the adoption of a particular construction of an instrument. But when, as in the case before us, these consequences are so serious, so far-reaching and pervading, so great a departure from the structure and spirit of our institutions; when the effect is to fetter and degrade the State governments by subjecting them to the control of Congress, in the exercise of powers heretofore universally conceded to them of the most ordinary and fundamental character; when in fact it radically changes the whole theory of the relations of the State and Federal governments to each other and of both these governments to the people; the argument has a force that is irresistible, in the absence of language which expresses such a purpose too clearly to admit of doubt.

We are convinced that no such results were intended by the Congress which proposed these amendments, nor by the legislatures of the States which ratified them.

Having shown that the privileges and immunities relied on in the argument are those which belong to citizens of the States as such, and that they are left to the State governments for security and protection, and not by this article placed under the special care of the Federal government, we may hold ourselves excused from defining the privileges and immunities of citizens of the United States which no State can abridge, until some case involving those privileges may make it necessary to do so.

But lest it should be said that no such privileges and immunities are to be found if those we have been considering are excluded, we venture to suggest some which owe their existence to the Federal government, its National character, its Constitution, or its laws.

One of these is well described in the case of *Crandall* v. *Nevada.* It is said to be the right of the citizen of this great country, protected by implied guarantees of its Constitution, "to come to the seat of government to assert any claim he may have upon that government, to transact any business he may have with it, to seek its protection, to share its offices, to engage in administering its functions. He has the right of free access to its seaports, through which all operations of foreign commerce are conducted, to the subtreasuries, land offices, and courts of justice in the several States." . . .

Another privilege of a citizen of the United States is to demand the care and protection of the Federal government over his life, liberty, and property when on the high seas or within the jurisdiction of a foreign government. Of this there can be no doubt, nor that the right depends upon his character as a citizen of the United States. The right to peaceably assemble and petition for redress of grievances, the privilege of the writ of *habeas corpus,* are rights of the citizen guaranteed by the Federal Constitution. The right to use the navigable waters of the United States, however they may penetrate the territory of the several States, all rights secured to our citizens by treaties with foreign nations, are dependent upon citizenship of the United States, and not citizenship of a State. One of these privileges is conferred by the very article under consideration. It is that a citizen of the United States can, of his own volition, become a citizen of any State of the Union by a *bonâ fide* residence therein, with the same rights as other citizens of that State. To these may be added the rights secured by the thirteenth and fifteenth articles of amendment, and by the other clause of the fourteenth, next to be considered.

But it is useless to pursue this branch of the inquiry, since we are of opinion that the rights claimed by these plaintiffs in error, if they have any existence, are not privileges and immunities of citizens of the United States within the meaning of the clause of the fourteenth amendment under consideration.

"All persons born or naturalized in the United States, and subject to the jurisdiction thereof, are citizens of the United States and of the State wherein they reside. No State shall make or enforce any law which shall abridge the privileges or immunities of citizens of the United States; nor shall any State deprive any person of life, liberty, or property without due process of law, nor deny to any person within its jurisdiction the equal protection of its laws."

The argument has not been much pressed in these cases that the defendant's charter deprives the plaintiffs of their property without due process of law, or that it denies to them the equal protection of the law. The first of these paragraphs has been in the Constitution since the adoption of the fifth amendment, as a restraint upon the Federal power. It is also to be found in some form of expression in the constitutions of nearly all the States, as a restraint upon the power of the States. This law, then, has practically been the same as it now is during the existence of the government, except so far as the present amendment may place the restraining power over the States in this matter in the hands of the Federal government.

We are not without judicial interpretation, therefore, both State and National, of the meaning of this clause. And it is sufficient to say that under no construction of that provision that we have ever seen, or any that we deem admissible, can the restraint imposed by the State of Louisiana upon the exercise of their trade by the butchers of New Orleans be held to be a deprivation of property within the meaning of that provision.

"Nor shall any State deny to any person within its jurisdiction the equal protection of the laws."

In the light of the history of these amendments, and the pervading purpose of them, which we have already discussed, it is not difficult to give a meaning to this clause. The existence of laws in the States where the newly emancipated negroes resided, which discriminated with gross injustice and hardship against them as a class, was the evil to be remedied by this clause, and by it such laws are forbidden.

If, however, the States did not conform their laws to its requirements, then by the fifth section of the article of amendment Congress was authorized to enforce it by suitable legislation. We doubt very much whether any action of a State not directed by way of discrimination against the negroes as a class, or on account of their race, will ever be held to come within the purview of this provision. It is so clearly a provision for that race and that emergency, that a strong case would be necessary for its application to any other. But as it is a State that is to be dealt with, and not alone the validity of its laws, we may safely leave that matter until Congress shall have exercised its power, or some case of State oppression, by denial of equal justice in its courts, shall have claimed a decision, at our hands. We find no such case in the one before us, and do not deem it necessary to go over the argument again, as it may have relation to this particular clause of the amendment.

In the early history of the organization of the government, its statesmen seem to have divided on the line which should separate the powers of the National government from those of the State governments, and though this line has never been very well defined in public opinion, such a division has continued from that day to this.

The adoption of the first eleven amendments to the Constitution so soon after the original instrument was accepted, shows a prevailing sense of danger at that time from the Federal power. And it cannot be denied that such a jealousy continued to exist with many patriotic men until the breaking out of the late civil war. It was then discovered that the true danger to the perpetuity of the Union was in the capacity of the State organizations to combine and concentrate all the powers of the State, and of contiguous States, for a determined resistance to the General Government.

Unquestionably this has given great force to the argument, and added largely to the number of those who believe in the necessity of a strong National government.

But, however pervading this sentiment, and however it may have contributed to the adoption of the amendments we have been considering, we do not see in those amendments any purpose to destroy the main features of the general system. Under the pressure of all the excited feeling growing out of the war, our statesmen have still believed that the existence of the States with powers for domestic and local government, including the regulation of civil rights—the rights of person and of property—was essential to the perfect working of our complex form of government, though they have thought proper to impose additional limitations on the States, and to confer additional power on that of the Nation.

But whatever fluctuations may be seen in the history of public opinion on this subject during the period of our national existence, we think it will be found that this court, so far as its functions required, has always held with a steady and an even hand the balance between State and Federal power, and we trust that such may continue to be the history of its relation to that subject so long as it shall have duties to perform which demand of it a construction of the Constitution, or of any of its parts.

The judgments of the Supreme Court of Louisiana in these cases are affirmed.

Mr. Justice Field, dissenting: I am unable to agree with the majority of the court in these cases . . . .

The act of Louisiana presents the naked case, unaccompanied by any public considerations, where a right to pursue a lawful and necessary calling, previously enjoyed by every citizen, and in connection with which a thousand persons were daily employed, is taken away and vested exclusively for twenty-five years, for an extensive district and a large population, in a single corporation, or its exercise is for that period restricted to the establishments of the corporation, and there allowed only upon onerous conditions.

If exclusive privileges of this character can be granted to a corporation of seventeen persons, they may, in the discretion of the legislature, be equally granted to a single individual. If they may be granted for twenty-five years they may be equally granted for a century, and in perpetuity. If they may be granted for the landing and keeping of animals intended for sale or slaughter they may be equally granted for the landing and storing of grain and other products of the earth, or for any article of commerce. If they may be granted for structures in which animal food is prepared for market they may be equally granted for structures in which farinaceous or vegetable food is prepared. They may be granted for any of the pursuits of human industry, even in its most simple and common forms. Indeed, upon the theory on which the exclusive privileges granted by the act in question are sustained, there is no monopoly, in the most odious form, which may not be upheld.

The question presented is, therefore, one of the gravest importance, not merely to the parties here, but to the whole country. It is nothing less than the question whether the recent amendments to the Federal Constitution protect the citizens of the United States against the deprivation of their common rights by State legislation. In my judgment the fourteenth amendment does afford such protection, and was so intended by the Congress which framed and the States which adopted it. . . .

It is not necessary, in my judgment, for the disposition of the present case in favor of the plaintiffs in error, to accept as entirely correct this conclusion of counsel. It, however, finds support in the act of Congress known as the Civil Rights Act, which was framed and adopted upon a construction of the thirteenth amendment, giving to its language a similar breadth. That amendment was ratified on the eighteenth of December, 1865, and in April of the following year the Civil Rights Act was passed. Its first section declares that all persons born in the United States, and not subject to any foreign power, excluding Indians not taxed, are "citizens of the United States," and that "such citizens, of every race and color, without regard to any previous condition of slavery, or involuntary servitude, except as a punishment for crime, whereof the party shall have been duly convicted, shall have the same right in every State and Territory in the United States, to make and enforce contracts, to sue, be parties, and give evidence, to inherit, purchase, lease, sell, hold, and convey real and personal property, and to full and equal benefit of all laws and proceedings for the security of person and property, as enjoyed by white citizens."

This legislation was supported upon the theory that citizens of the United States as such were entitled to the rights and privileges enumerated, and that to deny to any such citizen equality in these rights and privileges with others, was, to the extent of the denial, subjecting him to an involuntary servitude.

The first clause of the fourteenth amendment changes this whole subject, and removes it from the region of discussion and doubt. It recognizes in express terms, if it does not create, citizens of the United States, and it makes their citizenship dependent upon the place of their birth, or the fact of their adoption, and not upon the constitution or laws of any State or the condition of their ancestry. A citizen of a State is now only a citizen of the United States residing in that State. The fundamental rights, privileges, and immunities which belong to him as a free man and a free citizen, now belong to him as a citizen of the United States, and are not dependent upon his citizenship of any State. The exercise of these rights and privileges, and the degree of enjoyment received from such exercise, are always more or less affected by the condition and the local institutions of the State, or city, or town where he resides. They are thus affected in a State by the wisdom of its laws, the ability of its officers, the efficiency of its magistrates, the education and morals of its people, and by many other considerations. This is a result which follows from the constitution of society, and can never be avoided, but in no other way can they be affected by the action of the State, or by the residence of the citizen therein. They do not derive their existence from its legislation, and cannot be destroyed by its power.

The amendment does not attempt to confer any new privileges or immunities upon citizens, or to enumerate or define those already existing. It assumes that there are such privileges and immunities which belong of right to citizens as such, and ordains that they shall not be abridged by State legislation. If this inhibition has no reference to privileges and immunities of this character, but only refers, as held by the majority of the court in their opinion, to such privileges and immunities as were before its adoption specially designated in the Constitution or necessarily implied as belonging to citizens of the United States, it was a vain and idle enactment, which accomplished nothing, and most unnecessarily excited Congress and the people on its passage. With privileges and immunities thus designated or implied no State could ever have interfered by its laws, and no new constitutional provision was required to inhibit such interference. The supremacy of the Constitution and the laws of the United States always controlled any State legislation of that character. But if the amendment refers to the natural and inalienable rights which belong to all citizens, the inhibition has a profound significance and consequence.

What, then, are the privileges and immunities which are secured against abridgment by State legislation?

In the first section of the Civil Rights Act Congress has given its interpretation to these terms, or at least has stated some of the rights which, in its judgment, these terms include; it has there declared that they include the right "to make and enforce contracts, to sue, be parties and give evidence, to inherit, purchase, lease, sell, hold, and convey real and personal property, and to full and equal benefit of all laws and proceedings for the security of person and property." That act, it is true, was passed before the fourteenth amendment, but the amendment was adopted, as I have already said, to obviate objections to the act, or, speaking more accurately, I should say, to obviate objections to legislation of a similar character, extending the protection of the National government over the common rights of all citizens of the United States. Accordingly, after its ratification, Congress re-enacted the act under the belief that whatever doubts may have previously existed of its validity, they were removed by the amendment.

The terms, privileges and immunities, are not new in the amendment; they were in the Constitution before the amendment was adopted. They are found in the second section of the fourth article, which declares that "the citizens of each State shall be entitled to all privileges and immunities of citizens in the several States," and they have been the subject of frequent consideration in judicial decisions. In *Corfield* v. *Coryell,* Mr. Justice Washington said he had "no hesitation in confining these expressions to those privileges and immunities which were, in their nature, fundamental; which belong of right to citizens of all free governments, and which have at all times been enjoyed by the citizens of the several States which compose the Union, from the time of their becoming free, independent, and sovereign"; and, in considering what those fundamental privileges were, he said that perhaps it would be more tedious than difficult to enumerate them, but that they might be "all comprehended under the following general heads: protection by the government; the enjoyment of life and liberty, with the right to acquire and possess property of every kind, and to pursue and obtain happiness and safety, subject, nevertheless, to such restraints as the government may justly prescribe for the general good of the whole." This appears to me to be a sound construction of the clause in question. The privileges and immunities designated are those *which of right belong to the citizens of all free governments.* Clearly among these must be placed the right to pursue a lawful employment in a lawful manner, without other restraint than such as equally affects all persons. In the discussions in Congress upon the passage of the Civil Rights Act repeated reference was made to this language of Mr. Justice Washington. It was cited by Senator Trumbull with the observation that it enumerated the very rights belonging to a citizen of the United States set forth in the first section of the act, and with the statement that all persons born in the United States, being declared by the act citizens of the United States, would thenceforth be entitled to the rights of citizens, and that these were the great fundamental rights set forth in the act; and that they were set forth "as appertaining to every freeman."

The privileges and immunities designated in the second section of the fourth article of the Constitution are, then, according to the decision cited, those which of right belong to the citizens of all free governments, and they can be enjoyed under that clause by the citizens of each State in the several States upon the same terms and conditions as they are enjoyed by the citizens of the latter States. No discrimination can be made by one State against the citizens of other States in their enjoyment, nor can any greater imposition be levied than such as is laid upon its own citizens. It is a clause which insures equality in the enjoyment of these rights between citizens of the several States whilst in the same State. . . .

What the clause in question did for the protection of the citizens of one State against hostile and discriminating legislation of other States, the fourteenth amendment does for the protection of every citizen of the United States against hostile and discriminating legislation against him in favor of others, whether they reside in the same or in different States. If under the fourth article of the Constitution equality of privileges and immunities is secured between citizens of different States, under the fourteenth amendment the same equality is secured between citizens of the United States. . . .

This equality of right, with exemption from all disparaging and partial enactments, in the lawful pursuits of life, throughout the whole country, is the distinguishing privilege of citizens of the United States. To them, everywhere, all pursuits, all professions, all avocations are open without other restrictions than such as are imposed equally upon all others of the same age, sex, and condition. The State may prescribe such regulations for every pursuit and calling of life as will promote the public health, secure the good order and advance the general prosperity of society, but when once prescribed, the pursuit or calling must be free to be followed by every citizen who is within the conditions designated, and will conform to the regulations. This is the fundamental idea upon which our institutions rest, and unless adhered to in the legislation of the country our government will be a republic only in name. The fourteenth amendment, in my judgment, makes it essential to the validity of the legislation of every State that this equality of right should be respected. How widely this equality has been departed from, how entirely rejected and trampled upon by the act of Louisiana, I have already shown. And it is to me a matter of profound regret that its validity is recognized by a majority of this court, for by it the right of free labor, one of the most sacred and imprescriptible rights of man, is violated. . . .

I am authorized by the Chief Justice, Mr. Justice Swayne, and Mr. Justice Bradley, to state that they concur with me in this dissenting opinion.

Mr. Justice Bradley, also dissenting.   I concur in the opinion which has just been read by Mr. Justice Field; but desire to add a few observations for the purpose of more fully illustrating my views on the important question decided in these cases . . . .

First. Is it one of the rights and privileges of a citizen of the United States to pursue such civil employment as he may choose to adopt, subject to such reasonable regulations as may be prescribed by law?

Secondly. Is a monopoly, or exclusive right, given to one person to the exclusion of all others, to keep slaughter-houses, in a district of nearly twelve hundred square miles, for the supply of meat for a large city, a reasonable regulation of that employment which the legislature has a right to impose?

The first of these questions is one of vast importance, and lies at the very foundations of our government. The question is now settled by the fourteenth amendment itself, that citizenship of the United States is the primary citizenship in this country; and that State citizenship is secondary and derivative, depending upon citizenship of the United States and the citizen's place of residence. The States have not now, if they ever had, any power to restrict their citizenship to any classes or persons. A citizen of the

United States has a perfect constitutional right to go to and reside in any State he chooses, and to claim citizenship therein, and an equality of rights with every other citizen; and the whole power of the nation is pledged to sustain him in that right. He is not bound to cringe to any superior, or to pray for any act of grace, as a means of enjoying all the rights and privileges enjoyed by other citizens. And when the spirit of lawlessness, mob violence, and sectional hate can be so completely repressed as to give full practical effect to this right, we shall be a happier nation, and a more prosperous one than we now are. Citizenship of the United States ought to be, and, according to the Constitution, is, a sure and undoubted title to equal rights in any and every State in this Union, subject to such regulations as the legislature may rightfully prescribe. If a man be denied full equality before the law, he is denied one of the essential rights of citizenship as a citizen of the United States. . . .

The right of a State to regulate the conduct of its citizens is undoubtedly a very broad and extensive one, and not to be lightly restricted. But there are certain fundamental rights which this right of regulation cannot infringe. It may prescribe the manner of their exercise, but it cannot subvert the rights themselves. I speak now of the rights of citizens of any free government. Granting for the present that the citizens of one government cannot claim the privileges of citizens in another government; that prior to the union of our North American States the citizens of one State could not claim the privileges of citizens in another State; or, that after the union was formed the citizens of the United States, as such, could not claim the privileges of citizens in any particular State; yet the citizens of each of the States and the citizens of the United States would be entitled to certain privileges and immunities as citizens, at the hands of their own government—privileges and immunities which their own governments respectively would be bound to respect and maintain. In this free country, the people of which inherited certain traditionary rights and privileges from their ancestors, citizenship means something. It has certain privileges and immunities attached to it which the government, whether restricted by express or implied limitations, cannot take away or impair. It may do so temporarily by force, but it cannot do so by right. And thes privileges and immunities attach as well to citizenship of the United States as to citizenship of the States. . . .

The privileges and immunities of Englishmen were established and secured by long usage and by various acts of Parliament. But it may be said that the Parliament of England has unlimited authority, and might repeal the laws which have from time to time been enacted. Theoretically this is so, but practically it is not. England has no written constitution, it is true; but it has an unwritten one, resting in the acknowledged, and frequently declared, privileges of Parliament and the people, to violate which in any material respect would produce a revolution in an hour. A violation of one of the fundamental principles of that constitution in the Colonies, namely, the principle that recognizes the property of the people as their own, and which, therefore, regards all taxes for the support of government as gifts of the people through their representatives, and regards taxation without representation as subversive of free government, was the origin of our own revolution.

This, it is true, was the violation of a political right; but personal rights were deemed equally sacred, and were claimed by the very first Congress of the Colonies, assembled in 1774, as the undoubted inheritance of the people of this country; and the Declaration of Independence, which was the first political act of the American people in their independent sovereign capacity, lays the foundation of our National existence upon this broad proposition: "That all men are created equal; that they are endowed by their Creator with certain inalienable rights; that among these are life, liberty, and the pursuit of happiness." Here again we have the great threefold division of the rights of freemen, asserted as the rights of man. Rights to life, liberty, and the pursuit of happiness are equivalent to the rights of life, liberty, and property. These are the fundamental rights which can only be taken away by due process of law, and which can only be interfered with, or the enjoyment of which can only be modified, by lawful regulations necessary or proper for the mutual good of all; and these rights, I contend, belong to the citizens of every free government.

For the preservation, exercise, and enjoyment of these rights the individual citizen, as a necessity, must be left free to adopt such calling, profession, or trade as may seem to him most conducive to that end. Without this right he cannot be a freeman. This right to choose one's calling is an essential part of that liberty which it is the object of government to protect; and a calling, when chosen, is a man's property and right. Liberty and property are not protected where these rights are arbitrarily assailed.

I think sufficient has been said to show that citizenship is not an empty name, but that, in this country at least, it has connected with it certain incidental rights, privileges, and immunities of the greatest importance. And to say that these rights and immunities attach only to State citizenship, and not to citizenship of the United States, appears to me to evince a very narrow and insufficient estimate of constitutional history and the rights of men, not to say the rights of the American people.

On this point the often-quoted language of Mr. Justice Washington, in *Corfield* v. *Coryell,* is very instructive. Being called upon to expound that clause in the fourth article of the Constitution, which declares that "the citizens of each State shall be entitled to all the privileges and immunities of citizens in the several States," he says: "The inquiry is, what are the privileges and immunities of citizens in the several States? We feel no hesitation in confining these expressions to those privileges and immunities which are, in their nature, *fundamental*; which belong, of right, to the citizens of all free governments, and which have at all times been enjoyed by the citizens of the several States which compose this Union from the time of their becoming free, independent, and sovereign. What these fundamental privileges are it would perhaps be more tedious than difficult to enumerate. They may, however, be all comprehended under the following general heads: Protection by the government; the enjoyment of life and liberty, with the right to acquire and possess property of every kind, and to pursue and obtain happiness and safety, subject, nevertheless, to such restraints as the government may justly prescribe for the general good of the whole; the right of a citizen of one State to pass through, or to reside in, any other State for purposes of trade, agriculture, professional pursuits, or otherwise; to claim the benefit of the writ of *habeas corpus*; to institute and maintain actions of any kind in the courts of the State; to take, hold, and dispose of property, either real or personal; and an exemption from higher taxes or impositions than are paid by the other citizens of the State, may be mentioned as some of the particular privileges and immunities of citizens which are clearly embraced by the general description of privileges deemed to be fundamental."

It is pertinent to observe that both the clause of the Constitution referred to, and Justice Washington in his comment on it, speak of the privileges and immunities of citizens *in* a State; not of citizens *of* a State. It is the privileges and immunities of citizens, that is, of citizens as such, that are to be accorded to citizens of other States when they are found in any State; or, as Justice Washington says, "privileges and immunities which are, in their nature, fundamental; which belong, of right, to the citizens of all free governments."

It is true the courts have usually regarded the clause referred to as securing only an equality of privileges with the citizens of the State in which the parties are found. Equality before the law is undoubtedly one of the privileges and immunities of every citizen. I am not aware that any case has arisen in which it became necessary to vindicate any other fundamental privilege of citizenship; although rights have been claimed which were not deemed fundamental, and have been rejected as not within the protection of this clause. Be this, however, as it may, the language of the clause is as I have stated it, and seems fairly susceptible of a broader interpretation than that which makes it a guarantee of mere equality of privileges with other citizens.

But we are not bound to resort to implication, or to the constitutional history of England, to find an authoritative declaration of some of the most important privileges and immunities of citizens of the United States. It is in the Constitution itself. The Constitution, it is true, as it stood prior to the recent amendments, specifies, in terms, only a few of the personal privileges and immunities of citizens, but they are very comprehensive in their character. The States were merely prohibited from passing bills of attainder, *ex post facto* laws, laws impairing the obligation of contracts, and perhaps one or two more. But others of the greatest consequence were enumerated, although they were only secured, in express terms, from invasion by the Federal government; such as the right of *habeas corpus,* the right of trial by jury, or free exercise of religious worship, the right of free speech and a free press, the right peaceably to assemble for the discussion of public measures, the right to be secure against unreasonable searches and seizures, and above all, and including almost all the rest, the right of *not being deprived of life, liberty, or property, without due process of law.* These, and still others are specified in the original Constitution, or in the early amendments of it, as among the privileges and immunities of citizens of the United States, or, what is still stronger for the force of the argument, the rights of all persons, whether citizens or not.

But even if the Constitution were silent, the fundamental privileges and immunities of citizens, as such, would be no less real and no less inviolable than they now are. It was not necessary to say in words that the citizens of the United States should have and exercise all the privileges of citizens; the privilege of buying, selling, and enjoying property; the privilege of engaging in any lawful employment for a livelihood; the privilege of resorting to the laws for redress of injuries, and the like. Their very citizenship conferred these privileges, if they did not possess them before. And these privileges they would enjoy whether they were citizens of any State or not. Inhabitants of Federal territories and new citizens, made such by annexation of territory or naturalization, though without any status as citizens of a State, could, nevertheless, as citizens of the United States, lay claim to every one of the privileges and immunities which have been enumerated; and among these none is more essential and fundamental than the right to follow such profession or employment as each one may choose, subject only to uniform regulations equally applicable to all.

II. The next question to be determined in this case is: Is a monopoly or exclusive right, given to one person, or corporation, to the exclusion of all others, to keep slaughter-houses in a district of nearly twelve hundred square miles, for the supply of meat for a great city, a reasonable regulation of that employment which the legislature has a right to impose?

The keeping of a slaughter-house is part of, and incidental to, the trade of a butcher—one of the ordinary occupations of human life. To compel a butcher, or rather all the butchers of a large city and an extensive district, to slaughter their cattle in another person's slaughter-house and pay him a toll therefor, is such a restriction upon the trade as materially to interfere with its prosecution. It is onerous, unreasonable, arbitrary, and unjust. It has none of the qualities of a police regulation. If it were really a police regulation, it would undoubtedly be within the power of the legislature. That portion of the act which requires all slaughter-houses to be located below the city, and to be subject to inspection, &c., is clearly a police regulation. That portion which allows no one but the favored company to build, own, or have slaughter-houses is not a police regulation, and has not the faintest semblance of one. It is one of those arbitrary and unjust laws made in the interest of a few scheming individuals, by which some of the Southern States have, within the past few years, been so deplorably oppressed and impoverished. It seems to me strange that it can be viewed in any other light.

The granting of monopolies, or exclusive privileges to individuals or corporations, is an invasion of the right of others to choose a lawful calling, and an infringement of personal liberty. . . .

In my view, a law which prohibits a large class of citizens from adopting a lawful employment, or from following a lawful employment previously adopted, does deprive them of liberty as well as property, without due process of law. Their right of choice is a portion of their liberty; their occupation is their property. Such a law also deprives those citizens of the equal protection of the laws, contrary to the last clause of the section.

The constitutional question is distinctly raised in these cases; the constitutional right is expressly claimed; it was violated by State law, which was sustained by the State court, and we are called upon in a legitimate and proper way to afford redress. Our jurisdiction and our duty are plain and imperative.

It is futile to argue that none but the persons of the African race are intended to be benefited by this amendment. They may have been the primary cause of the amendment, but its language is general, embracing all citizens, and I think it was purposely so expressed.

The mischief to be remedied was not merely slavery and its incidents and consequences; but that spirit of insubordination and disloyalty to the National government which had troubled the country for so many years in some of the States, and that intolerance of free speech and free discussion which often rendered life and property insecure, and led to much unequal legislation. The amendment was an attempt to give voice to the strong National yearning for that time and that condition of things, in which American citizenship should be a sure guarantee of safety, and in which every citizen of the United States might stand erect on every portion of its soil, in the full enjoyment of every right and privilege belonging to a freeman, without fear of violence or molestation.

But great fears are expressed that this construction of the amendment will lead to enactments by Congress interfering with the internal affairs of the States, and establishing therein civil and criminal codes of law for the government of the citizens, and thus abolishing the State governments in everything but name; or else, that it will lead the Federal courts to draw to their cognizance the supervision of State tribunals on every subject of judicial inquiry, on the plea of ascertaining whether the privileges and immunities of citizens have not been abridged.

In my judgment no such practical inconveniences would arise. Very little, if any, legislation on the part of Congress would be required to carry the amendment into effect. Like the prohibition against passing a law impairing the obligation of a contract, it would execute itself. The point would be regularly raised, in a suit at law, and settled by final reference to the Federal court. As the privileges and immunities protected are only those fundamental ones which belong to every citizen, they would soon become so far defined as to cause but a slight accumulation of business in the Federal courts. Besides, the recognized existence of the law would prevent its frequent violation. But even if the business of the National courts should be increased, Congress could easily supply the remedy by increasing their number and efficiency. The great question is, What is the true construction of the amendment? When once we find that, we shall find the means of giving it effect. The argument from inconvenience ought not to have a very controlling influence in questions of this sort. The National will and National interest are of far greater importance.

In my opinion the judgment of the Supreme Court of Louisiana ought to be reversed.

The *Civil Rights Cases*, 1883

109 U.S. 3 (1883)

[8-1: Bradley, Waite, Gray, Woods, Miller, Blatchford, Matthews, Field; Harlan]

Justice Bradley Delivered the Opinion of the Court. The first section of the Fourteenth Amendment (which is the one relied on), after declaring who shall be citizens of the United States, and of the several States, is prohibitory in its character, and prohibitory upon the States. It declares that:

> "No State shall make or enforce any law which shall abridge the privileges or immunities of citizens of the United States; nor shall any State deprive any person of life, liberty, or property without due process of law; nor deny to any person within its jurisdiction the equal protection of the laws."

It is State action of a particular character that is prohibited. Individual invasion of individual rights is not the subject-matter of the amendment. It has a deeper and broader scope. It nullifies and makes void all State legislation, and State action of every kind, which impairs the privileges and immunities of citizens of the United States, or which injures them in life, liberty or property without due process of law, or which denies to any of them the equal protection of the laws. It not only does this, but, in order that the national will, thus declared, may not be a mere *brutum fulmen,* the last section of the amendment invests Congress with power to enforce it by appropriate legislation. To enforce what? To enforce the prohibition. To adopt appropriate legislation for correcting the effects of such prohibited State laws and State acts, and thus to render them effectually null, void, and innocuous. This is the legislative power conferred upon Congress, and this is the whole of it. It does not invest Congress with power to legislate upon subjects which are within the domain of State legislation; but to provide modes of relief against State legislation, or State action, of the kind referred to. It does not authorize Congress to create a code of municipal law for the regulation of private rights; but to provide modes of redress against the operation of State laws, and the action of State officers executive or judicial, when these are subversive of the fundamental rights specified in the amendment. Positive rights and privileges are undoubtedly secured by the Fourteenth Amendment; but they are secured by way of prohibition against State laws and State proceedings affecting those rights and privileges, and by power given to Congress to legislate for the purpose of carrying such prohibition into effect: and such legislation must necessarily be predicated upon such supposed State laws or State proceedings, and be directed to the correction of their operation and effect. . . .

And so in the present case, until some State law has been passed, or some State action through its officers or agents has been taken, adverse to the rights of citizens sought to be protected by the Fourteenth Amendment, no legislation of the United States under said amendment, nor any proceeding under such legislation, can be called into activity: for the prohibitions of the amendment are against State laws and acts done under State authority. Of course, legislation may, and should be, provided in advance to meet the exigency when it arises; but it should be adapted to the mischief and wrong which the amendment was intended to provide against; and that is, State laws, or State action of some kind, adverse to the rights of the citizen secured by the amendment. Such legislation cannot properly cover the whole domain of rights appertaining to life, liberty and property, defining them and providing for their vindication. That would be to establish a code of municipal law regulative of all private rights between man and man in society. It would be to make Congress take the place of the State legislatures and to supersede them. . . .

If this legislation is appropriate for enforcing the prohibitions of the amendment, it is difficult to see where it is to stop. Why may not Congress with equal show of authority enact a code of laws for the enforcement and vindication of all rights of life, liberty, and property? If it is supposable that the States may deprive persons of life, liberty, and property without due process of law (and the amendment itself does suppose this), why should not Congress proceed at once to prescribe due process of law for the protection of every one of these fundamental rights, in every possible case, as well as to prescribe equal privileges in inns, public conveyances, and theatres? The truth is, that the implication of a power to legislate in this manner is based upon the assumption that if the States are forbidden to legislate or act in a particular way on a particular subject, and power is conferred upon Congress to enforce the prohibition, this gives Congress power to legislate generally upon that subject, and not merely power to provide modes of redress against such State legislation or action. The assumption is certainly unsound. It is repugnant to the Tenth Amendment of the Constitution, which declares that powers not delegated to the United States by the Constitution, nor prohibited by it to the States, are reserved to the States respectively or to the people. . . .

In this connection it is proper to state that civil rights, such as are guaranteed by the Constitution against State aggression, cannot be impaired by the wrongful acts of individuals, unsupported by State authority in the shape of laws, customs, or judicial or executive proceedings. The wrongful act of an individual, unsupported by any such authority, is simply a private wrong, or a crime of that individual; an invasion of the rights of the injured party, it is true, whether they affect his person, his property, or his reputation; but if not sanctioned in some way by the State, or not done under State authority, his rights remain in full force, and may presumably be vindicated by resort to the laws of the State for redress. An individual cannot deprive a man of his right to vote, to hold property, to buy and sell, to sue in the courts, or to be a witness or a juror; he may, by force or fraud, interfere with the enjoyment of the right in a particular case; he may commit an assault against the person, or commit murder, or use ruffian violence at the polls, or slander the good name of a fellow citizen; but, unless protected in these wrongful acts by some shield of State law or State authority, he cannot destroy or injure the right; he will only render himself amenable to satisfaction or punishment; and amenable therefor to the laws of the State where the wrongful acts are committed. Hence, in all those cases where the Constitution seeks to protect the rights of the citizen against discriminative and unjust laws of the State by prohibiting such laws, it is not individual offences, but abrogation and denial of rights, which it denounces, and for which it clothes the Congress with power to provide a remedy. This abrogation and denial of rights, for which the States alone were or could be responsible, was the great seminal and fundamental wrong which was intended to be remedied. And the remedy to be provided must necessarily be predicated upon that wrong. It must assume that in the cases provided for, the evil or wrong actually committed rests upon some State law or State authority for its excuse and perpetration. . . .

It may be that by the Black Code (as it was called), in the times when slavery prevailed, the proprietors of inns and public conveyances were forbidden to receive persons of the African race, because it might assist slaves to escape from the control of their masters. This was merely a means of preventing such escapes, and was no part of the servitude itself. A law of that kind could not have any such object now, however justly it might be deemed an invasion of the party's legal right as a citizen, and amenable to the prohibitions of the Fourth Amendment.

The long existence of African slavery in this country gave us very distinct notions of what it was, and what were its necessary incidents. Compulsory service of the slave for the benefit of the master, restraint of his movements except by the master's will, disability to hold property, to make contracts, to have a standing in court, to be a witness against a white person, and such like burdens and incapacities, were the inseparable incidents of the institution. Severer punishments for crimes were imposed on the slave than on free persons guilty of the same offences. Congress, as we have seen, by the Civil Rights Bill of 1866, passed in view of the Thirteenth Amendment, before the Fourteenth was adopted, undertook to wipe out these burdens and disabilities, the necessary incidents of slavery, constituting its substance and visible form; and to secure to all citizens of every race and color, and without regard to previous servitude, those fundamental rights which are the essence of civil freedom, namely, the same right to make and enforce contracts, to sue, be parties, give evidence, and to inherit, purchase, lease, sell and convey property, as is enjoyed by white citizens. Whether this legislation was fully authorized by the Thirteenth Amendment alone, without the support which it afterward received from the Fourteenth Amendment, after the adoption of which it was re-enacted with some additions, it is not necessary to inquire. It is referred to for the purpose of showing that at that time (in 1866) Congress did not assume, under the authority given by the Thirteenth Amendment, to adjust what may be called the social rights of men and races in the community; but only to declare and vindicate those fundamental rights which appertain to the essence of citizenship, and the enjoyment or deprivation of which constitutes the essential distinction between freedom and slavery. . . .

When a man has emerged from slavery, and by the aid of beneficent legislation has shaken off the inseparable concomitants of that state, there must be some stage in the progress of his elevation when he takes the rank of a mere citizen, and ceases to be the special favorite of the laws, and when his rights as a citizen, or a man, are to be protected in the ordinary modes by which other men's rights are protected. There were thousands of free colored people in this country before the abolition of slavery, enjoying all the essential rights of life, liberty and property the same as white citizens; yet no one, at that time, thought that it was any invasion of his personal status as a freeman because he was not admitted to all the privileges enjoyed by white citizens, or because he was subjected to discriminations in the enjoyment of accommodations in inns, public conveyances and places of amusement. Mere discriminations on account of race or color were not regarded as badges of slavery. If, since that time, the enjoyment of equal rights in all these respects has become established by constitutional enactment, it is not by force of the Thirteenth Amendment (which merely abolishes slavery), but by force of the Thirteenth and Fifteenth Amendments.

On the whole we are of opinion, that no countenance of authority for the passage of the law in question can be found in either the Thirteenth or Fourteenth Amendment of the Constitution; and no other ground of authority for its passage being suggested, it must necessarily be declared void, at least so far as its operation in the several States is concerned. . . .

Justice Harlan Dissenting.   The opinion in these cases proceeds, it seems to me, upon grounds entirely too narrow and artificial. I cannot resist the conclusion that the substance and spirit of the recent amendments of the Constitution have been sacrificed by a subtle and ingenious verbal criticism. "It is not the words of the law but the internal sense of it that makes the law: the letter of the law is the body; the sense and reason of the law is the soul." Constitutional provisions, adopted in the interest of liberty, and for the purpose of securing, through national legislation, if need be, rights inhering in a state of freedom, and belonging to American citizenship, have been so construed as to defeat the ends the people desired to accomplish, which they attempted to accomplish, and which they supposed they had accomplished by changes in their fundamental law. By this I do not mean that the determination of these cases should have been materially controlled by considerations of mere expediency or policy. I mean only, in this form, to express an earnest conviction that the court has departed from the familiar rule requiring, in the interpretation of constitutional provisions, that full effect be given to the intent with which they were adopted. . . .

That there are burdens and disabilities which constitute badges of slavery and servitude, and that the power to enforce by appropriate legislation the Thirteenth Amendment may be exerted by legislation of a direct and primary character, for the eradication, not simply of the institution, but of its badges and incidents, are propositions which ought to be deemed indisputable. They lie at the foundation of the Civil Rights Act of 1866. Whether that act was authorized by the Thirteenth Amendment alone, without the support which it subsequently received from the Fourteenth Amendment, after the adoption of which it was re-enacted with some additions, my brethren do not consider it necessary to inquire. But I submit, with all respect to them, that its constitutionality is conclusively shown by their opinion. They admit, as I have said, that the Thirteenth Amendment established freedom; that these are burdens and disabilities, the necessary incidents of slavery, which constitute its substance and visible form; that Congress, by the act of 1866, passed in view of the Thirteenth Amendment, before the Fourteenth was adopted, undertook to remove certain burdens and disabilities, the necessary incidents of slavery, and to secure to all citizens of every race and color, and without regard to previous servitude, those fundamental rights which are the essence of civil freedom, namely, the same right to make and enforce contracts, to sue, be parties, give evidence, and to inherit, purchase, lease, sell, and convey property as is enjoyed by white citizens; that under the Thirteenth Amendment, Congress has to do with slavery and its incidents; and that legislation, so far as necessary or proper to eradicate all forms and incidents of slavery and involuntary servitude, may be direct and primary, operating upon the acts of individuals, whether sanctioned by State legislation or not. These propositions being conceded, it is impossible, as it seems to me, to question the constitutional validity of the Civil Rights Act of 1866. I do not contend that the Thirteenth Amendment invests Congress with authority, by legislation, to define and regulate the entire body of the civil rights which citizens enjoy, or may enjoy, in the several States. But I hold that since slavery, as the court has repeatedly declared, *Slaughter-House Cases,* 16 Wall. 36; *Strauder* v. *West Virginia,* 100 U.S. 303, was the moving or principal cause of the adoption of that amendment, and since that institution rested wholly upon the inferiority, as a race, of those held in bondage, their freedom necessarily involved immunity from, and protection against, all discrimination against them, because of their race, in respect of such civil rights as belong to freemen of other races. Congress, therefore, under its express power to enforce that amendment, by appropriate legislation, may enact laws to protect that people against the deprivation, *because of their race,* of any civil rights granted to other freemen in the same State; and such legislation may be of a direct and primary character, operating upon States, their officers and agents, and, also, upon, at least, such individuals and corporations as exercise public functions and wield power and authority under the State. . . .

Congress has not, in these matters, entered the domain of State control and supervision. It does not, as I have said, assume to prescribe the general conditions and limitations under which inns, public conveyances, and places of public amusement, shall be conducted or managed. It simply declares, in effect, that since the nation has established universal freedom in this country, for all time, there shall be no discrimination, based merely upon race or color, in respect of the accommodations and advantages of public conveyances, inns, and places of public amusement.

I am of the opinion that such discrimination practised by corporations and individuals in the exercise of their public or quasi-public functions is a badge of servitude the imposition of which Congress may prevent under its power, by appropriate legislation, to enforce the Thirteenth Amendment; and, consequently, without reference to its enlarged power under the Fourteenth Amendment, the act of March 1, 1875, is not, in my judgment, repugnant to the Constitution.

It remains now to consider these cases with reference to the power Congress has possessed since the adoption of the Fourteenth Amendment. Much that has been said as to the power of Congress under the Thirteenth Amendment is applicable to this branch of the discussion, and will not be repeated.

Before the adoption of the recent amendments, it had become, as we have seen, the established doctrine of this court that negroes, whose ancestors had been imported and sold as slaves, could not become citizens of a State, or even of the United States, with the rights and privileges guaranteed to citizens by the national Constitution; further, that one might have all the rights and privileges of a citizen of a State without being a citizen in the sense in which that word was used in the national Constitution, and without being entitled to the privileges and immunities of citizens of the several States. Still, further, between the adoption of the Thirteenth Amendment and the proposal by Congress of the Fourteenth Amendment, on June 16, 1866, the statute books of several of the States, as we have seen, had become loaded down with enactments which, under the guise of Apprentice, Vagrant, and Contract regulations, sought to keep the colored race in a condition, practically, of servitude. It was openly announced that whatever might be the rights which persons of that race had, as freemen, under the guarantees of the national Constitution, they could not become citizens of a State, with the privileges belonging to citizens, except by the consent of such State; consequently, that their civil rights, as citizens of the State, depended entirely upon State legislation. To meet this new peril to the black race, that the purposes of the nation might not be doubted or defeated, and by way of further enlargement of the power of Congress, the Fourteenth Amendment was proposed for adoption. . . .

But what was secured to colored citizens of the United States—as between them and their respective States—by the national grant to them of State citizenship? With what rights, privileges, or immunities did this grant invest them? There is one, if there be no other—exemption from race discrimination in respect of any civil right belonging to citizens of the white race in the same State. That, surely, is their constitutional privilege when within the jurisdiction of other States. And such must be their constitutional right, in their own State, unless the recent amendments be splendid baubles, thrown out to delude those who deserved fair and generous treatment at the hands of the nation. Citizenship in this country necessarily imports at least equality of civil rights among citizens of every race in the same State. It is fundamental in American citizenship that, in respect of such rights, there shall be no discrimination by the State, or its officers, or by individuals or corporations exercising public functions or authority, against any citizen because of his race or previous condition of servitude. . . .

But if it were conceded that the power of Congress could not be brought into activity until the rights specified in the act of 1875 had been abridged or denied by some State law or State action, I maintain that the decision of the court is erroneous. . . .

In every material sense applicable to the practical enforcement of the Fourteenth Amendment, railroad corporations, keepers of inns, and managers of places of public amusement are agents or instrumentalities of the State, because they are charged with duties to the public, and are amenable, in respect of their duties and functions, to governmental regulation. . . .

My brethren say, that when a man has emerged from slavery, and by the aid of beneficent legislation has shaken off the inseparable concomitants of that state, there must be some stage in the progress of his elevation when he takes the rank of a mere citizen, and ceases to be the special favorite of the laws, and when his rights as a citizen, or a man, are to be protected in the ordinary modes by which other men's rights are protected. It is, I submit, scarcely just to say that the colored race has been the special favorite of the laws. The statute of 1875, now adjudged to be unconstitutional, is for the benefit of citizens of every race and color. What the nation, through Congress, has sought to accomplish in reference to that race, is—what had already been done in every State of the Union for the white race—to secure and protect rights belonging to them as freemen and citizens; nothing more. It was not deemed enough "to help the feeble up, but to support him after." The one underlying purpose of congressional legislation has been to enable the black race to take the rank of mere citizens. The difficulty has been to compel a recognition of the legal right of the black race to take the rank of citizens, and to secure the enjoyment of privileges belonging, under the law, to them as a component part of the people for whose welfare and happiness government is ordained. At every step, in this direction, the nation has been confronted with class tyranny, which a contemporary English historian says is, of all tyrannies, the most intolerable, "for it is ubiquitous in its operation, and weighs, perhaps, most heavily on those whose obscurity or distance would withdraw them from the notice of a single despot." To-day, it is the colored race which is denied, by corporations and individuals wielding public authority, rights fundamental in their freedom and citizenship. At some future time, it may be that some other race will fall under the ban of race discrimination. If the constitutional amendments be enforced, according to the intent with which, as I conceive, they were adopted, there cannot be, in this republic, any class of human beings in practical subjection to another class, with power in the latter to dole out to the former just such privileges as they may choose to grant. The supreme law of the land has decreed that no authority shall be exercised in this country upon the basis of discrimination, in respect of civil rights, against freemen and citizens because of their race, color, or previous condition of servitude. To that decree—for the due enforcement of which, by appropriate legislation, Congress has been invested with express power—every one must bow, whatever may have been, or whatever now are, his individual views as to the wisdom or policy, either of the recent changes in the fundamental law, or of the legislation which has been enacted to give them effect.

For the reasons stated I feel constrained to withhold my assent to the opinion of the court.

Minor v. Happersett, 1875

21 WALLACE 163 (1875)

[Unanimous]

. . . The fourteenth amendment to the Constitution of the United States, in its first section, thus ordains:

> *All* persons born or naturalized in the United States, and subject to the jurisdiction thereof, are *citizens* of the United States, and of the State wherein they reside. No State shall make or enforce any law, which shall abridge the privileges or immunities of citizens of the United States. Nor shall any State deprive any person of life, liberty, or property, without due process of law; nor deny to any person within its jurisdiction, the equal protection of the laws.

And the constitution of the State of Missouri thus ordains:

> Every *male* citizen of the United States shall be entitled to vote.

Under a statute of the State all persons wishing to vote at any election, must previously have been registered in the manner pointed out by the statute, this being a condition precedent to the exercise of the elective franchise.

In this state of things, on the 15th of October, 1872 (one of the days fixed by law for the registration of voters), Mrs. Virginia Minor, a native born, free, white citizen of the United States, and of the State of Missouri, over the age of twenty-one years, wishing to vote for electors for President and Vice-President of the United States, and for a representative in Congress, and for other officers, at the general election held in November, 1872, applied to one Happersett, the registrar of voters, to register her as a lawful voter, which he refused to do, assigning for cause that she was not a "male citizen of the United States," but a woman. She thereupon sued him in one of the inferior State courts of Missouri, for wilfully refusing to place her name upon the list of registered voters, by which refusal she was deprived of her right to vote. . . .

[Chief Justice Waite for the Court].   The question is presented in this case, whether, since the adoption of the fourteenth amendment, a woman, who is a citizen of the United States and of the State of Missouri, is a voter in that State, notwithstanding the provision of the constitution and laws of the State, which confine the right of suffrage to men alone. . . .

It is contended that the provisions of the constitution and laws of the State of Missouri which confine the right of suffrage and registration therefore to men, are in violation of the Constitution of the United States, and therefore void. The argument is, that as a woman, born or naturalized in the United States and subject to the jurisdiction thereof, is a citizen of the United States and of the State in which she resides, she has the right of suffrage as one of the privileges and immunities of her citizenship, which the State cannot by its laws or constitution abridge.

There is no doubt that women may be citizens. They are persons, and by the fourteenth amendment "all persons born or naturalized in the United States and subject to the jurisdiction thereof" are expressly declared to be "citizens of the United States and of the State wherein they reside." But, in our opinion, it did not need this amendment to give them that position. Before its adoption the Constitution of the United States did not in terms prescribe who should be citizens of the United States or of the several States, yet there were necessarily such citizens without such provision. There cannot be a nation without a people. The very idea of a political community, such as a nation is, implies an association of persons for the promotion of their general welfare. Each one of the persons associated becomes a member of the nation formed by the association. He owes it allegiance and is entitled to its protection. Allegiance and protection are, in this connection, reciprocal obligations. The one is a compensation for the other; allegiance for protection and protection for allegiance.

For convenience it has been found necessary to give a name to this membership. The object is to designate by a title the person and the relation he bears to the nation. For this purpose the words "subject," "inhabitant," and "citizen" have been used, and the choice between them is sometimes made to depend upon the form of the government. Citizen is now more commonly employed, however, and as it has been considered better suited to the description of one living under a republican government, it was adopted by nearly all of the States upon their separation from Great Britain, and was afterwards adopted in the Articles of Confederation and in the Constitution of the United States. When used in this sense it is understood as conveying the idea of membership of a nation, and nothing more.

To determine, then, who were citizens of the United States before the adoption of the amendment it is necessary to ascertain what persons originally associated themselves together to form the nation, and what were afterwards admitted to membership.

Looking at the Constitution itself we find that it was ordained and established by "the people of the United States," and then going further back, we find that these were the people of the several States that had before dissolved the political bands which connected them with Great Britain, and assumed a separate and equal station among the powers of the earth, and that had by Articles of Confederation and Perpetual Union, in which they took the name of "the United States of America," entered into a firm league of friendship with each other for their common defence, the security of their liberties and their mutual and general welfare, binding themselves to assist each other against all force offered to or attack made upon them, or any of them, on account of religion, sovereignty, trade, or any other pretence whatever.

Whoever, then, was one of the people of either of these States when the Constitution of the United States was adopted, became *ipso facto* a citizen—a member of the nation created by its adoption. He was one of the persons associating together to form the nation, and was, consequently, one of its original citizens. As to this there has never been a doubt. Disputes have arisen as to whether or not certain persons or certain classes of persons were part of the people at the time, but never as to their citizenship if they were.

Additions might always be made to the citizenship of the United States in two ways: first, by birth, and second, by naturalization. This is apparent from the Constitution itself, for it provides that "no person except a natural-born citizen, or a citizen of the United States at the time of the adoption of the Constitution, shall be eligible to the office of President," and that Congress shall have power "to establish a uniform rule of naturalization." Thus new citizens may be born or they may be created by naturalization.

The Constitution does not, in words, say who shall be natural-born citizens. Resort must be had elsewhere to ascertain that. At common-law, with the nomenclature of which the framers of the Constitution were familiar, it was never doubted that all children born in a country of parents who were its citizens became themselves, upon their birth, citizens also. These were natives, or natural-born citizens, as distinguished from aliens or foreigners. Some authorities go further and include as citizens children born within the jurisdiction without reference to the citizenship of their parents. As to this class there have been doubts, but never as to the first. For the purposes of this case it is not necessary to solve these doubts. It is sufficient for everything we have now to consider that all children born of citizen parents within the jurisdiction are themselves citizens. The words "all children" are certainly as comprehensive, when used in this connection, as "all persons," and if females are included in the last they must be in the first. That they are included in the last is not denied. In fact the whole argument of the plaintiffs proceeds upon that idea.

Under the power to adopt a uniform system of naturalization Congress, as early . . . as 1804 . . . enacted . . . that when any alien who had declared his intention to become a citizen in the manner provided by law died before he was actually naturalized, his widow and children should be considered as citizens of the United States, and entitled to all rights and privileges as such upon taking the necessary oath; and in 1855 it was further provided that any woman who might lawfully be naturalized under the existing laws, married, or who should be married to a citizen of the United States, should be deemed and taken to be a citizen.

From this it is apparent that from the commencement of the legislation upon this subject alien women and alien minors could be made citizens by naturalization. . . .

But if more is necessary to show that women have always been considered as citizens the same as men, abundant proof is to be found in the legislative and judicial history of the country. Thus, by the Constitution, the judicial power of the United States is made to extend to controversies between citizens of different States. Under this it has been uniformly held that the citizenship necessary to give the courts of the United States jurisdiction of a cause must be affirmatively shown on the record. . . . Notwithstanding this the records of the courts are full of cases in which the jurisdiction depends upon the citizenship of women, and not one can be found, we think, in which objection was made on that account. Certainly none can be found in which it has been held that women could not sue or be sued in the courts of the United States. Again, at the time of the adoption of the Constitution, in many of the States (and in some probably now) aliens could not inherit or transmit inheritance. There are a multitude of cases to be found in which the question has been presented whether a woman was or was not an alien, and as such capable or incapable of inheritance, but in no one has it been insisted that she was not a citizen because she was a woman. On the contrary, her right to citizenship has been in all cases assumed. The only question has been whether, in the particular case under consideration, she had availed herself of the right.

In the legislative department of the government similar proof will be found. Thus, in the pre-emption laws, a widow, "being a citizen of the United States," is allowed to make settlement on the public lands and purchase upon the terms specified, and women, "being citizens of the United States," are permitted to avail themselves of the benefit of the homestead law.

Other proof of like character might be found, but certainly more cannot be necessary to establish the fact that sex has never been made one of the elements of citizenship in the United States. In this respect men have never had an advantage over women. The same laws precisely apply to both. The fourteenth amendment did not affect the citizenship of women any more than it did of men. In this particular, therefore, the rights of Mrs. Minor do not depend upon the amendment. She has always been a citizen from her birth, and entitled to all the privileges and immunities of citizenship. The amendment prohibited the State, of which she is a citizen, from abridging any of her privileges and immunities as a citizen of the United States; but it did not confer citizenship on her. That she had before its adoption.

If the right of suffrage is one of the necessary privileges of a citizen of the United States, then the constitution and laws of Missouri confining it to men are in violation of the Constitution of the United States, as amended, and consequently void. The direct question is, therefore, presented whether all citizens are necessarily voters.

The Constitution does not define the privileges and immunities of citizens. For that definition we must look elsewhere. In this case we need not determine what they are, but only whether suffrage is necessarily one of them.

It certainly is nowhere made so in express terms. The United States has no voters in the States of its own creation. The elective officers of the United

States are all elected directly or indirectly by State voters. The members of the House of Representatives are to be chosen by the people of the States, and the electors in each State must have the qualifications requisite for electors of the most numerous branch of the State legislature. Senators are to be chosen by the legislatures of the States, and necessarily the members of the legislature required to make the choice are elected by the voters of the State. Each State must appoint in such manner, as the legislature thereof may direct, the electors to elect the President and Vice-President. The times, places, and manner of holding elections for Senators and Representatives are to be prescribed in each State by the legislature thereof; but Congress may at any time, by law, make or alter such regulations, except as to the place of choosing Senators. It is not necessary to inquire whether this power of supervision thus given to Congress is sufficient to authorize any interference with the State laws prescribing the qualifications of voters, for no such interference has ever been attempted. The power of the State in this particular is certainly supreme until Congress acts.

The amendment did not add to the privileges and immunities of a citizen. It simply furnished an additional guarantee for the protection of such as he already had. No new voters were necessarily made by it. Indirectly it may have had that effect, because it may have increased the number of citizens entitled to suffrage under the constitution and laws of the States, but it operates for this purpose, if at all, through the States and the State laws, and not directly upon the citizen.

It is clear, therefore, we think, that the Constitution has not added the right of suffrage to the privileges and immunities of citizenship as they existed at the time it was adopted. This makes it proper to inquire whether suffrage was coextensive with the citizenship of the States at the time of its adoption. If it was, then it may with force be argued that suffrage was one of the rights which belonged to citizenship, and in the enjoyment of which every citizen must be protected. But if it was not, the contrary may with propriety be assumed.

When the Federal Constitution was adopted, all the States, with the exception of Rhode Island and Connecticut, had constitutions of their own. These two continued to act under their charters from the Crown. Upon an examination of those constitutions we find that in no State were all citizens permitted to vote. Each State determined for itself who should have that power. Thus, in New Hampshire, "every male inhabitant of each town and parish with town privileges, and places unincorporated in the State, of twenty-one years of age and upwards, excepting paupers and persons excused from paying taxes at their own request," were its voters; in Massachusetts "every male inhabitant of twenty-one years of age and upwards, having a freehold estate within the commonwealth of the annual income of three pounds, or any estate of the value of sixty pounds"; in Rhode Island "such as are admitted free of the company and society" of the colony; in Connecticut such persons as had "maturity in years, quiet and peaceable behavior, a civil conversation, and forty shillings freehold or forty pounds personal estate," if so certified by the selectmen; in New York "every male inhabitant of full age who shall have personally resided within one of the counties of the State for six months immediately preceding the day of election . . . if during the time aforesaid he shall have been a freeholder, possessing a freehold of the value of twenty pounds within the county, or have rented a tenement therein of the yearly value of forty shillings, and been rated and actually paid taxes to the State"; in New Jersey "all inhabitants . . . of full age who are worth fifty pounds, proclamation-money, clear estate in the same, and have resided in the county in which they claim a vote for twelve months immediately preceding the election"; in Pennsylvania "every freeman of the age of twenty-one years, having resided in the State two years next before the election, and within that time paid a State or county tax which shall have been assessed at least six months before the election"; in Delaware and Virginia "as exercised by law at present"; in Maryland "all freemen above twenty-one years of age having a freehold of fifty acres of land in the county in which they offer to vote and residing therein, and all freemen having property in the State above the value of thirty pounds current money, and having resided in the county in which they offer to vote one whole year next preceding the election"; in North Carolina, for senators, "all freemen of the age of twenty-one years who have been inhabitants of any one county within the State twelve months immediately preceding the day of election, and possessed of a freehold within the same county of fifty acres of land for six months next before and at the day of election," and for members of the house of commons "all freemen of the age of twenty-one years who have been inhabitants in any one county within the State twelve months immediately preceding the day of any election, and shall have paid public taxes"; in South Carolina "every free white man of the age of twenty-one years, being a citizen of the State and having resided therein two years previous to the day of election, and who hath a freehold of fifty acres of land, or a town lot of which he hath been legally seized and possessed at least six months before such election, or (not having such freehold or town lot), hath been a resident within the election district in which he offers to give his vote six months before said election, and hath paid a tax the pre-ceding year of three shillings sterling towards the support of the govern-ment"; and in Georgia such "citizens and inhabitants of the State as shall have attained to the age of twenty-one years, and shall have paid tax for the year next preceding the election, and shall have resided six months within the county."

In this condition of the law in respect to suffrage in the several States it cannot for a moment be doubted that if it had been intended to make all citizens of the United States voters, the framers of the Constitution would not have left it to implication. So important a change in the condition of citizenship as it actually existed, if intended, would have been expressly declared.

But if further proof is necessary to show that no such change was in-tended, it can easily be found both in and out of the Constitution. By Article 4, section 2, it is provided that "the citizens of each State shall be entitled to all the privileges and immunities of citizens in the several States." If suffrage is necessarily a part of citizenship, then the citizens of each State must be entitled to vote in the several States precisely as their citizens are. This is more than asserting that they may change their residence and become citizens of the State and thus be voters. It goes to the extent of insisting that while retaining their original citizenship they may vote in any State. This, we think, has never been claimed. And again, by the very terms of the amendment we have been considering (the fourteenth), "Representatives shall be apportioned among the several States according to their respective numbers, counting the whole number of persons in each State, excluding Indians not taxed. But when the right to vote at any election for the choice of electors for President and Vice-President of the United States, representatives in Congress, the executive and judicial officers of a State, or the members of the legislature thereof, is denied to any of the male inhabitants of such State, being twenty-one years of age and citizens of the United States, or in any way abridged, except for participation in the rebellion, or other crimes, the basis of representation therein shall be reduced in the proportion which the number of such male citizens shall bear to the whole number of male citizens twenty-one years of age in such State." Why this, if it was not in the power of the legislature to deny the right of suffrage to some male inhabitants? And if suffrage was necessarily one of the absolute rights of citizenship, why confine the operation of the limitation to male inhabitants? Women and children are, as we have seen, "persons." They are counted in the enumeration upon which the apportionment is to be made, but if they were necessarily voters because of their citizenship unless clearly excluded, why inflict the penalty for the exclusion of males alone? Clearly, no such form of words would have been selected to express the idea here indicated if suffrage was the absolute right of all citizens.

And still again, after the adoption of the fourteenth amendment, it was deemed necessary to adopt a fifteenth, as follows: "The right of citizens of the United States to vote shall not be denied or abridged by the United States, or by any State, on account of race, color, or previous condition of servitude." The fourteenth amendment had already provided that no State should make or enforce any law which should abridge the privileges or immunities of citizens of the United States. If suffrage was one of these privileges or immunities, why amend the Constitution to prevent its being denied on account of race, &c.? Nothing is more evident than that the greater must include the less, and if all were already protected why go through with the form of amending the Constitution to protect a part?

It is true that the United States guarantees to every State a republican form of government. It is also true that no State can pass a bill of attainder, and that no person can be deprived of life, liberty, or property without due process of law. All these several provisions of the Constitution must be construed in connection with the other parts of the instrument, and in the light of the surrounding circumstances.

The guarantee is of a republican form of government. No particular government is designated as republican, neither is the exact form to be guaranteed, in any manner especially designated. Here, as in other parts of the instrument, we are compelled to resort elsewhere to ascertain what was intended.

The guarantee necessarily implies a duty on the part of the States themselves to provide such a government. All the States had governments when the Constitution was adopted. In all the people participated to some extent, through their representatives elected in the manner specially provided. These governments the Constitution did not change. They were accepted precisely as they were, and it is, therefore, to be presumed that they were such as it was the duty of the States to provide. Thus we have unmistakable evidence of what was republican in form, within the meaning of that term as employed in the Constitution.

As has been seen, all the citizens of the States were not invested with the right of suffrage. In all, save perhaps New Jersey, this right was only bestowed upon men and not upon all of them. Under these circumstances it is certainly now too late to contend that a government is not republican, within the meaning of this guarantee in the Constitution, because women are not made voters.

The same may be said of the other provisions just quoted. Women were excluded from suffrage in nearly all the States by the express provision of their constitutions and laws. If that had been equivalent to a bill of attainder, certainly its abrogation would not have been left to implication. Nothing less than express language would have been employed to effect so radical a change. So also of the amendment which declares that no person shall be deprived of life, liberty, or property without due process of law, adopted as it was as early as 1791. If suffrage was intended to be included within its obligations, language better adapted to express that intent would most certainly have been employed. The right of suffrage, when granted, will be protected. He who has it can only be deprived of it by due process of law, but in order to claim protection he must first show that he has the right.

But we have already sufficiently considered the proof found upon the inside of the Constitution. That upon the outside is equally effective.

The Constitution was submitted to the States for adoption in 1787, and was ratified by nine States in 1788, and finally by the thirteen original States in 1790. Vermont was the first new State admitted to the Union, and it came in under a constitution which conferred the right of suffrage only upon men of the full age of twenty-one years, having resided in the State for the space of one whole year next before the election, and who were of quiet and peaceable behavior. This was in 1791. The next year, 1792, Kentucky followed with a constitution confining the right of suffrage to free male citizens of the age of twenty-one years who had resided in the State two years or in the county in which they offered to vote one year next before the election. Then followed Tennessee, in 1796, with voters of freemen of the age of twenty-one years and upwards, possessing a freehold in the county wherein they may vote, and being inhabitants of the State or freemen being inhabitants of any one county in the State six months immediately preceding the day of election. But we need not particularize further. No new State has ever been admitted to the Union which has conferred the right of suffrage upon women, and this has never been considered a valid objection to her admission. On the contrary, as is claimed in the argument, the right of suffrage was withdrawn from women as early as 1807 in the State of New Jersey, without any attempt to obtain the interference of the United States to prevent it. Since then the governments of the insurgent States have been reorganized under a requirement that before their representatives could be admitted to seats in Congress they must have adopted new constitutions, republican in form. In no one of these constitutions was suffrage conferred upon women, and yet the States have all been restored to their original position as States in the Union.

Besides this, citizenship has not in all cases been made a condition precedent to the enjoyment of the right of suffrage. Thus, in Missouri, persons of foreign birth, who have declared their intention to become citizens of the United States, may under certain circumstances vote. The same provision is to be found in the constitutions of Alabama, Arkansas, Florida, Georgia, Indiana, Kansas, Minnesota, and Texas.

Certainly, if the courts can consider any question settled, this is one. For nearly ninety years the people have acted upon the idea that the Constitution, when it conferred citizenship, did not necessarily confer the right of suffrage. If uniform practice long continued can settle the construction of so important an instrument as the Constitution of the United States confessedly is, most certainly it has been done here. Our province is to decide what the law is, not to declare what it should be.

We have given this case the careful consideration its importance demands. If the law is wrong, it ought to be changed; but the power for that is not with us. The arguments addressed to us bearing upon such a view of the subject may perhaps be sufficient to induce those having the power, to make the alteration, but they ought not to be permitted to influence our judgment in determining the present rights of the parties now litigating before us. No argument as to woman's need of suffrage can be considered. We can only act upon her rights as they exist. It is not for us to look at the hardship of withholding. Our duty is at an end if we find it is within the power of a State to withhold.

Being unanimously of the opinion that the Constitution of the United States does not confer the right of suffrage upon any one, and that the constitutions and laws of the several States which commit that important trust to men alone are not necessarily void, we affirm the judgment.

Bradwell v. Illinois, 1873

83 U.S. 130 (1873)

[8-1: Miller, Clifford, Bradley, Davis, Field,
Strong, Swayne, Hunt; Chase]

. . . Mrs. Myra Bradwell, residing in the State of Illinois, made application to the judges of the Supreme Court of that State for a license to practice law. . . .

The statute of Illinois on the subject of admissions to the bar, enacts that no person shall be permitted to practice as an attorney or counsellor-at-law, or to commence, conduct, or defend any action, suit, or plaint, in which he is not a party concerned, in any court of record within the State, either by using or subscribing his own name or the name of any other person, without having previously obtained a license for that purpose from some two of the justices of the Supreme Court, which license shall constitute the person receiving the same an attorney and counsellor-at-law, and shall authorize him to appear in all the courts of record within the State, and there to practice as an attorney and counsellor-at-law, according to the laws and customs thereof.

On Mrs. Bradwell's application first coming before the court, the license was refused, and it was stated as a sufficient reason that under the decisions of the Supreme Court of Illinois, the applicant—"as a married woman would be bound neither by her express contracts nor by those implied contracts which it is the policy of the law to create between attorney and client." After the announcement of this decision, Mrs. Bradwell, admitting that she was a married woman—though she expressed her belief that such fact did not appear in the record—filed a printed argument in which her right to admission, notwithstanding that fact, was earnestly and ably maintained. . . .

Mr. Justice Miller Delivered the Opinion of the Court. The record in this case is not very perfect, but it may be fairly taken that the plaintiff asserted her right to a license on the grounds, among others, that she was a citizen of the United States, and that having been a citizen of Vermont at one time, she was, in the State of Illinois, entitled to any right granted to citizens of the latter State.

The court having overruled these claims of right founded on the clauses of the Federal Constitution before referred to, those propositions may be considered as properly before this court.

As regards the provision of the Constitution that citizens of each State shall be entitled to all the privileges and immunities of citizens in the several States, the plaintiff in her affidavit has stated very clearly a case to which it is inapplicable.

The protection designed by that clause, as has been repeatedly held, has no application to a citizen of the State whose laws are complained of. If the plaintiff was a citizen of the State of Illinois, that provision of the Constitution gave her no protection against its courts or its legislation.

The plaintiff seems to have seen this difficulty, and attempts to avoid it by stating that she was born in Vermont.

While she remained in Vermont that circumstance made her a citizen of that State. But she states, at the same time, that she is a citizen of the United States, and that she is now, and has been for many years past, a resident of Chicago, in the State of Illinois.

The fourteenth amendment declares that citizens of the United States are citizens of the State within which they reside; therefore the plaintiff was, at the time of making her application, a citizen of the United States and a citizen of the State of Illinois.

We do not here mean to say that there may not be a temporary residence in one State, with intent to return to another, which will not create citizenship in the former. But the plaintiff states nothing to take her case out of the definition of citizenship of a State as defined by the first section of the fourteenth amendment.

In regard to that amendment counsel for the plaintiff in this court truly says that there are certain privileges and immunities which belong to a citizen of the United States as such; otherwise it would be nonsense for the fourteenth amendment to prohibit a State from abridging them, and he proceeds to argue that admission to the bar of a State of a person who possesses the requisite learning and character is one of those which a State may not deny.

In this latter proposition we are not able to concur with counsel. We agree with him that there are privileges and immunities belonging to citizens of the United States, in that relation and character, and that it is these and these alone which a State is forbidden to abridge. But the right to admission to practice in the courts of a State is not one of them. This right in no sense depends on citizenship of the United States. It has not, as far as we know, ever been made in any State, or in any case, to depend on citizenship at all. Certainly many prominent and distinguished lawyers have been admitted to practice, both in the State and Federal courts, who were not citizens of the United States or of any State. But, on whatever basis this right may be placed, so far as it can have any relation to citizenship at all, it would seem that, as to the courts of a State, it would relate to citizenship of the State, and as to Federal courts, it would relate to citizenship of the United States.

The opinion just delivered in the *Slaughter-House Cases* renders elaborate argument in the present case unnecessary; for, unless we are wholly and radically mistaken in the principles on which those cases are decided, the right to control and regulate the granting of license to practice law in the courts of a State is one of those powers which are not transferred for its protection to the Federal government, and its exercise is in no manner governed or controlled by citizenship of the United States in the party seeking such license.

It is unnecessary to repeat the argument on which the judgment in those cases is founded. It is sufficient to say they are conclusive of the present case.

Judgment affirmed.

Mr. Justice Bradley. I concur in the judgment of the court in this case, by which the judgment of the Supreme Court of Illinois is affirmed, but not for the reasons specified in the opinion just read. . . .

The claim that, under the fourteenth amendment of the Constitution, which declares that no State shall make or enforce any law which shall abridge the privileges and immunities of citizens of the United States, the statute law of Illinois, or the common law prevailing in that State, can no longer be set up as a barrier against the right of females to pursue any lawful employment for a livelihood (the practice of law included), assumes that it is one of the privileges and immunities of women as citizens to engage in any and every profession, occupation, or employment in civil life.

It certainly cannot be affirmed, as an historical fact, that this has ever been established as one of the fundamental privileges and immunities of the sex. On the contrary, the civil law, as well as nature herself, has always recognized a wide difference in the respective spheres and destinies of man and woman. Man is, or should be, woman's protector and defender. The natural and proper timidity and delicacy which belongs to the female sex evidently unfits it for many of the occupations of civil life. The constitution of the family organization, which is founded in the divine ordinance, as well as in the nature of things, indicates the domestic sphere as that which properly belongs to the domain and functions of womanhood. The harmony, not to say identity, of interests and views which belong, or should belong, to the family institution is repugnant to the idea of a woman adopting a distinct and independent career from that of her husband. So firmly fixed was this sentiment in the founders of the common law that it became a maxim of that system of jurisprudence that a woman had no legal existence separate from her husband, who was regarded as her head and representative in the social state; and, notwithstanding some recent modifications of this civil status, many of the special rules of law flowing from and dependent upon this cardinal principle still exist in full force in most States. One of these is, that a married woman is incapable, without her husband's consent, of making contracts which shall be binding on her or him. This very incapacity was one circumstance which the Supreme Court of Illinois deemed important in rendering a married woman incompetent fully to perform the duties and trusts that belong to the office of an attorney and counsellor.

It is true that many women are unmarried and not affected by any of the duties, complications, and incapacities arising out of the married state, but these are exceptions to the general rule. The paramount destiny and mission of woman are to fulfil the noble and benign offices of wife and mother. This is the law of the Creator. . . .

✣ E S S A Y S

Constitutional historians studying the Reconstruction era have produced an impressive but highly disputatious literature. The debate turns on several important interpretive matters, all of which boil down to two questions. First, did the framers of the Civil War amendments want to work an alteration in federalism and civil rights sufficient to bring about real equality in American life? Second, what is the appropriate yardstick by which to measure that effort—theirs or ours?

In the first essay, Robert J. Kaczorowski, a law professor at Fordham University, argues that Congress intended to work a revolutionary reconstruction in the scope of civil rights and in the authority of the federal government to protect those rights. Central to Kaczorowski's argument is the idea that the Fourteenth Amendment's framers defined natural rights as constitutionally recognized rights of American citizenship.

In the second essay, Michael Les Benedict, a historian from Ohio State University, takes a more skeptical view. He suggests that the Supreme Court under Chief Justice Morrison R. Waite (1874–1888) was more concerned with preserving federalism than with revolutionizing the scope of civil rights, whether for blacks or women. Nonetheless, Les Benedict concludes, the Waite Court ought to be credited for the civil-rights advances that it did promote rather than criticized for not acting the way modern-day civil-rights advocates believe it should have.

Professor Joan Hoff Wilson of Indiana University argues in the final essay that, where women were involved, both the framers of the Fourteenth Amendment and the justices of the Supreme Court came up short. From women's perspective, the Reconstruction era was neither revolutionary nor egalitarian. If anything, the constitutional status of women was more degraded after the Civil War.

A Revolution in Federal Civil Rights

ROBERT J. KACZOROWSKI

In 1857, the highest court in the United States held that blacks in America possessed no rights, could never become citizens of the United States, and that Congress was powerless to abolish slavery. In the aftermath of these pronouncements, this country fought one of the bloodiest wars in its history. Fewer than ten years after the *Dred Scott* decision, however, Congress and the Northern states accomplished precisely what the Supreme Court declared could not be done, through constitutional amendments and a civil rights statute. The Thirteenth Amendment abolished slavery everywhere in the United States. The Civil Rights Act of 1866 and the Fourteenth Amendment conferred citizenship on and secured the civil rights of all qualified, natural-born, and naturalized Americans, including former slaves and free blacks. The statute declared illegal infringements of certain civil rights made under the pretext of law or custom and authorized the removal of civil and criminal cases from the state to the federal courts whenever Americans were unable to enforce their rights in the state systems of justice. The Fourteenth Amendment also expressly prohibited the states from infringing the rights that Americans enjoyed as citizens of the United States and their rights to due process and equal protection of the law.

The meaning and scope of the Thirteenth and Fourteenth Amendments and the Civil Rights Act of 1866 have been almost as controversial among twentieth-century scholars as they were among the participants in Reconstruction. In 1947, Supreme Court Justice Hugo Black sparked a debate over the scope of a national authority to enforce civil rights when he held that the Fourteenth Amendment conferred on the national government the power to protect the Bill of Rights against state infringements. Charles Fairman quickly wrote a rebuttal, in which he insisted that the congressional framers intended to secure only an equality in state law among the few rights enumerated in Section 1 of the Civil Rights Act, a view he continued to

"To Begin the Nation Anew: Congress, Citizenship, and Civil Rights after the Civil War," by Robert J. Kaczorowski, *American Historical Review* 92 (February 1987): pp. 45–55, 66–68. Reprinted by permission of the American Historical Association and the author.

maintain. William Crosskey published a rejoinder to Fairman, in which Crosskey asserted his view of a nation-centered federalism that delegated to Congress the authority to enforce the Bill of Rights, a view he later elaborated in his three-volume history of the U.S. Constitution. The specific question whether or not the Fourteenth Amendment incorporates the Bill of Rights has been vigorously debated, most recently by Raoul Berger and Michael Curtis.

Other legal scholars and historians have focused on additional aspects of a national civil rights enforcement authority. Jacobus tenBroek and How-ard Jay Graham argued that the theory of the Reconstruction amendments derived from the natural rights ideology of the abolitionists, and that the amendments delegated to Congress an expansive authority to enforce fun-damental rights. They assumed that it was the Radicals who controlled Congress during Reconstruction and incorporated their expansive view into the Reconstruction amendments. Revisionist historians in the 1960s argued that the moderate Republicans, not the Radicals, controlled Congress and formulated Reconstruction policy.

Although revisionist political historians of the 1960s agreed that even moderate Republicans were committed to securing civil rights after the Civil War, revisionist legal historians in the 1970s argued that the Reconstruction amendments did not significantly alter American federal constitutionalism. Insisting that the moderates were legal conservatives who consciously in-tended to avoid a revolutionary restructuring of constitutional law and to retain a federalism based on states' rights, the revisionists concluded that the Civil Rights Act and the Fourteenth Amendment preserved in the states primary authority over citizenship and civil rights. The states therefore con-tinued to enjoy the authority to determine the status of Americans, define their rights, and provide for their protection. The framers of the legislation intended that citizens redress violations of civil rights and enforce their rights through state courts and law enforcement agencies. Conscious of the rev-olutionary implications for American federalism, the framers conferred on the national government merely the authority to prohibit the states from discriminating among citizens on the basis of race in matters relating to civil rights and to punish state officers who did so.

Congressional republicans believed that the Thirteenth and Fourteenth Amendments and the Civil Rights Act of 1866 represented a revolutionary change in American constitutionalism. A change in federalism was a pre-requisite for Congress to legislate for the protection of civil rights, in light of the nineteenth-century concept of federalism. If the status and funda-mental rights of citizenship were the rights that individuals enjoyed as citizens of the states, Congress would not have had the authority to legislate for their protection. These fundamental rights would be within the exclusive jurisdiction of the states. The proposal by Congress of a constitutional amendment and a statute that conferred on all Americans the precious status of citizen, enumerated some of the fundamental rights of citizenship, and extended to citizens federally enforceable guarantees for the protection of their civil rights was itself a revolutionary change in American federalism.

The radical change in American constitutionalism represented by the actions of Congress forced congressional Republicans to formulate a legal theory delegating to Congress the authority to secure the status and civil rights of Americans. Republicans explained that sovereignty resided in the national government and included the primary authority to determine the status and secure the rights of all Americans, white as well as black. They interpreted the Thirteenth Amendment as a constitutional guarantee of the status of Americans as free people and therefore as a delegation of authority to Congress to secure the fundamental rights of American citizens. Congressional Republicans reasoned that the amendment, in abolishing slavery, secured liberty and the rights of free people. They equated the status and rights of free people with the status and natural rights of citizens. Congressional Republicans understood the Thirteenth Amendment as a guarantee of the status and rights of citizenship. Applying a Hamiltonian, nationalistic interpretation of the Constitution, which attributed to Congress the authority to secure rights that are recognized or guaranteed by the Constitution, they concluded that the Thirteenth Amendment delegated to Congress the authority to prohibit slavery and, more important, the authority to secure inherent rights of all U.S. citizens against violation from any source in whatever manner Congress deemed appropriate. Thus, James F. Wilson, the representative from Iowa and the House floor manager of the Civil Rights Bill, introduced it with the explanation "that the possession of these rights by the citizen raises by necessary implication the power in Congress to protect them."

Republicans expressed in law their understanding of the scope of the Thirteenth Amendment when they enacted the Civil Rights Act of 1866 and the Fourteenth Amendment. Section 1 of the Civil Rights Act confers citizenship on all qualified American inhabitants and guarantees to all American citizens at least some of the rights the framers believed to be fundamental. They added a similar citizenship clause to the first section of the Fourteenth Amendment in the event that a subsequent Congress repealed the Civil Rights Act. The addition of this clause was also designed to prevent courts from declaring the statute unconstitutional by interpreting the Thirteenth Amendment as a mere abrogation of slavery. The citizenship clause of the Fourteenth Amendment makes explicit the constitutional recognition of the status and natural rights of citizens that its framers believed was implied in the Thirteenth Amendment. The ratification of the Fourteenth Amendment in 1868 thus completed the constitutional revolution regarding citizenship and civil rights. Congressional Republicans legislated to secure the civil rights of Americans in 1866 with the understanding that, with the Thirteenth and then the Fourteenth Amendment, the Constitution of the United States gave to all Americans the fundamental rights of citizenship and delegated to Congress the authority to protect citizens in their enjoyment of these rights.

A striking feature of the framers' intent in 1866 is their adoption of the most radical abolitionist theory of constitutionalism before the Civil War.

By 1866, not only radicals but all moderate and even some conservative Republicans supported the efforts of Congress to secure civil rights. This shift reveals the extent to which the Civil War radicalized American politics. A political and constitutional position regarded as extreme and embraced by a very small minority before the Civil War had become mainstream Republicanism by 1866. The position that contemporaries regarded as radical in 1866 was securing the voting rights of blacks. As a matter of law and as a matter of political objectives, most contemporaries distinguished between civil rights and voting rights. The essential reason that Radical Republicans criticized the Fourteenth Amendment as too moderate was its failure to provide the same protection for voting rights as for civil rights.

The full reach of this revolution in constitutionalism could have changed the nature of American government from a federal republic with divided authority to a unitary state. Democratic opponents in Congress recognized the implications of the Republicans' theory of constitutionalism. Democrats objected to the proposed Fourteenth Amendment and Civil Rights Bill precisely because the constitutional theory that these measures encompassed could be used by Congress to destroy the civil and criminal authority of states over their citizens. If, as proponents of civil rights insisted, the Constitution guaranteed the fundamental rights of citizenship, Congress could exercise exclusive jurisdiction over civil rights. National law could supplant state law and the national government could absorb "all reserved state sovereignty and rights." Senator Garret Davis, Democrat from Kentucky, was one of several opponents who objected that "the principles involved in this bill, if they are legitimate and constitutional, would authorize Congress to pass civil and criminal codes for every State of the Union." These views were echoed by the House of Representatives, the White House, and the press.

These positions were a continuation of a constitutional battle that had raged for many years. Before the Civil War, the states had defined the status and secured the rights of the inhabitants of the United States. They performed these functions through state legal institutions, statutes, and courts. Some antebellum legal theorists argued, however, that the primary authority to perform these functions rested with the national government. The question of whether the national or state governments possessed ultimate authority to determine the status and enforce the rights of American inhabitants produced a national political and constitutional debate that centered on slavery and culminated in the South's secession in 1861. Secession, based on the constitutional theory of state sovereignty, made the legal questions of federalism and the locus of sovereignty central issues of the Civil War. The North responded with Abraham Lincoln's theory of national sovereignty, which denied the existence of any state's right to secede. The Emancipation Proclamation added the other central question, namely, which government possessed the primary constitutional authority to determine the status of American inhabitants.

The antebellum constitutional questions of the nature of American federalism, the locus of sovereignty, and the primary authority over the status of Americans were thus joined as political issues in the Civil War. The causes of Unionism, national sovereignty, and emancipation were victorious on the battlefield. Northern Republicans believed that the Civil War had resolved these political and constitutional questions. They soon discovered they were mistaken. Former Confederates tenaciously adhered to a philosophy of state sovereignty and refused to respect national authority. They defiantly resisted the emancipation guaranteed blacks by the Thirteenth Amendment. Southern white supremacists denied the freedmen's freedom by continuing to treat them as if they were slaves. White supremacists frequently met the attempts of freed blacks to assert their constitutionally guaranteed freedom with violent repression and economic intimidation. Moreover, they treated white Unionists and federal officers with disrespect, and resorted to economic intimidation and violence toward them as well.

Local officials in the South sanctioned and legitimized the defiant behavior of individuals and the racial and political customs of communities dominated by whites. In their constitutions and laws, Southern states refused to recognize that blacks were citizens possessing the natural rights of free people. State officers commonly failed or refused to protect the personal safety and property of blacks. They similarly refused to extend this protection to whites who were political allies or federal agents of blacks. When Southern blacks and politically unpopular whites were the victims of crimes, they could not get sheriffs to arrest, courts to try, or juries to convict the perpetrators. When charged with crimes or sued in the civil courts, blacks seldom received impartial justice. Indeed, white Unionists and freed blacks were prosecuted and sent to prison during peacetime for aiding the U.S. forces during the war. Southern hostility persuaded Northern Republicans and Southern Unionists that secessionist and Confederate sentiments had survived the Civil War. By the end of 1865, the constitutional and political process of restoring the Southern states to the Union had become the problem of preserving the principles for which the war had been fought.

The Civil War had been a uniquely partisan war. Republicans stood for Union and emancipation; Democrats were associated with leniency toward Confederate secessionists and slavery. When President Andrew Johnson attempted a quick restoration of the Confederate states after the war, Democrats rallied behind him. Restoration by the president presented insuperable political problems, however. It preserved the political leadership of the same individuals and groups that had led the Southern states into secession and civil war. If Republicans acquiesced in Johnson's plan, their Democratic opponents would gain ascendancy by joining with the late belligerents of the South, an outcome unacceptable to Northern Republicans. It would condone "traitorism" and betray their Unionist allies in the South. But achievement of Republican political objectives in the South, which included a political power base of white Unionists and free blacks, would require a change in Southern political leadership. Political participation of the Republicans' Southern allies necessitated a federal presence to protect them from the hostility of the dominant Democratic Conservative white supremacists. As the Civil War was a partisan effort associated with and led by the Republican party, so Reconstruction was a partisan postwar readjustment controlled by and identified with Northern Republicans.

In 1866, the political context of civil rights deprivations compelled Congress to take effective measures to secure the fundamental rights of American citizens. Although Republicans shrank from providing freed blacks with economic independence through land redistribution, they did offer legal recognition of their liberty by securing important rights for their economic autonomy, such as the rights to enter into contracts and to buy and sell property. Congressional Republicans put aside racial prejudice that ordinarily would have precluded the legal enforcement of civil rights. The factors motivating them included the perceived need to preserve the objectives for which so many thousands gave their lives, the obligation to make effective the freedom they had promised to Southern blacks, a sense of elemental fairness and justice, as well as political self-interest. All these objectives were served by providing for the personal safety and security of Southern political allies—civilians of both races and federal officers. The political ideology of the Republican party further diminished the effects of Northern white racism on congressional Republicans. The central ideas of the party were the theory of natural rights, a classic liberalism, and a belief in equal opportunity. The combination served as a concept of American nationalism, distinguishing Republican notions of Unionism and American freedom from the Southern Democratic Conservative ideology of states' rights and slavery.

Northern Republicans decided that the preservation of American nationhood and freedom, as they understood them, required a strong central government to combat the danger posed by Southern recalcitrance. Republican William Lawrence of Ohio invoked political necessity when he warned the House that the congressional protection of civil rights was "essential to preserve national life, and the means of national existence." Withholding this protection would be tantamount to permitting the Southern states to divest citizens of their rights in the aftermath of Appomattox. The editor of the *Philadelphia American* echoed this theme in urging ratification of the Fourteenth Amendment: "If there be one lesson written in bloody letters by the [Civil] War, it is that the national citizenship must be paramount to that of the State. We propose to make it so . . . This citizenship provision is one of the most vital principles developed by the war. Without it we shall inevitably be exposed to new wars of Secession and States rights and nullification." The governor of Wisconsin, Lucius Fairchild, transmitted a copy of the proposed Fourteenth Amendment to the state legislature and urged ratification "because, in view of the terrible events of the past five years, we deem these guarantees necessary to the life of the nation, and we insist that those who saved that life have an undeniable right to demand full guarantees to its future preservation."

The conjunction of political ideology and political necessity resulted in congressional Republicans embracing a revolutionary theory of constitutionalism. To achieve political power in the South, to preserve their wartime objectives of Unionism and freedom for slaves, they insisted that sovereignty resided in the federal government and included primary authority to determine the status and secure the rights of all Americans, white and black. Republican supporters of the Reconstruction amendments and the civil rights statute acknowledged the revolutionary changes they had wrought in American federalism by delegating plenary authority over citizenship and civil rights to the national government. Before the Civil War, the states had exercised almost exclusive jurisdiction over fundamental rights. Under the Thirteenth and Fourteenth Amendments, as Republicans understood them, Congress could conceivably supplant the states in securing civil rights. By virtue of the Constitution's supremacy clause, Congress could exercise exclusive authority over citizenship and civil rights and thereby destroy state authority as a matter of constitutional law. Indeed, Congress exercised this authority when it determined by statute and constitutional amendment which people were citizens and what rights they were to enjoy. The states were deprived of their historical authority to make these decisions. Although congressional Republicans acknowledged the constitutional revolution in which they were engaged, they carefully avoided carrying this revolution to its ultimate conclusion of creating a unitary political structure. Republicans did not wish to supplant the states in providing a foundation for ordinary civil and criminal justice. On the contrary, they consciously preserved federalism by avoiding unnecessary intrusions on state authority over civil rights. Intentionally recognizing concurrent authority, Congress restricted its protection of fundamental rights to situations in which states and localities failed to protect them.

The decision of congressional Republicans to preserve state authority over ordinary civil and criminal justice has led legal historians to conclude that the Thirteenth and Fourteenth Amendments and the Civil Rights Act of 1866 were modest increases in national authority. The evidence, however, supports the belief of the framers that the Thirteenth and Fourteenth Amendments and the 1866 statute would bring about revolutionary changes in federal constitutionalism. The underlying constitutional authority to enforce civil rights stemmed from the constitutional recognition of the status and rights of free people as having the status and rights of U.S. citizens. Because the civil rights inherent in citizenship were constitutionally guaranteed, the framers believed that Congress, by statute and constitutional amendment, could require the states, the traditional guardians of these rights, to secure them for all Americans. Congress conferred citizenship on all qualified persons in Section 1 of the Civil Rights Act and the Fourteenth Amendment, the framers thereby forcing the states to recognize freed blacks as citizens both of the United States and of the states of their residence. The states no longer could decide state citizenship for themselves. They were prohibited from arbitrarily excluding any qualified persons from state citizenship and from refusing to secure the civil rights to which citizenship entitled them. By defining natural rights as constitutionally recognized rights of American citizenship, Republicans acknowledged that Americans possessed these rights independent of state law. That is, if the states were to repeal their legal recognition of these rights, citizens could still claim them as constitutionally recognized and secured rights of American citizenship. Indeed, James F. Wilson of Iowa made this precise point in arguing that the bill was needed because the Southern states failed to recognize and secure the rights of certain Americans. Congress had to provide this protection and had the power to do so independent of the states.

. . . Federal judges and legal officers interpreted the Thirteenth Amendment, the Fourteenth Amendment, and the Civil Rights Act of 1866 as conferring a broad authority to enforce civil rights directly, irrespective of the presence of discriminatory state action and regardless of the source of the violation, because these rights were the natural rights that belonged to all free citizens of a free republic. Indeed, the notion that a national civil rights enforcement authority was merely a guarantee of racially impartial government action was not judicially recognized in the federal courts until the Supreme Court's decisions in the 1870s.

The Supreme Court's decisions narrowing enforcement authority reflected the North's diminished interest in Reconstruction. By the 1870s, the Republican party, a coalition of diverse political groups, began to fragment further over the policies and corruption of Ulysses S. Grant's presidency. One group split away during Grant's first administration to form a separate party, the Liberal Republicans. They turned against Grant's Southern policy and resisted congressional interference in the South. Liberal Republicans also fought to curtail the size and power of the national government and to return political authority to local government. Their objectives indicated their desire for a return to normality and their interest in increasing states' rights for the purpose of controlling monopolies and the railroads. Some of the leaders of civil rights enforcement joined this movement. Lyman Trumbull was one. Reflecting these new political pressures, he changed his views regarding a national authority to enforce civil rights. By 1871, he was insisting that the 1866 Civil Rights Act and the Fourteenth Amendment applied only to racially discriminatory state action, and that they guaranteed no more than racial equality in state-conferred rights and a prohibition against racially discriminatory state laws. By July of 1873, the Grant administration also lost interest in Reconstruction and ended its policy of civil rights enforcement. Except for a few minor episodes of federal involvement in Southern affairs, black and white Republicans in the South were left on their own. Insofar as the enforcement of civil rights was concerned, Reconstruction ended long before the Compromise of 1877.

As the Republican framers understood them, the Thirteenth and Fourteenth Amendments were constitutionally revolutionary. These amendments delegated to Congress the authority to render a radical change in the role of the national government in American life. Congress and the federal courts had not participated to any great extent before 1860 in guaranteeing the fundamental and personal rights of citizens. Republicans chose to protect these rights in 1866 by enacting the Civil Rights Act, which conferred on the federal courts jurisdiction over and responsibility for enforcing the personal rights of citizens directly when citizens could not do so in the traditional institution, namely, the state and local courts.

This new role for national institutions involved radical changes in constitutional law. Fundamental rights were secured and enforced through state law before the Civil War, but, afterwards, the civil rights statutes made fundamental rights a matter of national jurisdiction. The fundamental rights of citizens were now defined as rights pertaining to U.S. citizenship and, as such, were recognized by the Constitution and laws of the United States. Although the states were expected to continue in their traditional function of securing civil rights, their authority was to be shared with Congress and the federal courts. Because federal law was supreme, Congress and the federal courts could supplant all state authority over personal rights. The framers' legal theory of citizenship and congressional authority over the rights of citizens held the potential of ending federalism and establishing a consolidated, unitary state. That the framers eschewed this extreme institutional arrangement should not deflect attention from the other ways in which civil rights amendments and laws of Reconstruction represented, to the framers and federal legal officers, a revolutionary constitutionalism and a new American federalism centered in national authority and national institutions.

In the 1870s, the Supreme Court rejected the revolutionary congressional Republican theory of constitutionalism and read into the Thirteenth and Fourteenth Amendments the theory of states' rights promoted by congressional Conservative Democrats. The Court explicitly rejected the broader theory of a congressional civil rights enforcement authority, precisely because it was revolutionary. The Supreme Court preserved a modified theory of state sovereignty, resurrected a theory of American federalism based on states' rights, and recognized primary authority over citizenship and civil rights as residing in the states. Although American law denied the right of secession, it adopted other important elements of the antebellum theory of constitutionalism. Congressional framers of the Fourteenth Amendment and the Civil Rights Act of 1866 may have thought they were reconstructing American government and basing it on a revolutionary constitutional foundation, but the Supreme Court decided against this revolutionary constitutionalism in a reactionary resurgence of states' rights that resulted in the virtual reenslavement of Southern black Americans.

Federalism and the Limits of Civil Rights

MICHAEL LES BENEDICT

. . . It has become a commonplace of American history that the Chase and Waite Courts subverted Congress's post–Civil War Reconstruction legislation. A typical reading is that the Court engaged in a "judicial counterrevo-

From "Preserving Federalism: Reconstruction and the Waite Court" by Michael Les Benedict, pp. 39–41, 45–47, 49, 56–61, 63–64, 67–70, 74–79 in *Supreme Court Review* 1978, edited by Phillip B. Kurland and Gerhard Casper, Copyright © 1979. Reprinted by permission of University of Chicago Press.

lution," a "judicially-directed perversion of what the abolitionists tried to write into the Constitution," the most "striking instance in American constitutional history of outright judicial disregard for congressional intent." Historians and legal scholars, in recognition that the postwar constitutional amendments were designed to write an antislavery theory of American rights into the Constitution, have damned the Court, essentially for two reasons. First, because the Court was so restrictive in its construction of the Fourteenth Amendment's Privileges and Immunities Clause. Second, because the Court gutted Republican efforts to make the national government the guarantor of citizens' rights. The vehicle for this subversion, it is charged, was the doctrine of "State action." While this criticism has flourished since the 1930s, John Mabry Matthews and Charles Warren had earlier described the same judicial misbehavior, except that, on the whole, Matthews and Warren approved of it.

No feat of revisionism can turn the Waite Court of the 1870s and 1880s into a firm and unflinching defender of black peoples' rights. But the fact is that the modern criticism distorts our constitutional history. It fails to distinguish the position of the Waite Court from its successors, accepting, for instance, the reactionary decisions of the Fuller Court in civil rights cases as logical extensions of Waite Court doctrines, which they were not. Moreover, the modern criticism proceeds from the assumptions of a constitutional theory of nationalism that is indigenous to our age, presumes that Reconstruction legislation proceeded upon the same theory, and judges the Supreme Court's nationalism against that standard. Historians of Reconstruction, however, are beginning to realize that Civil War–era Republicans adhered to a concept of nationalism far less expansive than what has since emerged. They fought for the Union they had known and loved, a Union in which the authority of the national government was balanced against the rights of the States. And they fought for freedom. After victory they wanted to make the rights inherent in that freedom secure, but they wanted to secure them within the old federal framework. As southern whites contested every inch of freedom's advance, it became ever more apparent that the Republicans' commitments both to federalism and to security of rights were in conflict, and they were forced to make an agonizing choice between them. The Supreme Court under Chase and Waite was faced with the same dilemma. Responding to it, the Justices did not bow to racism, betray nationalism, and revive discredited theories of federalism. They made the same effort as did the Republicans to preserve the balance of the old federal system, to protect the States' rights which had been an implicit element of nationalism as it had been understood for fifty years, and at the same time to recognize in Congress enough power to protect civil rights. In the process they reached surprisingly liberal conclusions about congressional power under the postwar Amendments, given the dominant ideas of federalism which provided the context in which they operated.

The essential difference between modern constitutional nationalism and that prevalent at the time of the Civil War was the latter's acceptance of the notion that there was a reserved area of State jurisdiction beyond the competence of national authority. Modern constitutional doctrine reflects the Supreme Court's conclusions in *United States* v. *Darby*—the deathblow to "dual federalism"—that the jurisdiction of the State governments is defined by that of the national, that the Tenth Amendment "states but a truism that all is retained which has not been surrendered."

The focus of our attention has shifted dramatically from where it was when Americans went to war in 1861. The earlier era was State centered. In practical terms this was reflected in the small effect of national government on Americans' daily lives. From birth to death the only federal officials most Americans were likely to see in peacetime were their postmaster and a pension agent. Both were local men appointed for political services rendered in their own communities. In political terms it was reflected in the continued domination from the 1830s to the eve of war of a political party founded upon a narrow conception of national power. And in legal-constitutional terms it was reflected in the acceptance, even among those who favored energetic national government, of the principles of what Edward S. Corwin identified as "dual federalism." . . .

It was not the doctrine of dual federalism, or "State rights," that threatened to disrupt the Union in 1861, but rather that of "State sovereignty." . . . When State sovereignty doctrines were expressed in the form of nullification and secession, the fundamental differences with even the most anti–national-power dual federalists became apparent, as northern Democrats rallied to the flag. In terms of constitutional theory, the Civil War was fought between the concepts of State sovereignty and what we would now identify as State rights.

Historians have accurately perceived in the legislation of the Civil War years an application of constitutional nationalism much more similar to our own than what had gone before . . . . Even as they fought to maintain national supremacy, northerners divided on whether the very existence of sovereign States imposed some limitation upon the jurisdiction of the national government. . . .

This commitment to State rights within the federal system seriously compromised Republican efforts to establish full freedom and equality for the newly freed slaves. Historians now recognize that every Reconstruction-era effort to protect the rights of citizens was tempered by the fundamental conviction that federalism required that the day-to-day protection of the citizen had to remain the duty of the States. . . .

Since Americans believed that the main purpose of government was to protect citizens against wrongs perpetrated by others, Republicans believed that by banning State discrimination they were guaranteeing positive protection to freed slaves. "The presumption was that these States would be obedient to the Constitution and the laws," James G. Blaine remembered. "But for this presumption, legislation would be but idle play, and a government of laws would degenerate at once into a government of force. In enacting the Reconstruction laws, Congress proceeded upon the basis of faith in Republican government." . . .

The Supreme Court's construction of the legislation and constitutional amendments of the Reconstruction era must be understood within the context of this State-centered nationalism. For if Republican legislators ultimately came to see that their desire to protect rights was at war with their desire to preserve federalism, the Court had to face that dilemma even earlier, and in its starkest aspect, in the *Slaughter-House Cases* of 1873.

The *Slaughter-House Cases* brought into focus the Fourteenth Amendment's potential for revolutionary change in American federalism in a way the black-rights-oriented legislation of Congress simply had not. The doctrines the lawyers for the New Orleans butchers advocated were aimed at more than the Crescent City Live-Stock and Slaughter-House Company's "monopoly" (which was in reality no monopoly at all). Their arguments attacked State legislation regulating the State lottery, municipal gas supply, levee repair, funding of the State debt, "prodigal expenditures and jobs innumerable." The Fourteenth Amendment was designed to protect individuals from State invasion of all citizens' fundamental rights and immunities, broadly construed, they insisted. Assume a narrower purpose and "the State may deny individual rights and liberties, and claim to perform all the offices and duties of society, and under the names of socialism, communism, and other specious pretences, control all the revenues and labor of the State." The argument for broad protection for citizens' privileges and immunities under the Fourteenth Amendment was no effort to secure the rights of black Americans. It was an invitation to the Court to write the "vested rights" doctrine into the Constitution through the Privileges and Immunities Clause in 1873 as they would write it into the Due Process Clause twenty years later. Defendant's counsel saw this clearly: "The result of the argument against the validity of this charter must . . . be this: that the 14th amendment does not prohibit State legislatures from passing acts of municipal legislation which abridge the privileges and immunities of citizens, provided such acts appear to be reasonable, but does prohibit the passing of acts which appear to be unreasonable; that it is for this court to determine whether such acts are reasonable or unreasonable."

Moreover, this proposition was being posited in an era of active congressional civil rights legislation, long before the Supreme Court became the most active protector of rights among the branches of the national government. Although the butchers' lawyers avoided the issue, there was no convincing reason why Congress should not accept the same invitation so temptingly offered the Justices. Even proponents of the broad view worried about such a revolution in the federal system. John Norton Pomeroy tried to demonstrate that the rights secured by the Privileges and Immunities Clause could be enforced only by the judiciary, but he was not very convincing. What was convincing was the terrible consequence he predicted from such an assumption of jurisdiction by Congress: "If the Democratic party should come to power, it is certainly within the range of possibilities that it should endeavor to uphold and sustain the liquor interest by Congressional legislation directed against State prohibitory and license laws. . . . [T]he State laws could be declared void; the States enacting and sustaining them could be described as 'abridging the privileges and immunities of citizens of the United States' . . . ." Likewise, Congress could protect privileges and immunities by nullifying Sabbath laws or restrictions against church endowments.

It is in light of the commitment of Americans generally to the idea that the States had a reserved area of jurisdiction that the query in Justice Miller's majority opinion must be read: "Was it the purpose of the fourteenth amendment . . . to transfer the security and protection of all the civil rights [broadly defined] . . . from the States to the Federal Government? . . . [W]as it intended to bring within the power of Congress the entire domain of civil rights heretofore belonging exclusively to the States?" If so, "Congress . . . may pass laws . . . limiting and restricting the exercise of legislative power by the States, in their most ordinary and usual functions," and the Supreme Court would be "constitute[d] a perpetual censor upon all legislation of the States, on the civil rights of their own citizens, with authority to nullify such as it did not approve as consistent with those rights."

Given such possibilities, it is not surprising that the majority of the Justices sought to avoid what seemed to many the obvious meaning of the Fourteenth Amendment's Privileges and Immunities Clause. And given the doctrines of dual federalism that the Court had already endorsed in *Collector* v. *Day,* it is not surprising that they found the way out in the notion that Americans held privileges and immunities as citizens of the United States different from those they held as citizens of the individual States.

Constitutional historians have severely criticized the *Slaughter-House* decision for nullifying the plain meaning of the Fourteenth Amendment's Privileges and Immunities Clause as defined by its framers. As early as 1879, a critic wondered what fiery old Thaddeus Stevens' reaction would have been if told that all he had intended to secure through that clause were the rights of ex-slaves to protection on the high seas, to travel freely between States, or to petition the government. There can be no doubt that the point was well made. Whatever Republicans intended "privileges and immunities of citizens of the United States" to mean, it was more than that. But Stevens would have been just as incredulous to learn that he had given Congress or the Supreme Court the power to nullify Louisiana's regulations of slaughterhouses, and that is the nub of the conundrum the Court faced. As the *American Law Review* understood, the problem in construing the Amendment's provisions was to "apply their letter . . . to new states of fact not contemplated by Congress nor the legislatures that made them."

Critics of the *Slaughter-House Cases* argue that the Court majority ignored the well-known intent of the Fourteenth Amendment and that Miller's eloquent articulation of its "one pervading purpose," to secure full liberty to blacks, was merely "a strategic obfuscation of the issues." But it was those who contended for the broad interpretation of privileges and immunities who had to concede they were innovating. "It is possible that those who framed the article were not themselves aware of the far reaching character of its terms," Justice Bradley admitted in his circuit court decision sustaining the butchers. "Yet, if the amendment, as framed and expressed, does in fact bear a broader meaning, and does extend its protecting shield over those who were never thought of when it was conceived and put in form . . . , it must be presumed that the American people, in giving it their imprimatur, understood what they were doing." The butchers' Democratic counsel insisted they were compelled on principle to "assume" a broader meaning for the Amendment than the merely "partisan" one that might be attributed to it. It was the Court majority and the defendant's lawyers, on the other hand, who argued, "So far as can be judged by the public debate upon the subject, it was certainly never intended or contemplated that this Amendment should receive such a construction." "Have Congress and the whole nation been deceived?" they asked. "Have they done what they did not intend to do?"

In virtually eliminating the Privileges and Immunities Clause as a source of national power to protect citizens' rights, Miller and the lawyers for the Slaughter-House "monopoly" insisted that they intended no subversion of black men's liberty. As noted, Miller was eloquent upon the "one pervading purpose" of the Amendment to protect black rights, and several of the "monopoly's" lawyers were active radical Republicans. Their conviction that the well-known purpose of the Amendment "was to secure all citizens and persons the same rights as white citizens and persons" suggests that they placed primary reliance upon its Equal Protection Clause. That ultimately proved to be a weak reed, but there is no reason to believe that a broader definition of the Privileges and Immunities Clause would have provided any stronger support for black rights. The real obstacle to protection for those rights was the Court's insistence that they were protected only against State infringement and not against individual violence. The Privileges and Immunities Clause was subject to the same limitation, and those who sustained a broad view of it made clear that they interpreted it the same way.

Moreover, those who advocated a broad interpretation of privileges and immunities intended to leave their definition to the vagaries of the judiciary, just as "due process of law" would be subject to judicial construction decades later. The implications are obvious in the result of *Bradwell* v. *Illinois,* decided only the next day. In that case three of the four Justices who advocated the broader view of privileges and immunities in Slaughter-House concluded that a regulation barring women from practicing law was a "reasonable" exercise of the State police power. It was consistent with "the divine law of the Creator," which made woman's "paramount destiny and mission . . . to fulfill the noble and benign offices of wife and mother." The same "divine law" could be—and would be—cited to ordain "reasonable" regulations of the privileges and immunities of freedmen. . . .

When one assesses the Supreme Court's decisions within the context of the doctrines of dual federalism accepted by most Americans in the nineteenth century, however, what is remarkable is the degree to which the Court sustained national authority to protect rights rather than the degree to which they restricted it. In fact, although the Justices found fault with indictments and ruled Reconstruction legislation unconstitutional for excessive breadth, they made clear that with the exception of a few of the *Civil Rights Cases,* every single prosecution brought before them could have been sustained by an appropriate national law. In the very decisions that released southern defendants as well as in those that affirmed their convictions, the Court rejected nearly all the arguments against national enforcement of rights put forward by its opponents. The Justices adhered to the doctrine of "state action" under the Fourteenth Amendment—the crucial element in the maintenance of the federal system they believed in. They repudiated every other restriction.

In Congress, in political platforms, campaign literature and oratory, and finally in legal briefs, arguments, and opinions, opponents of Reconstruction legislation developed a catalogue of limitations upon national authority to protect civil and political rights that truly would have nullified the constitutional amendments had it been accepted, and caused incalculable embarrassment to modern federal civil rights protection, much of which is still based upon the Reconstruction-era laws.

They insisted that the Thirteenth Amendment itself did no more than abolish the institution of slavery. Legislation authorized by its enforcement provision could reach nothing more than peonage and coolyism. Thus if the Fourteenth Amendment had not been passed, the Civil Rights Act of 1866 would have been unconstitutional. If the Thirteenth Amendment did not give Congress power to protect rights, the Fourteenth and Fifteenth Amendments did little more, according to the conservative argument. Not only were the prohibitions of the Fourteenth and Fifteenth Amendments aimed only at States, they were aimed at States only in their corporate capacities. Thus, they operated directly upon offending State laws, rendering them immediately null and void, but could not authorize criminal or civil action against State officers who carried out those laws. In a federal system in which State and nation were equally sovereign, neither government could impose duties on the officers of the other. And that was even more certainly true if the officer's act was not sanctioned by State law or was in actual contravention of it. Moreover, it was a plain violation of the Constitution to make the same act both a State and a national crime, so no offense against a State law could be prosecuted by the national government merely by giving it another name. . . .

A jurist's conviction that the Fourteenth Amendment restated the State's positive duty to provide full protection of the laws did not necessarily mean that he believed Congress could remedy its failure to fulfill it. The nationalist constitutional commentator Pomeroy, who did share this conviction, denied that State dereliction activated national authority. "If the good and valid laws which legislatures have enacted are not fully administered, there is no legal remedy to be obtained . . . from Congress . . . ; redress must be found alone in a change of officers through the ordinary processes of election and appointment," he insisted. While the Court never repudiated the notion in words as direct as David Dudley Field's—"State inaction . . . is no cause for federal action"—neither did it repeat Woods's dictum from his days as district judge that "denying includes inaction as well as action, . . . the omission to protect, as well as the omission to pass laws for protection." It would have been easy to do either.

The Court did, however, reject totally the contention that the Fourteenth Amendment referred to the action of States only in their corporate capacities. As early as 1870 federal judges were sustaining prosecutions of State officers for failures to administer State laws equally, whether or not the laws were discriminatory on their face. In circuit court in 1873 Justice Strong upheld the conviction of a tax collector who refused to accept a black man's tender of taxes required to vote under State law. Seven years later he delivered the Court's opinion that even State judges were liable to conviction for carrying out unfairly nonjudicial functions imposed by superficially equal State laws. Moreover, in a cognate case, Strong made clear that even if a State officer deprived a person of a right in direct contravention of State laws, such a violation would both make him "liable to punishment at the instance of the State and under the laws of the United States." At the same time the Court upheld congressional laws aimed directly at State officers' interference with voting rights at federal elections.

While we might take such decisions for granted today, within the context of nineteenth-century federalism these were bold rulings indeed. . . . The laws the Court thus sustained asserted "a power inconsistent with, and destructive of, the independence of the States," Field and Clifford insisted in dissent. "The right to control their own officers, to prescribe the duties they shall perform, without the supervision or interference of any other state authority . . . is essential to that independence." . . .

Even more enlightening is the reasoning by which the Supreme Court tried to sustain national authority to protect individual rights directly without permitting precedents that might later destroy the established lines between State and national power. The Justices did this through doctrines first propounded by Bradley in his circuit court opinion in *Cruikshank.* In that prosecution the United States district attorney for Louisiana, James Beckwith, sought the convictions of the Grant Parish rioters under section six of the Enforcement Act of 1870, which made it illegal for two or more people to injure or threaten any citizen "with intent to prevent or hinder his free exercise and enjoyment of any right or privilege granted or secured to him" by the United States Constitution or laws. The indictment alleged several counts of murder with the intent to deprive the victims of various rights secured by the Constitution—to bear arms, to assemble peaceably, to equal protection of the laws, to enjoyment of life and liberty unless deprived of them by due process of law, to rights secured by the State and national constitutions because of their color, the right to vote, and all the privileges and immunities of citizens of the United States.

The defendants' lawyers attacked the constitutionality of the law itself, insisting it usurped the States' jurisdiction over individual crimes. Bradley agreed that the Fourteenth Amendment prohibited State action only and that protection of rights was primarily the duty of the States. Any other holding "would be to clothe congress with power to pass laws for the general preservation of social order in every state." Yet despite these strictures, he upheld the law as an exercise of congressional power, not under the Fourteenth Amendment, but under the Thirteenth and Fifteenth.

The Thirteenth Amendment, Bradley asserted, involved more than the mere nullification of the formal institution of slavery. It implied the vesting of the positive rights of freedom. Therefore it authorized Congress "to make it a penal offense to conspire to deprive a person of, or hinder him in, the exercise and enjoyment of the rights and privileges conferred by the 13th amendment and the laws thus passed in pursuance thereof." So not only was Congress freed of the "State action" limitation by Bradley's construction, but the "rights and privileges" protected by the Enforcement Act were those of citizenship in general, not the limited ones the Supreme Court perceived incident to United States citizenship in *Slaughter-House*. . . .

It is not clear whether the whole Court immediately accepted Bradley's recognition of broad congressional power to enforce the Thirteenth Amendment. Bradley's colleagues certainly did not reject it when his *Cruikshank* opinion came before them a year later. Waite's majority opinion sustaining Bradley's circuit court judgment is unclear on the grounds on which the Justices upheld the constitutionality of the Enforcement Act provisions before them. Waite, however, followed Bradley's analysis of the specific counts closely, and Bradley did not write a separate opinion, suggesting that he saw nothing inconsistent between Waite's views and his own. In *United States v. Harris*, where a lynch mob was accused of killing their victims with intent to deny their right to equal protection of the laws, Justice Woods tested the provisions of the Enforcement Act against Congress's power to protect rights directly under the Thirteenth Amendment, but without committing the whole Court to Bradley's views. "Even if the Amendment is held to be directed against the action of private individuals," he wrote, "the law under consideration covers cases both within and without the provisions of the Amendment" because it does not require racial motivation for the offense. Therefore, under the rule of construction enunciated in *Reese*, the law fell.

But if the Court did not endorse Bradley's views unequivocally in *Cruikshank* or *Reese*, it certainly acquiesced in them when he wrote the opinion striking down the Civil Rights Act of 1875. In the famous (or perhaps infamous) *Civil Rights Cases*, Bradley tested the law against both the Fourteenth and the Thirteenth Amendments. Rejecting arguments that the businesses and institutions covered by the act were quasi–state agencies, he held the law unwarranted by the Fourteenth Amendment on State action grounds. But when it came to treating the Thirteenth Amendment, Bradley took advantage of the opportunity to write his expansive views of that Amendment—the heritage of the antislavery legal argument—squarely into the Court's opinion. "It is true, that . . . the Thirteenth Amendment may be regarded as nullifying all State laws which establish or uphold slavery. But it has a reflex character also, establishing and decreeing universal civil and political freedom throughout the United States; and it is assumed, [by those upholding the law,] that the power vested in Congress to enforce the article by appropriate legislation, clothes Congress with power to pass all laws necessary and proper for abolishing all badges and incidents of slavery in the United States." Bradley conceded the truth of the assumption, but then rejected the proposition that denial of equal accommodations and privileges was an incident of slavery.

Bradley's problem was that his own interpretation of the Thirteenth Amendment threatened to justify national punishment of any private invasion of a citizen's rights where race was the motive, to sustain a national criminal code protecting blacks against ordinary crimes against life and property. He apparently felt impelled to draw the line somewhere. In his cruel sentence—"When a man has emerged from slavery, . . . there must be some stage in the progress of his elevation when he takes the rank of a mere citizen, and ceases to be the special favorite of the laws, and when his rights as a . . . man, are to be protected in the ordinary modes by which other men's rights are protected"—Bradley, it would seem, was referring to stages of law, not time. Direct national legislation protecting basic rights inherent in freedom was legitimate; legislation protecting more elevated rights was not. Moreover, Bradley believed that State courts had held the common law to require equal access for all citizens to inns and public conveyances. Any change in that requirement would have to be made by statute. He implied that if such statute caused an injust discrimination, it would violate the Fourteenth Amendment. And he carefully avoided any suggestion that Congress lacked authority to pass a similar law restricted in its application to interstate conveyances and United States territory and the District of Columbia.

A recent analyst has stated aptly that "both the majority position in the *Civil Rights Cases* and the Harlan dissent . . . were fashioned by Joseph Bradley." Like Bradley, Harlan rejected the *Slaughter-House Cases'* narrow conception of congressional authority under the Fourteenth Amendment to protect rights of citizenship. But that was a lost cause. Harlan's dissent challenged Bradley most powerfully by accepting Bradley's own views of the Thirteenth Amendment. "The Thirteenth Amendment, it is conceded, did something more than to prohibit slavery as an *institution,* resting upon distinctions of race, and shielded by positive law," Harlan wrote. "My brethren admit that it established and decreed universal *civil freedom.* . . . They admit . . . that there are burdens and disabilities, the necessary incidents of slavery, which constitute its substance and visible form; that Congress, by the [Civil Rights] Act of 1866, passed in view of the Thirteenth Amendment, . . . undertook to remove certain burdens and disabilities . . . and secure to all citizens of every race and color . . . those fundamental rights which are the essence of civil freedom . . . ; that under the 13th Amendment . . . legislation, so far as necessary and proper to eradicate all forms and incidents of slavery and involuntary servitude may be direct and primary, operating upon the acts of individuals, whether sanctioned by state legislation or not." Harlan recognized what most scholars have not; to reverse Bradley's judgment it was not necessary to challenge his construction of the constitutional amendments. It was merely necessary to challenge his definition of the "incidents" of slavery.

In sum, then, the Supreme Court's construction of congressional power under the constitutional amendments hardly subverted Republican intent.

Committed, as were nearly all Americans of the time, to maintaining the State's primary jurisdiction over criminal offenses, endorsing the basic concepts of dual federalism, the Court still managed to sustain Congress's power to protect directly citizens' fundamental civil and political rights. . . .

Of course neither black Americans nor radical Republicans felt much like thanking the Waite Court for sustaining congressional power while they released southern killers and election riggers. Democrats and "liberal" or "Mugwump" Republicans demanding sectional reconciliation at the price of black rights praised Court decisions that protected "State rights" by releasing undoubted criminals upon technicalities of statutory construction. It was in their interests politically to ignore the fact that these decisions were based on technicalities, that beneath the surface most of Congress's power to protect rights remained unimpaired. But when one steps back from the immediate political circumstances of the decisions, when one assesses them in light of contemporary doctrines of federalism rather than our own, one reaches a more balanced conclusion. No one can accuse the Justices of the Waite Court of wearing their hearts upon the sleeves of their robes, but they left a heritage of sanctioned congressional power over civil rights that was ignored by their immediate successors and only recently resurrected, without credit to them, by the new abolitionists of the mid-twentieth century.

The Supreme Court's Denial of the Rights of Women

JOAN HOFF WILSON

The period 1865 to 1920 marks the first time that women systematically tried to obtain equality of treatment in the courts. While they did not succeed, in retrospect their attempts are interesting for a number of reasons. First, the few cases of major significance involving women clearly indicate the overwhelming legal obstacles that the several generations of women of these years faced, almost regardless of the issues being discussed. Second, judicial patterns or preferences that emerged by 1920 from these cases lingered for many years—some down to the [1970s]. Third, there was also a subtle interaction between the political and legal activities of women reformers during this period. Their relationship has been largely ignored by both legal historians and historians of women's history. . . .

In fact, the most overtly sexist decisions on the part of the Supreme Court occurred *after* the Civil War, as women attempted to improve their legal status under the fourteenth amendment. This is not to say that the Married Women's Property Acts, which were passed in nine states *before* the Civil War, were liberally interpreted by the lower courts. Professor Linda Kerber has referred to the conservative nature of these pre-war acts and the postwar ones were generally not more liberating in terms of either motivation of an expansion of married women's rights. The significance of these very

Joan Hoff Wilson, "The Legal Status of Women in the Late Nineteenth and Early Twentieth Centuries," from paper delivered at American Bar Association Meeting in Atlanta, 1976. Reprinted by permission of the author.

legally limited and narrowly interpreted Married Women's Property Acts lies in the fact that they represented one of the major traditional instruments whereby legal reform could be achieved for women, namely, through the passage of legislation at the state level. By 1900 they constituted the most significant advance in the status of married women with respect to property. They also represented the most viable legal alternative for women before the appearance of substantive due process, which did not occur until the early twentieth century when the Supreme Court adopted the use of "judicial notice" and accepted facts deemed "common knowledge."

In other words, all of the other legal means women pursued to obtain equality of treatment between 1865 and 1900 had failed. Let us review the major Supreme Court cases that arose after the passage of the Reconstruction Amendments. As I have said they are few in number and in some instances are well known for reasons other than their impact on women. They are: *Bradwell* v. *Illinois,* which held that the right to practice law was not a privilege and immunity of citizenship for a woman; the *Slaughter House Cases,* which also very narrowly interpreted the Privileges and Immunity clause of the fourteenth amendment and remains well known for its definition of national citizenship and the denial that the Equal Protection clause could be applied in other than race cases; *Minor* v. *Happersett,* which declared that historically women constituted a very special category of citizens whose inability to vote did not infringe upon their rights as citizens; and *Ex parte Yarbrough,* which technically overruled the *Minor* decision by setting the stage for the proposition that voting for a federal official was, indeed, a privilege and immunity of national citizenship.

Remember, that it was also during these years from 1865 to 1900, that in those states where the first women's rights movement was the most actively organized, Married Women's Property Acts were more comprehensive than before the Civil War. These statutes, however, were still subjected to severely restrictive judicial interpretations by the end of the century. These are the same years that women united around the long struggle for passage of women's suffrage at the state level. This effort finally led to the passage of the nineteenth amendment at the end of World War I. It was also the period in which the country celebrated its Centennial in 1876. Professor Kerber has alluded to the famous document that Susan B. Anthony and others insisted on presenting in Philadelphia that July 4—called a Women's Declaration of Rights. Beginning with the words: "The history of our country the past hundred years has been a series of assumptions and usurpations of power over woman, in direct opposition to the principles of just government . . . ," it called for the impeachment of American leaders. Thus, we can see that women reformers resorted to political activities when they failed to improve their legal status through the courts following the passage of the fourteenth and fifteenth amendments. These same women had unsuccessfully employed every effort to get Republican leaders to eliminate the word "male" from the first section of the former and to add the word "sex" to the latter. Taken together these two amendments to the Constitution of the United States implied that women were not citizens. Female activists lost no time testing both in the courts in some of the cases cited above. In a very real sense, therefore, passage of the fourteenth and fifteenth amendments, and their subsequent negative interpretation by courts, as far as women were concerned, forced all post-war female reformers—whether they considered themselves radical or moderates—to concentrate on what had never been their primary pre-war goal: suffrage.

So the legal and political implications of the Reconstruction Amendments for the first women's movement were enormous. The Civil War itself had disrupted the momentum of the women's rights movement since 1848. When the post-war political efforts of the more militant reformers, like Anthony and Stanton, failed to expressly include women in the fourteenth and fifteenth amendments, they immediately began the first of a series of systematic attempts by several generations of women to use the courts to improve their legal and political status—first through the Privileges and Immunities clause, then through the Due Process clause, and finally, continuing down to the present, through the Equal Protection clause. To date none of these efforts has been competely successful and the initial attempts, as reflected in the cases mentioned above, were particularly discouraging.

For example, one of the worst aspects of the Myra Colby Bradwell case was not simply that she was denied the right to practice as a lawyer in Illinois. Its worst feature was the language that Justice Bradley used in his concurring opinion. In the Blackstone tradition, Bradley insisted that women had no legal existence separate from that of their husbands, despite the passage of a number of Married Women's Property Acts. His opinion stated:

> The civil law, as well as nature itself, has always recognized a wide difference in the respective spheres and destinies of man and woman. Man is, or should be, woman's protector and defender. . . . The domestic sphere . . . properly belongs to the domain and functions of womanhood. The harmony . . . of interests and ties which belong, or should belong, to the family institution is repugnant to the idea of a woman adopting a distinct and independent career from that of her husband. . . . The paramount destiny and mission of woman are to fulfill the noble and benign offices of wife and mother. This is the law of the creator. And the rules of civil society must be adapted to the general constitution of things, and cannot be based upon exceptional cases.

Another interesting feature of *Bradwell* is its relationship to the *Slaughter House Cases.* Since both were considered by the Supreme Court during the same fourteen month period, it is entirely possible that the narrow interpretation of privileges and immunities with respect to a choice of occupation for the butchers in *Slaughter House* was probably "influenced by the Court's realization that a broad interpretation would necessarily change the status of women." Justice Bradley's position on these two cases is also noteworthy. He argued against Myra Bradwell's right of choice of occupation. But in his dissenting opinion in the *Slaughter House Cases,* he argued for the butchers having that same right, saying that a "law which prohibits a large class of citizens from adopting lawful employment . . . does deprive them of liberty as well as property without due process of law." Obviously by the word "citizens," Justice Bradley did not mean women. Mathew Carpenter, one of the best known advocates of the day, took similarly irreconcilable positions in these two cases. He was, unlike Bradley, arguing against the butchers and for Bradwell. His opinions were as inconsistent as Bradley's, albeit for different legal reasons. Nonetheless, both men used standard sexist arguments.

One might wonder why such inconsistencies were never seriously questioned by the Court or any historian until recently. Was Bradwell's case simply considered less important because of prevailing "natural male dominance" theories of the time? Did the general political climate of the Reconstruction Era play a more important role than gender discrimination in the *Bradwell* and *Slaughter House* decisions? Regardless of the exact reasons, one thing is clear. The decisions and precedents set in these two cases created insurmountable obstacles for a broadening of women's rights through the courts in the early post–Civil War decades.

About the same time that Bradwell was bringing suit to practice law, other women were taking more direct and disruptive action by actually trying to vote. In 1871 and 1872 over 100 women voted in nine different states. The most famous of all these attempts resulted in the trial of Susan B. Anthony, who with thirteen other women tried to vote on November 5, 1872, in Rochester, New York. All of the women were arrested under a provision of the Federal Civil Rights Act of 1870 which was designed to prevent white voters from cancelling out black votes by voting more than once. The misuse of this law against Anthony and other women in the 1870s brings to mind the parallel of the similarly novel use of federal statutes in the 1960s against demonstrators. It was also a clear indication of the political nature of her trial. The Anthony case never reached the Supreme Court because of two legal technicalities. Therefore, interest in the case today remains largely historical because of the increased interest in Anthony as a militant feminist. Moreover, the legal issues it raised were more clearly developed in *Minor* v. *Happersett* in 1875.

Using parallel reasoning to *Dred Scott* v. *Sandford,* the *Minor* court declared women a special category similar to that of children and specifically denied that the right to vote for national officials was a privilege and immunity of national citizenship as implied in the *Slaughter House Cases.* The *Minor* decision, like the *Dred Scott* decision of twenty years before, could only be bypassed by a constitutional amendment, even though the *Minor* case was unofficially overruled in the *Yarbrough* case of 1884. What is curious here is that *Dred Scott* has for some time been considered a blot on constitutional law, but *Minor* and *Bradwell* have yet to receive the same deserved castigation by the legal profession. Again, the question must be asked— why? Is it because of Reconstruction politics or judicial sexism, or both? Little wonder that Anthony and other radical women protested at the 1876 Centennial celebration in Philadelphia. These women knew what was happening to their rights in courts. Many, like Bradwell, were involved in writing and agitating for Married Women's Property Acts. So they took up the cause of suffrage with a vengeance and conservatism that had not generally characterized their court actions. . . .

✚ *F U R T H E R   R E A D I N G*

Herman Belz, *Emancipation and Equal Rights: Politics and Constitutionalism in the Civil War Era* (1978)

Raoul Berger, *Government by Judiciary: The Transformation of the Fourteenth Amendment* (1977)

Loren P. Beth, *The Development of the American Constitution, 1877–1917* (1971)

Michael Kent Curtis, *No State Shall Abridge: The Fourteenth Amendment and the Bill of Rights* (1986)

Charles Fairman, *Reconstruction and Reunion, 1864–88* (Part One), vol. 6 of *History of the Supreme Court of the United States,* P. Freund, ed. (1971)

Harold M. Hyman, *A More Perfect Union: The Impact of the Civil War and Reconstruction on the Constitution* (1973)

———and William M. Wiecek, *Equal Justice Under Law: Constitutional Development, 1835–1875* (1982)

Joseph B. James, *The Ratification of the Fourteenth Amendment* (1984).

Robert J. Kaczorowski, *The Politics of Judicial Interpretation: The Federal Courts, Department of Justice and Civil Rights, 1866–1876* (1985)

Michael Les Benedict, *A Compromise of Principle: Congressional Republicans and Reconstruction* (1974)

William E. Nelson, *The Fourteenth Amendment: From Political Principle to Judicial Doctrine* (1988)

Phillip S. Paludan, *A Covenant with Death: The Constitution, Law, and Equality in the Civil War Era* (1975)

Jacobus Ten Broek, *The Antislavery Origins of the Fourteenth Amendment* (1951)

The Articles of Confederation and Perpetual Union

Between the states of New Hampshire, Massachusetts Bay, Rhode Island and Providence Plantations, Connecticut, New York, New Jersey, Pennsylvania, Delaware, Maryland, Virginia, North Carolina, South Carolina, Georgia.*

Article I

The stile of this confederacy shall be "The United States of America."

Article II

Each State retains its sovereignty, freedom and independence, and every power, jurisdiction, and right, which is not by this confederation expressly delegated to the United States, in Congress assembled.

Article III

The said states hereby severally enter into a firm league of friendship with each other for their common defence, the security of their liberties and their mutual and general welfare; binding themselves to assist each other against all force offered to, or attacks made upon them, or any of them, on account of religion, sovereignty, trade, or any other pretence whatever.

Article IV

The better to secure and perpetuate mutual friendship and intercourse among the people of the different states in this union, the free inhabitants of each of these states, paupers, vagabonds, and fugitives from justice excepted, shall be entitled to all privileges and immunities of free citizens in the several states; and the people of each State shall have free ingress and regress to and from any other State, and shall enjoy therein all the privileges of trade and commerce, subject to the same duties, impositions, and restrictions, as the inhabitants thereof respectively; provided, that such restrictions shall not extend so far as to prevent the removal of property, imported into any State, to any other State of which the owner is an inhabitant; provided also, that no imposition, duties, or restriction, shall be laid by any State on the property of the United States, or either of them.

If any person guilty of, or charged with treason, felony, or other high misdemeanor in any State, shall flee from justice and be found in any of

---

* This copy of the final draft of the Articles of Confederation is taken from the *Journals,* 9:907–925, November 15, 1777.

the United States, he shall, upon demand of the governor or executive power of the State from which he fled, be delivered up and removed to the State having jurisdiction of his offence.

Full faith and credit shall be given in each of these states to the records, acts, and judicial proceedings of the courts and magistrates of every other State.

Article V

For the more convenient management of the general interests of the United States, delegates shall be annually appointed, in such manner as the legislature of each State shall direct, to meet in Congress, on the 1st Monday in November in every year, with a power reserved to each State to recall its delegates, or any of them, at any time within the year, and to send others in their stead for the remainder of the year.

No State shall be represented in Congress by less than two, nor by more than seven members; and no person shall be capable of being a delegate for more than three years in any term of six years; nor shall any person, being a delegate, be capable of holding any office under the United States, for which he, or any other for his benefit, receives any salary, fees, or emolument of any kind.

Each State shall maintain its own delegates in a meeting of the states, and while they act as members of the committee of the states.

In determining questions in the United States, in Congress assembled, each State shall have one vote.

Freedom of speech and debate in Congress shall not be impeached or questioned in any court or place out of Congress: and the members of Congress shall be protected in their persons from arrests and imprisonments, during the time of their going to and from, and attendance on Congress, *except for treason,* felony, or breach of the peace.

Article VI

No State, without the consent of the United States, in Congress assembled, shall send any embassy to, or receive any embassy from, or enter into any conference, agreement, alliance, or treaty with any king, prince, or state; nor shall any person, holding any office of profit or trust under the United States, or any of them, accept of any present, emolument, office or title, of any kind whatever, from any king, prince, or foreign state; nor shall the United States, in Congress assembled, or any of them, grant any title of nobility.

No two or more states shall enter into any treaty, confederation, or alliance, whatever, between them, without the consent of the United States, in Congress assembled, specifying accurately the purposes for which the same is to be entered into, and how long it shall continue.

No State shall lay any imposts or duties which may interfere with any stipulations in treaties entered into by the United States, in Congress assembled, with any king, prince, or state, in pursuance of any treaties already proposed by Congress to the courts of France and Spain.

No vessels of war shall be kept up in time of peace by any State, except such number only as shall be deemed necessary by the United States, in Congress assembled, for the defence of such State or its trade; nor shall any body of forces be kept up by any State, in time of peace, except such number only as, in the judgment of the United States, in Congress assembled, shall be deemed requisite to garrison the forts necessary for the defence of such State; but every State shall always keep up a well regulated and disciplined militia, sufficiently armed and accoutred, and shall provide, and constantly have ready for use, in public stores, a due number of field pieces and tents, and a proper quantity of arms, ammunition and camp equipage.

No State shall engage in any war without the consent of the United States, in Congress assembled, unless such State be actually invaded by enemies, or shall have received certain advice of a resolution being formed by some nation of Indians to invade such State, and the danger is so imminent as not to admit of a delay till the United States, in Congress assembled, can be consulted; nor shall any State grant commissions to any ships or vessels of war, nor letters of marque or reprisal, except it be after a declaration of war by the United States, in Congress assembled, and then only against the kingdom or state, and the subjects thereof, against which war has been so declared, and under such regulations as shall be established by the United States, in Congress assembled, unless such States be infested by pirates, in which case vessels of war may be fitted out for that occasion, and kept so long as the danger shall continue, or until the United States, in Congress assembled, shall determine otherwise.

Article VII

When land forces are raised by any State for the common defence, all officers of or under the rank of colonel, shall be appointed by the legislature of each State respectively, by whom such forces shall be raised, or in such manner as such State shall direct; and all vacancies shall be filled up by the State which first made the appointment.

Article VIII

All charges of war and all other expences, that shall be incurred for the common defence or general welfare, and allowed by the United States, in Congress assembled, shall be defrayed out of a common treasury, which shall be supplied by the several states, in proportion to the value of all land within each State, granted to or surveyed for any person, as such land and the buildings and improvements thereon shall be estimated according to such mode as the United States, in Congress assembled, shall, from time to time, direct and appoint.

The taxes for paying that proportion shall be laid and levied by the authority and direction of the legislatures of the several states, within the time agreed upon by the United States, in Congress assembled.

Article IX

The United States, in Congress assembled, shall have the sole and exclusive right and power of determining on peace and war, except in the cases mentioned in the 6th article; of sending and receiving ambassadors; entering into treaties and alliances, provided that no treaty of commerce shall be made, whereby the legislative power of the respective states shall be restrained from imposing such imposts and duties on foreigners as their own people are subjected to, or from prohibiting the exportation or importation of any species of goods or commodities whatsoever; of establishing rules for deciding, in all cases, what captures on land or water shall be legal, and in what manner prizes, taken by land or naval forces in the service of the United States, shall be divided or appropriated; of granting letters of marque and reprisal in times of peace; appointing courts for the trial of piracies and felonies committed on the high seas, and establishing courts for receiving and determining, finally, appeals in all cases of captures; provided, that no member of Congress shall be appointed a judge of any of the said courts.

The United States, in Congress assembled, shall also be the last resort on appeal in all disputes and differences now subsisting, or that hereafter may arise between two or more states concerning boundary, jurisdiction or any other cause whatever; which authority shall always be exercised in the manner following: whenever the legislative or executive authority, or lawful agent of any State, in controversy with another, shall present a petition to Congress, stating the matter in question, and praying for a hearing, notice thereof shall be given, by order of Congress, to the legislative or executive authority of the other State in controversy, and a day assigned for the appearance of the parties by their lawful agents, who shall then be directed to appoint, by joint consent, commissioners or judges to constitute a court for hearing and determining the matter in question; but, if they cannot agree, Congress shall name three persons out of each of the United States, and from the list of such persons each party shall alternately strike out one, in the petitioners beginning, until the number shall be reduced to thirteen; and from that number not less than seven, nor more than nine names, as Congress shall direct, shall, in the presence of Congress, be drawn out by lot; and the persons whose names shall be drawn, or any five of them, shall be commissioners or judges to hear and finally determine the controversy, so always as a major part of the judges who shall hear the cause shall agree in the determination; and if either party shall neglect to attend at the day appointed, without shewing reasons which Congress shall judge sufficient, or, being present, shall refuse to strike, the Congress shall proceed to nominate three persons out of each State, and the secretary of Congress shall strike in behalf of such party absent or refusing; and the judgment and sentence of the court to be appointed, in the manner before prescribed, shall be final and conclusive; and if any of the parties shall refuse to submit to the authority of such court, or to appear or defend their claim or cause, the court shall nevertheless proceed to pronounce sentence or judgment, which shall, in like manner, be final and decisive, the judgment or sentence and other proceedings being, in either case, transmitted to Congress, and lodged among the acts of Congress for the security of the parties concerned: provided, that every commissioner, before he sits in judgment, shall take an oath, to be administered by one of the judges of the supreme or superior court of the State where the cause shall be tried, "well and truly to hear and determine the matter in question, according to the best of his judgment, without favour, affection, or hope of reward": provided, also, that no State shall be deprived of territory for the benefit of the United States.

All controversies concerning the private right of soil, claimed under different grants of two or more states, whose jurisdictions, as they may respect such lands and the states which passed such grants, are adjusted, the said grants, or either of them, being at the same time claimed to have originated antecedent to such settlement of jurisdiction, shall, on the petition of either party to the Congress of the United States, be finally determined, as near as may be, in the same manner as is before prescribed for deciding disputes respecting territorial jurisdiction between different states.

The United States, in Congress assembled, shall also have the sole and exclusive right and power of regulating the alloy and value of coin struck by their own authority, or by that of the respective states; fixing the standard of weights and measures throughout the United States; regulating the trade and managing all affairs with the Indians not members of any of the states; provided that the legislative right of any State within its own limits be not infringed or violated; establishing and regulating post offices from one State to another throughout all the United States, and exacting such postage on the papers passing through the same as may be requisite to defray the expences of the said office; appointing all officers of the land forces in the service of the United States, excepting regimental officers; appointing all the officers of the naval forces, and commissioning all officers whatever in the service of the United States; making rules for the government and regulation of the said land and naval forces and directing their operations.

The United States, in Congress assembled, shall have authority to appoint a committee to sit in the recess of Congress, to be denominated "a Committee of the States," and to consist of one delegate from each State, and to appoint such other committees and civil officers as may be necessary for managing the general affairs of the United States, under their direction; to appoint one of their number to preside; provided that no person be allowed to serve in the office of president more than one year in any term of three years; to ascertain the necessary sums of money to be raised for the service of the United States, and to appropriate and apply the same for defraying the public expences; to borrow money or emit bills on the credit of the United States, transmitting, every half year, to the respective states, an account of the sums of money so borrowed or emitted; to build and equip a navy; to agree upon the number of land forces, and to make requisitions from each State for its quota, in proportion to the number of white inhabitants in such State; which requisitions shall be binding; and, thereupon, the legislature of each State shall appoint the regimental officers, raise the men, and cloathe, arm, and equip them in a soldier-like manner, at the expence of the United States; and the officers and men so cloathed, armed, and equipped, shall march to the place appointed and within the time agreed on by the United States, in Congress assembled; but if the United States, in Congress assembled, shall, on consideration of circumstances, judge proper that any State should not raise men, or should raise a smaller number than its quota, and that any other State should raise a greater number of men than the quota thereof, such extra number shall be raised, officered, cloathed, armed, and equipped in the same manner as the quota of such State, unless the legislature of such State shall judge that such extra number cannot be safely spared out of the same, in which case they shall raise, officer, cloathe, arm, and equip as many of such extra number as they judge can be safely spared. And the officers and men so cloathed, armed, and equipped, shall march to the place appointed and within the time agreed on by the United States, in Congress assembled.

The United States, in Congress assembled, shall never engage in a war, nor grant letters of marque and reprisal in time of peace, nor enter into any treaties or alliances, nor coin money, nor regulate the value thereof, nor ascertain the sums and expences necessary for the defence and welfare of the United States, or any of them: nor emit bills, nor borrow money on the credit of the United States, nor appropriate money, nor agree upon the number of vessels of war to be built or purchased, or the number of land or sea forces to be raised, nor appoint a commander in chief of the army or navy, unless nine states assent to the same; nor shall a question on any other point, except for adjourning from day to day, be determined, unless by the votes of a majority of the United States, in Congress assembled.

The Congress of the United States shall have power to adjourn to any time within the year, and to any place within the United States, so that no period of adjournment be for a longer duration than the space of six months, and shall publish the journal of their proceedings monthly, except such parts thereof, relating to treaties, alliances or military operations, as, in their judgment, require secrecy; and the yeas and nays of the delegates of each State on any question shall be entered on the journal, when it is desired by any delegate; and the delegates of a State, or any of them, at his, or their request, shall be furnished with a transcript of the said journal, except such parts as are above excepted, to lay before the legislatures of the several states.

Article X

The committee of the states, or any nine of them, shall be authorized to execute, in the recess of Congress, such of the powers of Congress as the United States, in Congress assembled, by the consent of nine states, shall, from time to time, think expedient to vest them with; provided, that no power be delegated to the said committee for the exercise of which, by the articles of confederation, the voice of nine states, in the Congress of the United States assembled, is requisite.

Article XI

Canada acceding to this confederation, and joining in the measures of the United States, shall be admitted into and entitled to all the advantages of this union; but no other colony shall be admitted into the same, unless such admission be agreed to by nine states.

Article XII

All bills of credit emitted, monies borrowed and debts contracted by, or under the authority of Congress before the assembling of the United States, in pursuance of the present confederation, shall be deemed and considered as a charge against the United States, for payment and satisfaction whereof the said United States and the public faith are hereby solemnly pledged.

Article XIII

Every State shall abide by the determinations of the United States, in Congress assembled, on all questions which, by this confederation, are submitted to them. And the articles of this confederation shall be inviolably observed by every State, and the union shall be perpetual; nor shall any alteration at any time hereafter be made in any of them, unless such alteration be agreed to in a Congress of the United States, and be afterwards confirmed by the legislatures of every State.

These articles shall be proposed to the legislatures of all the United States, to be considered, and if approved of by them, they are advised to authorize their delegates to ratify the same in the Congress of the United States; which being done, the same shall become conclusive.

Constitution of the United States of America

Preamble

We the people of the United States, in order to form a more perfect union, establish justice, insure domestic tranquillity, provide for the common defense, promote the general welfare, and secure the blessings of liberty to ourselves and our posterity, do ordain and establish this Constitution for the United States of America.

Article I

Section 1. All legislative powers herein granted shall be vested in a Congress of the United States, which shall consist of a Senate and a House of Representatives.

Section 2. The House of Representatives shall be composed of members chosen every second year by the people of the several States, and the electors in each State shall have the qualifications requisite for electors of the most numerous branch of the State Legislature.

No person shall be a Representative who shall not have attained to the age of twenty-five years, and been seven years a citizen of the United States, and who shall not, when elected, be an inhabitant of that State in which he shall be chosen.

Representatives and direct taxes shall be apportioned among the several States which may be included within this Union, according to their respective numbers, *which shall be determined by adding to the whole number of free persons, including those bound to service for a term of years and excluding Indians not taxed, three-fifths of all other persons.* The actual enumeration shall be made within three years after the first meeting of the Congress of the United States, and within every subsequent term of ten years, in such manner as they shall by law direct. The number of Representatives shall not exceed one for every thirty thousand, but each State shall have at least one Representative; *and until such enumeration shall be made, the State of New Hampshire shall be entitled to choose three, Massachusetts eight, Rhode Island and Providence Plantations one, Connecticut five, New York six, New Jersey four, Pennsylvania eight, Delaware one, Maryland six, Virginia ten, North Carolina five, South Carolina five, and Georgia three.*

When vacancies happen in the representation from any State, the Executive authority thereof shall issue writs of election to fill such vacancies.

The House of Representatives shall choose their Speaker and other officers; and shall have the sole power of impeachment.

Note: Passages that are no longer in effect are printed in italic type.

Section 3. The Senate of the United States shall be composed of two Senators from each State, *chosen by the legislature thereof,* for six years; and each Senator shall have one vote.

Immediately after they shall be assembled in consequence of the first election, they shall be divided as equally as may be into three classes. The seats of the Senators of the first class shall be vacated at the expiration of the second year, of the second class at the expiration of the fourth year, and of the third class at the expiration of the sixth year, so that one-third may be chosen every second year; *and if vacancies happen by resignation or otherwise, during the recess of the legislature of any State, the Executive thereof may make temporary appointments until the next meeting of the legislature, which shall then fill such vacancies.*

No person shall be a Senator who shall not have attained to the age of thirty years, and been nine years a citizen of the United States, and who shall not, when elected, be an inhabitant of that State for which he shall be chosen.

The Vice President of the United States shall be President of the Senate, but shall have no vote, unless they be equally divided.

The Senate shall choose their other officers, and also a President *pro tempore,* in the absence of the Vice President, or when he shall exercise the office of the President of the United States.

The Senate shall have the sole power to try all impeachments. When sitting for that purpose, they shall be on oath or affirmation. When the President of the United States is tried, the Chief Justice shall preside: and no person shall be convicted without the concurrence of two-thirds of the members present.

Judgment in cases of impeachment shall not extend further than to removal from the office, and disqualification to hold and enjoy any office of honor, trust or profit under the United States; but the party convicted shall nevertheless be liable and subject to indictment, trial, judgment and punishment, according to law.

Section 4. The times, places and manner of holding elections for Senators and Representatives shall be prescribed in each State by the legislature thereof; but the Congress may at any time by law make or alter such regulations, except as to the places of choosing Senators.

The Congress shall assemble at least once in every year, and such meeting *shall be on the first Monday in December, unless they shall by law appoint a different day.*

Section 5. Each house shall be the judge of the elections, returns and qualifications of its own members, and a majority of each shall constitute a quorum to do business; but a smaller number may adjourn from day to day, and may be authorized to compel the attendance of absent members, in such manner, and under such penalties, as each house may provide.

Each house may determine the rules of its proceedings, punish its members for disorderly behavior, and with the concurrence of two-thirds, expel a member.

Each house shall keep a journal of its proceedings, and from time to time publish the same, excepting such parts as may in their judgment require secrecy; and the yeas and nays of the members of either house on any question shall, at the desire of one-fifth of those present, be entered on the journal.

Neither house, during the session of Congress, shall, without the consent of the other, adjourn for more than three days, nor to any other place than that in which the two houses shall be sitting.

Section 6.   The Senators and Representatives shall receive a compensation for their services, to be ascertained by law and paid out of the treasury of the United States. They shall in all cases except treason, felony and breach of the peace, be privileged from arrest during their attendance at the session of their respective houses, and in going to and returning from the same; and for any speech or debate in either house, they shall not be questioned in any other place.

No Senator or Representative shall, during the time for which he was elected, be appointed to any civil office under the authority of the United States, which shall have been created, or the emoluments whereof shall have been increased, during such time; and no person holding any office under the United States shall be a member of either house during his continuance in office.

Section 7.   All bills for raising revenue shall originate in the House of Representatives; but the Senate may propose or concur with amendments as on other bills.

Every bill which shall have passed the House of Representatives and the Senate, shall, before it become a law, be presented to the President of the United States; if he approve he shall sign it, but if not he shall return it with objections to that house in which it originated, who shall enter the objections at large on their journal, and proceed to reconsider it. If after such reconsideration two-thirds of that house shall agree to pass the bill, it shall be sent, together with the objections, to the other house, by which it shall likewise be reconsidered, and, if approved by two-thirds of that house, it shall become a law. But in all such cases the votes of both houses shall be determined by yeas and nays, and the names of the persons voting for and against the bill shall be entered on the journal of each house respectively. If any bill shall not be returned by the President within ten days (Sundays excepted) after it shall have been presented to him, the same shall be a law, in like manner as if he had signed it, unless the Congress by their adjournment prevent its return, in which case it shall not be a law.

Every order, resolution, or vote to which the concurrence of the Senate and House of Representatives may be necessary (except on a question of adjournment) shall be presented to the President of the United States; and before the same shall take effect, shall be approved by him, or being disapproved by him, shall be repassed by two-thirds of the Senate and House of Representatives, according to the rules and limitations prescribed in the case of a bill.

Section 8.   The Congress shall have power

To lay and collect taxes, duties, imposts, and excises, to pay the debts and provide for the common defense and general welfare of the United States; but all duties, imposts and excises shall be uniform throughout the United States;

To borrow money on the credit of the United States;

To regulate commerce with foreign nations, and among the several States, and with the Indian tribes;

To establish an uniform rule of naturalization, and uniform laws on the subject of bankruptcies throughout the United States;

To coin money, regulate the value thereof, and of foreign coin, and fix the standard of weights and measures;

To provide for the punishment of counterfeiting the securities and current coin of the United States;

To establish post offices and post roads;

To promote the progress of science and useful arts by securing for limited times to authors and inventors the exclusive right to their respective writings and discoveries;

To constitute tribunals inferior to the Supreme Court;

To define and punish piracies and felonies committed on the high seas and offenses against the law of nations;

To declare war, grant letters of marque and reprisal, and make rules concerning captures on land and water;

To raise and support armies, but no appropriation of money to that use shall be for a longer term than two years;

To provide and maintain a navy;

To make rules for the government and regulation of the land and naval forces;

To provide for calling forth the militia to execute the laws of the Union, suppress insurrections, and repel invasions;

To provide for organizing, arming, and disciplining the militia, and for governing such part of them as may be employed in the service of the United States, reserving to the States respectively the appointment of the officers, and the authority of training the militia according to the discipline prescribed by Congress;

To exercise exclusive legislation in all cases whatsoever, over such district (not exceeding ten miles square) as may, by cession of particular States, and the acceptance of Congress, become the seat of government of the United States, and to exercise like authority over all places purchased by the consent of the legislature of the State, in which the same shall be, for erection of forts, magazines, arsenals, dock-yards, and other needful buildings;—and

To make all laws which shall be necessary and proper for carrying into execution the foregoing powers, and all other powers vested by this Constitution in the government of the United States, or in any department or officer thereof.

Section 9. *The migration or importation of such persons as any of the States now existing shall think proper to admit shall not be prohibited by the Congress prior to the year 1808; but a tax or duty may be imposed on such importation, not exceeding $10 for each person.*

The privilege of the writ of habeas corpus shall not be suspended, unless when in cases of rebellion or invasion the public safety may require it.

No bill of attainder or ex post facto law shall be passed.

No capitation, or other direct, tax shall be laid, unless in proportion to the census or enumeration herein before directed to be taken.

No tax or duty shall be laid on articles exported from any State.

No preference shall be given by any regulation of commerce or revenue to the ports of one State over those of another; nor shall vessels bound to, or from, one State, be obliged to enter, clear, or pay duties in another.

No money shall be drawn from the treasury, but in consequence of appropriations made by law; and a regular statement and account of the receipts and expenditures of all public money shall be published from time to time.

No title of nobility shall be granted by the United States: and no person holding any office of profit or trust under them, shall, without the consent of the Congress, accept of any present, emolument, office, or title, of any kind whatever, from any king, prince, or foreign state.

Section 10. No State shall enter into any treaty, alliance, or confederation; grant letters of marque and reprisal; coin money; emit bills of credit; make anything but gold and silver coin a tender in payment of debts; pass any bill of attainder, ex post facto law, or law impairing the obligation of contracts, or grant any title of nobility.

No State shall, without the consent of Congress, lay any imposts or duties on imports or exports, except what may be absolutely necessary for executing its inspection laws: and the net produce of all duties and imposts, laid by any State on imports or exports, shall be for the use of the treasury of the United States; and all such laws shall be subject to the revision and control of the Congress.

No State shall, without the consent of Congress, lay any duty of tonnage, keep troops or ships of war in time of peace, enter into any agreement or compact with another State, or with a foreign power, or engage in war, unless actually invaded, or in such imminent danger as will not admit of delay.

Article II

Section 1. The executive power shall be vested in a President of the United States of America. He shall hold his office during the term of four years, and, together with the Vice President, chosen for the same term, be elected as follows:

Each state shall appoint, in such manner as the legislature thereof may direct, a number of electors, equal to the whole number of Senators and Representatives to which the State may be entitled in the Congress; but no Senator or Representative, or person holding an office of trust or profit under the United States, shall be appointed an elector.

The electors shall meet in their respective States, and vote by ballot for two persons, of whom one at least shall not be an inhabitant of the same State with themselves. And they shall make a list of all the persons voted for, and of the number of votes for each; which list they shall sign and certify, and transmit sealed to the seat of government of the United States, directed to the President of the Senate. The President of the Senate shall, in the presence of the Senate and the House of Representatives, open all the certificates, and the votes shall then be counted. The person having the greatest number of votes shall be the President, if such number be a majority of the whole number of electors appointed; and if there be more than one who have such majority, and have an equal number of votes, then the House of Representatives shall immediately choose by ballot one of them for President; and if no person have a majority, then from the five highest on the list said house shall in like manner choose the President. But in choosing the President the votes shall be taken by States, the representation from each State having one vote; a quorum for this purpose shall consist of a member or members from two-thirds of the States, and a majority of all the States shall be necessary to a choice. In every case, after the choice of the President, the person having the greatest number of votes of the electors shall be the Vice President. But if there should remain two or more who have equal votes, the Senate shall choose from them by ballot the Vice President.

The Congress may determine the time of choosing the electors and the day on which they shall give their votes; which day shall be the same throughout the United States.

No person except a natural-born citizen, *or a citizen of the United States at the time of the adoption of this Constitution,* shall be eligible to the office of President; neither shall any person be eligible to that office who shall not have attained to the age of thirty-five years, and been fourteen years a resident within the United States.

In case of the removal of the President from office or of his death, resignation, or inability to discharge the powers and duties of the said office, the same shall devolve on the Vice President, and the Congress may by law provide for the case of removal, death, resignation, or inability, both of the President and Vice President, declaring what officer shall then act as President, and such officer shall act accordingly, until the disability be removed, or a President shall be elected.

The President shall, at stated times, receive for his services a compensation, which shall neither be increased nor diminished during the period for which he shall have been elected, and he shall not receive within that period any other emolument from the United States, or any of them.

Before he enter on the execution of his office, he shall take the following oath or affirmation:—"I do solemnly swear (or affirm) that I will faithfully execute the office of the President of the United States, and will to the best of my ability preserve, protect and defend the Constitution of the United States."

Section 2. The President shall be commander in chief of the army and navy of the United States, and of the militia of the several States, when called into the actual service of the United States; he may require the opinion, in writing, of the principal officer in each of the executive departments, upon any subject relating to the duties of their respective offices, and he shall have power to grant reprieves and pardons for offenses against the United States, except in cases of impeachment.

He shall have power, by and with the advice and consent of the Senate, to make treaties, provided two-thirds of the Senators present concur; and he shall nominate, and by and with the advice and consent of the Senate, shall appoint ambassadors, other public ministers and consuls, judges of the Supreme Court, and all other officers of the United States, whose appointments are not herein otherwise provided for, and which shall be established by law: but Congress may by law vest the appointment of such inferior officers, as they think proper, in the President alone, in the courts of law, or in the heads of departments.

The President shall have power to fill up all vacancies that may happen during the recess of the Senate, by granting commissions which shall expire at the end of their next session.

Section 3. He shall from time to time give to the Congress information of the state of the Union, and recommend to their consideration such measures as he shall judge necessary and expedient; he may, on extraordinary occasions, convene both houses, or either of them, and in case of disagreement between them, with respect to the time of adjournment, he may adjourn them to such time as he shall think proper; he shall receive ambassadors and other public ministers; he shall take care that the laws be faithfully executed, and shall commission all the officers of the United States.

Section 4. The President, Vice President and all civil officers of the United States shall be removed from office on impeachment for, and on conviction of, treason, bribery, or other high crimes and misdemeanors.

Article III

Section 1. The judicial power of the United States shall be vested in one Supreme Court, and in such inferior courts as the Congress may from time to time ordain and establish. The judges, both of the Supreme and inferior courts, shall hold their offices during good behavior, and shall, at stated times, receive for their services a compensation which shall not be diminished during their continuance in office.

Section 2. The judicial power shall extend to all cases, in law and equity, arising under this Constitution, the laws of the United States, and treaties made, or which shall be made, under their authority;—to all cases affecting ambassadors, other public ministers and consuls;—to all cases of admiralty and maritime jurisdiction;—to controversies to which the United States shall be a party;—to controversies between two or more States;—*between a State and citizens of another State;*—between citizens of different States;—between citizens of the same State claiming lands under grants of different States, and between a State, or the citizens thereof, and foreign states, citizens or subjects.

In all cases affecting ambassadors, other public ministers and consuls, and those in which a State shall be party, the Supreme Court shall have original jurisdiction. In all the other cases before mentioned, the Supreme Court shall have appellate jurisdiction, both as to law and fact, with such exceptions, and under such regulations, as the Congress shall make.

The trial of all crimes, except in cases of impeachment, shall be by jury; and such trial shall be held in the State where said crimes shall have been committed; but when not committed within any State, the trial shall be at such place or places as the Congress may by law have directed.

Section 3. Treason against the United States shall consist only in levying war against them, or in adhering to their enemies, giving them aid and comfort. No person shall be convicted of treason unless on the testimony of two witnesses to the same overt act, or on confession in open court.

The congress shall have power to declare the punishment of treason, but no attainder of treason shall work corruption of blood, or forfeiture except during the life of the person attainted.

Article IV

Section 1. Full faith and credit shall be given in each State to the public acts, records, and judicial proceedings of every other State. And the Congress may by general laws prescribe the manner in which such acts, records, and proceedings shall be proved, and the effect thereof.

Section 2. The citizens of each State shall be entitled to all privileges and immunities of citizens in the several States.

A person charged in any State with treason, felony, or other crime, who shall flee from justice, and be found in another State, shall on demand of the executive authority of the State from which he fled, be delivered up, to be removed to the State having jurisdiction of the crime.

No person held to service or labor in one State, under the laws thereof, escaping into another, shall, in consequence of any law or regulation therein, be discharged from such service or labor, but shall be delivered up on claim of the party to whom such service or labor may be due.

Section 3. New States may be admitted by the Congress into this Union; but no new State shall be formed or erected within the jurisdiction of any other State; nor any State be formed by the junction of two or more States, or parts of States, without the consent of the legislatures of the States concerned as well as of the Congress.

The Congress shall have power to dispose of and make all needful rules and regulations respecting the territory or other property belonging to the United States; and nothing in this Constitution shall be so construed as to prejudice any claims of the United States, or of any particular State.

Section 4. The United States shall guarantee to every State in this Union a republican form of government, and shall protect each of them against invasion; and on application of the legislature, or of the executive (when the legislature cannot be convened), against domestic violence.

Article V

The Congress, whenever two-thirds of both houses shall deem it necessary, shall propose amendments to this Constitution, or, on the application of the legislatures of two-thirds of the several States, shall call a convention for proposing amendments, which, in either case, shall be valid to all intents and purposes, as part of this Constitution, when ratified by the legislatures of three-fourths of the several States, or by conventions in three-fourths thereof, as the one or the other mode of ratification may be proposed by the Congress; provided *that no amendments which may be made prior to the year one thousand eight hundred and eight shall in any manner affect the first and fourth clauses in the ninth section of the first article;* and that no State, without its consent, shall be deprived of its equal suffrage in the Senate.

Article VI

All debts contracted and engagements entered into, before the adoption of this Constitution, shall be as valid against the United States under this Constitution, as under the Confederation.

This Constitution, and the laws of the United States which shall be made in pursuance thereof; and all treaties made, or which shall be made, under the authority of the United States, shall be the supreme law of the land; and the judges in every State shall be bound thereby, anything in the Constitution or laws of any State to the contrary notwithstanding.

The Senators and Representatives before mentioned, and the members of the several State legislatures, and all executive and judicial officers, both of the United States and of the several States, shall be bound by oath or affirmation to support this Constitution; but no religious test shall ever be required as a qualification to any office or public trust under the United States.

Article VII

The ratification of the conventions of nine States shall be sufficient for the establishment of this Constitution between the States so ratifying the same.

Done in Convention by the unanimous consent of the States present, the seventeenth day of September in the year of our Lord one thousand seven hundred and eighty-seven and of the Independence of the United States of American the twelfth. In witness whereof we have hereunto subscribed our names.

[Signed by]
G° WASHINGTON
Presidt and Deputy from Virginia
[*and thirty-eight others*]

Amendments to the Constitution

Amendment I*

Congress shall make no law respecting an establishment of religion, or prohibiting the free exercise thereof; or abridging the freedom of speech, or of the press; or the right of the people peaceably to assemble, and to petition the government for a redress of grievances.

Amendment II

A well-regulated militia being necessary to the security of a free State, the right of the people to keep and bear arms shall not be infringed.

Amendment III

No soldier shall, in time of peace, be quartered in any house without the consent of the owner, nor in time of war, but in a manner to be prescribed by law.

Amendment IV

The right of the people to be secure in their persons, houses, papers, and effects, against unreasonable searches and seizures, shall not be violated, and no warrants shall issue but upon probable cause, supported by oath or affirmation, and particularly describing the place to be searched, and the persons or things to be seized.

Amendment V

No person shall be held to answer for a capital, or otherwise infamous crime, unless on a presentment or indictment of a grand jury, except in cases arising in the land or naval forces, or in the militia, when in actual service in time

---

* The first ten Amendments (Bill of Rights) were adopted in 1791.

of war or public danger; nor shall any person be subject for the same offense to be twice put in jeopardy of life or limb; nor shall be compelled in any criminal case to be a witness against himself, nor be deprived of life, liberty, or property, without due process of law; nor shall private property be taken for public use without just compensation.

Amendment VI

In all criminal prosecutions, the accused shall enjoy the right to a speedy and public trial, by an impartial jury of the State and district wherein the crime shall have been committed, which district shall have been previously ascertained by law, and to be informed of the nature and cause of the accusation; to be confronted with the witnesses against him; to have compulsory process for obtaining witnesses in his favor, and to have the assistance of counsel for his defense.

Amendment VII

In suits at common law, where the value in controversy shall exceed twenty dollars, the right of trial by jury shall be preserved, and no fact tried by a jury shall be otherwise reexamined in any court of the United States, than according to the rules of the common law.

Amendment VIII

Excessive bail shall not be required, nor excessive fines imposed, nor cruel and unusual punishments inflicted.

Amendment IX

The enumeration in the Constitution, of certain rights, shall not be construed to deny or disparage others retained by the people.

Amendment X

The powers not delegated to the United States by the Constitution, nor prohibited by it to the States, are reserved to the States respectively, or to the people.

Amendment XI
[*Adopted 1798*]

The judicial power of the United States shall not be construed to extend to any suit in law or equity, commenced or prosecuted against one of the United States by citizens of another State, or by citizens or subjects of any foreign state.

Amendment XII
[Adopted 1804]

The electors shall meet in their respective States, and vote by ballot for President and Vice President, one of whom, at least, shall not be an inhabitant of the same State with themselves; they shall name in their ballots the person voted for as President, and in distinct ballots the person voted for as Vice President, and they shall make distinct lists of all persons voted for as President, and of all persons voted for as Vice President, and of the number of votes for each, which lists they shall sign and certify, and transmit sealed to the seat of government of the United States, directed to the President of the Senate;—the President of the Senate shall, in the presence of the Senate and House of Representatives, open all the certificates and the votes shall then be counted;—the person having the greatest number of votes for President shall be the President, if such number be a majority of the whole number of electors appointed; and if no person have such majority, then from the persons having the highest numbers not exceeding three on the list of those voted for as President, the House of Representatives shall choose immediately, by ballot, the President. But in choosing the President, the votes shall be taken by States, the representation from each State having one vote; a quorum for this purpose shall consist of a member or members from two-thirds of the States, and a majority of all the States shall be necessary to a choice. And if the House of Representatives shall not choose a President whenever the right of choice shall devolve upon them, before *the fourth day of March* next following, then the Vice President shall act as President, as in the case of the death or other constitutional disability of the President.

The person having the greatest number of votes as Vice President shall be the Vice President, if such a number be a majority of the whole number of electors appointed; and if no person have a majority, then from the two highest numbers on the list the Senate shall choose the Vice President; a quorum for the purpose shall consist of two-thirds of the whole number of Senators, and a majority of the whole number shall be necessary to a choice. But no person constitutionally ineligible to the office of President shall be eligible to that of Vice President of the United States.

Amendment XIII
[Adopted 1865]

Section 1.   Neither slavery nor involuntary servitude, except as a punishment for crime whereof the party shall have been duly convicted, shall exist within the United States, or any place subject to their jurisdiction.

Section 2.   Congress shall have power to enforce this article by appropriate legislation.

Amendment XIV
[*Adopted 1868*]

Section 1.   All persons born or naturalized in the United States, and subject to the jurisdiction thereof, are citizens of the United States and of the State wherein they reside. No State shall make or enforce any law which shall abridge the privileges or immunities of citizens of the United States; nor shall any State deprive any person of life, liberty, or property, without due process of law; nor deny to any person within its jurisdiction the equal protection of the laws.

Section 2.   Representatives shall be apportioned among the several States according to their respective numbers, counting the whole number of persons in each State, excluding Indians not taxed. But when the right to vote at any election for the choice of Electors for President and Vice President of the United States, Representatives in Congress, the executive and judicial officers of a State, or the members of the legislature thereof, is denied to any of the male inhabitants of such State, being twenty-one years of age and citizens of the United States, or in any way abridged, except for participation in rebellion, or other crime, the basis of representation therein shall be reduced in the proportion which the number of such male citizens shall bear to the whole number of male citizens twenty-one years of age in such State.

Section 3.   No person shall be a Senator or Representative in Congress or Elector of President and Vice President, or hold any office, civil or military, under the United States, or under any State, who, having previously taken an oath, as a member of Congress, or as an officer of the United States, or as a member of any State legislature, or as an executive or judicial officer of any State, to support the Constitution of the United States, shall have engaged in insurrection or rebellion against the same, or given aid and comfort to the enemies thereof. Congress may, by a vote of two-thirds of each house, remove such disability.

Section 4.   The validity of the public debt of the United States, authorized by law, including debts incurred for payment of pensions and bounties for services in suppressing insurrection or rebellion, shall not be questioned. But neither the United States nor any State shall assume or pay any debt or obligation incurred in aid of insurrection or rebellion against the United States, or any claim for the loss or emancipation of any slave; but all such debts, obligations, and claims shall be held illegal and void.

Section 5.   The Congress shall have the power to enforce, by appropriate legislation, the provisions of this article.

Amendment XV
[Adopted 1870]

Section 1. The right of citizens of the United States to vote shall not be denied or abridged by the United States or by any State on account of race, color, or previous condition of servitude.

Section 2. The Congress shall have power to enforce this article by appropriate legislation.

Amendment XVI
[Adopted 1913]

The Congress shall have power to lay and collect taxes on incomes, from whatever source derived, without apportionment among the several States, and without regard to any census or enumeration.

Amendment XVII
[Adopted 1913]

Section 1. The Senate of the United States shall be composed of two Senators from each State, elected by the people thereof, for six years; and each Senator shall have one vote. The electors in each State shall have the qualifications requisite for electors of [voters for] the most numerous branch of the State legislatures.

Section 2. When vacancies happen in the representation of any State in the Senate, the executive authority of such State shall issue writs of election to fill such vacancies: Provided, that the Legislature of any State may empower the executive thereof to make temporary appointments until the people fill the vacancies by election as the Legislature may direct.

Section 3. This amendment shall not be so construed as to affect the election or term of any Senator chosen before it becomes valid as part of the Constitution.

Amendment XVIII
[Adopted 1919; repealed 1933]

Section 1. *After one year from the ratification of this article the manufacture, sale, or transportation of intoxicating liquors within, the importation thereof into, or the exportation thereof from the United States and all territory subject to the jurisdiction thereof, for beverage purposes, is hereby prohibited.*

Section 2. *The Congress and the several States shall have concurrent power to enforce this article by appropriate legislation.*

Section 3. *This article shall be inoperative unless it shall have been ratified as an amendment to the Constitution by the legislatures of the several States, as provided by the Constitution, within seven years from the date of the submission thereof to the States by the Congress.*

Amendment XIX
[Adopted 1920]

Section 1. The right of citizens of the United States to vote shall not be denied or abridged by the United States or by any State on account of sex.

Section 2. The Congress shall have the power to enforce this article by appropriate legislation.

Amendment XX
[Adopted 1933]

Section 1. The terms of the President and Vice President shall end at noon on the 20th day of January, and the terms of Senators and Representatives at noon on the 3d day of January, of the years in which such terms would have ended if this article had not been ratified; and the terms of their successors shall then begin.

Section 2. The Congress shall assemble at least once in every year, and such meeting shall begin at noon on the 3d of January, unless they shall by law appoint a different day.

Section 3. If, at the time fixed for the beginning of the term of the President, the President-elect shall have died, the Vice President-elect shall become President. If a President shall not have been chosen before the time fixed for the beginning of his term, or if the President-elect shall have failed to qualify, then the Vice President-elect shall act as President until a President shall have qualified; and the Congress may by law provide for the case wherein neither a President-elect nor a Vice President-elect shall have qualified, declaring who shall then act as President, or the manner in which one who is to act shall be selected, and such persons shall act accordingly until a President or Vice President shall have qualified.

Section 4. The Congress may by law provide for the case of the death of any of the persons from whom the House of Representatives may choose a President whenever the right of choice shall have devolved upon them, and for the case of the death of any of the persons from whom the Senate may choose a Vice President whenever the right of choice shall have devolved upon them.

Section 5. Sections 1 and 2 shall take effect on the 15th day of October following the ratification of this article.

Section 6. This article shall be inoperative unless it shall have been ratified as an amendment to the Constitution by the Legislatures of three-fourths of the several States within seven years from the date of its submission.

Amendment XXI
[Adopted 1933]

Section 1. The eighteenth article of amendment to the Constitution of the United States is hereby repealed.

Section 2. The transportation or importation into any State, Territory, or Possession of the United States for delivery or use therein of intoxicating liquors, in violation of the laws thereof, is hereby prohibited.

Section 3. This article shall be inoperative unless it shall have been ratified as an amendment to the Constitution by conventions in the several States, as provided in the Constitution, within seven years from the date of submission thereof to the States by the Congress.

Amendment XXII
[Adopted 1951]

Section 1. No person shall be elected to the office of President more than twice, and no person who has held the office of President, or acted as President, for more than two years of a term to which some other person was elected President shall be elected to the office of President more than once. But this article shall not apply to any person holding the office of President when this article was proposed by the Congress, and shall not prevent any person who may be holding the office of President, or acting as President, during the term within which this article becomes operative from holding the office of President or acting as President during the remainder of such term.

Section 2. This article shall be inoperative unless it shall have been ratified as an amendment to the Constitution by the legislatures of three-fourths of the several States within seven years from the date of its submission to the States by the Congress.

Amendment XXIII
[Adopted 1961]

Section 1. The District constituting the seat of Government of the United States shall appoint in such manner as the Congress may direct:

A number of electors of President and Vice President equal to the whole number of Senators and Representatives in Congress to which the District would be entitled if it were a State, but in no event more than the least populous State; they shall be in addition to those appointed by the States, but they shall be considered for the purposes of the election of President and Vice President, to be electors appointed by a State; and they shall meet in the District and perform such duties as provided by the twelfth article of amendment.

Section 2. The Congress shall have the power to enforce this article by appropriate legislation.

Amendment XXIV
[*Adopted 1964*]

Section 1. The right of citizens of the United States to vote in any primary or other election for President or Vice President, for electors for President or Vice President, or for Senator or Representative in Congress, shall not be denied or abridged by the United States or any State by reason of failure to pay any poll tax or other tax.

Section 2. The Congress shall have the power to enforce this article by appropriate legislation

Amendment XXV
[*Adopted 1967*]

Section 1. In case of the removal of the President from office or of his death or resignation, the Vice President shall become President.

Section 2. Whenever there is a vacancy in the office of the Vice President, the President shall nominate a Vice President who shall take office upon confirmation by a majority vote of both Houses of Congress.

Section 3. Whenever the President transmits to the President pro tempore of the Senate and the Speaker of the House of Representatives his written declaration that he is unable to discharge the powers and duties of his office, and until he transmits to them a written declaration to the contrary, such powers and duties shall be discharged by the Vice President as Acting President.

Section 4. Whenever the Vice President and a majority of either the principal officers of the executive departments or of such other body as Congress may by law provide, transmit to the President pro tempore of the Senate and the Speaker of the House of Representatives their written declaration that the President is unable to discharge the powers and duties of his office, the Vice President shall immediately assume the powers and duties of the office as Acting President.

Thereafter, when the President transmits to the President pro tempore of the Senate and the Speaker of the House of Representatives his written declaration that no inability exists, he shall resume the powers and duties of his office unless the Vice President and a majority of either the principal officers of the executive department[s] or of such other body as Congress may by law provide, transmit within four days to the President pro tempore of the Senate and the Speaker of the House of Representatives their written declaration that the President is unable to discharge the powers and duties of his office. Thereupon Congress shall decide the issue, assembling within forty-eight hours for that purpose if not in session. If the Congress, within twenty-one days after receipt of the latter written declaration, or, if Congress is not in session, within twenty-one days after Congress is required to assemble, determines by two-thirds vote of both Houses that the President is unable to discharge the powers and duties of his office, the Vice President shall continue to discharge the same as Acting President; otherwise, the President shall resume the powers and duties of his office.

Amendment XXVI
[Adopted 1971]

Section 1. The right of citizens of the United States, who are eighteen years of age or older, to vote shall not be denied or abridged by the United States or by any State on account of age.

Section 2. The Congress shall have power to enforce this article by appropriate legislation.

The Constitution of the Confederate States
of America

We, the people of the Confederate States, each State acting in its sovereign and independent character, in order to form a permanent federal government, establish justice, insure domestic tranquillity, and secure the blessings of liberty to ourselves and our posterity—invoking the favor and guidance of Almighty God—do ordain and establish this Constitution for the Confederate States of America.

Article I

Section 1.   All legislative powers herein delegated shall be vested in a Congress of the Confederate States, which shall consist of a Senate and House of Representatives.

Section 2.   (1) The House of Representatives shall be chosen every second year by the people of the several States; and the electors in each State shall be citizens of the Confederate States, and have the qualifications requisite for electors of the most numerous branch of the State Legislature; but no person of foreign birth, not a citizen of the Confederate States, shall be allowed to vote for any officer, civil or political, State or Federal.

(2) No person shall be a Representative who shall not have attained the age of twenty-five years, and be a citizen of the Confederate States, and who shall not, when elected, be an inhabitant of that State in which he shall be chosen.

(3) Representatives and direct taxes shall be apportioned among the several States which may be included within this Confederacy, according to their respective numbers, which shall be determined by adding to the whole number of free persons, including those bound to service for a term of years, and excluding Indians not taxed, three-fifths of all slaves. The actual enumeration shall be made within three years after the first meeting of the Congress of the Confederate States, and within every subsequent term of ten years, in such manner as they shall by law direct. The number of Representatives shall not exceed one for every fifty thousand, but each State shall have at least one Representative; and until such enumeration shall be made, the State of South Carolina shall be entitled to choose six; the State of Georgia ten; the State of Alabama nine; the State of Florida two; the State of Mississippi seven; the State of Louisiana six; and the State of Texas six.

(4) When vacancies happen in the representation of any State, the Executive authority thereof shall issue writs of election to fill such vacancies.

(5) The House of Representatives shall choose their Speaker and other officers; and shall have the sole power of impeachment; except that any judicial or other federal officer resident and acting solely within the limits of any State, may be impeached by a vote of two-thirds of both branches of the Legislature thereof.

Section 3. (1) The Senate of the Confederate States shall be composed of two Senators from each State, chosen for six years by the Legislature thereof, at the regular session next immediately preceding the commencement of the term of service; and each Senator shall have one vote.

(2) Immediately after they shall be assembled, in consequence of the first election, they shall be divided as equally as may be into three classes. The seats of the Senators of the first class shall be vacated at the expiration of the second year; of the second class at the expiration of the fourth year; and of the third class at the expiration of the sixth year; so that one-third may be chosen every second year; and if vacancies happen by resignation or otherwise during the recess of the Legislature of any State, the Executive thereof may make temporary appointments until the next meeting of the Legislature, which shall then fill such vacancies.

(3) No person shall be a Senator, who shall not have attained the age of thirty years, and be a citizen of the Confederate States; and who shall not, when elected, be an inhabitant of the State for which he shall be chosen.

(4) The Vice-President of the Confederate States shall be President of the Senate, but shall have no vote, unless they be equally divided.

(5) The Senate shall choose their other officers, and also a President *pro tempore,* in the absence of the Vice-President, or when he shall exercise the office of President of the Confederate States.

(6) The Senate shall have sole power to try all impeachments, When sitting for that purpose they shall be on oath or affirmation. When the President of the Confederate States is tried, the Chief-Justice shall preside; and no person shall be convicted without the concurrence of two-thirds of the members present.

(7) Judgment in cases of impeachment shall not extend further than removal from office, and disqualification to hold and enjoy any office of honor, trust, or profit, under the Confederate States; but the party convicted shall, nevertheless, be liable to and subject to indictment, trial, judgment, and punishment according to law.

Section 4. (1) The times, places, and manner of holding elections for Senators and Representatives, shall be prescribed in each State by the Legislature thereof, subject to the provisions of this Constitution; but the Congress may, at any time, by law, make or alter such regulations, except as to the times and places of choosing Senators.

(2) The Congress shall assemble at least once in every year; and such meeting shall be on the first Monday in December, unless they shall, by law, appoint a different day.

Section 5. (1) Each House shall be the judge of the elections, returns, and qualifications of its own members, and a majority of each shall constitute a quorum to do business; but a smaller number may adjourn from day to day, and may be authorized to compel the attendance of absent members, in such manner and under such penalties as each House may provide.

(2) Each House may determine the rules of its proceedings, punish its

members for disorderly behavior, and, with the concurrence of two-thirds of the whole number, expel a member.

(3) Each House shall keep a journal of its proceedings, and from time to time publish the same, excepting such part as may in its judgment require secrecy, and the ayes and nays of the members of either House, on any question, shall, at the desire of one-fifth of those present, be entered on the journal.

(4) Neither House, during the session of Congress, shall, without the consent of the other, adjourn for more than three days, nor to any other place than that in which the two Houses shall be sitting.

Section 6. (1) The Senators and Representatives shall receive a compensation for their services, to be ascertained by law, and paid out of the Treasury of the Confederate States. They shall, in all cases except treason and breach of the peace, be privileged from arrest during their attendance at the session of their respective Houses, and in going to and returning from the same; and for any speech or debate in either House, they shall not be questioned in any other place.

(2) No Senator or Representative shall, during the time for which he was elected, be appointed to any civil office under the authority of the Confederate States, which shall have been created, or the emoluments whereof shall have been increased during such time; and no person holding any office under the Confederate States shall be a member of either House during his continuance in office. But Congress may, by law, grant to the principal officer in each of the Executive Departments a seat upon the floor of either house, with the privilege of discussing any measure appertaining to his department.

Section 7. (1) All bills for raising revenue shall originate in the House of Representatives; but the Senate may propose or concur with amendments as on other bills.

(2) Every bill which shall have passed both houses shall, before it becomes a law, be presented to the President of the Confederate States; if he approve he shall sign it; but if not, he shall return it with his objections to that House in which it shall have originated, who shall enter the objections at large on their journal, and proceed to reconsider it. If, after such reconsideration, two-thirds of that House shall agree to pass the bill, it shall be sent, together with the objections, to the other House, by which it shall likewise be reconsidered, and if approved by two-thirds of that House, it shall become a law. But in all such cases, the votes of both Houses shall be determined by yeas and nays, and the names of the persons voting for and against the bill shall be entered on the journal of each House respectively. If any bill shall not be returned by the President within ten days (Sundays excepted) after it shall have been presented to him, the same shall be a law, in like manner as if he had signed it, unless the Congress, by their adjournment, prevent its return; in which case it shall not be a law. The President may approve any appropriation and disapprove any other appro-

priation in the same bill. In such case he shall, in signing the bill, designate the appropriations disapproved; and shall return a copy of such appropriations, with his objections, to the House in which the bill shall have originated; and the same proceedings shall then be had as in case of other bills disapproved by the President.

(3) Every order, resolution, or vote, to which the concurrence of both Houses may be necessary (except on question of adjournment) shall be presented to the President of the Confederate States; and before the same shall take effect shall be approved by him; or being disapproved by him, may be repassed by two-thirds of both Houses, according to the rules and limitations prescribed in case of a bill.

Section 8.   —The Congress shall have power—

(1) To lay and collect taxes, duties, imposts, and excises, for revenue necessary to pay the debts, provide for the common defence, and carry on the Government of the Confederate States; but no bounties shall be granted from the treasury; nor shall any duties or taxes on importations from foreign nations be laid to promote or foster any branch of industry; and all duties, imposts, and excises shall be uniform throughout the Confederate States.

(2) To borrow money on the credit of the Confederate States.

(3) To regulate commerce with foreign nations, and among the several States, and with the Indian tribes; but neither this, nor any other clause contained in the Constitution shall be construed to delegate the power to Congress to appropriate money for any internal improvement intended to facilitate commerce; except for the purpose of furnishing lights, beacons, and buoys, and other aids to navigation upon the coasts, and the improvement of harbors, and the removing of obstructions in river navigation, in all which cases, such duties shall be laid on the navigation facilitated thereby, as may be necessary to pay the costs and expenses thereof.

(4) To establish uniform laws of naturalization, and uniform laws on the subject of bankruptcies throughout the Confederate States, but no law of Congress shall discharge any debt contracted before the passage of the same.

(5) To coin money, regulate the value thereof, and of foreign coin, and fix the standard of weights and measures.

(6) To provide for the punishment of counterfeiting the securities and current coin of the Confederate States.

(7) To establish post-offices and post-routes; but the expenses of the Post-office Department, after the first day of March, in the year of our Lord eighteen hundred and sixty-three, shall be paid out of its own revenues.

(8) To promote the progress of science and useful arts, by securing for limited times to authors and inventors the exclusive right to their respective writings and discoveries.

(9) To constitute tribunals inferior to the Supreme Court.

(10) To define and punish piracies and felonies committed on the high seas, and offences against the law of nations.

(11) To declare war, grant letters of marque and reprisal, and make rules concerning captures on land and water.

(12) To raise and support armies; but no appropriation of money to that use shall be for a longer term than two years.

(13) To provide and maintain a navy.

(14) To make rules for government and regulation of the land and naval forces.

(15) To provide for calling forth the militia to execute the laws of the Confederate States; suppress insurrections, and repel invasions.

(16) To provide for organizing, arming, and disciplining the militia, and for governing such part of them as may be employed in the service of the Confederate States; reserving to the States, respectively, the appointment of the officers, and the authority of training the militia according to the discipline prescribed by Congress.

(17) To exercise exclusive legislation, in all cases whatsoever, over such district (not exceeding ten miles square) as may, by cession of one or more States, and the acceptance of Congress, become the seat of the Government of the Confederate States; and to exercise a like authority over all places purchased by the consent of the Legislature of the State in which the same shall be, for the erection of forts, magazines, arsenals, dock-yards, and other needful buildings, and

(18) To make all laws which shall be necessary and proper for carrying into execution the foregoing powers, and all other powers vested by this Constitution in the Government of the Confederate States, or in any department or officer thereof.

Section 9. (1) The importation of negroes of the African race, from any foreign country, other than the slaveholding States or Territories of the United States of America, is hereby forbidden; and Congress is required to pass such laws as shall effectually prevent the same.

(2) Congress shall also have power to prohibit the introduction of slaves from any State not a member of, or Territory not belonging to, this Confederacy.

(3) The privilege of the writ of *habeas corpus* shall not be suspended, unless when in cases of rebellion or invasion the public safety may require it.

(4) No bill of attainder, or *ex post facto* law, or law denying or impairing the right of property in negro slaves shall be passed.

(5) No capitation or other direct tax shall be laid unless in proportion to the census or enumeration hereinbefore directed to be taken.

(6) No tax or duty shall be laid on articles exported from any State, except by a vote of two-thirds of both Houses.

(7) No preference shall be given by any regulation of commerce or revenue to the ports of one State over those of another.

(8) No money shall be drawn from the treasury but in consequence of appropriations made by laws; and a regular statement and account of the

receipts and expenditures of all public money shall be published from time to time.

(9) Congress shall appropriate no money from the treasury except by a vote of two-thirds of both Houses, taken by yeas and nays, unless it be asked and estimated for by some one of the heads of departments, and submitted to Congress by the President; or for the purpose of paying its own expenses and contingencies; or for the payment of claims against the Confederate States, the justice of which shall have been judicially declared by a tribunal for the investigation of claims against the Government, which it is hereby made the duty of Congress to establish.

(10) All bills appropriating money shall specify in federal currency the exact amount of each appropriation and the purposes for which it is made; and Congress shall grant no extra compensation to any public contractor, officer, agent, or servant, after such contract shall have been made or such service rendered.

(11) No title of nobility shall be granted by the Confederate States; and no person holding any office of profit or trust under them shall, without the consent of the Congress, accept of any present, emoluments, office, or title of any kind whatever, from any king, prince, or foreign state.

(12) Congress shall make no law respecting an establishment of religion, or prohibiting the free exercise thereof; or abridging the freedom of speech or of the press; or the right of the people peaceably to assemble and petition the Government for a redress of grievances.

(13) A well-regulated militia being necessary to the security of a free State, the right of the people to keep and bear arms shall not be infringed.

(14) No soldier shall, in time of peace, be quartered in any house without the consent of the owner; nor in time of war, but in a manner prescribed by law.

(15) The right of the people to be secure in their persons, houses, papers, and against unreasonable searches and seizures, shall not be violated; and no warrant shall issue but upon probable cause, supported by oath or affirmation, and particularly describing the place to be searched, and the person or things to be seized.

(16) No person shall be held to answer for a capital or otherwise infamous crime, unless on a presentment or indictment of a grand jury, except in cases arising in the land or naval forces, or in the militia, when in actual service, in time of war, or public danger; nor shall any person be subject for the same offence to be twice put in jeopardy of life or limb; nor be compelled in any criminal case to be a witness against himself; nor be deprived of life, liberty, or property, without due process of law; nor shall any private property be taken for public use without just compensation.

(17) In all criminal prosecutions the accused shall enjoy the right to a speedy and public trial, by an impartial jury of the State and district wherein the crime shall have been committed, which district shall have been previously ascertained by law, and to be informed of the nature and cause of the accusation; to be confronted with the witnesses against him; to have com-

pulsory process for obtaining witnesses in his favor; and to have the assistance of counsel for his defence.

(18) In suits at common law, where the value in controversy shall exceed twenty dollars, the right of trial by jury shall be preserved; and no fact so tried by a jury shall be otherwise re-examined in any court of the Confederacy, than according to the rules of the common law.

(19) Excessive bail shall not be required, nor excessive fines imposed, nor cruel or unusual punishment inflicted.

(20) Every law, or resolution having the force of law, shall relate to but one subject, and that shall be expressed in the title.

Section 10. (1) No State shall enter into any treaty, alliance, or confederation; grant letters of marque and reprisals; coin money; make any thing but gold and silver coin a tender in payment of debts; pass any bill of attainder, or *ex post facto* law, or law impairing the obligation of contracts; or grant any title of nobility.

(2) No State shall, without the consent of Congress, lay any imposts or duties on imports or exports, except what may be absolutely necessary for executing its inspection laws; and the net produce of all duties and imposts, laid by any State on imports or exports, shall be for the use of the Treasury of the Confederate States; and all such laws shall be subject to the revision and control of Congress.

(3) No state shall, without the consent of Congress, lay any duty of tonnage, except on sea-going vessels, for the improvement of its rivers and harbors navigated by the said vessels; but such duties shall not conflict with any treaties of the Confederate States with foreign nations; and any surplus of revenue, thus derived, shall, after making such improvement, be paid into the common treasury; nor shall any State keep troops or ships of war in time of peace, enter into any agreement or compact with another State, or with a foreign power, or engage in war, unless actually invaded, or in such imminent danger as will not admit of delay. But when any river divides or flows through two or more States, they may enter into compacts with each other to improve the navigation thereof.

Article II

Section 1. (1) The Executive power shall be vested in a President of the Confederate States of America. He and the Vice-President shall hold their offices for the term of six years; but the President shall not be reëligible. The President and Vice-President shall be elected as follows:

(2) Each State shall appoint, in such manner as the Legislature thereof may direct, a number of electors equal to the whole number of Senators and Representatives to which the State may be entitled in Congress; but no Senator or Representative, or person holding an office of trust or profit under the Confederate States, shall be appointed an elector.

(3) The electors shall meet in their respective States and vote by ballot

for President and Vice-President, one of whom, at least, shall not be an inhabitant of the same State with themselves; they shall name in their ballots the person voted for as President, and in distinct ballots the person voted for as Vice-President, and they shall make distinct lists of all persons voted for as President, and of all persons voted for as Vice-President, and of the number of votes for each; which list they shall sign, and certify, and transmit, sealed, to the Government of the Confederate States, directed to the President of the Senate. The President of the Senate shall, in the presence of the Senate and House of Representatives, open all the certificates, and the votes shall then be counted; the person having the greatest number of votes for President shall be the President, if such number be a majority of the whole number of electors appointed; and if no person shall have such a majority, then, from the persons having the highest numbers, not exceeding three, on the list of those voted for as President, the House of Representatives shall choose immediately, by ballot, the President. But, in choosing the President, the votes shall be taken by States, the Representative from each State having one vote; a quorum for this purpose shall consist of a member or members from two-thirds of the States, and a majority of all the States shall be necessary to a choice. And if the House of Representatives shall not choose a President, whenever the right of choice shall devolve upon them, before the fourth day of March next following, then the Vice-President shall act as President, as in case of the death, or other constitutional disability of the President.

(4) The person having the greatest number of votes as Vice-President shall be the Vice-President, if such number be a majority of the whole number of electors appointed; and if no person have a majority, then from the two highest numbers on the list, the Senate shall choose the Vice-President; a quorum for the purpose shall consist of two-thirds of the whole number of Senators, and a majority of the whole number shall be necessary for a choice.

(5) But no person constitutionally ineligible to the office of President shall be eligible to that of Vice-President of the Confederate States.

(6) The Congress may determine the time of choosing the electors, and the day on which they shall give their votes; which day shall be the same throughout the Confederate States.

(7) No person except a natural born citizen of the Confederate States, or a citizen thereof, at the time of the adoption of this Constitution, or a citizen thereof born in the United States prior to the 20th December, 1860, shall be eligible to the office of President; neither shall any person be eligible to that office who shall not have attained the age of thirty-five years, and been fourteen years a resident within the limits of the Confederate States, as they may exist at the time of his election.

(8) In case of the removal of the President from office, or of his death, resignation, or inability to discharge the powers and duties of the said office, the same shall devolve on the Vice-President; and the Congress may, by law, provide for the case of the removal, death, resignation, or inability both of the President and the Vice-President, declaring what officer shall

then act as President, and such officer shall then act accordingly until the disability be removed or a President shall be elected.

(9) The President shall, at stated times, receive for his services a compensation, which shall neither be increased nor diminished during the period for which he shall have been elected; and he shall not receive within that period any other emolument from the Confederate States, or any of them.

(10) Before he enters on the execution of the duties of his office, he shall take the following oath or affirmation:

"I do solemnly swear (or affirm) that I will faithfully execute the office of President of the Confederate States, and will, to the best of my ability, preserve, protect, and defend the Constitution thereof."

Section 2. (1) The President shall be commander-in-chief of the army and navy of the Confederate States, and of the militia of the several States, when called into the actual service of the Confederate States; he may require the opinion, in writing, of the principal officer in each of the Executive Departments, upon any subject relating to the duties of their respective offices; and he shall have power to grant reprieves and pardons for offences against the Confederate States, except in cases of impeachment.

(2) He shall have power, by and with the advice and consent of the Senate, to make treaties, provided two-thirds of the Senators present concur; and he shall nominate, and, by and with the advice and consent of the Senate, shall appoint ambassadors, other public ministers, and consuls, Judges of the Supreme Court, and all other officers of the Confederate States, whose appointments are not herein otherwise provided for, and which shall be established by law; but the Congress may by law vest the appointment of such inferior officers, as they think proper, in the President alone, in the courts of law, or in the heads of departments.

(3) The principal officer in each of the Executive Departments, and all persons connected with the diplomatic service, may be removed from office at the pleasure of the President. All other civil officers of the Executive Department may be removed at any time by the President, or other appointing power, when their services are unnecessary, or for dishonesty, incapacity, inefficiency, misconduct, or neglect of duty; and when so removed, the removal shall be reported to the Senate, together with the reasons therefor.

(4) The President shall have power to fill all vacancies that may happen during the recess of the Senate, by granting commissions which shall expire at the end of the next session; but no person rejected by the Senate shall be reappointed to the same office during their ensuing recess.

Section 3. (1) The President shall, from time to time, give to the Congress information of the state of the Confederacy, and recommend to their consideration such measures as he shall judge necessary and expedient; he may, on extraordinary occasions, convene both Houses, or either of them; and, in case of disagreement between them, with respect to the time of adjournment he may adjourn them to such time as he shall think proper; he shall receive ambassadors and other public ministers; he shall take care that the laws be faithfully executed, and shall commission all the officers of the Confederate States.

Section 4. (1) The President and Vice-President, and all civil officers of the Confederate States, shall be removed from office on impeachment for, or conviction of, treason, bribery, or other high crimes and misdemeanors.

Article III

Section 1. (1) The judicial power of the Confederate States shall be vested in one Superior Court, and in such inferior courts as the Congress may from time to time ordain and establish. The judges, both of the Supreme and inferior courts, shall hold their offices during good behavior, and shall, at stated times, receive for their services a compensation, which shall not be diminished during their continuance in office.

Section 2. (1) The judicial power shall extend to all cases arising under the Constitution, the laws of the Confederate States, or treaties made or which shall be made under their authority; to all cases affecting ambassadors, other public ministers, and consuls; to all cases of admiralty or maritime jurisdiction; to controversies to which the Confederate States shall be a party; to controversies between two or more States; between a State and citizens of another State, where the State is plaintiff; between citizens claiming lands under grants of different States, and between a State or the citizens thereof, and foreign States, citizens, or subjects; but no State shall be sued by a citizen or subject of any foreign State.

(2) In all cases affecting ambassadors, other public ministers, and consuls, and those in which a State shall be a party, the Supreme Court shall have original jurisdiction. In all the other cases before mentioned, the Supreme Court shall have appellate jurisdiction, both as to law and fact, with such exceptions, and under such regulations as the Congress shall make.

(3) The trial of all crimes, except in cases of impeachment, shall be by jury, and such trial shall be held in the State where the said crimes shall have been committed; but when not committed within any State, the trial shall be at such place or places as the Congress may by law have directed.

Section 3. (1) Treason against the Confederate States shall consist only in levying war against them, or in adhering to their enemies, giving them aid and comfort. No person shall be convicted of treason unless on the testimony of two witnesses to the same overt act, or on confession in open court.

(2) The Congress shall have power to declare the punishment of treason, but no attainder of treason shall work corruption of blood, or forfeiture, except during the life of the person attainted.

Article IV

Section 1. (1) Full faith and credit shall be given in each State to the public acts, records, and judicial proceedings of every other State. And the Congress may, by general laws, prescribe the manner in which such acts, records, and proceedings shall be proved, and the effect thereof.

Section 2. (1) The citizens of each State shall be entitled to all the privileges and immunities of citizens of the several States, and shall have the right of transit and sojourn in any State of this Confederacy, with their slaves and other property; and the right of property in said slaves shall not be thereby impaired.

(2) A person charged in any State with treason, felony, or other crime against the laws of such State, who shall flee from justice, and be found in another State, shall, on demand of the executive authority of the State from which he fled, be delivered up to be removed to the State having jurisdiction of the crime.

(3) No slave or other person held to service or labor in any State or Territory of the Confederate States, under the laws thereof, escaping or unlawfully carried into another, shall, in consequence of any law or regulation therein, be discharged from such service or labor; but shall be delivered up on claim of the party to whom such slave belongs, or to whom such service or labor may be due.

Section 3. (1) Other States may be admitted into this Confederacy by a vote of two-thirds of the whole House of Representatives, and two-thirds of the Senate, the Senate voting by States; but no new State shall be formed or erected within the jurisdiction of any other State; nor any State be formed by the junction of two or more States, or parts of States, without the consent of the Legislatures of the States concerned as well as of the Congress.

(2) The Congress shall have power to dispose of and make all needful rules and regulations concerning the property of the Confederate States, including the lands thereof.

(3) The Confederate States may acquire new territory; and Congress shall have power to legislate and provide governments for the inhabitants of all territory belonging to the Confederate States, lying without the limits of the several States, and may permit them, at such times, and in such manner as it may by law provide, to form States to be admitted into the Confederacy. In all such territory, the institution of negro slavery, as it now exists in the Confederate States, shall be recognized and protected by Congress and by the territorial government; and the inhabitants of the several Confederate States and Territories shall have the right to take to such territory any slaves lawfully held by them in any of the States or Territories of the Confederate States.

(4) The Confederate States shall guarantee to every State that now is or hereafter may become a member of this Confederacy, a Republican form of Government, and shall protect each of them against invasion; and on

application of the Legislature, (or of the Executive when the Legislature is not in session,) against domestic violence.

Article V

Section 1. (1) Upon the demand of any three States, legally assembled in their several Conventions, the Congress shall summon a Convention of all the States, to take into consideration such amendments to the Constitution as the said States shall concur in suggesting at the time when the said demand is made; and should any of the proposed amendments to the Constitution be agreed on by the said Convention—voting by States—and the same be ratified by the Legislatures of two-thirds of the several States, or by conventions in two-thirds thereof—as the one or the other mode of ratification may be proposed by the general convention—they shall thenceforward form a part of this Constitution. But no State shall, without its consent, be deprived of its equal representation in the Senate.

Article VI

1.—The Government established by this Constitution is the successor of the Provisional Government of the Confederate States of America, and all the laws passed by the latter shall continue in force until the same shall be repealed or modified; and all the officers appointed by the same shall remain in office until their successors are appointed and qualified, or the offices abolished.

2. All debts contracted and engagements entered into before the adoption of this Constitution, shall be as valid against the Confederate States under this Constitution as under the Provisional Government.

3. This Constitution, and the laws of the Confederate States, made in pursuance thereof, and all treaties made, or which shall be made, under the authority of the Confederate States, shall be the supreme law of the land; and the judges in every State shall be bound thereby, any thing in the Constitution or laws of any State to the contrary notwithstanding.

4. The Senators and Representatives before mentioned, and the members of the several State Legislatures, and all executive and judicial offices, both of the Confederate States and of the several States, shall be bound, by oath or affirmation, to support this Constitution; but no religious test shall ever be required as a qualification to any office or public trust under the Confederate States.

5. The enumeration, in the Constitution, of certain rights, shall not be construed to deny or disparage others retained by the people of the several States.

6. The powers not delegated to the Confederate States by the Constitution, nor prohibited by it to the States, are reserved to the States, respectively, or to the people thereof.

Article VII

1.—The ratification of the conventions of five States shall be sufficient for the establishment of this Constitution between the States so ratifying the same.

2. When five States shall have ratified this Constitution in the manner before specified, the Congress, under the provisional Constitution, shall prescribe the time for holding the election of President and Vice-President, and for the meeting of the electoral college, and for counting the votes and inaugurating the President. They shall also prescribe the time for holding the first election of members of Congress under this Constitution, and the time for assembling the same. Until the assembling of such Congress, the Congress under the provisional Constitution shall continue to exercise the legislative powers granted them; not extending beyond the time limited by the Constitution of the Provisional Government.

Adopted unanimously by the Congress of the Confederate States of South Carolina, Georgia, Florida, Alabama, Mississippi, Louisiana, and Texas, sitting in convention at the capitol, in the city of Montgomery, Ala., on the eleventh day of March, in the year eighteen hundred and sixty-one.

Howard Cobb
President of the Congress.

[Signatures]

Supreme Court Nominations, 1789–1990

Name	State	Date of Birth	To Replace	Date of Appointment	Confirmation or Other Action*	Date Resigned	Date of Death	Years of Service
WASHINGTON								
John Jay	N.Y.	12/12/1745		9/24/1789	9/26/1789	6/29/1795	5/17/1829	6
John Rutledge	S.C.	9/1739		9/24/1789	9/26/1789	3/5/1791	7/18/1800	1
William Cushing	Mass.	3/1/1732		9/24/1789	9/26/1789		9/13/1810	21
Robert H. Harrison	Md.	1745		9/24/1789	9/26/1789 (D)		4/20/1790	
James Wilson	Pa.	9/14/1742		9/24/1789	9/26/1789		8/21/1798	9
John Blair	Va.	1732		9/24/1789	9/26/1789	1/27/1796	8/31/1800	6
James Iredell	N.C.	10/5/1751	Harrison	2/8/1790	2/10/1790		10/20/1799	9
Thomas Johnson	Md.	11/4/1732	Rutledge	11/1/1791	11/7/1791	3/4/1793	10/26/1819	1
William Paterson	N.J.	12/24/1745	Johnson	2/27/1793	2/28/1793 (W)			
William Paterson †			Johnson	3/4/1793	3/4/1793		9/9/1806	13
John Rutledge ‡			Jay	7/1/1795	12/15/1795 (R, 10-14)			
William Cushing ‡			Jay	1/26/1796	1/27/1796 (D)			
Samuel Chase	Md.	4/17/1741	Blair	1/26/1796	1/27/1796		6/19/1811	15
Oliver Ellsworth	Conn.	4/29/1745	Jay	3/3/1796	3/4/1796 (21-1)	12/25/1800	11/26/1807	4

Boldface—Chief Justice
Italics—Did not serve
‡ Earlier court service. See above.
† Earlier nomination not confirmed. See above.
D Declined

W Withdrawn
P Postponed
R Rejected
*Where no vote is listed, confirmation was by voice vote or otherwise recorded.

				Nominated	Confirmed	Resigned	Died	No.
ADAMS								
Bushrod Washington	Va.	6/5/1762	Wilson	12/19/1798	12/20/1798		11/26/1829	31
Alfred Moore	N.C.	5/21/1755	Iredell	12/6/1799	12/10/1799	1/26/1804	10/15/1810	4
John Jay ‡			Ellsworth	12/18/1800	12/19/1800 (D)			
John Marshall	Va.	9/24/1755	Ellsworth	1/20/1801	1/27/1801		7/6/1835	34
JEFFERSON								
William Johnson	S.C.	12/27/1771	Moore	3/22/1804	3/24/1804		8/4/1834	30
H. Brockholst Livingston	N.Y.	11/25/1757	Paterson	12/13/1806	12/17/1806		3/18/1823	16
Thomas Todd	Ky.	1/23/1765	New seat	2/28/1807	3/3/1807		2/7/1826	19
MADISON								
Levi Lincoln	Mass.	5/15/1749	Cushing	1/2/1811	1/3/1811 (D)		4/14/1820	
Alexander Wolcott	Conn.	9/15/1758	Cushing	2/4/1811	2/13/1811 (R, 9-24)		6/26/1828	
John Quincy Adams	Mass.	7/11/1767	Cushing	2/21/1811	2/22/1811 (D)		2/23/1848	
Joseph Story	Mass.	9/18/1779	Cushing	11/15/1811	11/18/1811		9/10/1845	34
Gabriel Duvall	Md.	12/6/1752	Chase	11/15/1811	11/18/1811	1/14/1835	3/6/1844	23
MONROE								
Smith Thompson	N.Y.	1/17/1768	Livingston	12/8/1823	12/19/1823		12/18/1843	20
J. Q. ADAMS								
Robert Trimble	Ky.	11/17/1776	Todd	4/11/1826	5/9/1826 (27-5)		8/25/1828	2
John J. Crittenden	Ky.	9/10/1787	Trimble	12/17/1828	2/12/1829 (P)		7/26/1863	
JACKSON								
John McLean	Ohio	3/11/1785	Trimble	3/6/1829	3/7/1829		4/4/1861	32
Henry Baldwin	Pa.	1/14/1780	Washington	1/4/1830	1/6/1830 (41-2)		4/21/1844	14
James M. Wayne	Ga.	1790	Johnson	1/7/1835	1/9/1835		7/5/1867	32
Roger H. Taney	Md.	3/17/1777	Duvall	1/15/1835	3/3/1835 (P)			

Name	State	Date of Birth	To Replace	Date of Appointment	Confirmation or Other Action*	Date Resigned	Date of Death	Years of Service
Roger B. Taney †			Marshall	12/28/1835	3/15/1836 (29-15)		10/12/1864	28
Philip P. Barbour	Va.	5/25/1783	Duvall	12/28/1835	3/15/1836 (30-11)		2/25/1841	5
William Smith	Ala.	1762	New seat	3/3/1837	3/8/1837 (23-18) (D)		6/10/1840	
John Catron	Tenn.	1786	New seat	3/3/1837	3/8/1837 (28-15)		5/30/1865	28
VAN BUREN								
John McKinley	Ala.	5/1/1780	New seat	9/18/1837	9/25/1837		7/19/1852	15
Peter V. Daniel	Va.	4/24/1784	Barbour	2/26/1841	3/2/1841 (22-5)		5/31/1860	19
TYLER								
John C. Spencer	N.Y.	1/8/1788	Thompson	1/9/1844	1/31/1844 (R, 21-26)		5/18/1855	
Reuben H. Walworth	N.Y.	10/26/1788	Thompson	3/13/1844	6/17/1844 (W)		11/27/1867	
Edward King	Pa.	1/31/1794	Baldwin	6/5/1844	6/15/1844 (P)			
Edward King †			Baldwin	12/4/1844	2/7/1845 (W)		5/8/1873	
Samuel Nelson	N.Y.	11/10/1792	Thompson	2/4/1845	2/14/1845	11/28/1872	12/13/1873	27
John M. Read	Pa.	2/21/1797	Baldwin	2/7/1845	No action		11/29/1874	
POLK								
George W. Woodward	Pa.	3/26/1809	Baldwin	12/23/1845	1/22/1846 (R, 20-29)		5/10/1875	
Levi Woodbury	N.H.	12/22/1789	Story	12/23/1845	1/3/1846		9/4/1851	5
Robert C. Grier	Pa.	3/5/1794	Baldwin	8/3/1846	8/4/1846	1/31/1870	9/25/1870	23
FILLMORE								
Benjamin R. Curtis	Mass.	11/4/1809	Woodbury	12/11/1851	12/29/1851	9/30/1857	9/15/1874	5
Edward A. Bradford	La.	9/27/1813	McKinley	8/16/1852	No action		11/22/1872	
George E. Badger	N.C.	4/13/1795	McKinley	1/10/1853	2/11/1853 (P)		5/11/1866	
William C. Micou	La.	1806	McKinley	2/24/1853	No action		4/16/1854	

PIERCE									
John A. Campbell	Ala.	6/24/1811	McKinley	3/22/1853	3/25/1853		4/30/1861	3/12/1889	8
BUCHANAN									
Nathan Clifford	Maine	8/18/1803	Curtis	12/9/1857	1/12/1858	(26-23)		7/25/1881	23
Jeremiah S. Black	Pa.	1/10/1810	Daniel	2/5/1861	2/21/1861	(R, 25-26)		8/19/1883	
LINCOLN									
Noah H. Swayne	Ohio	12/7/1804	McLean	1/21/1862	1/24/1862	(38-1)	1/24/1881	6/8/1884	19
Samuel F. Miller	Iowa	4/5/1816	Daniel	7/16/1862	7/16/1862			10/13/1890	28
David Davis	Ill.	3/9/1815	Campbell	12/1/1862	12/8/1862		3/4/1877	6/26/1886	14
Stephen J. Field	Calif.	11/4/1816	New seat	3/6/1863	3/10/1863		12/1/1897	4/9/1899	34
Salmon P. Chase	Ohio	1/13/1808	Taney	12/6/1864	12/6/1864			5/7/1873	8
JOHNSON									
Henry Stanbery	Ohio	2/20/1803	Catron	4/16/1866	No action			6/26/1881	
GRANT									
Ebenezer R. Hoar	Mass.	2/21/1816	New seat	12/15/1869	2/3/1870	(R, 24-33)		1/31/1895	
Edwin M. Stanton	Pa.	12/19/1814	Grier	12/20/1869	12/20/1869	(46-11)		12/24/1869	
William Strong	Pa.	5/6/1808	Grier	2/7/1870	2/18/1870		12/14/1880	8/19/1895	10
Joseph B. Bradley	N.J.	3/14/1813	New seat	2/7/1870	3/21/1870	(46-9)		1/22/1892	21
Ward Hunt	N.Y.	6/14/1810	Nelson	12/3/1872	12/11/1872		1/27/1882	3/24/1886	9
George H. Williams	Ore.	3/23/1823	Chase	12/1/1873	1/8/1874	(W)		4/4/1910	
Caleb Cushing	Mass.	1/17/1800	Chase	1/9/1874	1/13/1874	(W)		1/2/1879	
Morrison R. Waite	Ohio	11/29/1816	Chase	1/19/1874	1/21/1874	(63-0)		3/23/1888	14
HAYES									
John M. Harlan	Ky.	6/1/1833	Davis	10/17/1877	11/29/1877			10/14/1911	34

Name	State	Date of Birth	To Replace	Date of Appointment	Confirmation or Other Action*	Date Resigned	Date of Death	Years of Service
William B. Woods	Ga.	8/3/1824	Strong	12/15/1880	12/21/1880 (39-8)		5/14/1887	6
Stanley Matthews	Ohio	7/21/1824	Swayne	1/26/1881	No action			
GARFIELD								
Stanley Matthews †			Swayne	3/14/1881	5/12/1881 (24-23)		3/22/1889	7
ARTHUR								
Horace Gray	Mass.	3/24/1828	Clifford	12/19/1881	12/20/1881 (51-5)		9/15/1902	20
Roscoe Conkling	N.Y.	10/30/1829	Hunt	2/24/1882	3/2/1882 (39-12) (D)		4/18/1888	
Samuel Blatchford	N.Y.	3/9/1820	Hunt	3/13/1882	3/27/1882		7/7/1893	11
CLEVELAND								
Lucius Q. C. Lamar	Miss.	9/17/1825	Woods	12/6/1887	1/16/1888 (32-28)		1/23/1893	5
Melville W. Fuller	Ill.	2/11/1833	Waite	4/30/1888	7/20/1888 (41-20)		7/4/1910	22
HARRISON								
David J. Brewer	Kan.	6/20/1837	Matthews	12/4/1889	12/18/1889 (53-11)		3/28/1910	20
Henry B. Brown	Mich.	3/2/1836	Miller	12/23/1890	12/29/1890	5/28/1906	9/4/1913	15
George Shiras, Jr.	Pa.	1/26/1832	Bradley	7/19/1892	7/26/1892	2/23/1903	8/2/1924	10
Howell E. Jackson	Tenn.	4/8/1832	Lamar	2/2/1893	2/18/1893		8/8/1895	2
CLEVELAND								
William B. Hornblower	N.Y.	5/13/1851	Blatchford	9/19/1893	1/15/1894 (R, 24-30)		6/16/1914	
Wheeler H. Peckham	N.Y.	1/1/1833	Blatchford	1/22/1894	2/16/1894 (R, 32-41)		9/27/1905	
Edward D. White	La.	11/3/1845	Blatchford	2/19/1894	2/19/1894		5/19/1921	17
Rufus W. Peckham	N.Y.	11/8/1838	Jackson	12/3/1895	12/9/1895		10/24/1909	13

MCKINLEY								
Joseph McKenna	Calif.	8/10/1843	Field	12/16/1897	1/21/1898		1/5/1925	11/21/1926	26
ROOSEVELT								
Oliver W. Holmes	Mass.	3/8/1841	Gray	12/2/1902	12/4/1902		1/12/1932	3/6/1935	29
William R. Day	Ohio	4/17/1849	Shiras	2/19/1903	2/23/1903		11/13/1922	7/9/1923	19
William H. Moody	Mass.	12/23/1853	Brown	12/3/1906	12/12/1906		11/20/1910	7/2/1917	3
TAFT								
Horace H. Lurton	Tenn.	2/26/1844	Peckham	12/13/1909	12/20/1909			7/12/1914	4
Charles E. Hughes	N.Y.	4/11/1862	Brewer	4/25/1910	5/2/1910		6/10/1916	8/27/1948	6
Edward D. White ‡			Fuller	12/12/1910	12/12/1910				10 ‡
Willis Van Devanter	Wyo.	4/17/1859	White	12/12/1910	12/15/1910		6/2/1937	2/8/1941	26
Joseph R. Lamar	Ga.	10/14/1857	Moody	12/12/1910	12/15/1910			1/2/1916	5
Mahlon Pitney	N.J.	2/5/1858	Harlan	2/19/1912	3/13/1912	(50-26)	12/31/1922	12/29/1924	10
WILSON								
James C. McReynolds	Tenn.	2/3/1862	Lurton	8/19/1914	8/29/1914	(44-6)	1/31/1941	8/24/1946	26
Louis D. Brandeis	Mass.	11/13/1856	Lamar	1/28/1916	6/1/1916	(47-22)	2/13/1939	10/5/1941	22
John H. Clarke	Ohio	9/18/1857	Hughes	7/14/1916	7/24/1916		9/18/1922	3/22/1945	6
HARDING								
William H. Taft	Ohio	9/15/1857	White	6/30/1921	6/30/1921		2/3/1930	3/8/1930	8
George Sutherland	Utah	3/25/1862	Clarke	9/5/1922	9/5/1922		1/17/1938	7/18/1942	15
Pierce Butler	Minn.	3/17/1866	Day	11/23/1922	12/21/1922	(61-8)		11/16/1939	17
Edward T. Sanford	Tenn.	7/23/1865	Pitney	1/24/1923	1/29/1923			3/8/1930	7
COOLIDGE								
Harlan F. Stone	N.Y.	10/11/1872	McKenna	1/5/1925	2/5/1925	(71-6)		4/22/1946	16

Name	State	Date of Birth	To Replace	Date of Appointment	Confirmation or Other Action*	Date Resigned	Date of Death	Years of Service
HOOVER								
Charles E. Hughes ‡			Taft	2/3/1930	2/13/1930 (52-26)	7/1/1941		11 ‡
John J. Parker	N.C.	11/20/1885	Sanford	3/21/1930	5/7/1930 (R, 39-41)		3/17/1958	
Owen J. Roberts	Pa.	5/2/1875	Sanford	5/9/1930	5/20/1930	7/31/1945	5/17/1955	15
Benjamin N. Cardozo	N.Y.	5/24/1870	Holmes	2/15/1932	2/24/1932		7/9/1938	6
ROOSEVELT								
Hugo L. Black	Ala.	2/27/1886	Van Devanter	8/12/1937	8/17/1937 (63-16)	9/17/1971	10/25/1971	34
Stanley F. Reed	Ky.	12/31/1884	Sutherland	1/15/1938	1/25/1938	2/25/1957	4/2/1980	19
Felix Frankfurther	Mass.	11/15/1882	Cardozo	1/5/1939	1/17/1939	8/28/1962	2/22/1965	23
William O. Douglas	Conn.	10/16/1898	Brandeis	3/20/1939	4/4/1939 (62-4)	11/12/1975		36
Frank Murphy	Mich.	4/13/1890	Butler	1/4/1940	1/15/1940		7/19/1949	9
Harlan F. Stone ‡			Hughes	6/12/1941	6/27/1941		4/22/1946	5 ‡
James F. Byrnes	S.C.	5/2/1879	McReynolds	6/12/1941	6/12/1941	10/3/1942	4/9/1972	1
Robert H. Jackson	N.Y.	2/13/1892	Stone	6/12/1941	7/7/1941		10/9/1954	13
Wiley B. Rutledge	Iowa	7/20/1894	Byrnes	1/11/1943	2/8/1943		9/10/1949	6
TRUMAN								
Harold H. Burton	Ohio	6/22/1888	Roberts	9/19/1945	9/19/1945	10/13/1958	10/28/1964	13
Fred M. Vinson	Ky.	1/22/1890	Stone	6/6/1946	6/20/1946		9/8/1953	7
Tom C. Clark	Texas	9/23/1899	Murphy	8/2/1949	8/18/1949 (73-8)	6/12/1967	6/13/1977	18
Sherman Minton	Ind.	10/20/1890	Rutledge	9/15/1949	10/4/1949 (48-16)	10/15/1956	4/9/1965	7
EISENHOWER								
Earl Warren	Calif.	3/19/1891	Vinson	9/30/1953	3/1/1954	6/23/1969	6/9/1974	15
John M. Harlan	N.Y.	5/20/1899	Jackson	1/10/1955	3/16/1955 (71-11)	9/23/1971	12/29/1971	16

Name	State	Birth	Replaced	Nominated	Confirmed/Action	Vote	Left Court	Died	No.
William J. Brennan, Jr.	N.J.	4/25/1906	Minton	1/14/1957	3/19/1957		7/20/1990		5
Charles E. Whittaker	Mo.	2/22/1901	Reed	3/2/1957	3/19/1957		3/31/1962	11/26/1973	22
Potter Stewart	Ohio	1/23/1915	Burton	1/17/1959	5/5/1959	(70-17)	7/3/1981	12/7/1985	
KENNEDY									
Byron R. White	Colo.	6/8/1917	Whittaker	3/30/1962	4/11/1962				3
Arthur J. Goldberg	Ill.	8/8/1908	Frankfurter	8/29/1962	9/25/1962		7/25/1965		
JOHNSON									
Abe Fortas	Tenn.	6/19/1910	Goldberg	7/28/1965	8/11/1965		5/14/1969	4/5/1982	4
Thurgood Marshall	N.Y.	6/2/1908	Clark	6/13/1967	8/30/1967	(69-11)			
Abe Fortas ‡			Warren	6/26/1968	10/4/1968	(W)			
Homer Thornberry	Texas	1/9/1909	Fortas	6/26/1968	No action				
NIXON									
Warren E. Burger	Minn.	9/17/1907	Warren	5/21/1969	6/9/1969	(74-3)	9/26/1986		17
Clement Haynsworth Jr.	S.C.	10/30/1912	Fortas	8/18/1969	11/21/1969	(R, 45-55)			
G. Harrold Carswell	Fla.	12/22/1919	Fortas	1/19/1970	4/8/1970	(R, 45-51)			
Harry A. Blackmun	Minn.	11/12/1908	Fortas	4/14/1970	5/12/1970	(94-0)			
Lewis F. Powell, Jr.	Va.	9/19/1907	Black	10/21/1971	12/6/1971	(89-1)	6/26/1987		16
William H. Rehnquist	Ariz.	10/1/1924	Harlan	10/21/1971	12/10/1971	(68-26)			
FORD									
John Paul Stevens	Ill.	4/20/1920	Douglas	11/28/1975	12/17/1975	(98-0)			
REAGAN									
Sandra Day O'Connor	Ariz.	3/26/1930	Stewart	8/19/1981	9/21/1981	(99-0)			
William H. Rehnquist ‡			Burger	6/20/1986	9/17/1986	(65-33)			
Antonin Scalia	Va.	3/11/1936	Rehnquist	6/24/1986	9/17/1986	(98-0)			

Name	State	Date of Birth	To Replace	Date of Appointment	Confirmation or Other Action*	Date Resigned	Date of Death	Years of Service
Robert H. Bork	D.C.	3/1/1927	Powell	7/1/1987	10/23/1987 (R, 42–58)			
Anthony M. Kennedy	Calif.	7/23/1936	Powell	11/30/1987	2/3/1988 (97–0)			
BUSH								
David H. Souter	N.H.	9/17/1939	Brennan	7/23/1990	10/6/1990 (90–9)		·	

Sources: Leon Friedman and Fred L. Israel, eds., *The Justice of the United States Supreme Court, 1789–1969*; Executive Journal of the U.S. Senate, 1789–1975; Congressional Quarterly *Almanacs*, 1971, 1975, 1981, 1986, and 1987.

Reprinted with permission of Congressional Quarterly, Inc.